# C# 7.1 and .NET Co Modern Cross-Platform Development

## *Third Edition*

Create powerful applications with .NET Standard 2.0, ASP.NET Core 2.0, and Entity Framework Core 2.0, using Visual Studio 2017 or Visual Studio Code

**Mark J. Price**

BIRMINGHAM - MUMBAI

# C# 7.1 and .NET Core 2.0 – Modern Cross-Platform Development

## *Third Edition*

Copyright © 2017 Packt Publishing

All rights reserved. No part of this book may be reproduced, stored in a retrieval system, or transmitted in any form or by any means, without the prior written permission of the publisher, except in the case of brief quotations embedded in critical articles or reviews.

Every effort has been made in the preparation of this book to ensure the accuracy of the information presented. However, the information contained in this book is sold without warranty, either express or implied. Neither the author, nor Packt Publishing, and its dealers and distributors will be held liable for any damages caused or alleged to be caused directly or indirectly by this book.

Packt Publishing has endeavored to provide trademark information about all of the companies and products mentioned in this book by the appropriate use of capitals. However, Packt Publishing cannot guarantee the accuracy of this information.

First published: March 2016

Second edition: March 2017

Third edition: November 2017

Production reference: 1291117

Published by Packt Publishing Ltd.
Livery Place
35 Livery Street
Birmingham
B3 2PB, UK.
ISBN 978-1-78839-807-7

www.packtpub.com

# Credits

**Author**
Mark J. Price

**Reviewers**
Dustin Heffron
Efraim Kyriakidis

**Acquisition Editor**
Ben Renow-Clarke

**Project Editor**
Radhika Atitkar

**Content Development Editor**
Chris Nelson

**Technical Editors**
Bhagyashree Rai
Gaurav Gavas

**Copy Editor**
Tom Jacob

**Proofreader**
Safis Editing

**Indexer**
Rekha Nair

**Graphics**
Kirk D'Penha

**Production Coordinator**
Shantanu Zagade

# About the Author

**Mark J. Price** is a Microsoft Certified Solutions Developer (MCSD), Microsoft Specialist: Programming in C#, and Episerver Certified Developer, with more than 20 years of educational and programming experience.

Microsoft
CERTIFIED
Solutions Developer
App Builder

Microsoft
Specialist
Programming in C#

Episerver CMS
Certified Developer

Since 1993, Mark has passed more than 80 Microsoft programming exams, and he specializes in preparing others to pass them too. His students range from professionals with decades of experience to 16-year-old apprentices with none. He successfully guides all of them by combining educational skills with real-world experience in consulting and developing systems for enterprises worldwide.

Between 2001 and 2003, Mark was employed full-time to write official courseware for Microsoft in Redmond, USA. His team wrote the first training courses for C# while it was still an early alpha version. While with Microsoft, he taught "train-the-trainer" classes to get Microsoft Certified Trainers up-to-speed on C# and .NET.

Currently, Mark creates and delivers classroom and e-learning training courses for Episerver's Digital Experience Cloud, the best .NET CMS for Digital Marketing and E-commerce. He is an Episerver Certified Developer (ECD) on Episerver CMS.

In 2010, Mark studied for a Postgraduate Certificate in Education (PGCE). He taught GCSE and A-Level mathematics in two London secondary schools. He holds a Computer Science BSc Hons. degree from the University of Bristol, UK.

*Thank you to my parents, Pamela and Ian, for raising me to be polite, hardworking, and curious about the world. Thank you to my sisters, Emily and Juliet, for loving me despite being their awkward older brother. Thank you to my friends and colleagues who inspire me technically and creatively. Lastly, thanks to all the students I have taught over the years for motivating me to be the best teacher that I can be.*

# About the Reviewers

**Dustin Heffron** is a software engineer by day and an independent game developer by night. He has over 10 years of experience programming in various languages, eight of which have been in working with C# and .NET.

Currently, Dustin develops tools to automate and test medical instruments at Becton Dickinson. He is also the cofounder and CEO for SunFlake Studios.
Dustin has a long history of reviewing for Packt, including *XNA 4.0 Game Development by Example: Beginner's Guide, C# 6 and .NET Core 1.0: Modern Cross-Platform Development*, and the video tutorial series *XNA 3D Programming by Example*. He also coauthored the video tutorial series *XNA 3D Toolkit* with *Larry Louisiana*.

*I'd like to thank my wife for helping to push me to be the best that I can be, every day.*

**Efraim Kyriakidis** is a skilled software engineer with over 10 years of experience on developing and delivering software solutions for diverse customers and projects. He's well-versed in all stages of the software development life cycle. His first acquaintance with computers and programming was a state of the art Commodore 64, back in the '80s as a kid. Since then he has grown and received his Diploma from Aristotle University Thessaloniki in Greece. Throughout his career, he mainly worked with Microsoft technologies, using C# and .NET since .NET 1.0. He currently works for Siemens AG in Germany as a software developer.

# www.PacktPub.com

For support files and downloads related to your book, please visit www.PacktPub.com. Did you know that Packt offers eBook versions of every book published, with PDF and ePub files available? You can upgrade to the eBook version at www.PacktPub.com and as a print book customer, you are entitled to a discount on the eBook copy. Get in touch with us at service@packtpub.com for more details. At www.PacktPub.com, you can also read a collection of free technical articles, sign up for a range of free newsletters and receive exclusive discounts and offers on Packt books and eBooks.

https://www.packtpub.com/mapt

Get the most in-demand software skills with Mapt. Mapt gives you full access to all Packt books and video courses, as well as industry-leading tools to help you plan your personal development and advance your career.

## Why subscribe?

- Fully searchable across every book published by Packt
- Copy and paste, print, and bookmark content
- On demand and accessible via a web browser

# Customer Feedback

Thanks for purchasing this Packt book. At Packt, quality is at the heart of our editorial process. To help us improve, please leave us an honest review on this book's Amazon page at `https://www.amazon.com/dp/1788398076`.

If you'd like to join our team of regular reviewers, you can email us at `customerreviews@packtpub.com`. We award our regular reviewers with free eBooks and videos in exchange for their valuable feedback. Help us be relentless in improving our products!

# Table of Contents

## Chapter 16: Building Web Services and Applications Using ASP.NET Core 611

# Preface

There are C# books that are thousands of pages long that aim to be comprehensive references to the C# programming language and the .NET Framework.

This book is different. It is concise and aims to be a fast-paced read that is packed with hands-on walkthroughs. I wrote this book to be the best step-by-step guide to learning modern cross-platform C# proven practices using .NET Core.

I will point out the cool corners and gotchas of C#, so you can impress colleagues and employers and get productive fast. Rather than slowing down and boring some readers by explaining every little thing, I will assume that if a term I use is new to you, then you will know how to Google an answer.

At the end of each chapter is a section titled *Practice and explore*, in which you will complete hands-on practical exercises and explore topics deeper on your own with a little nudge in the right direction from me.

You can download solutions for the exercises from the following GitHub repository. I will provide instructions on how to do this using Visual Studio 2017 and Visual Studio Code at the end of `Chapter 1`, *Hello, C#! Welcome, .NET Core!*

`https://github.com/markjprice/cs7dotnetcore2`

## What this book covers

`Chapter 1`, *Hello, C#! Welcome, .NET Core!*, is about setting up your development environment and using various tools to create the simplest application possible with C#. You will learn how to write and compile code using Visual Studio 2017 on Windows; Visual Studio Code on macOS, Linux, or Windows; or Visual Studio for Mac on macOS. You will learn the different .NET technologies: .NET Framework, .NET Core, .NET Standard, and .NET Native.

# Part 1 – C# 7.1

`Chapter 2`, *Speaking C#*, explains the grammar and vocabulary that you will use every day to write the source code for your applications. In particular, you will learn how to declare and work with variables of different types.

`Chapter 3`, *Controlling the Flow and Converting Types*, talks about writing code that makes decisions, repeats a block of statements, and converts between types, and writing code defensively to handle errors when they inevitably occur. You will also learn the best places to look for help.

`Chapter 4`, *Writing, Debugging, and Testing Functions*, is about following the Don't Repeat Yourself (DRY) principle by writing reusable functions, and learning how to use debugging tools to track down and remove bugs, monitoring your code while it executes to diagnose problems, and rigorously testing your code to remove bugs and ensure stability and reliability before it gets deployed into production.

`Chapter 5`, *Building Your Own Types with Object-Oriented Programming*, discusses all the different categories of members that a type can have, including fields to store data and methods to perform actions. You will use OOP concepts, such as aggregation and encapsulation. You will learn the C# 7 language features such as tuple syntax support and out variables, and C# 7.1 language features such as default literals and inferred tuple names.

`Chapter 6`, *Implementing Interfaces and Inheriting Classes*, explains deriving new types from existing ones using object-oriented programming (OOP). You will learn how to define operators and C# 7 local functions, delegates and events, how to implement interfaces about base and derived classes, how to override a type member, how to use polymorphism, how to create extension methods, and how to cast between classes in an inheritance hierarchy.

# Part 2 – .NET Core 2.0 and .NET Standard 2.0

`Chapter 7`, *Understanding and Packaging .NET Standard Types*, presents .NET Core 2.0 types that are part of .NET Standard 2.0, and how they are related to C#. You will learn how to deploy and package your own apps and libraries.

`Chapter 8`, *Using Common .NET Standard Types*, discusses the .NET Standard types that allow your code to perform common practical tasks, such as manipulating numbers and text, storing items in collections, and implementing internationalization.

`Chapter 9`, *Working with Files, Streams, and Serialization*, talks about interacting with the filesystem, reading and writing to files and streams, text encoding, and serialization.

`Chapter 10`, *Protecting Your Data and Applications*, is about protecting your data from being viewed by malicious users using encryption and from being manipulated or corrupted using hashing and signing. You will also learn about authentication and authorization to protect applications from unauthorized uses.

`Chapter 11`, *Working with Databases Using Entity Framework Core*, explains reading and writing to databases, such as Microsoft SQL Server and SQLite, using the object-relational mapping technology named Entity Framework Core.

`Chapter 12`, *Querying and Manipulating Data Using LINQ*, teaches you Language INtegrated Query (LINQ)—language extensions that add the ability to work with sequences of items and filter, sort, and project them into different outputs.

`Chapter 13`, *Improving Performance and Scalability Using Multitasking*, discusses allowing multiple actions to occur at the same time to improve performance, scalability, and user productivity. You will learn about the C# 7.1 `async Main` feature, and how to use types in the `System.Diagnostics` namespace to monitor your code to measure performance and efficiency.

# Part 3 – App Models

`Chapter 14`, *Building Web Sites Using ASP.NET Core Razor Pages*, is about learning the basics of building websites with a modern HTTP architecture on the server-side using ASP.NET Core. You will learn the new ASP.NET Core feature known as Razor Pages that simplifies creating web pages for small web sites.

`Chapter 15`, *Building Web Sites Using ASP.NET Core MVC*, is about learning how to build large, complex websites in a way that is easy to unit test and manage with teams of programmers using ASP.NET Core. You will learn about startup configuration, authentication, routes, models, views, and controllers in ASP.NET Core MVC.

`Chapter 16`, *Building Web Services and Applications Using ASP.NET Core*, explains building web applications with a combination of a modern frontend technology, such as Angular or React, and a backend REST architecture web service using ASP.NET Core Web API.

`Chapter 17`, *Building Windows Apps Using XAML and Fluent Design*, talks about learning the basics of XAML that can be used to define the user interface for a graphical app for the Universal Windows Platform (UWP), and applying principles and features of Fluent Design to light it up. This app can then run on any device running Windows 10, Xbox One, and even Mixed Reality devices such as HoloLens.

`Chapter 18`, *Building Mobile Apps Using XAML and Xamarin.Forms*, discusses introducing you to taking C# mobile by building a cross-platform app for iOS and Android. The client-side mobile app will be created with Visual Studio for Mac using XAML and Xamarin.Forms.

`Appendix`, *Answers to the Test Your Knowledge Questions*, has the answers to the test questions at the end of each chapter.

# What you need for this book

You can develop and deploy C# on many platforms, including Windows, macOS, and many varieties of Linux. For the best programming experience, and to reach the most platforms, I recommend that you learn the basics of all members of the Visual Studio family: Visual Studio 2017, Visual Studio Code, and Visual Studio for Mac.

My recommendation for the operating system and development tool combinations is as follows:

- Visual Studio 2017 on Windows 10
- Visual Studio for Mac on macOS
- Visual Studio Code on Windows 10 or macOS

The best version of Windows to use is Microsoft Windows 10 because you will need this version to create Universal Windows Platform apps in `Chapter 17`, *Building Windows Apps Using XAML and Fluent Design*. Earlier versions of Windows, such as 7 or 8.1, will work for the other chapters.

The best version of macOS to use is Sierra or High Sierra because you will need macOS to build iOS mobile apps in `Chapter 18`, *Building Mobile Apps Using XAML and Xamarin.Forms*. Although you can use Visual Studio 2017 on Windows to write the code for iOS and Android mobile apps, you must have macOS and Xcode to compile them.

# Who this book is for

If you have heard that C# is a popular general-purpose programming language used to create every type of software, ranging from web applications and services, to business applications and games, then this book is for you.

If you have heard that C# can create software that runs on a wide range of devices, from desktop to server, from mobile to gaming systems such as Xbox One, then this book is for you.

If you have heard that .NET Core is Microsoft's bet on a cross-platform .NET future, optimized for server-side web development in the cloud, and Augmented Reality (AR) or Virtual Reality (VR) devices such as HoloLens, then this book is for you.

If you have heard that Microsoft has a popular cross-platform developer tool named Visual Studio Code that creates these cross-platform apps, and you are curious to try it, then this book is for you.

# Conventions

In this book, you will find a number of text styles that distinguish between different kinds of information. Here are some examples of these styles and an explanation of their meaning.

Code words in text, database table names, folder names, filenames, file extensions, pathnames, dummy URLs, user input, and Twitter handles are shown as follows: "The `Controllers`, `Models`, and `Views` folders contain ASP.NET Core classes and the `.cshtml` files for execution on the server."

A block of code is set as follows:

```
// storing items at index positions
names[0] = "Kate";
names[1] = "Jack";
names[2] = "Rebecca";
names[3] = "Tom";
```

When we wish to draw your attention to a particular part of a code block, the relevant lines or items are set in bold:

```
// storing items at index positions
names[0] = "Kate";
names[1] = "Jack";
names[2] = "Rebecca";
names[3] = "Tom";
```

Any command-line input or output is written as follows:

```
dotnet new console
```

**New terms** and **important words** are shown in bold. Words that you see on the screen, for example, in menus or dialog boxes, appear in the text like this: "Clicking on the **Next** button moves you to the next screen."

Warnings or important notes appear in a box like this.

**Good Practice**

Recommendations for how to program like an expert appear like this.

# Reader feedback

Feedback from our readers is always welcome. Let us know what you think about this book—what you liked or disliked. Reader feedback is important for us as it helps us develop titles that you will really get the most out of.

To send us general feedback, simply email `feedback@packtpub.com`, and mention the book's title in the subject of your message.

If there is a topic that you have expertise in and you are interested in either writing or contributing to a book, see our author guide at `www.packtpub.com/authors`.

# Customer support

Now that you are the proud owner of a Packt book, we have a number of things to help you to get the most from your purchase.

## Downloading the example code

You can download the example code files for this book from your account at `http://www.packtpub.com`. If you purchased this book elsewhere, you can visit `http://www.packtpub.com/support` and register to have the files emailed directly to you.

You can download the code files by following these steps:

1. Log in or register to our website using your email address and password.
2. Hover the mouse pointer on the SUPPORT tab at the top.
3. Click on Code Downloads & Errata.
4. Enter the name of the book in the Search box.
5. Select the book for which you're looking to download the code files.
6. Choose from the drop-down menu where you purchased this book from.
7. Click on Code Download.

Once the file is downloaded, please make sure that you unzip or extract the folder using the latest version of:

- WinRAR / 7-Zip for Windows
- Zipeg / iZip / UnRarX for Mac
- 7-Zip / PeaZip for Linux

The code bundle for the book is also hosted on GitHub at `https://github.com/PacktPublishing/CSharp-7.1-and-.NET-Core-2.0-Modern-Cross-Platform-Development-Third-Edition`. We also have other code bundles from our rich catalog of books and videos available at `https://github.com/PacktPublishing/`. Check them out!

## Downloading the color images of this book

We also provide you with a PDF file that has color images of the screenshots/diagrams used in this book. The color images will help you better understand the changes in the output. You can download this file from https://www.packtpub.com/sites/default/files/downloads/CSharp71andNETCore20ModernCrossPlatformDevelopmentThirdEdition_ColorImages.pdf.

## Errata

Although we have taken every care to ensure the accuracy of our content, mistakes do happen. If you find a mistake in one of our books—maybe a mistake in the text or the code—we would be grateful if you could report this to us. By doing so, you can save other readers from frustration and help us improve subsequent versions of this book. If you find any errata, please report them by visiting http://www.packtpub.com/submit-errata, selecting your book, clicking on the Errata Submission Form link, and entering the details of your errata. Once your errata are verified, your submission will be accepted and the errata will be uploaded to our website or added to any list of existing errata under the Errata section of that title.

To view the previously submitted errata, go to https://www.packtpub.com/books/content/support and enter the name of the book in the search field. The required information will appear under the Errata section.

## Piracy

Piracy of copyrighted material on the Internet is an ongoing problem across all media. At Packt, we take the protection of our copyright and licenses very seriously. If you come across any illegal copies of our works in any form on the Internet, please provide us with the location address or website name immediately so that we can pursue a remedy.

Please contact us at copyright@packtpub.com with a link to the suspected pirated material.

We appreciate your help in protecting our authors and our ability to bring you valuable content.

## Questions

If you have a problem with any aspect of this book, you can contact us at questions@packtpub.com, and we will do our best to address the problem.

# 1
# Hello, C#! Welcome, .NET Core!

This chapter is about setting up your development environment, understanding the similarities and differences between .NET Core, .NET Framework, .NET Standard, and .NET Native, and using various tools to create the simplest application possible with C# and .NET Core.

Most people learn complex topics by imitation and repetition rather than reading a detailed explanation of theory. So, I will not explain every keyword and step. The idea is to get you to write some code, build an application, and see it run. You don't need to know the details of how it all works yet.

In the words of Samuel Johnson, author of the English dictionary in 1755, I have likely committed "a few wild blunders, and risible absurdities, from which no work of such multiplicity is free." I take sole responsibility for these and hope you appreciate the challenge of my attempt to *lash the wind* by writing this book about .NET Core and its command-line tooling during its rocky birth during 2016 and 2017.

This chapter covers the following topics:

- Setting up your development environment
- Understanding .NET
- Writing and compiling code using the .NET Core CLI tool
- Writing and compiling code using Visual Studio 2017
- Writing and compiling code using Visual Studio Code
- Writing and compiling code using Visual Studio for Mac
- Managing source code with GitHub

# Setting up your development environment

Before you start programming, you will need to choose an **Integrated Development Environment** (**IDE**) that includes a code editor for C#. Microsoft has a family of IDEs:

- Visual Studio 2017
- Visual Studio for Mac
- Visual Studio Code

The most mature and fully-featured IDE to choose is **Microsoft Visual Studio 2017**, but it only runs on the Windows operating system.

The most modern and lightweight IDE to choose, and the only one from Microsoft that is cross-platform, is **Microsoft Visual Studio Code**, and it will run on all common operating systems, including Windows, macOS, and many varieties of Linux, such as **Red Hat Enterprise Linux** (**RHEL**) and Ubuntu.

To help you decide if Visual Studio Code is right for you, I recommend that you watch the following video, *Beginner's Guide to VS Code: Up and Running in Ten Minutes*: `https://channel9.msdn.com/Blogs/raw-tech/Beginners-Guide-to-VS-Code`

The most suitable IDE to choose for mobile development is **Visual Studio for Mac**. To create apps for iOS (iPhone and iPad), tvOS, macOS, and watchOS, you must have macOS and Xcode. Although you can use Visual Studio 2017 with its Xamarin extensions to *write* a cross-platform mobile app, you still need macOS and Xcode to *compile* it.

The following table shows which IDE and operating systems can or must be used for each of the chapters in this book:

| **Chapters** | **IDE** | **Operating systems** |
|---|---|---|
| Chapters 1 to 16 | Visual Studio 2017 | Windows 7 SP1 or later |
| Chapters 1 to 16 | Visual Studio Code | Windows, macOS, Linux |
| Chapters 1 to 16 | Visual Studio for Mac | macOS |
| Chapter 17 | Visual Studio 2017 | Windows 10 |
| Chapter 18 | Visual Studio for Mac | macOS |

**Good Practice**
If you have the option, then I recommend that you try all the coding exercises with Visual Studio 2017 on Windows, Visual Studio Code on macOS, Linux, or Windows, and Visual Studio for Mac. It will be good for you to get experience with C# and .NET Core on a variety of operating systems and development tools.

To write the third edition of this book, I used the following listed software, as shown in the following screenshot:

- Visual Studio 2017 on Windows 10 in a virtual machine
- Visual Studio for Mac on macOS
- Visual Studio Code on macOS
- Visual Studio Code on RHEL (not shown in screenshot)

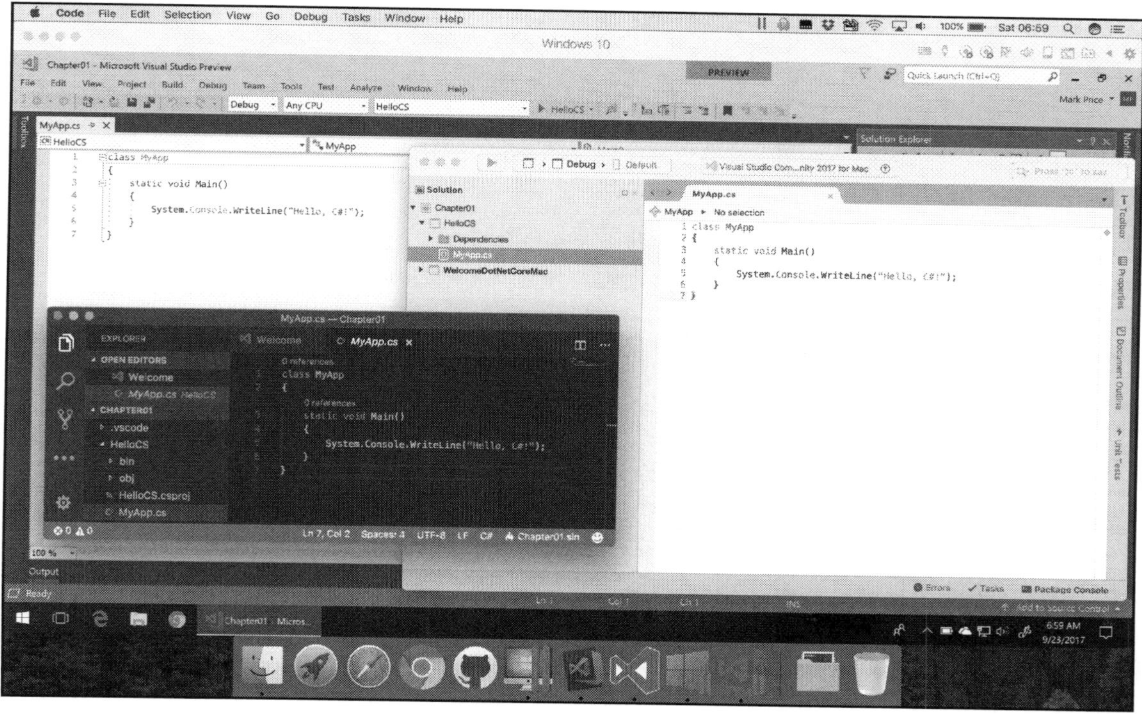

## Using alternative C# IDEs

There are alternative IDEs for C#, for example, **MonoDevelop** and **JetBrains Rider**. You can install either of these two IDEs with the help of the following URLs:

- For MonoDevelop IDE, visit `http://www.monodevelop.com/`
- For JetBrains Rider, visit `https://www.jetbrains.com/rider/`

**Cloud9** is a web browser-based IDE, so it's even more cross-platform than the others. It is growing in popularity. Here is the link: `https://c9.io/web/sign-up/free`

## Deploying cross-platform

Your choice of IDE and operating system for development does not limit where your code gets deployed. .NET Core 2.0 supports the following platforms for deployment:

- Windows 7 SP1, or later
- Windows Server 2008 R2 SP1, or later
- Windows IoT 10, or later
- macOS Sierra (version 10.12), or later
- RHEL 7.3, or later
- Ubuntu 14.04, or later
- Fedora 25, or later
- Debian 8.7, or later
- openSUSE 42.2, or later
- Tizen 4, or later

Linux OSes are popular server host platforms because they are relatively lightweight and more cost-effectively scalable when compared to operating system platforms such as Windows and macOS.

In the next section, you will install Microsoft Visual Studio 2017 for Windows. If you prefer to use Microsoft Visual Studio Code, jump ahead to the *Installing Microsoft Visual Studio Code for Windows, macOS, or Linux* section. If you prefer to use Microsoft Visual Studio for Mac, jump ahead to the *Installing Microsoft Visual Studio for Mac* section.

# Installing Microsoft Visual Studio 2017

You can use Windows 7 SP1 or later to complete most of the chapters in this book, but you will have a better experience if you use Windows 10 Fall Creators Update.

Since October 2014, Microsoft has made a professional-quality edition of Visual Studio available to everyone for free. It is called **Community Edition**.

Download and install **Microsoft Visual Studio 2017 version 15.4 or later** from the following link:

`https://www.visualstudio.com/downloads/`

You must install version 15.4 or later of Visual Studio 2017 to be able to work with .NET Core for UWP. You must install version 15.3 or later of Visual Studio 2017 to be able to work with .NET Core 2.0. Older versions of Visual Studio 2017 only support .NET Core 1.0 and 1.1.

## Choosing workloads

On the **Workloads** tab, choose the following, as partially shown in the following screenshot:

- **Universal Windows Platform development**
- **.NET desktop development**
- **ASP.NET and web development**
- **Azure development**
- **Node.js development**

- **.NET Core cross-platform development**

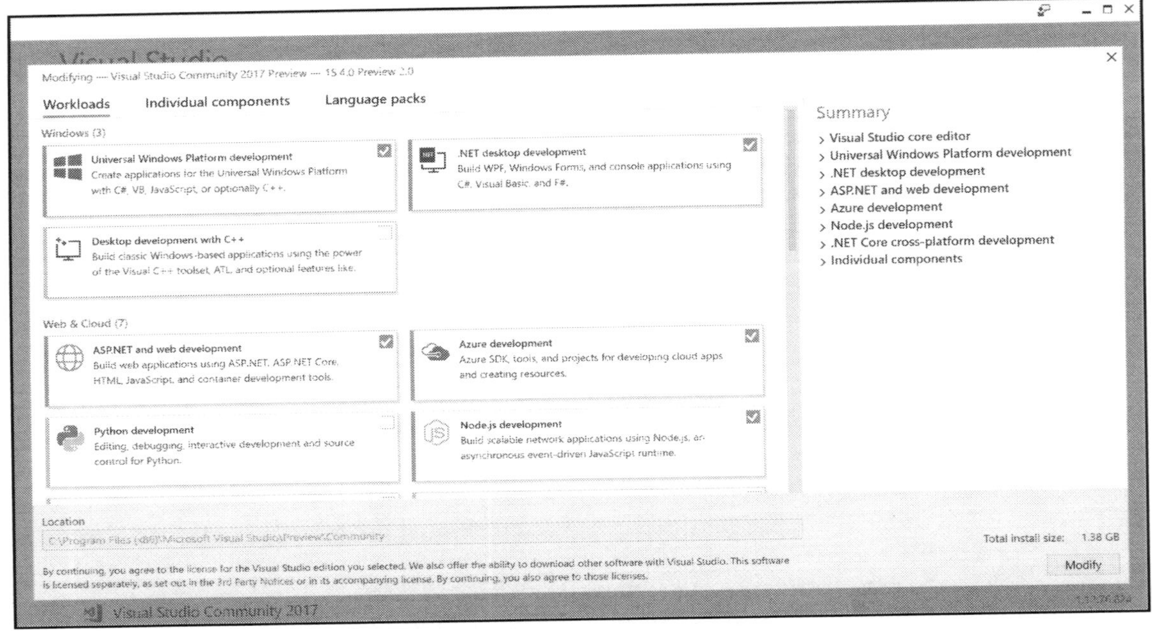


## Choosing additional components

On the **Individual components** tab, choose the following additional components:

- **Class Designer**
- **GitHub extension for Visual Studio**
- **PowerShell tools**

Click on **Install**, and wait for the installer to acquire the selected software, and install it. When the installation is complete, click on **Launch**.

While you wait for Visual Studio 2017 to install, you can jump ahead to the *Understanding .NET* section in this chapter.

The first time that you run Visual Studio 2017, you will be prompted to sign in. If you have a Microsoft account, you can use that account. If you don't, then register for a new one at the following link:

```
https://signup.live.com/
```

When starting Visual Studio 2017 for the first time, you will be prompted to configure your environment. For **Development Settings**, choose **Visual C#**. For the color theme, I chose **Blue**, but you can choose whatever tickles your fancy.

You will see the Microsoft Visual Studio user interface with the **Start Page** open in the central area. Like most Windows desktop applications, Visual Studio has a menu bar, a toolbar for common commands, and a status bar at the bottom. On the right is the **Solution Explorer** that will list your open projects:

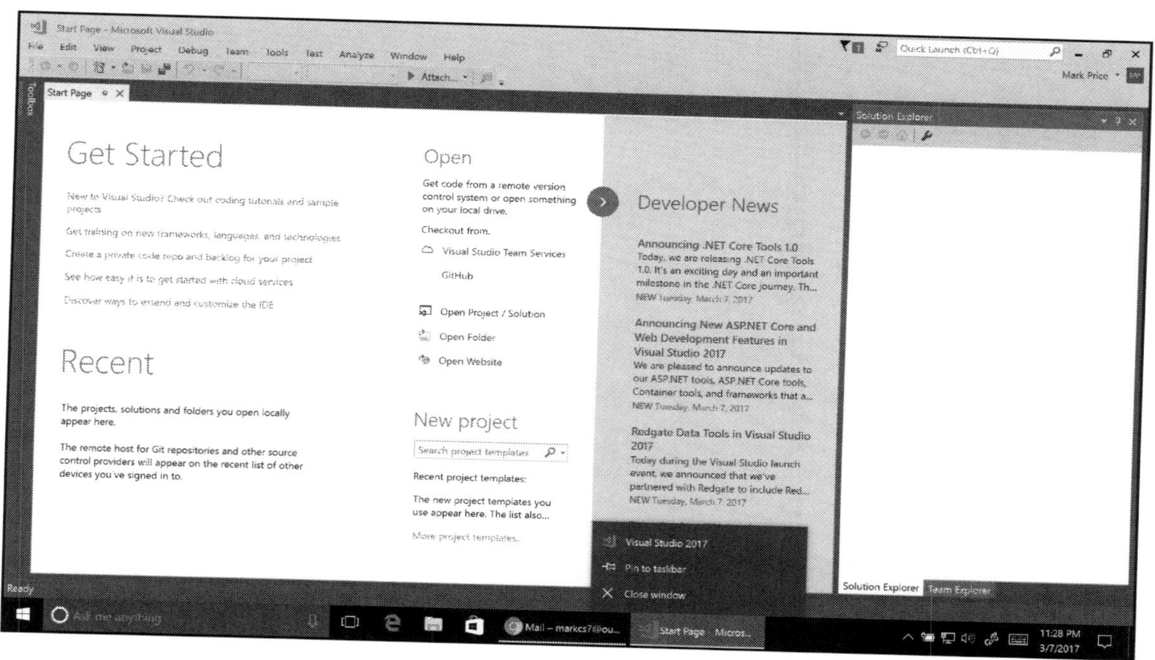

To have quick access to Visual Studio in the future, right-click on its entry in the Windows taskbar and select **Pin this program to taskbar**.

In `Chapter 14`, *Building Web Sites Using ASP.NET Core Razor Pages*, `Chapter 15`, *Building Web Sites Using ASP.NET Core MVC*, and `Chapter 16`, *Building Web Services and Applications Using ASP.NET Core*, you will need Node.js and NPM installed.

Download the Node.js installer for Windows from the following link:

`https://nodejs.org/en/download/`

Run the Node.js installer, as shown in the following screenshot:

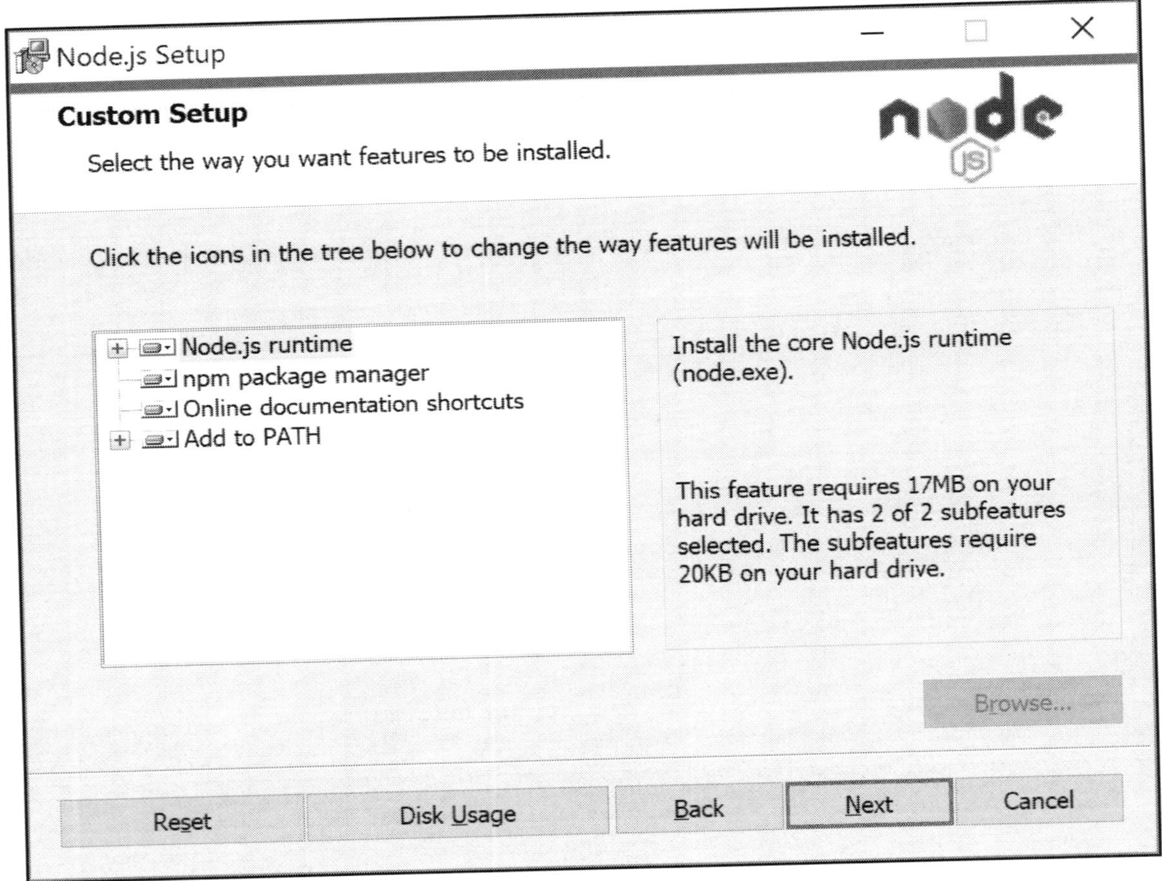

# Installing Microsoft Visual Studio Code

Between June 2015 and September 2017, Microsoft released a new version of **Visual Studio Code** almost every month. Visual Studio Code has rapidly improved and surprised Microsoft with its popularity. Even if you plan to use Visual Studio 2017 or Visual Studio for Mac as your primary development tool, I recommend that you learn how to use Visual Studio Code and the .NET Core command-line tool as well.

You can download Visual Studio Code from the following link:

`https://code.visualstudio.com/`

You can read about Microsoft's plans for Visual Studio Code in 2018 at the following link:
`https://github.com/Microsoft/vscode/wiki/Roadmap`

## Installing Microsoft Visual Studio Code for macOS

In this book, I will show examples and screenshots of Visual Studio Code using the version for macOS. The steps for doing the same with Visual Studio Code for Windows and variants of Linux is very similar, so I will not repeat the instructions for every platform.

After downloading Visual Studio Code for macOS, drag and drop it to your `Applications` folder, as shown in the following screenshot:

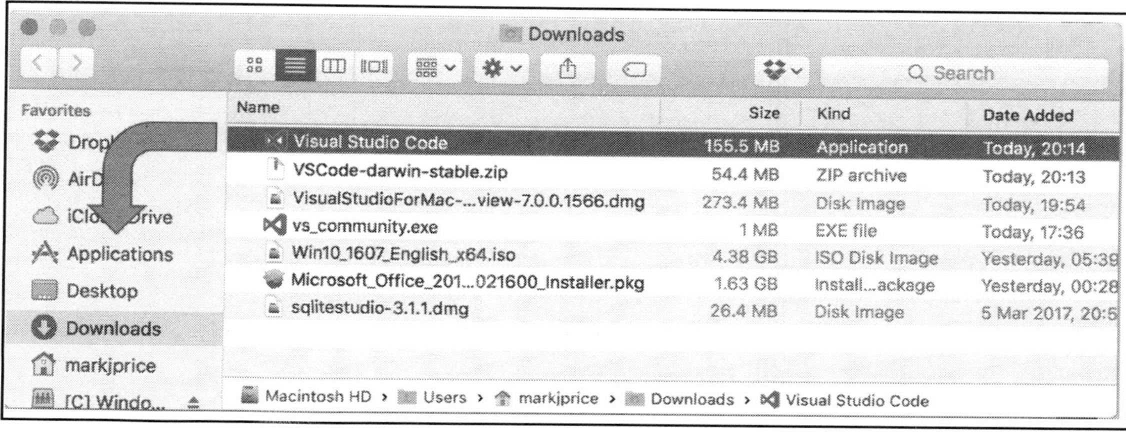

You will now need to install the .NET Core SDK for macOS. The full instructions, including a video to watch, are described at the following link, and I have included the basic steps in this book for your convenience:
`https://www.microsoft.com/net/core#macos`

The first step is to install Homebrew (if you don't already have it).

Start macOS's **Terminal** app and enter the following command at the prompt:

```
/usr/bin/ruby -e "$(curl -fsSL
https://raw.githubusercontent.com/Homebrew/install/master/install)"
```

Terminal will prompt you to press *Enter* to continue and then prompt for your password.

If you are using .NET Core 1.0 or 1.1, then at this point you will need to use Homebrew to install OpenSSL, which is a dependency of older versions of .NET Core on macOS.

## Installing .NET Core SDK for macOS

The next step is to download the **.NET Core SDK** installer for macOS (x64) from the following link:

`https://www.microsoft.com/net/download/core`

Run the `dotnet-sdk-2.0.0-sdk-osx-x64.pkg` installer package, as shown in the following screenshot:

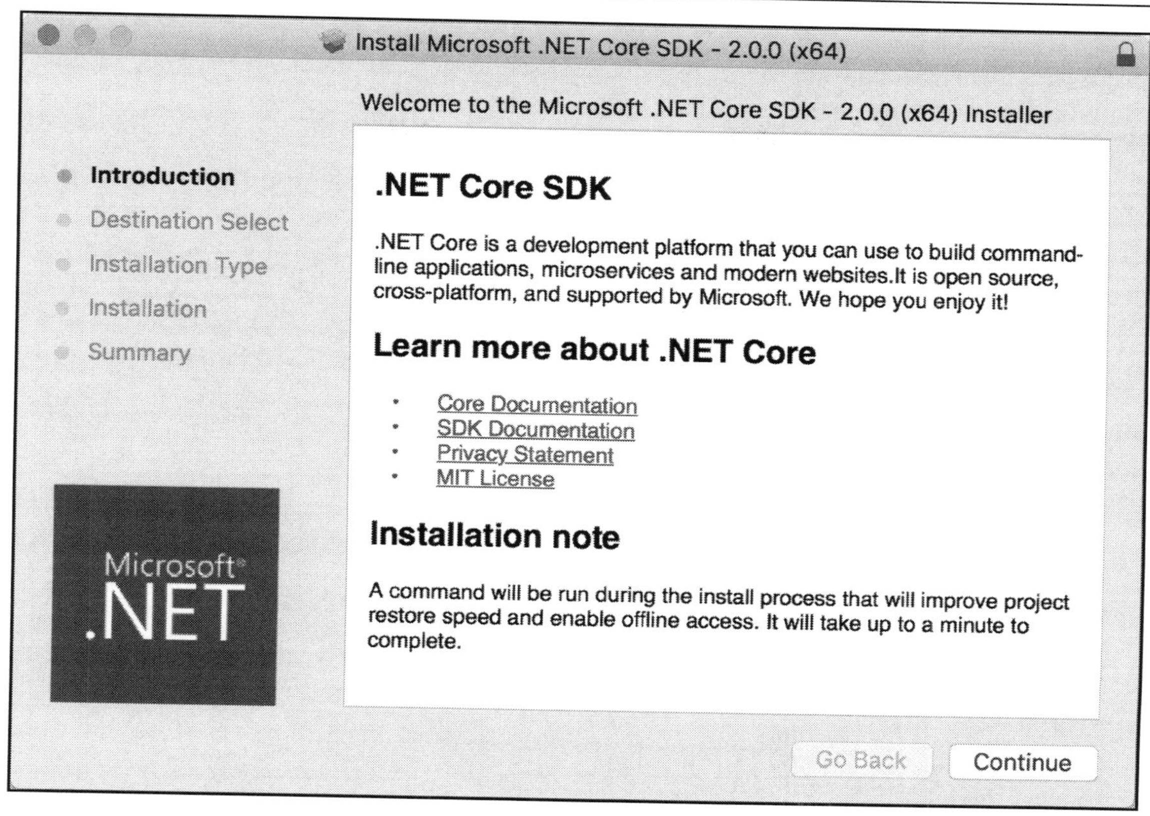


Click on **Continue**, accept the license agreement, click on **Install**, and then, once it has finished, click on **Close.**

## Installing Node Package Manager for macOS

In `Chapter 14`, *Building Web Sites Using ASP.NET Core Razor Pages*, `Chapter 15`, *Building Web Sites Using ASP.NET Core MVC*, and `Chapter 16`, *Building Web Services and Applications Using ASP.NET Core*, you will need Node.js and NPM installed.

In Terminal, enter commands to install Node.js and NPM, and then check their versions, which at the time I wrote this book, were Node.js version 8.4 and NPM version 5.3, as shown in the following screenshot:

```
brew install node
node -v
npm -v
```

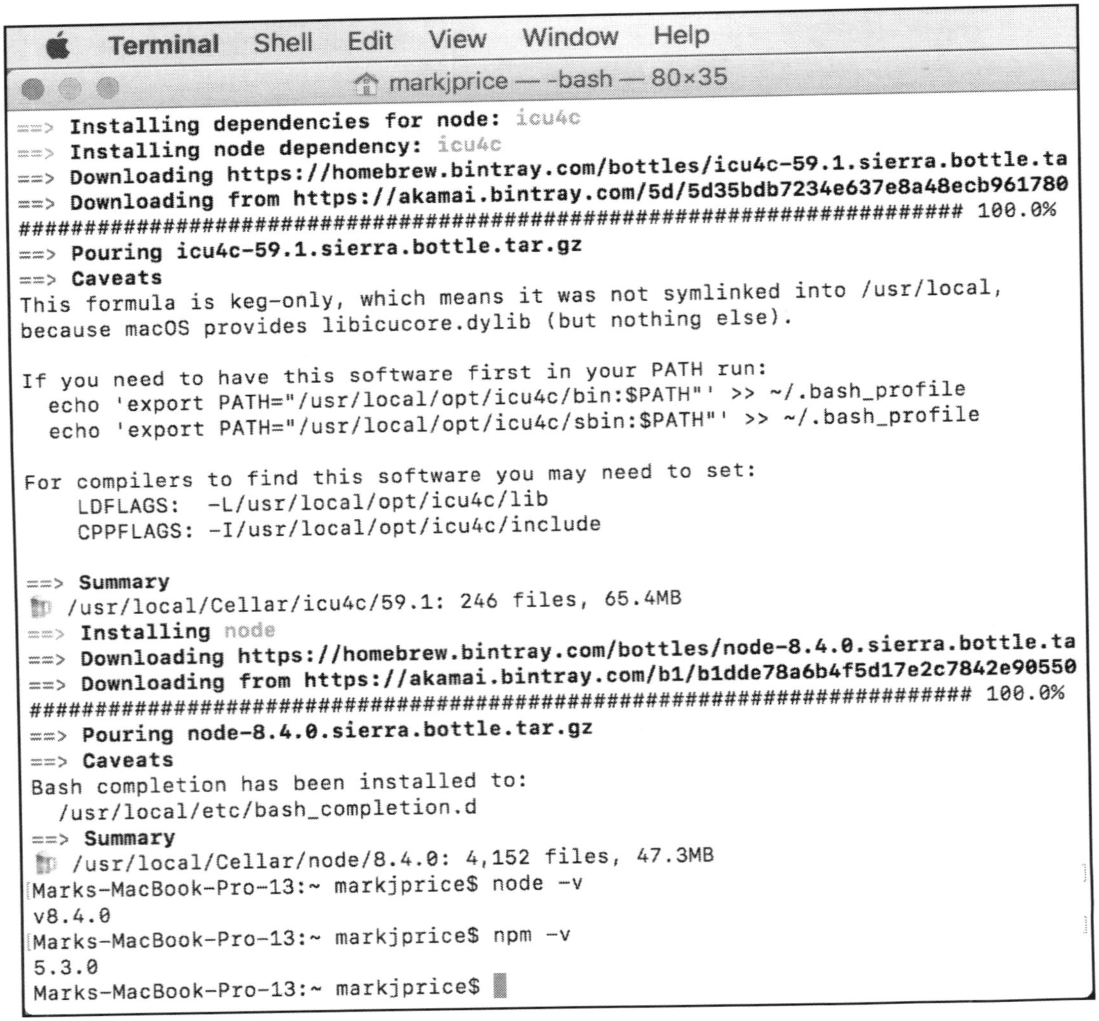

```
Terminal  Shell  Edit  View  Window  Help
markjprice — -bash — 80×35
==> Installing dependencies for node: icu4c
==> Installing node dependency: icu4c
==> Downloading https://homebrew.bintray.com/bottles/icu4c-59.1.sierra.bottle.ta
==> Downloading from https://akamai.bintray.com/5d/5d35bdb7234e637e8a48ecb961780
######################################################################## 100.0%
==> Pouring icu4c-59.1.sierra.bottle.tar.gz
==> Caveats
This formula is keg-only, which means it was not symlinked into /usr/local,
because macOS provides libicucore.dylib (but nothing else).

If you need to have this software first in your PATH run:
  echo 'export PATH="/usr/local/opt/icu4c/bin:$PATH"' >> ~/.bash_profile
  echo 'export PATH="/usr/local/opt/icu4c/sbin:$PATH"' >> ~/.bash_profile

For compilers to find this software you may need to set:
    LDFLAGS:  -L/usr/local/opt/icu4c/lib
    CPPFLAGS: -I/usr/local/opt/icu4c/include

==> Summary
/usr/local/Cellar/icu4c/59.1: 246 files, 65.4MB
==> Installing node
==> Downloading https://homebrew.bintray.com/bottles/node-8.4.0.sierra.bottle.ta
==> Downloading from https://akamai.bintray.com/b1/b1dde78a6b4f5d17e2c7842e90550
######################################################################## 100.0%
==> Pouring node-8.4.0.sierra.bottle.tar.gz
==> Caveats
Bash completion has been installed to:
  /usr/local/etc/bash_completion.d
==> Summary
/usr/local/Cellar/node/8.4.0: 4,152 files, 47.3MB
Marks-MacBook-Pro-13:~ markjprice$ node -v
v8.4.0
Marks-MacBook-Pro-13:~ markjprice$ npm -v
5.3.0
Marks-MacBook-Pro-13:~ markjprice$
```

## Installing the Visual Studio Code extension for C#

The C# for Visual Studio Code extension is not necessary, but it provides IntelliSense as you type, so it's very handy to install.

Launch **Visual Studio Code** and click on the **Extensions** icon, or go to **View** | **Extensions**, or press *Cmd* + *Shift* + *X*.

C# is the most popular extension, so you should see it at the top of the list, as shown in the following screenshot:

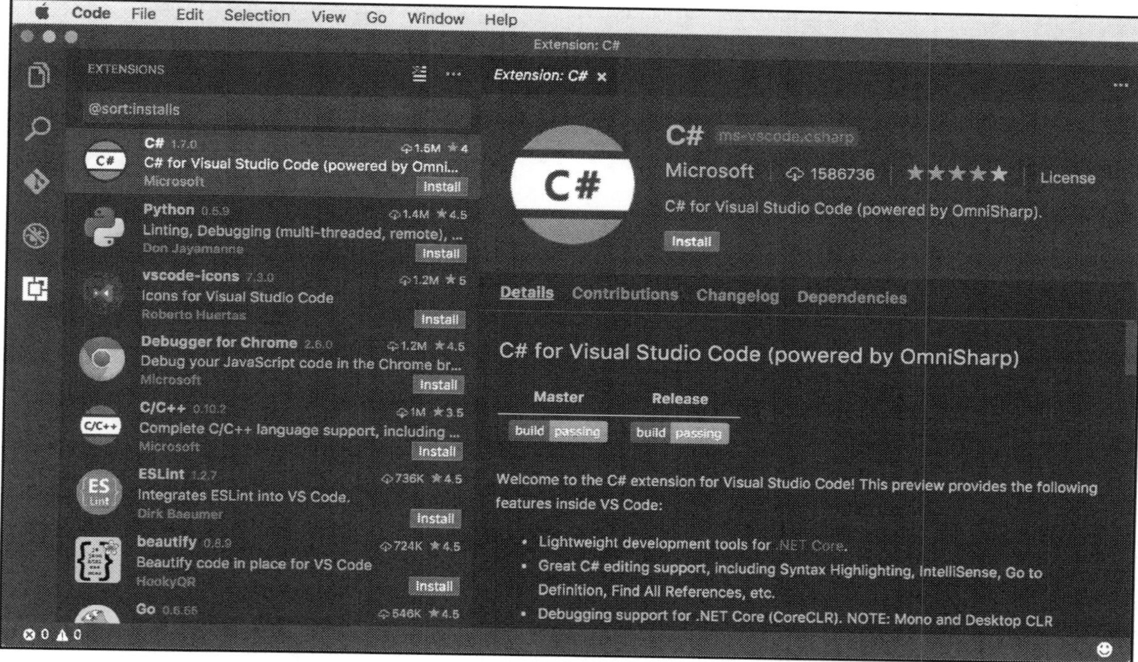


Click on **Install**, and then click on **Reload**, to reload the window and activate the extension.

## Installing Visual Studio for Mac

In November 2016, Microsoft released a preview version of Visual Studio for Mac. Initially, it could only be used to create Xamarin mobile apps, because it is a fork of the Xamarin Studio product. The final release version, available since May 2017, has support for creating .NET Standard 2.0 class libraries, ASP.NET Core web applications and services, and console apps, so it can be used to complete (almost) all of the exercises in this book.

Although Visual Studio 2017 on Windows can be used to create mobile apps for iOS and Android, only Xcode running on macOS or OS X can compile iOS apps, so it is my opinion that a developer might as well use the native Visual Studio for Mac to create mobile apps.

### Installing Xcode

If you have not already installed Xcode on your Mac, install it now from the App Store.

On the Apple menu, choose **App Store...**.

In the **App Store**, enter `xcode` in the **Search** box, and one of the first results will be **Xcode**, as shown in the following screenshot:

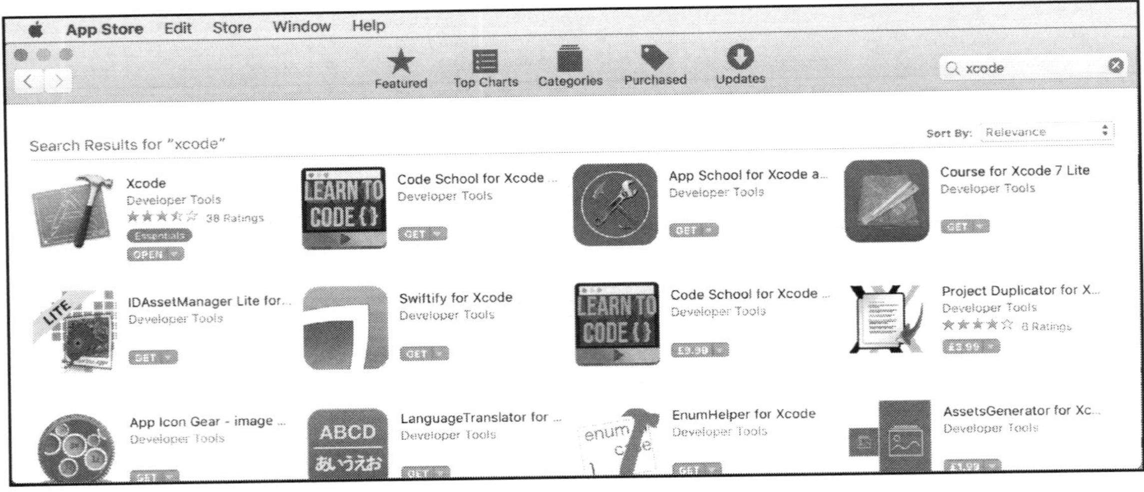


Click on **Get**, and wait for Xcode to install.

# Downloading and installing Visual Studio for Mac

You can download and install Visual Studio for Mac from the following link:

`https://www.visualstudio.com/vs/visual-studio-mac/`

In the **Visual Studio for Mac Installer**, accept the License Terms and the Privacy Statement, choose to install all components, and then click on **Continue**, as shown in the following screenshot:

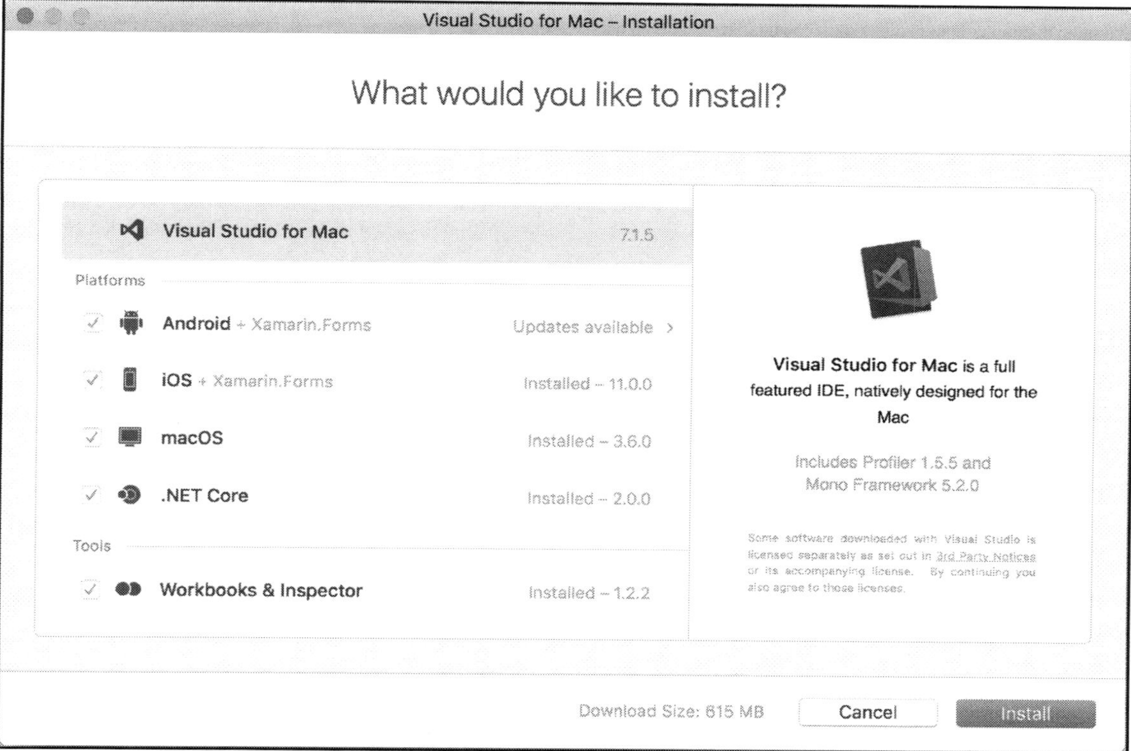


Click on **Continue**, and then click on **Install**.

Agree to the license terms for the components, such as the Android SDK, click on **Continue**, and wait for Visual Studio for Mac to fully install.

Start Visual Studio for Mac to see the **Welcome Page**, as shown in the following screenshot:

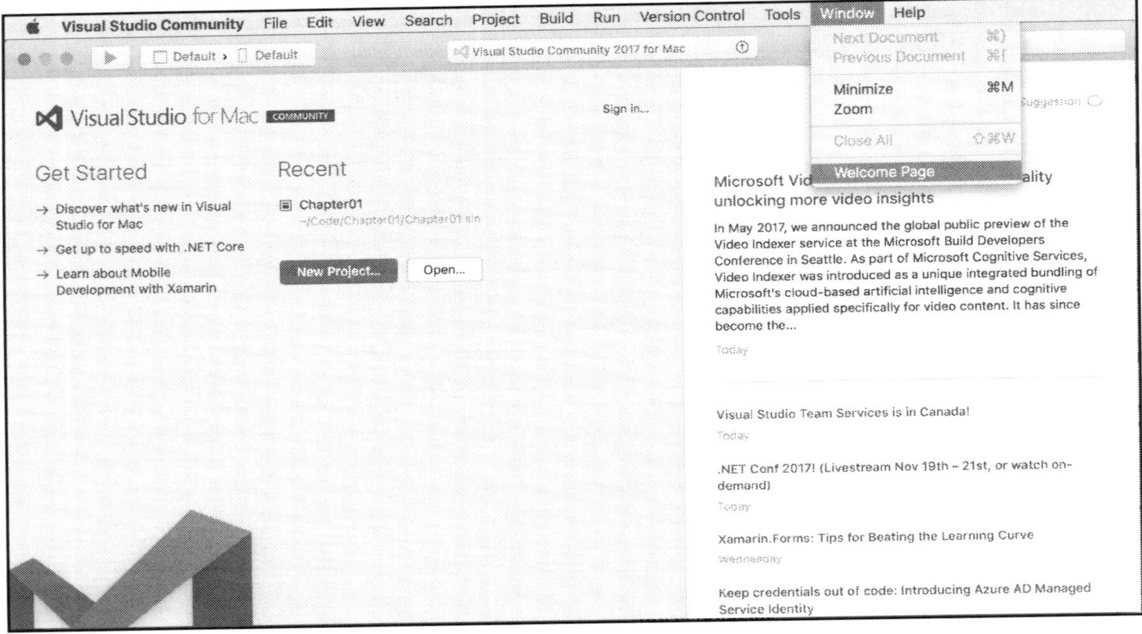


If you are prompted to update components, then click on **Restart and Install Updates**.

Now that you have installed and set up your development environment, you will learn some background about .NET before diving in to writing code.

# Understanding .NET

.NET Framework, .NET Core, .NET Standard, and .NET Native are related and overlapping platforms for developers to build applications and services upon.

# Understanding .NET Framework

Microsoft's .NET Framework is a development platform that includes a **Common Language Runtime (CLR)** that manages the execution of code, and provides a rich library of classes to build applications.

Microsoft designed .NET Framework to have the possibility of being cross-platform, but Microsoft put their implementation effort into making it work best with Windows.

Practically speaking, .NET Framework is Windows-only, and a legacy platform.

## Understanding the Mono and Xamarin projects

Third parties developed a .NET implementation named the Mono project that you can read more about at the following link:
`http://www.mono-project.com/`

**Mono** is cross-platform, but it fell well behind the official implementation of .NET Framework. It has found a niche as the foundation of the **Xamarin** mobile platform.

Microsoft purchased Xamarin in 2016 and now gives away what used to be an expensive Xamarin extension for free with Visual Studio 2017. Microsoft renamed the **Xamarin Studio** development tool to **Visual Studio for Mac**, and has given it the ability to create ASP.NET Core Web API services. Xamarin is targeted at mobile development and building cloud services to support mobile apps.

## Understanding .NET Core

Today, we live in a truly cross-platform world. Modern mobile and cloud development has made Windows a much less important operating system. So, Microsoft has been working on an effort to decouple .NET from its close ties with Windows.

While rewriting .NET to be truly cross-platform, Microsoft has taken the opportunity to refactor .NET to remove major parts that are no longer considered **core**.

This new product is branded as **.NET Core**, which includes a cross-platform implementation of the CLR known as **CoreCLR**, and a streamlined library of classes known as **CoreFX**.

Scott Hunter, Microsoft Partner Director Program Manager for .NET, says, "Forty percent of our .NET Core customers are brand-new developers to the platform, which is what we want with .NET Core. We want to bring new people in."

The following table shows when important versions of .NET Core were released, and Microsoft's schedule for the next major release:

| Version | Released |
| --- | --- |
| .NET Core RC1 | November 2015 |
| .NET Core 1.0 | June 2016 |
| .NET Core 1.1 | November 2016 |
| .NET Core 1.0.4 and .NET Core 1.1.1 | March 2017 |
| .NET Core 2.0 | August 2017 |
| .NET Core for UWP in Windows 10 Fall Creators Update | October 2017 |
| .NET Core 2.1 | Q1 2018 |

If you need to work with .NET Core 1.0 and 1.1, then I recommend that you read the announcement for .NET Core 1.1, although the information at the following URL is useful for all .NET Core developers: `https://blogs.msdn.microsoft.com/dotnet/2016/11/16/announcing-net-core-1-1/`

.NET Core is much smaller than the current version of .NET Framework because a lot has been removed.

For example, **Windows Forms** and **Windows Presentation Foundation** (**WPF**) can be used to build **graphical user interface** (**GUI**) applications, but they are tightly bound to Windows, so they have been removed from .NET Core. The latest technology used to build Windows apps is **Universal Windows Platform** (**UWP**), and UWP is built on a custom version of .NET Core. You will learn about it in `Chapter 17`, *Building Windows Apps Using XAML and Fluent Design*.

**ASP.NET Web Forms** and **Windows Communication Foundation** (**WCF**) are old web application and service technologies that fewer developers choose to use for new development projects today, so they have also been removed from .NET Core. Instead, developers prefer to use ASP.NET MVC and ASP.NET Web API. These two technologies have been refactored and combined into a new product that runs on .NET Core, named **ASP.NET Core**. You will learn about **ASP.NET Core MVC** in `Chapter 15`, *Building Web Sites Using ASP.NET Core MVC*, **ASP.NET Core Razor Pages** in `Chapter 14`, *Building Web Sites Using ASP.NET Core Razor Pages*, and **ASP.NET Core Web API** and **Single Page Applications** (**SPAs**) such as Angular and React in `Chapter 16`, *Building Web Services and Applications Using ASP.NET Core*.

The **Entity Framework** (**EF**) 6 is an object-relational mapping technology to work with data stored in relational databases such as Oracle and Microsoft SQL Server. It has gained baggage over the years, so the cross-platform version has been slimmed down and named **Entity Framework Core**. You will learn about it in `Chapter 11`, *Working with Databases Using Entity Framework Core*.

In addition to removing large pieces from .NET Framework to make .NET Core, Microsoft has componentized .NET Core into NuGet packages: small chunks of functionality that can be deployed independently.

Microsoft's primary goal is not to make .NET Core smaller than .NET Framework. The goal is to componentize .NET Core to support modern technologies and to have fewer dependencies, so that deployment requires only those packages that your application needs.

# Understanding .NET Standard

The situation with .NET today is that there are three forked .NET platforms, all controlled by Microsoft:

- .NET Framework
- .NET Core
- Xamarin

Each have different strengths and weaknesses because they are designed for different scenarios. This has led to the problem that a developer must learn three platforms, each with annoying quirks and limitations.

So, Microsoft defined .NET Standard 2.0: a specification for a set of APIs that all .NET platforms must implement. You cannot install .NET Standard 2.0 in the same way that you cannot install HTML5. To use HTML5, you must install a web browser that implements the HTML5 specification. To use .NET Standard 2.0, you must install a .NET platform that implements the .NET Standard 2.0 specification.

.NET Standard 2.0 is implemented by the latest versions of .NET Framework, .NET Core, and Xamarin. .NET Standard 2.0 makes it much easier for developers to share code between any flavor of .NET.

For .NET Core 2.0, this adds many of the missing APIs that developers need to port old code written for .NET Framework to the cross-platform .NET Core. However, some APIs are *implemented*, but throw an exception to indicate to a developer that they should not actually be used! This is usually due to differences in the operating system on which you run .NET Core. You will learn how to handle these exceptions in `Chapter 2`, *Speaking C#*.

The following diagram summarizes how the three variants of .NET (sometimes known as App Models) will share the common .NET Standard 2.0 and infrastructure:

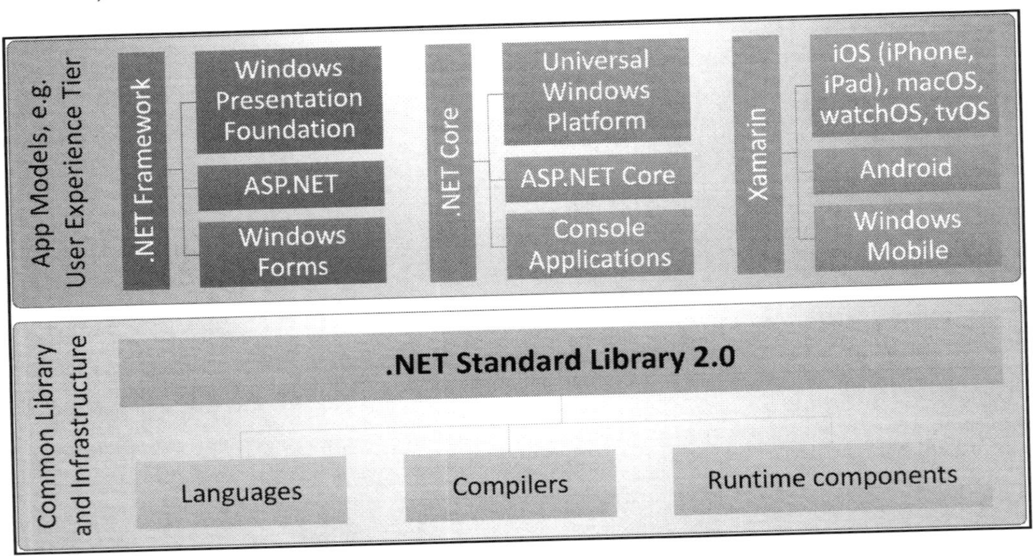


The first edition of this book focused on .NET Core, but used .NET Framework when important or useful features had not yet been implemented in .NET Core. Visual Studio 2015 was used for most examples, with Visual Studio Code shown only briefly.

The second edition was almost completely purged of all .NET Framework code examples.

The third edition completes the job. It has been rewritten so that all of the code is pure .NET Core and can be written with Visual Studio 2017, Visual Studio for Mac, or Visual Studio Code on any supported operating system. The only exceptions are the last two chapters. In `Chapter 17`, *Building Windows Apps Using XAML and Fluent Design*, you will use .NET Core for UWP, which requires Visual Studio 2017 running on Windows 10, and in `Chapter 18`, *Building Mobile Apps Using XAML and Xamarin.Forms*, you will use Xamarin instead of .NET Core.

## Understanding .NET Native

Another .NET initiative is .NET Native. This compiles C# code to native CPU instructions **ahead-of-time (AoT)**, rather than using the CLR to compile **intermediate language (IL)** code **just-in-time (JIT)** to native code later.

.NET Native improves execution speed and reduces the memory footprint for applications. It supports the following:

- UWP apps for Windows 10, Windows 10 Mobile, Xbox One, HoloLens, and **Internet of Things (IoT)** devices such as Raspberry Pi
- Server-side web development with ASP.NET Core
- Console applications for use on the command line

## Comparing .NET technologies

The following table summarizes and compares .NET technologies:

| Technology | Feature set | Compiles to | Host OSes |
|---|---|---|---|
| .NET Framework | Both legacy and modern | IL code | Windows only |
| Xamarin | Mobile only | IL code | iOS, Android, Windows Mobile |
| .NET Core | Modern only | IL code | Windows, macOS, Linux |
| .NET Native | Modern only | Native code | Windows, macOS, Linux |

# Writing and compiling code using the .NET Core CLI tool

When you install Visual Studio 2017, Visual Studio for Mac, or the .NET Core SDK, a **Command-Line Interface (CLI)** tool named `dotnet` is installed, as well as the .NET Core runtime.

Before we use CLI tools, such as `dotnet`, we need to write some code!

# Writing code using a simple text editor

If you are using Windows, start Notepad.

If you are using macOS, launch TextEdit. Navigate to **TextEdit | Preferences**, clear the **Smart quotes** check box, and then close the dialog. Navigate to **Format | Make Plain Text**.

Alternatively, run your favorite plain text editor.

Enter the following code:

```
class MyApp { static void Main() {
 System.Console.WriteLine("Hello, C#!"); } }
```

C# is case sensitive, meaning that you must type uppercase and lowercase characters exactly as shown in the preceding code. C# is not whitespace sensitive, meaning that it does not care if you use tabs, spaces, or carriage-returns to layout your code however you like.

You can type the code all in one line, or spread it out over multiple lines and indent your lines. For example, the following code would also compile and have the same output:

```
class
      MyApp       {
 static                    void
Main          (){System.       Console.
    WriteLine(       "Hello, C#!");         }       }
```

Of course, it's best to write your code in a way that other programmers, and yourself months or years later, can clearly read!

## If you are using Windows Notepad

In Notepad, navigate to **File | Save As...**.

In the **Save As** dialog, change to drive `C:` (or any drive which you want to use to save your projects), click on the **New folder** button, and name the folder `Code`. Open the `Code` folder, and click on the **New folder** button, and name the folder `Chapter01`. Open the `Chapter01` folder, and click on the **New folder** button, and name the folder `HelloCS`. Open the `HelloCS` folder.

In the **Save as type** field, select **All Files** from the drop-down list to avoid appending the `.txt` file extension, and enter the filename as `MyApp.cs`, as shown in the following screenshot:

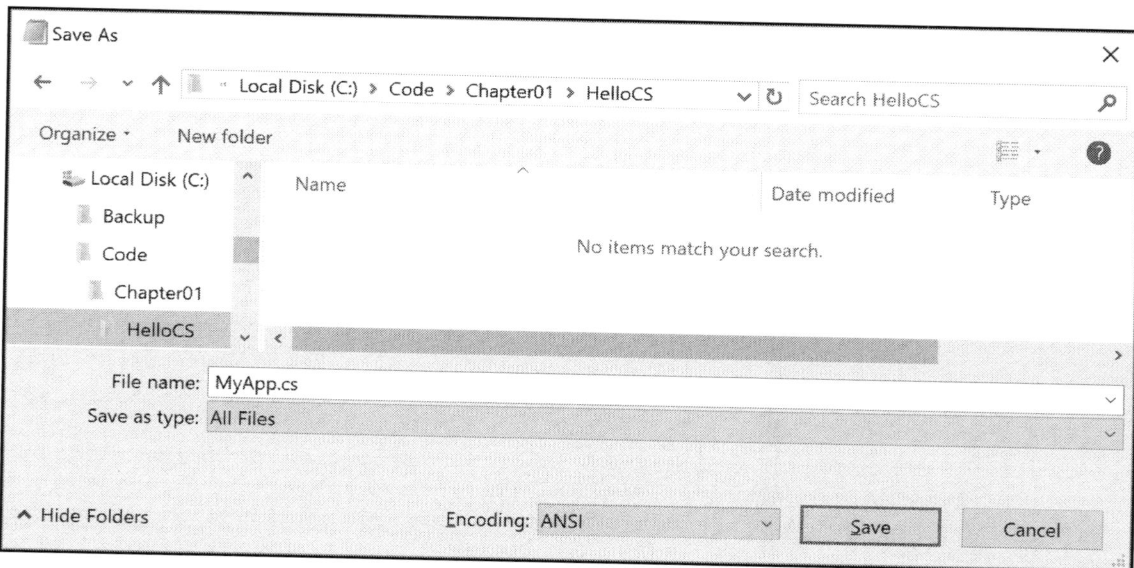


Your code in Notepad should look something like the following screenshot:

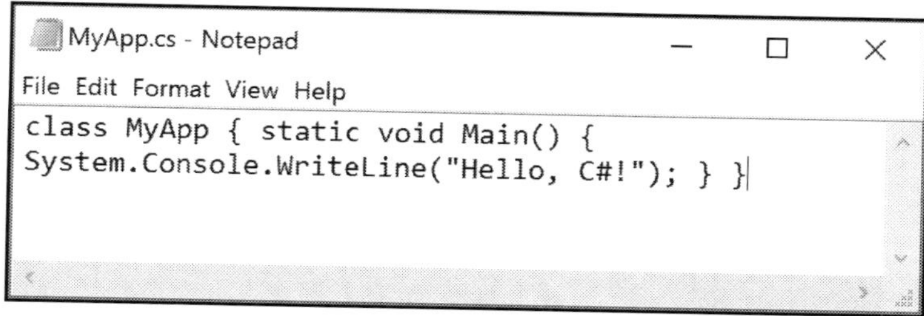

## If you are using macOS TextEdit

In TextEdit, navigate to **File** | **Save...**, or press *Cmd* + *S*.

In the **Save** dialog, change to your *user* folder (mine is named `markjprice`) or any directory in which you want to use to save your projects, click on the **New Folder** button, and name the folder `Code`. Open the `Code` folder, and click on the **New Folder** button, and name the folder `Chapter01`. Open the `Chapter01` folder, and click on the **New Folder** button, and name the folder `HelloCS`. Open the `HelloCS` folder.

In the **Plain Text Encoding** field, select **Unicode (UTF-8)** from the drop-down list, uncheck the box for **If no extension is provided, use ".txt"** to avoid appending the `.txt` file extension, enter the filename as `MyApp.cs`, and click on **Save**.

# Creating and compiling apps using the .NET Core CLI tool

If you are using Windows, start **Command Prompt**.

If you are using macOS, launch **Terminal**.

At the prompt, enter the `dotnet` command and note the output, as shown in the following screenshot on macOS:

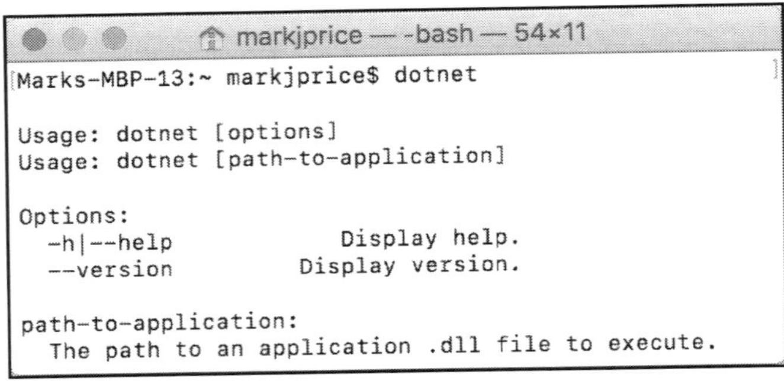

The output from the `dotnet` command-line tool will be identical on Windows, macOS, and Linux.

## Creating a console application at Command Prompt

Enter the following commands at the prompt to do the following:

- Change to the folder for the project
- Create a new console application in the directory
- List the files that the `dotnet` command-line tool created

If you are using Windows, in **Command Prompt**, enter the following:

```
cd C:\Code\Chapter01\HelloCS
dotnet new console
dir
```

If you are using macOS, in **Terminal**, enter this:

```
cd Code/Chapter01/HelloCS
dotnet new console
ls
```

You should see that the `dotnet` tool has created two new files for you, as shown in the following screenshot on Windows:

- `Program.cs`: Source code for a simple console application
- `HelloCS.csproj`: A project file that lists dependencies and project-related configuration:

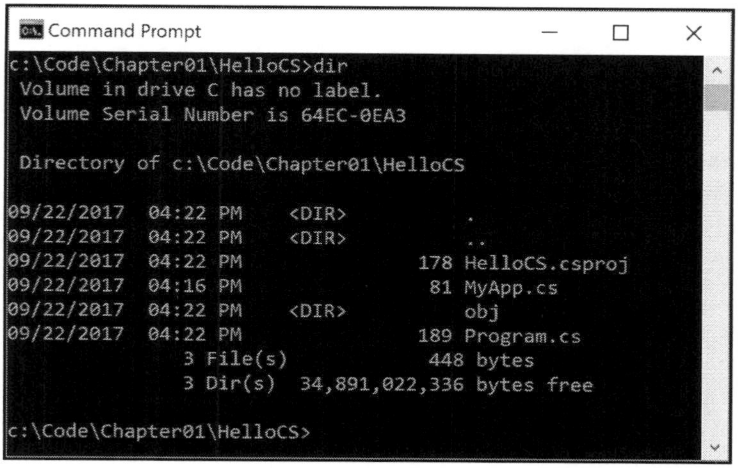

```
Command Prompt
c:\Code\Chapter01\HelloCS>dir
 Volume in drive C has no label.
 Volume Serial Number is 64EC-0EA3

 Directory of c:\Code\Chapter01\HelloCS

09/22/2017  04:22 PM    <DIR>          .
09/22/2017  04:22 PM    <DIR>          ..
09/22/2017  04:22 PM               178 HelloCS.csproj
09/22/2017  04:16 PM                81 MyApp.cs
09/22/2017  04:22 PM    <DIR>          obj
09/22/2017  04:22 PM               189 Program.cs
               3 File(s)            448 bytes
               3 Dir(s)  34,891,022,336 bytes free

c:\Code\Chapter01\HelloCS>
```

For this example, we must delete the file named `Program.cs`, since we have already created our own class in the file named `MyApp.cs`.

If you are using Windows, in **Command Prompt**, enter the following command:

```
del Program.cs
```

If you are using macOS, in **Terminal**, enter this:

```
rm Program.cs
```

In all future examples, we will use the `Program.cs` file generated by the tool rather than manually create our own.

## Restoring packages, compiling code, and running the application

At the prompt, enter the `dotnet run` command.

After a few seconds, all the packages needed by our code will be downloaded, the source code will be compiled, and your application will run, as shown in the following screenshot on macOS:

```
HelloCS — -bash — 80×6
Marks-MBP-13:hellocs markjprice$ ls
HelloCS.csproj  MyApp.cs        Program.cs      obj
Marks-MBP-13:hellocs markjprice$ rm Program.cs
Marks-MBP-13:hellocs markjprice$ dotnet run
Hello, C#!
Marks-MBP-13:hellocs markjprice$
```

Your source code, the `MyApp.cs` file, has been compiled into an assembly named `HelloCS.dll` in the `bin/Debug/netcoreapp2.0` subfolder. (Browse your filesystem for it if you like, I'll be waiting here for you to come back and continue.)

For now, this assembly can only be executed by the `dotnet run` command. In `Chapter 7`, *Understanding and Packaging .NET Standard Types*, you will learn how to package your compiled assemblies for use on any operating system that supports .NET Core.

## Fixing compiler errors

If the compiler displays errors, read them carefully, and fix them in your text editor. Save your changes and try again.

At the prompt, you can press the up and down arrows on your keyboard to cycle through previous commands you have entered.

A typical error might be using the wrong case, a missing semicolon at the end of a line, or a mismatched pair of curly braces. For example, if you mistyped a lowercase `m` for the `Main` method, you would see the following error message:

```
error CS5001: Program does not contain a static 'Main' method
suitable for an entry point
```

## Understanding intermediate language

The C# compiler (named **Roslyn**) used by the `dotnet` CLI tool converts your C# source code into IL code, and stores the IL in an **assembly** (a DLL or EXE file).

IL code statements are like assembly language instructions, but they are executed by .NET Core's virtual machine, known as the **CoreCLR**.

At runtime, the CoreCLR loads the IL code from the assembly, JIT compiles it into native CPU instructions, and then it is executed by the CPU on your machine.

The benefit of this two-step compilation process is that Microsoft can create CLRs for Linux and macOS as well as for Windows. The same IL code runs everywhere because of the second compilation process that generates code for the native operating system and CPU instruction set.

Regardless of which language the source is written in, for example, C# or F#, all .NET applications use IL code for their instructions stored in an assembly. Microsoft and others provide disassembler tools that can open an assembly and reveal this IL code.

Actually, not all .NET applications use IL code! Some use .NET Native's compiler to generate native code instead of IL code, improving performance and reducing memory footprint, but at the cost of portability.

# Writing and compiling code using Visual Studio 2017

We will now create a similar application using Visual Studio 2017. If you have chosen to use Visual Studio for Mac or Visual Studio Code, I still recommend that you review these instructions and screenshots because Visual Studio for Mac and Visual Studio Code have similar, although not as extensive, features.

I have been training students to use Visual Studio for over a decade, and I am always surprised at how many programmers fail to use the tool to their advantage.

Over the next few pages, I will walk you through typing a line of code. It may seem redundant, but you will benefit from seeing what help and information Visual Studio provides as you enter your code. If you want to become a fast and accurate coder, letting Visual Studio write most of your code for you is a huge benefit!

## Writing code using Microsoft Visual Studio 2017

Start Visual Studio 2017.

Navigate to **File** | **New** | **Project...** or press *Ctrl* + *Shift* + *N*.

From the **Installed** list on the left, expand **Visual C#**, and choose **.NET Core**. In the list at the center, choose **Console App (.NET Core)**. Enter the name `WelcomeDotNetCore`, set the location to `C:\Code`, enter `Chapter01` as the solution name, and click on **OK** or press *Enter*, as shown in the following screenshot:

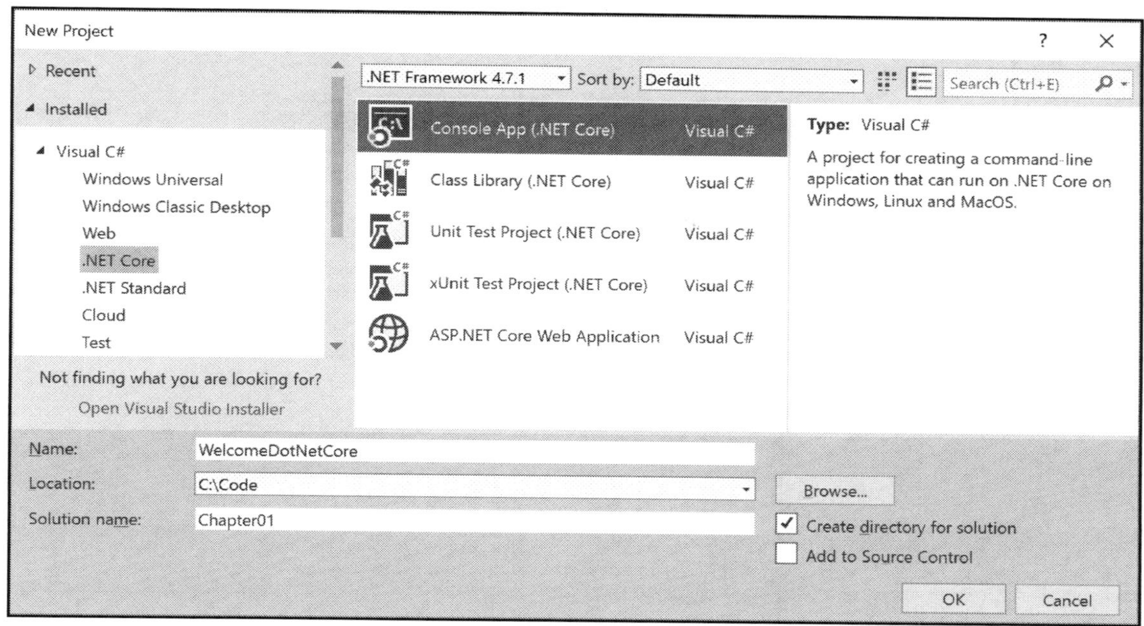

Ignore the target set to .NET Framework 4.7.1. That drop-down list box does not affect .NET Core projects!

In the code editor, delete the statement on line **9** that says the following: `Console.WriteLine("Hello World!");`

Inside the `Main` method, type the letters `sy`, as shown in the following screenshot, and note the IntelliSense menu that appears:

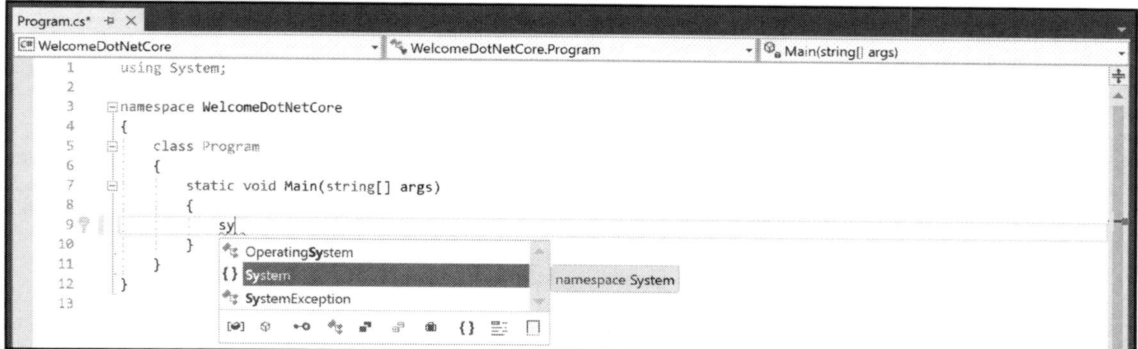

IntelliSense shows a filtered list of **keywords**, **namespaces**, and **types** that contain the letters `sy` and highlights the one that starts with `sy`, which happens to be the namespace that we want—`System`.

Type a dot (also known as decimal point or full stop).

IntelliSense automatically completes the word `System` for you, enters the dot, and displays a list of types, such as `AggregateException` and `Action`, in the `System` namespace, as shown in the following screenshot:

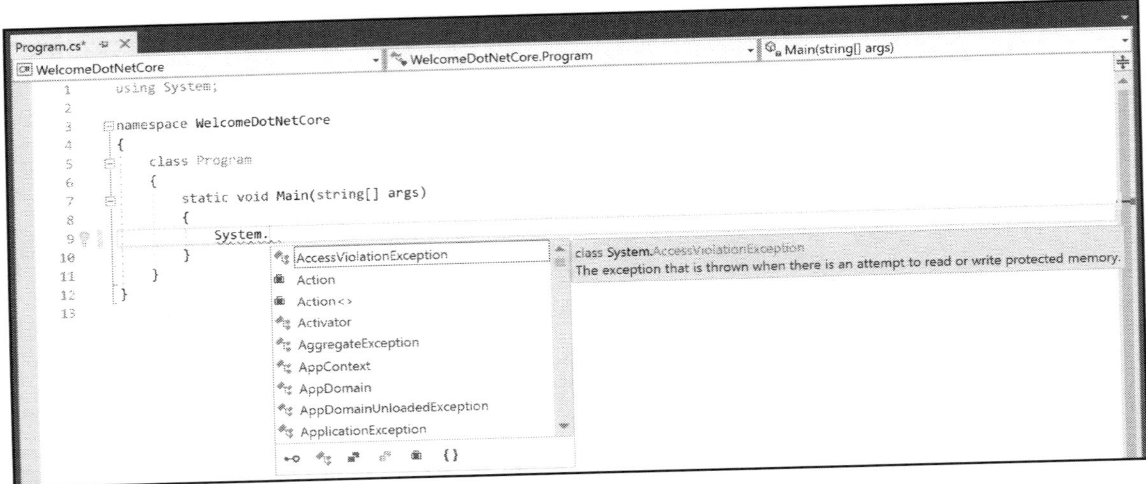


Type the letters `con`, IntelliSense shows a list of matching types and namespaces, as shown in the following screenshot:

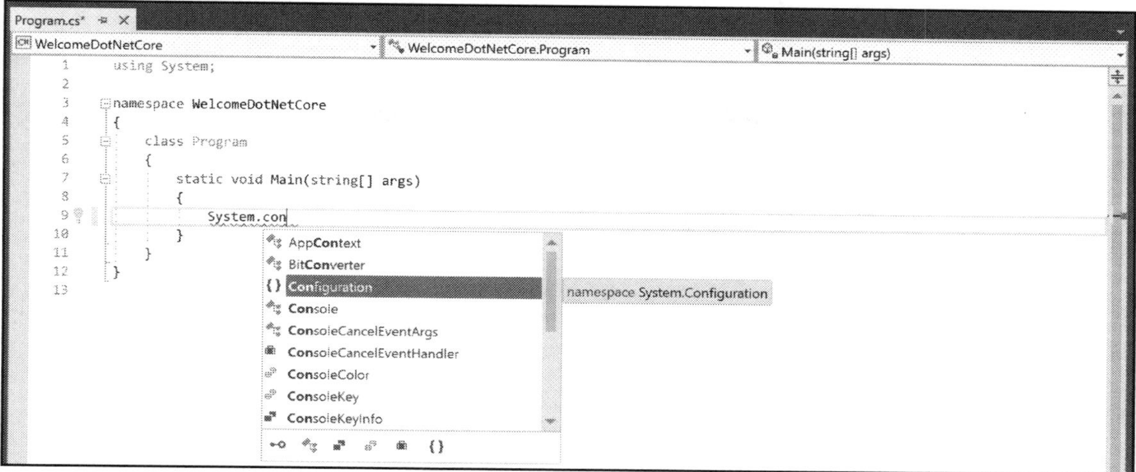


We want `Console`. Press the down arrow on your keyboard to highlight it. When `Console` is selected, type a dot.

IntelliSense shows a list of the **members** of the `Console` class, as shown in the following screenshot:

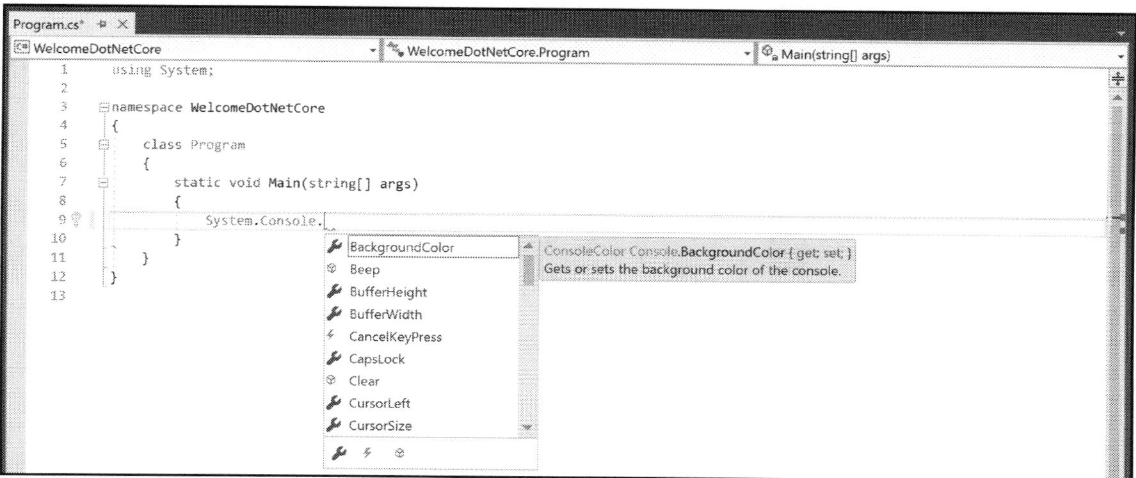

**Members** include **properties** (attributes of an object, such as `BackgroundColor`), **methods** (actions the object can perform, such as `Beep`), **events**, and other related things.

Type the letters `wl`. IntelliSense shows two matching members containing these letters in title case, `WindowLeft` and `WriteLine`, as shown in the following screenshot:

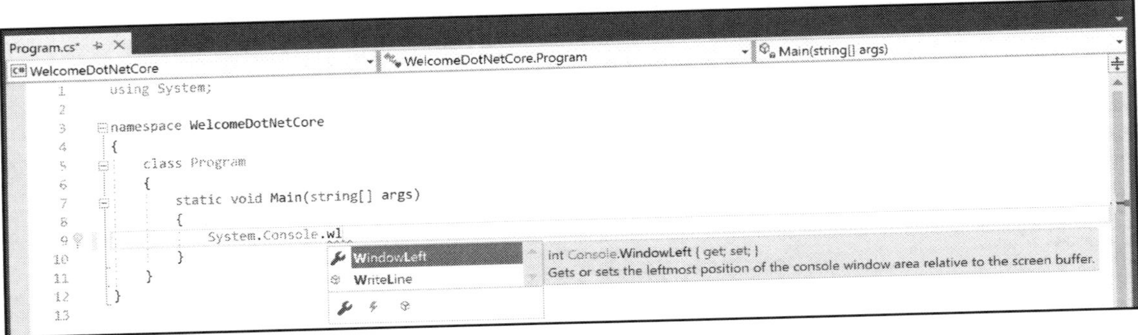


Use the down arrow to highlight `WriteLine` and then type an open parenthesis `(`.

IntelliSense autocompletes `WriteLine` and enters a pair of parentheses.

You will also see a tooltip telling you that the `WriteLine` method has 18 variations, as shown in the following screenshot:

```
Program.cs*
WelcomeDotNetCore    WelcomeDotNetCore.Program    Main(string[] args)
using System;

namespace WelcomeDotNetCore
{
    class Program
    {
        static void Main(string[] args)
        {
            System.Console.WriteLine()
        }   ▲ 1 of 18 ▼ void Console.WriteLine()
    }               Writes the current line terminator to the standard output stream.
}
```

Type a double quote (`"`). IntelliSense enters a pair of double quotes for you and leaves the keyboard cursor in between them.

Type the text `Welcome, .NET Core!`, as shown in the following screenshot:

```
Program.cs*  WelcomeDotNetCore  WelcomeDotNetCore.Program  Main(string[] args)
using System;

namespace WelcomeDotNetCore
{
    class Program
    {
        static void Main(string[] args)
        {
            System.Console.WriteLine("Welcome, .NET Core!")
        }
    }
}
```

The red squiggle at the end of the line indicates an error because every C# statement must end in a semicolon. Move the cursor to the end of the line and type a semicolon to fix the error.

# Compiling code using Visual Studio 2017

Navigate to **Debug** | **Start Without Debugging** or press *Ctrl* + *F5*.

Visual Studio's status bar tells us that **Build started...**, then **Build succeeded**, and then your console application runs in a Command Prompt window, as shown in the following screenshot:

To save space in this book and to make the output clearer, I will usually not include screenshots of output from console applications as I did in the previous screenshot. Instead, I will show the output like this:

```
Welcome, .NET Core!
```

# Fixing mistakes with the error list

Let's make two deliberate errors:

- Change the `M` of the `Main` method to the lowercase letter `m`
- Delete the `e` at the end of the method name, `WriteLine`

Navigate to **Debug** | **Start Without Debugging** or press *Ctrl* + *F5*.

After a few seconds, the status bar tells us that **Build failed** and an error message appears. Click on **No**.

**Error List** becomes active, as shown in the following screenshot:

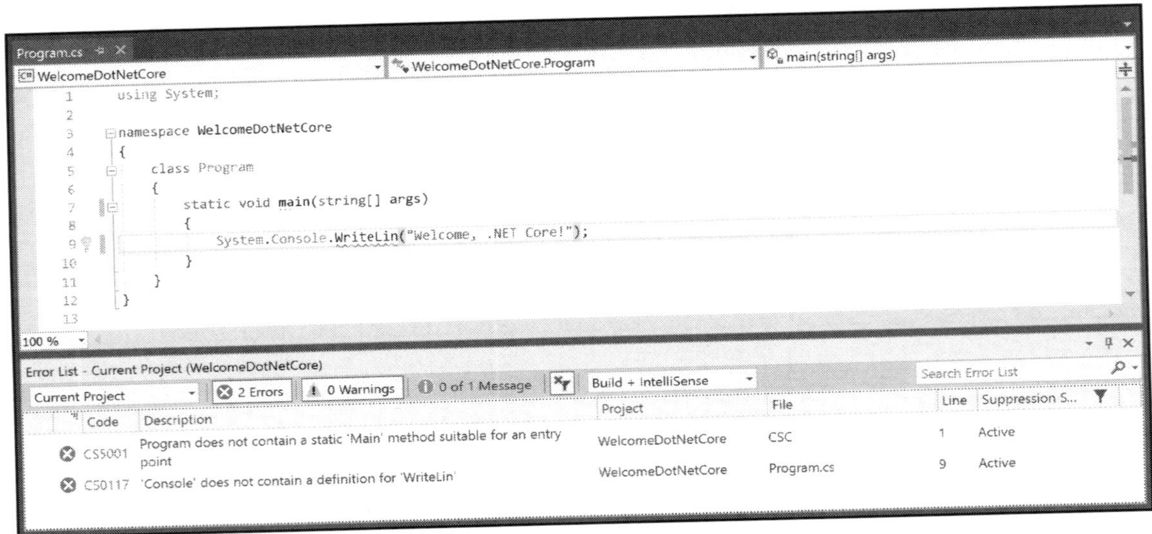


The list can be filtered to show **Errors**, **Warnings**, and **Messages** by clicking on the toggle buttons in the toolbar at the top of the **Error List** window.

If an error shows a file and a line number, for example **File**: **Program.cs** and **Line**: **9**, then you can double-click on the error to jump to that line causing the problem.

If it's a more general error, such as the missing `Main` method, the compiler can't tell you a useful line number. You might want a method named `main` as well as a method named `Main` (remember that C# is case sensitive, so you're allowed to do that).

However, Visual Studio can also analyze your code and highlight suggestions with three small grey dots under a potential problem. When you click on the dotted statement, a light bulb appears, and if you click on it, it provides suggestions for improvements, such as telling you that method names should begin with an uppercase character, as shown in the following screenshot:

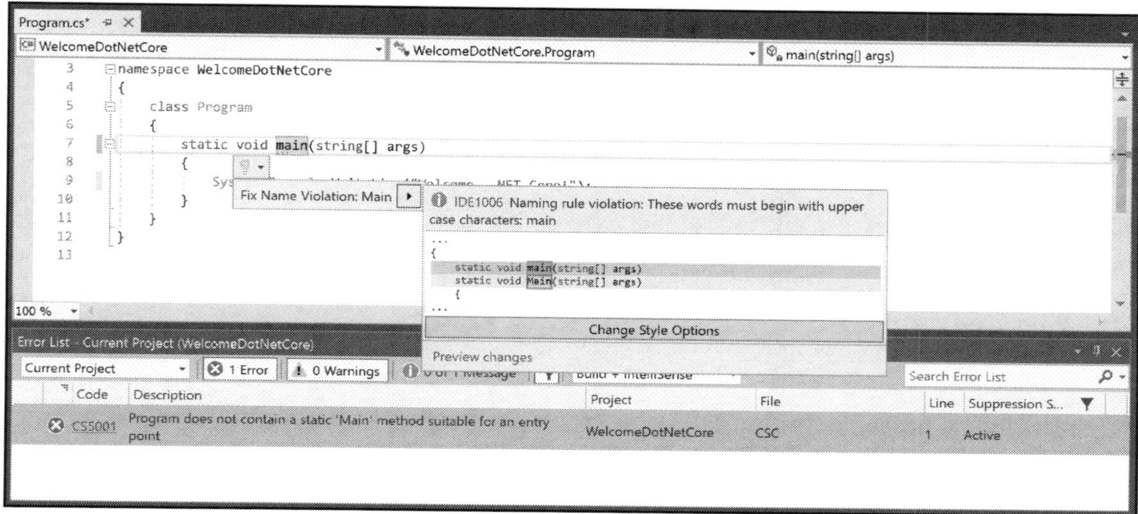


As shown in the preceding screenshot, fix the two errors, and rerun the application to ensure that it works before you continue. Note that the **Error List** window updates to show no errors.

# Adding existing projects to Visual Studio 2017

Earlier, you created a project using the `dotnet` CLI tool. Now that you have a solution in Visual Studio 2017, you might want to add the earlier project to the solution.

Navigate to **File** | **Add** | **Existing Project...**, browse to the `C:\Code\Chapter01\HelloCS` folder, and select the `HelloCS.csproj` file.

To be able to run this project, in **Solution Explorer**, right-click on **Solution 'Chapter01' (2 projects)**, and choose **Properties** or press *Alt* + *Enter*.

For the **Startup Project** option, click on **Current selection**, and then click on **OK**.

In **Solution Explorer**, click on any file inside the `HelloCS` project, and then press *Ctrl* + *F5*, or navigate to **Debug** | **Start Without Debugging**.

## Autoformatting code

Code is easier to read and understand if it is consistently indented and spaced out.

If your code can compile, then Visual Studio 2017 can automatically format it, nicely spaced and indented for you.

In **Solution Explorer**, double-click on the file named `MyApp.cs`, as shown in the following screenshot:

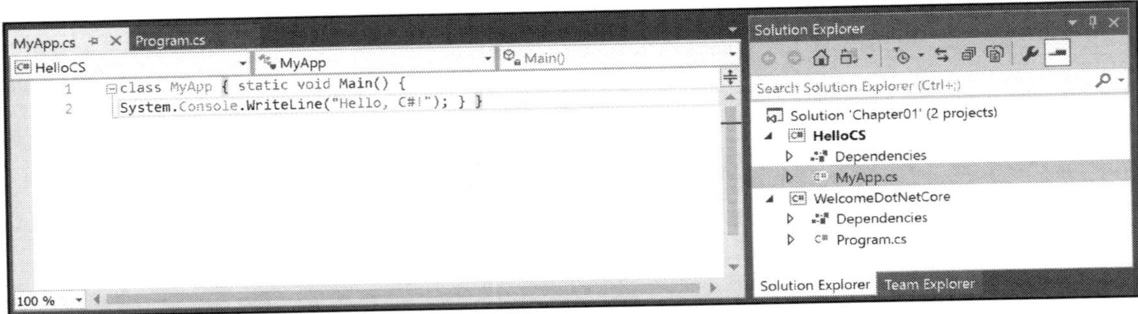


Navigate to **Build** | **Build HelloCS** or press *Shift* + *F6*, wait for your code to build, and then navigate to **Edit** | **Advanced** | **Format Document**, or press *Ctrl* + *E*, *D*. Your code will be autoformatted, as shown in the following screenshot:

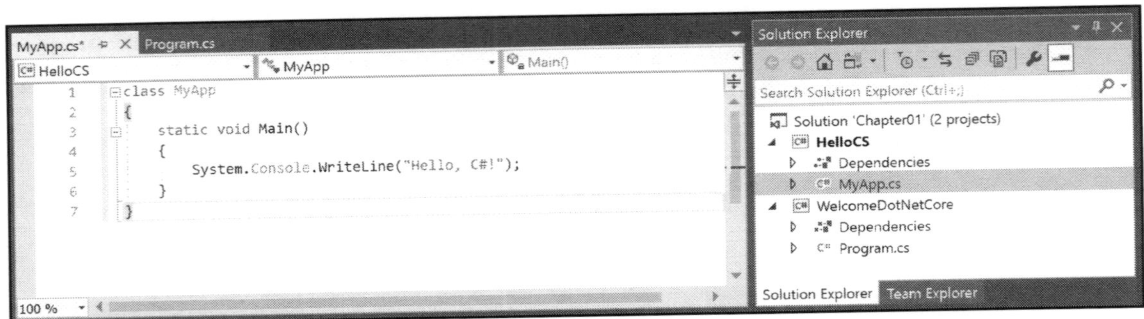

# Experimenting with C# Interactive

Although Visual Studio has always had an **Immediate** window with limited **Read-eval-print loop (REPL)** support, Visual Studio 2017 includes an enhanced window with full IntelliSense and color syntax code named **C# Interactive**.

In Visual Studio 2017, navigate to **View** | **Other Windows** | **C# Interactive**.

We will write some interactive code to download the **About** page from Microsoft's public website.

This is just an example. You don't need to understand the code yet!

At the **C# Interactive** prompt, we will enter commands to do the following:

- Reference the `System.Net.Http` assembly
- Import the `System.Net.Http` namespace
- Declare and instantiate an HTTP client variable
- Set the client's base address to Microsoft's website
- Asynchronously wait for a response to a GET request for the **About** page
- Read the status code returned by the web server
- Read the content type header
- Read the contents of the HTML page as a string

Type each of the following commands after the > prompt, and then press *Enter*:

```
> #r "System.Net.Http"
> using System.Net.Http;
> var client = new HttpClient();
> client.BaseAddress = new Uri("http://www.microsoft.com/");
> var response = await client.GetAsync("about");
> response.StatusCode
OK
> response.Content.Headers.GetValues("Content-Type")
string[1] { "text/html" }
> await response.Content.ReadAsStringAsync()
"<!DOCTYPE html ><html
xmlns:mscom="http://schemas.microsoft.com/CMSvNext"
xmlns:md="http://schemas.microsoft.com/mscom-data" lang="en"
xmlns="http://www.w3.org/1999/xhtml"><head><meta http-equiv="X-UA-
Compatible" content="IE=edge" /><meta charset="utf-8" /><meta
```

```
name="viewport" content="width=device-width, initial-scale=1.0"
/><link rel="shortcut icon"
href="//www.microsoft.com/favicon.ico?v2" /><script
type="text/javascript"
src="http://ajax.aspnetcdn.com/ajax/jQuery/jquery-
1.7.2.min.js">rn // Third party scripts and code linked to
or referenced from this website are licensed to you by the parties
that own such code, not by Microsoft. See ASP.NET Ajax CDN Terms of
Use - http://www.asp.net/ajaxlibrary/CDN.ashx.rn
</script><script type="text/javascript"
language="javascript">/*<![CDATA[*/if($(document).bind("mobileinit
",function(){$.mobile.autoInitializePage=!1}),navigator.userAgent.ma
tch(/IEMobile\/10\.0/)){var
msViewportStyle=document.createElement("style ...
```

The following screenshot shows what Visual Studio 2017 should look like after you've entered the preceding commands into the **C# Interactive** window:

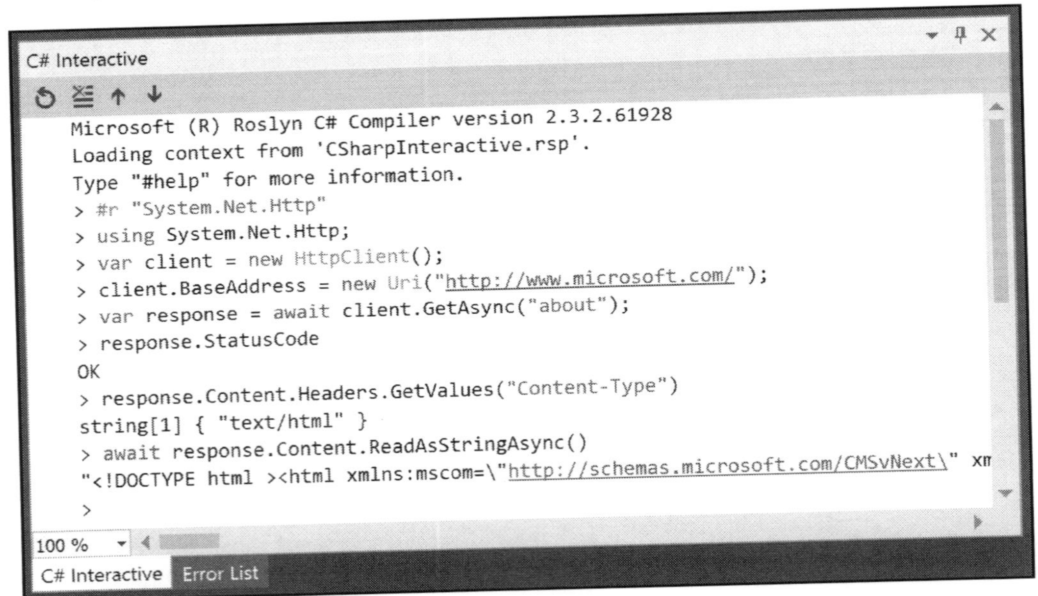

Roslyn is the name of the C# compiler. Roslyn version 1.0 was for C# 6. Roslyn version 2.0 was for C# 7. Roslyn 2.3 and later is for C# 7.1.

# Other useful windows

Visual Studio 2017 has lots of other useful windows, including the following:

- **Solution Explorer** for managing projects and files
- **Team Explorer** for source code management tools
- **Server Explorer** for managing database connections and resources to manage in Microsoft Azure

If you can't see a window you need, go to the **View** menu to make it reappear or learn its keyboard shortcut, few of such shortcuts are shown in the following screenshot:

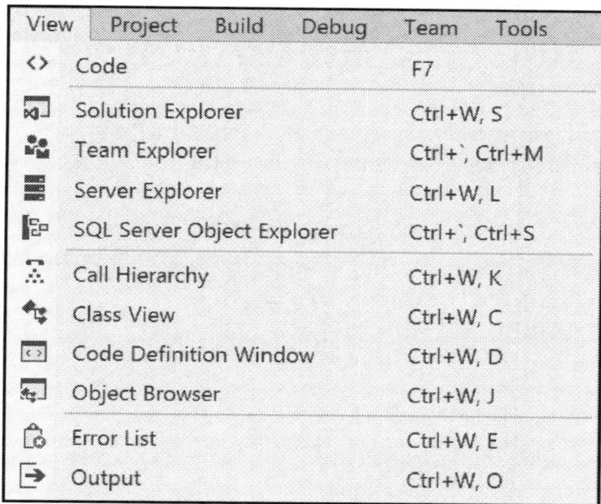

If your keyboard shortcuts are different from the ones in the preceding screenshot, it is because you picked a different set when you installed Visual Studio. You can reset your keyboard shortcuts to match the ones used in this book by clicking on the **Tools** menu, then clicking on **Import and Export Settings...**, choosing **Reset all settings**, and then choosing to reset to the **Visual C#** settings collection.

# Writing and compiling code using Visual Studio Code

The instructions and screenshots in this section are for macOS, but the same actions will work with Visual Studio Code on either Windows or Linux. The main differences will be native command-line actions such as deleting a file: both the command and the path are likely to be different. The `dotnet` CLI tool will be identical on all platforms.

## Writing code using Visual Studio Code

Start Visual Studio Code.

Navigate to **File** | **Open...**, or press *Cmd* + *O*.

In the dialog, open the `Code` folder, select the `Chapter01` folder, click on the **New Folder** button, enter the name `WelcomeDotNetCore`, and click on **Create**. Select the **WelcomeDotNetCore** folder, and click on **Open** or press *Enter*.

In Visual Studio Code, navigate to **View** | **Integrated Terminal**, or press *Ctrl* + `.

At the **TERMINAL** prompt, enter the following command:

```
dotnet new console
```

You will see that the `dotnet` command-line tool creates a new console application project for you in the current folder, and the **Explorer** window shows the two files created, as shown in the following screenshot:

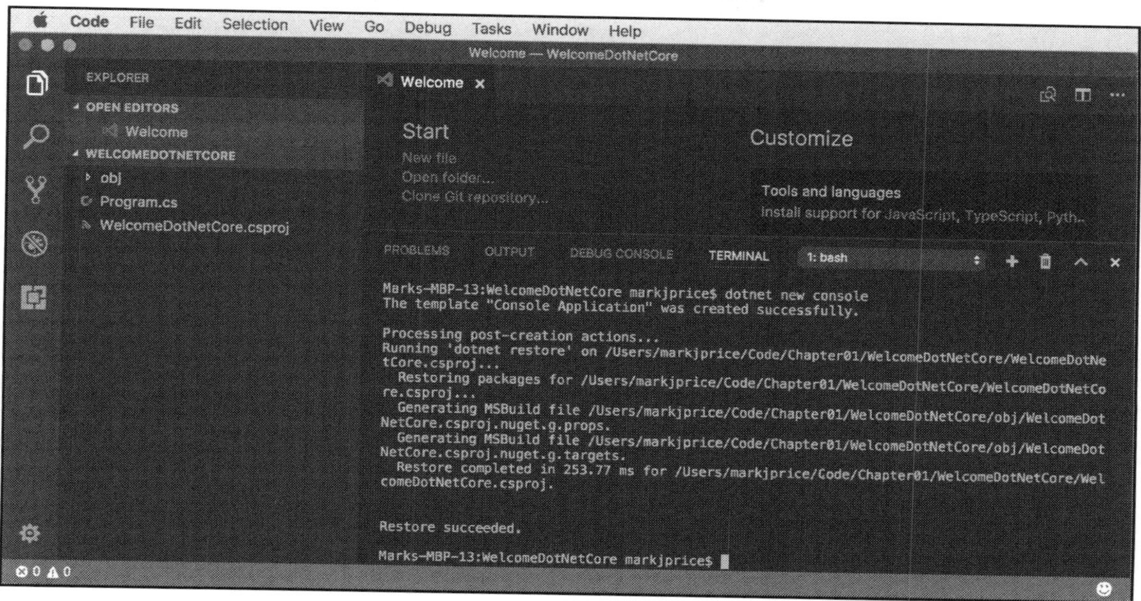


In the **EXPLORER** window, click on the file named `Program.cs` to open it in the editor window.

If you see the warnings mentioning that the required assets are missing, click on **Yes**, as shown in the following screenshot:

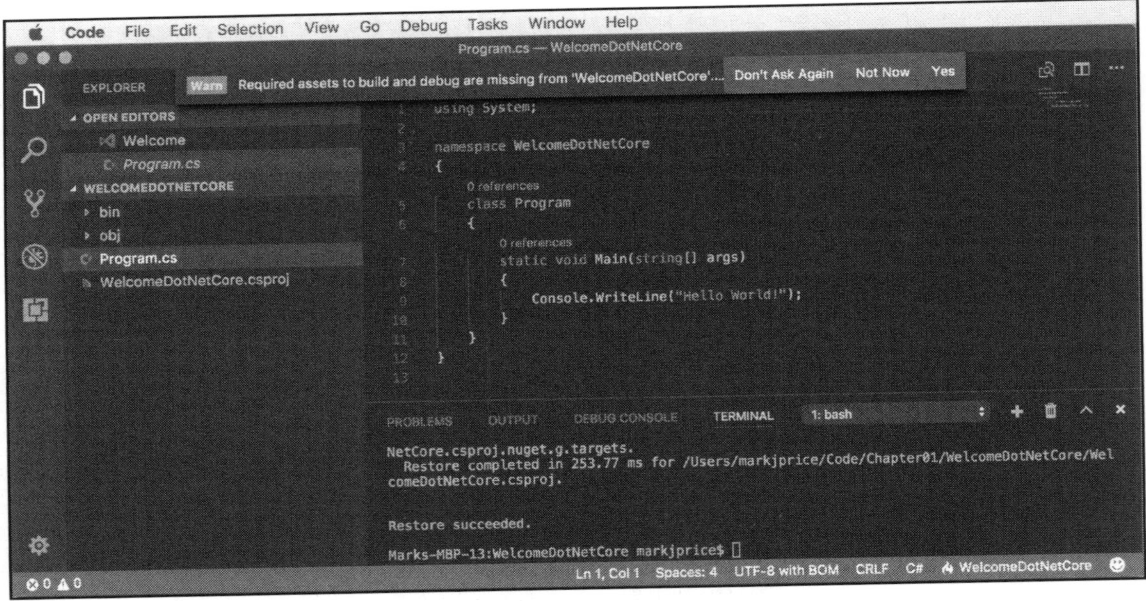

Modify the text that is being written to the console to say, `Welcome, .NET Core!`

Navigate to **File** | **Auto Save**. This toggle will save the annoyance of remembering to save before rebuilding your application each time!

## Compiling code using Visual Studio Code

Navigate to **View** | **Integrated Terminal** or press *Ctrl* + `, and enter the following command:

```
dotnet run
```

The output in the **TERMINAL** window will show the result of running your application.

## Autoformatting code

In Visual Studio Code, navigate to **File** | **Open**, and open the `Chapter01` folder.

In **Explorer**, expand **HelloCS**, and select **MyApp.cs**.

Click on **Yes**, when prompted to add required assets.

In Visual Studio Code, either right-click and choose **Format Document**, or press *Alt* + *Shift* + *F*, as shown in the following screenshot:

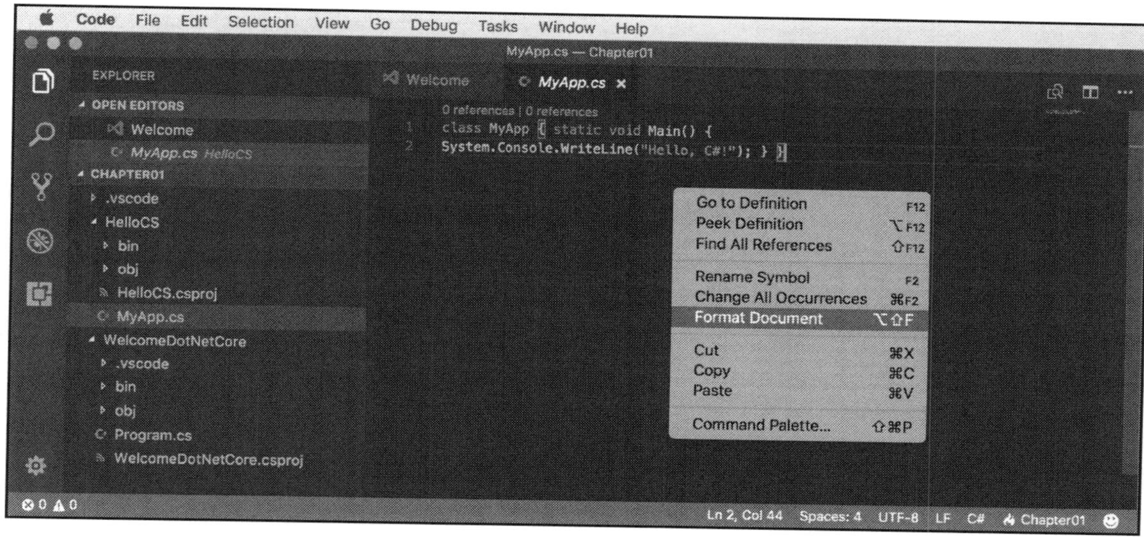


Visual Studio Code is rapidly approaching feature parity with Visual Studio 2017 on Windows.

## Writing and compiling code using Visual Studio for Mac

Start Visual Studio for Mac, and navigate to **File** | **New Solution**.

In the list on the left, in the **.NET Core** section, select **App**.

In the project template list in the middle, select **Console Application**, and then click on **Next**, as shown in the following screenshot:

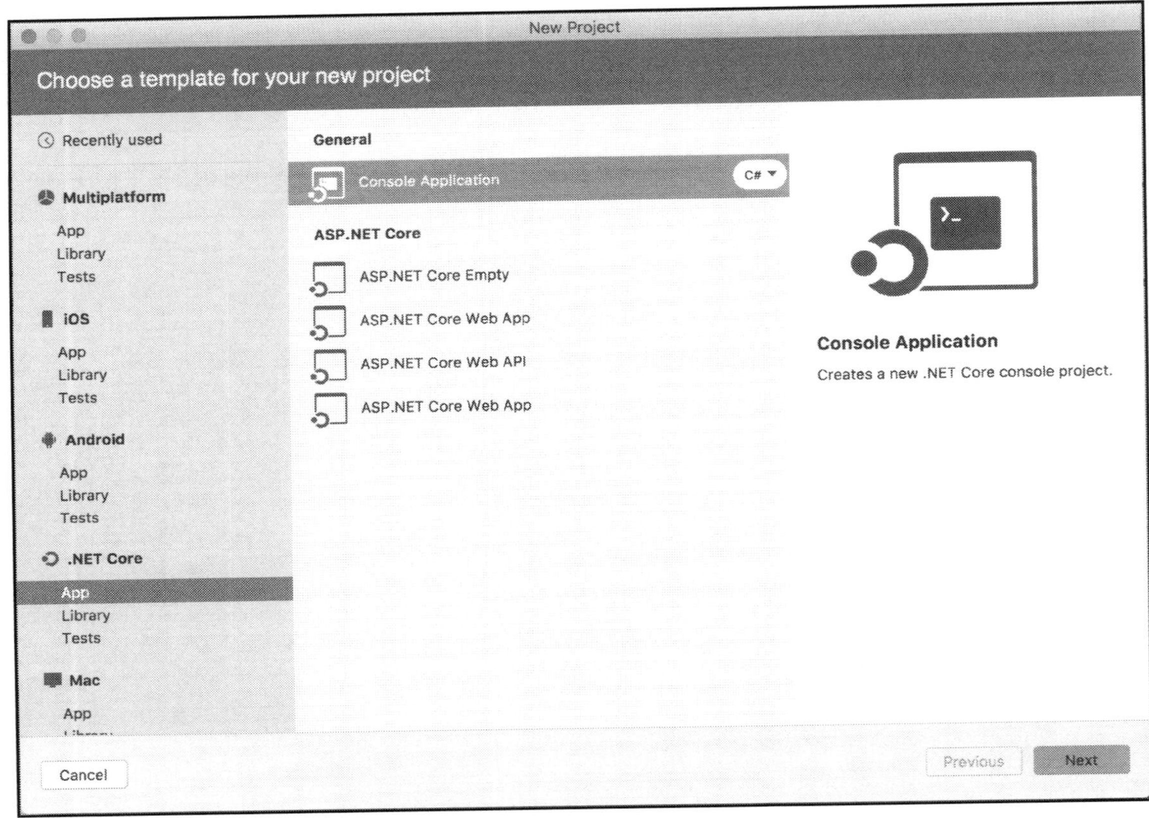


In the **Configure your new Console Application** step, select a **Target Framework** of **.NET Core 2.0**, and click on **Next**.

In the **Configure your new Console Application** step, enter **Project Name** as `WelcomeDotNetCoreMac`, enter **Solution Name** as `Chapter01`, set the **Location** to your `Code` folder, and click on **Create**, as shown in the following screenshot:

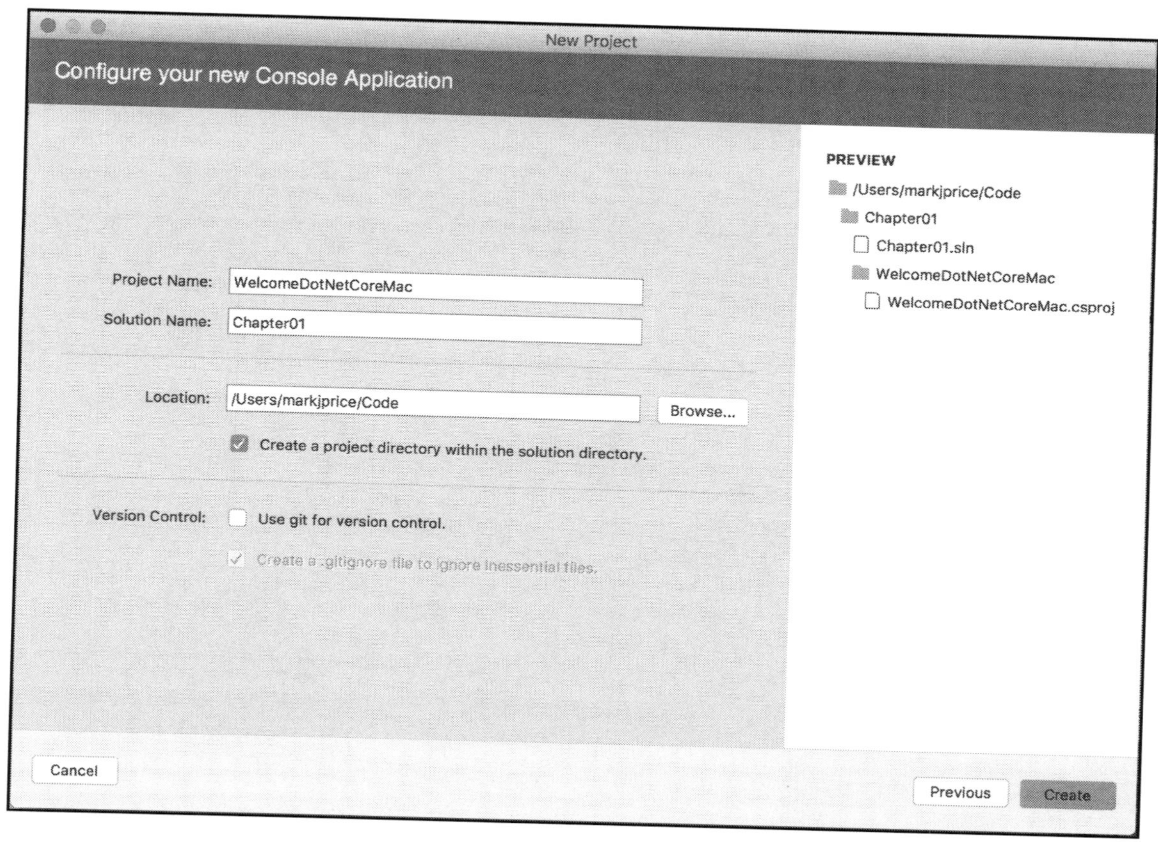

Modify the text that is being written to the console to say, `Welcome, .NET Core on the Mac!`

In Visual Studio for Mac, navigate to **Run** | **Start Without Debugging**, or press *Cmd* + *Option* + *Enter*.

The output in **Terminal** will show the result of running your application.

In the **Solution** pad, right-click on **Chapter01**, and go to **Add** | **Add Existing Project...**.

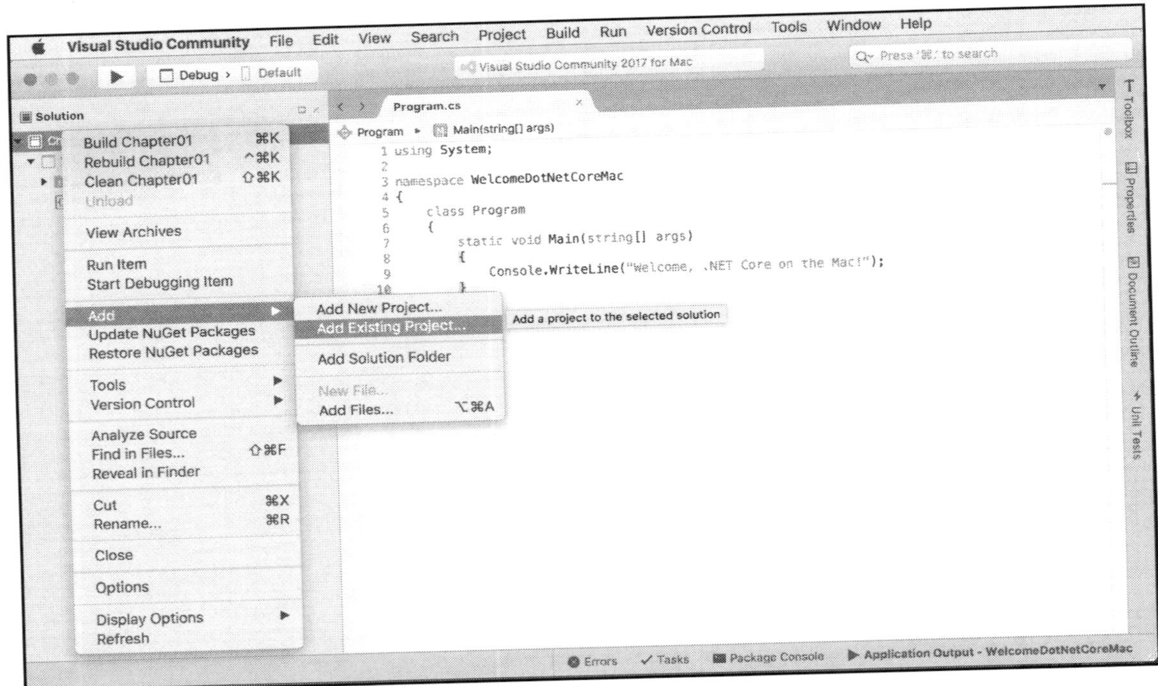


In the **HelloCS** folder, select `HelloCS.cs.proj`.

In the **Solution** pad, right-click on **HelloCS**, and select **Run Item**, as shown in the following screenshot:

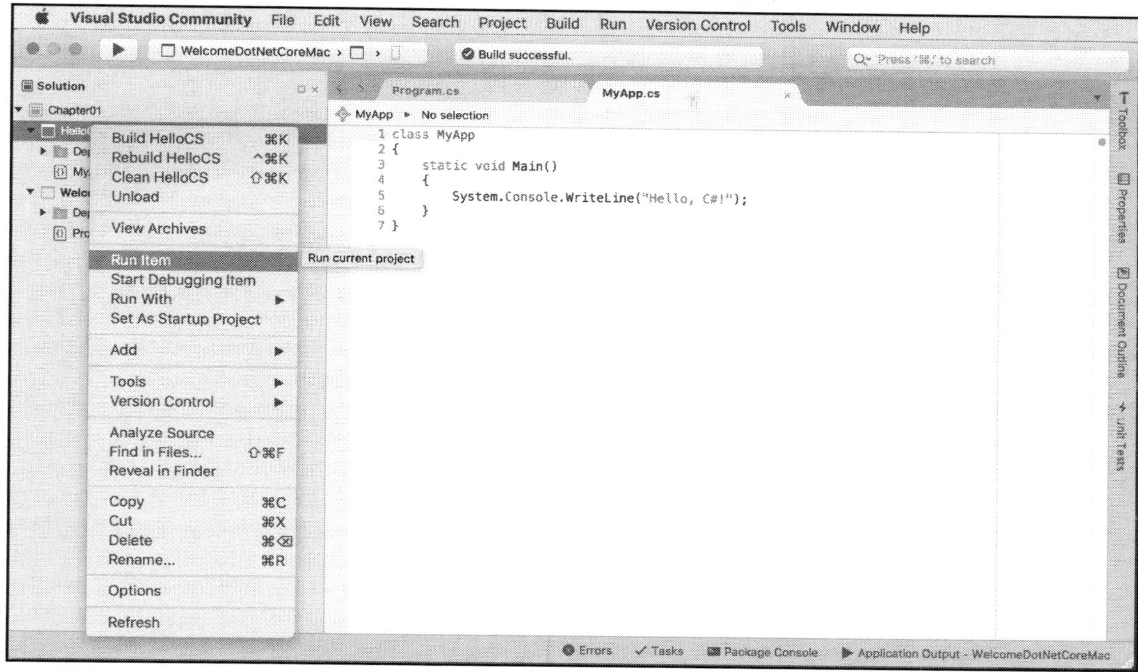


## Next steps

You now know how to create and build simple .NET Core applications for Windows and macOS (and Linux is just as easy).

You will be able to complete almost all of the chapters in this book using Visual Studio 2017 on Windows, Visual Studio for Mac, or Visual Studio Code on Windows, macOS, or Linux.

# Managing source code with GitHub

**Git** is a commonly used source code management system. **GitHub** is a company, website, and desktop application that makes it easier to manage Git.

I used GitHub to store solutions to all the practical exercises at the end of each chapter at the following URL:

`https://github.com/markjprice/cs7dotnetcore2`

# Using Git with Visual Studio 2017

Visual Studio 2017 has built-in support for using Git with GitHub as well as Microsoft's own source code management system named **Visual Studio Team Services (VSTS)**.

## Using the Team Explorer window

In Visual Studio 2017, navigate to **View** | **Team Explorer**, as shown in the following screenshot:

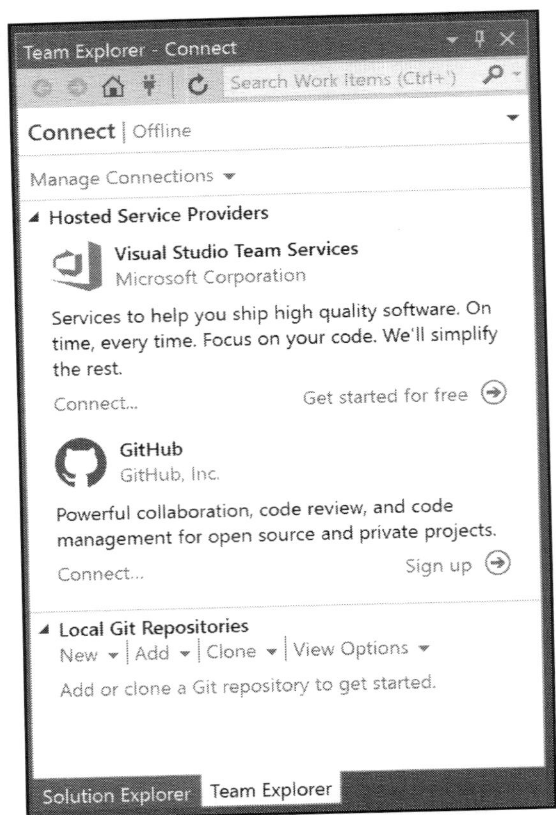

Although it is a good idea to sign up with an online source code management system provider, you can clone a GitHub repository without signing up for an account.

## Cloning a GitHub repository

In the **Team Explorer** window, expand **Local Git Repositories**, click on the **Clone** menu, and then enter the following URL of a Git repository to clone it:

```
https://github.com/markjprice/cs7dotnetcore2.git
```

Enter a path for the cloned Git repository:

```
C:\Code\Repos\cs7dotnetcore2
```

Click on the **Clone** button, as shown in the following screenshot:

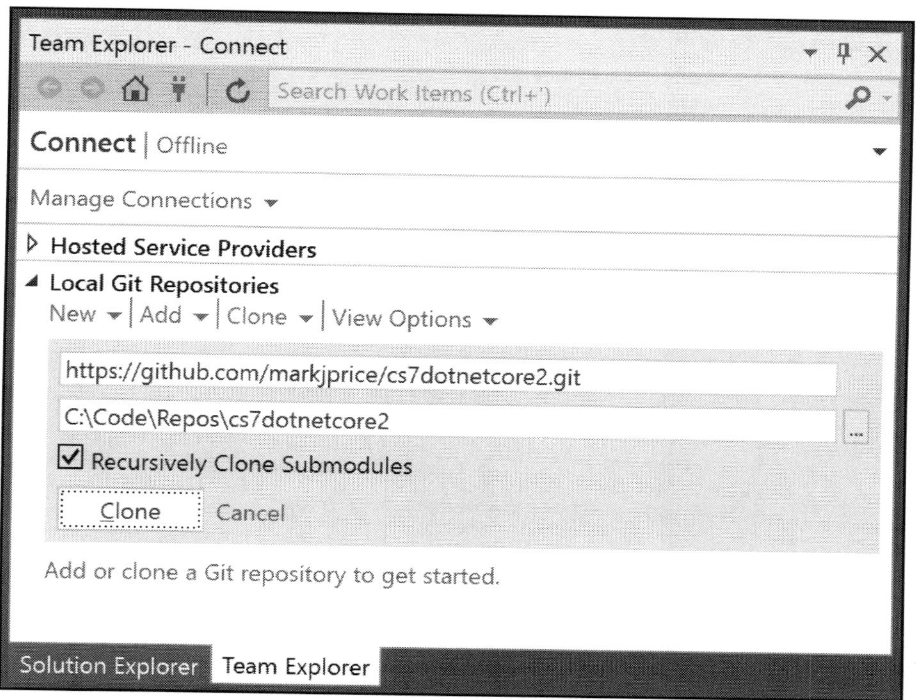


Wait for the Git repository to clone locally.

You will now have a local copy of the complete solutions to all of the hands-on practice exercises for this book.

### Managing a GitHub repository

Double-click on the `cs7dotnetcore2` repo to open a detail view.

You can click on the options in the **Project** section to view **Pull Requests** and **Issues**, and other aspects of a repository.

You can double-click on an entry in the **Solutions** section to open it in **Solution Explorer**.

## Using Git with Visual Studio Code

Visual Studio Code has support for Git, but it will use your OS's Git installation, so you must install Git 2.0 or later first before you get these features. You can install Git from the following link:

`https://git-scm.com/download`

If you like to use a GUI, you can download GitHub Desktop from the following link:
`https://desktop.github.com`

### Configuring Git at the command line

Launch **Terminal**, and enter the following command to check your configuration:

```
git config --list
```

The output should include your username and email address, because these will be used with every commit that you make:

```
...other congfiguration...
user.name=Mark J. Price
user.email=markjprice@gmail.com
```

If your username and email has not been set, to set your username and email, enter the following commands, using your own name and email, not mine:

```
git config --global user.name "Mark J. Price"
git config --global user.email markjprice@gmail.com
```

You can check an individual configuration setting like this:

```
git config user.name
```

## Managing Git with Visual Studio Code

Launch Visual Studio Code, and open the `Code` folder.

Navigate to **View** | **Integrated Terminal** or press *Ctrl* + `, and enter the following commands:

```
mkdir Repos
cd Repos
git clone https://github.com/markjprice/cs7dotnetcore2.git
```

Cloning all of the solutions for all of the chapters to your local drive will take a minute, as shown in the following screenshot:

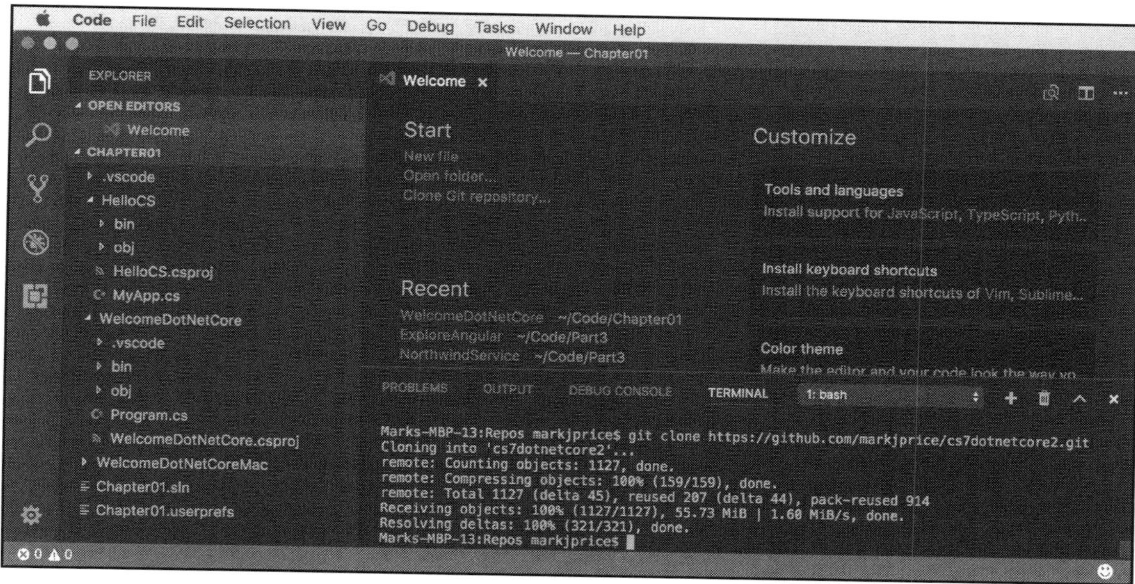

For more information about source code version control with Visual Studio Code, visit the following link:
https://code.visualstudio.com/Docs/editor/versioncontrol

# Practicing and exploring

Test your knowledge and understanding by answering some questions, get some hands-on practice, and explore with deeper research into the topics covered in this chapter.

## Exercise 1.1 – Test your knowledge

Answer the following questions:

1. Why can a programmer use different languages, for example C# and F#, to write applications that run on .NET Core?
2. What do you type at the prompt to build and execute C# source code?
3. What is the Visual C# developer settings keyboard shortcut to save, compile, and run an application without attaching the debugger?
4. What is the Visual Studio Code keyboard shortcut to view Integrated Terminal?
5. Is Visual Studio 2017 better than Visual Studio Code?
6. Is .NET Core better than .NET Framework?
7. How is .NET Native different from .NET Core?
8. What is .NET Standard and why is it important?
9. What is the difference between Git and GitHub?
10. What is the name of the entry-point method of a .NET console application and how should it be declared?

## Exercise 1.2 – Practice C# anywhere

You do not need Visual Studio 2017, Visual Studio for Mac, or Visual Studio Code to practice writing C#.

Go to one of the following websites and start coding:

- **.NET Fiddle**: `https://dotnetfiddle.net/`
- **Cloud9**: `https://c9.io/web/sign-up/free`

## Exercise 1.3 – Explore topics

Use the following links to read more details about the topics covered in this chapter:

- **Welcome to .NET Core**: `http://dotnet.github.io`
- **.NET Core Command Line Interface (CLI) tool**: `https://github.com/dotnet/cli`
- **.NET Core runtime, CoreCLR**: `https://github.com/dotnet/coreclr/`
- **.NET Core Roadmap**: `https://github.com/dotnet/core/blob/master/roadmap.md`
- **.NET Standard FAQ**: `https://github.com/dotnet/standard/blob/master/docs/faq.md`
- **Visual Studio Documentation**: `https://docs.microsoft.com/en-us/visualstudio/`
- **Visual Studio Blog**: `https://blogs.msdn.microsoft.com/visualstudio/`
- **Git and Team Services**: `https://www.visualstudio.com/en-us/docs/git/overview`
- **The easiest way to connect to your GitHub repositories in Visual Studio**: `https://visualstudio.github.com/`

# Summary

In this chapter, we set up the development environment, used Windows' Command Prompt and macOS's Terminal to compile and run a console application, used Visual Studio 2017, Visual Studio for Mac, and Visual Studio Code to create a similar application, and discussed the differences between .NET Framework, .NET Core, .NET Standard, and .NET Native.

In the next chapter, you will learn to speak C#.

# Part 1

## C# 7.1

This part of the book is about the C# language—the grammar and vocabulary that you will use every day to write the source code for your applications.

Programming languages have many similarities to human languages, except that in programming languages, we can make up our own words, just like Dr. Seuss!

In a book written by Dr. Seuss in 1950, *If I Ran the Zoo*, he states this:

> *And then, just to show them, I'll sail to Ka-Troo And Bring Back an It-Kutch a Preep and a Proo A Nerkle, a Nerd and a Seersucker, too!*

This book covers C# 7.1. Microsoft has plans for future versions of C#, as shown in the following table:

| Version | Features |
|---|---|
| C# 7.2 | ref readonly, blittable, strongname, interior pointer, nontrailing named arguments, private protected, Digit separator after base specifier |
| C# 7.3 | Range with double-dot operator, for example, `1..10` |
| C# 8.0 | Default interface methods, nullable reference types |

You can learn more at this link:
`https://github.com/dotnet/roslyn/blob/master/docs/Language%20Feature%20Status.md`

Just as we were going to press for the third edition, Microsoft released C# 7.2. Look out for a blog article about the improvements in C# 7.2 on Packt's website at the following link:
`https://www.packtpub.com/books/content/exploring-language-improvements-c-72-and-73`
I will update this blog with the details of the improvements in C# 7.3, once it is released.

To learn C#, you will need to create some simple applications. To avoid overloading you with too much information too soon, the chapters in the first part of this book will use the simplest type of application: a console application.

In the following chapters, you will learn these topics:

2. The grammar and vocabulary of C#.
3. The branching and looping statements of C#, and how to convert between C# types.
4. How to reuse code with C# functions, and how to debug and test C# code.
5. How to use object-oriented features of C#.
6. How to use advanced object-oriented features of C#.

# 2
# Speaking C#

This chapter is about the basics of the C# programming language. You will learn how to write statements using the grammar of C#, some of the common vocabulary that you will use every day, how to temporarily store information in your computer's memory, and how to perform simple operations on that information.

This chapter covers the following topics:

- Understanding C# basics
- Declaring variables
- Building console applications
- Operating on variables

## Understanding C# basics

Let's start by looking at the basics of the grammar and vocabulary of C#. In this chapter, you will create multiple console applications, each showing a feature of the C# language.

Each console application requires a project. Often developers want to open multiple projects at the same time. You can do this by adding projects to a solution.

To manage these projects with Visual Studio 2017, we will put them all in a single solution. Visual Studio 2017 can only have one solution open at any one time, but each solution can group together multiple projects. A project can build a console application, a Windows desktop application, a web application, and dozens of others.

To manage these projects with Visual Studio Code, which does not support solutions, we will manually create a container folder named `Chapter02`. If you would like to use Visual Studio Code, skip to the section titled *Using Visual Studio Code on macOS, Linux, or Windows*.

## Using Visual Studio 2017

Start Microsoft Visual Studio 2017. In Visual Studio, press *Ctrl* + *Shift* + *N* or navigate to **File** | **New** | **Project...**.

In the **New Project** dialog, in the **Installed** list, expand **Other Project Types** and select **Visual Studio Solutions**. In the list at the center, select **Blank Solution**, type the name `Chapter02`, change the location to `C:\Code`, and then click on **OK**, as shown in the following screenshot:

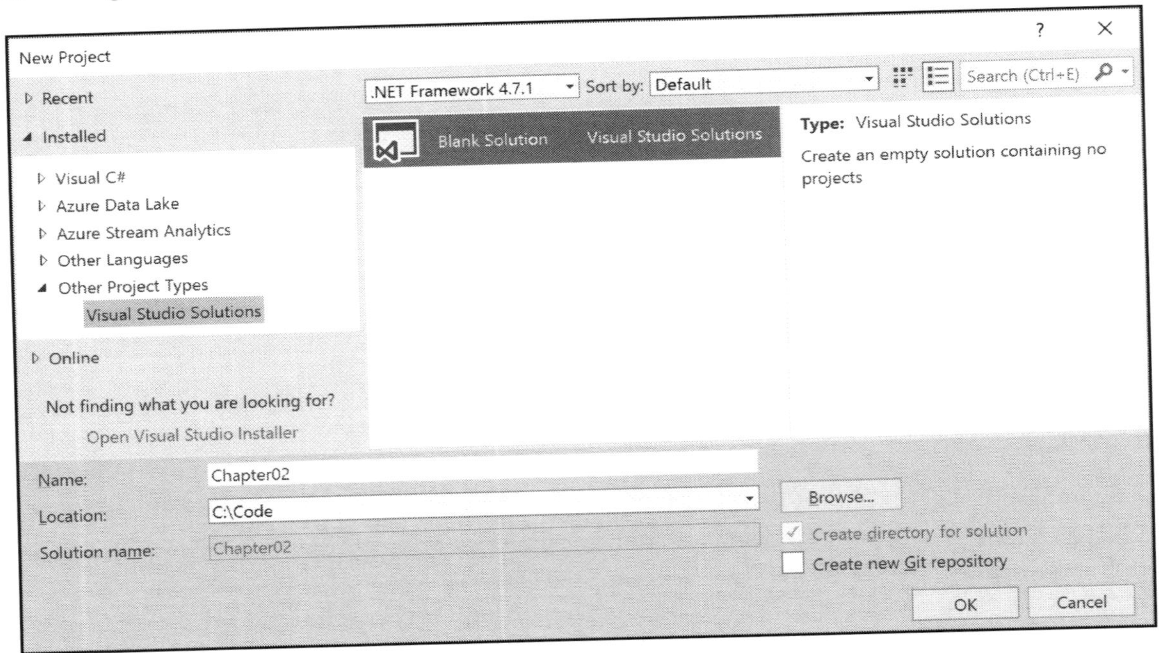

If you were to run **File Explorer**, you would see that Visual Studio has created a folder named `Chapter02` with a Visual Studio solution named `Chapter02` inside it, as shown in the following screenshot:

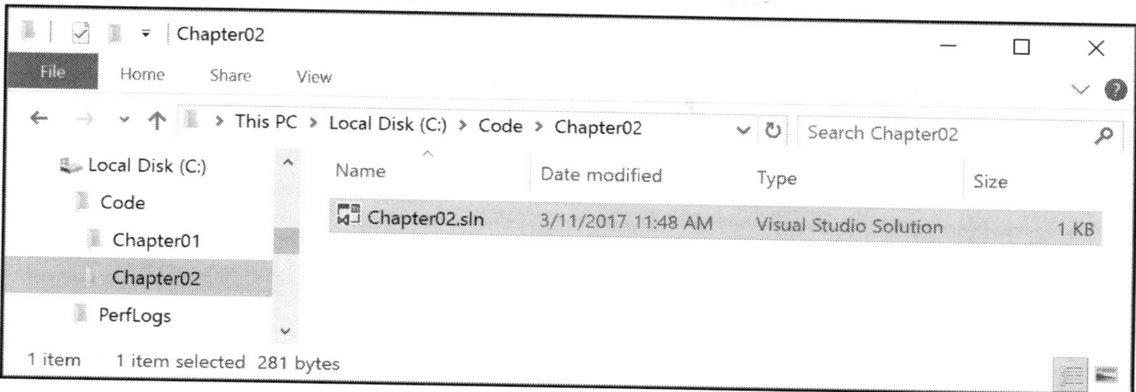


In Visual Studio, navigate to **File** | **Add** | **New Project...**, as shown in the following screenshot. This will add a new project to the blank solution:

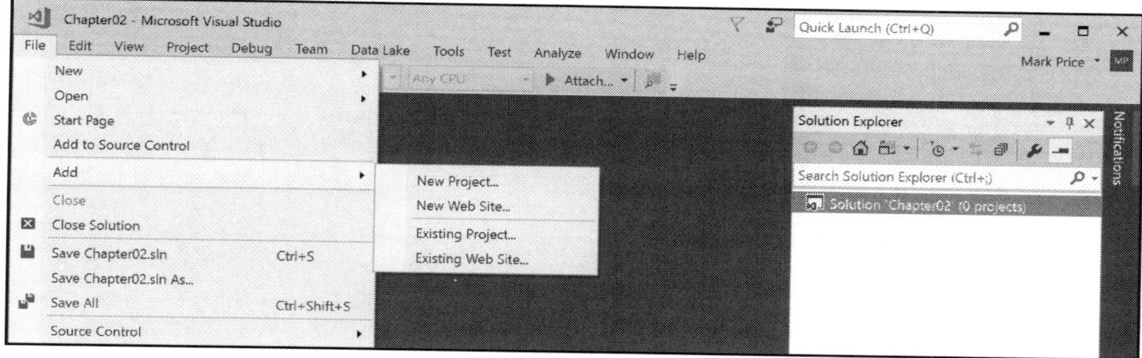

In the **Add New Project** dialog, in the **Installed** list, expand **Visual C#**, and select **.NET Core**. In the list at the center, select **Console App (.NET Core)**, type the name `Basics`, and then click on **OK**, as shown in the following screenshot:

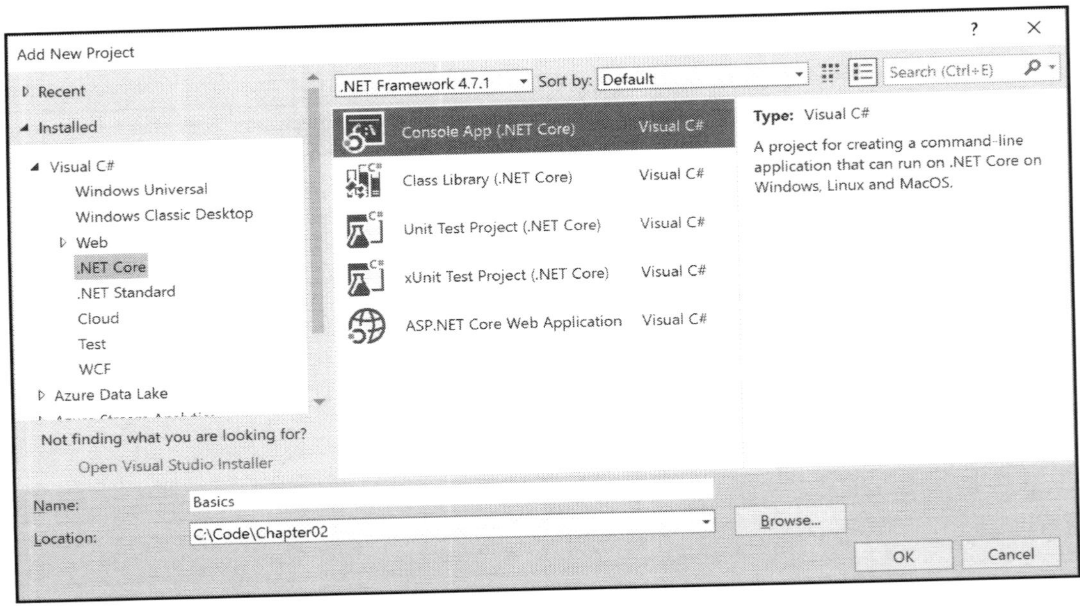


If you were to run **File Explorer**, you would see that Visual Studio has created a new folder with some files and subfolders inside it. You don't need to know what all these do yet. The code you will write will be stored in the file named `Program.cs`, as shown in the following screenshot:

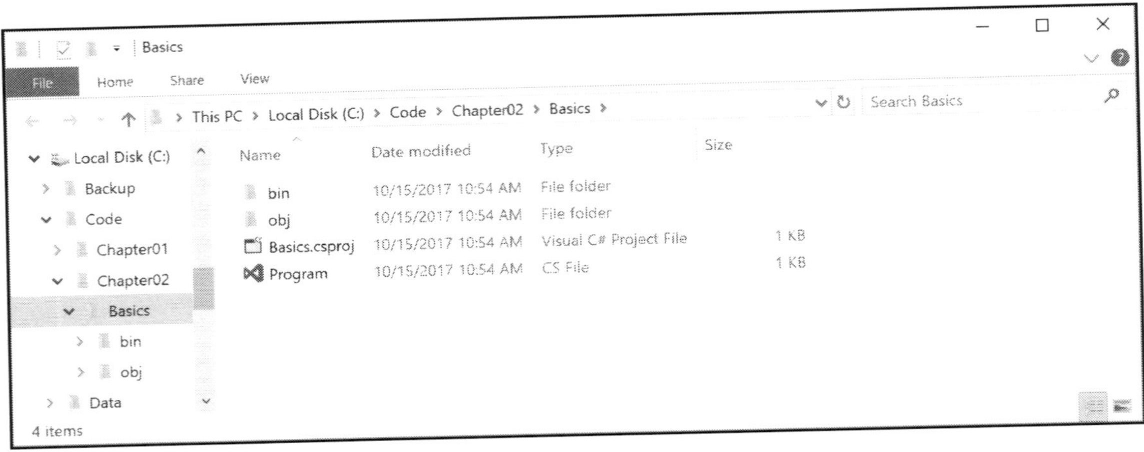

In Visual Studio, **Solution Explorer** shows the same files as the ones in the preceding screenshot of the file system.

Some folders and files, for example, the `bin` folder, are hidden by default in **Solution Explorer**. At the top of the window is a toolbar button named **Show All Files**. Toggle this button to show and hide folders and files, as shown in the following screenshot:

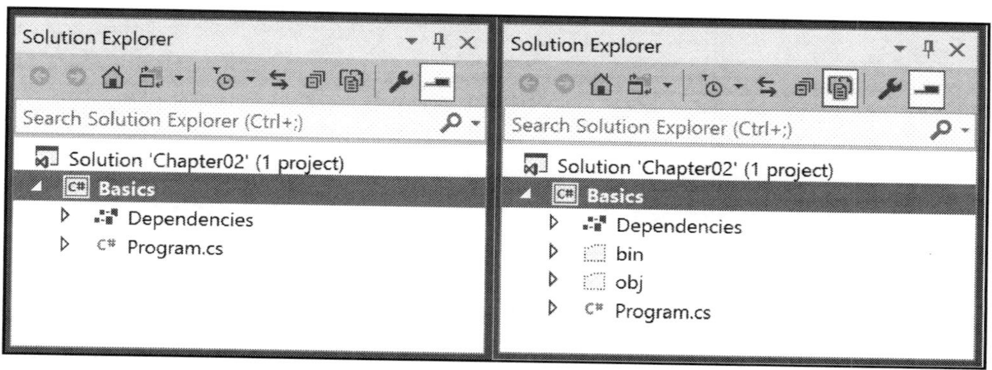


# Using Visual Studio Code on macOS, Linux, or Windows

If you completed `Chapter 1`, *Hello, C#! Welcome, .NET Core!*, then you will already have a `Code` folder in your user folder. If not, create it, and then create a subfolder named `Chapter02` and a sub-subfolder named `Basics`, as shown in the following screenshot:

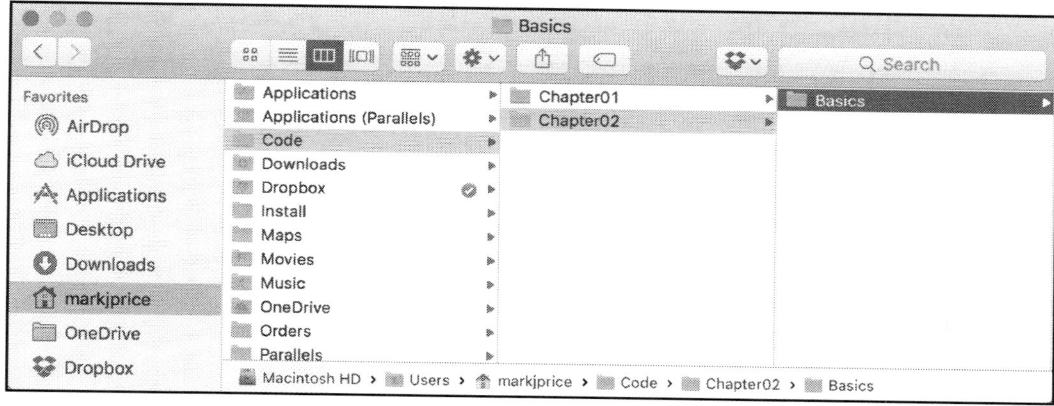

Start Visual Studio Code and open the `/Chapter02/Basics/` folder.

In Visual Studio Code, navigate to **View** | **Integrated Terminal**, and enter the following command:

```
dotnet new console
```

In the **EXPLORER**, click the `Program.cs` file, and then click on **Yes** to add the missing required assets, as shown in the following screenshot:

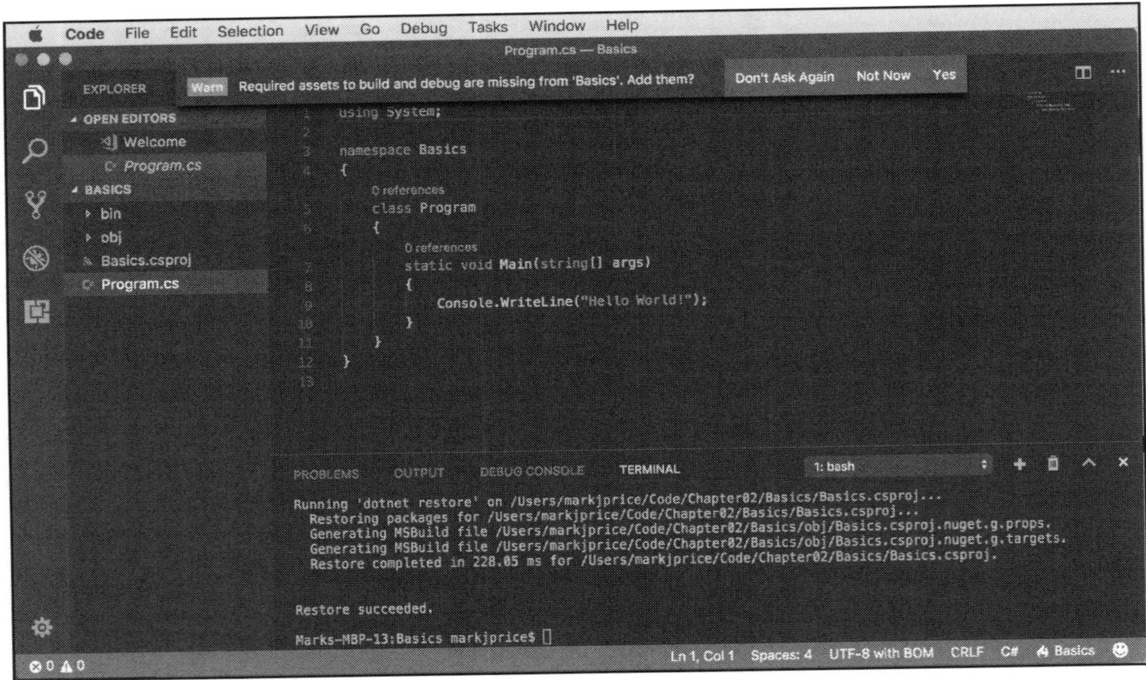


# C# grammar

The grammar of C# includes **statements** and **blocks**. To document your code, you use **comments**.

## Statements

In English, we indicate the end of a sentence with a full stop. A sentence can be composed of multiple words and phrases. The order of words is part of grammar. For example, in English, we say: "the black cat." The adjective, black, comes before the noun, cat. French grammar has a different order; the adjective comes after the noun, "le chat noir." The order matters.

C# indicates the end of a **statement** with a semicolon. A statement can be composed of multiple **variables** and **expressions**.

In the following statement, `fullName` is a variable and `firstName + lastName` is an expression:

```
var fullName = firstName + lastName;
```

The expression is made up of an **operand** (`firstName`), an **operator** (+), and another operand (`lastName`). The order matters.

## Comments

You can add comments to explain your code using a double slash `//`.

The compiler ignores everything after the `//` until the end of the line; for example:

```
var totalPrice = cost + tax; // tax is 20% of the cost
```

In Windows, Visual Studio 2017 and Visual Studio Code will add or remove the comment (double slashes) at the start of the currently selected line(s) if you press *Ctrl* + *K* + *C* or *Ctrl* + *K* + *U*. In macOS, Visual Studio Code will do the same if you press *Cmd* instead of *Ctrl*.

To write a multiline comment, use `/*` at the beginning and `*/` at the end of the comment, as shown in the following code:

```
/*
This is a multi-line
comment.
*/
```

## Blocks

In English, we indicate a paragraph by starting a new line. C# indicates a **block** of code with curly brackets `{ }`. Blocks start with a declaration to indicate what it is defining. For example, a block can define a **namespace**, a **class**, a **method**, or a **statement**. You will learn what these are later.

In your current project, note the grammar of C# written for you by the Visual Studio template or by the `dotnet` CLI tool.

In the following example, I have added some comments to describe the code:

```
using System; // a semicolon indicates the end of a statement

class Program
{
   static void Main(string[] args)
   { // the start of a block
      Console.WriteLine("Hello World!"); // a statement
   } // the end of a block
}
```

## C# vocabulary

C# vocabulary is made up of keywords, symbols, and types.

Some of the 79 predefined, reserved keywords that you will see in this chapter include `using`, `namespace`, `class`, `static`, `int`, `string`, `double`, `bool`, `var`, `if`, `switch`, `break`, `while`, `do`, `for`, and `foreach`.

Visual Studio 2017 shows C# keywords in blue to make them easier to spot. In the following screenshot, `using`, `namespace`, `class`, `static`, `void`, and `string` are part of the vocabulary of C#:

```
using System;

namespace Basics
{
    class Program
    {
        static void Main(string[] args)
        {
            Console.WriteLine("Hello World!");
        }
    }
}
```

The equivalent for Visual Studio Code is shown in the following screenshot:

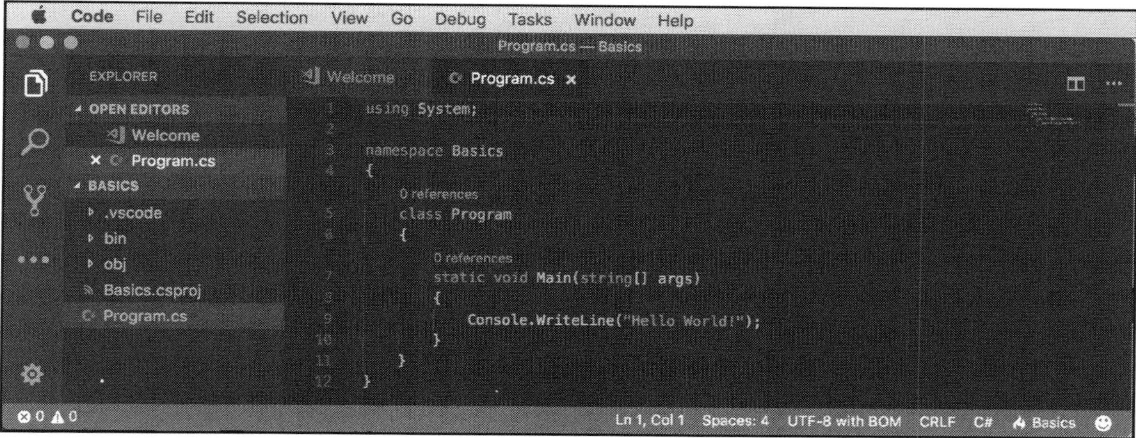

Both Visual Studio 2017 and Visual Studio Code allow you to customize the color scheme. In Visual Studio 2017, navigate to **Tools** | **Options** | **Environment** | **Fonts and Colors**. In Visual Studio Code, navigate to **Code** | **Preferences** | **Color Theme**.

There are another 25 contextual keywords that only have a special meaning in a specific context. However, that still means that there are only 104 actual C# keywords in the language.

English has more than 250,000 distinct words. How does C# get away with only having 104 keywords? Why is C# so difficult to learn if it has so few words?

One of the key differences between a human language and a programming language is that developers need to be able to define new "words" with new meanings.

Apart from the 104 keywords in the C# language, this book will teach you about some of the hundreds of thousands of "words" that other developers have defined. You will also learn how to define your own "words."

Programmers all over the world must learn English because most programming languages use English words such as `namespace` and `class`. There are programming languages that use other human languages, such as Arabic, but they are rare. This YouTube video shows a demonstration of an Arabic programming language: `https://www.youtube.com/watch?v=77KAHPZUR8g`

## Help for writing correct code

Plain text editors such as Notepad don't help you write correct English, as shown in the following screenshot:

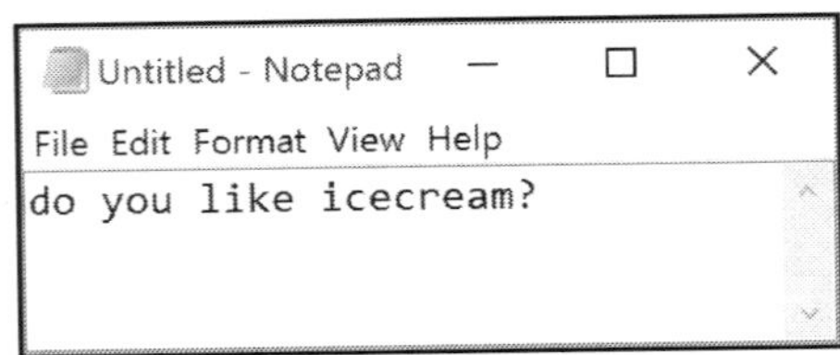


Notepad won't help you write correct C# either:

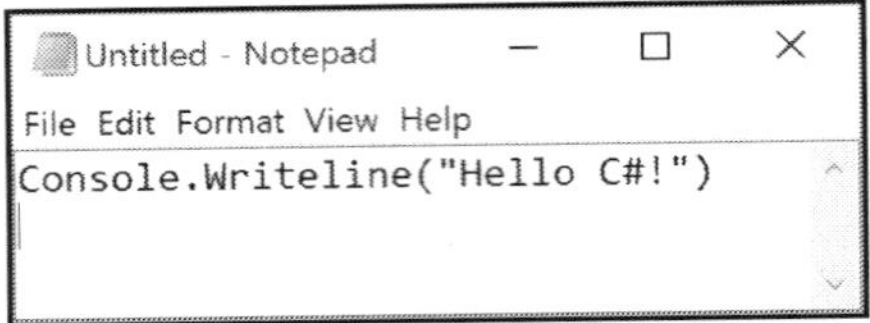


Microsoft Word helps you write English by highlighting spelling mistakes with red squiggles (Microsoft Word says it should be *ice-cream* or *ice cream*) and grammatical errors with blue squiggles (sentences should have an uppercase first letter):

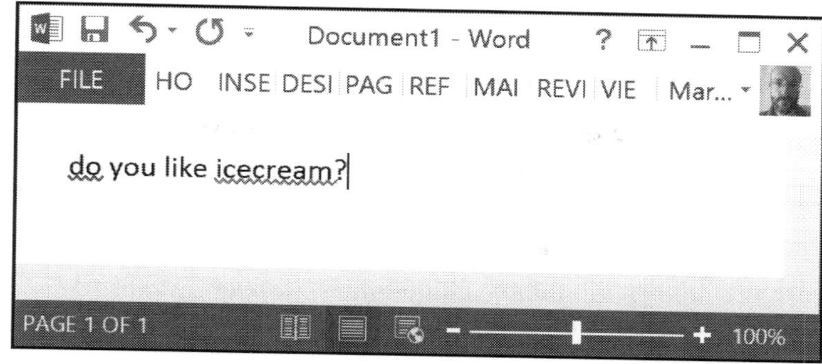


Similarly, Visual Studio 2017 and Visual Studio Code help you write C# code by highlighting spelling mistakes (the method name should be `WriteLine` with an uppercase `L`) and grammatical errors (statements must end with a semicolon).

Visual Studio 2017 constantly watches what you type and gives you feedback by highlighting problems with colored squiggly lines under your code and showing the **Error List** window (known as the **PROBLEMS** window in Visual Studio Code), as you can see in the following screenshot:

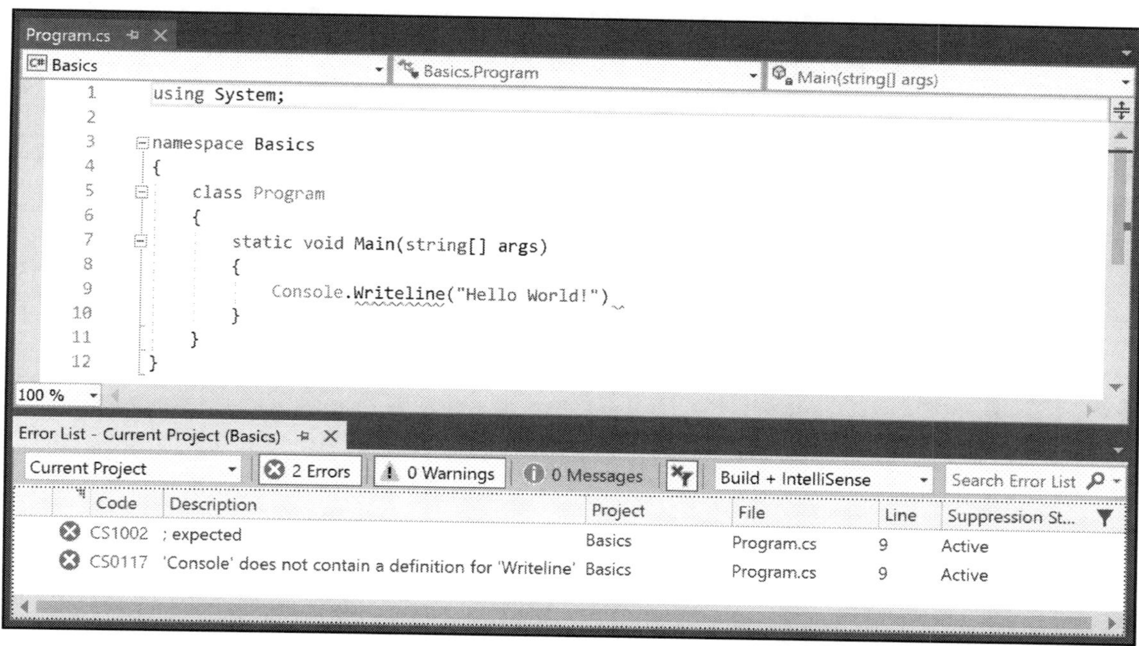

You can ask Visual Studio 2017 to do a complete check of all the projects in a solution by going to **Build | Build Solution** or pressing *F6*. For Visual Studio Code, enter the following command in Integrated Terminal:
`dotnet build`

Visual Studio Code has a similar **PROBLEMS** window, as shown in the following screenshot:

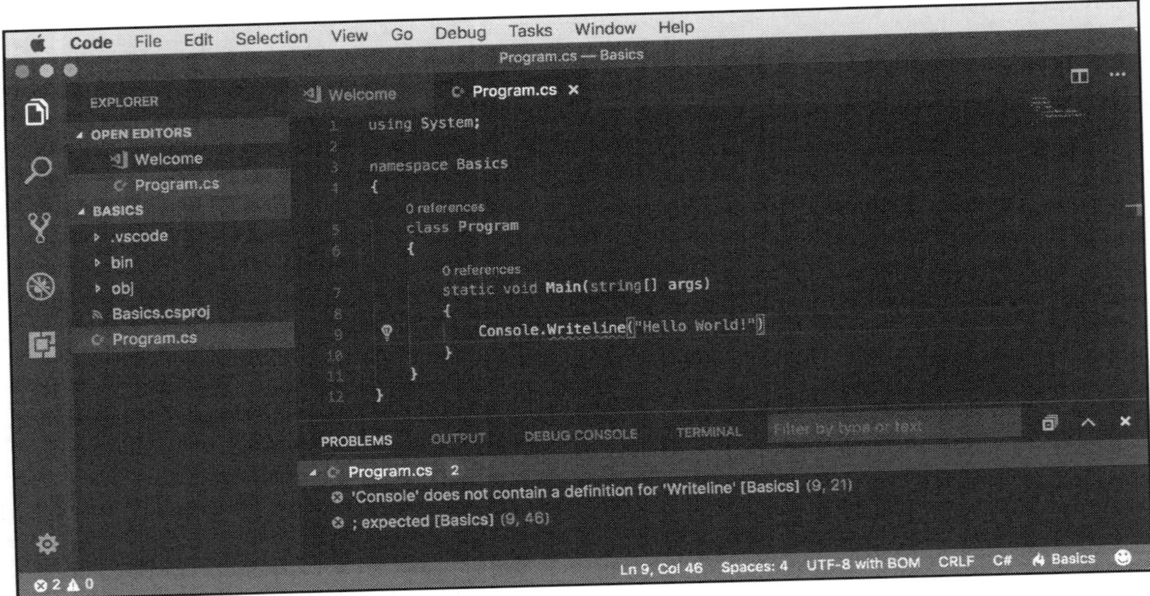


## Verbs are methods

In English, verbs are doing or action words. In C#, doing or action words are called **methods**. There are literally hundreds of thousands of methods available to C#.

In English, verbs change how they are written based on when in time the action happens. For example, Amir *was jumping* in the past, Beth *jumps* in the present, they *jumped* in the past, and Charlie *will jump* in the future.

In C#, methods such as `WriteLine` change how they are called or executed based on the specifics of the action. This is called overloading, which we will cover in more detail in `Chapter 5`, *Building Your Own Types with Object-Oriented Programming*. Consider the following example:

```
// outputs a carriage-return
Console.WriteLine();
// outputs the greeting and a carriage-return
Console.WriteLine("Hello Ahmed");
// outputs a formatted number and date and a carriage-return
Console.WriteLine("Temperature on {0:D} is {1}°C.",
DateTime.Today, 23.4);
```

A different analogy is that some words are spelled the same, but have different meanings depending on the context.

## Nouns are types, fields, and variables

In English, nouns are names that refer to things. For example, Fido is the name of a dog. The word "dog" tells us the type of thing that Fido is. To order Fido to fetch a ball, we would use his name.

In C#, their equivalents are **types**, **fields**, and **variables**. For example, `Animal` and `Car` are types, that is, nouns for categorizing things. `Head` and `Engine` are fields, that is, nouns that belong to `Animal` and `Car`. `Fido` and `Bob` are variables, that is, nouns for referring to a specific thing.

There are tens of thousands of types available *to* C#. Note that I don't say, "There are tens of thousands of types *in* C#."

The difference is subtle but important. C# (the language) only has a few keywords for types, such as `string` and `int`. Strictly speaking, C# doesn't define any types. Keywords such as `string` that look like types are **aliases**. Those aliases represent types provided by the platform on which C# runs.

C# cannot exist alone. It is a language that runs on variants of .NET. In theory, someone could write a compiler for C# that uses a different platform, with different underlying types. In practice, the platform for C# is one of the .NET platforms. It is .NET that provides the tens of thousands of types to C#. Those types include `System.Int32`, which the C# keyword alias `int` maps to, as well as much more complex types, such as `System.Xml.Linq.XDocument`.

Note that the term *type* is often confused with `class`. Have you ever played the parlor game, *Twenty Questions*, also known as *Animal, Vegetable, or Mineral?* In the game, every thing can be categorized as an animal, vegetable, or mineral. In C#, every type can be categorized as a `class`, `struct`, `enum`, `interface`, or `delegate`. The C# keyword `string` is a `class`, but `int` is a `struct`. So, it is best to use the term *type* to include both.

# Revealing the extent of the C# vocabulary

We know that there are 104 keywords in C#, but how many types are there? Let's write some code to find out how many types (and their methods) are available to C# in our simple console application.

Don't worry about how this code works for now; it uses a technique called **reflection**.

Start by adding the following statements at the top of the `Program.cs` file:

```
using System.Linq;
using System.Reflection;
```

Inside the `Main` method, delete the statement that writes `Hello World!`, and replace it with the following code:

```
// loop through the assemblies that this application references
foreach (var r in Assembly.GetEntryAssembly()
  .GetReferencedAssemblies())
{
    // load the assembly so we can read its details
    var a = Assembly.Load(new AssemblyName(r.FullName));
    // declare a variable to count the total number of methods
    int methodCount = 0;
    // loop through all the types in the assembly
    foreach (var t in a.DefinedTypes)
    {
        // add up the counts of methods
        methodCount += t.GetMethods().Count();
    }
    // output the count of types and their methods
    Console.WriteLine($"{a.DefinedTypes.Count():N0} types " +
     $"with {methodCount:N0} methods in {r.Name} assembly.");
}
```

## Building and running with Visual Studio 2017

Press *Ctrl* + *F5* to save, compile, and run your application without the debugger attached, or click on the **Debug** menu and then on **Start Without Debugging**.

You will see the following output that shows the actual number of types and methods that are available to you in the simplest application when running on Windows:

```
25 types with 290 methods in System.Runtime assembly.
95 types with 1,029 methods in System.Linq assembly.
43 types with 652 methods in System.Console assembly.
```

## Building and running with Visual Studio Code

At **Integrated Terminal**, enter the following command:

```
dotnet run
```

You will see the following output that shows the actual number of types and methods that are available to you in the simplest application when running on macOS:

```
25 types with 290 methods in System.Runtime assembly.
95 types with 1,029 methods in System.Linq assembly.
53 types with 691 methods in System.Console assembly.
```

The numbers of types and methods displayed may be different depending on the platform that you are using. For example, although the `System.Runtime` and `System.Linq` assemblies have the same number of types and methods on Windows and macOS, `System.Console` on macOS has 10 more types and 39 more methods.

## Adding more types with Visual Studio 2017 and Visual Studio Code

Add the following statements at the top of the `Main` method. By declaring variables that use types in other assemblies, those assemblies are loaded with our application. This allows our code to see all the types and methods in them:

```
static void Main(string[] args)
{
    System.Data.DataSet ds;
    System.Net.Http.HttpClient client;
```

Visual Studio 2017 **Error List** and Visual Studio Code **PROBLEMS** will show warnings about variables that are declared but never used. You can safely ignore these warnings.

In Visual Studio 2017, press *Ctrl* + *F5*.

In Visual Studio Code, enter `dotnet run` in **Integrated Terminal**.

View your output, which should look similar to the following output on Windows:

```
25 types with 290 methods in System.Runtime assembly.
349 types with 6,327 methods in System.Data.Common assembly.
169 types with 1,882 methods in System.Net.Http assembly.
95 types with 1,029 methods in System.Linq assembly.
43 types with 652 methods in System.Console assembly.
```

Now, you have a better sense of why learning C# is a challenge. There are many types, with many methods to learn, and methods are only one category of member that a type can have, and other programmers are constantly defining new members!

# Declaring variables

All applications process data. Data comes in, data is processed, and data goes out.

Data usually comes into our program from files, databases, or user input. Data can be put temporarily in variables that will be stored in the memory of the running program. When the program ends, the data in memory is lost. Data is usually output to files and databases, or to the screen or a printer.

When using variables, you should think about, first, how much space it takes in memory, and, second, how fast it can be processed.

We control this by picking an appropriate type. You can think of simple common types such as `int` and `double` as being different sized storage boxes. A smaller box would take less memory, but may not be as fast at being processed. Some of these boxes may be stacked close by, and some may be thrown into a big heap further away.

# Naming variables

There are naming conventions for variables, and it is good practice to follow them, as shown in the following table:

| Naming convention | Examples | Use for |
|---|---|---|
| Camel case | `cost, orderDetail, dateOfBirth` | Local variables and private members. |
| Pascal (aka title) case | `Cost, OrderDetail, DateOfBirth` | Type names and non-private members. |

**Good Practice**
Following a consistent set of naming conventions will enable your code to be easily understood by other developers (and yourself in the future!).
**Naming Guidelines**:
`https://msdn.microsoft.com/en-us/library/ms229002(v=vs.110).aspx`

The following code block shows an example of declaring and initializing a local variable by assigning a value to it. Note that you can output the name of a variable using a keyword introduced in C# 6, that is, `nameof`:

```
// let the heightInMetres variable become equal to the value 1.88
double heightInMetres = 1.88;
Console.WriteLine($"The variable {nameof(heightInMetres)} has the
value {heightInMetres}.");
```

The message in double quotes in the preceding code wraps onto a second line because the width of a printed page is too narrow. When entering a statement like this in your code editor, type it all in a single line.

# Literal values

When you assign to a variable, you often, but not always, assign a **literal** value. A literal is a notation that represents a fixed value. Data types have different notations for their literal values. In the next few sections, you will see examples of using literal notation to assign values to variables.

## Storing text

For text, a single letter, such as `A`, is stored as a `char` type and is assigned using single quotes around the literal value, or the return value of a function call:

```
char letter = 'A';
char digit = '1';
char symbol = '$';
char userChoice = GetCharacterFromUser();
```

For text, multiple letters, such as `Bob`, are stored as a `string` type and are assigned using double quotes around the literal value, or the return value of a function call:

```
string firstName = "Bob";
string lastName = "Smith";
string phoneNumber = "(215) 555-4256";
string address = GetAddressFromDatabase(id: 563);
```

## Storing numbers

Numbers are data that we want to perform an arithmetic calculation on, for example, multiplying.

A telephone number is not a number. To decide whether a variable should be stored as a number or not, ask yourself whether you need to multiply two telephone numbers together or whether the number includes special characters such as (414) 555-1234. In these cases, the number is a sequence of characters, so it should be stored as a string.

Numbers can be natural numbers, such as 42, used for counting (also called whole numbers); they can also be negative numbers, such as -42 (called **integers**); or, they can be **real** numbers, such as 3.9 (with a fractional part), which are called **single** or **double-precision floating point** numbers in computing:

```
uint naturalNumber = 23; // unsigned integer means positive whole number
int integerNumber = -23; // integer means negative or positive whole number
double realNumber = 2.3; // double means double-precision floating point
```

You might know that computers store everything as bits. A **bit** is either 0 or 1. This is called a **binary** number system. Humans use a **decimal** number system.

The decimal number system has ten as its base. Although it is the number base most commonly used by human civilizations, other number-base systems are popular in science, engineering, and computing.

## Storing whole numbers

The following table shows how computers store the number 10. Note the 1 bits in the 8 and the 2 columns; *8 + 2 = 10*:

| 128 | 64 | 32 | 16 | 8 | 4 | 2 | 1 |
|---|---|---|---|---|---|---|---|
| 0 | 0 | 0 | 0 | 1 | 0 | 1 | 0 |

So, 10 in decimal is 00001010 in binary.

## C# 7 improvements

Two of the improvements in C# 7 are the use of the underscore character (_) as a **digit separator** and support for **binary literals**.

You can insert underscores anywhere into the digits of a number literal, including decimal, binary, or hexadecimal notation, to improve legibility. For example, you could write the value for one million in decimal notation (Base 10) as: 1_000_000.

To use binary notation (Base 2), using only 1s and 0s, start the number literal with `0b`. To use hexadecimal notation (Base 16), using 0 to 9 and A to F, start the number literal with `0x`, as shown in the following code:

```
int decimalNotation = 2_000_000; // 2 million
int binaryNotation = 0b0001_1110_1000_0100_1000_0000; // 2 million
int hexadecimalNotation = 0x001E_8480; // 2 million
Console.WriteLine($"{decimalNotation == binaryNotation}"); // => true
Console.WriteLine($"{decimalNotation == hexadecimalNotation}"); // => true
```

Computers can always exactly represent integers (positive and negative whole numbers) using the `int` type or one of its sibling types such as `short`.

## Storing real numbers

Computers cannot always exactly represent floating point numbers. The `float` and `double` types store real numbers using single and double precision floating points.

The following table shows how a computer stores the number 12.75. Note the 1 bits in the 8, 4, ½, and ¼ columns.

*8 + 4 + ½ + ¼ = 12¾ = 12.75.*

| 128 | 64 | 32 | 16 | 8 | 4 | 2 | 1 | . | ½ | ¼ | 1/8 | 1/16 |
|---|---|---|---|---|---|---|---|---|---|---|---|---|
| 0 | 0 | 0 | 0 | 1 | 1 | 0 | 0 | . | 1 | 1 | 0 | 0 |

So, 12.75 in decimal is 00001100.1100 in binary.

As you can see, the number 12.75 can be exactly represented using bits. However, some numbers can't, as you will see shortly.

## Using Visual Studio 2017

In Visual Studio 2017, go to **File** | **Add** | **New Project...**. In the **Add New Project** dialog, in **Installed** list, select **Visual C#**. In the list at the center, select **Console App (.NET Core)**, type the name `Numbers`, and then click on **OK**.

In **Solution Explorer**, right-click on the solution and select **Properties** or press *Alt* + *Enter*. For **Startup Project**, select **Current selection**. From now on, you can simply click on a project in **Solution Explorer** and then press *Ctrl* + *F5* to save, compile, and run that project, as shown in the following screenshot:

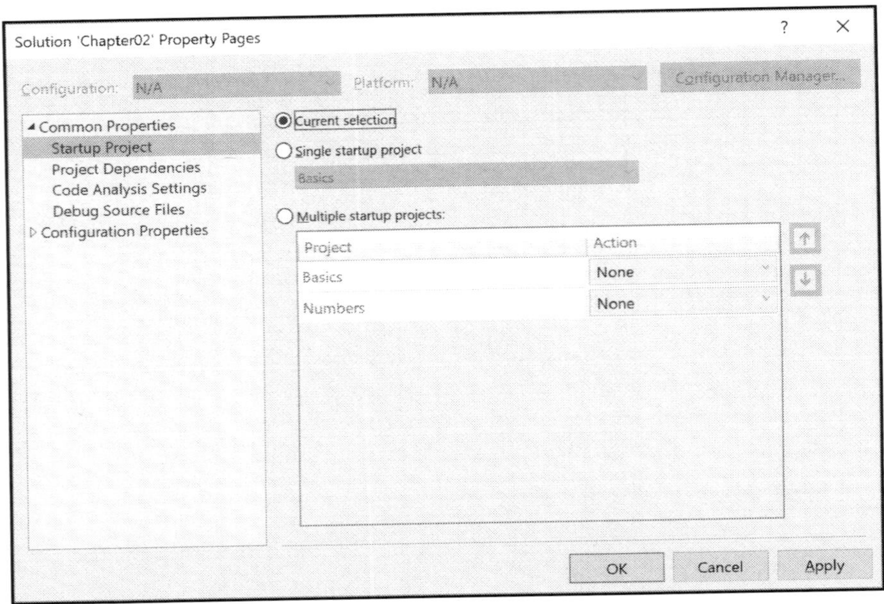

### Using Visual Studio Code

Create a new folder inside the `Chapter02` folder named `Numbers`.

In Visual Studio Code, open the `Numbers` folder and use Integrated Terminal to create a new console application using the `dotnet new console` command. When you open the `Program.cs` file, you will be prompted to restore packages.

## Writing code to explore numbers

Type the following code inside the `Main` method:

```
Console.WriteLine($"int uses {sizeof(int)} bytes and can store
numbers in the range {int.MinValue:N0} to {int.MaxValue:N0}.");
Console.WriteLine($"double uses {sizeof(double)} bytes and can
store numbers in the range {double.MinValue:N0} to
{double.MaxValue:N0}.");
Console.WriteLine($"decimal uses {sizeof(decimal)} bytes and can
store numbers in the range {decimal.MinValue:N0} to
{decimal.MaxValue:N0}.");
```

Remember to enter the statements that use double-quotes in a single line.

Run the console application by pressing *Ctrl* + *F5*, or entering `dotnet run`, and view the output:

```
int uses 4 bytes and can store numbers in the range -2,147,483,648 to
2,147,483,647.
double uses 8 bytes and can store numbers in the range -
179,769,313,486,232,000,000,000,000,000,000,000,000,000,000,000,000,0
00,000,000,000,000,000,000,000,000,000,000,000,000,000,000,000,000,00
0,000,000,000,000,000,000,000,000,000,000,000,000,000,000,000,000,000
,000,000,000,000,000,000,000,000,000,000,000,000,000,000,000,000,000,
000,000,000,000,000,000,000,000,000,000,000,000,000,000,000,000,000,0
00,000,000,000,000,000,000,000,000,000,000,000,000,000,000,000,000 to
179,769,313,486,232,000,000,000,000,000,000,000,000,000,000,000,000,0
00,000,000,000,000,000,000,000,000,000,000,000,000,000,000,000,000,00
0,000,000,000,000,000,000,000,000,000,000,000,000,000,000,000,000,000
,000,000,000,000,000,000,000,000,000,000,000,000,000,000,000,000,000,
000,000,000,000,000,000,000,000,000,000,000,000,000,000,000,000,000,0
00,000,000,000,000,000,000,000,000,000,000,000,000,000,000,000,000.
decimal uses 16 bytes and can store numbers in the range -
```

**79,228,162,514,264,337,593,543,950,335 to 79,228,162,514,264,337,593,543,950,335.**

An `int` variable uses four bytes of memory and can store positive or negative numbers up to about 2 billion. A `double` variable uses eight bytes of memory and can store much bigger values! A `decimal` variable uses 16 bytes of memory and can store big numbers, but not as big as a `double` type.

Why might a `double` variable be able to store bigger numbers than a `decimal` variable, yet use half the space in memory? Let's find out!

## Comparing double and decimal types

Under the previous statements, enter the following code. Do not worry about understanding the syntax right now, although it isn't too hard to follow:

```
double a = 0.1;
double b = 0.2;
if (a + b == 0.3)
{
   Console.WriteLine($"{a} + {b} equals 0.3");
}
else
{
   Console.WriteLine($"{a} + {b} does NOT equal 0.3");
}
```

Run the console application and view the output:

```
0.1 + 0.2 does NOT equal 0.3
```

The `double` type is not guaranteed to be accurate. Only use `double` when accuracy, especially when comparing two numbers, is not important; for example, when measuring a person's height.

The problem with the preceding code is how the computer stores the number 0.1 or multiples of 0.1. To represent 0.1 in binary, the computer stores 1 in the 1/16 column, 1 in the 1/128 column, 1 in the 1/1024 column, and so on. The number 0.1 in decimal is 0.0001001001001 repeating forever:

| 4 | 2 | 1 | . | ½ | ¼ | 1/8 | 1/16 | 1/32 | 1/64 | 1/128 | 1/256 | 1/512 | 1/1024 | 1/2048 |
|---|---|---|---|---|---|---|---|---|---|---|---|---|---|---|
| 0 | 0 | 0 | . | 0 | 0 | 0 | 1 | 0 | 0 | 1 | 0 | 0 | 1 | 0 |

**Good Practice**

Never compare double values using ==. During the First Gulf War, an American Patriot missile battery used double values in its calculations. The inaccuracy caused it to fail to track and intercept an incoming Iraqi Scud missile, and 28 soldiers were killed; you can read about this at: `https://www.ima.umn.edu/~arnold/disasters/patriot.html`

Copy and paste the code you wrote before that used `double` variables and then modify it to look like the following code:

```
decimal c = 0.1M; // M indicates a decimal literal value
decimal d = 0.2M;
if (c + d == 0.3M)
{
   Console.WriteLine($"{c} + {d} equals 0.3");
}
else
{
   Console.WriteLine($"{c} + {d} does NOT equal 0.3");
}
```

Run the console application and view the output:

```
0.1 + 0.2 equals 0.3
```

The `decimal` type is accurate because it stores the number as a large integer and shifts the decimal point. For example, 0.1 is stored as 1, with a note to shift the decimal point one place to the left. 12.75 is stored as 1275, with a note to shift the decimal point two places to the left.

**Good Practice**

Use `int` for whole numbers and `double` for real numbers. Use `decimal` for money, CAD drawings, general engineering, and wherever accuracy of a real number is important.

The `double` type has some useful special values; `double.NaN` means not-a-number, `double.Epsilon` is the smallest positive number that can be stored in a double, and `double.Infinity` means an infinitely large value. You can use these special values when comparing `double` values.

## Storing Booleans

Booleans can only contain one of the two values: `true` or `false`, as shown in the following code. They are most commonly used to branch and loop, as you will see in `Chapter 3`, *Controlling the Flow and Converting Types*:

```
bool happy = true;
bool sad = false;
```

## The object type

There is a special type named `object` that can store any type of data, but its flexibility comes at the cost of messier code and poor performance due to boxing and unboxing operations when storing a value type. You should avoid it whenever possible.

From now on, I will assume that you know how to create a new console application using either Visual Studio 2017 or Visual Studio Code, so I will only give general instructions.

Add a new console application project named `Variables` and add the following code to the `Main` method:

```
object height = 1.88; // storing a double value in an object
object name = "Amir"; // storing a string value in an object
int length1 = name.Length; // gives compile error!
int length2 = ((string)name).Length; // cast to access members
```

The `object` type has been available since the first version of C#, but C# 2 and higher versions have a better alternative called **generics**, which we will cover later, that provide the flexibility we want without the performance overhead.

## The dynamic type

There is another special type named `dynamic` that can also store any type of data, and like `object`, its flexibility comes at the cost of performance. Unlike `object`, the value stored in the variable can have its members invoked without an explicit cast, as shown in the following code:

```
// storing a string in a dynamic object
dynamic anotherName = "Ahmed";
// this compiles but might throw an exception at run-time!
int length = anotherName.Length;
```

The limitation of `dynamic` is that Visual Studio cannot show IntelliSense to help you write the code because the compiler doesn't check at build time. Instead, the CLR checks for the member at runtime. The `dynamic` keyword was introduced in C# 4.

# Local variables

Local variables are declared inside methods and they only exist during the call to that method. Once the method returns, the memory allocated to any local variables is released.

Strictly speaking, value types are released while reference types must wait for a garbage collection. You will learn about the difference between value types and reference types later.

## Specifying the type of a local variable

Enter the following code to declare and assign values to some local variables inside the `Main` method. Note that we specify the type before the name of each variable:

```
int population = 66_000_000; // 66 million in UK
double weight = 1.88; // in kilograms
decimal price = 4.99M; // in pounds sterling
string fruit = "Apples"; // strings use double-quotes
char letter = 'Z'; // chars use single-quotes
bool happy = true; // Booleans have value of true or false
```

Visual Studio 2017 and Visual Studio Code will show green squiggles under each of the variable names to warn you that the variable is assigned, but its value is never used.

## Inferring the type of a local variable

You can use the `var` keyword to declare local variables. The compiler will infer the type from the literal value you assign after the assignment (=) operator.

A literal number without a decimal point is inferred as an `int` variable unless you add the `L` suffix, in which case, it infers a `long` variable. A literal number with a decimal point is inferred as `double` unless you add the `M` suffix, in which case, it infers a `decimal` variable, or the `F` suffix, in which case, it infers a `float` variable. Double quotes indicate a `string` variable, single quotes indicate a `char` variable, and the `true` and `false` values infer a `bool` type.

Modify your code to use `var`:

```
var population = 66_000_000; // 66 million in UK
var weight = 1.88; // in kilograms
var price = 4.99M; // in pounds sterling
var fruit = "Apples"; // strings use double-quotes
var letter = 'Z'; // chars use single-quotes
var happy = true; // Booleans have value of true or false
```

**Good Practice**
Although using `var` is convenient, some developers avoid using it, to make it easier for a code reader to understand the types in use. Personally, I use it only when the type is obvious. For example, in the following code statements, the first statement is just as clear as the second in stating what the type of the `xml` variable is, but it is shorter. However, the third statement isn't clear, so the fourth is better. If in doubt, spell it out!

```
// good use of var
var xml1 = new XmlDocument();
// unnecessarily verbose repeating XmlDocument
XmlDocument xml2 = new XmlDocument();

// bad use of var; what data type is file1?
var file1 =
  File.CreateText(@"C:\something.txt");
// good use of a specific type declaration
StreamWriter file2 =
File.CreateText(@"C:\something.txt");
```

# Making a value type nullable

Most of the primitive types except `string` are **value types**. This means they must have a value. You can determine the default value of a type using the `default()` operator. The default value of an `int` variable is `0` (zero):

```
Console.WriteLine($"{default(int)}"); // 0
Console.WriteLine($"{default(bool)}"); // False
Console.WriteLine($"{default(DateTime)}"); // 1/01/0001 00:00:00
```

Strings are **reference types**. This means that they contain the memory address of a variable, not the value of the variable itself. A reference type variable can have a `null` value. The `null` value is a special literal value that indicates that the variable does not reference anything (yet).

You will learn more about value types and reference types in `Chapter 6`, *Implementing Interfaces and Inheriting Classes*.

Sometimes, for example, when reading values stored in a database that allows null values, it is convenient to allow a value type to be `null`. We call this a **nullable** value type. You can do this by adding a question mark as a suffix to the type when declaring a variable, as shown in the following code:

```
int ICannotBeNull = 4;
int? ICouldBeNull = null;
Console.WriteLine(ICouldBeNull.GetValueOrDefault()); // 0
ICouldBeNull = 4;
Console.WriteLine(ICouldBeNull.GetValueOrDefault()); // 4
```

# Understanding nullable reference types

Arguably, the most significant change to the language that Microsoft plans for C# 8.0 is the introduction of nullable reference types. "But wait!", you are probably thinking, "Reference types are already nullable!" And you would be right, but in C# 8.0, references types will no longer allow the null value by default. In C# 8.0, if you want a reference type to be assigned the null value, then you will have to use the same syntax as making a value type nullable, that is, add a `?` symbol after the type declaration.

This will be a big change that affects all code built with the C# 8.0 compiler, so Microsoft needs lots of testing done before the release of C# 8.0, and as early as possible in the process. They have made a preview of the feature available a year before the expected final release of C# 8.0. You can learn about the preview and download it for testing at the following link:
`https://github.com/dotnet/csharplang/wiki/Nullable-Reference-Types-Preview`

## The billion-dollar mistake

The use of the null value is so common, in so many languages, that many experienced programmers never question the need for its existence. But there are many scenarios where we could write better, simpler code, if a variable is not allowed to have a null value. You can find out more at the following link where the inventor of null, Sir Charles Antony Richard Hoare, admits his mistake in a recorded hour-long talk:
`https://www.infoq.com/presentations/Null-References-The-Billion-Dollar-Mistake-Tony-Hoare`

## Changing the defaults for nullable types in C# 8.0

Microsoft could decide to leave the default for reference types as allowing nulls for compatibility with how it is today, and add new syntax to indicate that a reference type is non-nullable. However, Microsoft is planning something more radical; a change that will cause more pain initially, but will reorient C# better for the long term. This change will also align reference and value types with the same defaults and behavior, making the syntax simpler, and learning and using the language, easier.

So, how will nullable reference types work? Let's look at an example. When storing information about an address, you might want to force a value for the street, city, and region, but building can be left blank (that is, null), as shown in the following code:

```
class Address
{
   string? Building; // can be null
   string Street;    // must have a value
   string City;      // must have a value
   string Region;    // must have a value
}
```

So, this is why the new language feature is named nullable reference types. Starting with C# 8.0, unadorned reference types become non-nullable by default, and the same syntax is used to make a reference type nullable, as is used for value types.

## Checking for null

Checking whether a reference type or nullable value type variable currently contains `null` is important because if you do not, a `NullReferenceException` can be thrown, causing an error in your code:

```
// check is myVariable is not null before using it
if (ICouldBeNull != null)
{
    // do something with ICouldBeNull
}
```

If you are trying to get a field or property from a variable that might be `null`, use the null check operator (`?.`), as shown in the following code:

```
string authorName = null;
// if authorName is null, instead of throwing an exception,
// null is returned
int? howManyLetters = authorName?.Length;
```

Sometimes you want to either assign a variable to a result, or use an alternative value, such as zero, if the variable is null. You do this using the null-coalescing operator (`??`), as shown in the following code:

```
// result will be three if howManyLetters is null
var result = howManyLetters ?? 3;
Console.WriteLine(result);
```

# Storing multiple values in an array

When you need to store multiple values of the same type, you can declare an **array**. For example, you might need to store four names in a `string` array.

The following code declares an array for storing four `string` values. Then, it stores the `string` values at index positions 0 to 3 (arrays count from zero, so the last item is one less than the length of the array). Finally, it loops through each item in the array using a `for` statement that we will cover in more detail in `Chapter 3`, *Controlling the Flow and Converting Types*.

Add the following lines of code to the end of the `Main` method:

```
// declaring the size of the array
string[] names = new string[4];
// storing items at index positions
names[0] = "Kate";
names[1] = "Jack";
names[2] = "Rebecca";
names[3] = "Tom";
for (int i = 0; i < names.Length; i++)
{
   Console.WriteLine(names[i]); // read the item at this index
}
```

Arrays are always of a fixed size at the time of creation, so you need to decide how many items you want to store before instantiating them. An array variable can later be assigned to a new array of a different size. Arrays are useful for temporarily storing multiple items, but collections are more flexible when adding and removing items dynamically. We will cover collections in `Chapter 8`, *Using Common .NET Standard Types*.

# Exploring console applications further

We have already created and used basic console applications, but now we should delve into them more deeply.

Console applications are text-based and are run at Command Prompt. They typically perform simple tasks that need to be scripted, such as compiling a file or encrypting a section of a configuration file. They can have arguments passed to them to control their behavior; for example, to encrypt the database connection strings section in a `Web.config` file, use the following command line:

```
aspnet_regiis -pdf "connectionStrings" "c:\mywebsite"
```

## Displaying output to the user

The two most common tasks that a console application performs are writing and reading data. We have already been using the `WriteLine` method to output. If we didn't want a carriage return at the end of the lines, we could have used the `Write` method.

C# 6 and later has a handy feature named **string interpolation**. This allows us to easily output one or more variables in a nicely formatted manner. A string prefixed with `$` can use curly braces around the name of a variable to output the current value of that variable at that position in the string.

In the `Variables` project, enter the following statements at the bottom of the `Main` method:

```
Console.WriteLine($"The UK population is {population}.");
Console.Write($"The UK population is {population:N0}. ");
Console.WriteLine($"{weight}kg of {fruit} costs {price:C}.");
```

Run the console application and view the output:

```
The UK population is 66000000.
The UK population is 66,000,000. 1.88kg of Apples costs £4.99.
```

A variable can be formatted using special pieces of code. `N0` means a number with commas for thousands and no decimal places. `C` means currency. The currency format will be determined by the current thread. If you run this code on a PC in the UK, you get pounds sterling. If you run this code on a PC in Germany, you would get Euros.

# Getting input from the user

We can get input from the user using the `ReadLine` method. This method waits for the user to type some text. As soon as the user presses *Enter*, whatever the user has typed is returned as a `string` type.

Let's ask the user for their name and age. Later, we will convert the age into a number, but we will leave it as a `string` type for now:

```
Console.Write("Type your first name and press ENTER: ");
string firstName = Console.ReadLine();
Console.Write("Type your age and press ENTER: ");
string age = Console.ReadLine();
Console.WriteLine($"Hello {firstName}, you look good for {age}.");
```

Run the console application and view the output.

Enter `name` and `age`, as shown in the following output:

```
Type your name and press ENTER: Gary
Type your age and press ENTER: 34
Hello Gary, you look good for 34.
```

## Importing a namespace

You might have noticed that unlike our very first application, we have not been typing `System` before `Console`.

`System` is a namespace. Namespaces are like an address for a type. To refer to someone exactly, you might use *Oxford.HighStreet.BobSmith*, which tells us to look for a person named Bob Smith on the High Street in the city of Oxford.

The `System.Console.WriteLine` line tells the compiler to look for a method named `WriteLine` in a type named `Console` in a namespace named `System`.

To simplify our code, Visual Studio 2017, or the `dotnet new console` command when using Visual Studio Code, added a statement at the top of the code file to tell the compiler to always look in the `System` namespace for types that haven't been prefixed with their namespace, as shown in the following code:

```
using System;
```

We call this **importing the namespace**. The effect of importing a namespace is that all available types in that namespace will be available to your program and will be seen in IntelliSense while you write code.

## Simplifying the usage of the console

In C# 6 and later, the `using` statement can be used to further simplify our code.

Add the following line to the top of the file:

```
using static System.Console;
```

Now, we don't need to enter the `Console` type throughout our code. We can use **Find and Replace** to remove it.

Select the first `Console.` line in your code (ensure that you select the dot after the word `Console`).

In Visual Studio 2017, press *Ctrl* + *H* to do a quick replace (ensure that the **Replace...** box is empty), as shown in the following screenshot:

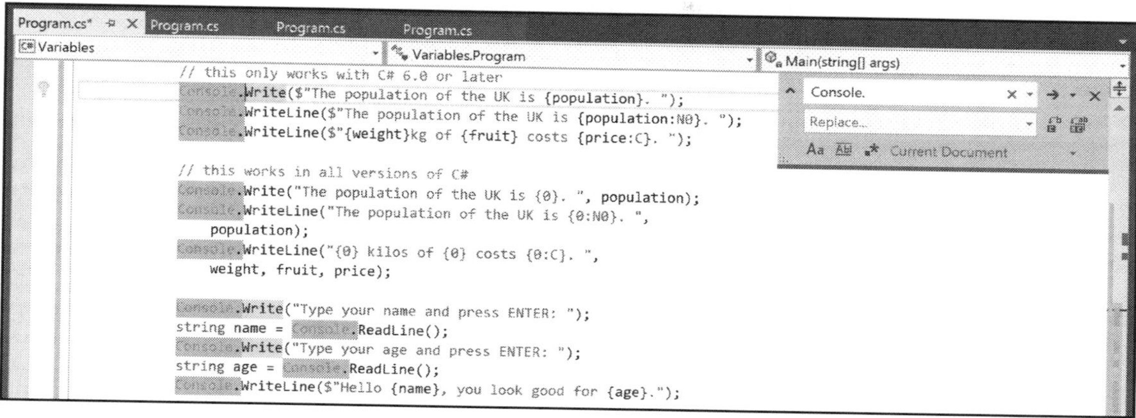


In Visual Studio Code, choose **Edit**, and then **Replace**, as shown in the following screenshot:

```
// declaring the size of the array
string[] names = new string[4];
// storing items at index positions
names[0] = "Kate";
names[1] = "Jack";
names[2] = "Rebecca";
names[3] = "Tom";
for (int i = 0; i < names.Length; i++)
{
    Console.WriteLine(names[i]); // read the item at this index
}

Console.Write($"The population of the UK is {population}. ");
Console.WriteLine($"The population of the UK is {population:N0}. ");
```

In both Visual Studio 2017 and Visual Studio Code, click on the **Replace All** button or press *Alt* + *A* or *Alt* + *Cmd* + *Enter* to replace all; click on **OK**, and then close the replace box by clicking on the cross in its top-right corner.

# Reading arguments and working with arrays

You have probably been wondering what the `string[] args` argument is in the `Main` method. It is an array used to pass arguments into a console application.

Add a new console application project named `Arguments`.

Imagine that we want to be able to enter the following command at Command Prompt:

```
Arguments apples bananas cherries
```

We would be able to read the fruit names by reading them from the `args` array that is always passed into the `Main` method of a console application.

Remember that arrays use the square bracket syntax to indicate multiple values. Arrays have a property named `Length` that tells us how many items are currently in the array. If there is at least one item, then we can access it by knowing its index. Indexes start counting from zero, so the first item in an array is item 0.

Add a statement to statically import the `System.Console` type. Write a statement to output the number of arguments passed to the application. Remove the unnecessary `using` statements. Your code should now look like this:

```
using static System.Console;

namespace Arguments
{
   class Program
   {
      static void Main(string[] args)
      {
         WriteLine($"There are {args.Length} arguments.");
      }
   }
}
```

Remember to statically import the `System.Console` type in future projects to simplify your code, as these instructions will not be repeated.

Run the console application and view the output:

```
There are 0 arguments.
```

## Passing arguments with Visual Studio 2017

In **Solution Explorer**, right-click on the `Arguments` project, and choose **Properties**.

In the **Properties** window, select the **Debug** tab, and in the **Application arguments** box, enter a space-separated list of four arguments, as shown in the following code and screenshot:

```
firstarg second-arg third:arg "fourth arg"
```

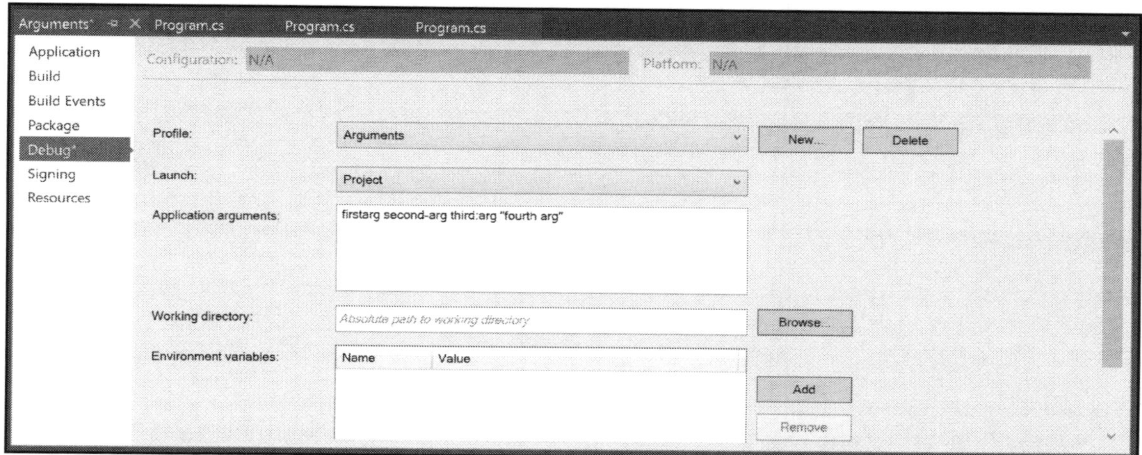

You can use almost any character in an argument, including hyphens and colons. If you need to use a space inside an argument, you must wrap it in double quotes.

## Passing arguments with Visual Studio Code

Type arguments after the `dotnet run` command, as shown in the following example:

```
dotnet run firstarg second-arg third:arg "fourth arg"
```

## Viewing the output

Run the console application with passed arguments, and view the output:

```
There are 4 arguments.
```

# Enumerating arguments

To enumerate or iterate (that is, loop through) the values of those four arguments, add the following lines of highlighted code after outputting the length of the array:

```
WriteLine($"There are {args.Length} arguments.");
foreach (string arg in args)
{
   WriteLine(arg);
}
```

We will now use these arguments to allow the user to pick a color for the background, foreground, width, and height of the console window.

Change the argument values to the following:

```
red yellow 50 10
```

Import the `System` namespace by adding the following line to the top of the code file if it is not already there:

```
using System;
```

We need to import the `System` namespace so that the compiler knows about the `ConsoleColor` and `Enum` types. If you cannot see either of these types in the IntelliSense list, it is because you are missing the `using System;` statement.

Add the highlighted code on top of the existing code like this:

```
ForegroundColor = (ConsoleColor)
  Enum.Parse(typeof(ConsoleColor), args[0], true);
BackgroundColor = (ConsoleColor)
  Enum.Parse(typeof(ConsoleColor), args[1], true);
WindowWidth = int.Parse(args[2]);
WindowHeight = int.Parse(args[3]);

WriteLine($"There are {args.Length} arguments.");
foreach (var arg in args)
{
   WriteLine(arg);
}
```

## Running on Windows

In Visual Studio 2017, press *Ctrl* + *F5*. The console window is now a different size and uses different colors for the foreground and background text, as shown in the following screenshot:

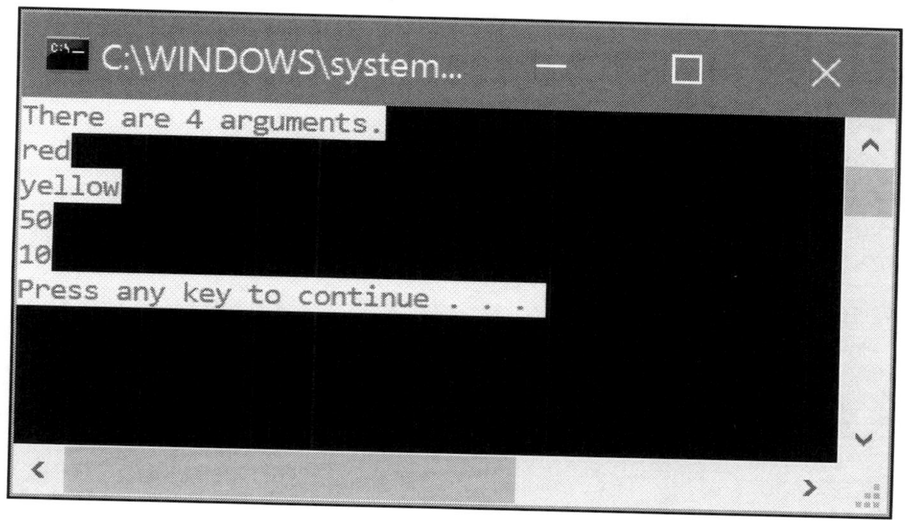


## Running on macOS

In Visual Studio Code, enter the following command at the Terminal:

```
dotnet run red yellow 50 10
```

You will see an error dialog, and details of the error in **Terminal**, as shown in the following screenshot:

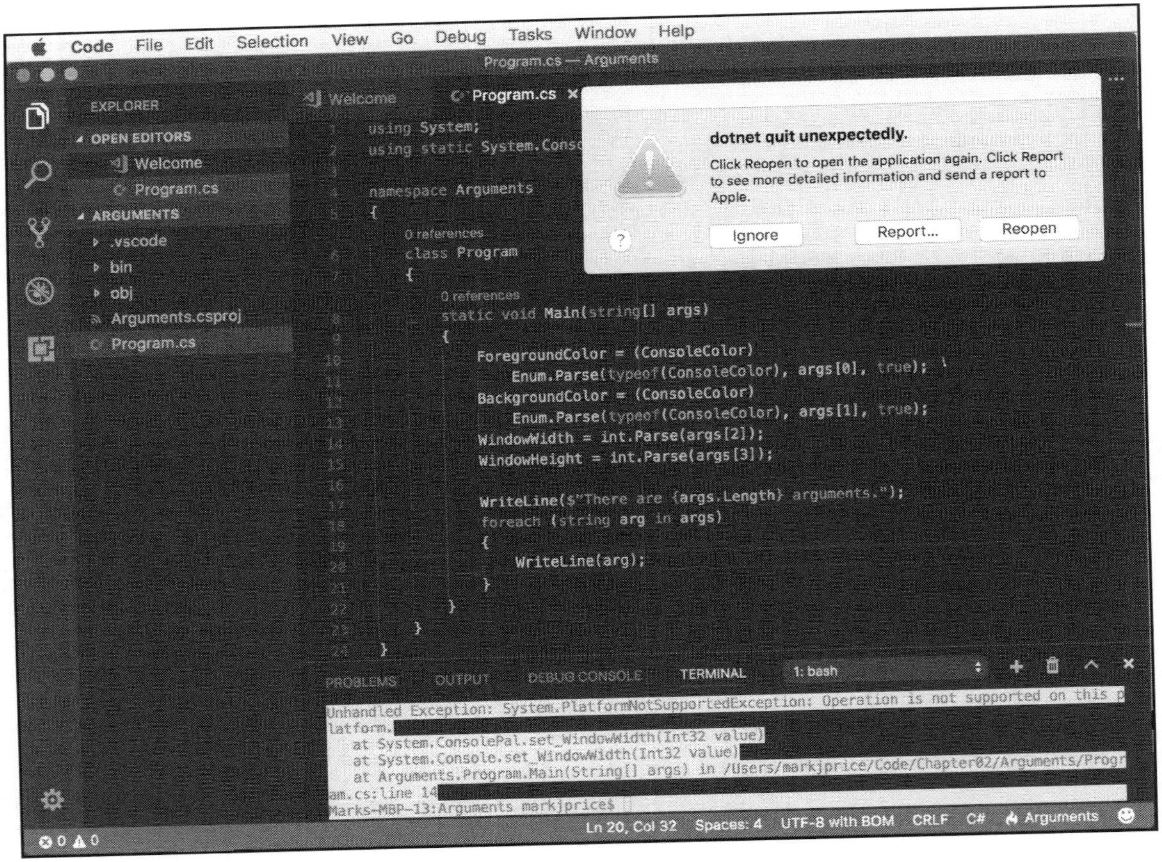

Click on **Ignore**.

Although the compiler did not give an error or warning, at runtime some API calls may fail on some platforms. Although a console application running on Windows can change its size, on macOS it cannot.

## Handling platforms that do not support an API

We can solve this problem using an exception handler. You will learn more details about the `try...catch` statement in `Chapter 3`, *Controlling the Flow and Converting Types*, so for now, just enter the code.

Modify the code to wrap the lines that change the height and width in a `try` statement, as shown in the following code:

```
try
{
    WindowWidth = int.Parse(args[2]);
    WindowHeight = int.Parse(args[3]);
}
catch(PlatformNotSupportedException)
{
    WriteLine("The current platform does not support changing the
    size of a console window.");
}
```

If you rerun the console application, you will see the exception is caught and a friendly message is shown to the user.

# Operating on variables

**Operators** apply simple operations such as addition and multiplication to operands such as numbers. They usually return a new value that is the result of the operation.

Most operators are **binary**, meaning that they work on two operands, as shown in the following pseudocode:

```
var resultOfOperation = firstOperand operator secondOperand;
```

Some operators are **unary**, meaning they work on a single operand, as shown in the following pseudocode:

```
var resultOfOperation = onlyOperand operator;
```

A **ternary** operator works on three operands, as shown in the following pseudocode:

```
var resultOfOperation =
  firstOperand firstOperator secondOperand secondOperator thirdOperand;
```

# Experimenting with unary operators

Two common unary operators are used to increment `++` and decrement `--` a number.

In Visual Studio 2017, navigate to **View** | **Other Windows** | **C# Interactive**.

In Visual Studio Code, create a new console application and write your own statements to output the results using `Console.WriteLine()`.

Enter the following code:

```
> int i = 3;
> i
3
```

Note that when you enter a full statement ending in a semicolon, it is executed when you press *Enter*.

The first statement uses the assignment operator `=` to assign the value `3` to the variable `i`. When you enter a variable name at the prompt, it returns the variable's current value.

Enter the following statements, and before pressing *Enter*, try to guess what the value of `x` and `y` will be:

```
> int x = 3;
> int y = x++;
```

Now check the values of `x` and `y`. You might be surprised to see that `y` has the value `3`:

```
> x
4
> y
3
```

The variable `y` has the value `3` because the `++` operator executes after the assignment. This is known as **postfix**. If you need to increment before assignment, use **prefix**, as shown in the following code:

```
> int x = 3;
> int y = ++x;
> x
4
> y
4
```

You can decrement the value using the `--` operator.

**Good Practice**
Due to the confusion between prefix and postfix for the increment and decrement operators when combined with assignment, the Swift programming language designers plan to drop support for this operator in version 3. My recommendation for usage in C# is to never combine the use of `++` and `--` operators with an assignment `=`. Perform the operations as separate statements.

# Experimenting with arithmetic operators

Arithmetic operators allow you to perform arithmetic operations on numbers.

Enter the following in the **C# Interactive** window:

```
> 11 + 3
14
> 11 - 3
8
> 11 * 3
33
> 11 / 3
3
> 11 % 3
2
> 11.0 / 3
3.6666666666666665
```

To understand the divide (`/`) and modulus (`%`) operators when applied to integers (whole numbers), you need to think back to primary school.

Imagine you have eleven sweets and three friends. How can you divide the sweets between your friends? You can give three sweets to each of your friends and there will be two left over. Those two are the modulus, also known as remainder. If you have twelve sweets, then each friend gets four of them and there are none left over. So, the remainder is 0.

If you start with a real number, such as `11.0`, then the divide operator returns a floating point value, such as `3.6666666666665`, rather than a whole number.

## Comparison and Boolean operators

Comparison and Boolean operators either return `true` or `false`. In the next chapter, we will use comparison operators in the `if` and `while` statements to check for conditions, and the ternary operator.

# Practicing and exploring

Test your knowledge and understanding by answering some questions, get some hands-on practice, and explore the topics covered in this chapter with deeper research.

## Exercise 2.1 – Test your knowledge

What type would you choose for the following "numbers"?

1. A person's telephone number.
2. A person's height.
3. A person's age.
4. A person's salary.
5. A book's ISBN.
6. A book's price.
7. A book's shipping weight.
8. A country's population.
9. The number of stars in the Universe.
10. The number of employees in each of the small or medium businesses in the UK (up to about 50,000 employees per business).

## Exercise 2.2 – Practice number sizes and ranges

Create a console application project named `Exercise02` that outputs the number of bytes in memory that each of the following number types use and the minimum and maximum possible values they can have: `sbyte`, `byte`, `short`, `ushort`, `int`, `uint`, `long`, `ulong`, `float`, `double`, and `decimal`.

Read the online MSDN documentation, available at `https://msdn.microsoft.com/en-us/library/txafckwd(v=vs.110).aspx` for *Composite Formatting* to learn how to align text in a console application.

The output of your application should look something like the following screenshot:

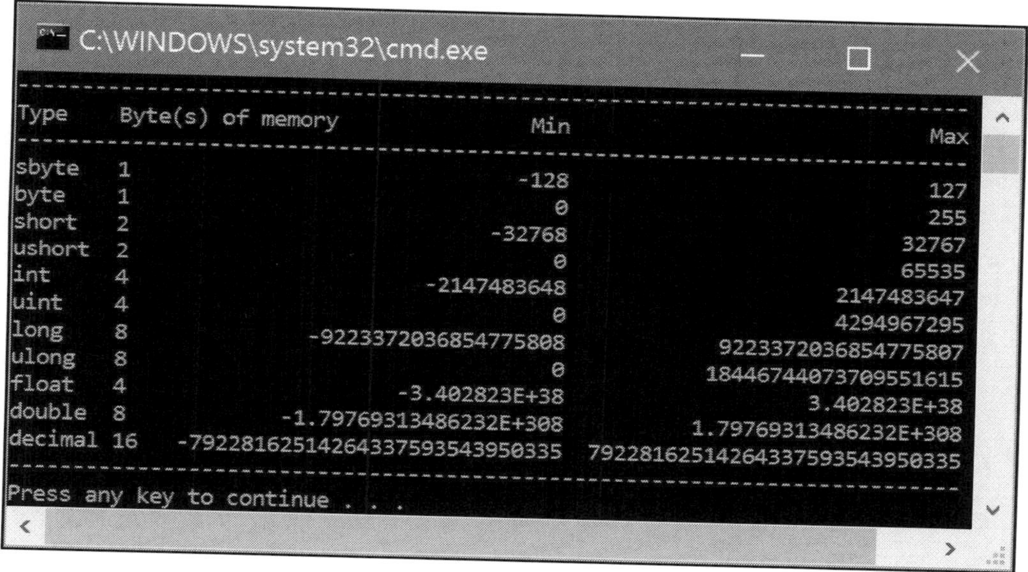


## Exercise 2.3 – Explore topics

Use the following links to read more about the topics covered in this chapter:

- **C# Keywords**: `https://docs.microsoft.com/en-us/dotnet/csharp/language-reference/keywords/index`
- **Main() and command-line arguments (C# Programming Guide)**: `https://docs.microsoft.com/en-us/dotnet/csharp/programming-guide/main-and-command-args/`
- **Types (C# Programming Guide)**: `https://docs.microsoft.com/en-us/dotnet/csharp/programming-guide/types/`
- **Statements, Expressions, and Operators (C# Programming Guide)**: `https://docs.microsoft.com/en-us/dotnet/csharp/programming-guide/statements-expressions-operators/`

- **Strings (C# Programming Guide):** https://docs.microsoft.com/en-us/dotnet/csharp/programming-guide/strings/
- **Nullable Types (C# Programming Guide):** https://docs.microsoft.com/en-us/dotnet/csharp/programming-guide/nullable-types/
- **Console Class**: https://msdn.microsoft.com/en-us/library/system.console(v=vs.110).aspx
- **C# Operators**: https://msdn.microsoft.com/en-us/library/6a71f45d.aspx

# Summary

In this chapter, you learned how to declare variables with a specified or an inferred type; we discussed some of the built-in types for numbers, text, and Booleans; we covered how to choose between number types; and we experimented with some operators.

In the next chapter, you will learn about branching, looping, and converting between types.

# 3
# Controlling the Flow and Converting Types

This chapter is about writing code that makes decisions, repeats blocks of statements, converts between types, handling exceptions, and checking for overflows in number variables.

This chapter covers the following topics:

- Selection statements
- Iteration statements
- Casting and converting between types
- Handling exceptions
- Checking for overflow

## Selection statements

Every application needs to be able to select from choices and branch along different code paths. The two selection statements in C# are `if` and `switch`. You can use `if` for all your code, but `switch` can simplify your code in some common scenarios.

## Using Visual Studio 2017

Start Microsoft Visual Studio 2017. In Visual Studio, press *Ctrl* + *Shift* + *N* or choose **File** | **New** | **Project...**.

In the **New Project** dialog, in the **Installed** list, select **Visual C#**. In the list at the center, select **Console App (.NET Core)**, type the name `SelectionStatements`, change the location to `C:\Code`, type the solution name `Chapter03`, and then click on **OK**.

# Using Visual Studio Code on macOS, Linux, or Windows

If you have completed the previous chapters, then you will already have a `Code` folder in your user folder. If not, create it, and then create a subfolder named `Chapter03`, and then a sub-subfolder named `SelectionStatements`.

Start Visual Studio Code and open the `/Chapter03/SelectionStatements/` folder.

In Visual Studio Code, navigate to **View** | **Integrated Terminal**, and then enter the following command:

```
dotnet new console
```

# The if statement

The `if` statement determines which branch to follow by evaluating a Boolean expression. The `else` block is optional. The `if` statement can be nested and combined. Each Boolean expression can be independent of the others.

## The code

Add the following statements inside the `Main` method to check whether this console application has any arguments passed to it:

```
if (args.Length == 0)
{
   WriteLine("There are no arguments.");
}
else
{
   WriteLine("There is at least one argument.");
}
```

As there is only a single statement inside each block, this code *can* be written without the curly braces, as shown in the following code:

```
if (args.Length == 0)
  WriteLine("There are no arguments.");
else
  WriteLine("There is at least one argument.");
```

This style of the `if` statement is not recommended because it can introduce serious bugs, for example, the infamous *#gotofail* bug in Apple's iPhone operating system. For 18 months after Apple's iOS 6 was released, it had a bug in its **Secure Sockets Layer** (**SSL**) encryption code, which meant that any user running Safari to connect to secure websites, such as their bank, were not properly secure because an important check was being accidentally skipped: `https://gotofail.com/`

Just because you can leave out the curly braces, doesn't mean you should. Your code is not "more efficient" without them, instead, it is less maintainable and potentially more dangerous, as this tweet points out:

Chris Adamson @invalidname · May 26
Had a colleague remove my {} surrounding a 1-line if clause today. No, not angry. It's on his conscience now. **#gotofail**
10 15

## Pattern matching with the if statement

A feature introduced with C# 7 is **pattern matching**. The `if` statement can use the `is` keyword in combination with declaring a local variable to make your code safer.

Add the following statements to the end of the `Main` method. If the value stored in the variable named `o` is an `int`, then the value is assigned to the local variable named `i`, which can then be used inside the `if` statement. This is safer than using the variable named `o` because we know for sure that `i` is an `int` variable and not something else:

```
object o = "3";
int j = 4;

if(o is int i)
{
   WriteLine($"{i} x {j} = {i * j}");
}
else
```

```
{
    WriteLine("o is not an int so it cannot multiply!");
}
```

Run the console application and view the output:

```
o is not an int so it cannot multiply!
```

Delete the double-quote characters around the "3" value so that the value stored in the variable named o is an int type instead of a string type and then rerun the console application and view the output:

```
3 x 4 = 12
```

# The switch statement

The switch statement is different from the if statement because it compares a single expression against a list of multiple possible cases. Every case is related to the single expression. Every case must end with the break keyword (like case 1 in the following code) or the goto case keywords (like case 2 in the following code), or they should have no statements (like case 3 in the following code).

## The code

Enter the following code after the if statements that you wrote previously. Note that the first line is a label that can be jumped to and the second line generates a random number. The switch statement branches based on the value of this random number:

```
A_label:
  var number = (new Random()).Next(1, 7);
  WriteLine($"My random number is {number}");
  switch (number)
  {
      case 1:
        WriteLine("One");
        break; // jumps to end of switch statement
      case 2:
        WriteLine("Two");
        goto case 1;
      case 3:
      case 4:
        WriteLine("Three or four");
        goto case 1;
      case 5:
```

```
        // go to sleep for half a second
        System.Threading.Thread.Sleep(500);
        goto A_label;
      default:
        WriteLine("Default");
        break;
    } // end of switch statement
```

**Good Practice**
You can use the `goto` keyword to jump to another case or a label. The `goto` keyword is frowned upon by most programmers but can be a good solution to code logic in some scenarios. Use it sparingly.

In Visual Studio 2017, run the program by pressing *Ctrl* + *F5*.

In Visual Studio Code, run the program by entering the following command into **Integrated Terminal**:

```
dotnet run
```

Run the program multiple times to see what happens in various cases of random numbers, as shown in the following output from Visual Studio Code:

```
bash-3.2$ dotnet run
My random number is 4
Three or four
One
bash-3.2$ dotnet run
My random number is 2
Two
One
bash-3.2$ dotnet run
My random number is 1
One
```

## Pattern matching with the switch statement

Like the `if` statement, the `switch` statement supports pattern matching in C# 7. The case values no longer need to be literal values. They can be patterns.

Add the following statement to the top of the file:

```
using System.IO;
```

Add the following statements to the end of the `Main` method:

If you are using macOS, then swap the commented statement that sets the `path` variable and replace my username with your user folder name.

```
// string path = "/Users/markjprice/Code/Chapter03";
// macOS
string path = @"C:\Code\Chapter03"; // Windows
Stream s = File.Open(
  Path.Combine(path, "file.txt"),
  FileMode.OpenOrCreate);

switch(s)
{
   case FileStream writeableFile when s.CanWrite:
     WriteLine("The stream is to a file that I can write to.");
     break;
   case FileStream readOnlyFile:
     WriteLine("The stream is to a read-only file.");
     break;
   case MemoryStream ms:
     WriteLine("The stream is to a memory address.");
     break;
   default: // always evaluated last despite its current position
     WriteLine("The stream is some other type.");
     break;
   case null:
     WriteLine("The stream is null.");
     break;
}
```

Note that the variable named `s` is declared as a `Stream` type.

You will learn more about the `System.IO` namespace and the `Stream` type in `Chapter 9`, *Working with Files, Streams, and Serialization*. You can read more about pattern matching at the following link: `https://docs.microsoft.com/en-us/dotnet/csharp/pattern-matching`

In .NET, there are multiple subtypes of `Stream`, including `FileStream` and `MemoryStream`. In C# 7 and later, your code can more concisely both branch, based on the subtype of stream, and declare and assign a local variable to safely use it.

Also, note that the `case` statements can include a `when` keyword to perform more specific pattern matching. In the first `case` statement in the preceding code, `s` would only be a match if the stream was `FileStream` and its `CanWrite` property was true.

# Iteration statements

Iteration statements repeat a block either while a condition is true or for each item in a group. The choice of which statement to use is based on a combination of ease of understanding to solve the logic problem and personal preference.

Use either Visual Studio 2017 or Visual Studio Code to add a new console application project named `IterationStatements`.

In Visual Studio 2017, you can set the solution's start up project to be the current selection so that the current project runs when you press *Ctrl* + *F5*.

## The while statement

The `while` statement evaluates a Boolean expression and continues to loop while it is true.

Type the following code inside the `Main` method:

```
int x = 0;
while (x < 10)
{
   WriteLine(x);
   x++;
}
```

Run the console application and view the output:

```
0
1
2
3
4
5
6
7
8
9
```

## The do statement

The `do` statement is like `while`, except the Boolean expression is checked at the bottom of the block instead of the top, which means that it always executes at least once.

Type the following code at the end of the `Main` method and run it:

```
string password = string.Empty;
do
{
   Write("Enter your password: ");
   password = ReadLine();
} while (password != "secret");
WriteLine("Correct!");
```

You will be prompted to enter your password repeatedly until you enter it correctly, as shown in the following output:

```
Enter your password: password
Enter your password: 12345678
Enter your password: ninja
Enter your password: asdfghjkl
Enter your password: secret
Correct!
```

As an optional exercise, add statements so that the user can only make ten attempts before an error message is displayed.

## The for statement

The `for` statement is like `while`, except that it is more succinct. It combines an initializer statement that executes once at the start of the loop, a Boolean expression to check whether the loop should continue, and an incrementer that executes at the bottom of the loop. The `for` statement is commonly used with an integer counter, as shown in the following code:

```
for (int y = 1; y <= 10; y++)
{
   WriteLine(y);
}
```

Run the console application and view the output, which should be the numbers 1 to 10.

# The foreach statement

The `foreach` statement is a bit different from the other three iteration statements. It is used to perform a block of statements on each item in a sequence, for example, an array or collection. Each item is read-only, and if the sequence is modified during iteration, for example, by adding or removing an item, then an exception will be thrown.

Type the following code inside the `Main` method, which creates an array of string variables and then outputs the length of each of them:

```
string[] names = { "Adam", "Barry", "Charlie" };
foreach (string name in names)
{
   WriteLine($"{name} has {name.Length} characters.");
}
```

Run the console application and view the output:

```
Adam has 4 characters.
Barry has 5 characters.
Charlie has 7 characters.
```

Technically, the `foreach` statement will work on any type that implements an interface called `IEnumerable`. An interface is a contract and you will learn more about them in `Chapter 6`, *Implementing Interfaces and Inheriting Classes*.

The compiler turns the `foreach` statement in the preceding code into something like this:

```
IEnumerator e = names.GetEnumerator();
while (e.MoveNext())
{
   string name = (string)e.Current; // Current is read-only!
   WriteLine($"{name} has {name.Length} characters.");
}
```

Due to the use of an iterator, the variable declared in a `foreach` statement cannot be used to modify the value of the current item.

# Casting and converting between types

You will often need to convert between different types. For example, data input is often done into a text field, so it is initially stored in a variable of the `string` type, but it then needs to be converted into a date, or time, or number, or some other data type, depending on how it should be stored and processed.

Casting has two varieties: **implicit** and **explicit**. Implicit casting happens automatically and it is safe, meaning that you will not lose any information. Explicit casting must be performed manually because it may lose information, for example, the accuracy of a number. By explicitly casting, you are telling the C# compiler that you understand and accept the risk.

Add a new console application project named `CastingConverting`.

## Casting from numbers to numbers

Implicitly casting an `int` variable into a `double` variable is safe.

### Casting numbers implicitly

In the `Main` method, enter the following statements:

```
int a = 10;
double b = a; // an int can be stored in a double
WriteLine(b);
```

You cannot implicitly cast a `double` variable into an `int` variable because it is potentially unsafe and would lose data.

In the `Main` method, enter the following statements:

```
double c = 9.8;
int d = c; // compiler gives an error for this line
WriteLine(d);
```

In Visual Studio 2017, press *Ctrl* + *W*, *E* to view the **Error List**, as shown in the following screenshot:

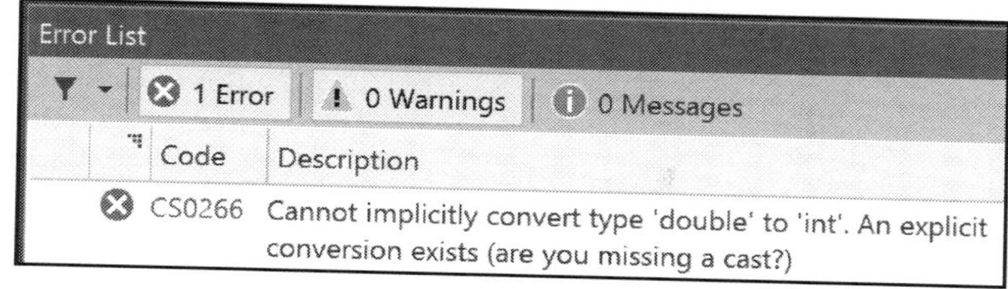


In Visual Studio Code, either view the **PROBLEMS** window, or enter the `dotnet run` command, which will give the following output:

```
Compiling Ch03_CastingConverting for .NETCoreApp,Version=v1.1
/usr/local/share/dotnet/dotnet compile-csc
@/Users/markjprice/Code/Chapter03/Ch03_CastingConverting/obj/
Debug/netcoreapp1.1/dotnet-compile.rsp returned Exit Code 1
/Users/markjprice/Code/Chapter03/Ch03_CastingConverting/Program.cs(14
,21): error CS0266: Cannot implicitly convert type 'double' to 'int'.
An explicit conversion exists (are you missing a cast?)
Compilation failed.
    0 Warning(s)
    1 Error(s)
Time elapsed 00:00:01.0461813
```

## Casting numbers explicitly

You must explicitly cast a `double` variable into an `int` variable using a pair of round brackets around the type you want to cast the `double` type into. The pair of round brackets is the **cast operator**. Even then, you must beware that the part after the decimal point will be trimmed off without warning.

Modify the assignment statement for the `d` variable, as shown in the following code:

```
double c = 9.8;
int d = (int)c;
WriteLine(d); // d is 9 losing the .8 part
```

Run the console application and view the output:

```
10
9
```

We must perform a similar operation when moving values between larger integers and smaller integers. Again, beware that you might lose information because any value too big will get set to `-1`!

Enter the following code:

```
long e = 10;
int f = (int)e;
WriteLine($"e is {e} and f is {f}");
e = long.MaxValue;
f = (int)e;
WriteLine($"e is {e} and f is {f}");
```

Run the console application and view the output:

```
e is 10 and f is 10
e is 9223372036854775807 and f is -1
```

# Using the convert type

An alternative to using the casting operator is to use the `System.Convert` type.

At the top of the `Program.cs` file, type the following code:

```
using static System.Convert;
```

Add the following statements to the bottom of the `Main` method:

```
double g = 9.8;
int h = ToInt32(g);
WriteLine($"g is {g} and h is {h}");
```

Run the console application and view the output:

```
g is 9.8 and h is 10
```

One difference between casting and converting is that converting rounds the double value up to `10` instead of trimming the part after the decimal point.

The `System.Convert` type can convert to and from all the C# number types as well as Booleans, strings, and date and time values.

## Rounding numbers

You have now seen that the cast operator trims the decimal part of a real number and that the convert methods round up or down. However, what is the rule for rounding?

In British primary schools, children are taught to round *up* if the decimal part is `.5` or higher and round *down* if the decimal part is less.

Enter the following code:

```
double i = 9.49;
double j = 9.5;
double k = 10.49;
double l = 10.5;
WriteLine($"i is {i}, ToInt(i) is {ToInt32(i)}");
WriteLine($"j is {j}, ToInt(j) is {ToInt32(j)}");
WriteLine($"k is {k}, ToInt(k) is {ToInt32(k)}");
WriteLine($"l is {l}, ToInt(l) is {ToInt32(l)}");
```

Run the console application and view the output:

```
i is 9.49, ToInt(i) is 9
j is 9.5, ToInt(j) is 10
k is 10.49, ToInt(k) is 10
l is 10.5, ToInt(l) is 10
```

Note that the rule for rounding in C# is subtly different. It will round *up* if the decimal part is `.5` or higher and the nondecimal part is odd, but it will round *down* if the nondecimal part is even. It always rounds *down* if the decimal part is less than `.5`.

This rule is known as **Banker's Rounding**, and it is preferred because it reduces bias. Sadly, other languages such as JavaScript use the primary school rule.

**Good Practice**
For every programming language that you use, check its rounding rules. They may not work the way you expect!

# Converting from any type to a string

The most common conversion is from any type into a `string` variable, so all types have a method named `ToString` that they inherit from the `System.Object` class.

The `ToString` method converts the current value of any variable into a textual representation. Some types can't be sensibly represented as text so they return their namespace and type name.

Add the following statements to the bottom of the `Main` method:

```
int number = 12;
WriteLine(number.ToString());
bool boolean = true;
WriteLine(boolean.ToString());
DateTime now = DateTime.Now;
WriteLine(now.ToString());
object me = new object();
WriteLine(me.ToString());
```

Run the console application and view the output:

```
12
True
27/01/2017 13:48:54
System.Object
```

# Converting from a binary object to a string

When you have a binary object that you want to store or transmit, it is best not to send the raw bits, because you never know how those bits could be misinterpreted, for example, by the network protocol transmitting them or another operating system that is reading the store binary object.

The safest thing to do is to convert the binary object into a string of safe characters. Programmers call this **Base64** encoding.

The `Convert` type has a pair of methods, `ToBase64String` and `FromBase64String`, that perform this conversion for you.

Add the following statements to the end of the `Main` method:

```
// allocate array of 128 bytes
byte[] binaryObject = new byte[128];

// populate array with random bytes
(new Random()).NextBytes(binaryObject);

WriteLine("Binary Object as bytes:");
for(int index = 0; index < binaryObject.Length; index++)
{
   Write($"{binaryObject[index]:X} ");
}
WriteLine();

// convert to Base64 string
string encoded = Convert.ToBase64String(binaryObject);

WriteLine($"Binary Object as Base64: {encoded}");
```

By default, an `int` value would output assuming decimal notation, that is, base10. You can use format codes such as `index:X` to format the value using hexadecimal notation.

Run the console application and view the output:

```
Binary Object as bytes:
B3 4D 55 DE 2D E BB CF BE 4D E6 53 C3 C2 9B 67 3 45 F9 E5 20 61 7E 4F 7A 81
EC 49 F0 49 1D 8E D4 F7 DB 54 AF A0 81 5 B8 BE CE F8 36 90 7A D4 36 42 4 75
81 1B AB 51 CE 5 63 AC 22 72 DE 74 2F 57 7F CB E7 47 B7 62 C3 F4 2D 61 93
85 18 EA 6 17 12 AE 44 A8 D B8 4C 89 85 A9 3C D5 E2 46 E0 59 C9 DF 10 AF ED
EF 8AA1 B1 8D EE 4A BE 48 EC 79 A5 A 5F 2F 30 87 4A C7 7F 5D C1 D 26 EE
Binary Object as Base64:
s01V3i0Ou8++TeZTw8KbZwNF+eUgYX5PeoHsSfBJHY7U99tUr6CBBbi+zvg2kHrUNkIEdYEbq1H
OBWOsInLedC9Xf8vnR7diw/QtYZOFGOoGFxKuRKgNuEyJhak81eJG4FnJ3xCv7e+KobGN7kq+SO
x5pQpfLzCHSsd/XcENJu4=
```

# Parsing from strings to numbers or dates and times

The second most common conversion is from strings to numbers or date and time values. The opposite of `ToString` is `Parse`. Only a few types have a `Parse` method, including all the number types and `DateTime`.

Add the following statements to the `Main` method:

```
int age = int.Parse("27");
DateTime birthday = DateTime.Parse("4 July 1980");
WriteLine($"I was born {age} years ago.");
WriteLine($"My birthday is {birthday}.");
WriteLine($"My birthday is {birthday:D}.");
```

Run the console application and view the output:

```
I was born 27 years ago.
My birthday is 04/07/1980 00:00:00.
My birthday is 04 July 1980.
```

By default, a date and time value outputs with the short date and time format. You can use format codes such as `D` to output only the date part using long date format. There are many other format codes for common scenarios.

One problem with the `Parse` method is that it gives errors if the string cannot be converted.

Add the following statements to the bottom of the `Main` method:

```
int count = int.Parse("abc");
```

Run the console application and view the output:

```
Unhandled Exception: System.FormatException: Input string was not in
a correct format.
```

To avoid errors, you can use the `TryParse` method instead. `TryParse` attempts to convert the input string and returns `true` if it can convert it and `false` if it cannot. The `out` keyword is required to allow the `TryParse` method to set the count variable when the conversion works.

Replace the `int count` declaration with the following statements:

```
Write("How many eggs are there? ");
int count;
string input = Console.ReadLine();
if (int.TryParse(input, out count))
{
   WriteLine($"There are {count} eggs.");
}
else
{
```

```
    WriteLine("I could not parse the input.");
}
```

Run the application twice. The first time, enter `12`. You will see the following output:

```
How many eggs are there? 12
There are 12 eggs.
```

The second time, enter `twelve`. You will see the following output:

```
How many eggs are there? twelve
I could not parse the count.
```

You can also use the `Convert` type; however, like the `Parse` method, it gives an error if it cannot convert.

# Handling exceptions when converting types

You've seen several scenarios when errors have occurred when converting types. C# calls this, *an exception has been thrown.*

Good practice is to avoid writing code that will throw an exception whenever possible, perhaps by performing `if` statement checks, but sometimes you can't. In those scenarios, you must catch the exception and handle it.

As you have seen, the default behavior of a console application is to display details about the exception in the output and then stop running the application.

You can take control over how to handle exceptions using the `try` statement.

## The try statement

Add a new console application project named `HandlingExceptions`.

When you know that a statement can cause an error, you should wrap that statement in a `try` block. For example, parsing from a string to a number can cause an error. We do not have to do anything inside the `catch` block. When the following code executes, the error will get caught and will not be displayed, and the console application will continue running.

In the `Main` method, add the following statements:

```
WriteLine("Before parsing");
Write("What is your age? ");
string input = Console.ReadLine();
try
{
    int age = int.Parse(input);
    WriteLine($"You are {age} years old.");
}
catch
{

}
WriteLine("After parsing");
```

Run the console application and enter a valid age, for example, `43`:

```
Before parsing
What is your age? 43
You are 43 years old.
After parsing
```

Run the console application again and enter an invalid age, for example, `kermit`;

```
Before parsing
What is your age? kermit
After parsing
```

The exception was caught, but it might be useful to see the type of error that occurred.

## Catching all exceptions

Modify the `catch` statement to look like this:

```
catch(Exception ex)
{
    WriteLine($"{ex.GetType()} says {ex.Message}");
}
```

Run the console application and again enter an invalid age, for example, `kermit`:

```
Before parsing
What is your age? kermit
System.FormatException says Input string was not in a correct format.
After parsing
```

## Catching specific exceptions

Now that we know which specific type of exception occurred, we can improve our code by catching just that type of exception and customizing the message that we display to the user.

Leave the existing `catch` block, but add the following code above it:

```
catch (FormatException)
{
   WriteLine("The age you entered is not a valid number format.");
}
catch (Exception ex)
{
   WriteLine($"{ex.GetType()} says {ex.Message}");
}
```

Run the program and again enter an invalid age, for example, `kermit`:

```
Before parsing
What is your age? kermit
The age you entered is not a valid number format.
After parsing
```

The reason we want to leave the more general `catch` below is because there might be other types of exceptions that can occur. For example, run the program and enter a number that is too big for an integer, for example, `9876543210`:

```
Before parsing
What is your age? 9876543210
System.OverflowException says Value was either too large or too small  for
an
Int32.
After parsing
```

Let's add another catch for this new type of exception:

```
catch(OverflowException)
{
   WriteLine("Your age is a valid number format but it is either too big or
small.");
}
catch (FormatException)
{
   WriteLine("The age you entered is not a valid number format.");
}
```

Rerun the program one more time and enter a number that is too big:

```
Before parsing
What is your age? 9876543210
Your age is a valid number format but it is either too big or small.
After parsing
```

The order in which you catch exceptions is important. The correct order is related to the inheritance hierarchy of the exception types. You will learn about inheritance in `Chapter 5`, *Building Your Own Types with Object-Oriented Programming*. However, don't worry too much about this—the compiler will give you build errors if you get exceptions in the wrong order anyway.

# Checking for overflow

Earlier, we saw that when casting between number types, it was possible to lose information, for example, when casting from a `long` variable to an `int` variable. If the value stored in a type is too big, it will overflow.

Add a new console application project named `CheckingForOverflow`.

# The checked statement

The `checked` statement tells .NET to throw an exception when an overflow happens instead of allowing it to happen silently.

We set the initial value of an `int` variable to its maximum value minus one. Then, we increment it several times, outputting its value each time. Note that once it gets above its maximum value, it overflows to its minimum value and continues incrementing from there.

Type the following code in the `Main` method and run the program:

```
int x = int.MaxValue - 1;
WriteLine(x);
x++;
WriteLine(x);
x++;
WriteLine(x);
x++;
WriteLine(x);
```

Run the console application and view the output:

```
2147483646
2147483647
-2147483648
-2147483647
```

Now, let's get the compiler to warn us about the overflow using the `checked` statement:

```
checked
{
   int x = int.MaxValue - 1;
   WriteLine(x);
   x++;
   WriteLine(x);
   x++;
   WriteLine(x);
   x++;
   WriteLine(x);
}
```

Run the console application and view the output:

```
2147483646
2147483647
Unhandled Exception: System.OverflowException: Arithmetic operation
resulted in an overflow.
```

Just like any other exception, we should wrap these statements in a `try` block and display a nicer error message for the user:

```
try
{
   // previous code goes here
}
catch(OverflowException)
{
```

```
    WriteLine("The code overflowed but I caught the exception.");
}
```

Run the console application and view the output:

```
2147483646
2147483647
The code overflowed but I caught the exception.
```

# The unchecked statement

A related keyword is `unchecked`. This keyword switches off overflow checks within a block of code.

Type the following statement at the end of the previous statements. The compiler will not compile this statement because it knows it would overflow:

```
int y = int.MaxValue + 1;
```

Press *F6* or enter the `dotnet run` command to build and notice the error, as shown in the following screenshot from Visual Studio 2017:

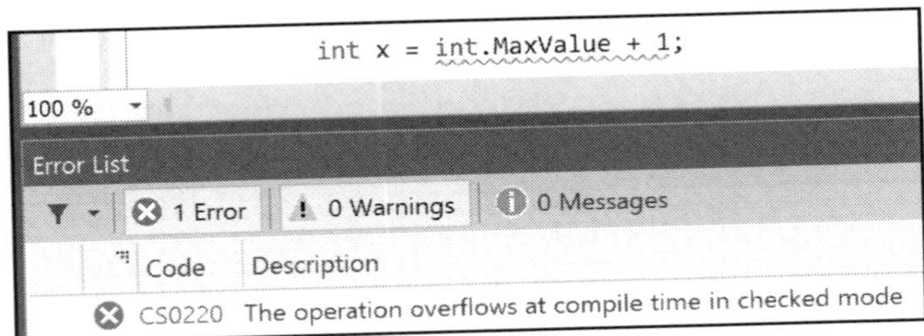


Note that this is a **compile-time** check. To disable compile-time checks, we can wrap the statement in an `unchecked` block, as shown in the following code:

```
unchecked
{
    int y = int.MaxValue + 1;
    WriteLine(y); // this will output -2147483648
    y--;
    WriteLine(y); // this will output 2147483647
    y--;
    WriteLine(y); // this will output 2147483646
}
```

Run the console application and view the output:

```
2147483646
2147483647
The code overflowed but I caught the exception.
-2147483648
2147483647
2147483646
```

Of course, it would be rare that you would want to explicitly switch off a check like this because it allows an overflow to occur. But, perhaps, you can think of a scenario where you might want that behavior.

# Looking for help

This section is about how to find quality information about programming on the web.

## Microsoft Docs and MSDN

The definitive resource for getting help with Microsoft developer tools and platforms used to be **Microsoft Developer Network** (**MSDN**). Now, it is **Microsoft Docs**: `https://docs.microsoft.com/`

Visual Studio 2017 is integrated with MSDN and Docs, so if you press *F1* inside a C# keyword or type, then it will open your browser and take you to the official documentation.

In Visual Studio Code, pressing *F1* shows the **Command Palette**. It does not support context sensitive help.

# Go to definition

Another useful keystroke in both Visual Studio 2017 and Visual Studio Code is *F12*. This will show what the public definition of the type looks like by reading the metadata in the compiled assembly. Some tools will even reverse-engineer from the metadata and IL code back into C# for you.

Enter the following code, click inside `int`, and then press *F12* (or right-click and choose **Go To Definition**):

```
int z;
```

In the new code window that appears, you can see that `int` is in the `mscorlib.dll` assembly; it is named `Int32`; it is in the `System` namespace; and `int` is therefore an alias for `System.Int32`, as shown in the following screenshot:

```
MetadataAsSourceProject                    System.Int32
Assembly mscorlib, Version=4.0.0.0, Culture=neutral, PublicKeyToken=b77a5c561934e089

using ...

namespace System
{
    ...public struct Int32 : IComparable, IFormattable, IConvertible, IComparable<Int32>
    {
        ...public const Int32 MaxValue = 2147483647;
        ...public const Int32 MinValue = -2147483648;
```

>

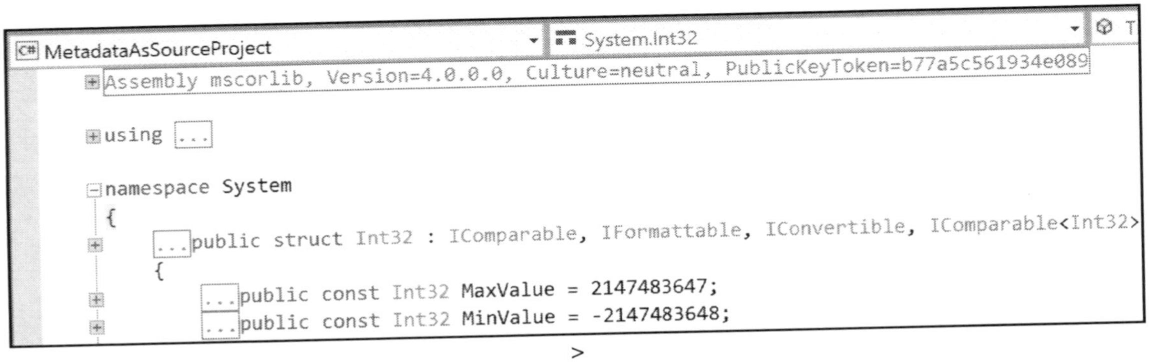

Microsoft defined `int` using a `struct` keyword, meaning that `int` is a value type stored on the stack. You can also see that `int` implements interfaces such as `IComparable` and has constants for its maximum and minimum values.

In the code editor window, scroll down to find the `Parse` methods and in Visual Studio 2017, you will need to click on the small box with a plus symbol in them to expand the code like I have done in the following screenshot:

```
//
// Summary:
//     Converts the string representation of a number to its 32-bit signed integer equivalent.
//
// Parameters:
//   s:
//     A string containing a number to convert.
//
// Returns:
//     A 32-bit signed integer equivalent to the number contained in s.
//
// Exceptions:
//   T:System.ArgumentNullException:
//     s is null.
//
//   T:System.FormatException:
//     s is not in the correct format.
//
//   T:System.OverflowException:
//     s represents a number less than System.Int32.MinValue or greater than System.Int32.MaxValue.
public static Int32 Parse(string s);
```

In the comment, you will see that Microsoft has documented what exceptions might occur if you call this method (`ArgumentNullException`, `FormatException`, and `OverflowException`).

Now, we know that we need to wrap a call to this method in a `try` statement and which exceptions to catch.

# Stack Overflow

**Stack Overflow** is the most popular third-party website for getting answers to difficult programming questions. It is so popular that search engines such as DuckDuckGo have a special way to write a query to search the site.

Go to `DuckDuckGo.com` and enter the following query:

```
!so securestring
```

You will get the following results:

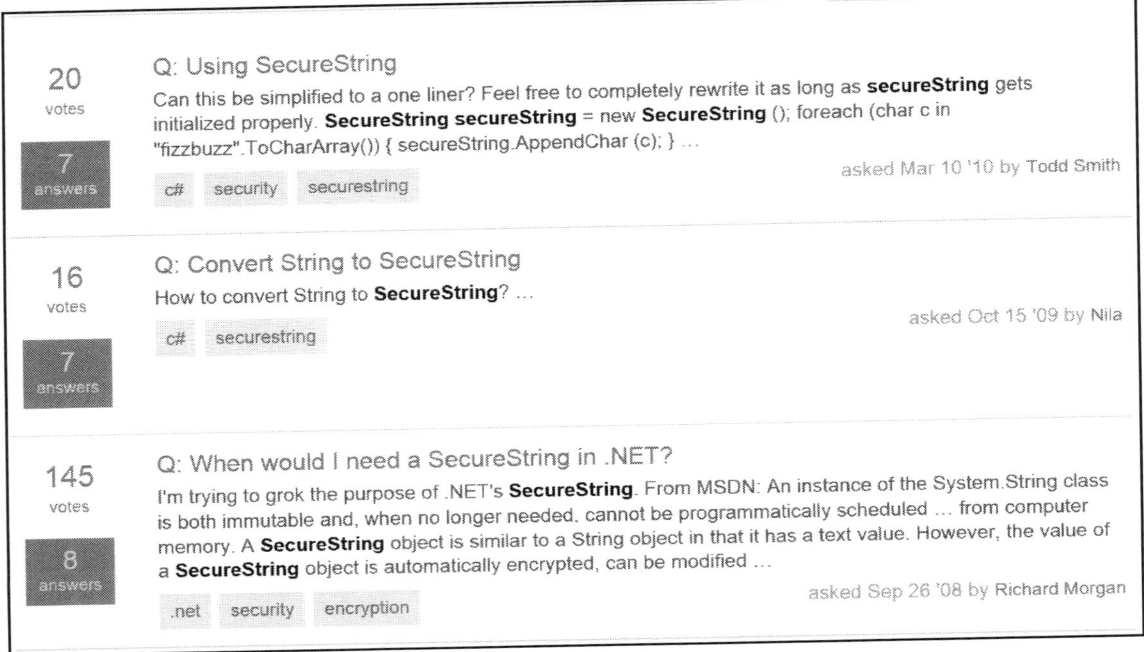


# Google

You can search **Google** with advanced search options to increase the likelihood of finding what you need.

For example, if you are searching for information about `garbage collection` using a simple Google query, you will see a Wikipedia definition of garbage collection in computer science, and then a list of garbage collection services in your local area, as shown in the following screenshot:

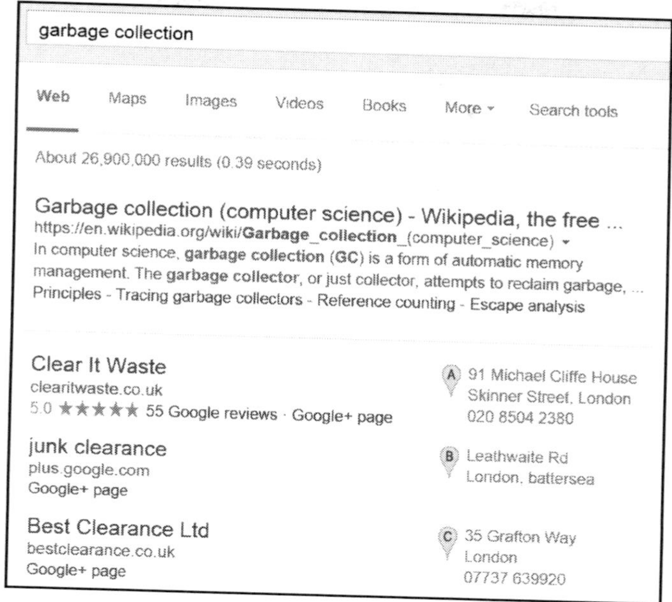


We can improve the search by restricting it to a useful site such as Stack Overflow, as shown in the following screenshot:

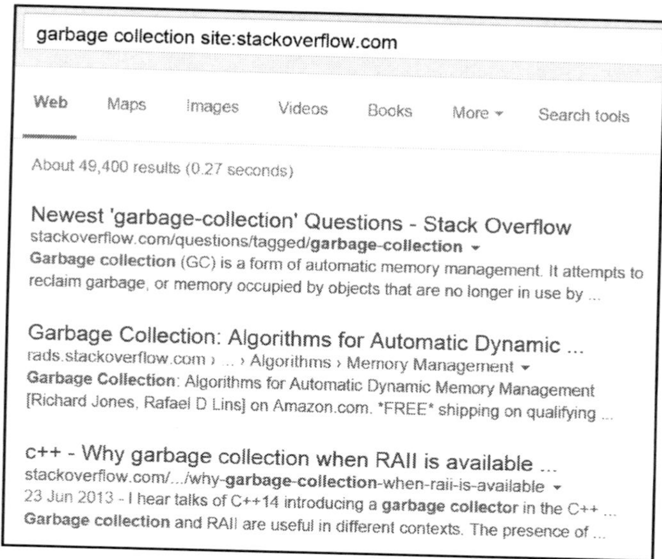

We can improve the search even more by removing languages that we might not care about such as C++, as shown in the following screenshot:

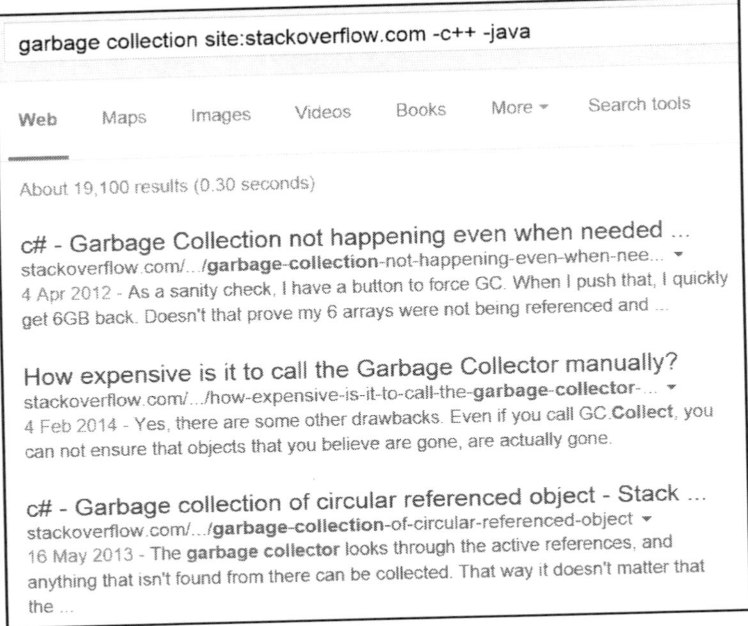


# Subscribing to blogs

To keep up to date with .NET, an excellent blog to subscribe to is the official *.NET Blog* written by the .NET engineering teams. This blog has a tag, *Week in .NET*, which is a summary of interesting news that has happened in the world of .NET in the previous week (`https://blogs.msdn.microsoft.com/dotnet/`).

# Design patterns

A **design pattern** is a general solution to a common problem. Programmers have been solving the same problems over and over. When the community discovers a good reusable solution, we call it a design pattern. Many design patterns have been documented over the years.

Navigate to the following link to read about common design patterns:

https://en.wikipedia.org/wiki/Software_design_pattern#Classification_and_list

Microsoft has a group called *patterns & practices* that specializes in documenting and promoting design patterns for Microsoft products.

**Good Practice**
Before writing new code, search to see if someone else has already solved the problem in a general way.

## Singleton pattern

One of the most common patterns is the **Singleton** pattern. Examples of Singleton in .NET are the `Console` and `Math` types.

Read more about the Singleton pattern at:
https://en.wikipedia.org/wiki/Singleton_pattern

# Practicing and exploring

Test your knowledge and understanding by answering some questions, get some hands-on practice, and explore with deeper research into this chapter's topics.

## Exercise 3.1 – Test your knowledge

Answer the following questions:

1. Where would you look for help about a C# keyword?
2. Where would you look for solutions to common programming problems?
3. What happens when you divide an `int` variable by `0`?
4. What happens when you divide a `double` variable by `0`?
5. What happens when you overflow an `int` variable, that is, set it to a value beyond its range?
6. What is the difference between `x = y++;` and `x = ++y;`?

7. What is the difference between `break`, `continue`, and `return` when used inside a loop statement?
8. What are the three parts of a `for` statement and which of them are required?
9. What is the difference between the = and == operators?
10. Does the following statement compile? `for ( ; true; ) ;`

## Exercise 3.2 – Explore loops and overflow

What will happen if this code executes?

```
int max = 500;
for (byte i = 0; i < max; i++)
{
  WriteLine(i);
}
```

Add a new console application in `Chapter03` named `Exercise02` and enter the preceding code. Run the console application and view the output. What happens?

What code could you add (don't change any of the preceding code) to warn us about the problem?

## Exercise 3.3 – Practice loops and operators

FizzBuzz is a group word game for children to teach them about division. Players take turns to count incrementally, replacing any number divisible by three with the word *fizz*, any number divisible by five with the word *buzz*, and any number divisible by both with *fizzbuzz*.

Some interviewers give applicants simple FizzBuzz-style problems to solve during interviews. Most good programmers should be able to write out on paper or whiteboard a program to output a simulated FizzBuzz game in under a couple of minutes.

Want to know something worrisome? Many computer science graduates can't. You can even find senior programmers who take more than 10-15 minutes to write a solution.

> *"199 out of 200 applicants for every programming job can't write code at all. I repeat: they can't write any code whatsoever."*
>
> *– Reginald Braithwaite*

This quote is taken from the following website:

`http://blog.codinghorror.com/why-cant-programmers-program/`

Refer to the following link for more information:

`http://imranontech.com/2007/01/24/using-fizzbuzz-to-find-developers-who-grok-coding/`

Create a console application in `Chapter03` named `Exercise03` that outputs a simulated FizzBuzz game counting up to 100. The output should look something like this:

```
1, 2, Fizz, 4, Buzz, Fizz, 7, 8, Fizz, Buzz, 11, Fizz, 13, 14,  FizzBuzz,
16, 17,
Fizz, 19, Buzz, Fizz, 22, 23, Fizz, Buzz, 26, Fizz,  28, 29, FizzBuzz, 31,
32,
Fizz, 34, Buzz, Fizz, 37, 38, Fizz, Buzz,  41, Fizz, 43, 44, FizzBuzz, 46,
47,
Fizz, 49, Buzz, Fizz, 52, 53,  Fizz, Buzz, 56, Fizz, 58, 59, FizzBuzz, 61,
62,
Fizz, 64, Buzz, Fizz,  67, 68, Fizz, Buzz, 71, Fizz, 73, 74, FizzBuzz, 76,
77,
Fizz, 79,  Buzz, Fizz, 82, 83, Fizz, Buzz, 86, Fizz, 88, 89, FizzBuzz, 91,
92,
Fizz, 94, Buzz, Fizz, 97, 98, Fizz, Buzz
```

# Exercise 3.4 – Practice exception handling

Create a console application in `Chapter03` named `Exercise04` that asks the user for two numbers in the range 0-255 and then divides the first number by the second:

```
Enter a number between 0 and 255: 100
Enter another number between 0 and 255: 8
100 divided by 8 is 12
```

Write exception handlers to catch any thrown errors:

```
Enter a number between 0 and 255: apples
Enter another number between 0 and 255: bananas
FormatException: Input string was not in a correct format.
```

## Exercise 3.5 – Explore topics

Use the following links to read in more detail about the topics covered in this chapter:

- **Selection Statements (C# Reference)**: https://docs.microsoft.com/en-us/dotnet/articles/csharp/language-reference/keywords/selection-statements
- **Iteration Statements (C# Reference)**: https://docs.microsoft.com/en-us/dotnet/articles/csharp/language-reference/keywords/iteration-statements
- **Jump Statements (C# Reference)**: https://docs.microsoft.com/en-us/dotnet/articles/csharp/language-reference/keywords/jump-statements
- **Casting and Type Conversions (C# Programming Guide)**: https://docs.microsoft.com/en-us/dotnet/articles/csharp/programming-guide/types/casting-and-type-conversions
- **Exception Handling Statements (C# Reference)**: https://docs.microsoft.com/en-us/dotnet/articles/csharp/language-reference/keywords/exception-handling-statements
- **Stack Overflow**: http://stackoverflow.com/
- **Google Advanced Search**: http://www.google.com/advanced_search
- **Microsoft Virtual Academy**: https://mva.microsoft.com/
- **Microsoft Channel 9: Developer Videos**: https://channel9.msdn.com/
- **Design Patterns**: https://msdn.microsoft.com/en-us/library/ff649977.aspx
- **patterns & practices**: https://msdn.microsoft.com/en-us/library/ff921345.aspx

# Summary

In this chapter, you learned how to branch and loop, how to convert between types, how to catch exceptions, and most importantly, how to find help.

You are now ready to learn how to track down bugs in your code and squash them!

# 4
# Writing, Debugging, and Testing Functions

This chapter is about writing functions to reuse code, debugging logic errors during development, logging exceptions during runtime, and unit testing your code to remove bugs and ensure stability and reliability.

This chapter covers the following topics:

- Writing functions
- Debugging during development
- Logging during runtime
- Unit testing

## Writing functions

A fundamental principle of programming is **Don't Repeat Yourself** (**DRY**).

While programming, if you find yourself writing the same statements over and over, then turn those statements into a function. Functions are like tiny programs that complete one small task. For example, you might write a function to calculate sales tax and then reuse that function in many places in a financial application.

Like programs, functions usually have inputs and outputs. They are sometimes described as black boxes, where you feed some raw materials in one end and a manufactured item emerges at the other. Once created, you don't need to think about how they work.

Let's say that you want to help your child learn their times tables, so you want to make it easy to generate a times table for a number, such as the 12 times table:

```
1 x 12 = 12
2 x 12 = 24
...
12 x 12 = 144
```

You previously learned about the `for` statement, so you know that `for` can be used to generate repeated lines of output when there is a regular pattern, like the 12 times table, as shown in the following code:

```
for (int row = 1; row <= 12; row++)
{
   Console.WriteLine($"{row} x 12 = {row * 12}");
}
```

However, instead of outputting the 12 times table, we want to make this more flexible, so it could output the times table for any number. We can do this by creating a function, also known as a **method**.

# Writing a times table function

Create a solution/folder named `Chapter04`, and add a new console application project named `WritingFunctions`.

Modify the template file as shown in the following code:

```
using static System.Console;

namespace WritingFunctions
{
   class Program
   {
      static void TimesTable(byte number)
      {
         WriteLine($"This is the {number} times table");
         for (int row = 1; row <= 12; row++)
         {
           WriteLine(
             $"{row} x {number} = {row * number}");
         }
      }

      static void RunTimesTable()
```

```
        {
            Write("Enter a number between 0 and 255: ");
            if (byte.TryParse(ReadLine(), out byte number))
            {
                TimesTable(number);
            }
            else
            {
                WriteLine("You did not enter a valid number!");
            }
        }

        static void Main(string[] args)
        {
            RunTimesTable();
        }
    }
}
```

Note the following:

- We have statically imported the `Console` type so that we can simplify calls to its methods such as `WriteLine`.
- We have written a function named `TimesTable` that can have a `byte` value passed to it named `number`.
- The `TimesTable` function uses a `for` statement to output the times table for the number passed to it.
- We have written a function named `RunTimesTable` that prompts the user to enter a number, and then calls the `TimesTable` method, passing it the entered number. It includes handling for dealing with the scenario where the user does not enter a valid number.
- We call the `RunTimeTable` function in the `Main` method.

The function named `TimesTable` has one input: a parameter named `number` that must be a `byte` value. `TimesTable` does not return a value to the caller, so it is declared with the `void` keyword before its name.

Run the console application, enter a number, for example, 6, and view the output:

```
Enter a number between 0 and 255: 6
This is the 6 times table:
1 x 6 = 6
2 x 6 = 12
3 x 6 = 18
4 x 6 = 24
5 x 6 = 30
6 x 6 = 36
7 x 6 = 42
8 x 6 = 48
9 x 6 = 54
10 x 6 = 60
11 x 6 = 66
12 x 6 = 72
```

# Writing a function that returns a value

The previous function performed actions (looping and writing to the console), but it did not return a value.

Let's say that you need to calculate sales tax or **valued-added tax (VAT)**. In Europe, VAT rates range from 8% in Switzerland to 27% in Hungary. In the United States, state sales taxes range from 0% in Oregon to 8.25% in California.

Add another function to the `Program` class named `SalesTax`, with a function to run it, as shown in the following code, and note the following:

- The `SalesTax` function has two inputs: a parameter named `amount` that will be the amount of money spent, and a parameter named `twoLetterRegionCode` that will be the region the amount is spent in
- The `SalesTax` function will perform a calculation using a `switch` statement, and then return the sales tax owed on the amount as a `decimal` value; so, before the name of the function, we have declared the data type of the return value
- The `RunSalesTax` function prompts the user to enter an amount and a region code, and then calls `SalesTax` and outputs the result.

```
static decimal SalesTax(
  decimal amount, string twoLetterRegionCode)
{
   decimal rate = 0.0M;
   switch (twoLetterRegionCode)
   {
```

```
        case "CH": // Switzerland
          rate = 0.08M;
          break;
        case "DK": // Denmark
        case "NO": // Norway
          rate = 0.25M;
          break;
        case "GB": // United Kingdom
        case "FR": // France
          rate = 0.2M;
          break;
        case "HU": // Hungary
          rate = 0.27M;
          break;
        case "OR": // Oregon
        case "AK": // Alaska
        case "MT": // Montana
          rate = 0.0M;
          break;
        case "ND": // North Dakota
        case "WI": // Wisconsin
        case "ME": // Maryland
        case "VA": // Virginia
          rate = 0.05M;
          break;
        case "CA": // California
          rate = 0.0825M;
          break;
        default: // most US states
          rate = 0.06M;
          break;
    }
    return amount * rate;
}

static void RunSalesTax()
{
    Write("Enter an amount: ");
    string amountInText = ReadLine();
    Write("Enter a two letter region code: ");
    string region = ReadLine();
    if (decimal.TryParse(amountInText, out decimal amount))
    {
        decimal taxToPay = SalesTax(amount, region);
        WriteLine($"You must pay {taxToPay} in sales tax.");
    }
    else
    {
```

```
            WriteLine("You did not enter a valid amount!");
        }
    }
```

In the `Main` method, comment the `RunTimesTable` method call, and call the `RunSalesTax` method, as shown in the following code:

```
// RunTimesTable();

RunSalesTax();
```

Run the console application, enter an amount and a region code, and view the output:

```
Enter an amount: 149
Enter a two letter region code: FR
You must pay 29.8 in sales tax.
```

Can you think of any problems with the `SalesTax` function as written? What would happen if the user enters a code of UK? How could you rewrite the function to improve it?

# Writing mathematical functions

Although you might never create an application that needs to have mathematical functionality, everyone studies mathematics at school, so using mathematics is a common way to learn about functions.

## Formatting numbers for output

Numbers that are used to count are called **cardinal** numbers, for example, 1, 2, and 3. Numbers that are used to order are **ordinal** numbers, for example, 1$^{st}$, 2$^{nd}$, and 3$^{rd}$.

We will write a function named `CardinalToOrdinal` that converts a cardinal `int` value into an ordinal `string` value; for example, it converts `1` into `1st`, `2` into `2nd`, and so on, as shown in the following code:

```
static string CardinalToOrdinal(int number)
{
    switch (number)
    {
        case 11:
        case 12:
        case 13:
```

```
            return $"{number}th";
          default:
            string numberAsText = number.ToString();
            char lastDigit =
              numberAsText[numberAsText.Length - 1];
            string suffix = string.Empty;
            switch (lastDigit)
            {
              case '1':
                suffix = "st";
                break;
              case '2':
                suffix = "nd";
                break;
              case '3':
                suffix = "rd";
                break;
              default:
                suffix = "th";
                break;
            }
            return $"{number}{suffix}";
      }
    }

    static void RunCardinalToOrdinal()
    {
      for (int number = 1; number <= 40; number++)
      {
        Write($"{CardinalToOrdinal(number)} ");
      }
    }
```

Note the following:

- The `CardinalToOrdinal` function has one input: a parameter of the `int` type named `number`, and one output: a return value of the `string` type
- A `switch` statement is used to handle the special cases of `11`, `12`, and `13`
- A nested `switch` statement then handles all other cases: if the last digit is `1`, then use `st` as the suffix, if the last digit is `2`, then use `nd` as the suffix, if the last digit is `3`, then use `rd` as the suffix, and if the last digit is anything else, then use `th` as the suffix
- The `RunCardinalToOrdinal` function uses a `for` statement to loop from 1 to 40, calling the `CardinalToOrdinal` function for each number and writing the returned string to the console, separated by a space character

In the `Main` method, comment the `RunSalesTax` method call, and call the `RunCardinalToOrdinal` method, as shown in the following code:

```
// RunTimesTable();
// RunSalesTax();

RunCardinalToOrdinal();
```

Run the console application and view the output:

```
1st 2nd 3rd 4th 5th 6th 7th 8th 9th 10th 11th 12th 13th 14th 15th 16th 17th
18th 19th 20th 21st 22nd 23rd 24th 25th 26th 27th 28th 29th 30th 31st 32nd
33rd 34th 35th 36th 37th 38th 39th 40th
```

## Calculating factorials with recursion

The factorial of 5 is 120, because factorials are calculated by multiplying the starting number by one less than itself, and then by one less again, and so on, until the number is reduced to 1, like this: *5 x 4 x 3 x 2 x 1 = 120*.

We will write a function named `Factorial` that calculates the factorial for an `int` passed to it as a parameter. We will use a clever technique called **recursion**, which means a function that calls itself.

Recursion is clever, but it can lead to problems, such as a stack overflow due to too many function calls. Iteration is a more practical, if less succinct, solution in languages like C#. You can read more about this at the following link: `https://en.wikipedia.org/wiki/Recursion_(computer_science)#Recursion_versus_iteration`

Add a function named `Factorial`, as shown in the following code:

```
static int Factorial(int number)
{
   if (number < 1)
   {
      return 0;
   }
   else if (number == 1)
   {
      return 1;
   }
   else
   {
```

```
            return number * Factorial(number - 1);
        }
    }

    static void RunFactorial()
    {
        Write("Enter a number: ");
        if (int.TryParse(ReadLine(), out int number))
        {
            WriteLine(
              $"{number:N0}! = {Factorial(number):N0}");
        }
        else
        {
            WriteLine("You did not enter a valid number!");
        }
    }
```

Note the following:

- If the input number is zero or negative, `Factorial` returns `0`.
- If the input number is `1`, `Factorial` returns `1`, and therefore stops calling itself.
- If the input number is larger than one, `Factorial` multiplies the number by the result of calling itself and passing one less than the number. This makes the function recursive.
- `RunFactorial` prompts the user to enter a number, calls the `Factorial` function, and then outputs the result, formatted using the code `N0`, which means number format and use commas to show thousands with zero decimal places.

In the `Main` method, comment the `RunCardinalToOrdinal` method call, and call the `RunFactorial` method.

Run the console application several times, entering various numbers, and view the output:

```
Enter a number: 3
3! = 6
Enter a number: 5
5! = 120
Enter a number: 31
31! = 738,197,504
Enter a number: 32
32! = -2,147,483,648
```

Factorials are written like this: 5!, where the exclamation mark is read as *bang*, so 5! = 120, that is, *five bang equals one hundred and twenty*. Bang is a good name for factorials because they increase in size very rapidly, just like an explosion. As you can see in the previous output, factorials of 32 and higher will overflow the `int` type because they are so big.

# Debugging an application during development

In this section, you will learn how to debug problems at development time.

## Creating an application with a deliberate bug

Add a new console application project named `Debugging`.

Modify the template code to look like this:

```
using static System.Console;

namespace Debugging
{
   class Program
   {
      static double Add(double a, double b)
      {
         return a * b; // deliberate bug!
      }

      static void Main(string[] args)
      {
         double a = 4.5; // or use var
         double b = 2.5;
         double answer = Add(a, b);
         WriteLine($"{a} + {b} = {answer}");
         ReadLine(); // wait for user to press ENTER
      }
   }
}
```

Run the console application and view the output:

```
4.5 + 2.5 = 11.25
```

There is a bug: `4.5` added to `2.5` should be `7` and not `11.25`!

We will use the debugging tools in Visual Studio 2017 or Visual Studio Code to squash the bug.

## Setting a breakpoint

Breakpoints allow us to mark a line of code that we want to pause at to find bugs. Click on the open curly brace at the beginning of the `Main` method and press *F9*.

A red circle will appear in the margin bar on the left-hand side to indicate that a breakpoint has been set, as shown in the following screenshot:

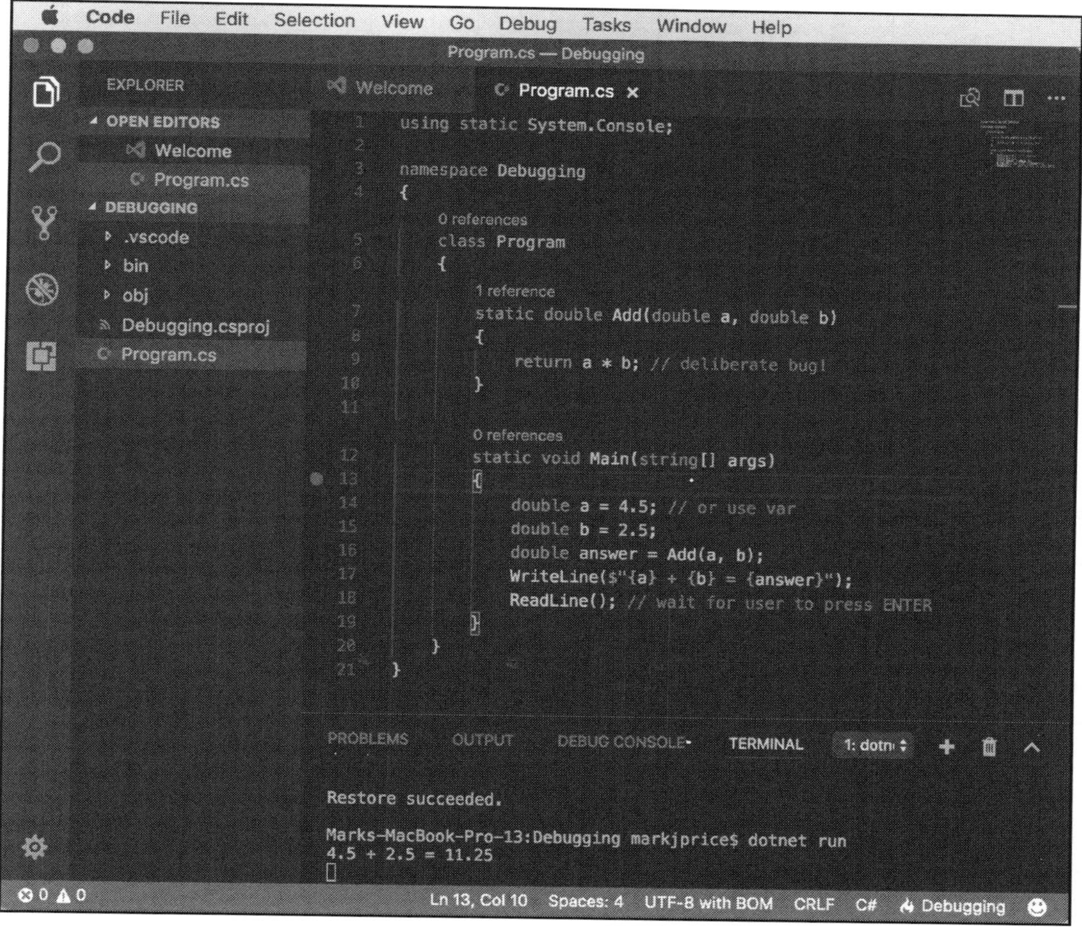

Breakpoints can be toggled with *F9*. You can also left-click in the margin to toggle the breakpoint on and off, or right-click to see more options, such as remove, disable, or edit the breakpoint.

In Visual Studio 2017, go to **Debug** | **Start Debugging**, or click on the **Start** toolbar button, or press *F5*.

In Visual Studio Code, go to **View** | **Debug**, or press *Shift* + *Cmd* + *D*, and then click on the **Start Debugging** button, or press *F5*.

Visual Studio starts the console application executing and then pauses when it hits the breakpoint. This is known as **break mode**. The line that will be executed next is highlighted in yellow, and a yellow arrow points at the line from the gray margin bar, as shown in the following screenshot:

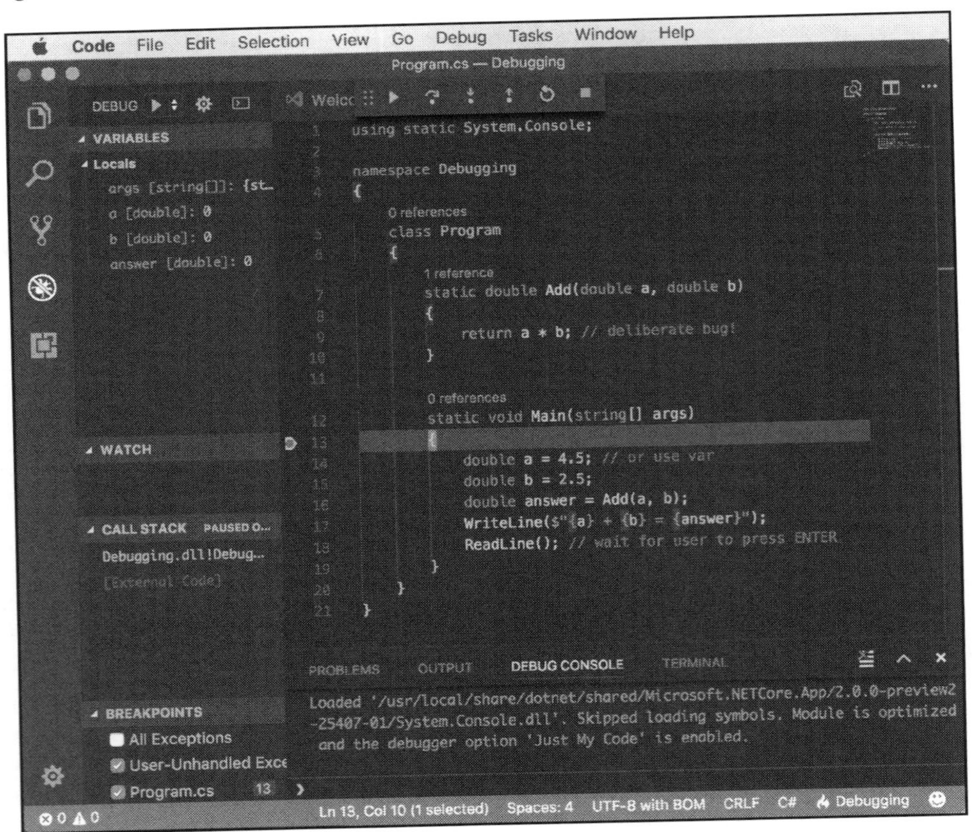

# The debugging toolbar

Visual Studio 2017 enables some extra toolbar buttons to make it easy to access debugging features. Here are a few of those:

- **Continue**/*F5* (green triangle): This button will run the code at full speed from the current position
- **Stop Debugging** / *Shift* + *F5* (red square): This button will stop the program
- **Restart**/*Ctrl* or *Cmd* + *Shift* + *F5* (circular black arrow): This button will stop and then immediately restart the program
- **Step Into** / *F11*, **Step Over** / *F10*, and **Step Out** / *Shift* + *F11* (blue arrows over dots): This button will step through the code in various ways

The following screenshot illustrates Visual Studio 2017's extra toolbar buttons:

The following screenshot illustrates Visual Studio Code's extra toolbar buttons:

# Debugging windows

Visual Studio 2017 makes some extra windows visible so that you can monitor useful information, such as variables, while you step through your code. If you cannot find one of these windows, then, in Visual Studio 2017, navigate to **Debug** | **Windows**, and then select the window you want to view, as shown in the following screenshot:

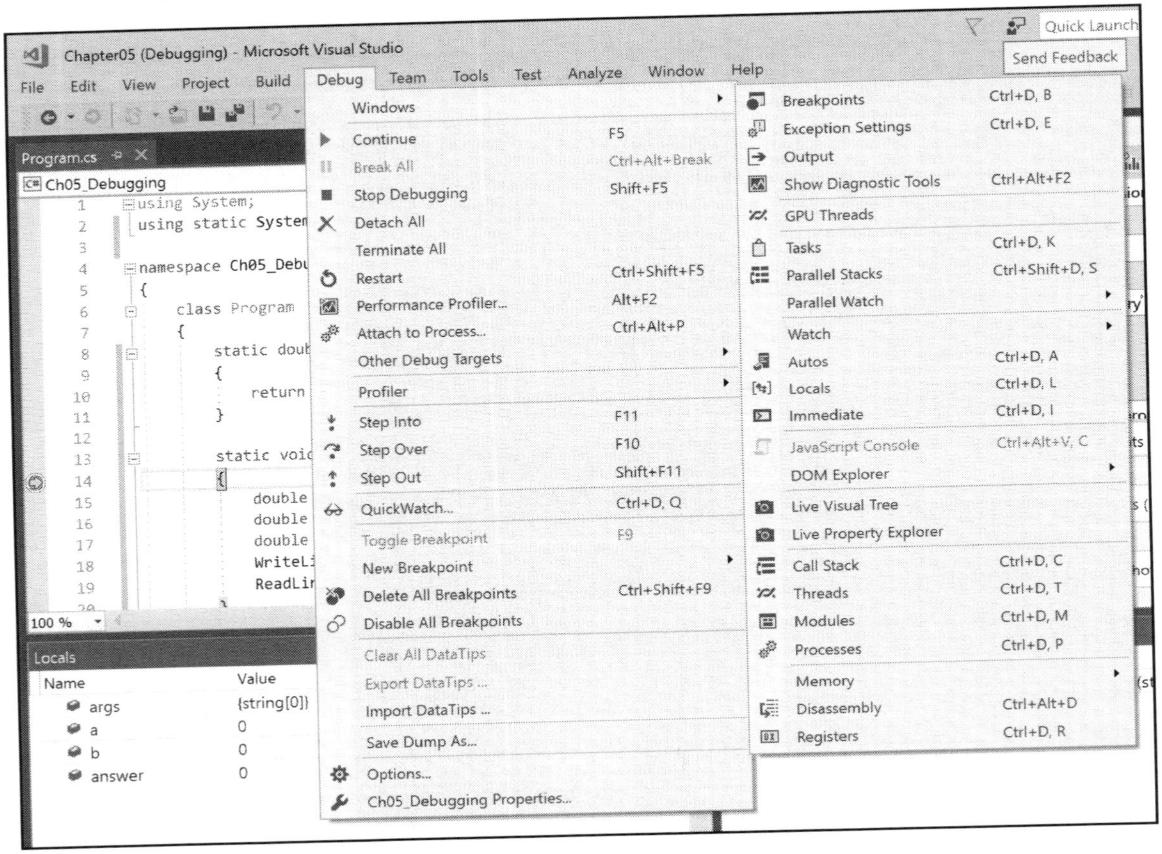

Most of the debug windows are only available when you are in the break mode.

In Visual Studio Code, the windows are all in the **Debug** view on the left-hand side, as shown in the earlier screenshot.

The **Locals** windows in Visual Studio 2017 and Visual Studio Code, show the name, value, and type for any local variables. Keep an eye on this window while you step through your code, as shown in the following screenshots:

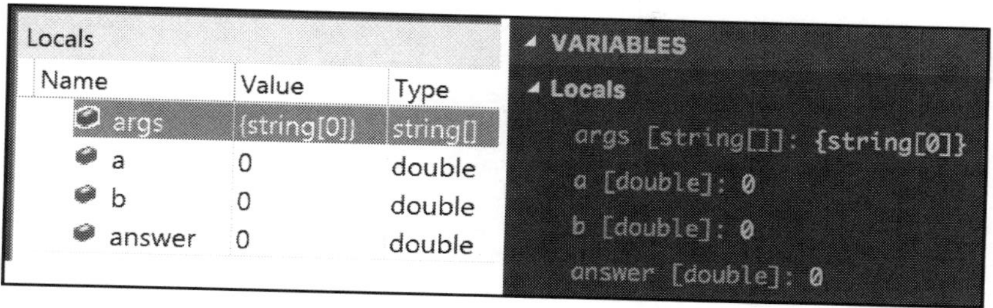


In `Chapter 1`, *Hello, C#! Welcome, .NET Core!*, I introduced you to the **C# Interactive** window. The similar but more basic Visual Studio 2017 **Immediate Window** and Visual Studio Code **DEBUG CONSOLE** also allow live interaction with your code.

For example, you can ask a question such as, "What is 1+2?" by typing `1+2` and pressing *Enter*, as shown in the following screenshot:

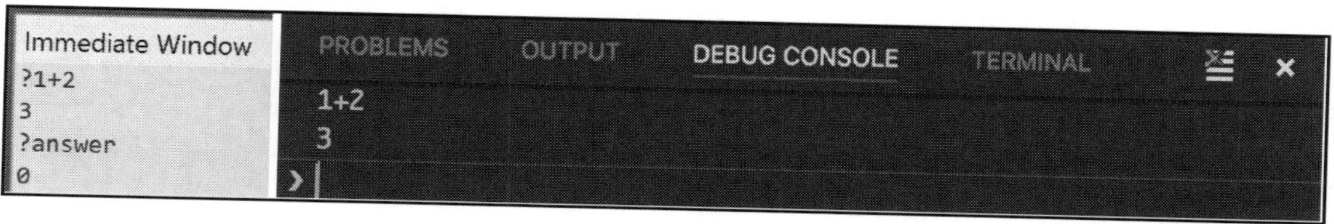


## Stepping through code

In Visual Studio 2017, navigate to **Debug** | **Step Into**, or in both Visual Studio 2017 and Visual Studio Code, click on the **Step Into** button in the toolbar, or press *F11*.

The yellow highlight steps forward one line, as shown in the following screenshot:

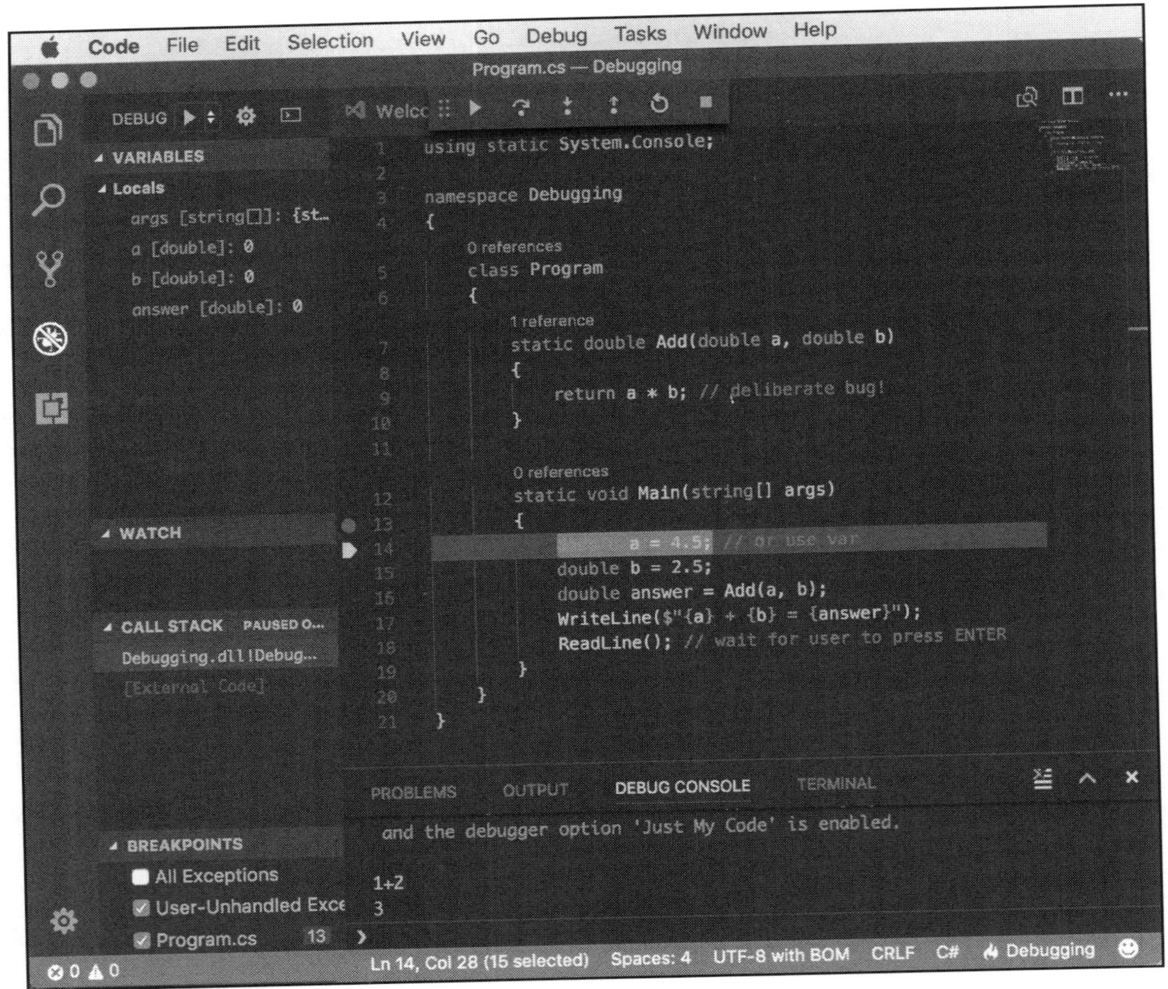

Go to **Debug** | **Step Over** or press *F10*. The yellow highlight steps forward one line. At the moment, you can see that there is no difference between using **Step Into** or **Step Over**.

Press *F10* again so that the yellow highlight is on the line that calls the `Add` method:

```
0 references
static void Main(string[] args)
{
    double a = 4.5; // or use var
    double b = 2.5;
    answer = Add(a, b);
    WriteLine($"{a} + {b} = {answer}");
    ReadLine(); // wait for user to press ENTER
}
    }
}
```

The difference between **Step Into** and **Step Over** can be seen when you are about to execute a method call. If you click on **Step Into**, the debugger steps *into* the method so that you can step through every line in that method. If you click on **Step Over**, the whole method is executed in one go; it does *not* skip over the method.

Click on **Step Into** to step inside the method. If you are using Visual Studio 2017, hover your mouse over the multiply (`*`) operator. A tooltip will appear, showing that this operator is multiplying `a` by `b` to give the result `11.25`. We can see that this is the bug. You can pin the tooltip by clicking on the pin icon, as I have done here:

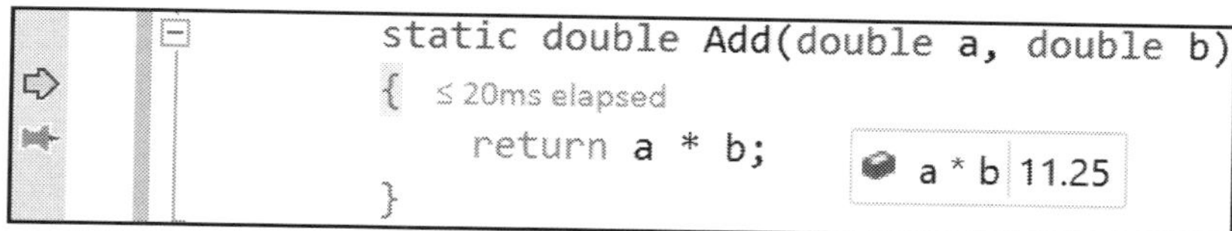

Visual Studio Code does not have the hover-over-operator and pin features, but it does have a hover-over-variable feature. If you hover your mouse pointer over the `a` or `b` parameters, a tooltip appears showing the current value.

Fix the bug by changing `*` to `+`.

We now need to stop, recompile, and restart, so click on the red square **Stop** button or press *Shift* + *F5*.

If you rerun the console application, you will find that it now calculates correctly.

## Customizing breakpoints

In Visual Studio 2017, you can right-click on a breakpoint and choose advanced options, such as **Conditions...**, as shown in the following screenshot:

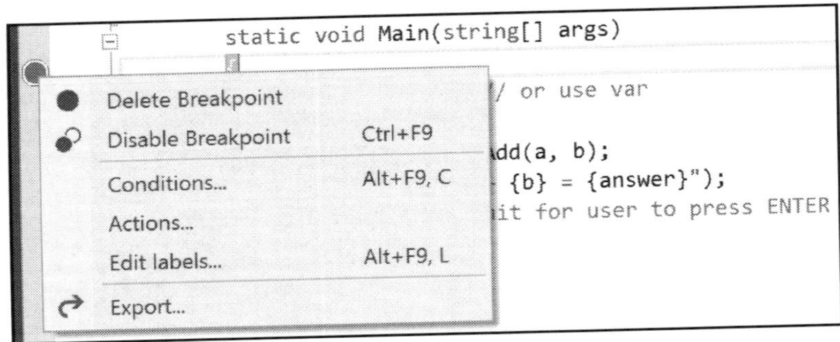


The conditions for a breakpoint include an expression that must be true and a hit count to reach for the breakpoint to apply.

In the example, as you can see in the following screenshot, I have set a condition to only apply the breakpoint if both the answer variable is greater than 9 and we have hit the breakpoint three times:

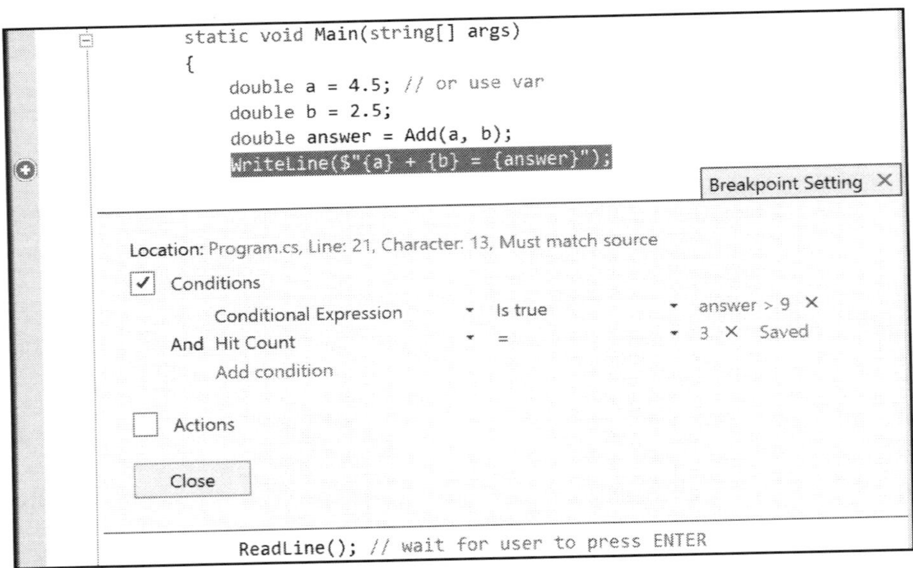

Visual Studio Code has similar, but more limited customization options.

You have now fixed a bug using some debugging tools.

# Logging during development and runtime

Once you believe that all the bugs have been removed from your code, you would then compile a release version and deploy the application so people can use it. But no code is bug free, and during runtime unexpected errors can occur.

End users are notoriously bad about noticing what they were doing when an error occurs, so you should not rely on them accurately providing useful information to fix the problem.

Therefore, it is good practice to add code throughout your application to log what is happening, and especially when exceptions occur, so that you can review the logs and use them to trace the issue and fix the problem.

There are two types that can be used to add simple logging to your code: `Debug` and `Trace`. `Debug` is used to add logging that gets written during development. `Trace` is used to add logging that gets written during both development and runtime.

## Instrumenting with Debug and Trace

You have seen the use of the `Console` type and its `WriteLine` method to provide output to the console window. We also have a pair of types named `Debug` and `Trace` that have more flexibility in where they write out to.

The `Debug` and `Trace` classes can write to any **trace listener**. A trace listener is a type that can be configured to write output anywhere you like when the `Trace.WriteLine` method is called. There are several trace listeners provided by .NET Core, and you can even make your own by inheriting from the `TraceListener` type.

## Writing to the default trace listener

One trace listener, the `DefaultTraceListener` class, is configured automatically and writes to Visual Studio 2017's **Output** pane, or to Visual Studio Code's **Debug** pane. You can configure others manually using code.

Add a new console application project named `Instrumenting`.

Modify the template code, as shown in the following code:

```
using System.Diagnostics;

namespace Instrumenting
{
    class Program
    {
        static void Main(string[] args)
        {
            Debug.WriteLine("Debug says, I am watching!");
            Trace.WriteLine("Trace says, I am watching!");
        }
    }
}
```

Start the console application with the debugger attached.

In Visual Studio 2017's **Output** window, you will see the two messages. If you cannot see the **Output** window, press *Ctrl* + *W* + *O* or navigate to **View** | **Output**. Ensure that you select the **Show output from: Debug** option, as shown in the following screenshot:

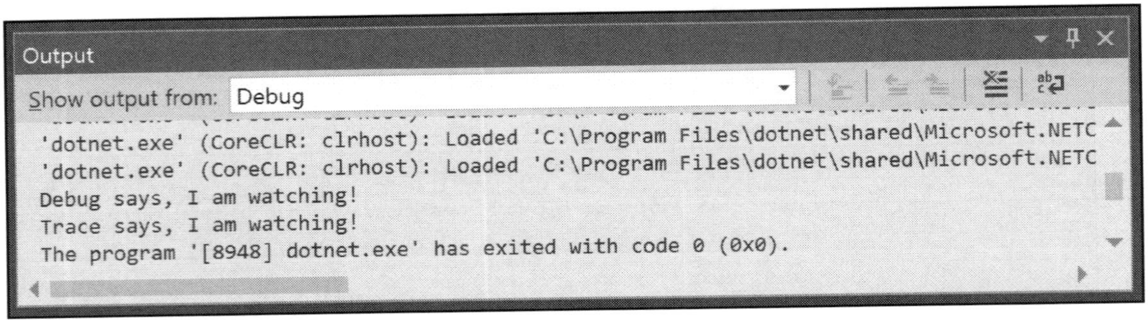

In Visual Studio Code, the **DEBUG CONSOLE** will output the same two messages, mixed with other debugging information like loaded assembly DLLs, as shown in the following screenshot:

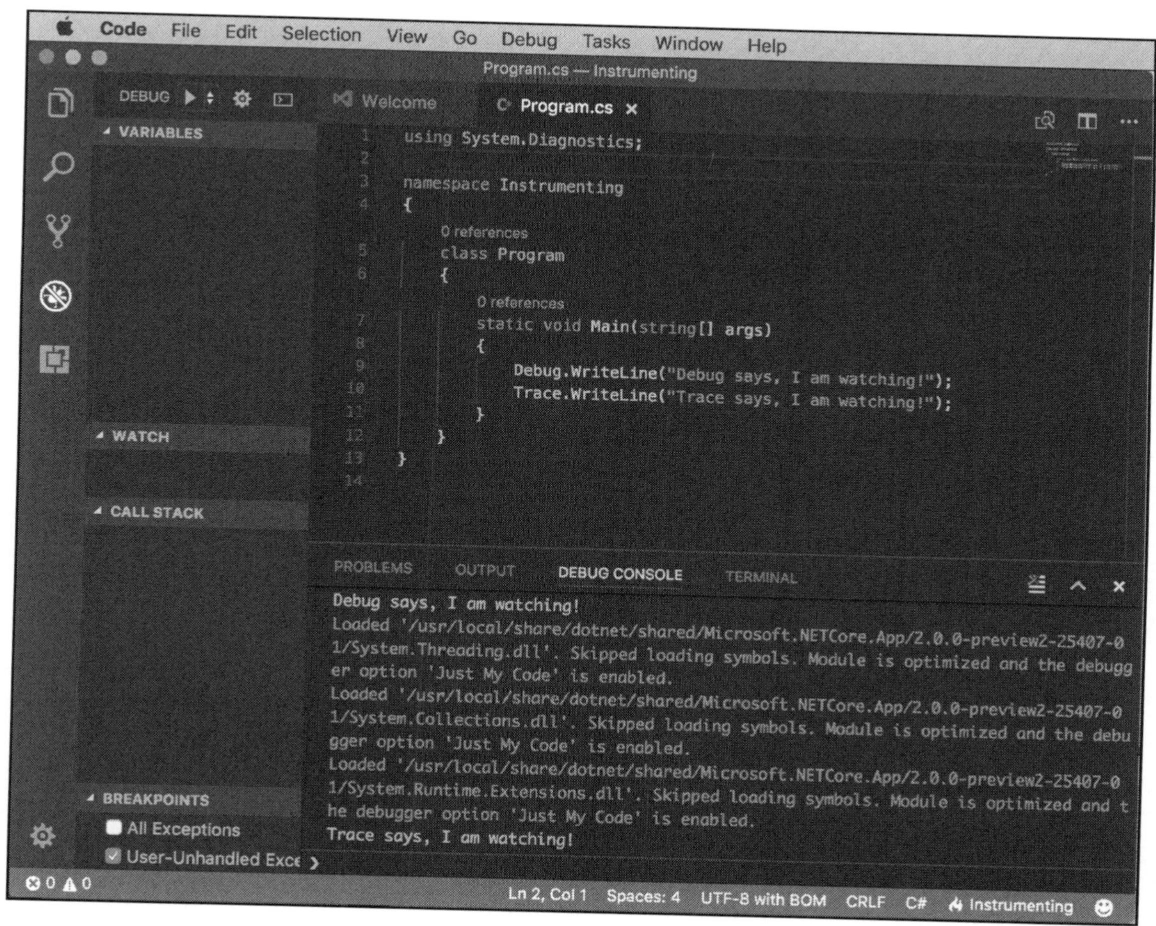


## Configuring trace listeners

Now, we will configure another trace listener that will write to a text file.

Modify the template code to look like this:

```
using System.Diagnostics;
using System.IO;

namespace Instrumenting
{
   class Program
   {
      static void Main(string[] args)
      {
        // write to a text file in the project folder
        Trace.Listeners.Add(new TextWriterTraceListener(
        File.CreateText("log.txt")));

        // text writer is buffered, so this option calls
        // Flush() on all listeners after writing
        Trace.AutoFlush = true;
        Debug.WriteLine("Debug says, I am watching!");
        Trace.WriteLine("Trace says, I am watching!");
      }
   }
}
```

Run the console application without the debugger, and open the file named `log.txt`, as shown in the following screenshot:

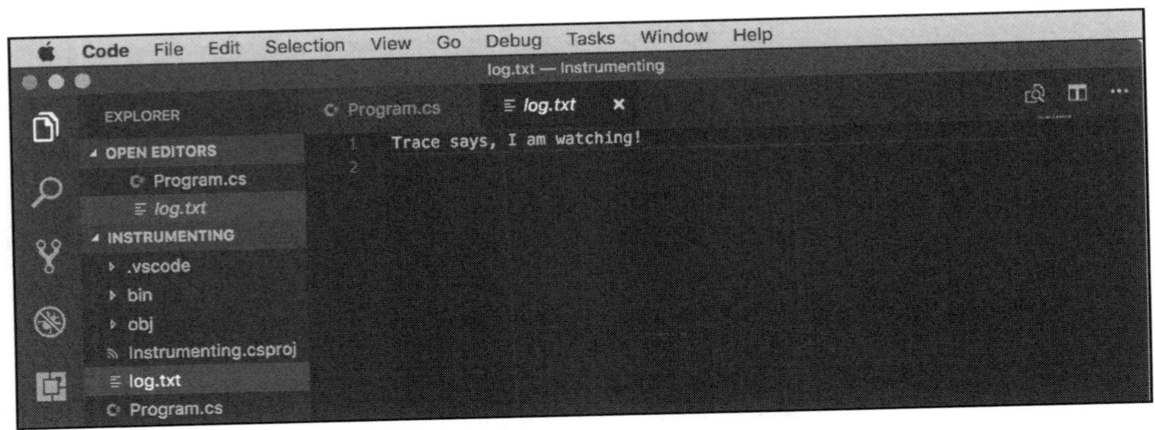

When debugging, both `Debug` and `Trace` are active and will show their output in the **Output / DEBUG CONSOLE** window. When running without debugging, only the `Trace` output is shown. You can therefore use the `Debug.WriteLine` calls liberally throughout your code, knowing they will be stripped out automatically when you compile the release version of your application.

## Switching trace levels

The `Trace.WriteLine` calls are left in your code even after release. So, we need a way to control when they are output. We can do this with a trace switch.

The value of a trace switch can be set using a number or a word. For example, the number 3 can be replaced with the word Info, as shown in the following table:

| Number | Word | Description |
|---|---|---|
| 0 | Off | This will output nothing |
| 1 | Error | This will output only errors |
| 2 | Warning | This will output errors and warnings |
| 3 | Info | This will output errors, warnings, and information |
| 4 | Verbose | This will output all levels |

Add some statements to the end of the `Main` method to create a trace switch, set its level using a passed command line parameter, and then output the four trace switch levels, as shown in the following code:

```
var ts = new TraceSwitch("PacktSwitch",
  "This switch is set via a command line argument.");

if (args.Length > 0)
{
   if (System.Enum.TryParse<TraceLevel>(args[0],
       ignoreCase: true, result: out TraceLevel level))
   {
      ts.Level = level;
   }
}

Trace.WriteLineIf(ts.TraceError, "Trace error");
Trace.WriteLineIf(ts.TraceWarning, "Trace warning");
```

```
Trace.WriteLineIf(ts.TraceInfo, "Trace information");
Trace.WriteLineIf(ts.TraceVerbose, "Trace verbose");
```

In Visual Studio Code, in **Integrated Terminal**, enter `dotnet run info` to run the console application and ask to output up to Info (3) level, and then open the file named `log.txt`, as shown in the following screenshot:

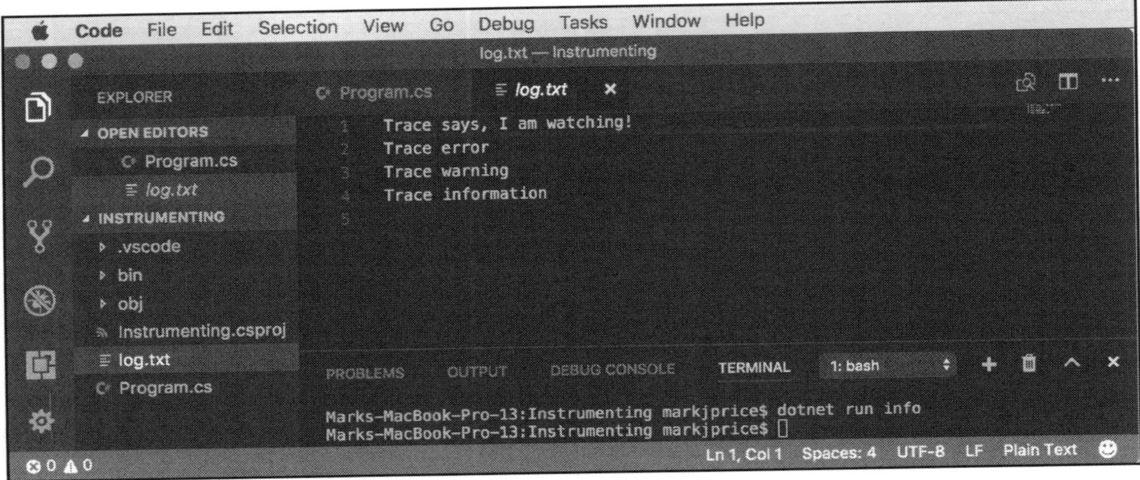


In Visual Studio Code, in **Integrated Terminal**, enter `dotnet run 1`, to run the console application and ask to output up to Error (1) level, and then open the file named `log.txt`, and note that this time, only `Trace error` is output from the four levels.

In Visual Studio 2017, in **Solution Explorer**, right-click on **Instrumenting** project, and click on **Properties**. Click on the **Debug** tab, and enter `info` in the **Application arguments** box, as shown in the following screenshot:

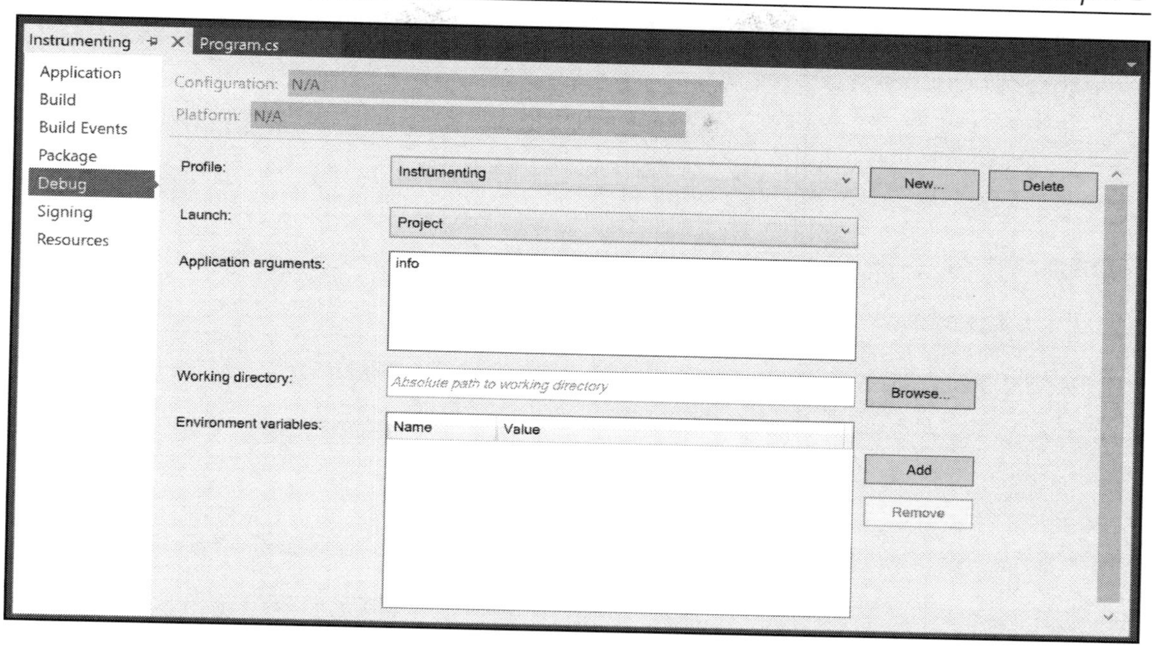


Press *Ctrl* + *F5* to run the console application, and then open the file named `log.txt`, as shown in the following screenshot:

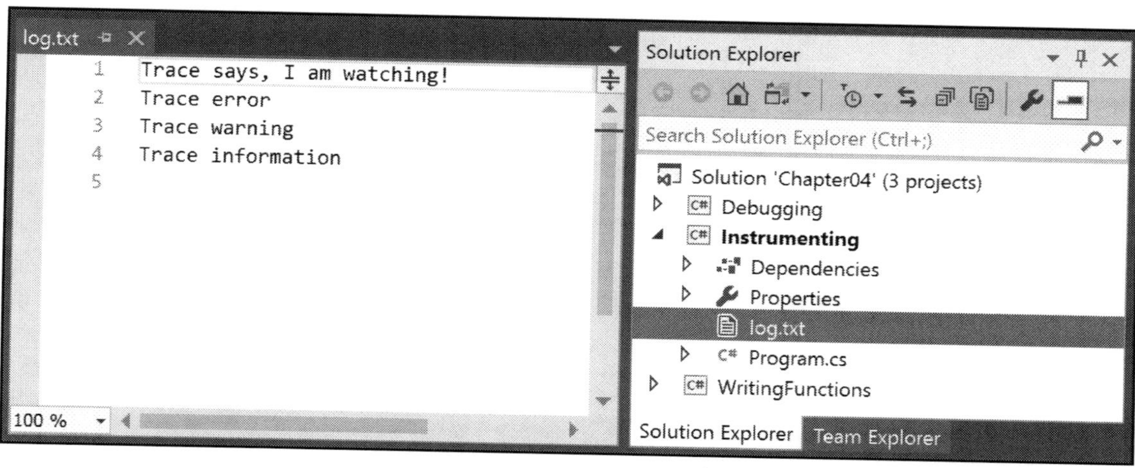

If no argument is passed, the default trace switch level is Off (0), so nothing is output.

# Unit testing functions

Fixing bugs in code is costly. The earlier a bug is discovered, the less expensive it will be to fix. Unit testing is a great way to find bugs early in the development process. Some developers even follow the principle that programmers should create unit tests before they write code. This is called **Test Driven Development** (**TDD**).

You can learn more about unit testing at the following link:
`https://docs.microsoft.com/en-us/dotnet/core/testing/`
You can learn more about TDD at the following link:
`https://en.wikipedia.org/wiki/Test-driven_development`

Microsoft has a proprietary unit testing framework known as MS Test, which is closely integrated with Visual Studio. However, to use a unit testing framework that is compatible with .NET Core, we will use the third-party framework **xUnit.net**.

## Creating a class library that needs testing with Visual Studio 2017

In Visual Studio 2017, add a new **Class Library (.NET Standard)** project named `CalculatorLib`, as shown in the following screenshot:

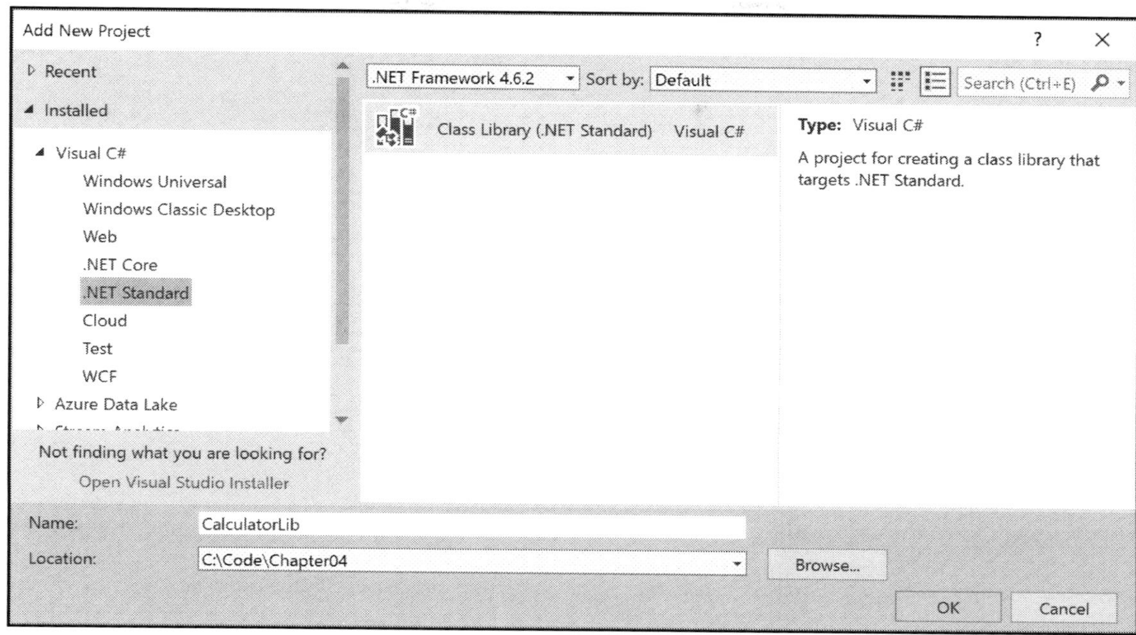


In Visual Studio 2017, in the **Solution Explorer** window, right-click on the `Class1.cs` file and choose **Rename**. Change its name to `Calculator`. You will be prompted to rename all references. Click on **Yes**.

Modify the code to look like this (note the deliberate bug!):

```
namespace Packt.CS7
{
   public class Calculator
   {
      public double Add(double a, double b)
      {
         return a * b;
      }
   }
}
```

# Creating a unit test project with Visual Studio 2017

In Visual Studio 2017, add a new **xUnit Test Project (.NET Core)** project named `CalculatorLibUnitTests`, as shown in the following screenshot:

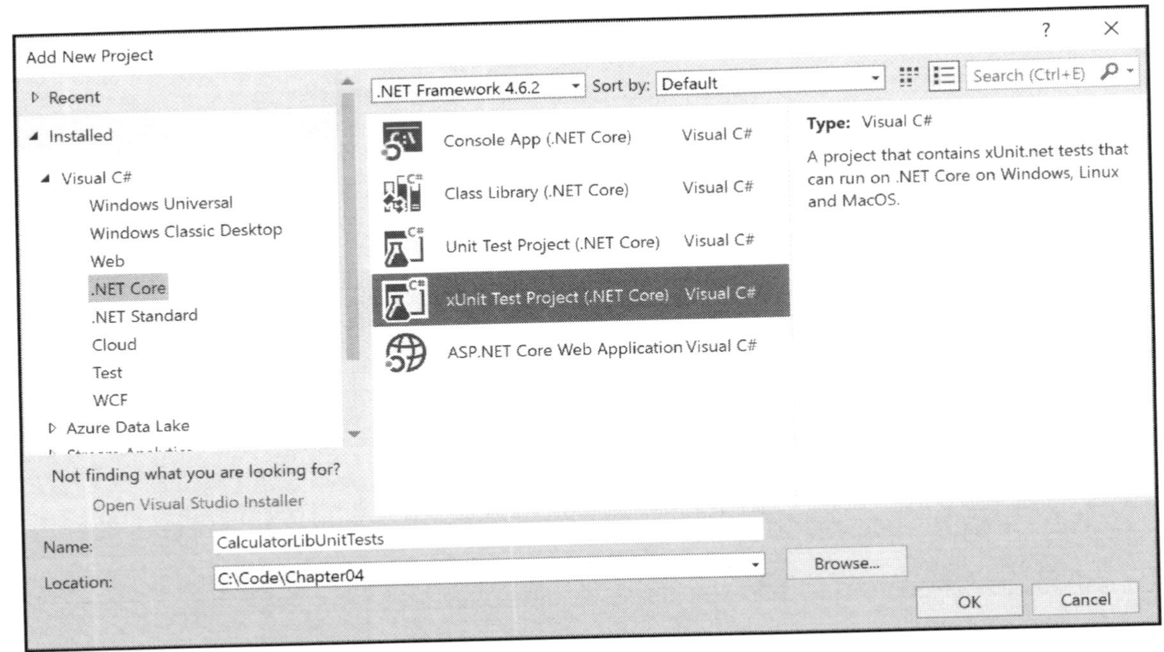


In **Solution Explorer**, in the `CalculatorLibUnitTests` project, right-click on **Dependencies**, and choose **Add Reference...**. In the **Reference Manager** window, select the checkbox for `CalculatorLib`, and then click on **OK**, as shown in the following screenshot:

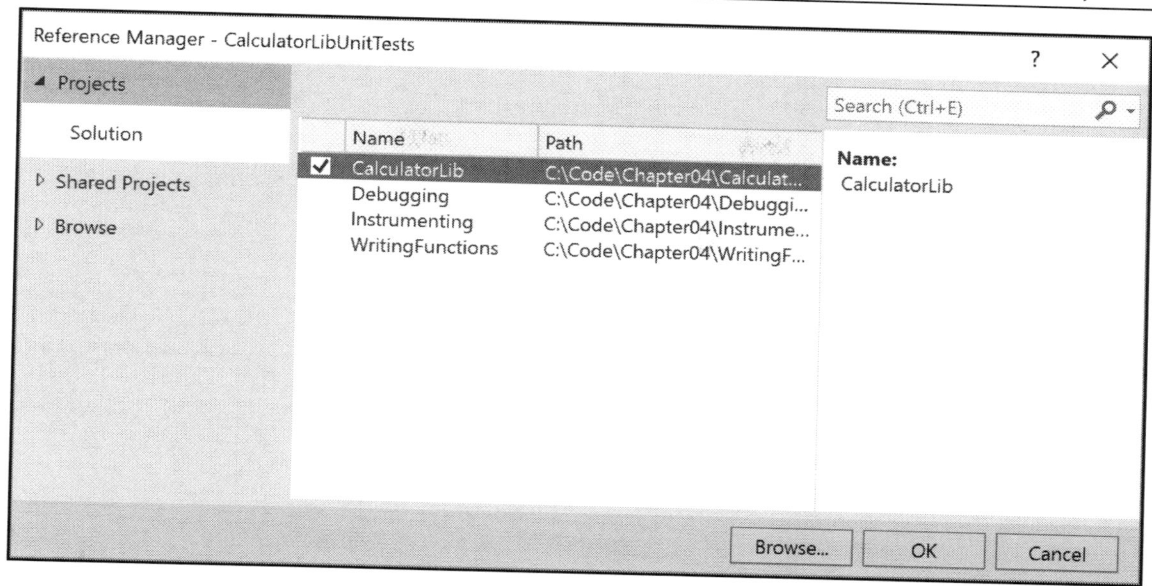


In the **Solution Explorer** window, right-click on the `UnitTest1.cs` file and choose **Rename**. Change its name to `CalculatorUnitTests`. Click on **Yes** when prompted.

## Creating a class library that needs testing with Visual Studio Code

Inside the `Chapter04` folder, create subfolders named `CalculatorLib` and `CalculatorLibUnitTests`.

In Visual Studio Code, open the `CalculatorLib` folder, and enter the following command in the **Integrated Terminal** window:

```
dotnet new classlib
```

Rename the file named `Class1.cs` to `Calculator.cs`, and modify the file to look like the following code (note the deliberate bug!):

```
namespace Packt.CS7
{
   public class Calculator
   {
      public double Add(double a, double b)
      {
```

```
            return a * b;
        }
    }
}
```

Enter the following command in the **Integrated Terminal** window:

```
dotnet build
```

Open the `CalculatorLibUnitTests` folder, and enter the following command in the **Integrated Terminal** window:

```
dotnet new xunit
```

Click on the file named `CalculatorLibUnitTests.csproj`, and modify the configuration to add an item group with a project reference to the `CalculatorLib` project, as shown highlighted in the following markup:

```
<Project Sdk="Microsoft.NET.Sdk">

  <PropertyGroup>
    <TargetFramework>netcoreapp2.0</TargetFramework>
    <IsPackable>false</IsPackable>
  </PropertyGroup>

  <ItemGroup>
    <PackageReference Include="Microsoft.NET.Test.Sdk"
                      Version="15.5.0-preview-20171012-09" />
    <PackageReference Include="xunit" Version="2.3.0" />
    <PackageReference Include="xunit.runner.visualstudio"
                      Version="2.3.0" />
  </ItemGroup>

  <ItemGroup>
    <ProjectReference Include=
      "..\CalculatorLib\CalculatorLib.csproj" />
  </ItemGroup>

</Project>
```

You can search Microsoft's NuGet feed for the latest `Microsoft.NET.Test.Sdk` at the following link: `https://www.nuget.org/packages?q=Microsoft.NET.Test.Sdk`

Rename the file named `UnitTest1.cs` to `CalculatorUnitTests.cs` and the class to `CalculatorUnitTests`.

## Writing unit tests

In Visual Studio 2017 or Visual Studio Code, open the file named `CalculatorUnitTests.cs`, and then modify the code to look like this:

```
using Packt.CS7;
using Xunit;

namespace CalculatorLibUnitTests
{
    public class CalculatorUnitTests
    {
        [Fact]
        public void TestAdding2And2()
        {
            // arrange
            double a = 2;
            double b = 2;
            double expected = 4;
            var calc = new Calculator();
            // act
            double actual = calc.Add(a, b);
            // assert
            Assert.Equal(expected, actual);
        }
        [Fact]
        public void TestAdding2And3()
        {
            // arrange
            double a = 2;
            double b = 3;
            double expected = 5;
            var calc = new Calculator();
            // act
            double actual = calc.Add(a, b);
            // assert
            Assert.Equal(expected, actual);
        }
    }
}
```

A well-written unit test will have three parts:

- **Arrange**: This part will declare and instantiate variables for input and output
- **Act**: This part will execute the unit that you are testing
- **Assert**: This part will make one or more assertions about the output

# Running unit tests with Visual Studio 2017

In Visual Studio 2017, navigate to **Test** | **Windows** | **Test Explorer**, and then navigate to **Build** | **Build Solution**, or press *F6*. Note that two tests have been discovered but not yet run, as shown in the following screenshot:

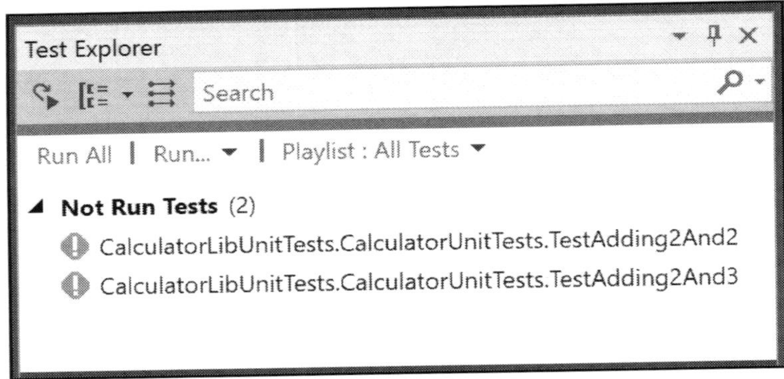


In **Test Explorer**, click on **Run All**.

Wait for a few seconds for the tests to complete, as shown in the following screenshot. Note that one test passed and the other failed. This is why it is good to write multiple tests for each unit:

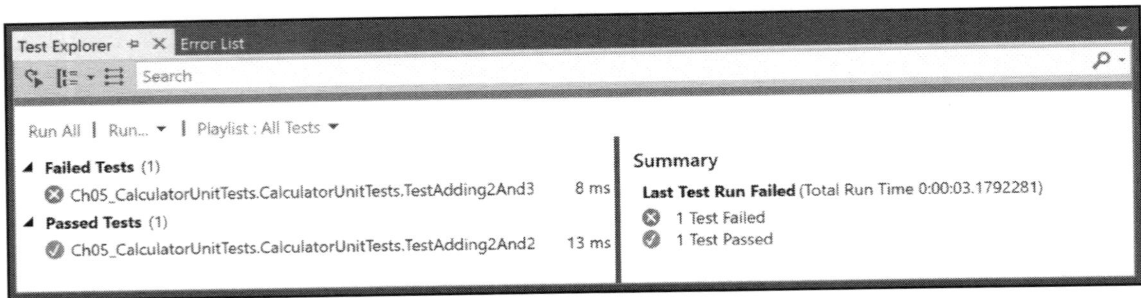


Clicking on a test shows more details and, from there, we should be able to diagnose the bug and fix it:

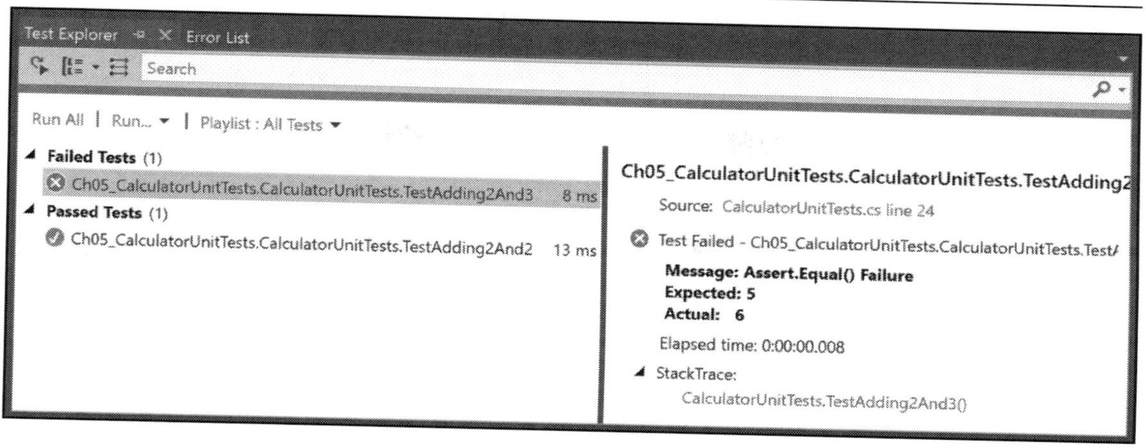


Fix the bug in the `Add` method, and then rerun the unit tests to see that the bug is now fixed, as shown in the following screenshot:

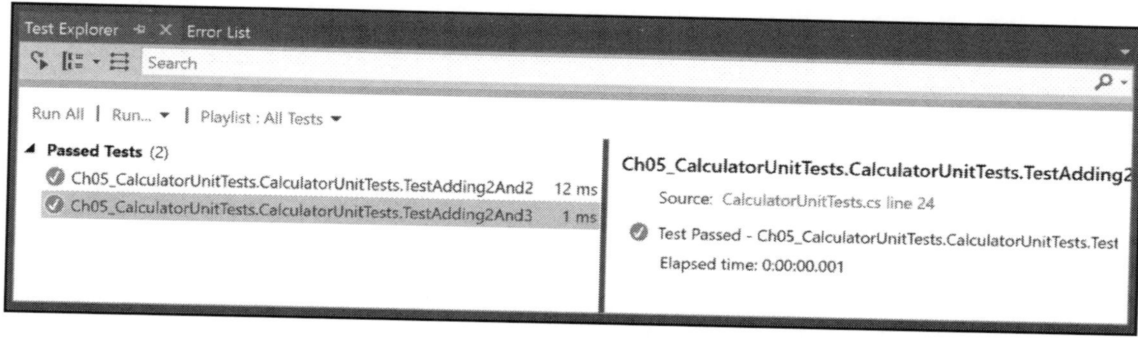


# Running unit tests with Visual Studio Code

In Visual Studio Code, open the `Chapter04` folder.

In **Integrated Terminal**, enter the following command:

```
cd CalculatorLibUnitTest
dotnet test
```

You should see the following results:

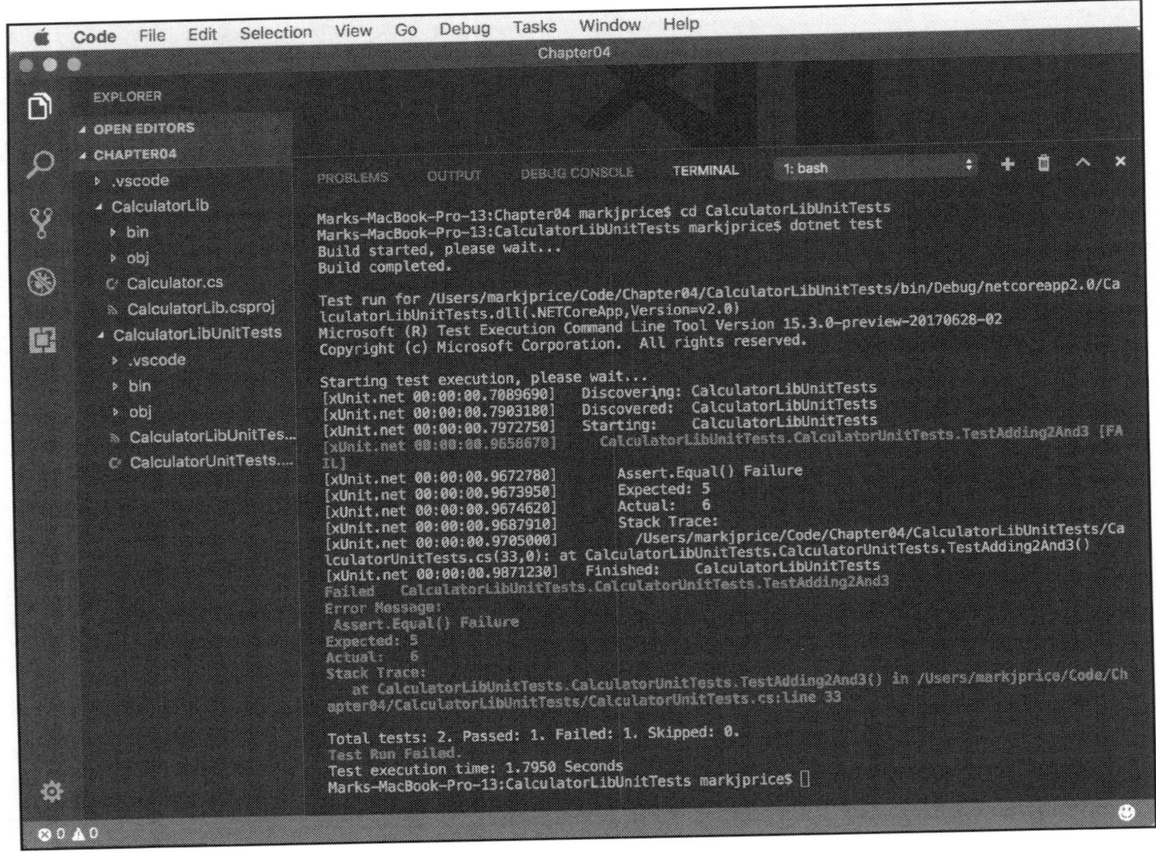

Fix the bug in the `Add` method, and then rerun the unit tests to see that the bug is now fixed, as shown in the following screenshot:

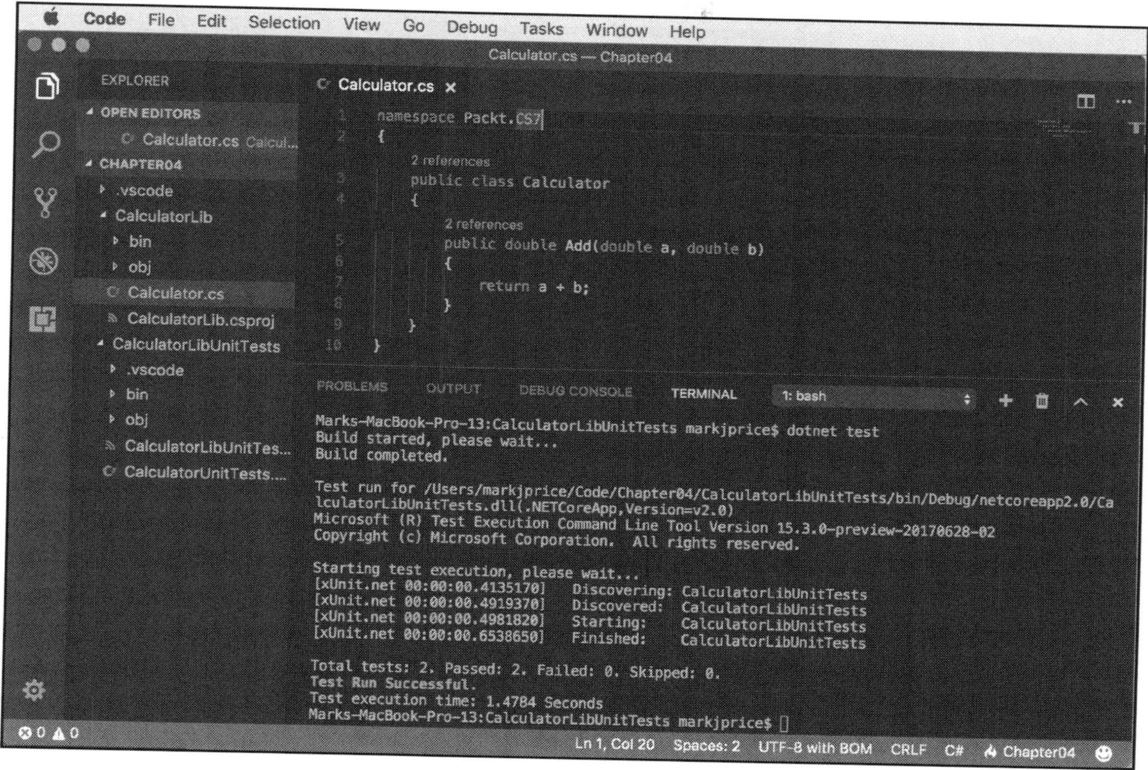

# Practicing and exploring

Test your knowledge and understanding by answering some questions, get some hands-on practice, and explore with deeper research into the topics covered in this chapter.

# Exercise 4.1 – Test your knowledge

Answer the following questions, by Googling the answers if necessary:

1. What does the C# keyword `void` mean?
2. How many parameters can a C# method have?
3. In Visual Studio 2017, what is the difference between pressing *F5*, *Ctrl* + *F5*, *Shift* + *F5*, and *Ctrl* + *Shift* + *F5*?
4. Where does the `Trace.WriteLine` method write its output to?
5. What are the five trace levels?
6. What is the difference between `Debug` and `Trace`?
7. When writing a unit test, what are the three As?
8. When writing a unit test using xUnit, what attribute must you decorate the test methods with?
9. What `dotnet` command executes xUnit tests?
10. What is TDD?

# Exercise 4.2 – Practice writing functions with debugging and unit testing

Prime factors are the combination of the smallest prime numbers, that, when multiplied together, will produce the original number. Consider the following example:

- Prime factors of 4 are: 2 x 2
- Prime factors of 7 are: 7
- Prime factors of 30 are: 2 x 3 x 5
- Prime factors of 40 are: 2 x 2 x 2 x 5
- Prime factors of 50 are: 2 x 5 x 5

Create a console application named `Exercise02` with a method named `PrimeFactors` that, when passed an `int` variable as a parameter, returns a string showing its prime factors.

Use the debugging tools and write unit tests to ensure that your function works correctly with multiple inputs and returns the correct output.

## Exercise 4.3 – Explore topics

Use the following links to read more about the topics covered in this chapter:

- **Debugging in Visual Studio Code:** `https://code.visualstudio.com/docs/editor/debugging`
- **System.Diagnostics Namespaces**: `https://docs.microsoft.com/en-us/dotnet/core/api/system.diagnostics`
- **Debugger Basics**: `https://docs.microsoft.com/en-us/visualstudio/debugger/debugger-basics`
- **xUnit.net**: `http://xunit.github.io/`

# Summary

In this chapter, you learned how to use the Visual Studio debugging and diagnostic features, and unit tested your code.

In the next chapter, you will learn how to build your own types using object-oriented programming techniques.

# 5
# Building Your Own Types with Object-Oriented Programming

This chapter is about making your own types using **object-oriented programming** (**OOP**). You will learn about all the different categories of members that a type can have, including fields to store data and methods to perform actions. You will use OOP concepts such as aggregation and encapsulation. You will also learn about C# 7 language features, such as tuple syntax support and `out` variables, and C# 7.1 language features, like inferred tuple names and default literals.

This chapter will cover the following topics:

- Talking about OOP
- Building class libraries
- Storing data with fields
- Writing and calling methods
- Controlling how parameters are passed
- Splitting classes using partial
- Controlling access with properties and indexers

# Talking about OOP

An object in the real world is a thing, such as a car or a person. An object in programming often represents something in the real world, such as a product or bank account, but can also be something more abstract.

In C#, we use `class` (usually) or `struct` (rarely) to define each type of object. You can think of a type as being a blueprint or template for an object.

Object-oriented programming concepts are briefly described here:

- **Encapsulation** is the combination of the data and actions that are related to an object. For example, a `BankAccount` type might have data, such as `Balance` and `AccountName`, as well as actions, such as `Deposit` and `Withdraw`. When encapsulating, you often want to control what can access those actions and the data.
- **Composition** is about what an object is made of. For example, a car is composed of different parts, such as four wheels, several seats, and an engine.
- **Aggregation** is about what is related to an object. For example, a person could sit in the driver's seat and then becomes the car's driver.
- **Inheritance** is about reusing code by having a subclass derive from a **base** or **super** class. All functionality in the base class becomes available in the derived class.
- **Abstraction** is about capturing the core idea of an object and ignoring the details or specifics. Abstraction is a tricky balance. If you make a class more abstract, more classes would be able to inherit from it, but there will be less functionality to share.
- **Polymorphism** is about allowing a derived class to override an inherited action to provide custom behavior.

# Building class libraries

Class library assemblies group types together into easily deployable units (DLL files). Apart from when you learned about unit testing, you have only created console applications to contain your code. To make the code that you write reusable across multiple projects, you should put it in class library assemblies, just like Microsoft does.

**Good Practice**
Put types that you might reuse in a .NET Standard class library to enable them to be reused in .NET Core, .NET Framework, and Xamarin projects.

# Creating a class library with Visual Studio 2017

Start Microsoft Visual Studio 2017. In Visual Studio, press *Ctrl* + *Shift* + *N*, or go to **File** | **New** | **Project....**

In the **New Project** dialog, in the **Installed** list, expand **Visual C#**, and select **.NET Standard**. In the center list, select **Class Library (.NET Standard)**, type **Name** as `PacktLibrary`, change **Location** to `C:\Code`, type **Solution name** as `Chapter05`, and then click on **OK**, as shown in the following screenshot:

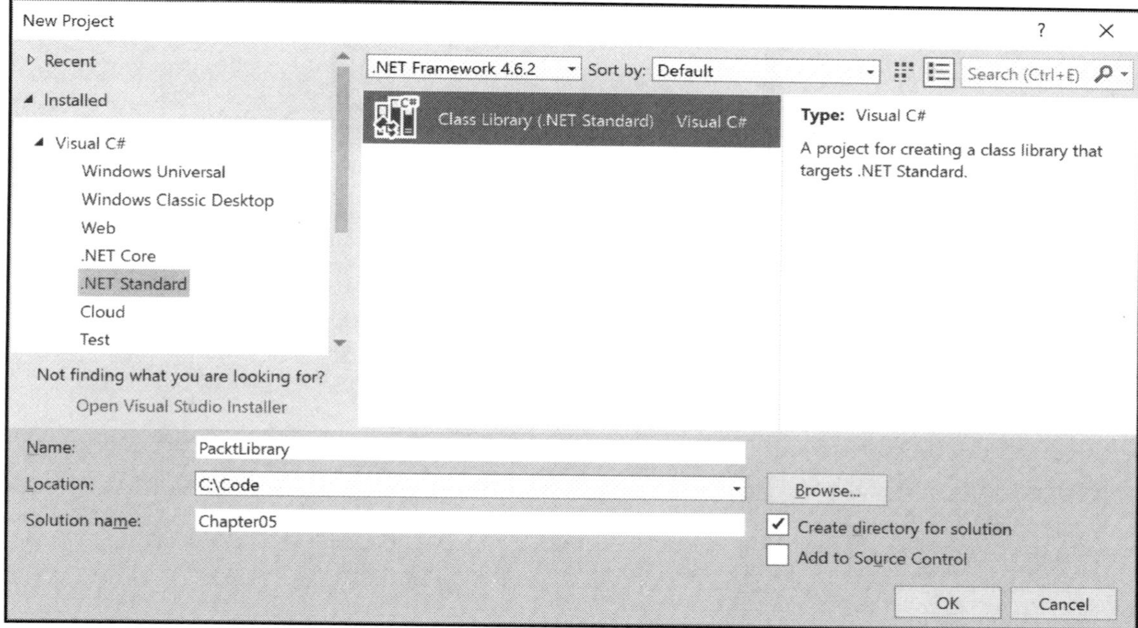

Make sure you choose a **Class Library (.NET Standard)** and *not* a **Console App (.NET Core)**!

In **Solution Explorer**, right-click on the file named `Class1.cs` and choose **Rename**. Type the name as `Person`. When you are prompted to rename all other references to the class, click on **Yes**.

# Creating a class library with Visual Studio Code

To create a class library with Visual Studio Code, follow these steps:

1. Create a folder named `Chapter05` with a subfolder named `PacktLibrary`.
2. Start Visual Studio Code and open the `PacktLibrary` folder.
3. View **Integrated Terminal** and enter the following command:

```
dotnet new classlib
```

4. In the **EXPLORER** pane, rename the file named `Class1.cs` to `Person.cs`.
5. Click on `Person.cs` to open it, restore packages, and change the class name to `Person`.

# Defining a class

In either Visual Studio 2017 or Visual Studio Code, change the namespace to `Packt.CS7`, because it is important to put your classes in a logically named namespace. In this, and the next chapter, we will learn about OOP and most of the new language features of C# 7.0 and 7.1.

Your class file should now look like the following code:

```
using System;

namespace Packt.CS7
{
   public class Person
   {
   }
}
```

Note that the C# keyword `public` is applied before `class`. This keyword is called an **access modifier**, and it allows all code to access this class. If you do not explicitly apply the `public` keyword, then it would only be accessible within the assembly that defined it. We need it to be accessible outside the assembly too. This type does not yet have any members encapsulated within it. We will create some soon.

Members can be fields, methods, or specialized versions of both. They are described here:

- **Fields** are used to store data. There are also three specialized categories of field, as shown in the following bullets:
    - **Constants**: The data in this field never changes
    - **Read-only fields**: The data in this field cannot change after the class is instantiated
    - **Events**: This refers to methods that you want to call automatically when something happens, such as clicking on a button
- **Methods** are used to execute statements. You saw some examples when you learned about functions in `Chapter 4`, *Writing, Debugging, and Testing Functions*. There are also four specialized categories of method, as shown in the following bullets:
    - **Constructors**: These are the methods that execute when you use the `new` keyword to allocate memory and instantiate a class
    - **Properties**: These are the methods that execute when you want to access data
    - **Indexers**: These are the methods that execute when you want to access data
    - **Operators**: These are the methods that execute when you want to apply an operator

# Instantiating a class

In this section, we will make an **instance** of the `Person` class, which is known as **instantiating** a class.

## Referencing an assembly using Visual Studio 2017

In Visual Studio 2017, add a new console application project named `PeopleApp` to your existing `Chapter05` solution.

Make sure you add a **Console App (.NET Core)** and *not* a **Class Library (.NET Core)**!

Right-click on the solution, choose **Properties**, set **Startup Project** to **Single startup project**, and choose **PeopleApp**.

This project needs a reference to the class library we just made.

In **Solution Explorer**, in the **PeopleApp** project, right-click on **Dependencies** and choose **Add Reference...**.

In the **Reference Manager - PeopleApp** dialog box, in the list on the left-hand side, go to **Projects** | **Solution**, select the `PacktLibrary` assembly, and then click on **OK**, as shown in the following screenshot:

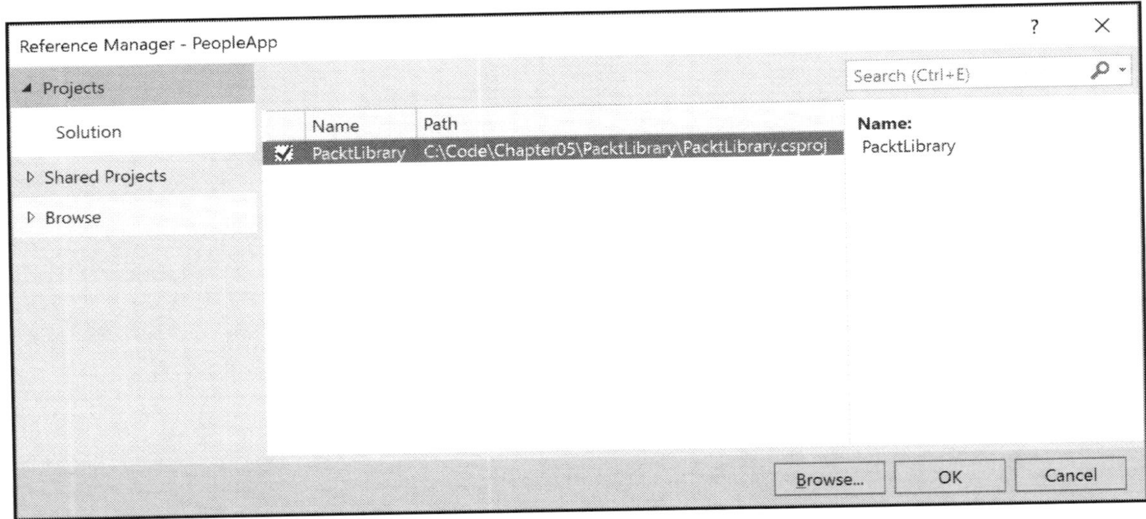


In **Solution Explorer**, expand **Dependencies** in both projects to show the class library's dependence on .NET Standard, and the console application's dependence on **PacktLibrary** and .NET Core, as shown in the following screenshot:

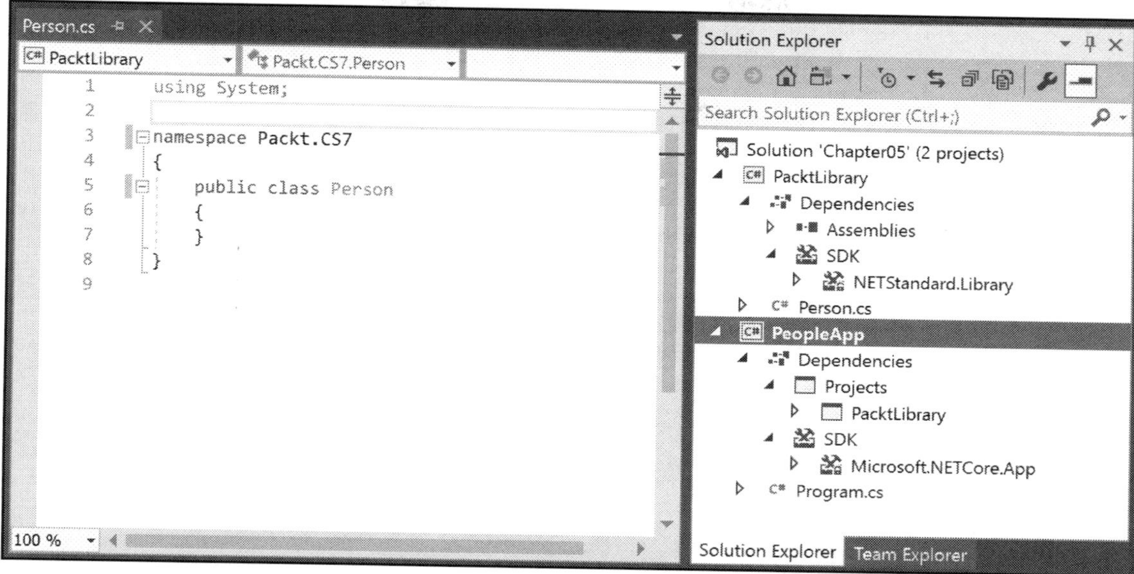


## Referencing an assembly using Visual Studio Code

Create a subfolder under `Chapter05` named `PeopleApp`.

In Visual Studio Code, open the `PeopleApp` folder.

In **Integrated Terminal**, enter the following command:

```
dotnet new console
```

In the **EXPLORER** pane, click on the file named `PeopleApp.csproj` and add a project reference to `PacktLibrary`, as shown highlighted in the following markup:

```
<Project Sdk="Microsoft.NET.Sdk>

  <PropertyGroup>
    <OutputType>Exe</OutputType>
      <TargetFramework>netcoreapp2.0</TargetFramework>
  </PropertyGroup>

  <ItemGroup>
    <ProjectReference
```

```
      Include="../PacktLibrary/PacktLibrary.csproj" />
  </ItemGroup>

</Project>
```

In Visual Studio Code, in **Integrated Terminal**, enter the following commands:

```
dotnet restore
dotnet build
```

Both the `PacktLibrary` and `PeopleApp` projects will compile into DLL assemblies, as shown in the following screenshot:

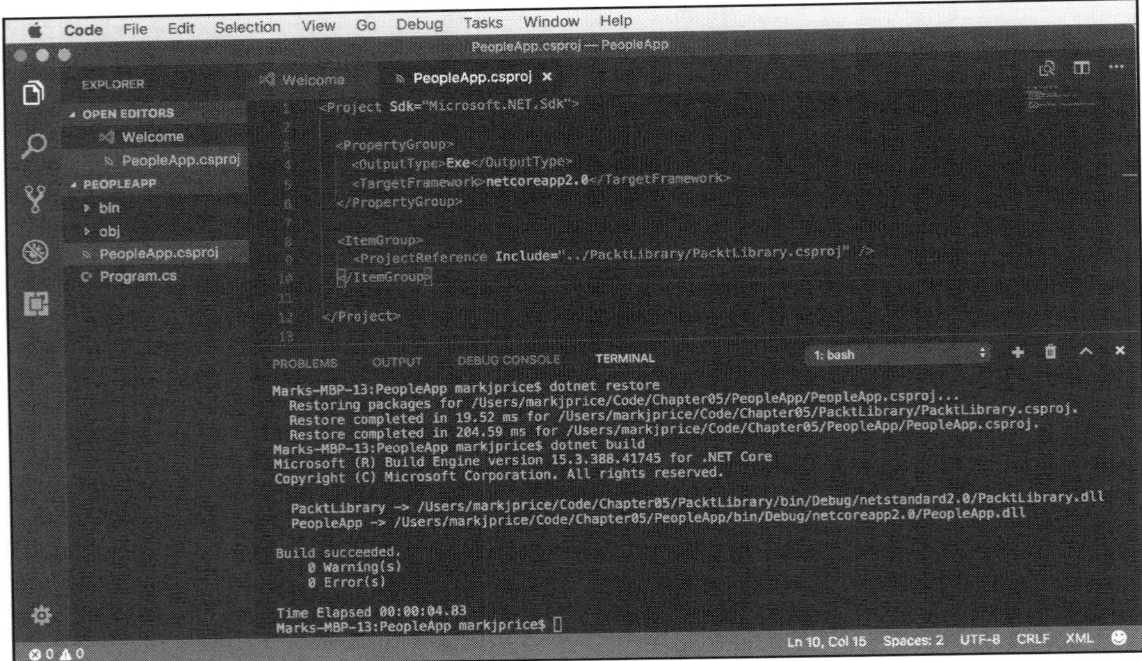

## Importing a namespace

In both Visual Studio 2017 and Visual Studio Code, at the top of the `Program.cs` file, type the following code to import the namespace for our class and statically import the `Console` class:

```
using Packt.CS7;
using static System.Console;
```

In the `Main` method, type the following code to create an instance of the `Person` type using the `new` keyword. The `new` keyword allocates memory for the object and initializes any internal data. We could use `Person` in place of the `var` keyword, but the use of `var` involves less typing and is still just as clear:

```
var p1 = new Person();
WriteLine(p1.ToString());
```

You might be wondering, "Why does the `p1` variable have a method named `ToString`? The `Person` class is empty!" You are about to find out.

Run the console application, using *Ctrl* + *F5* in Visual Studio 2017, or entering `dotnet run` in Visual Studio Code, and view the output:

```
Packt.CS7.Person
```

# Managing multiple projects with Visual Studio Code

If you have multiple projects that you want to work with at the same time, either open a new window by navigating to **File** | **New Window** or press *Shift* + *Cmd* + *N*, or open a parent folder that contains the project folders that you want to work with.

If you choose to open a parent folder, be careful when executing commands in the Terminal because they will apply to whatever the current folder is.

In Visual Studio Code, open the `Chapter05` folder, and then in Terminal, enter the following command to change the directory to the console application project, as shown in the following screenshot:

```
cd PeopleApp
```

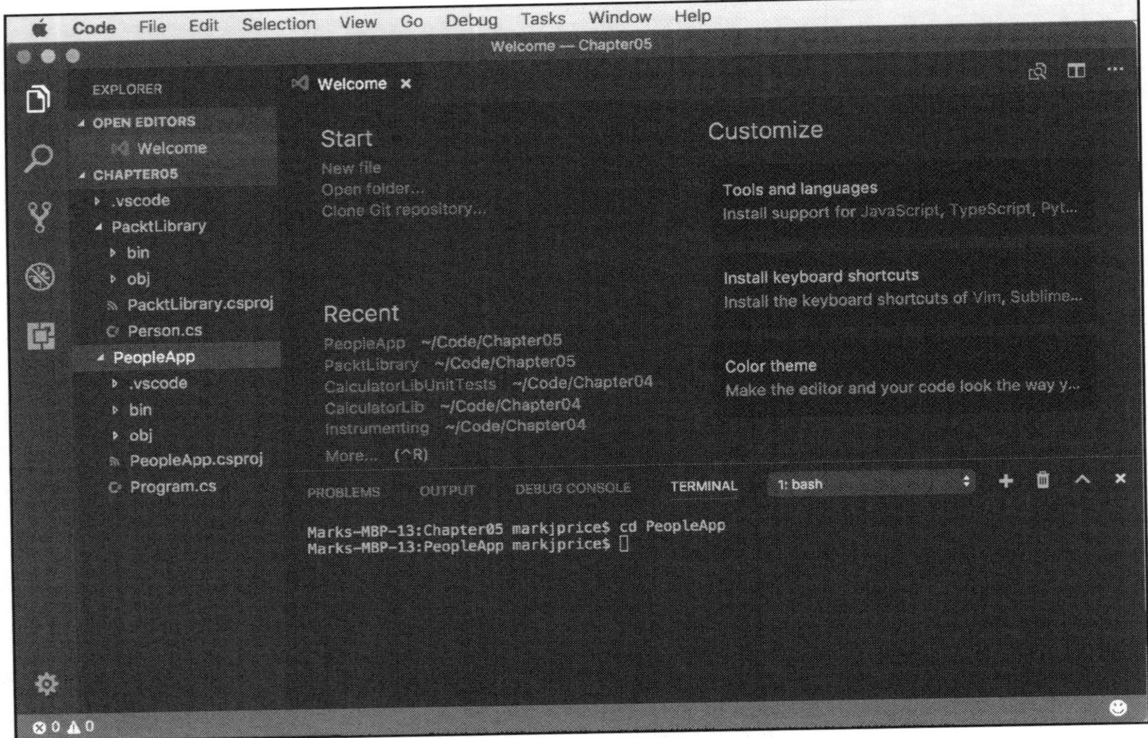


# Inheriting from System.Object

Although our `Person` class did not explicitly choose to inherit from a type, all types indirectly inherit from a special type named `System.Object`. The implementation of the `ToString` method in the `System.Object` type simply outputs the full namespace and type name, as shown in the preceding output.

Back in the original `Person` class, we could have explicitly told the compiler that `Person` inherits from the `System.Object` type, like this:

```
public class Person : System.Object
```

When class B **inherits** from class A, we say that A is the **base** or **super** class and B is the **derived** or **subclass**. In this case, `System.Object` is the base or super class and `Person` is the derived or subclass.

You can also use the C# type alias keyword `object`:

```
public class Person : object
```

Modify your `Person` class to explicitly inherit from `object`. Then, click inside the keyword and press *F12*, or right-click on the `object` keyword and choose **Go to Definition**.

You will see the Microsoft-defined `System.Object` type and its members. You do not need to understand any of this yet, but notice that it has a method named `ToString`, as shown in the following screenshot:

```
namespace System
{
    [...]public class Object
    {
        [...]public Object();

        [...]~Object();

        [...]public static bool Equals(Object objA, Object objB);
        [...]public static bool ReferenceEquals(Object objA, Object objB);
        [...]public virtual bool Equals(Object obj);
        [...]public virtual int GetHashCode();
        [...]public Type GetType();
        [...]public virtual string ToString();
        [...]protected Object MemberwiseClone();
    }
}
```

**Good Practice**
Assume other programmers know that if inheritance is not specified, the class will inherit from `System.Object`.

# Storing data with fields

Next, we will define some fields in the class to store information about a person.

## Defining fields

Inside the `Person` class, write the following code. At this point, we have decided that a person is composed of a name and a date of birth. We have encapsulated these two values inside the person. We have also made the fields public so that they are visible outside the class itself:

```
public class Person : object
{
    // fields
    public string Name;
    public DateTime DateOfBirth;
}
```

You can use any type for a field, including arrays and collections such as lists and dictionaries. These would be used if you need to store multiple values in one named field.

In Visual Studio 2017, you might want to click, hold, and drag the tabs for one of your open files to arrange them so that you can see both `Person.cs` and `Program.cs` at the same time, as shown in the following screenshot:

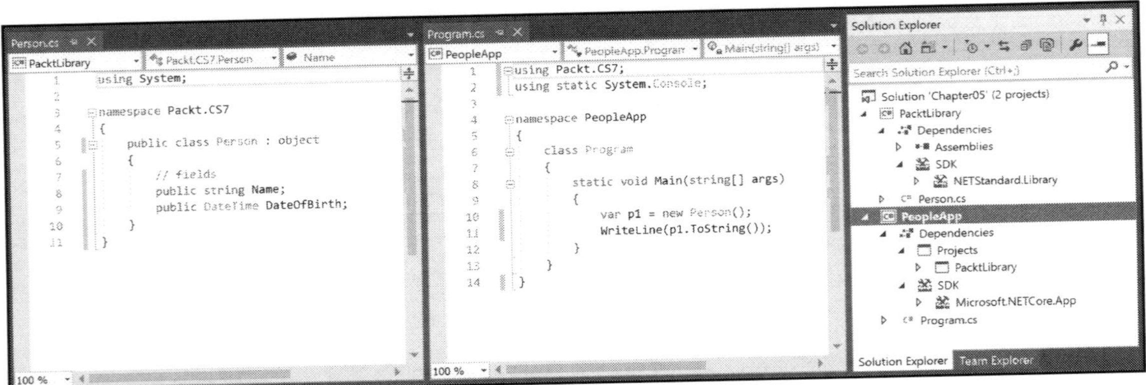

In Visual Studio Code, you can click on the **Split Editor** button or press *Cmd* + \, and then close one copy of the duplicated file editor so that you have two files open side by side, as shown in the following screenshot:

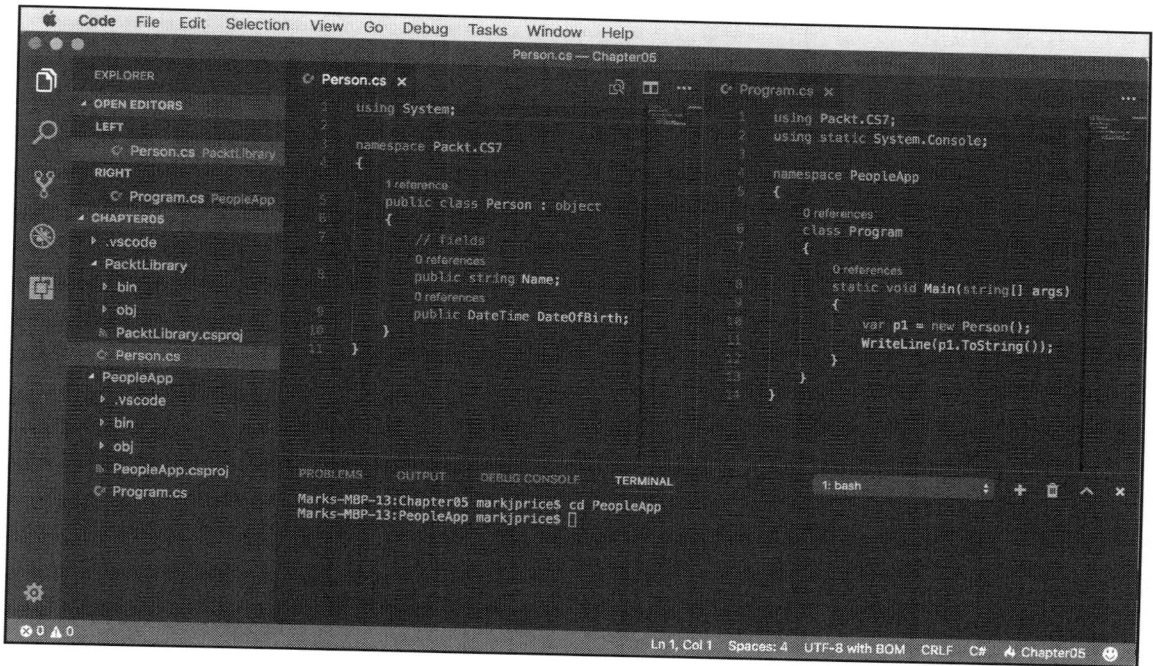

## Understanding access modifiers

Note that, like we did with the class, we applied the `public` keyword to these fields. If we hadn't, then they would be `private` to the class, which means they are accessible only inside the class.

There are four access modifier keywords, and one combination of keywords, that you can apply to a class member, such as a field or method. Part of encapsulation is choosing how visible the members are:

| Access Modifier | Description |
|---|---|
| `private` | Member is accessible inside the type only. This is the default. |
| `internal` | Member is accessible inside the type and any type in the same assembly. |
| `protected` | Member is accessible inside the type and any type that inherits from the type. |
| `public` | Member is accessible everywhere. |
| `internal protected` | Member is accessible inside the type, any type in the same assembly, and any type that inherits from the type. |

**Good Practice**
Explicitly apply one of the access modifiers to all type members, even if you want to use the default, which is `private`. Also, fields should usually be `private` or `protected`, and you should then create `public` properties to get or set the field values. This provides more control.

At the top of `Program.cs`, import the `System` namespace, if it is missing, as shown in the following code:

```
using System;
```

Inside the `Main` method, change the code to look like this:

```
var p1 = new Person();
p1.Name = "Bob Smith";
p1.DateOfBirth = new System.DateTime(1965, 12, 22);
WriteLine($"{p1.Name} was born on {p1.DateOfBirth:dddd, d MMMM  yyyy}");
```

Run the application and view the output:

```
Bob Smith was born on Wednesday, 22 December 1965
```

You can also initialize fields using a shorthand object initializer syntax using curly braces.

Add the following code underneath the existing code to create another new person. Notice the different format code for the date of birth when writing to the console:

```
var p2 = new Person
{
    Name = "Alice Jones",
    DateOfBirth = new  DateTime(1998, 3, 17)
};
WriteLine($"{p2.Name} was born on {p2.DateOfBirth:d MMM yy}");
```

Run the application and view the output:

```
Bob Smith was born on Wednesday, 22 December 1965
Alice Jones was born on 17 Mar 98
```

## Storing a value using the enum keyword

Sometimes, a value needs to be one of a limited list of options. For example, a person may have a favorite ancient world wonder. Sometimes, a value needs to be a combination of a limited list of options. For example, a person may have a bucket list of ancient world wonders they want to visit. We can store this data using an `enum` type.

An `enum` type is a very efficient way of storing one or more choices because, internally, it uses the `int` values in combination with a lookup table of string descriptions.

In Visual Studio 2017, add a new class to the `PacktLibrary` project named `WondersOfTheAncientWorld` by pressing *Shift* + *Alt* + *C* or going to **Project** | **Add Class....**

In Visual Studio Code, add a new class to the project by selecting `PacktLibrary`, clicking on the **New File** button in the mini toolbar, and entering the name `WondersOfTheAncientWorld.cs`, as shown in the following screenshot:

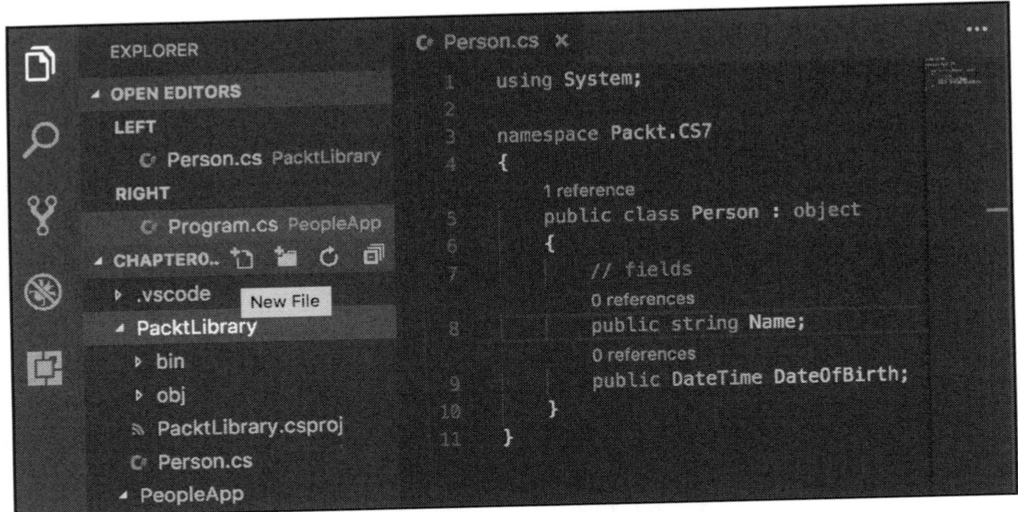


Modify the `WondersOfTheAncientWorld.cs` class file to make it look like this:

```
namespace Packt.CS7
{
    public enum WondersOfTheAncientWorld
    {
        GreatPyramidOfGiza,
        HangingGardensOfBabylon,
        StatueOfZeusAtOlympia,
        TempleOfArtemisAtEphesus,
        MausoleumAtHalicarnassus,
        ColossusOfRhodes,
        LighthouseOfAlexandria
    }
}
```

In the `Person` class, add the following statement to your list of fields:

```
public WondersOfTheAncientWorld FavouriteAncientWonder;
```

Back in the `Main` method of `Program.cs`, add the following statements:

```
p1.FavouriteAncientWonder =
  WondersOfTheAncientWorld.StatueOfZeusAtOlympia;
WriteLine($"{p1.Name}'s favourite wonder is {p1.FavouriteAncientWonder}");
```

Run the application and view the additional output:

```
Bob Smith's favourite wonder is StatueOfZeusAtOlympia
```

For the bucket list, we could create a collection of instances of the enum, but there is a better way. We can combine multiple choices into a single value using **flags**.

Modify the enum to look as shown in the following code. Note that I have used the left shift operator (<>) to set individual bits within the flag. I could also have set the values to 1, 2, 4, 8, 16, 32, and so on:

```
namespace Packt.CS7
{
   [System.Flags]
   public enum WondersOfTheAncientWorld : byte
   {
      None = 0,
      GreatPyramidOfGiza = 1,
      HangingGardensOfBabylon = 1 << 1, // i.e. 2
      StatueOfZeusAtOlympia = 1 << 2, // i.e. 4
      TempleOfArtemisAtEphesus = 1 << 3, // i.e. 8
      MausoleumAtHalicarnassus = 1 << 4, // i.e. 16
      ColossusOfRhodes = 1 << 5, // i.e. 32
      LighthouseOfAlexandria = 1 << 6 // i.e. 64
   }
}
```

We are assigning explicit values for each choice that would not overlap when looking at the bits stored in memory. We must also mark the `enum` type with the `System.Flags` attribute. Normally, an `enum` type uses an `int` variable internally, but since we don't need values that big, we can make it more efficient by telling it to use a `byte` variable.

If we want to indicate that our bucket list includes the *Hanging Gardens* and *Mausoleum at Halicarnassus* ancient world wonders, then we would want the 16 and 2 bits set to `1`. In other words, we would store the value `18`:

| 64 | 32 | 16 | 8 | 4 | 2 | 1 | 0 |
|---|---|---|---|---|---|---|---|
| 0 | 0 | 1 | 0 | 0 | 1 | 0 | 0 |

In the `Person` class, add the following statement to your list of fields:

```
public WondersOfTheAncientWorld BucketList;
```

Back in the `Main` method of `PeopleApp`, add the following statements to set the bucket list using the `|` operator (logical OR) to combine the `enum` values. We could also set the value using the number `18` cast into the `enum` type, as in the comment:

```
p1.BucketList = WondersOfTheAncientWorld.HangingGardensOfBabylon |
WondersOfTheAncientWorld.MausoleumAtHalicarnassus;
// p1.BucketList = (WondersOfTheAncientWorld)18;
WriteLine($"{p1.Name}'s bucket list is {p1.BucketList}");
```

Run the application and view the additional output:

```
Bob Smith's bucket list is HangingGardensOfBabylon,
MausoleumAtHalicarnassus
```

**Good Practice**
Use the `enum` values to store combinations of discreet options. Derive an `enum` type from `byte` if there are up to eight options, from `short` if there are up to 16 options, from `int` if there are up to 32 options, and from `long` if there are up to 64 options.

# Storing multiple values using collections

Let's add a field to store a person's children. This is an example of aggregation because children are instances of a class that is related to the current person, but are not part of the person itself.

We will use a generic `List<T>` collection type, so we need to import the `System.Collections.Generic` namespace at the top of the `Person.cs` class file:

```
using System.Collections.Generic;
```

The angle brackets after the `List<T>` type is a feature of C# called **generics** that was introduced in 2005 with C# 2.0. It's just a fancy term for making a collection **strongly typed**, that is, the compiler knows more specifically what type of object can be stored in the collection. Generics improve the performance and correctness of your code. Strong typed is different from **statically typed**. The old `System.Collection` types are statically typed to contain weakly typed `System.Object` items. The newer `System.Collection.Generic` types introduced in 2005 are statically typed to contain strongly typed `<T>` instances. Ironically, the term *generics* means a more specific static type!

Then, we can declare a new field in the `Person` class:

```
public List<Person> Children = new List<Person>();
```

Notice that we need to ensure the collection is initialized to a new instance of a collection before we can add items to the collection.

In the `Main` method, add the following code:

```
p1.Children.Add(new Person { Name = "Alfred" });
p1.Children.Add(new Person { Name = "Zoe" });
WriteLine(
  $"{p1.Name} has {p1.Children.Count} children:");
for (int child = 0; child < p1.Children.Count; child++)
{
   WriteLine($"  {p1.Children[child].Name}");
}
```

Run the application and view the output:

```
Bob Smith has 2 children:
  Alfred
  Zoe
```

## Making a field static

The fields that we have created so far have all been instance members, meaning that a copy of each field exists for each instance of the class that is created.

Sometimes, you want to define a field that only has one copy that is shared across all instances. These are called **static** members.

In the `PacktLibrary` project, add a new class named `BankAccount`. Modify the class, as shown in the following code:

```
namespace Packt.CS7
{
   public class BankAccount
   {
      public string AccountName;
      public decimal Balance;
      public static decimal InterestRate;
   }
}
```

Each instance of `BankAccount` will have its own `AccountName` and `Balance` values, but all instances will share a single `InterestRate` value.

In `Program.cs` and its `Main` method, add the following code, where we will set the shared interest rate and then create two instances of the `BankAccount` type:

```
BankAccount.InterestRate = 0.012M;
var ba1 = new BankAccount();
ba1.AccountName = "Mrs. Jones";
ba1.Balance = 2400;
WriteLine($"{ba1.AccountName} earned {ba1.Balance *
BankAccount.InterestRate:C} interest.");
var ba2 = new BankAccount();
ba2.AccountName = "Ms. Gerrier";
ba2.Balance = 98;
WriteLine($"{ba2.AccountName} earned {ba2.Balance *
BankAccount.InterestRate:C} interest.");
```

Run the application and view the additional output:

```
Mrs. Jones earned £28.80 interest.
Ms. Gerrier earned £1.18 interest.
```

`:C` is a format code that tells .NET to use the currency format for the numbers. In `Chapter 8`, *Using Common .NET Standard Types*, you will learn how to control the culture that determines the currency symbol. For now, it will use the default for your operating system installation. I live in London, UK, hence my output shows British Pounds (£).

# Making a field constant

If the value of a field will never *ever* change, you can use the `const` keyword and assign the value at compile time.

Inside the `Person` class, add the following code:

```
// constants
public const string Species = "Homo Sapien";
```

Inside the `Main` method, change the code to look like this. Note that, to read a constant field, you must write the name of the class, not the name of an instance of the class:

```
WriteLine($"{p1.Name} is a {Person.Species}");
```

Run the application and view the additional output:

```
Bob Smith is a Homo Sapien
```

Examples of the `const` fields in Microsoft types include `System.Int32.MaxValue` and `System.Math.PI` because neither value will ever change, as you can see in the following screenshot:

(constant) int int.MaxValue = 2147483647
Represents the largest possible value of an int. This field is constant.

(constant) double Math.PI = 3.1415926535897931
Represents the ratio of the circumference of a circle to its diameter, specified by the constant, π.

**Good Practice**
Constants should be avoided for two important reasons: the value must be known at compile time, and it must be expressible as a literal string, Boolean, or number value. Every reference to the `const` field is replaced with the literal value at compile time, which will, therefore, not be reflected if the value changes in a future version.

# Making a field read-only

A better choice for fields that should not change is to mark them as read-only.

Inside the `Person` class, write the following code:

```
// read-only fields
public readonly string HomePlanet = "Earth";
```

Inside the `Main` method, add the following code statement. Notice that, to get a read-only field, you must write the name of an instance of the class, not the type name, unlike `const`:

```
WriteLine($"{p1.Name} was born on {p1.HomePlanet}");
```

Run the application and view the output:

```
Bob Smith was born on Earth
```

**Good Practice**
Use read-only fields over the `const` fields for two important reasons: the value can be calculated or loaded at runtime and can be expressed using any executable statement. So, a read-only field can be set using a constructor or a field assignment. Every reference to the field is a live reference, so any future changes will be correctly reflected by calling code.

# Initializing fields with constructors

Fields often need to be initialized at runtime. You do this in a constructor that will be called when you make an instance of the class using the `new` keyword. Constructors execute before any fields are set by the code that is using the type.

Inside the Person class, add the following highlighted code after the existing read-only HomePlanet field:

```
// read-only fields
public readonly string HomePlanet = "Earth";
public readonly DateTime Instantiated;

// constructors
public Person()
{
   // set default values for fields
   // including read-only fields
   Name = "Unknown";
   Instantiated = DateTime.Now;
}
```

Inside the Main method, add the following code:

```
var p3 = new Person();
WriteLine($"{p3.Name} was instantiated at  {p3.Instantiated:hh:mm:ss} on
{p3.Instantiated:dddd, d MMMM  yyyy}");
```

Run the application and view the output:

```
Unknown was instantiated at 11:58:12 on Sunday, 12 March 2017
```

You can have multiple constructors in a type. This is especially useful to encourage developers to set initial values for fields.

Inside the Person class, add the following code:

```
public Person(string initialName)
{
   Name = initialName;
   Instantiated = DateTime.Now;
}
```

Inside the Main method, add the following code:

```
var p4 = new Person("Aziz");
WriteLine($"{p4.Name} was instantiated at
{p4.Instantiated:hh:mm:ss} on {p4.Instantiated:dddd, d MMMM yyyy}");
```

Run the application and view the output:

```
Aziz was instantiated at 11:59:25 on Sunday, 4 June 2017
```

# Setting fields with default literal

A new language feature introduced in C# 7.1 is default literals. In Chapter 2, *Speaking C#*, you learned about the `default(type)` keyword.

For example, if you had some fields in a class that you wanted to initial to their default type values in a constructor, you could use `default(type)`, as shown in the following code:

```
using System;
using System.Collections.Generic;
using Packt.CS7;

public class ThingOfDefaults
{
   public int Population;
   public DateTime When;
   public string Name;
   public List<Person> People;

   public ThingOfDefaults()
   {
      Population = default(int); // C# 2.0 and later
      When = default(DateTime);
      Name = default(string);
      People = default(List<Person>);
   }
}
```

You might think that the compiler ought to be able to work out what type we mean without being explicitly told, and you'd be right, but for the first 15 years of the C# compiler's life, it didn't.

Finally, with the C# 7.1 compiler, it does, as shown in the following code:

```
using System;
using System.Collections.Generic;
using Packt.CS7;

public class ThingOfDefaults
{
   public int Population;
   public DateTime When;
```

```
        public string Name;
        public List<Person> People;

        public ThingOfDefaults()
        {
            Population = default; // C# 7.1 and later
            When = default;
            Name = default;
            People = default;
        }
    }
```

But if you try to use this new C# 7.1 keyword, Visual Studio 2017 and Visual Studio Code both currently give a compile error, as shown in the following screenshot:

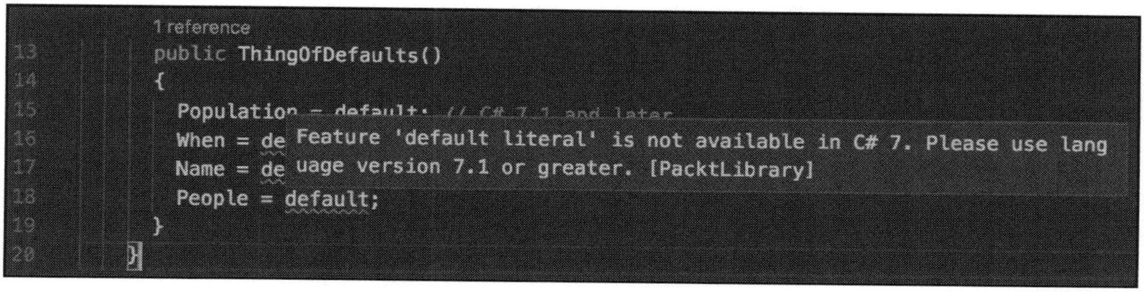

To tell the Visual Studio 2017 and Visual Studio Code to use the C# 7.1 compiler, open `PacktLibrary.csproj`, and add a pair of `<PropertyGroup>` elements for the `Release` and `Debug` configurations, as shown in the following markup:

```
<PropertyGroup
Condition="'$(Configuration)|$(Platform)'=='Release|AnyCPU'">
  <LangVersion>7.1</LangVersion>
</PropertyGroup>

<PropertyGroup Condition="'$(Configuration)|$(Platform)'=='Debug|AnyCPU'">
  <LangVersion>7.1</LangVersion>
</PropertyGroup>
```

You can replace `<LangVersion>7.1</LangVersion>` with `<LangVersion>latest</LangVersion>` if you always want to use the latest C# compiler for a project. For example, early in 2018, Microsoft plans to release C# 7.2.

Constructors are a special category of method. Let's look at methods in more detail.

# Writing and calling methods

**Methods** are type members that execute a block of statements.

A method that performs some actions, but does not return a value indicates this by showing that it returns the `void` type before the name of the method. A method that performs some actions and returns a value indicates this by showing that it returns the type of that value before the name of the method.

For example, you will create two methods:

- `WriteToConsole`: This will perform an action (writing a line), but it will return nothing from the method, indicated by the `void` keyword
- `GetOrigin`: This will return a string value, indicated by the `string` keyword

Inside the `Person` class, statically import `System.Console`, and then add the following code:

```
// methods
public void WriteToConsole()
{
   WriteLine($"{Name} was born on {DateOfBirth:dddd, d MMMM yyyy}");
}

public string GetOrigin()
{
   return $"{Name} was born on {HomePlanet}";
}
```

Inside the `Main` method, add the following code:

```
p1.WriteToConsole();
WriteLine(p1.GetOrigin());
```

Run the application and view the output:

```
Bob Smith was born on Wednesday, 22 December 1965
Bob Smith was born on Earth
```

# Combining multiple values with tuples

Each method can only return a single value that has a single type. That type could be a simple type, such as `string` in the previous example, a complex type, such as `Person`, or a collection type, such as `List<Person>`.

Imagine that we want to define a method named `GetTheData` that returns both a `string` value and an `int` value. We could define a new class named `TextAndNumber` with a `string` field and an `int` field, and return an instance of that complex type, as shown in the following code:

```
public class TextAndNumber
{
   public string Text;
   public int Number;
}

public class Processor
{
   public TextAndNumber GetTheData()
   {
      return new TextAndNumber
      {
         Text = "What's the mean of life?",
         Number = 42
      };
   }
}
```

Alternatively, we could use tuples.

Tuples have been a part of some languages such as F# since their first version, but .NET only added support for them in .NET 4.0 with the `System.Tuple` type. It was only in C# 7 that the C# language added syntax support for tuples.

While adding tuple support to the C# 7 language, .NET also added a new `System.ValueTuple` type that is more efficient in some common scenarios than the old .NET 4.0 `System.Tuple` type.

`System.ValueTuple` is not part of .NET Standard 1.6, and therefore not available by default in .NET Core 1.0 or 1.1 projects. `System.ValueTuple` is built-in with .NET Standard 2.0, and therefore, .NET Core 2.0.

## Defining methods with tuples

First, we will define a method that would work in C# 4 or later. Then we will use the new C# 7 language support.

Inside the `Person` class, add the following code to define two methods, the first with a return type of `System.Tuple<string, int>` and the second with a return type using C# 7 syntax:

```
// the old C# 4 and .NET 4.0 System.Tuple type
public Tuple<string, int> GetFruitCS4()
{
   return Tuple.Create("Apples", 5);
}

// the new C# 7 syntax and new System.ValueTuple type
public (string, int) GetFruitCS7()
{
   return ("Apples", 5);
}
```

Inside the `Main` method, add the following code:

```
Tuple<string, int> fruit4 = p1.GetFruitCS4();
WriteLine($"There are {fruit4.Item2} {fruit4.Item1}.");

(string, int) fruit7 = p1.GetFruitCS7();
WriteLine($"{fruit7.Item1}, {fruit7.Item2} there are.");
```

Run the application and view the output:

```
There are 5 Apples.
Apples, 5 there are.
```

## Naming the fields of a tuple

To access the fields of a tuple, the default names are `Item1`, `Item2`, and so on.

You can explicitly specify the field names. Inside the `Person` class, add the following code to define a method:

```
public (string Name, int Number) GetNamedFruit()
{
   return (Name: "Apples", Number: 5);
}
```

Inside the `Main` method, add the following code:

```
var fruitNamed = p1.GetNamedFruit();
WriteLine($"Are there {fruitNamed.Number} {fruitNamed.Name}?");
```

Run the application and view the output:

```
Are there 5 Apples?
```

## Inferring tuple names

If you are constructing a tuple from another object, you can use a new feature introduced in C# 7.1 called **tuple name inference**.

Let's create two tuple things, made of a `string` and `int` value each, as shown in the following code:

```
var thing1 = ("Neville", 4);
WriteLine(
  $"{thing1.Item1} has {thing1.Item2} children.");
var thing2 = (p1.Name, p1.Children.Count);
WriteLine(
  $"{thing2.Item1} has {thing2.Item2} children.");
```

In C# 7, both things use the `Item1` and `Item2` naming schemes. In C# 7.1, the second thing would infer the names `Name` and `Count`, as shown in the following code:

```
var thing2 = (p1.Name, p1.Children.Count);
WriteLine(
  $"{thing2.Name} has {thing2.Count} children.");
```

Just like all C# 7.1 language features, you will need to modify `PeopleApp.csproj` to instruct the compiler to use 7.1 or latest.

## Deconstructing tuples

You can also deconstruct tuples into separate variables. The deconstructing declaration has the same syntax as named field tuples, but without a variable name for the whole tuple. This has the effect of splitting the tuple into its parts and assigning those parts to new variables.

Inside the `Main` method, add the following code:

```
(string fruitName, int fruitNumber) = p1.GetFruitCS7();
WriteLine($"Deconstructed: {fruitName}, {fruitNumber}");
```

Run the application and view the output:

```
Deconstructed: Apples, 5
```

Deconstruction is not just for tuples. Any type can be deconstructed if it has a **Deconstructor** method. You can read about this at the following link: `https://docs.microsoft.com/en-us/dotnet/csharp/tuples#deconstruction`

# Defining and passing parameters to methods

Methods can have parameters passed to them to change their behavior. Parameters are defined a bit like variable declarations, but inside the parentheses of the method.

Inside the `Person` class, add the following code to define two methods, the first without parameters and the second with one parameter:

```
public string SayHello()
{
   return $"{Name} says 'Hello!'";
}

public string SayHelloTo(string name)
{
   return $"{Name} says 'Hello {name}!'";
}
```

Inside the `Main` method, add the following code:

```
WriteLine(p1.SayHello());
WriteLine(p1.SayHelloTo("Emily"));
```

Run the application and view the output:

```
Bob Smith says 'Hello!'
Bob Smith says 'Hello Emily!'
```

# Overloading methods

When typing a statement that calls a method, IntelliSense should show useful tooltips in both Visual Studio 2017 and Visual Studio Code, with the appropriate language extension installed.

In Visual Studio 2017, you can press *Ctrl* + *K*, *I* or go to **Edit** | **IntelliSense** | **Quick Info** to see quick info of a method, as shown in the following screenshot:

```
SayHello());
string Person.SayHello()
```

Here is the `SayHelloTo` method's quick info:

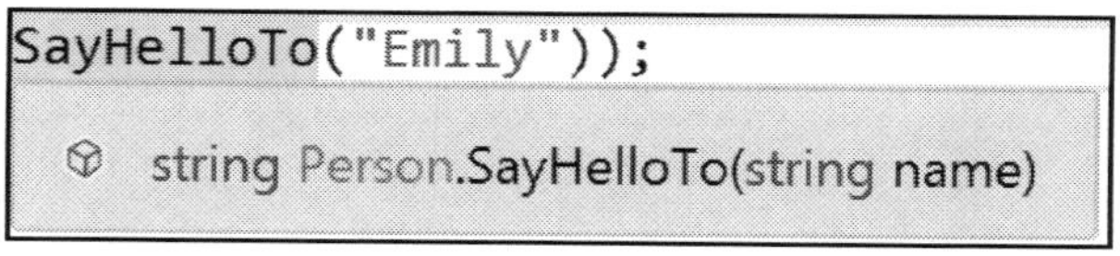

```
SayHelloTo("Emily"));
string Person.SayHelloTo(string name)
```

Instead of having two different method names, we could give both methods the same name. This is allowed because the methods each have a different signature. A **method signature** is a list of parameter types that can be passed when calling the method.

In the `Person` class, change the name of the `SayHelloTo` method to `SayHello`. Now, when you view the quick info for the method, it tells you that it has one additional overload:

```
SayHello("Emily"));
string Person.SayHello(string name) (+ 1 overload)
```

**Good Practice**
Use overloaded methods to simplify your class by making it appear to have fewer methods.

# Optional parameters and named arguments

Another way to simplify methods is to make parameters optional. You make a parameter optional by assigning a default value inside the method parameter list. Optional parameters must always come last in the list of parameters.

There is one exception to optional parameters always coming last. C# has a `params` keyword that allows you to pass a comma-separated list of parameters of any length as an array. You can read about `params` at the following link:
https://docs.microsoft.com/en-us/dotnet/csharp/language-reference/keywords/params

You will now create a method with three optional parameters.

Inside the `Person` class, add the following code:

```
public string OptionalParameters(string command = "Run!",
  double number = 0.0, bool active = true)
{
   return $"command is {command}, number is {number}, active is {active}";
}
```

Inside the `Main` method, add the following code:

```
WriteLine(p1.OptionalParameters());
```

Watch IntelliSense's **Quick Info** appear as you type the code, and you will see a tooltip, showing the three optional parameters with default values, as shown in the following screenshot:

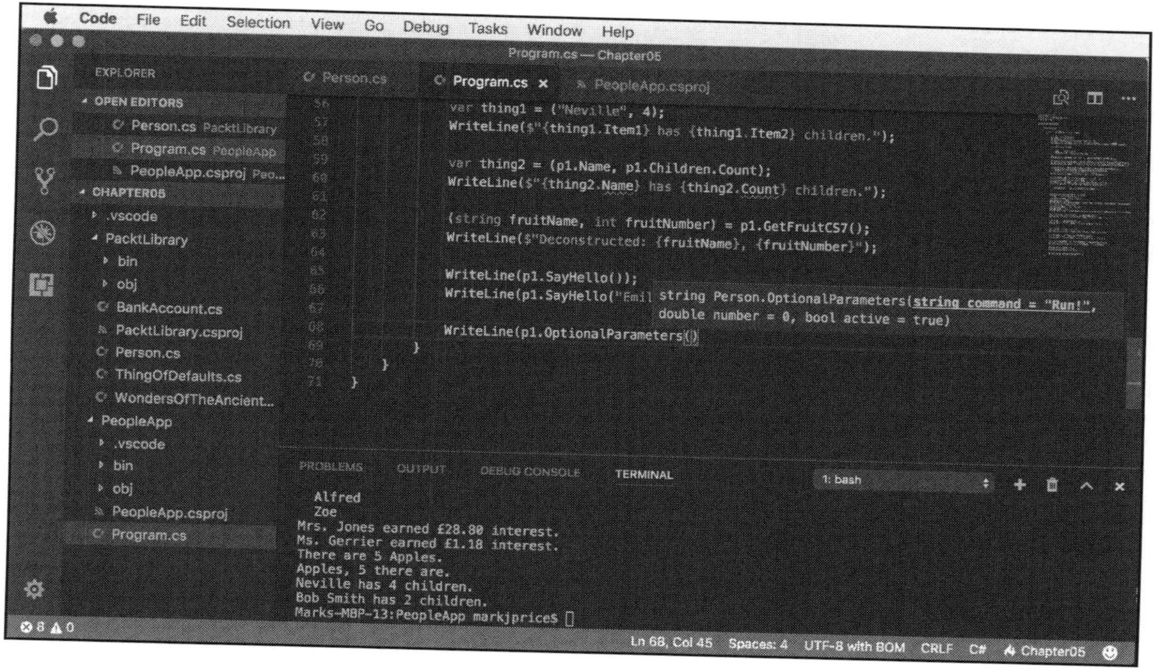

When you run the application, you will see the following output:

```
command is Run!, number is 0, active is True
```

In the `Main` method, add the following line, which passes a `string` value for the `command` parameter and a `double` value for the `number` parameter:

```
p1.OptionalParameters("Jump!", 98.5);
```

Run the application and see the output:

```
command is Jump!, number is 98.5, active is True
```

The default values for `command` and `number` have been replaced, but the default for `active` is still `true`.

Optional parameters are often combined with naming parameters when you call the method, because naming a parameter allows the values to be passed in a different order than how they were declared.

In the `Main` method, add the following line, which passes a `string` value for the `command` parameter and a `double` value for the `number` parameter but using named parameters, so that the order they are passed through can be swapped around:

```
p1.OptionalParameters(number: 52.7, command: "Hide!");
```

Run the application and see the output:

```
command is Hide!, number is 52.7, active is True
```

You can even use named parameters to skip over optional parameters.

In the `Main` method, add the following line that passes a `string` value for the `command` parameter using positional order, skips the `number` parameter, and uses the named `active` parameter:

```
p1.OptionalParameters("Poke!", active: false);
```

Run the application and see the output:

```
command is Poke!, number is 0, active is False
```

# Controlling how parameters are passed

When a parameter is passed into a method, it can be passed in one of three ways:

- By **value** (this is the default): Think of these as being *in-only*
- By **reference** as a `ref` parameter: Think of these as being *in-and-out*
- As an `out` parameter: Think of these as being *out-only*

In the Person class, add the following method:

```
public void PassingParameters(int x, ref int y, out int z)
{
    // out parameters cannot have a default
    // AND must be initialized inside the method
    z = 99;

    // increment each parameter
    x++;
    y++;
    z++;
}
```

In the Main method, add the following statements to declare some int variables and pass them into the method:

```
int a = 10;
int b = 20;
int c = 30;
WriteLine($"Before: a = {a}, b = {b}, c = {c}");
p1.PassingParameters(a, ref b, out c);
WriteLine($"After: a = {a}, b = {b}, c = {c}");
```

Run the application and see the output:

```
Before: a = 10, b = 20, c = 30
After: a = 10, b = 21, c = 100
```

When passing a variable as a parameter by default, its current *value* gets passed, *not* the variable itself. Therefore, x is a copy of the a variable. The a variable retains its original value of 10. When passing a variable as a ref parameter, a *reference* to the variable gets passed into the method. Therefore, y is a reference to b. The b variable gets incremented when the y parameter gets incremented. When passing a variable as an out parameter, a *reference* to the variable gets passed into the method. Therefore, z is a reference to c. The c variable gets replaced by whatever code executes inside the method. We could simplify the code in the Main method by not assigning the value 30 to the c variable, since it will always be replaced anyway.

In C# 7, we can simplify code that uses the out variables.

Add the following statements to the `Main` method:

```
// simplified C# 7 syntax for out parameters
int d = 10;
int e = 20;
WriteLine($"Before: d = {d}, e = {e}, f doesn't exist yet!");
p1.PassingParameters(d, ref e, out int f);
WriteLine($"After: d = {d}, e = {e}, f = {f}");
```

In C# 7, the `ref` keyword is not just for passing parameters into a method, it can also be applied to the return value. This allows an external variable to reference an internal variable and modify its value after the method call. This might be useful in advanced scenarios, for example, passing around placeholders into big data structures, but it's beyond the scope of this book.

# Splitting classes using partial

When working on large projects with multiple team members, it is useful to be able to split the definition of a complex class across multiple files. You do this using the `partial` keyword.

Imagine we want to add a new method to the `Person` class without having to ask another programmer to close the `Person.cs` file. If the class is defined as `partial`, then we can split it over as many separate files as we like.

In the `Person` class, add the `partial` keyword, as shown highlighted in the following code:

```
namespace Packt.CS7
{
   public partial class Person
   {
```

In Visual Studio 2017, navigate to **Project | Add Class...** or press *Shift* + *Alt* + *C*. Enter the name `Person2`. We cannot enter `Person` because Visual Studio 2017 isn't smart enough to understand what we want to do. Instead, we must now rename the new class to `Person`, change the namespace, and add the `public partial` keywords, as shown in the following code:

```
namespace Packt.CS7
{
   public partial class Person
   {
```

In Visual Studio Code, click on the **New File** button in the `PacktLibrary` folder in the **Explorer** pane and enter a name of `Person2.cs`. Add statements to the new file, as shown in the following code:

```
namespace Packt.CS7
{
   public partial class Person
   {
   }
}
```

The rest of the code we write for this chapter will be written in the `Person2.cs` file.

# Controlling access with properties and indexers

Earlier, you created a method named `GetOrigin` that returned a `string` containing the name and origin of the person. Languages such as Java do this a lot. C# has a better way: **properties**.

A property is simply a method (or a pair of methods) that acts and looks like a field when you want to get or set a value, thereby simplifying the syntax.

# Defining read-only properties

In the `Person2.cs` file, inside the `Person` class, add the following code to define three properties:

- The first property will perform the same role as the `GetOrigin` method using the property syntax that works with all versions of C# (although, it uses the C# 6 and later string interpolation syntax)
- The second property will return a greeting message using the C# 6 and later, the lambda expression (=>) syntax
- The third property will calculate the person's age

Here is the code:

```
// property defined using C# 1 - 5 syntax
public string Origin
{
   get
   {
      return $"{Name} was born on {HomePlanet}";
   }
}

// two properties defined using C# 6+ lambda expression syntax
public string Greeting => $"{Name} says 'Hello!'";

public int Age => (int)(System.DateTime.Today
  .Subtract(DateOfBirth).TotalDays / 365.25);
```

In the `Main` method, add the following code. You can see that, to set or get a property, you treat it like a field:

```
var sam = new Person
{
   Name = "Sam",
   DateOfBirth = new DateTime(1972, 1, 27)
};
WriteLine(sam.Origin);
WriteLine(sam.Greeting);
WriteLine(sam.Age);
```

Run the application and view the output:

```
Sam was born on Earth
Sam says 'Hello!'
46 // if executed between 27 January 2018 and 27 January 2019
```

# Defining settable properties

To create a settable property, you must use the older syntax and provide a pair of methods—not just a `get` part, but also a `set` part.

In the `Person2.cs` file, add the following code to define a `string` property that has both a `get` and `set` method (also known as *getter* and *setter*). Although you have not manually created a field to store the person's favorite ice-cream, it is there, automatically created by the compiler for you:

```
public string FavoriteIceCream { get; set; } // auto-syntax
```

Sometimes, you need more control over what happens when a property is set. In this scenario, you must use a more detailed syntax and manually create a `private` field to store the value for the property:

```
private string favoritePrimaryColor;
public string FavoritePrimaryColor
{
    get
    {
        return favoritePrimaryColor;
    }
    set
    {
        switch (value.ToLower())
        {
            case "red":
            case "green":
            case "blue":
                favoritePrimaryColor = value;
                break;
            default:
                throw new System.ArgumentException($"{value} is not a
                primary color. Choose from: red, green, blue.");
        }
    }
}
```

In the `Main` method, add the following code:

```
sam.FavoriteIceCream = "Chocolate Fudge";
WriteLine($"Sam's favorite ice-cream flavor is  {sam.FavoriteIceCream}.");
sam.FavoritePrimaryColor = "Red";
WriteLine($"Sam's favorite primary color is  {sam.FavoritePrimaryColor}.");
```

Run the application and view the output:

```
Sam's favorite ice-cream flavor is Chocolate Fudge.
Sam's favorite primary color is Red.
```

If you try to set the color to any value other than red, green, or blue, then the code will throw an exception. The calling code could then use a `try` statement to display the error message.

**Good Practice**
Use properties instead of fields when you want to validate what value can be stored, when you want to data bind in XAML (we will cover this in `Chapter 17`, *Building Windows Apps Using XAML and Fluent Design*), and when you want to read and write to fields without using methods. You can read more about encapsulation of fields using properties at the following link: `https://www.microsoft.com/net/tutorials/csharp/getting-started/encapsulation-oop`

## Defining indexers

Indexers allow the calling code to use the array syntax to access a property. For example, the `string` type defines an **indexer** so that the calling code can access individual characters in the string individually. We will define an indexer to simplify access to the children of a person.

In the `Person2.cs` file, add the following code to define an indexer to get and set a child using the index (position) of the child:

```
// indexers
public Person this[int index]
{
   get
   {
      return Children[index];
   }
   set
```

```
        {
            Children[index] = value;
        }
    }
```

You can overload indexers so that different types can be used to call them. For example, as well as passing an `int` value, you could also pass a `string` value.

In the `Main` method, add the following code. After adding to the children, we will access the first and second child using the longer `Children` field and the shorter indexer syntax:

```
sam.Children.Add(new Person { Name = "Charlie" });
sam.Children.Add(new Person { Name = "Ella" });
WriteLine($"Sam's first child is {sam.Children[0].Name}");
WriteLine($"Sam's second child is {sam.Children[1].Name}");
WriteLine($"Sam's first child is {sam[0].Name}");
WriteLine($"Sam's second child is {sam[1].Name}");
```

Run the application and view the output:

```
Sam's first child is Charlie
Sam's second child is Ella
Sam's first child is Charlie
Sam's second child is Ella
```

**Good Practice**
Only use indexers if it makes sense to use the square bracket/array syntax. As you can see from the preceding example, indexers rarely add much value.

# Practicing and exploring

Test your knowledge and understanding by answering some questions, get some hands-on practice, and explore this chapter's topics with deeper research.

# Exercise 5.1 – Test your knowledge

Answer the following questions:

1. What are the four access modifiers and what do they do?
2. What is the difference between the `static`, `const`, and `readonly` keywords?
3. What does a constructor do?
4. Why do you need to apply the `[Flags]` attribute to an `enum` keyword when you want to store combined values?
5. Why is the `partial` keyword useful?
6. What is a tuple?
7. What does the C# `ref` keyword do?
8. What does overloading mean?
9. What is the difference between a field and a property?
10. How do you make a method parameter optional?

# Exercise 5.2 – Explore topics

Use the following links to read more about this chapter's topics:

- **Fields (C# programming guide):** `https://docs.microsoft.com/en-us/dotnet/articles/csharp/programming-guide/classes-and-structs/fields`
- **Access modifiers (C# programming guide):** `https://docs.microsoft.com/en-us/dotnet/articles/csharp/language-reference/keywords/access-modifiers`
- **Constructors (C# programming guide):** `https://docs.microsoft.com/en-us/dotnet/articles/csharp/programming-guide/classes-and-structs/constructors`
- **Methods (C# programming guide):** `https://docs.microsoft.com/en-us/dotnet/articles/csharp/methods`
- **Properties (C# programming guide):** `https://docs.microsoft.com/en-us/dotnet/articles/csharp/properties`

# Summary

In this chapter, you learned about making your own types using OOP. You learned about some of the different categories of members that a type can have, including fields to store data and methods to perform actions. You used OOP concepts, such as aggregation and encapsulation, and explored some of the new language syntax features in C# 7.0 and 7.1.

In the next chapter, you will take these concepts further by defining delegates and events, implementing interfaces, and inheriting from existing classes.

# 6
# Implementing Interfaces and Inheriting Classes

This chapter is about deriving new types from existing ones using **object-oriented programming** (**OOP**). You will learn about defining operators and C# 7 local functions for performing simple actions, delegates and events for exchanging messages between types, implementing interfaces for common functionality, inheriting from a base class to create a derived class to reuse functionality, overriding a type member, using polymorphism, creating extension methods, and casting between classes in an inheritance hierarchy.

This chapter covers the following topics:

- Setting up a class library and console application
- Simplifying methods with operators
- Defining local functions
- Raising and handling events
- Implementing interfaces
- Making types more reusable with generics
- Managing memory with reference and value types
- Inheriting from classes
- Casting within inheritance hierarchies
- Inheriting and extending .NET types

# Setting up a class library and console application

We will start by defining a solution with two projects like the one created in `Chapter 5`, *Building Your Own Types with Object-Oriented Programming*. If you completed all the exercises in that chapter, then you can open it and continue with it. Otherwise, follow the instructions for your preferred development tool given here.

## Using Visual Studio 2017

In Visual Studio 2017, press *Ctrl* + *Shift* + *N* or go to **File** | **New** | **Project....**

In the **New Project** dialog, in the **Installed** list, expand **Visual C#**, and select **.NET Standard**. In the center list, select **Class Library (.NET Standard)**, type **Name** as `PacktLibrary`, change **Location** to `C:\Code`, type **Solution name** as `Chapter06`, and then click on **OK**.

In **Solution Explorer**, right-click on the file named `Class1.cs` and choose **Rename**. Type the name as `Person`. Modify the contents like this:

```
namespace Packt.CS7
{
   public class Person
   {
   }
}
```

Add a new console application project named `PeopleApp`.

In the solution's properties, set the startup project to be the `PeopleApp` project.

In **Solution Explorer**, in the `PeopleApp` project, right-click on **Dependencies** and choose **Add Reference....**

In the **Reference Manager - PeopleApp** dialog box, in the list on the left-hand side, choose **Projects**, select the `PacktLibrary` assembly, and then click on **OK**.

## Using Visual Studio Code

Create a folder named `Chapter06` with two subfolders named `PacktLibrary` and `PeopleApp`, as shown in this hierarchy:

- `Chapter06`
    - `PacktLibrary`
    - `PeopleApp`

Start Visual Studio Code and open the `Chapter06` folder.

In **Integrated Terminal**, enter the following commands:

```
cd PacktLibrary
dotnet new classlib
cd ..
cd PeopleApp
dotnet new console
```

In the **EXPLORER** pane, in the `PacktLibrary` project, rename the file named `Class1.cs` to `Person.cs`.

Modify the class file contents, as shown in the following code:

```
namespace Packt.CS7
{
   public class Person
   {
   }
}
```

In the **EXPLORER** pane, expand the folder named `PeopleApp` and click on the file named `PeopleApp.csproj`.

Add a project reference to `PacktLibrary`, as shown in the following markup:

```
<Project Sdk="Microsoft.NET.Sdk">
  <PropertyGroup>
    <OutputType>Exe</OutputType>
    <TargetFramework>netcoreapp2.0</TargetFramework>
  </PropertyGroup>

  <ItemGroup>
```

```
    <ProjectReference Include="..\PacktLibrary\PacktLibrary.csproj" />
  </ItemGroup>

</Project>
```

In **Integrated Terminal**, note that you are in the `PeopleApp` folder, enter the `dotnet build` command, and note the output indicating that both projects have been built successfully, as shown in the following screenshot:

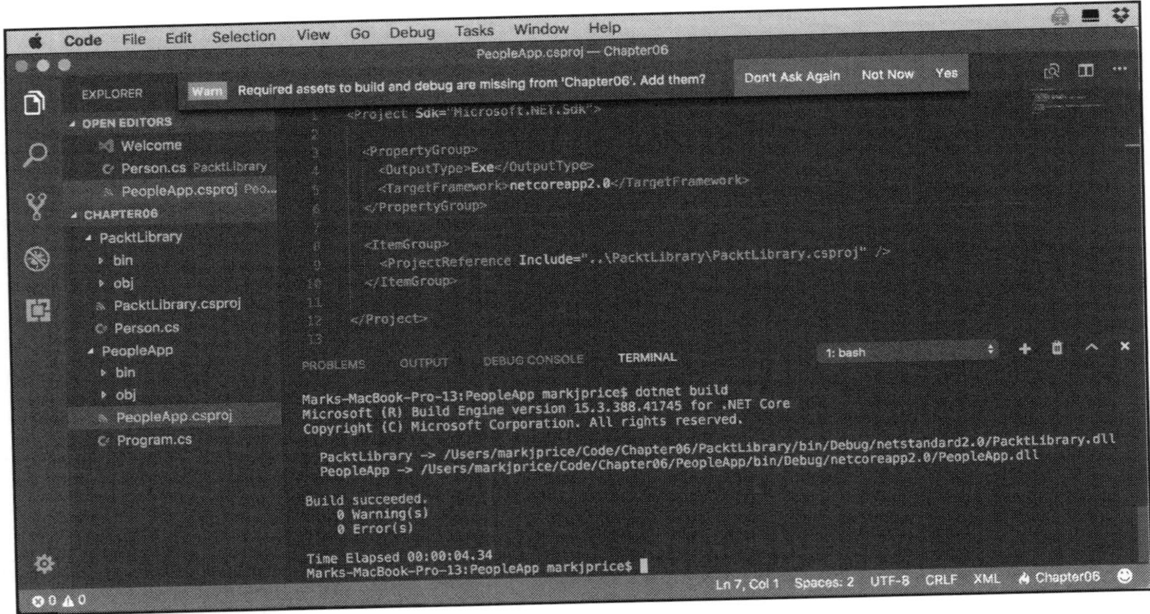

If prompted, click on **Yes** to add required assets.

## Defining the classes

In either Visual Studio 2017 or Visual Studio Code, add statements to the `Person` class, as shown in the following code:

```
using System;
using System.Collections.Generic;
using static System.Console;

namespace Packt.CS7
{
  public partial class Person
```

```
    {
        // fields
        public string Name;
        public DateTime DateOfBirth;
        public List<Person> Children = new List<Person>();

        // methods
        public void WriteToConsole()
        {
            WriteLine($"{Name} was born on {DateOfBirth:dddd, d MMMM yyyy}");
        }
    }
}
```

# Simplifying methods with operators

We might want two instances of a person to be able to procreate. We can implement this by writing methods. Instance methods are actions an object does to itself; static methods are actions the type does. Which you choose depends on what makes sense for the action.

**Good Practice**
Having both the static and instance methods to perform similar actions often makes sense. For example, `string` has both a `Compare` static method and a `CompareTo` instance method. This makes the functionality more visible to programmers using the type.

# Implementing some functionality with a method

Add two methods to the `Person` class that will allow two `Person` objects to procreate, as shown in the following code:

```
// methods to "multiply"
public static Person Procreate(Person p1, Person p2)
{
    var baby = new Person
    {
        Name = $"Baby of {p1.Name} and {p2.Name}"
    };
    p1.Children.Add(baby);
    p2.Children.Add(baby);
    return baby;
}
```

```
public Person ProcreateWith(Person partner)
{
   return Procreate(this, partner);
}
```

Note the following:

- In the `static` method named `Procreate`, the `Person` objects to procreate are passed as parameters named `p1` and `p2`
- A new `Person` class named `baby` is created with a name made of a combination of the two people who have procreated
- The `baby` object is added to the `Children` collection of both parents and then returned
- In the instance method named `ProcreateWith`, the `Person` object to procreate with is passed as a parameter named `partner`, and it along with `this` are passed to the static `Procreate` method

**Good Practice**
A method that creates a new object, or modified an existing object, should return that object so that the caller can see the results.

In the `PeopleApp` project, at the top of the `Program.cs` file, import the namespace for our class and statically import the `Console` type, as shown in the following code:

```
using System;
using Packt.CS7;
using static System.Console;
```

In the `Main` method, create three people and have them procreate, as shown in the following code:

```
var harry = new Person { Name = "Harry" };
var mary = new Person { Name = "Mary" };
var jill = new Person { Name = "Jill" };

// call instance method
var baby1 = mary.ProcreateWith(harry);

// call static method
var baby2 = Person.Procreate(harry, jill);

WriteLine($"{mary.Name} has {mary.Children.Count} children.");
```

```
WriteLine($"{harry.Name} has {harry.Children.Count} children.");
WriteLine($"{jill.Name} has {jill.Children.Count} children.");
WriteLine($"{mary.Name}'s first child is named
\"{mary.Children[0].Name}\".");
```

Run the console application and view the output:

```
Mary has 1 children.
Harry has 2 children.
Jill has 1 children.
Mary's first child is named "Baby of Harry and Mary".
```

# Implementing some functionality with an operator

The `System.String` class has a static method named `Concat` that concatenates two `string` values, as shown in the following code:

```
string s1 = "Hello ";
string s2 = "World!";
string s3 = string.Concat(s1, s2);
WriteLine(s3); // => Hello World!
```

Calling a method like `Concat` works, but it might be more natural for a programmer to use the + symbol to *add* two `string` values together, as shown in the following code:

```
string s1 = "Hello ";
string s2 = "World!";
string s3 = s1 + s2;
WriteLine(s3); // => Hello World!
```

A well-known phrase is *Go forth and multiply*, meaning to procreate. So let's write code so that the `*` (multiply) symbol will allow two `Person` objects to procreate.

We do this by defining a `static` operator for a symbol like `*`. The syntax is rather like a method, because in effect, an operator is a method, but using a symbol instead of a method name.

The list of symbols that your types can use as operators are listed at this link:
`https://docs.microsoft.com/en-us/dotnet/csharp/programming-guide/statements-expressions-operators/overloadable-operators`

In the `PacktLibrary` project, in the `Person` class, create a `static` operator for the `*` symbol, as shown in the following code:

```
// operator to "multiply"
public static Person operator *(Person p1, Person p2)
{
   return Person.Procreate(p1, p2);
}
```

**Good Practice**
Unlike methods, operators do not appear in IntelliSense lists for a type. For every operator you define, make a method as well, because it may not be obvious to a programmer that the operator is available. The implementation of the operator can then call the method, reusing the code you have written. A second reason for providing a method is that operators can be slower than method calls. If performance is a priority, then a programmer can call your method at the cost of readability.

In the `Main` method, after calling the static `Procreate` method, use the `*` operator to make another baby, as shown in the following highlighted code:

```
// call static method
var baby2 = Person.Procreate(harry, jill);

// call an operator
var baby3 = harry * mary;
```

Run the application and view the output:

```
Mary has 2 children.
Harry has 3 children.
Jill has 1 children.
Mary's first child is named "Baby of Harry and Mary".
```

# Defining local functions

A language feature introduced in C# 7 is the ability to define a local function. Local functions are the method equivalent to local variables. In other words, they are methods that are only visible and callable from within the containing method in which they have been defined. In other languages, they are sometimes called **nested** or **inner** functions.

We will use a local function to implement a factorial calculation.

Add the following code to the `Person` class:

```
// method with a local function
public static int Factorial(int number)
{
  if (number < 0)
  {
    throw new ArgumentException(
      $"{nameof(number)} cannot be less than zero.");
  }
  return localFactorial(number);

  int localFactorial(int localNumber)
  {
    if (localNumber < 1) return 1;
    return localNumber * localFactorial(localNumber - 1);
  }
}
```

Local functions can be defined anywhere inside a method: the top, the bottom, or even somewhere in the middle!

In the `Program.cs` file, in the `Main` method, add the following statement:

```
WriteLine($"5! is {Person.Factorial(5)}");
```

Run the console application and view the output:

```
5! is 120
```

# Raising and handling events

**Methods** are often described as *actions that an object can do*. For example, a `List` class can add an item to itself or clear itself.

**Events** are often described as *actions that happen to an object*. For example, in a user interface, `Button` has a `Click` event, click being something that happens to a button.

Another way of thinking of events is that they provide a way of exchanging messages between two objects.

# Calling methods using delegates

You have already seen the most common way to call or execute a method: use the **dot** syntax to access the method using its name. For example, `Console.WriteLine` tells the `Console` type to write out the message to the console window or Terminal.

The other way to call or execute a method is to use a **delegate**. If you have used languages that support function pointers, then think of a delegate as being a type-safe method pointer. In other words, a delegate is the memory address of a method that matches the same signature as the delegate so that it can be safely called.

For example, imagine there is a method that must have a `string` datatype passed as its only parameter and it returns an `int` datatype:

```
public int MethodIWantToCall(string input)
{
   return input.Length; // it doesn't matter what this does
}
```

I can call this method directly like this:

```
int answer = p1.MethodIWantToCall("Frog");
```

Alternatively, I can define a delegate with a matching signature to call the method indirectly. Notice that the names of the parameters do not have to match. Only the types of parameters and return values must match:

```
delegate int DelegateWithMatchingSignature(string s);
```

Now, I can create an instance of the delegate, point it at the method, and finally, call the delegate (which calls the method!), as shown here:

```
var d = new DelegateWithMatchingSignature(p1.MethodIWantToCall);
int answer2 = d("Frog");
```

You are probably thinking, "What's the point of that?" Well, it provides flexibility.

We could use delegates to create a queue of methods that need to be called in order. Delegates have built-in support for asynchronous operations that run on a different thread for better performance. Most importantly, delegates allow us to create events.

Delegates and events are one of the most advanced features of C# and can take a few attempts to understand, so don't worry if you feel lost!

# Defining events

Microsoft has two predefined delegates for use as events. They look like this:

```
public delegate void EventHandler(object sender, EventArgs e);
public delegate void EventHandler<TEventArgs>(object sender, TEventArgs e);
```

**Good Practice**
When you want to define an event in your own type, you should use one of these two predefined delegates.

Add the following code to the `Person` class. The code defines an event named `Shout`. It also defines a field to store `AngerLevel` and a method named `Poke`. Each time a person is poked, their anger level increments. Once their anger level reaches three, they raise the `Shout` event, but only if the event delegate is pointing at a method defined somewhere else in code, that is, not null:

```
// event
public event EventHandler Shout;

// field
public int AngerLevel;

// method
public void Poke()
{
   AngerLevel++;
   if (AngerLevel >= 3)
   {
      // if something is listening...
      if (Shout != null)
      {
         // ...then raise the event
         Shout(this, EventArgs.Empty);
```

```
        }
    }
}
```

Checking if an object is null before calling one of its methods is very common. C# allows these statements to be simplified like this: `Shout?.Invoke(this, EventArgs.Empty);`

## Using Visual Studio 2017

In Visual Studio 2017, in the `Main` method, start typing the following code to assign an event handler:

```
harry.Shout +=
```

Notice the IntelliSense that appears when you enter the `+=` operator, as shown in the following screenshot:

Press *Tab*. You will see a preview of what Visual Studio 2017 would like to do for you.

Press *Enter* to accept the name of the method.

Visual Studio 2017 inserts a method that correctly matches the signature of the event delegate. This method will be called when the event is raised.

Scroll down to find the method Visual Studio 2017 created for you, and delete the statement that throws `NotImplementedException`.

## Using Visual Studio Code

In Visual Studio Code, you must write the method and assign its name yourself. The name can be anything, but `Harry_Shout` is sensible.

In the Program class, add a method, as shown in the following code:

```
private static void Harry_Shout(object sender, System.EventArgs e)
{
}
```

In the Main method, add the following statement to assign the method to the event:

```
harry.Shout += Harry_Shout;
```

## Using Visual Studio 2017 or Visual Studio Code

Add statements to the Harry_Shout method to get a reference to the Person object and output some information about them, as shown in the following code:

```
private static void Harry_Shout(object sender, EventArgs e)
{
    Person p = (Person)sender;
    WriteLine($"{p.Name} is this angry: {p.AngerLevel}.");
}
```

Back in the Main method, add the following statements to call the Poke method four times, after assigning the method to the Shout event:

```
harry.Shout += Harry_Shout;
harry.Poke();
harry.Poke();
harry.Poke();
harry.Poke();
```

Run the application and view the output. Note that Harry only gets angry enough to shout once he's been poked at least three times:

```
Harry is this angry: 3.
Harry is this angry: 4.
```

You can define your own custom EventArgs-derived types so that you can pass additional information into an event handler method. You can read more at the following link: https://docs.microsoft.com/en-us/dotnet/standard/events/how-to-raise-and-consume-events

# Implementing interfaces

**Interfaces** are a way of connecting different types together to make new things. Think of them like the studs on top of LEGO™ bricks that allow them to "stick" together, or electrical standards for plugs and sockets.

If a type implements an interface, then it is making a promise to the rest of .NET that it supports a certain feature.

## Common interfaces

Here are some common interfaces that your types might want to implement:

| Interface | Method(s) | Description |
|---|---|---|
| `IComparable` | `CompareTo` (other) | This defines a comparison method that a type implements to order or sort its instances. |
| `IComparer` | `Compare` (first, second) | This defines a comparison method that a secondary type implements to order or sort instances of a primary type. |
| `IDisposable` | `Dispose()` | This defines a disposal method to release unmanaged resources more efficiently than waiting for a finalizer. |
| `IFormattable` | `ToString` (format, culture) | This defines a culture-aware method to format the value of an object into a string representation. |
| `IFormatter` | `Serialize` (stream, object), `Deserialize` (stream) | This defines methods to convert an object to and from a stream of bytes for storage or transfer. |
| `IFormatProvider` | `GetFormat` (Type) | This defines a method to format inputs based on a language and region. |

# Comparing objects when sorting

One of the most common interfaces that you will want to implement is `IComparable`. It allows arrays and collections of your type to be sorted.

## Attempting to sort objects without a method to compare

Add the following code to the `Main` method, which creates an array of the `Person` instances, outputs the array, attempts to sort it, and then outputs the sorted array:

```
Person[] people =
{
    new Person { Name = "Simon" },
    new Person { Name = "Jenny" },
    new Person { Name = "Adam" },
    new Person { Name = "Richard" }
};

WriteLine("Initial list of people:");
foreach (var person in people)
{
    WriteLine($"{person.Name}");
}

WriteLine("Use Person's IComparable implementation to sort:");
Array.Sort(people);
foreach (var person in people)
{
    WriteLine($"{person.Name}");
}
```

Run the application, and you will see this runtime error:

```
Unhandled Exception: System.InvalidOperationException: Failed to compare
two elements in the array. ---> System.ArgumentException: At least one
object must implement IComparable.
```

As the error explains, to fix the problem, our type must implement `IComparable`.

## Defining a method to compare

In the `PacktLibrary` project, in the `Person` class, after the class name, add a colon and enter `IComparable<Person>`, as shown in the following code:

```
public partial class Person : IComparable<Person>
```

Visual Studio 2017 and Visual Studio Code will draw a red squiggle under the new code to warn you that you have not yet implemented the method you have promised to.

Visual Studio 2017 and Visual Studio Code can write the skeleton implementation for you if you click on the light bulb and choose the **Implement interface** option, as shown in the following screenshot:

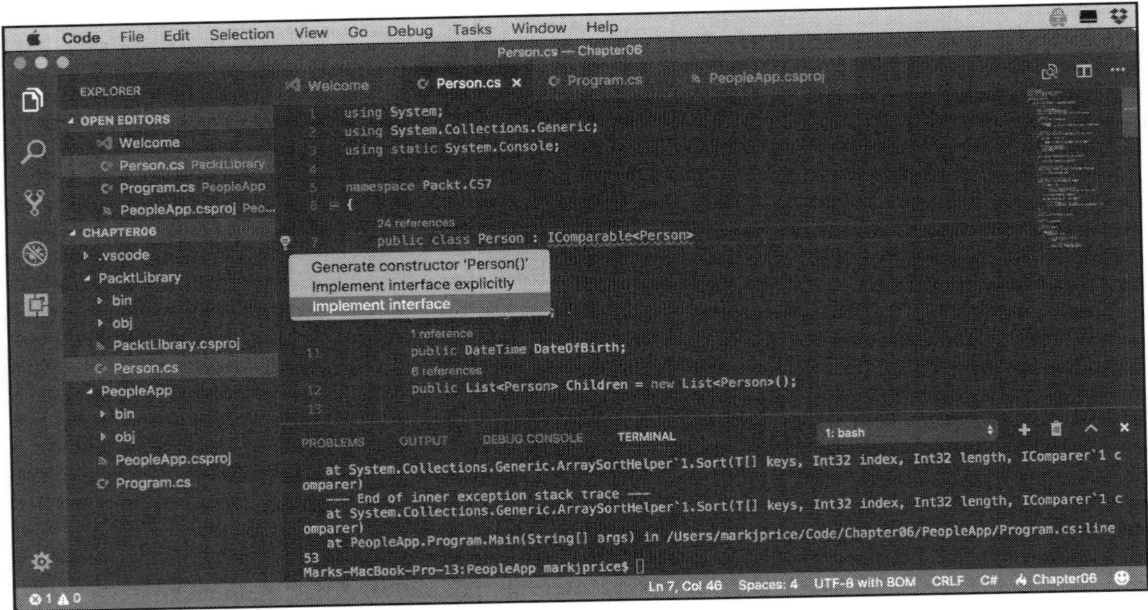

Interfaces can be implemented implicitly and explicitly. Implicit implementations are simpler. Explicit implementations are only necessary if a type must have multiple methods with the same name. For example, both `IGamePlayer` and `IKeyHolder` might have a method called `Lose`. In a type that must implement both interfaces, only one implementation of `Lose` can be the implicit method. The other `Lose` method would have to be implemented, and called, explicitly. You can read more at the following link:
https://docs.microsoft.com/en-us/dotnet/csharp/programming-guide/interfaces/explicit-interface-implementation

Scroll down to find the method that was written for you and delete the statement that throws the `NotImplementedException` error. Add a statement to call the `CompareTo` method of the `Name` field, which uses the `string` type's implementation of `CompareTo`, as shown in the following code:

```
public int CompareTo(Person other)
{
   return Name.CompareTo(other.Name);
}
```

We have chosen to compare two `Person` instances by comparing their `Name` fields. People will, therefore, be sorted alphabetically by their name.

Run the application. This time, it works:

```
Initial list of people:
Simon
Jenny
Adam
Richard
Use Person's IComparable implementation to sort:
Adam
Jenny
Richard
Simon
```

# Defining a separate comparer

Sometimes, you won't have access to the source code for a type, and it might not implement the `IComparable` interface. Luckily, there is another way to sort instances of a type. You can create a secondary type that implements a slightly different interface, named `IComparer`.

In the `PacktLibrary` project, add a new class named `PersonComparer` that implements the `IComparer` interface, as shown in the following block of code. It will compare two people by comparing the length of their `Name` field, or if the names are the same length, then by comparing the names alphabetically:

```
using System.Collections.Generic;

namespace Packt.CS7
{
   public class PersonComparer : IComparer<Person>
   {
      public int Compare(Person x, Person y)
      {
         // Compare the Name lengths...
         int temp = x.Name.Length.CompareTo(y.Name.Length);

         /// ...if they are equal...
         if (temp == 0)
         {
            // ...then sort by the Names...
            return x.Name.CompareTo(y.Name);
         }
         else
         {
            // ...otherwise sort by the lengths.
            return temp;
         }
      }
   }
}
```

In `PeopleApp`, in the `Program` class, in the `Main` method, add the following code:

```
WriteLine("Use PersonComparer's IComparer implementation to sort:");
Array.Sort(people, new PersonComparer());
foreach (var person in people)
{
   WriteLine($"{person.Name}");
}
```

Run the application and view the output.

This time, when we sort the people array, we explicitly ask the sorting algorithm to use the `PersonComparer` type instead, so that the people are sorted with the shortest names first, and when the lengths of two or more names are equal, to sort them alphabetically:

```
Use Person's IComparable implementation to sort:
Adam
Jenny
Richard
Simon
Use PersonComparer's IComparer implementation to sort:
Adam
Jenny
Simon
Richard
```

**Good Practice**
If anyone would want to sort an array or collection of instances of your type, then implement the `IComparable` interface.

# Making types more reusable with generics

In 2005, with C# and .NET Framework 2.0, Microsoft introduced a feature named **generics** that enables your types to be more reusable, by allowing a programmer to pass types as parameters similar to how you can pass objects as parameters.

## Making a generic type

First, let's see an example of a non-generic type, so that you can understand the problem that generics is designed to solve.

In the `PacktLibrary` project, add a new class named `Thing`, as shown in the following code, and note the following:

- `Thing` has a field named `Data` of the `object` type
- `Thing` has a method named `Process` that accepts an input parameter of the `string` type, and returns a `string` value

If we wanted the `Thing` type to be flexible in .NET Framework 1.0, we would have to use the `object` type for the field.

```
using System;

namespace Packt.CS7
{
   public class Thing
   {
      public object Data = default(object);

      public string Process(string input)
      {
         if (Data == input)
         {
            return Data.ToString() + Data.ToString();
         }
         else
         {
            return Data.ToString();
         }
      }
   }
}
```

In the `PeopleApp` project, add some statements to the end of `Main`, as shown in the following code:

```
var t = new Thing();
t.Data = 42;
WriteLine($"Thing: {t.Process("42")}");
```

Run the console application and view the output, and note the warning:

```
Thing.cs(11,17): warning CS0252: Possible unintended reference comparison;
to get a value comparison, cast the left hand side to type 'string'
[/Users/markjprice/Code/Chapter06/PacktLibrary/PacktLibrary.csproj]
```

`Thing` is currently flexible, because any type can be set for the `Data` field. But there is no type checking, so inside the `Process`, method we cannot safely do much beyond calling `ToString`.

In the PacktLibrary project, add a new class named GenericThing, as shown in the following code:

```
using System;

namespace Packt.CS7
{
    public class GenericThing<T> where T : IComparable, IFormattable
    {
        public T Data = default(T);

        public string Process(string input)
        {
            if (Data.ToString().CompareTo(input) == 0)
            {
                return Data.ToString() + Data.ToString();
            }
            else
            {
                return Data.ToString();
            }
        }
    }
}
```

Note the following:

- GenericThing has a generic type parameter named T, that can be any type that implements IComparable and IFormattable, so it must have methods named CompareTo and ToString. By convention, use the type parameter name T if there is only one type parameter
- GenericThing has a field named Data of the T type
- GenericThing has a method named Process that accepts an input parameter of the string type, and returns a value of the string type

In the PeopleApp project, add some statements to the end of Main, as shown in the following code, and note the following:

- When instantiating an instance of a generic type, the developer must pass a type parameter. In this example, we pass int as the type, so wherever T appears in the GenericThing class, it is replaced with int.

- When setting the `Data` field, we must use an `int` value, like `42`:

```
var gt = new GenericThing<int>();
gt.Data = 42;
WriteLine($"GenericThing: {gt.Process("42")}");
```

Run the console application and view the output, and note the logic of the `Process` method correctly works for `GenericThing`, but not `Thing`:

```
Thing: 42
GenericThing: 4242
```

# Making a generic method

Generics can be used for methods, even inside a non-generic type.

In `PacktLibrary`, add a new class named `Squarer`, with a generic method named `Square`, as shown in the following code:

```
using System;
using System.Threading;

namespace Packt.CS7
{
   public static class Squarer
   {
      public static double Square<T>(T input)
      where T : IConvertible
      {
         double d = input.ToDouble(
         Thread.CurrentThread.CurrentCulture);
         return d * d;
      }
   }
}
```

Note the following:

- The static `Squarer` class is non-generic.
- The static `Square` method is generic, and its type parameter `T` must implement `IConvertible`, so we know it has a `ToDouble` method. `T` is used as the type for the `input` parameter.

- `ToDouble` requires a parameter that implements `IFormatProvider` for understanding the format of numbers for a language and region. We can pass the `CurrentCulture` property of the current thread to specify the language and region used by your computer. You will learn about cultures in `Chapter 8`, *Using Common .NET Standard Types*.
- The return value is the input value multiplied by itself.

In `PeopleApp`, in the `Program` class, at the bottom of the `Main` method, add the following code. Note that when calling a generic method, you can specify the type parameter to make it clearer, although the compiler can usually work it out without you telling it the type:

```
string number1 = "4";
WriteLine($"{number1} squared is {Squarer.Square<string>(number1)}");

byte number2 = 3;
WriteLine($"{number2} squared is {Squarer.Square<byte>(number2)}");
```

Run the console application and view the output:

```
4 squared is 16
3 squared is 9
```

# Managing memory with reference and value types

There are two categories of memory: **stack** memory and **heap** memory. Stack memory is fast but limited, and heap memory is slow but plentiful.

There are two C# keywords that you can use to create object types: `class` and `struct`. Both can have the same members. The difference between the two is how memory is allocated.

When you define a type using class, you are defining a reference type. This means that the memory for the object itself is allocated on the heap, and only the memory address of the object (and a little overhead) is stored on the stack.

When you define a type using `struct`, you are defining a value type. This means that the memory for the object itself is allocated on the stack.

If a `struct` uses types that are not of the `struct` type for any of its fields, then those fields will be stored on the heap!

These are the most common `struct` types in .NET Core:

- **Numbers**: `byte`, `sbyte`, `short`, `ushort`, `int`, `uint`, `long`, `ulong`, `float`, `double`, and `decimal`
- **Miscellaneous**: `char` and `bool`
- **System.Drawing**: `Color`, `Point`, and `Rectangle`

Almost all the other types in .NET Core are the `class` types, including `string`.

You cannot inherit from `struct`.

## Defining a struct type

Add a class file named `DisplacementVector.cs` to the `PacktLibrary` project.

There isn't an item template in Visual Studio 2017 for `struct`, so you must use `class` and then change it manually.

Modify the file, as shown in the following code, and note the following:

- The type is a `struct` value type instead of a `class` reference type
- It has two fields of type `int`, named `X` and `Y`
- It has a constructor for setting initial values for `X` and `Y`
- It has an operator for adding two instances together that returns a new instance with `X` added to `X`, and `Y` added to `Y`

```
namespace Packt.CS7
{
   public struct DisplacementVector
   {
      public int X;
      public int Y;
```

```
        public DisplacementVector(int initialX, int initialY)
        {
            X = initialX;
            Y = initialY;
        }

        public static DisplacementVector operator
            +(DisplacementVector vector1, DisplacementVector vector2)
        {
            return new DisplacementVector(
              vector1.X + vector2.X,vector1.Y + vector2.Y);
        }
    }
}
```

In the `PeopleApp` project, in the `Program` class, in the `Main` method, add the following code to create two new instances of `DisplacementVector`, add them together, and output the result:

```
var dv1 = new DisplacementVector(3, 5);
var dv2 = new DisplacementVector(-2, 7);
var dv3 = dv1 + dv2;
WriteLine($"({dv1.X}, {dv1.Y}) + ({dv2.X}, {dv2.Y}) = ({dv3.X},{dv3.Y})");
```

Run the application and view the output:

```
(3, 5) + (-2, 7) = (1, 12)
```

**Good Practice**
If all the fields in your type use 16 bytes or less of stack memory, your type only uses the `struct` types for its fields, and you will never want to derive from your type, then Microsoft recommends that you use a `struct` type. If your type uses more than 16 bytes of stack memory, or if it uses class types for its fields, or if you might want to inherit from it, then use `class`.

# Releasing unmanaged resources

In the previous chapter, we saw that constructors can be used to initialize fields and that a type may have multiple constructors.

Imagine that a constructor allocates an unmanaged resource, that is, anything that is not controlled by .NET. The unmanaged resource must be manually released because .NET cannot do it for us.

For this topic, I will show some code examples, but you do not need to create them in your current project.

Each type can have a single **finalizer** (aka destructor) that will be called by the CLR when the resources need to be released. A finalizer has the same name as a constructor, that is, the type name, but it is prefixed with a tilde (~), as shown in the following example:

```
public class Animal
{
   public Animal()
   {
      // allocate an unmanaged resource
   }
   ~Animal() // Finalizer aka destructor
   {
      // deallocate the unmanaged resource
   }
}
```

Do not confuse a finalizer (aka **destructor**) with a **deconstructor**. A destructor releases resources, that is, it destroys an object. A deconstructor returns an object split up into its constituent parts and uses the new C# 7 deconstruction syntax.

This is the minimum you should do in this scenario. The problem with just providing a finalizer is that the .NET garbage collector requires two garbage collections to completely release the allocated resources for this type.

Though optional, it is recommended to also provide a method to allow a developer who uses your type to explicitly release resources so that the garbage collector can then release the object in a single collection.

There is a standard mechanism to do this in .NET by implementing the `IDisposable` interface, as shown in the following example:

```
public class Animal : IDisposable
{
   public Animal()
   {
      // allocate unmanaged resource
   }

   ~Animal() // Finalizer
   {
      if(disposed) return;
      Dispose(false);
   }

   bool disposed = false; // have resources been released?

   public void Dispose()
   {
      Dispose(true);
      GC.SuppressFinalize(this);
   }

   protected virtual void Dispose(bool disposing)
   {
      if (disposed) return;
      // deallocate the *unmanaged* resource
      // ...
      if (disposing)
      {
        // deallocate any other *managed* resources
        // ...
      }
      disposed = true;
   }
}
```

There are two `Dispose` methods. The `public` method will be called by a developer using your type. The `Dispose` method with a `bool` parameter is used internally to implement the deallocation of resources, both unmanaged and managed. When the public `Dispose` method is called, both unmanaged and managed resources need to be deallocated, but when the finalizer runs, only unmanaged resources need to be deallocated.

Also, note the call to `GC.SuppressFinalize(this)` is what notifies the garbage collector that it no longer needs to run the finalizer, and removes the need for a second collection.

# Ensuring that dispose is called

When someone uses a type that implements `IDisposable`, they can ensure that the public `Dispose` method is called with the `using` statement, as shown in the following code:

```
using(Animal a = new Animal())
{
   // code that uses the Animal instance
}
```

The compiler converts your code into something like the following, which guarantees that even if an exception occurs, the `Dispose` method will still be called:

```
Animal a = new Animal();
try
{
   // code that uses the Animal instance
}
finally
{
   if (a != null) a.Dispose();
}
```

You will see practical examples of releasing unmanaged resources with `IDisposable`, the `using` statements, and the `try...finally` blocks in `Chapter 9`, *Working with Files, Streams, and Serialization*.

# Inheriting from classes

The `Person` type we created earlier is implicitly derived (inherited) from `System.Object`. Now, we will create a new class that inherits from `Person`.

Add a new class named `Employee.cs` to the `PacktLibrary` project.

Modify its code as shown in the following code:

```
using System;

namespace Packt.CS7
{
    public class Employee : Person
    {
    }
}
```

Add statements to the `Main` method to create an instance of the `Employee` class:

```
Employee e1 = new Employee
{
    Name = "John Jones",
    DateOfBirth = new DateTime(1990, 7, 28)
};
e1.WriteToConsole();
```

Run the console application and view the output:

```
John Jones was born on Saturday, 28 July 1990
```

Note that the `Employee` class has inherited all the members of `Person`.

# Extending classes

Now, we will add some employee-specific members to extend the class.

In the `Employee` class, add the following code to define two properties:

```
public string EmployeeCode { get; set; }
public DateTime HireDate { get; set; }
```

Back in the `Main` method, add the following code:

```
e1.EmployeeCode = "JJ001";
e1.HireDate = new DateTime(2014, 11, 23);
WriteLine($"{e1.Name} was hired on {e1.HireDate:dd/MM/yy}");
```

Run the console application and view the output:

```
John Jones was hired on 23/11/14
```

## Hiding members

So far, the `WriteToConsole` method is being inherited from `Person`, and it only outputs the employee's name and date of birth. We might want to change what this method does for an employee.

In the `Employee` class, add the following highlighted code to redefine the `WriteToConsole` method:

Note that you will need to statically import `System.Console`.

```
using System;
using static System.Console;

namespace Packt.CS7
{
   public class Employee : Person
   {
      public string EmployeeCode { get; set; }
      public DateTime HireDate { get; set; }

      public void WriteToConsole()
      {
         WriteLine($"{Name}'s birth date is {DateOfBirth:dd/MM/yy} and hire
date was {HireDate:dd/MM/yy}");
      }
   }
}
```

Run the application and view the output:

```
John Jones's birth date is 28/07/90 and hire date was 01/01/01
John Jones was hired on 23/11/14
```

Both Visual Studio 2017 and Visual Studio Code warn you that your method now hides the method with the same name that you inherited from the `Person` class by drawing a green squiggle under the method name, as shown in the following screenshot:

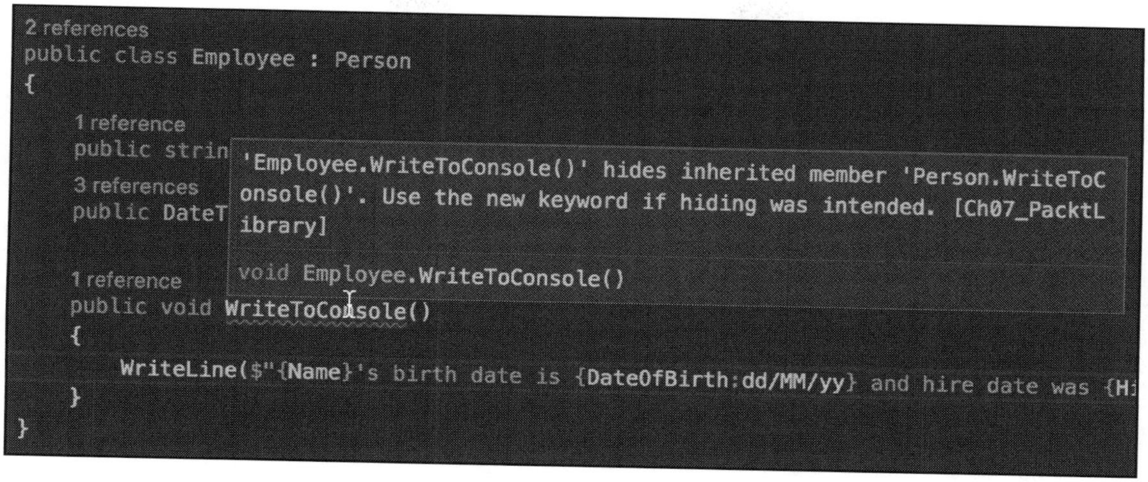

```
2 references
public class Employee : Person
{
    1 reference
    public strin 'Employee.WriteToConsole()' hides inherited member 'Person.WriteToC
    3 references  onsole()'. Use the new keyword if hiding was intended. [Ch07_PacktL
    public DateT  ibrary]

    1 reference   void Employee.WriteToConsole()
    public void WriteToConsole()
    {
        WriteLine($"{Name}'s birth date is {DateOfBirth:dd/MM/yy} and hire date was {Hi
    }
}
```

You can remove this warning by applying the `new` keyword to the method, to indicate that you are deliberately replacing the old method, as shown in the following code:

```
public new void WriteToConsole()
```

# Overriding members

Rather than hiding a method, it is usually better to override it. You can only override members if the base class chooses to allow overriding, by applying the `virtual` keyword.

In the `Main` method, add the following statement:

```
WriteLine(e1.ToString());
```

Run the application. The `ToString` method is inherited from `System.Object`. The implementation outputs the namespace and type name, as follows:

```
Packt.CS7.Employee
```

Let's override this behavior for the `Person` class.

Make this change to the `Person` class, not the `Employee` class.

## Using Visual Studio 2017

In Visual Studio 2017, open the `Person.cs` file, and at the bottom (but inside the class brackets), type the keyword `override` and enter a space after the word. You will see that Visual Studio shows a list of methods that have been marked as `virtual` so that they can be overridden, as shown in the following screenshot:

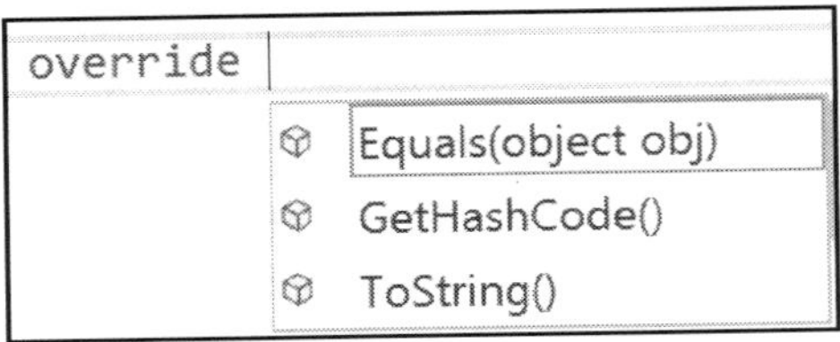


Use the arrow keys on your keyboard to choose `ToString` and then press *Enter*.

## Using Visual Studio 2017 or Visual Studio Code

In Visual Studio 2017, add a `return` statement to the method, or in Visual Studio Code, write the whole method, as shown in the following code:

```
// overridden methods
public override string ToString()
{
    return $"{Name} is a {base.ToString()}";
}
```

Run the console application and view the output. Now, when the `ToString` method is called, it outputs the person's name, as well as the base classes implementation of `ToString`, as shown in the following output:

```
John Jones is a Packt.CS7.Employee
```

**Good Practice**
Many real-world APIs, for example, Microsoft's Entity Framework Core, Castle's DynamicProxy, and Episerver's content models, require the properties that you define in your classes to be marked as `virtual`. Unless you have a good reason, mark your method and property members as `virtual`.

# Preventing inheritance and overriding

You can prevent someone from inheriting from your class by applying the `sealed` keyword to its definition. No one can inherit from Scrooge McDuck:

```
public sealed class ScroogeMcDuck
{
}
```

An example of `sealed` in the real world is the `string` class. Microsoft has implemented some extreme optimizations inside the `string` class that could be negatively affected by your inheritance; so, Microsoft prevents that.

You can prevent someone from overriding a method in your class by applying the `sealed` keyword to the method. No one can change the way Lady Gaga sings:

```
public class LadyGaga
{
    public sealed void Sing()
    {
    }
}
```

# Polymorphism

You have now seen two ways to change the behavior of an inherited method. We can hide it using `new` (known as **non polymorphic inheritance**), or we can override it (**polymorphic inheritance**).

Both ways can call the base class using the `base` keyword, so what is the difference?

It all depends on the type of the variable holding a reference to the object. For example, a variable of the `Person` type can hold a reference to a `Person` class, *or any type that derives* from `Person`.

In the `Employee` class, add the following code:

```
public override string ToString()
{
   return $"{Name}'s code is {EmployeeCode}";
}
```

In the `Main` method, write the following code:

```
Employee aliceInEmployee = new Employee { Name = "Alice", EmployeeCode =
"AA123" };
Person aliceInPerson = aliceInEmployee;
aliceInEmployee.WriteToConsole();
aliceInPerson.WriteToConsole();
WriteLine(aliceInEmployee.ToString());
WriteLine(aliceInPerson.ToString());
```

Run the console application and view the output:

```
Alice's birth date is 01/01/01 and hire date was 01/01/01
Alice was born on Monday, 1 January 0001
Alice's code is AA123
Alice's code is AA123
```

Note that when a method is hidden with `new`, the compiler is not smart enough to know that the object is an employee, so it calls the `WriteToConsole` method in `Person`.

When a method is overridden with `virtual` and `override`, the compiler is smart enough to know that although the variable is declared as a `Person` class, the object itself is an `Employee` class and, therefore, the `Employee` implementation of `ToString` is called.

The access modifiers and the affect they have is summarized in the following table:

| Variable type | Access modifier | Method executed | In class |
|---|---|---|---|
| `Person` | | `WriteToConsole` | `Person` |
| `Employee` | `new` | `WriteToConsole` | `Employee` |
| `Person` | `virtual` | `ToString` | `Employee` |
| `Employee` | `override` | `ToString` | `Employee` |

Polymorphism is literally academic to most programmers. If you get the concept, that's fine; but, if not, I suggest that you don't worry about it. Some people like to make others feel inferior by saying understanding polymorphism is important, but IMHO it's not. You can have a successful career with C# and never need to be able to explain polymorphism, just as a racing car driver doesn't need to be able to explain the engineering behind fuel injection.

# Casting within inheritance hierarchies

Casting is subtly different from converting between types.

## Implicit casting

In the previous example, you saw how an instance of a derived type can be stored in a variable of its base type (or its base's base type, and so on). When we do this, it is called **implicit casting**.

## Explicit casting

Going the other way is an explicit cast, and you must use parentheses to do it.

In the `Main` method, add the following code:

```
Employee e2 = aliceInPerson;
```

Visual Studio 2017 and Visual Studio Code display a red squiggle and a compile error in the **Error List** and **Problems** windows, as shown in the following screenshot:

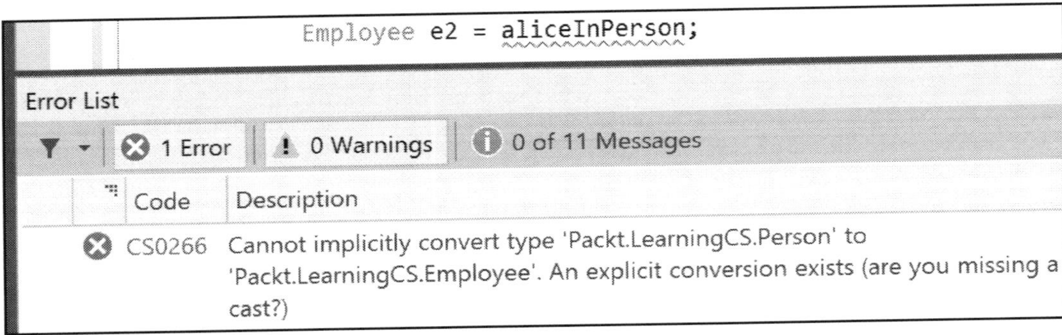


Change the code as follows:

```
Employee e2 = (Employee)aliceInPerson;
```

## Handling casting exceptions

The compiler is now happy; *but*, because `aliceInPerson` might be a different derived type, like `Student` instead of `Employee`, we need to be careful. This statement might throw an `InvalidCastException` error.

We can handle this by writing a `try` statement, but there is a better way. We can check the current type of the object using the `is` keyword.

Wrap the explicit cast statement in an `if` statement, as follows:

```
if (aliceInPerson is Employee)
{
   WriteLine($"{nameof(aliceInPerson)} IS an Employee");
   Employee e2 = (Employee)aliceInPerson;
   // do something with e2
}
```

Run the console application and view the output:

```
aliceInPerson IS an Employee
```

Alternatively, you can use the `as` keyword to cast. Instead of throwing an exception, the `as` keyword returns `null` if the type cannot be cast.

Add the following statements to the end of the `Main` method:

```
Employee e3 = aliceInPerson as Employee;
if (e3 != null)
{
   WriteLine($"{nameof(aliceInPerson)} AS an Employee");
   // do something with e3
}
```

Since accessing a `null` variable can throw a `NullReferenceException` error, you should always check for `null` before using the result.

Run the console application and view the output:

```
aliceInPerson AS an Employee
```

**Good Practice**
Use the `is` and `as` keywords to avoid throwing exceptions when casting between derived types.

# Inheriting and extending .NET types

.NET has prebuilt class libraries containing hundreds of thousands of types. Rather than creating your own completely new types, you can often start by inheriting from one of Microsoft's.

# Inheriting from an exception

In the `PacktLibrary` project, add a new class named `PersonException`, as shown in the following code:

```
using System;

namespace Packt.CS7
{
   public class PersonException : Exception
   {
      public PersonException() : base() { }
      public PersonException(string message) : base(message) { }
```

```
        public PersonException(string message, Exception innerException) :
        base(message, innerException) { }
    }
}
```

Unlike ordinary methods, constructors are not inherited, so we must explicitly declare and explicitly call the base constructor implementations in `System.Exception` to make them available to programmers who might want to use those constructors in our custom exception.

In the `Person` class, add the following method:

```
public void TimeTravel(DateTime when)
{
   if (when <= DateOfBirth)
   {
      throw new PersonException("If you travel back in time to a
      date earlier than your own birth then the universe will
      explode!");
   }
   else
   {
      WriteLine($"Welcome to {when:yyyy}!");
   }
}
```

In the `Main` method, add the following statements to test what happens when we try to time travel too far back:

```
try
{
   e1.TimeTravel(new DateTime(1999, 12, 31));
   e1.TimeTravel(new DateTime(1950, 12, 25));
}
catch (PersonException ex)
{
   WriteLine(ex.Message);
}
```

Run the console application and view the output:

```
Welcome to 1999!
If you travel back in time to a date earlier than your own birth then the
universe will explode!
```

**Good Practice**
When defining your own exceptions, give them the same three constructors.

# Extending types when you can't inherit

Earlier, we saw how the `sealed` modifier can be used to prevent inheritance.

Microsoft has applied the `sealed` keyword to the `System.String` class so that no one can inherit and potentially break the behavior of strings.

Can we still add new methods to strings? Yes, if we use a language feature named **extension methods**, which was introduced with C# 3.

## Using static methods to reuse functionality

Since the first version of C#, we could create the `static` methods to reuse functionality, such as the ability to validate that a string contains an email address.

In the `PacktLibrary` project, add a new class named `StringExtensions.cs`, as shown in the following code, and note the following:

- The class imports a namespace for handling regular expressions
- The `IsValidEmail` static method uses the `Regex` type to check for matches against a simple email pattern that looks for valid characters before and after the `@` symbol

You will learn about regular expressions in `Chapter 8`, *Using Common .NET Standard Types*.

```
using System.Text.RegularExpressions;

namespace Packt.CS7
{
   public class StringExtensions
   {
      public static bool IsValidEmail(string input)
      {
         // use simple regular expression to check
```

```
            // that the input string is a valid email
            return Regex.IsMatch(input, @"[a-zA-Z0-9\.-_]+@[a-zA-Z0-9\.-_]+");
        }
    }
}
```

Add the following statements to the bottom of the `Main` method to validate two examples of email addresses:

```
string email1 = "pamela@test.com";
string email2 = "ian&test.com";

WriteLine($"{email1} is a valid e-mail address:
{StringExtensions.IsValidEmail(email1)}.");
WriteLine($"{email2} is a valid e-mail address:
{StringExtensions.IsValidEmail(email2)}.");
```

Run the application and view the output:

```
pamela@test.com is a valid e-mail address: True.
ian&test.com is a valid e-mail address: False.
```

This works, but extension methods can reduce the amount of code we must type and simplify the usage of this function.

# Using extension methods to reuse functionality

In the `StringExtensions` class, add the `static` modifier before the class, and add the `this` modifier before the `string` type, as highlighted in the following code:

```
public static class StringExtensions
{
    public static bool IsValidEmail(this string input)
    {
```

These two changes inform the compiler that it should treat the method as a method that extends the `string` type.

Back in the `Program` class, add some new statements to use the extension method for strings:

```
WriteLine($"{email1} is a valid e-mail address:{email1.IsValidEmail()}.");
WriteLine($"{email2} is a valid e-mail address:{email2.IsValidEmail()}.");
```

Note the subtle change in the syntax. The `IsValidEmail` method now appears to be an instance member of the `string` type, as shown in the following screenshot:

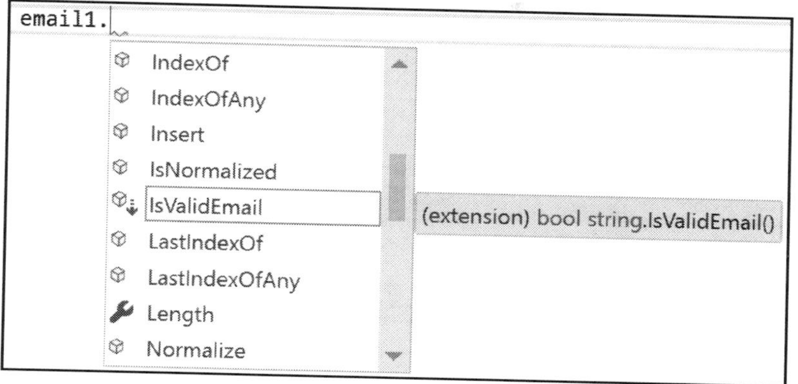

Extension methods cannot replace or override existing instance methods, so you cannot, for example, redefine the `Insert` method of a `string` variable. The extension method will appear as an overload, but the instance method will be called in preference to the extension method with the same name and signature.

Although extension methods might not seem to give a big benefit compared to simply using `static` methods, in `Chapter 12`, *Querying and Manipulating Data Using LINQ*, you will see some extremely powerful uses of extension methods.

# Practicing and exploring

Test your knowledge and understanding by answering some questions. Get some hands-on practice and explore with deeper research into this chapter's topics.

## Exercise 6.1 – Test your knowledge

Answer the following questions:

1. What is a delegate?
2. What is an event?
3. How are a base class and a derived class related?
4. What is the difference between `is` and `as`?

5. Which keyword is used to prevent a class from being derived from, or a method from being overridden?
6. Which keyword is used to prevent a class from being instantiated with the `new` keyword?
7. Which keyword is used to allow a member to be overridden?
8. What's the difference between a destructor and a deconstructor?
9. What are the signatures of the constructors that all exceptions should have?
10. What is an extension method and how do you define one?

## Exercise 6.2 – Practice creating an inheritance hierarchy

Add a new console application named `Exercise02`.

Create a class named `Shape` with properties named `Height`, `Width`, and `Area`.

Add three classes that derive from it—`Rectangle`, `Square`, and `Circle`—with any additional members you feel are appropriate and that override and implement the `Area` property correctly.

## Exercise 6.3 – Explore topics

Use the following links to read more about the topics covered in this chapter:

- **Operator (C# reference)**: `https://docs.microsoft.com/en-us/dotnet/articles/csharp/language-reference/keywords/operator`
- **Delegates**: `https://docs.microsoft.com/en-us/dotnet/articles/csharp/tour-of-csharp/delegates`
- **Events (C# programming guide)**: `https://docs.microsoft.com/en-us/dotnet/articles/csharp/language-reference/keywords/event`
- **Interfaces**: `https://docs.microsoft.com/en-us/dotnet/articles/csharp/tour-of-csharp/interfaces`

- **Generics (C# Programming Guide)**: https://docs.microsoft.com/en-us/dotnet/csharp/programming-guide/generics
- **Reference Types (C# Reference)**: https://docs.microsoft.com/en-us/dotnet/articles/csharp/language-reference/keywords/reference-types
- **Value Types (C# Reference)**: https://docs.microsoft.com/en-us/dotnet/articles/csharp/language-reference/keywords/value-types
- **Inheritance (C# Programming Guide)**: https://docs.microsoft.com/en-us/dotnet/articles/csharp/programming-guide/classes-and-structs/inheritance
- **Destructors (C# Programming Guide)**: https://docs.microsoft.com/en-us/dotnet/articles/csharp/programming-guide/classes-and-structs/destructors

# Summary

In this chapter, you learned about delegates and events, implementing interfaces, generics, and deriving types using inheritance and OOP. You also learned about base and derived classes, how to override a type member, use polymorphism, and cast between types.

In the next part, you will learn about .NET Core 2.1 and .NET Standard 2.0, and the types that they provide you with to implement common functionality such as file handling, database access, encryption, and multitasking.

# Part 2

## .NET Core 2.0 and .NET Standard 2.0

This part of the book is about the functionality in the APIs provided by .NET Core 2.0, and how to reuse functionality cross-platform using .NET Standard 2.0.

.NET Core 2.0's support for .NET Standard 2.0 is important because it provides many of the .NET Framework APIs that are missing in the first versions of .NET Core. The 15 years' worth of libraries and applications that .NET Framework developers had created for Windows can now be migrated to .NET Core 2.0 and run cross-platform on macOS and Linux variants, as well as on Windows.

API support has increased by 142% with .NET Core 2.0. The number of available APIs is now 32,638, versus only 13,501 with .NET Core 1.1!

The full list of .NET Standard 2.0 APIs is documented at the following link:
`https://github.com/dotnet/standard/blob/master/docs/versions/netstandard2.0.md`

To search and browse all .NET APIs, use the following link, as shown in the following screenshot:
`https://docs.microsoft.com/en-us/dotnet/api/`

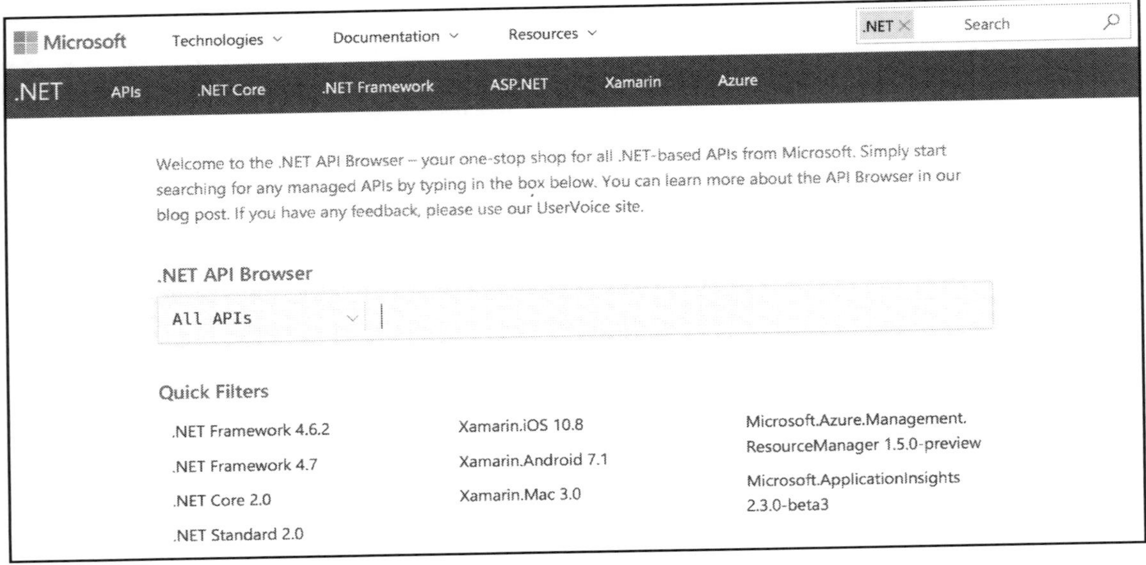


In the following chapters, you will learn how to do the following:

7. Use .NET Standard 2.0 types, and how to build and package your own.
8. Implement some .NET Standard 2.0 types that are commonly used in applications.
9. Work with files and the streams of bytes in them.
10. Protect your data with encryption and other techniques.
11. Work with databases.
12. Query and manipulate data.
13. Improve the performance, scalability, and resource usage of your code.

# 7
# Understanding and Packaging .NET Standard Types

This chapter is about .NET Core 2.0 and how it implements the types that are defined in .NET Standard 2.0. You will learn how C# keywords are related to .NET types, and about the relationship between namespaces and assemblies. You will learn how to package and publish your .NET Core apps and libraries for use cross-platform, how to use existing .NET Framework libraries in .NET Standard libraries, and the possibility of porting .NET Framework code bases to .NET Core.

This chapter covers the following topics:

- Understanding assemblies and namespaces
- Sharing code cross-platform with .NET Standard class libraries
- Understanding NuGet packages
- Publishing your applications for deployment
- Packaging your libraries for NuGet distribution
- Porting from .NET Framework to .NET Core

# Understanding assemblies and namespaces

.NET Core is made up of several pieces, which are as follows:

- **Language compilers**: These turn your source code (written with languages such as C#, F#, and Visual Basic) into **intermediate language** (**IL**) code stored in assemblies (applications and class libraries). C# 6 introduced a completely rewritten compiler known as Roslyn.
- **Common Language Runtime (CoreCLR)**: The runtime loads assemblies, compiles the IL code stored in them into native code instructions for your computer's CPU, and executes the code within an environment that manages resources such as threads and memory.
- **Base Class Libraries (BCL) and NuGet packages (CoreFX)**: These are prebuilt assemblies of types for performing common tasks when building applications. You can use them to quickly build anything you want, rather like combining LEGO™ pieces. .NET Core 2.0 is based on .NET Standard 2.0, which is a superset of all previous versions of .NET Standard, and lifts .NET Core up to parity with the modern parts of .NET Framework and Xamarin.

## Base Class Libraries and CoreFX

.NET Framework's BCL and .NET Core's CoreFX are libraries of prebuilt code that are divided into assemblies and namespaces that make it easier to manage the tens of thousands of types available. It is important to understand the difference between an assembly and a namespace.

## Assemblies, NuGet packages, and platforms

An **assembly** is where a type is stored in the filesystem. Assemblies are a mechanism for deploying code. For example, the `System.Data.dll` assembly contains types for managing data. To use types in other assemblies, they must be referenced.

Assemblies are often distributed as **NuGet packages**, which can contain multiple assemblies and other resources. You will also hear the talk about **metapackages** and **platforms**, which are combinations of NuGet packages.

## Namespaces

A **namespace** is the address of a type. Namespaces are a mechanism to uniquely identify a type by requiring a full address rather than just a short name.

In the real world, *Bob of 34 Sycamore Street* is different from *Bob of 12 Willow Drive*.

In .NET Core, the `IActionFilter` interface of the `System.Web.Mvc` namespace is different from the `IActionFilter` interface of the `System.Web.Http.Filters` namespace.

# Understanding dependent assemblies

If an assembly is compiled as a **class library** (it provides types for other assemblies to use), then it has the file extension `.dll` (**dynamic link library**) and it cannot be executed standalone. It must be executed by the `dotnet run` command.

If an assembly is compiled as an **application**, then it has the file extension `.exe` (executable) and can be executed standalone.

Any assembly (both EXE applications and DLL class libraries) can reference one or more DLL class library assemblies as dependencies, but you cannot have circular references, so assembly *B* cannot reference assembly *A*, if assembly *A* already references assembly *B*. Visual Studio will warn you if you attempt to add a dependency reference that would cause a circular reference.

**Good Practice**

Circular references are often a warning sign of poor code design. If you are sure that you need a circular reference, then use an interface to solve it, as explained in the Stack Overflow answer at the following link: `https://stackoverflow.com/questions/6928387/how-to-solve-circular-reference`

Every application created for .NET Core has a dependency reference to the **Microsoft .NET Core App platform**. This special platform contains thousands of types in NuGet packages that almost all applications would need, such as the `int` and `string` variables.

## Using Visual Studio 2017

In Visual Studio 2017, press *Ctrl* + *Shift* + *N* or navigate to **File** | **New** | **Project...**.

In the **New Project** dialog, in the **Installed** list, expand **Visual C#** and select **.NET Core**. In the list at the center, select **Console App (.NET Core)**, type the name `Assemblies`, change the location to `C:\Code`, type the solution name `Chapter07`, and then click on **OK**.

In **Solution Explorer**, right-click **Assemblies** project, and choose **Edit Assemblies.csproj**.

## Using Visual Studio Code

In Visual Studio Code, use **Integrated Terminal** to create a folder named `Chapter07` with a subfolder named `Assemblies`.

Use `dotnet new console` to create a console application.

Open `Assemblies.csproj`.

## Using Visual Studio 2017 and Visual Studio Code

When using .NET Core, you reference the dependency assemblies, NuGet packages, and platforms that your application needs in a project file.

The original project file for .NET Core 1.0 was a JSON format file named `project.json`. The *newer* format for .NET Core 1.1 and later is an XML file with the `.csproj` extension. I say *newer*, because it is actually an older format that has been used since the beginning of .NET in 2002. Microsoft changed their mind after the release of .NET Core 1.0!

`Assemblies.csproj` is a typical project file for a .NET Core application, as shown in the following markup:

```
<Project Sdk="Microsoft.NET.Sdk">

  <PropertyGroup>
    <OutputType>Exe</OutputType>
    <TargetFramework>netcoreapp2.0</TargetFramework>
  </PropertyGroup>

</Project>
```

# Relating assemblies and namespaces

To understand the relationship between assemblies and namespaces, we will use a tool available in Visual Studio 2017. If you are using Visual Studio Code, just look at the screenshots.

## Browsing assemblies with Visual Studio 2017

Using Visual Studio 2017, navigate to **View** | **Object Browser**, or press *Ctrl* + *W*, *J*, and you will see that your solution has dependencies on assemblies such as `System.Console`, used in all the coding exercises so far, as shown in the following screenshot:

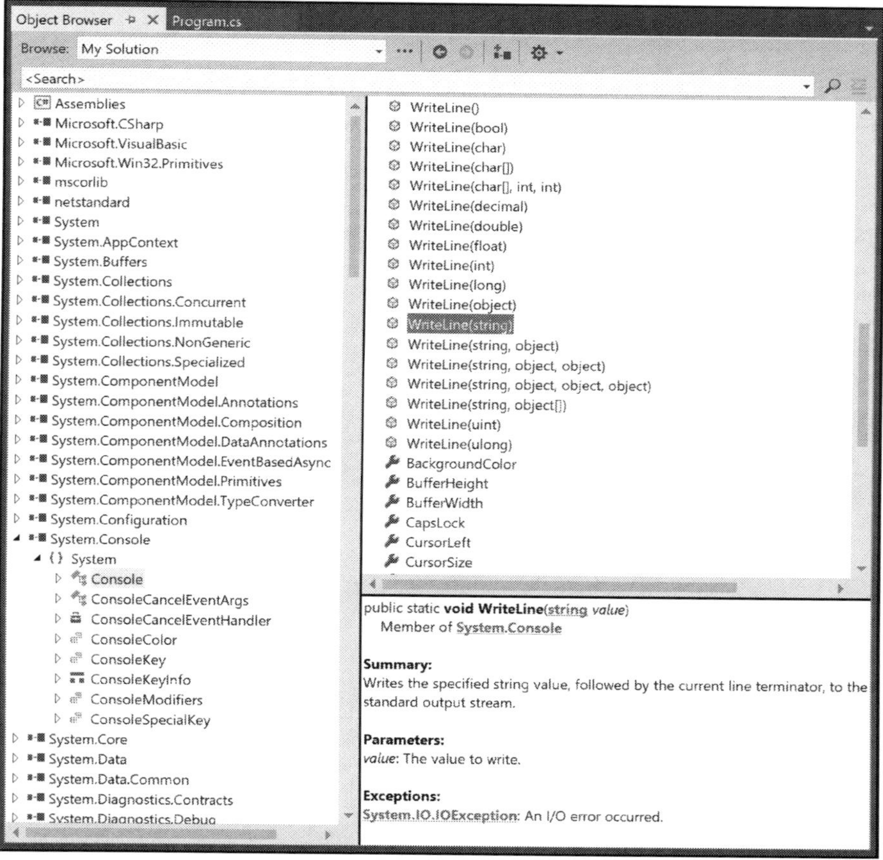

**Object Browser** can be used to learn about the assemblies and namespaces that .NET Core uses to logically and physically group types together.

For types that are only used in some scenarios, for example, the `Console` type is only used in console applications, not in web applications or mobile apps, there is an assembly for just that one type and its supporting types. The `System.Console.dll` assembly is located in the filesystem, as shown in the following screenshot:

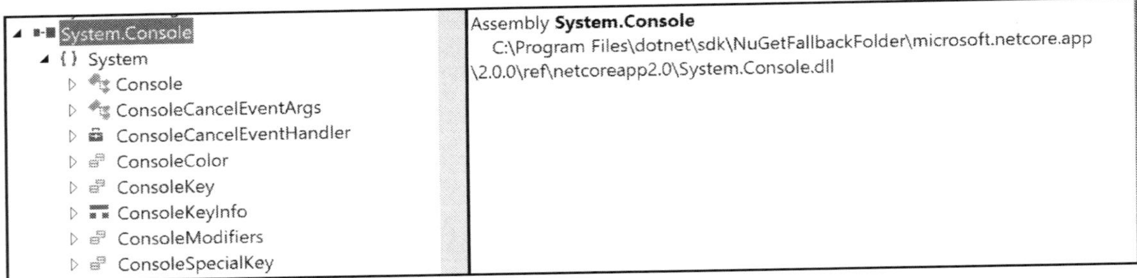


The `System.Console.dll` assembly only contains eight types, all of them in the `System` namespace, and all to support the `Console` type, as shown in the following screenshot:

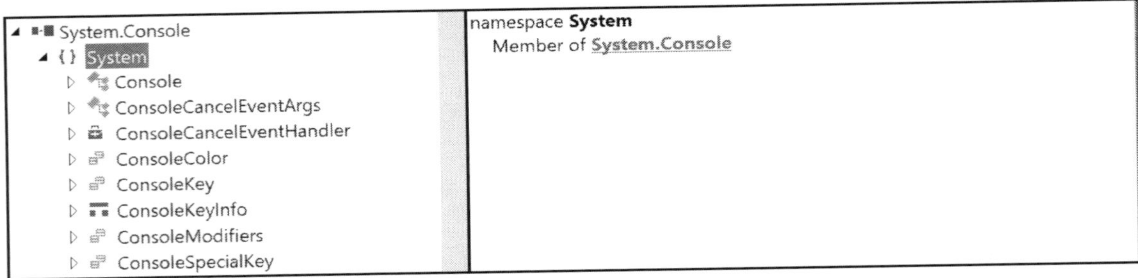


By default, **Object Browser** shows types grouped by assembly, that is, the file that *contains* the namespaces and types in the filesystem. Sometimes, it is more useful to ignore the *physical* location of a type and focus on its *logical* grouping, that is, its namespace.

In its toolbar, click on **Object Browser Settings** (the last button that looks like a gear icon), and select **View Namespaces**, as shown in the following screenshot:

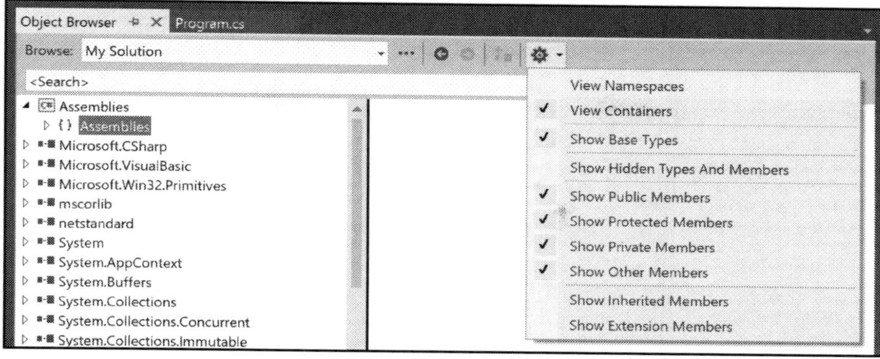


Now, **Object Browser** shows types grouped by their namespace, and when a namespace is selected, for example `System`, it shows a list of the assemblies that have types in that namespace, as shown in the following screenshot:

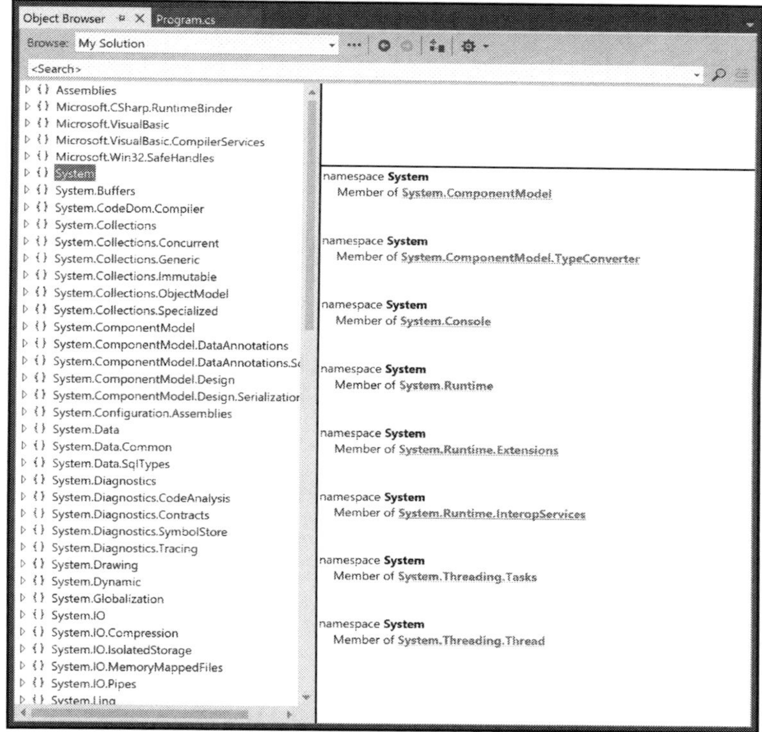

Most common .NET Core types are in the `System.Runtime.dll` assembly. You can see the relationship between some assemblies and the namespaces that they supply types for, and note that there is not always a one-to-one mapping between assemblies and namespaces, as shown in the following table:

| **Assembly** | **Example namespaces** | **Example types** |
|---|---|---|
| `System.Runtime.dll` | `System`, `System.Collections`, `System.Collections.Generics` | `Int32`, `String`, `List<T>` |
| `System.Console.dll` | `System` | `Console` |
| `System.Threading.dll` | `System.Threading` | `Interlocked`, `Monitor`, `Mutex` |
| `System.Xml.XDocument.dll` | `System.Xml.Linq` | `XDocument`, `XElement`, `XNode` |

## Using Visual Studio 2017 or Visual Studio Code

In either Visual Studio 2017 or Visual Studio Code, inside the `Main` method, enter the following code:

```
var doc = new XDocument();
```

The `XDocument` type is not recognized because we have not told the compiler what the namespace of the type is. Although this project already has a reference to the assembly that contains the type, we also need to either prefix the type name with its namespace or to import the namespace.

## Importing a namespace

Click inside the `XDocument` class name. Visual Studio 2017 and Visual Studio Code both display a light bulb, showing that it recognizes the type and can automatically fix the problem for you.

Click on the light bulb, or in Windows, press *Ctrl* + . (dot), or in macOS, press *Cmd* + . (dot).

Visual Studio 2017 shows an explanation of your choices, and a preview of its suggested changes, as shown in the following screenshot:

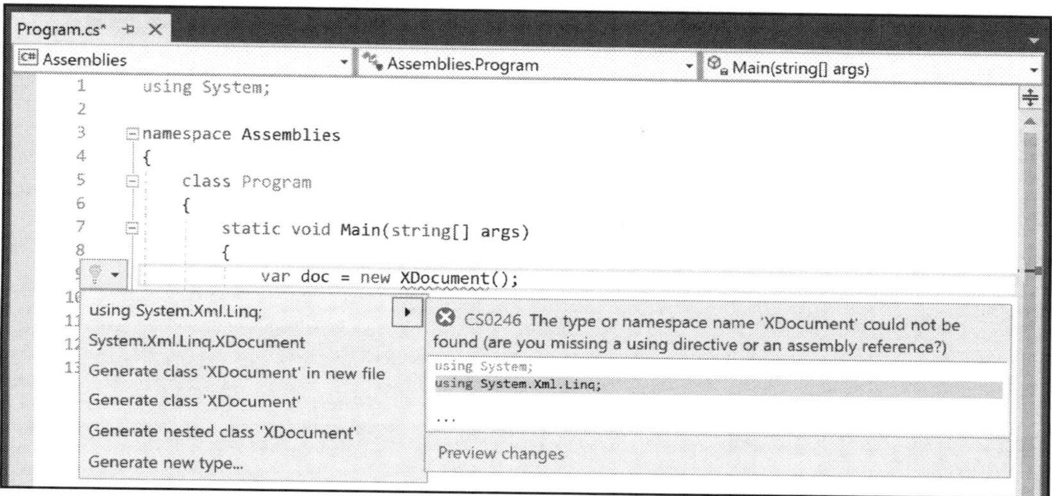

Visual Studio Code has no explanation and preview, but it does have almost the same choices, as shown in the following screenshot:

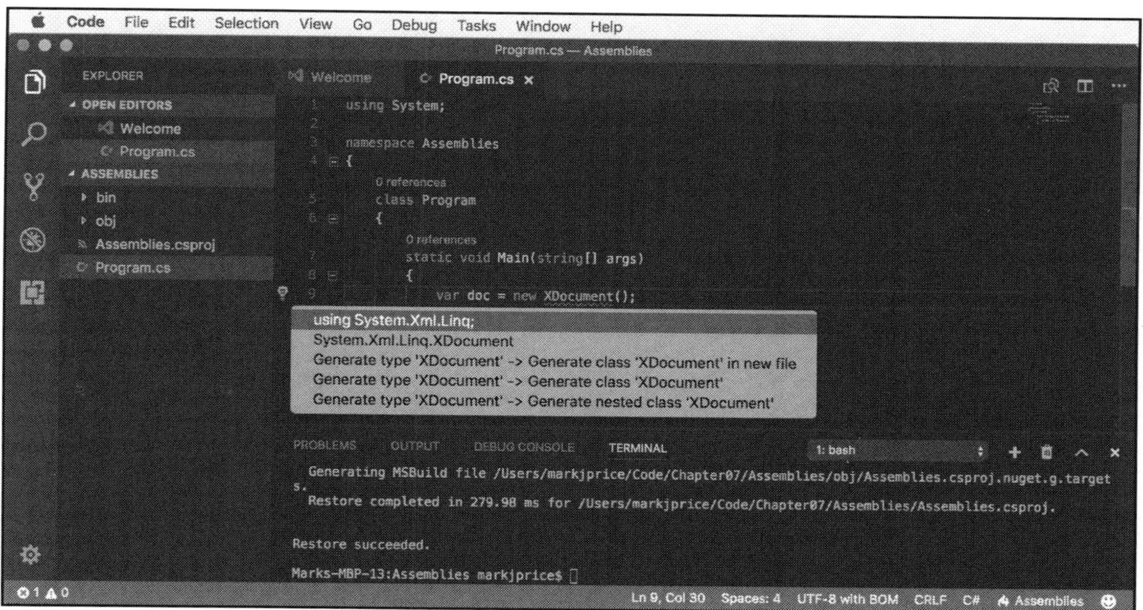

Select `using System.Xml.Linq;` from the menu. This will *import the namespace* by adding a `using` statement to the top of the file.

Once a namespace is imported at the top of a code file, then all the types within the namespace are available for use in that code file by just typing their name.

# Relating C# keywords to .NET types

One of the common questions I get from new C# programmers is, *What is the difference between* `string` *with a lowercase and* `String` *with an uppercase*?

The short answer is easy: none.

The long answer is that all C# type keywords are aliases for a .NET type in a class library assembly.

When you use the `string` keyword, the compiler turns it into a `System.String` type. When you use the `int` type, the compiler turns it into a `System.Int32` type. You can even see this if you hover your mouse over an `int` type, as shown in the following screenshot:

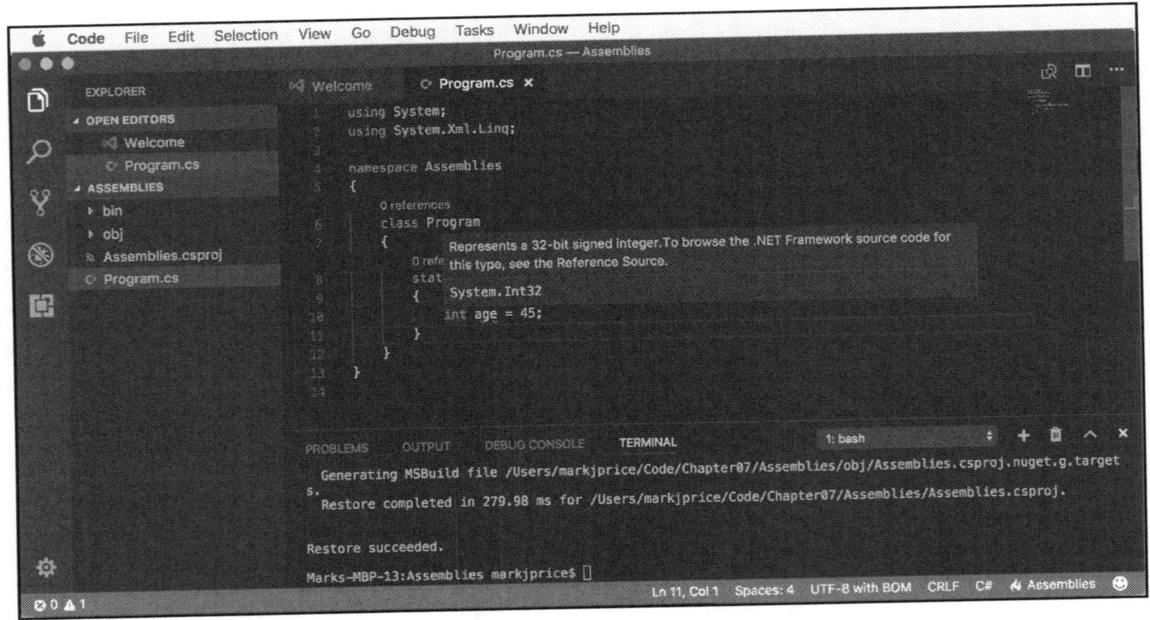

**Good Practice**
Use the C# keyword instead of the actual type because the keywords do not need the namespace imported.

The following table shows the 16 C# type keywords and their actual .NET types:

| Keyword | .NET type | Keyword | .NET type |
|---|---|---|---|
| `string` | `System.String` | `char` | `System.Char` |
| `sbyte` | `System.SByte` | `byte` | `System.Byte` |
| `short` | `System.Int16` | `ushort` | `System.UInt16` |
| `int` | `System.Int32` | `uint` | `System.UInt32` |
| `long` | `System.Int64` | `ulong` | `System.UInt64` |
| `float` | `System.Single` | `double` | `System.Double` |
| `decimal` | `System.Decimal` | `bool` | `System.Boolean` |
| `object` | `System.Object` | `dynamic` | `System.Dynamic.DynamicObject` |

Other .NET programming language compilers can do the same thing. For example, the Visual Basic .NET language has a type named `Integer` that is its alias for `System.Int32`.

# Sharing code cross-platform with .NET Standard 2.0 class libraries

Before .NET Standard 2.0, there was **Portable Class Libraries** (**PCL**). With PCLs, you can create a library of code and explicitly specify which platforms you want the library to support, such as Xamarin, Silverlight, and Windows 8. Your library can then use the intersection of APIs that are supported by the specified platforms.

Microsoft realized that this is unsustainable, so they have been working on .NET Standard 2.0—a single API that all future .NET platforms will support. There are older versions of .NET Standard, but they are not supported by multiple .NET platforms.

.NET Standard 2.0 is similar to HTML5 in that they are both standards that a platform should support. Just as Google's Chrome browser and Microsoft's Edge browser implement HTML5 standard, so .NET Core and Xamarin implement .NET Standard 2.0.

If you want to create a library of types that will work across .NET Framework (on Windows), .NET Core (on Windows, macOS, and Linux), and Xamarin (on iOS, Android, and Windows Mobile), you can do so most easily with .NET Standard 2.0.

The following table summarizes versions of .NET Standard, and which platforms they support:

| **Platform** | **1.1** | **1.2** | **1.3** | **1.4** | **1.5** | **1.6** | **2.0** |
|---|---|---|---|---|---|---|---|
| .NET Core | → | → | → | → | → | 1.0, 1.1 | 2.0 |
| .NET Framework | 4.5 | 4.5.1 | 4.6 | → | → | → | 4.6.1 |
| Xamarin/Mono | → | → | → | → | → | 4.6 | 5.4 |
| UWP | → | → | → | 10 | → | → | 6.0 |

# Creating a .NET Standard 2.0 class library

We will create a class library using .NET Standard 2.0 so that it can be used cross-platform on Windows, macOS, and Linux.

## Using Visual Studio 2017

Start Microsoft Visual Studio 2017.

In Visual Studio, press *Ctrl* + *Shift* + *N* or go to **File** | **Add** | **New Project...**.

In the **New Project** dialog, in the **Installed** list, expand **Visual C#**, and then select **.NET Standard**. In the list at the center, select **Class Library (.NET Standard)**, type the name `SharedLibrary`, and then click on **OK**, as shown in the following screenshot:

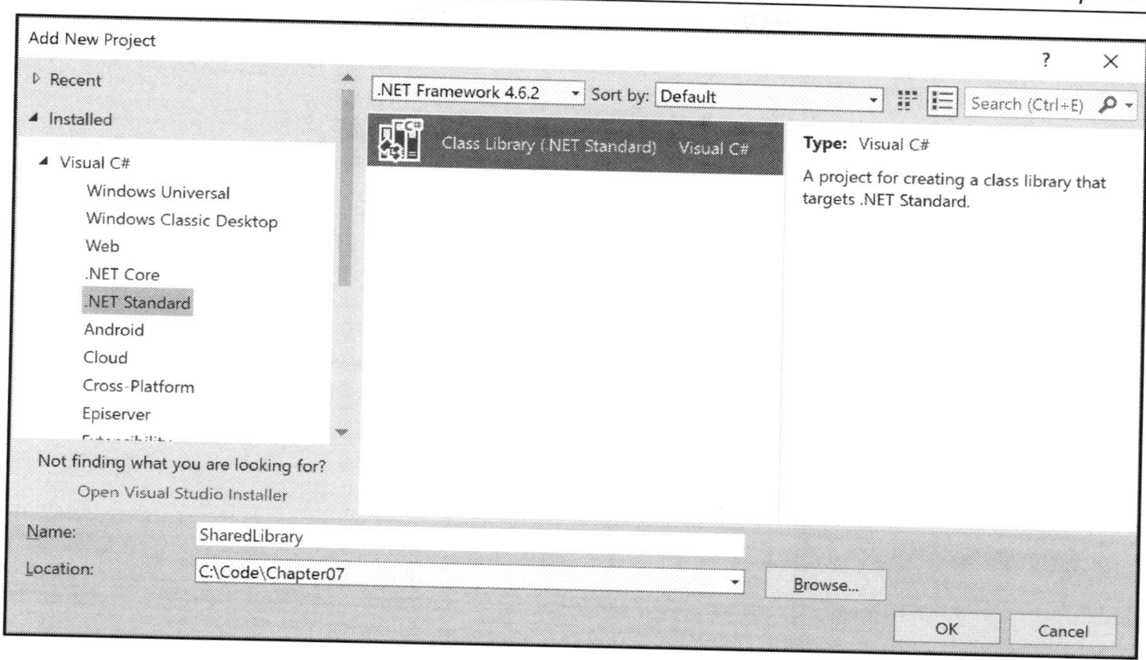


In **Solution Explorer**, right-click on the **SharedLibrary** project, and choose **Edit SharedLibrary.csproj**.

A **Class Library (.NET Standard)** project will target version 2.0 by default, as shown in the following markup:

```
<Project Sdk="Microsoft.NET.Sdk">

  <PropertyGroup>
    <TargetFramework>netstandard2.0</TargetFramework>
  </PropertyGroup>

</Project>
```

## Using Visual Studio Code

In the `Code/Chapter07` folder, create a subfolder named `SharedLibrary`.

In Visual Studio Code, open the `SharedLibrary` folder.

In Visual Studio Code, navigate to **View** | **Integrated Terminal**, and then enter the following command:

```
dotnet new classlib
```

Click on `SharedLibrary.csproj` and note that a class library generated by the `dotnet` CLI targets version 2.0 by default, as shown in the following markup:

```
<Project Sdk="Microsoft.NET.Sdk">

  <PropertyGroup>
    <TargetFramework>netstandard2.0</TargetFramework>
  </PropertyGroup>

</Project>
```

# Understanding NuGet packages

.NET Core is split into a set of packages, distributed using a Microsoft-defined package management technology named NuGet. Each of these packages represents a single assembly of the same name. For example, the `System.Collections` package contains the `System.Collections.dll` assembly.

The following are the benefits of packages:

- Packages can ship on their own schedule
- Packages can be tested independently of other packages
- Packages can support different OSes and CPUs
- Packages can have dependencies specific to only one library
- Apps are smaller because unreferenced packages aren't part of the distribution

The following table lists some of the more important packages:

| **Package** | **Important types** |
|---|---|
| `System.Runtime` | `Object`, `String`, `Int32`, `Array` |
| `System.Collections` | `List<T>`, `Dictionary<TKey, TValue>` |
| `System.Net.Http` | `HttpClient`, `HttpResponseMessage` |
| `System.IO.FileSystem` | `File`, `Directory` |
| `System.Reflection` | `Assembly`, `TypeInfo`, `MethodInfo` |

# Understanding metapackages

**Metapackages** describe a set of packages that are used together. Metapackages are referenced just like any other NuGet package. By referencing a metapackage, you have, in effect, added a reference to each of its dependent packages.

Older versions of Visual Studio 2017 nicely showed the relationship between metapackages, packages, and assemblies, as shown in the following screenshot:

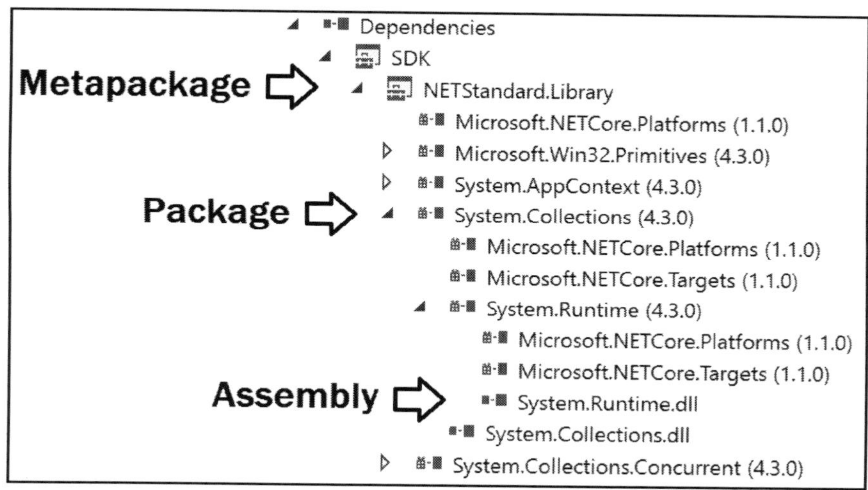

Metapackages are often just referred to as packages in Microsoft's documentation, as you are about to see.

The following list contains links to some common metapackages and packages, including an official list of their dependencies:

- `https://www.nuget.org/packages/Microsoft.NETCore.App`
- `https://www.nuget.org/packages/NETStandard.Library`
- `https://www.nuget.org/packages/Microsoft.NETCore.Runtime.CoreCLR`
- `https://www.nuget.org/packages/System.IO`
- `https://www.nuget.org/packages/System.Collections`
- `https://www.nuget.org/packages/System.Runtime`

If you were to go to the link for the `Microsoft.NETCore.App` metapackage, you would see information about the metapackage, including how to install it, dependencies, version history, and how many downloads it has had, as shown in the following screenshot:

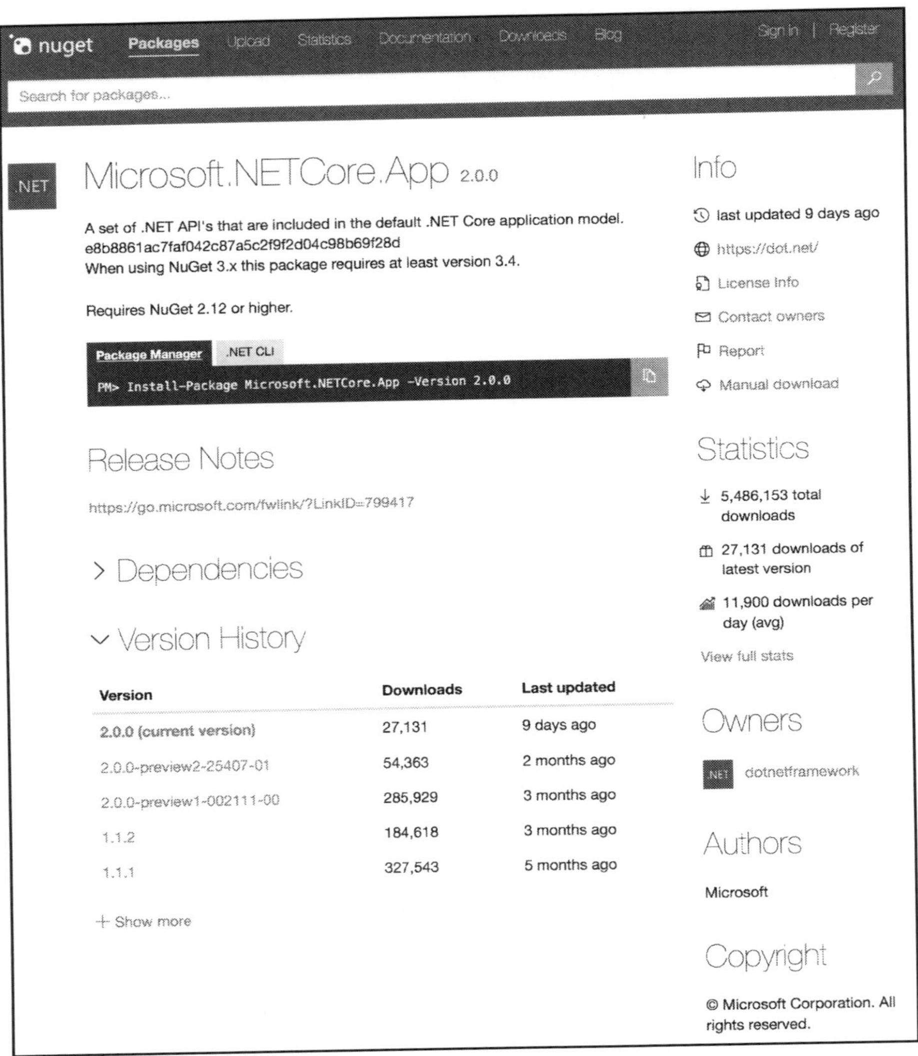

If you were to expand **Dependencies**, you would see the list of dependencies for the metapackage, as shown in the following screenshot:

.NETCoreApp 2.0

Microsoft.NETCore.DotNetHostPolicy (>= 2.0.0)
Microsoft.NETCore.Platforms (>= 2.0.0)
NETStandard.Library (>= 2.0.0)

`Microsoft.NETCore.App` version 2.0.0 has a dependency on `NETStandard.Library` version 2.0.0.

# Understanding frameworks

There is a two-way relationship between frameworks and packages. Packages define the APIs, frameworks group packages. A framework without any packages would not define any APIs.

If you have a strong understanding of interfaces and types that implement them, you might find the following URL useful for grasping how packages and their APIs relate to frameworks such as the various .NET Standard versions: `https://gist.github.com/davidfowl/8939f305567e1755412d6dc0b8baf1b7`

.NET Core packages each support a set of frameworks. For example, the `System.IO.FileSystem` package supports the following frameworks, as shown in the following screenshot:

- .NETStandard, version 1.3
- .NETFramework, version 4.6

- Six Xamarin platforms (for example, Xamarin.iOS 1.0)

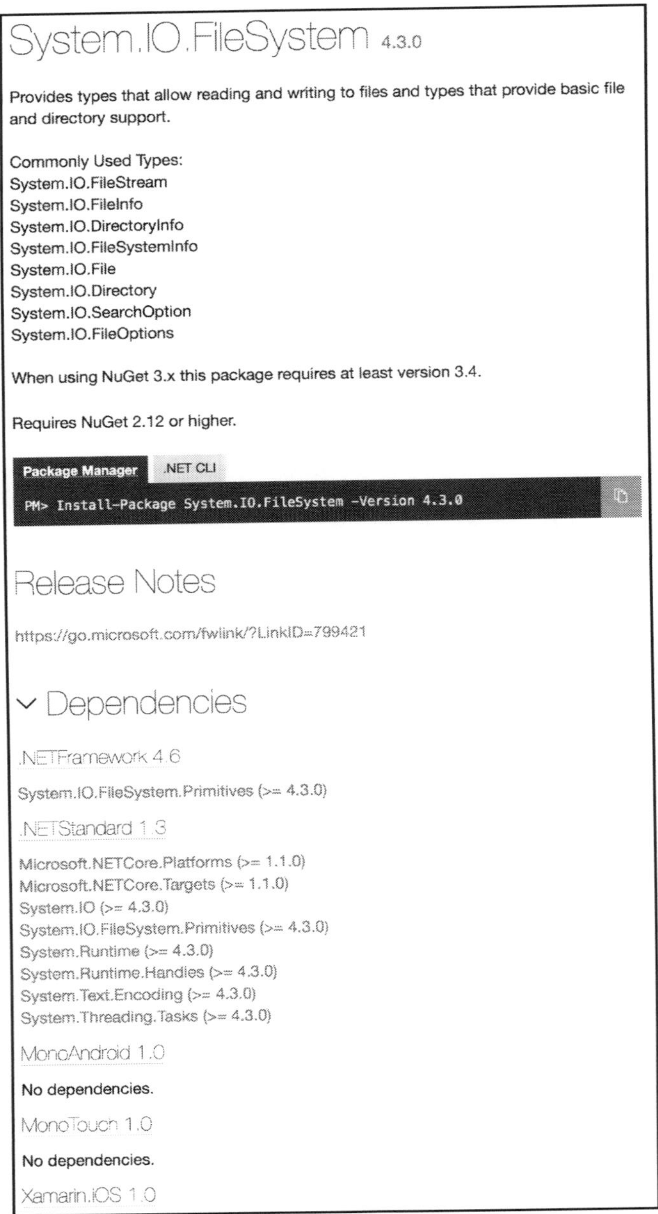

# System.IO.FileSystem 4.3.0

Provides types that allow reading and writing to files and types that provide basic file and directory support.

Commonly Used Types:
System.IO.FileStream
System.IO.FileInfo
System.IO.DirectoryInfo
System.IO.FileSystemInfo
System.IO.File
System.IO.Directory
System.IO.SearchOption
System.IO.FileOptions

When using NuGet 3.x this package requires at least version 3.4.

Requires NuGet 2.12 or higher.

Package Manager | .NET CLI

```
PM> Install-Package System.IO.FileSystem -Version 4.3.0
```

## Release Notes

https://go.microsoft.com/fwlink/?LinkID=799421

## Dependencies

.NETFramework 4.6

System.IO.FileSystem.Primitives (>= 4.3.0)

.NETStandard 1.3

Microsoft.NETCore.Platforms (>= 1.1.0)
Microsoft.NETCore.Targets (>= 1.1.0)
System.IO (>= 4.3.0)
System.IO.FileSystem.Primitives (>= 4.3.0)
System.Runtime (>= 4.3.0)
System.Runtime.Handles (>= 4.3.0)
System.Text.Encoding (>= 4.3.0)
System.Threading.Tasks (>= 4.3.0)

MonoAndroid 1.0

No dependencies.

MonoTouch 1.0

No dependencies.

Xamarin.iOS 1.0

**Good Practice**
Choose `NETStandard.Library` if you are creating a class library that is intended to be referenced by multiple platforms, such as .NET Framework and Xamarin, as well as .NET Core.

# Fixing dependencies

To consistently restore packages and write reliable code, it's important that you fix your dependencies. Fixing dependencies means you are using the same family of packages released for a specific version of .NET Core, for example, 1.0.

To fix dependencies, every package should have a single version with no additional qualifiers. Additional qualifiers include release candidates (`rc4`) and wildcards (`*`). Wildcards allow future versions to be automatically referenced and used because they always represent the most recent release. But wildcards are therefore dangerous, because it could result in the restoration of future incompatible packages that break your code.

The following dependencies are NOT fixed and should be avoided:

```
<PackageReference Include="System.Net.Http" Version="4.1.0-*" />
<PackageReference Include="Microsoft.NETCore.App" Version="1.0.0-
rc4-00454-00" />
```

**Good Practice**
Microsoft guarantees that if you fixed your dependencies to what ships with a specific version of .NET Core, for example, 2.0, those packages will all work together. Always fix your dependencies.

# Publishing your applications for deployment

There are two ways to publish and deploy a .NET Core application:

- Framework-dependent
- Self-contained

If you choose to deploy your application and its dependencies, but not .NET Core itself, then you rely on .NET Core already being on the target computer. This works well for web applications deployed to a server because .NET Core and lots of other web applications are likely already on the server.

Sometimes, you want to be able to give someone a USB stick containing your application and know that it can execute on their computer. You want to perform a self-contained deployment. The size of the deployment files will be larger, but you will know that it will work.

# Creating a console application to publish

Add a new console application project named DotNetCoreEverywhere.

Modify the code to look like this:

```
using static System.Console;

namespace DotNetCoreEverywhere
{
   class Program
   {
      static void Main(string[] args)
      {
         WriteLine("I can run everywhere!");
      }
   }
}
```

Open DotNetCoreEverywhere.csproj, and add the runtime identifiers to target four operating systems, inside the <PropertyGroup> element, as shown in the following markup:

```
<Project Sdk="Microsoft.NET.Sdk">

  <PropertyGroup>
    <OutputType>Exe</OutputType>
    <TargetFramework>netcoreapp2.0</TargetFramework>
    <RuntimeIdentifiers>
      win10-x64;osx.10.12-x64;rhel.7-x64;ubuntu.14.04-x64
    </RuntimeIdentifiers>
  </PropertyGroup>

</Project>
```

The `win10-x64` RID value means Windows 10 or Windows Server 2016. The `osx.10.12-x64` RID value means macOS Sierra. You can find the full list of currently supported **Runtime IDentifier (RID)** values at the following link: `https://docs.microsoft.com/en-us/dotnet/articles/core/rid-catalog`

# Publishing with Visual Studio 2017 on Windows

In Visual Studio 2017, right-click on **DotNetCoreEverywhere**, and choose **Publish...**, then select **Folder**, and then click on **Publish**, as shown in the following screenshot:

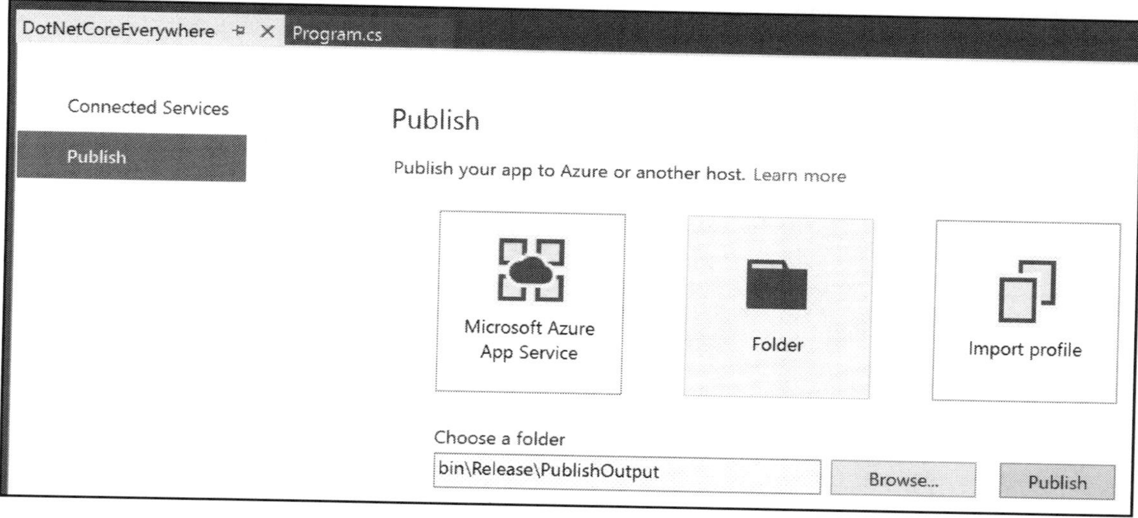

By default, you have now published the Windows 10 64-bit version, as shown in the following screenshot:

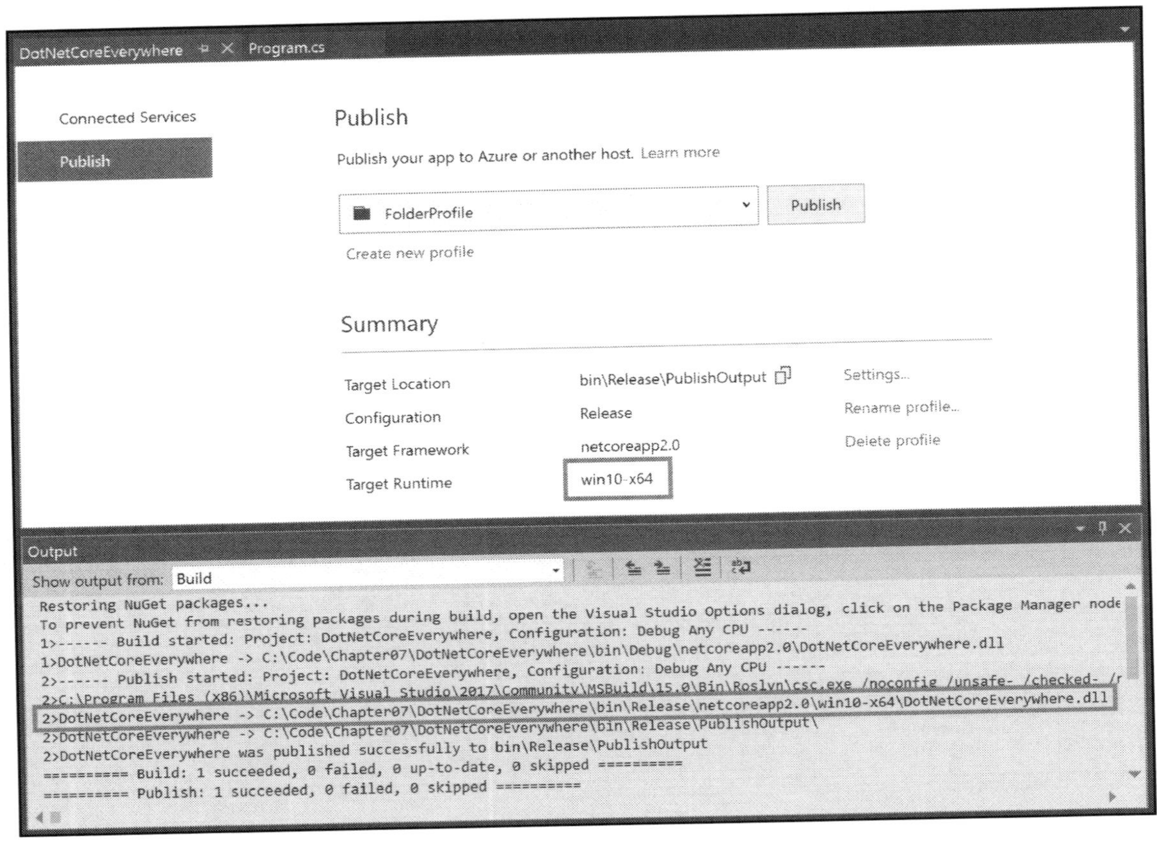

Click on **Settings...**, and change **Target Runtime** to **osx.10.12-x64**, as shown in the following screenshot, and then click on **Save**:

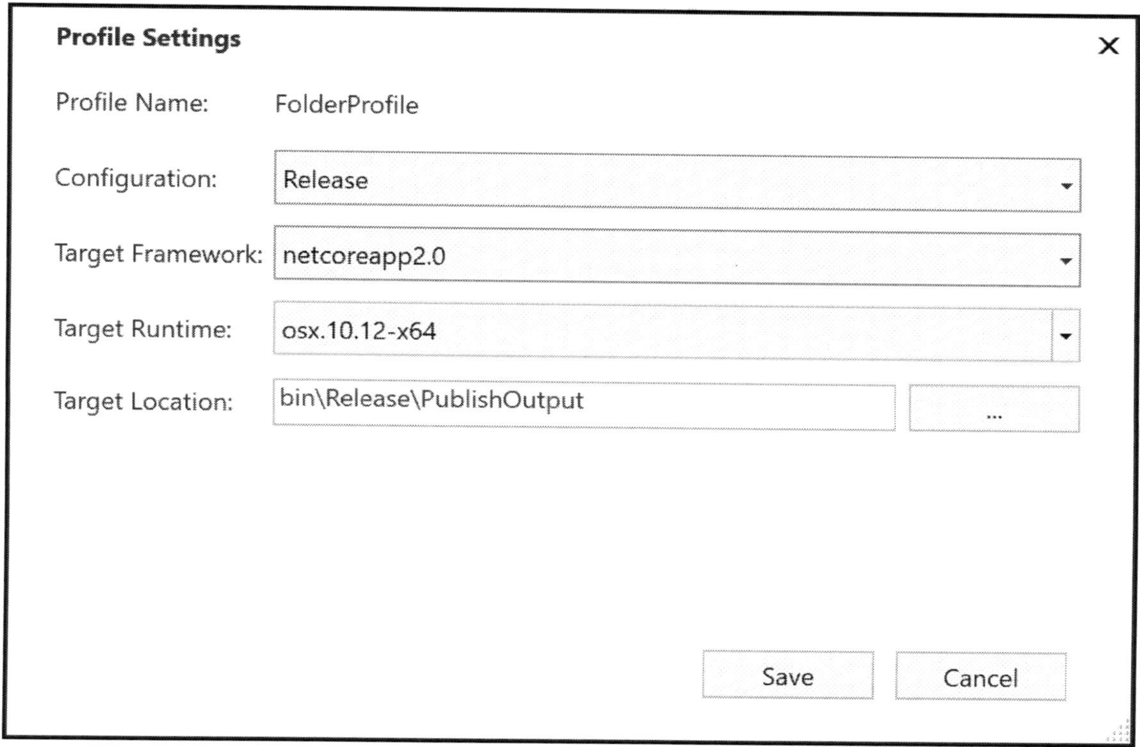


Next, click on **Publish**.

In **Solution Explorer**, show all files, expand **bin**, **Release**, **netcoreapp2.0**, **osx.10.12-x64**, and **win10-x64**, as shown in the following screenshot, and note the application files:

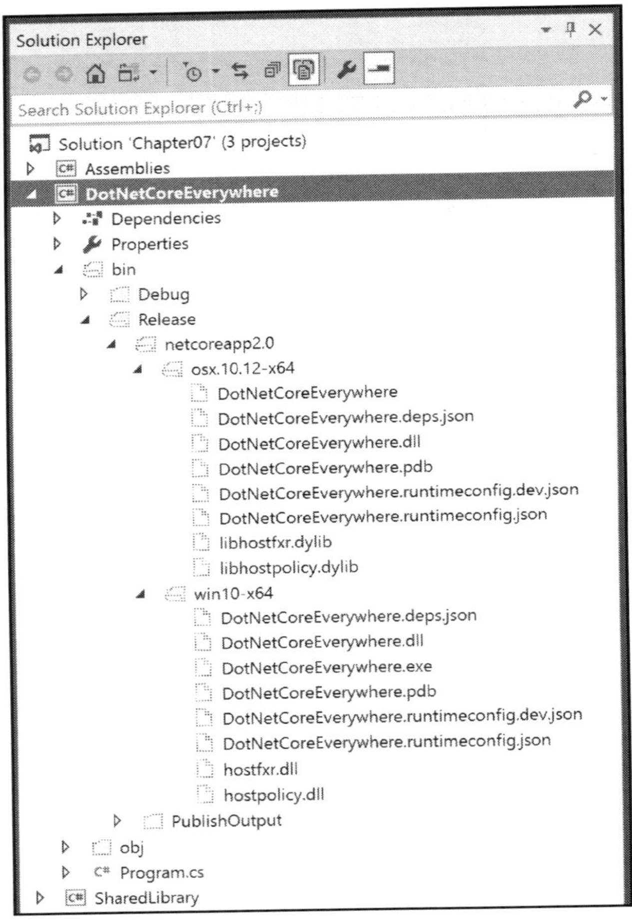


# Publishing with Visual Studio Code on macOS

In Visual Studio Code, in **Integrated Terminal**, enter the following command to build the release version of the console application for Windows 10:

```
dotnet publish -c Release -r win10-x64
```

Microsoft Build Engine will compile and publish the console application, as shown in the following screenshot:

In **Integrated Terminal**, enter the following commands to build release versions for macOS, **Red Hat Enterprise Linux** (**RHEL**), and Ubuntu Linux:

```
dotnet publish -c Release -r osx.10.12-x64
dotnet publish -c Release -r rhel.7-x64
dotnet publish -c Release -r ubuntu.14.04-x64
```

Open a macOS **Finder** window, navigate to `DotNetCoreEverywhere\bin\Release\netcoreapp2.0`, and note the output folders for the four operating systems and the files, including a Windows executable named `DotNetCoreEverywhere.exe`, as shown in the following screenshot:

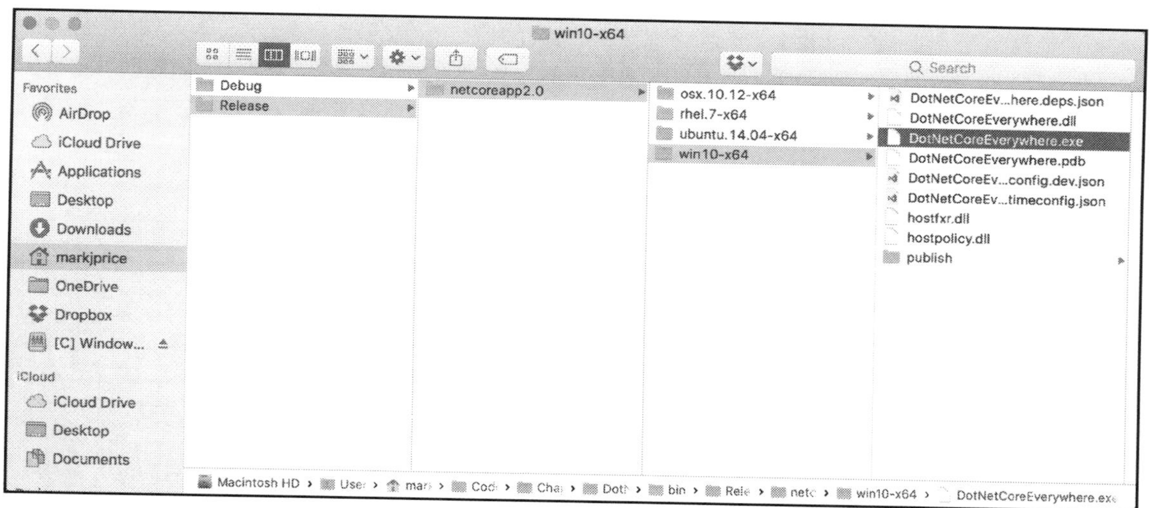

If you copy any of those folders to the appropriate operating system, the console application will run because it is a self-contained deployable .NET Core application.

# Packaging your libraries for NuGet distribution

When you install .NET Core SDK, it includes the **command-line interface (CLI)** named `dotnet`.

## Understanding dotnet commands

The `dotnet` command-line interface has commands that work on the current folder to create a new project using templates, some of which are listed here:

- `dotnet new console`: This creates a new console application project
- `dotnet new classlib`: This creates a new assembly library project
- `dotnet new web`: This creates a new empty ASP.NET Core project
- `dotnet new mvc`: This creates a new ASP.NET Core MVC project
- `dotnet new razor`: This creates a new ASP.NET Core MVC project with support for Razor Pages
- `dotnet new angular`: This creates a new ASP.NET Core MVC project with support for an Angular Single Page Application as the frontend
- `dotnet new react`: This creates a new ASP.NET Core MVC project with support for an React **Single Page Application (SPA)** as the frontend
- `dotnet new webapi`: This creates a new ASP.NET Core Web API project

You can install additional templates from the following link: `https://github.com/dotnet/templating/wiki/Available-templates-for-dotnet-new`
You can define your own project templates, as explained in the official documentation for the `dotnet new` command at the following link: `https://docs.microsoft.com/en-us/dotnet/core/tools/dotnet-new?tabs=netcore2x`

Enter the `dotnet new -l` command to list your currently installed templates, as shown in the following screenshot:

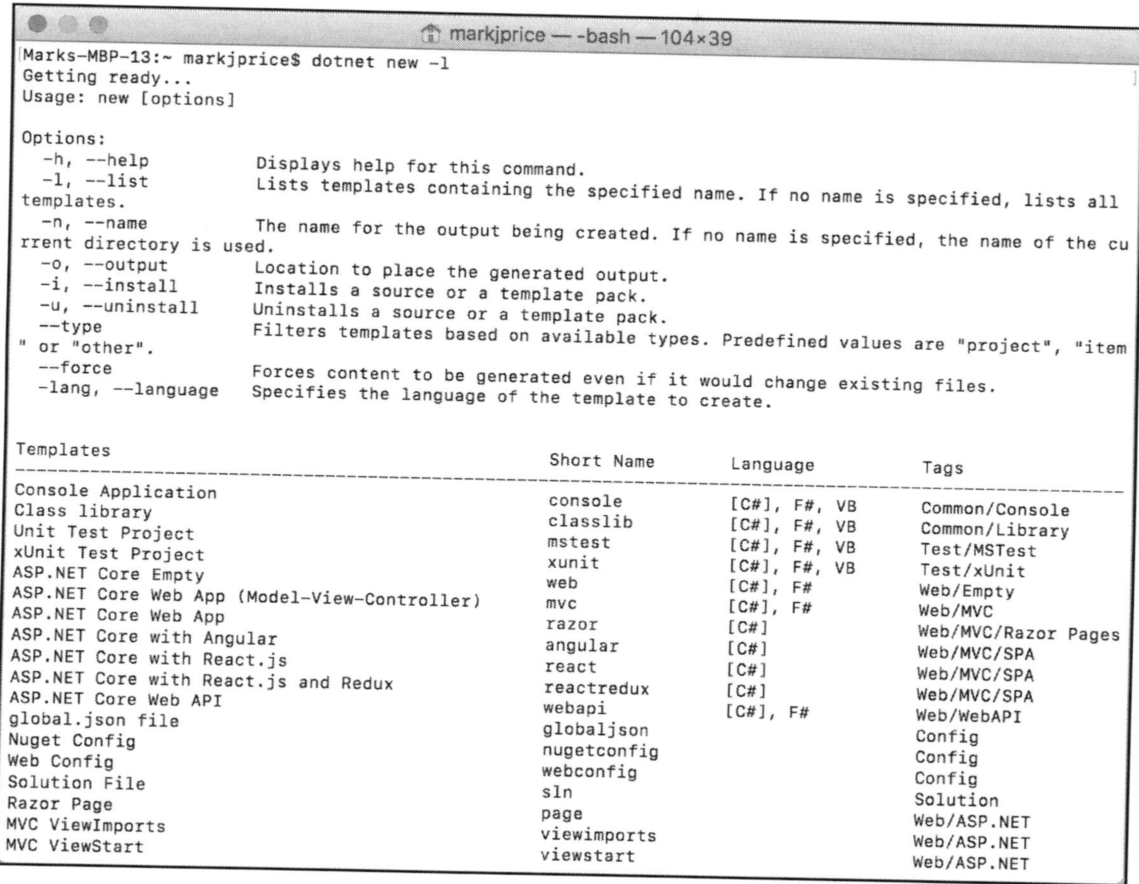
```
Marks-MBP-13:~ markjprice$ dotnet new -l
Getting ready...
Usage: new [options]

Options:
  -h, --help          Displays help for this command.
  -l, --list          Lists templates containing the specified name. If no name is specified, lists all
templates.
  -n, --name          The name for the output being created. If no name is specified, the name of the cu
rrent directory is used.
  -o, --output        Location to place the generated output.
  -i, --install       Installs a source or a template pack.
  -u, --uninstall     Uninstalls a source or a template pack.
  --type              Filters templates based on available types. Predefined values are "project", "item
" or "other".
  --force             Forces content to be generated even if it would change existing files.
  -lang, --language   Specifies the language of the template to create.

Templates                                         Short Name       Language        Tags
-----------------------------------------------------------------------------------------------------
Console Application                               console          [C#], F#, VB    Common/Console
Class library                                     classlib         [C#], F#, VB    Common/Library
Unit Test Project                                 mstest           [C#], F#, VB    Test/MSTest
xUnit Test Project                                xunit            [C#], F#, VB    Test/xUnit
ASP.NET Core Empty                                web              [C#], F#        Web/Empty
ASP.NET Core Web App (Model-View-Controller)      mvc              [C#], F#        Web/MVC
ASP.NET Core Web App                              razor            [C#]            Web/MVC/Razor Pages
ASP.NET Core with Angular                         angular          [C#]            Web/MVC/SPA
ASP.NET Core with React.js                        react            [C#]            Web/MVC/SPA
ASP.NET Core with React.js and Redux              reactredux       [C#]            Web/MVC/SPA
ASP.NET Core Web API                              webapi           [C#], F#        Web/WebAPI
global.json file                                  globaljson                       Config
Nuget Config                                      nugetconfig                      Config
Web Config                                        webconfig                        Config
Solution File                                     sln                              Solution
Razor Page                                        page                             Web/ASP.NET
MVC ViewImports                                   viewimports                      Web/ASP.NET
MVC ViewStart                                     viewstart                        Web/ASP.NET
```

The `dotnet` CLI has the following commands that work on the project in the current folder, to manage the project:

- `dotnet restore`: This downloads dependencies for the project
- `dotnet build`: This compiles the project
- `dotnet test`: This runs unit tests on the project
- `dotnet run`: This runs the project
- `dotnet migrate`: This migrates a .NET Core project created with the preview CLI tools to the current CLI tool MS Build format
- `dotnet pack`: This creates a NuGet package for the project

- `dotnet publish`: This compiles and publishes the project, either with dependencies or as a self-contained application
- `add`: This adds a reference to a package to the project
- `remove`: This removes a reference to a package from the project
- `list`: This lists the package references for the project

## Adding a package reference

Let's say that you want to add a package created by a third-party developer, for example, Newtonsoft.Json, a popular package for working with the **JavaScript Object Notation (JSON)** serialization format.

### Using Visual Studio Code

In Visual Studio Code, open the `Chapter07/Assemblies` folder that you created earlier, and then enter the following command in **Integrated Terminal**:

```
dotnet add package newtonsoft.json
```

Visual Studio Code outputs information about adding the reference, as shown in the following output:

```
info : Adding PackageReference for package 'newtonsoft.json' into project
'/Users/markjprice/Code/Chapter07/Assemblies/Assemblies.csproj'.
log : Restoring packages for
/Users/markjprice/Code/Chapter07/Assemblies/Assemblies.csproj...
info : GET
https://api.nuget.org/v3-flatcontainer/newtonsoft.json/index.json
info : OK https://api.nuget.org/v3-flatcontainer/newtonsoft.json/index.json
485ms
info : GET
https://api.nuget.org/v3-flatcontainer/newtonsoft.json/10.0.3/newtonsoft.js
on.10.0.3.nupkg
info : OK
https://api.nuget.org/v3-flatcontainer/newtonsoft.json/10.0.3/newtonsoft.js
on.10.0.3.nupkg 602ms
log : Installing Newtonsoft.Json 10.0.3.
info : Package 'newtonsoft.json' is compatible with all the specified
frameworks in project
'/Users/markjprice/Code/Chapter07/Assemblies/Assemblies.csproj'.
info : PackageReference for package 'newtonsoft.json' version '10.0.3'
added to file
'/Users/markjprice/Code/Chapter07/Assemblies/Assemblies.csproj'.
```

Open `Assemblies.csproj`, and you will see the package reference has been added, as shown in the following markup:

```
<Project Sdk="Microsoft.NET.Sdk">
  <PropertyGroup>
    <OutputType>Exe</OutputType>
    <TargetFramework>netcoreapp2.0</TargetFramework>
  </PropertyGroup>
  <ItemGroup>
    <PackageReference Include="newtonsoft.json" Version="10.0.3" />
  </ItemGroup>
</Project>
```

## Using Visual Studio 2017

In Visual Studio 2017, right-click on a project in **Solution Explorer**, and select **Manage NuGet Packages...**, and then use **NuGet Package Manager** to search for the **Newtonsoft.Json** package, as shown in the following screenshot:

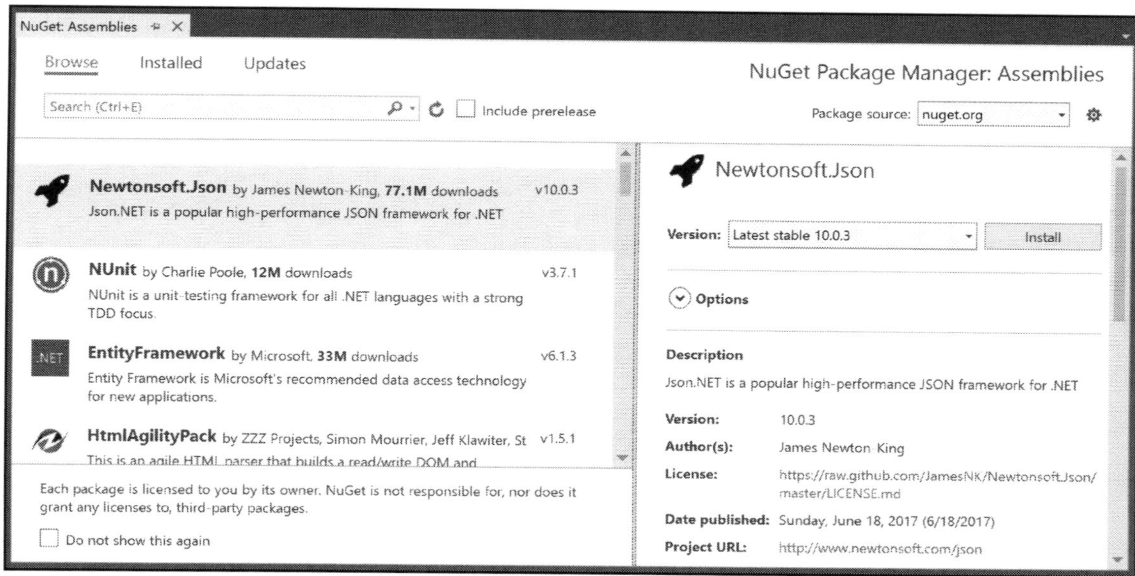


Click on **Install**, and accept the license agreement.

Right-click on the **Assemblies** project, select **Edit Assemblies.csproj**, and note the change to the file, as shown earlier for Visual Studio Code.

In Visual Studio 2017, you can navigate to **Tools | NuGet Package Manager | Package Manager Console** to use a command line for installing, updating, and removing package references, in a similar way to Visual Studio Code's **Integrated Terminal**.

# Packaging a library for NuGet

Now, let's package the `SharedLibrary` project that you created earlier.

In the `SharedLibrary` project, rename `Class1.cs` to `StringExtensions.cs`, and modify its contents, as shown in the following code:

```
using System.Text.RegularExpressions;

namespace Packt.CS7
{
   public static class StringExtensions
   {
      public static bool IsValidXmlTag(this string input)
      {
         return Regex.IsMatch(input,
           @"^<([a-z]+)([^<]+)*(?:>(.*)<\/\1>|\s+\/>)$");
      }

      public static bool IsValidPassword(this string input)
      {
         // minimum of eight valid characters
         return Regex.IsMatch(input, "^[a-zA-Z0-9_-]{8,}$");
      }

      public static bool IsValidHex(this string input)
      {
         // three or six valid hex number characters
         return Regex.IsMatch(input,
           "^#?([a-fA-F0-9]{3}|[a-fA-F0-9]{6})$");
      }
   }
}
```

These extension methods use regular expressions to validate the `string` value. You will learn how to write regular expressions in `Chapter 8`, *Using Common .NET Standard Types*.

Edit `SharedLibrary.csproj`, and modify its contents, as shown in the following markup, and note the following:

- `PackageId` must be globally unique, so you must use a different value if you want to publish this NuGet package to the `https://www.nuget.org/` public feed for others to reference and download
- All the other elements are self-explanatory:

```
<Project Sdk="Microsoft.NET.Sdk">

<PropertyGroup>
  <TargetFramework>netstandard2.0</TargetFramework>
  <GeneratePackageOnBuild>true</GeneratePackageOnBuild>
  <PackageId>Packt.CS7.SharedLibrary</PackageId>
  <PackageVersion>1.0.0.0</PackageVersion>
  <Authors>Mark J Price</Authors>
  <PackageLicenseUrl>
    http://opensource.org/licenses/MS-PL
  </PackageLicenseUrl>
  <PackageProjectUrl>
    http://github.com/markjprice/cs7dotnetcore2
  </PackageProjectUrl>
  <PackageIconUrl>
    http://github.com/markjprice/cs7dotnetcore2/nuget.png
  </PackageIconUrl>
  <PackageRequireLicenseAcceptance>true</PackageRequireLicenseAcceptance>
  <PackageReleaseNotes>
    Example shared library packaged for NuGet.
  </PackageReleaseNotes>
  <Description>
    Three extension methods to validate a string value.
  </Description>
  <Copyright>
    Copyright ©2017 Packt Publishing Limited
  </Copyright>
  <PackageTags>string extension packt cs7</PackageTags>
  </PropertyGroup>

</Project>
```

In Visual Studio 2017, right-click on the **SharedLibrary** project, and select **Pack**.

In Visual Studio Code, in **Integrated Terminal**, enter a command to generate a NuGet package, as shown here:

```
dotnet pack -c Release
```

Visual Studio 2017 and Visual Studio Code display output indicating success, as shown in the following screenshot:

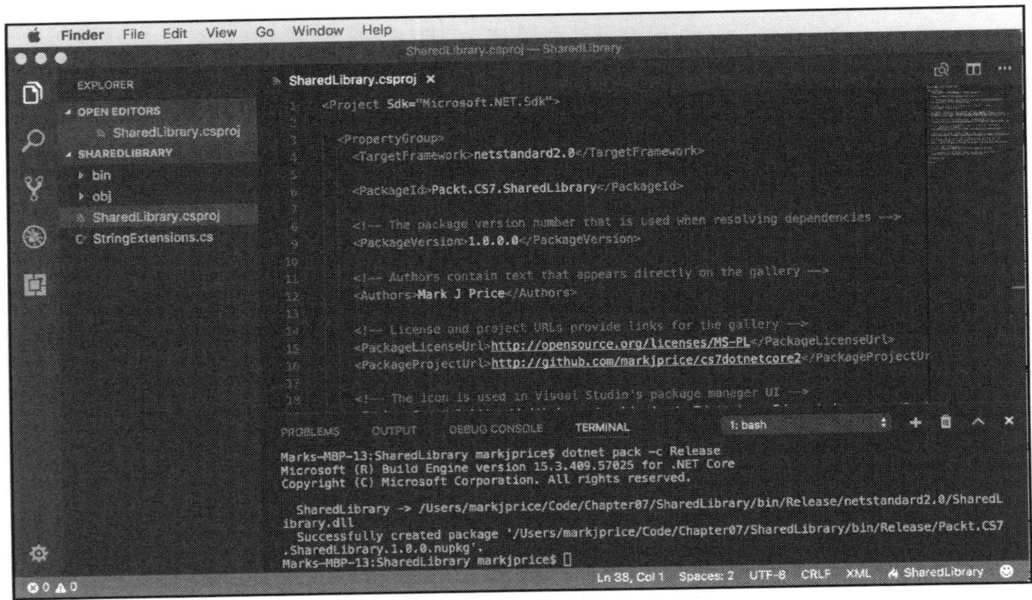


Start your favorite browser and navigate to the following link: `https://www.nuget.org/packages/manage/upload`

You will need to register with `https://www.nuget.org/` if you want to upload a NuGet package for other developers to reference as a dependency package.

Click on **Browse...** and select the `.nupkg` file that was created by the `pack` command, as shown in the following screenshot:

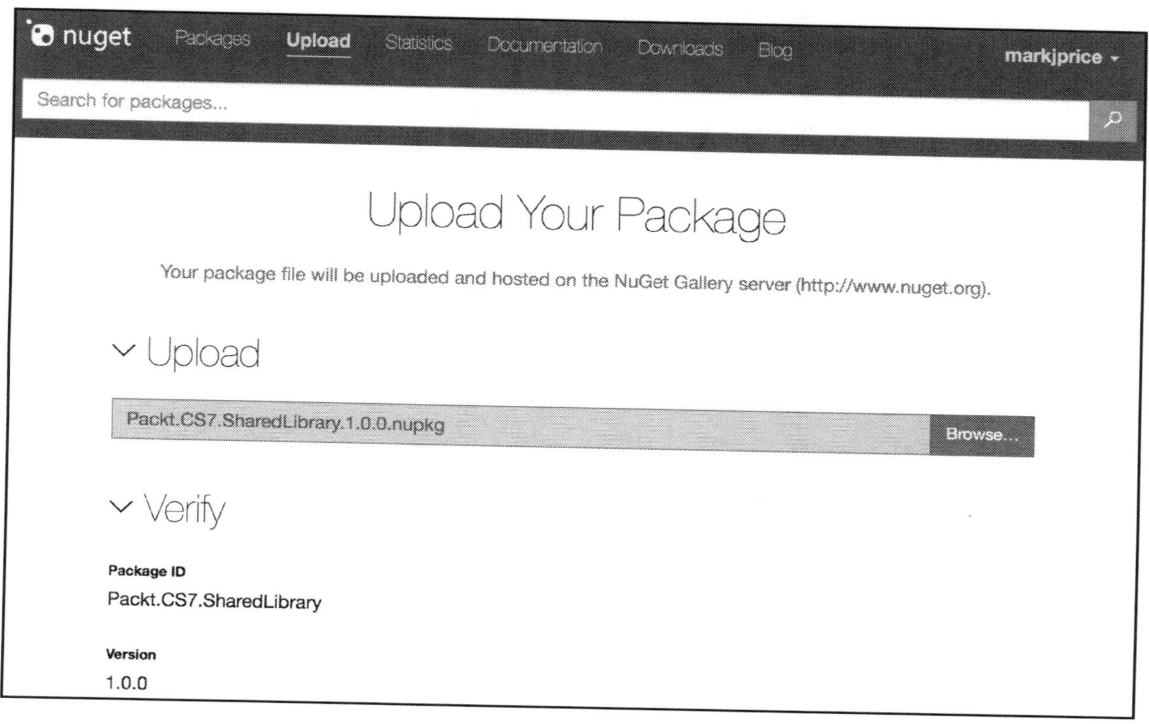


Verify that the information you entered in the `SharedLibrary.csproj` file has been correctly filled in, and then click on **Submit**.

After a few seconds, you will see a success message and you will see your package has been uploaded, as shown in the following screenshot:

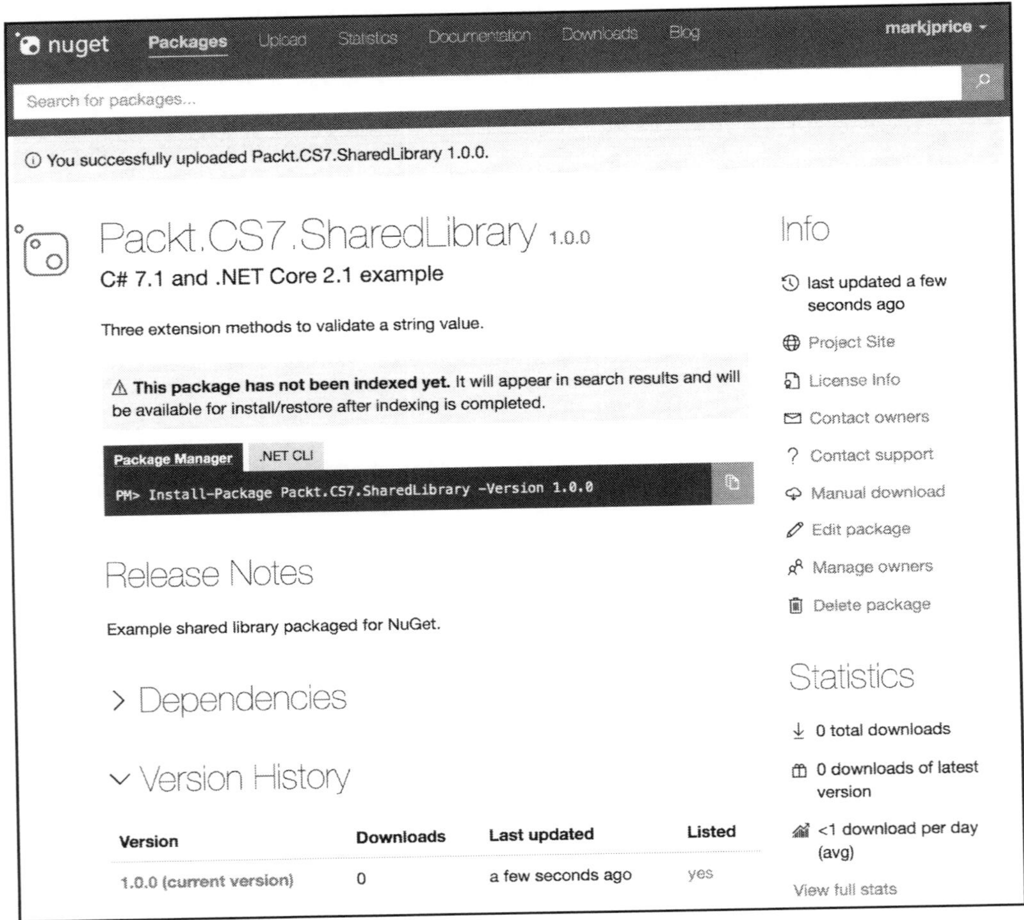


## Testing your package

You will now test your uploaded package by referencing it in the `Assemblies` project.

## Using Visual Studio Code

In Visual Studio Code, open the `Assemblies` project, and modify the project file to reference your package, as shown in the following markup:

```
<Project Sdk="Microsoft.NET.Sdk">
  <PropertyGroup>
    <OutputType>Exe</OutputType>
    <TargetFramework>netcoreapp2.0</TargetFramework>
  </PropertyGroup>
  <ItemGroup>
    <PackageReference Include="newtonsoft.json" Version="10.0.3" />
    <PackageReference Include="packt.cs7.sharedlibrary" Version="1.0.0" />
  </ItemGroup>
</Project>
```

## Using Visual Studio 2017

In Visual Studio 2017, use **NuGet Package Manager** to search for the package and install it, as shown in the following screenshot:

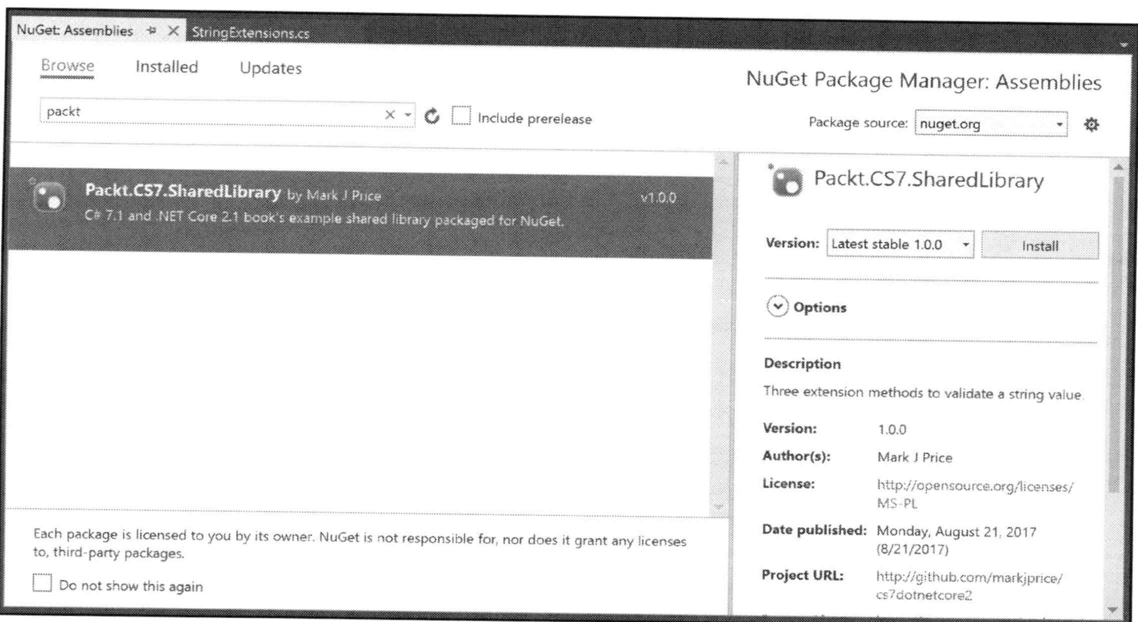

## Using Visual Studio 2017 and Visual Studio Code

Edit `Program.cs` to import the `Packt.CS7` namespace, and in the `Main` method, prompt the user to enter some string values, and then validate them using the extension methods in the package, as shown in the following code:

```
using static System.Console;
using Packt.CS7;

namespace Assemblies
{
   class Program
   {
      static void Main(string[] args)
      {
         Write("Enter a valid color value in hex: ");
         string hex = ReadLine();
         WriteLine($"Is {hex} a valid color value:
         {hex.IsValidHex()}");

         Write("Enter a valid XML tag: ");
         string xmlTag = ReadLine();
         WriteLine($"Is {xmlTag} a valid XML tag:
         {xmlTag.IsValidXmlTag()}");

         Write("Enter a valid password: ");
         string password = ReadLine();
         WriteLine($"Is {password} a valid password:
         {password.IsValidPassword()}");
      }
   }
}
```

Run the console application and view the output:

```
Enter a valid color value in hex: 00ffc8
Is 00ffc8 a valid color value: True
Enter a valid XML tag: <h1 class="<" />
Is <h1 class="<" /> a valid XML tag: False
Enter a valid password: secretsauce
Is secretsauce a valid password: True
```

# Porting from .NET Framework to .NET Core

If you are an existing .NET Framework developer, then you may have existing applications that you are wondering if you should port to .NET Core. You should consider if porting is the right choice for your code. Sometimes, the best choice is not to port.

## Could you port?

.NET Core has great support for the following types of applications:

- **ASP.NET Core MVC** web applications
- **ASP.NET Core Web API** web services (REST/HTTP)
- **Universal Windows Platform** (**UWP**) applications
- **Console** applications

.NET Core does not support the following types of applications:

- **ASP.NET Web Forms** web applications
- **Windows Forms** desktop applications
- **Windows Presentation Foundation** (**WPF**) desktop applications
- **Silverlight** applications

Luckily, WPF and Silverlight applications use a dialect of XAML, which is like the XAML dialect used by UWP and Xamarin.Forms.

## Should you port?

Even if you *could* port, *should* you? What benefits do you gain? Some common benefits include the following:

- **Deployment to Linux or Docker**: These OSes are lightweight and cost-effective as web application and web service platforms, especially when compared to Windows Server

- **Removal of dependency on IIS and System.Web.dll**: Even if you continue to deploy to Windows Server, ASP.NET Core can be hosted on lightweight, higher performance Kestrel (or other) web servers
- **Command-line tools**: These include those tools that developers and administrators use to automate their tasks are written as console applications. The ability to run a single tool cross-platform is very useful.

# Differences between .NET Framework and .NET Core

There are three key differences, as shown in the following table:

| .NET Core | .NET Framework |
|---|---|
| Distributed as NuGet packages, so each application can be deployed with its own app-local copy of the version of .NET Core that it needs. | Distributed as a system-wide, shared set of assemblies (literally, in the **Global Assembly Cache (GAC)**). |
| Split into small, layered components, so a minimal deployment can be performed. | Single, monolithic deployment. |
| Removes older technologies, such as Windows Forms and Web Forms, and noncross-platform features, such as AppDomains, .NET Remoting, and binary serialization. | Retains some older technologies such as Windows Forms, WPF, and ASP.NET Web Forms. |

# Understanding the .NET Portability Analyzer

Microsoft has a useful tool that you can run against your existing applications to generate a report for porting. You can watch a demonstration of the tool at the following link: `https://channel9.msdn.com/Blogs/Seth-Juarez/A-Brief-Look-at-the-NET-Portability-Analyzer`

# Using non-.NET Standard libraries

70% of existing NuGet packages can be used with .NET Core 2.0, even if they are not compiled for .NET Standard 2.0.
To search for useful NuGet packages, follow this link:
https://www.nuget.org/packages

For example, there is a package of custom collections for handling matrices created by Dialect Software LLC, documented at the following link:
https://www.nuget.org/packages/DialectSoftware.Collections.Matrix/

The package was last updated in 2013, as shown in the following screenshot:

2013 was long before .NET Core existed, so this package was built for .NET Framework. As long as an assembly package like this only uses APIs available in .NET Standard 2.0, it can be used in a .NET Core 2.0 project.

Open `Assemblies.csproj`, and add `<PackageReference>` for Dialect Software's package, as shown in the following markup:

```
<PackageReference Include="dialectsoftware.collections.matrix"
Version="1.0.0" />
```

Open `Program.cs`, add statements to import the `DialectSoftware.Collections` and `DialectSoftware.Collections.Generics` namespaces, and add statements to create instances of `Axis` and `Matrix<T>`, populate them with values, and output them, as shown in the following code:

```
var x = new Axis("x", 0, 10, 1);
var y = new Axis("y", 0, 4, 1);

var matrix = new Matrix<long>(new[] { x, y });
int i = 0;
for (; i < matrix.Axes[0].Points.Length; i++)
{
   matrix.Axes[0].Points[i].Label = "x" + i.ToString();
}
```

```
i = 0;
for (; i < matrix.Axes[1].Points.Length; i++)
{
    matrix.Axes[1].Points[i].Label = "y" + i.ToString();
}

foreach (long[] c in matrix)
{
    matrix[c] = c[0] + c[1];
}

foreach (long[] c in matrix)
{
    WriteLine("{0},{1} ({2},{3}) = {4}", matrix.Axes[0].Points[c[0]].Label,
    matrix.Axes[1].Points[c[1]].Label, c[0], c[1], matrix[c]);
}
```

Run the console application, view the output, and note the warning message:

```
/Users/markjprice/Code/Chapter07/Assemblies/Assemblies.csproj : warning
NU1701: Package 'DialectSoftware.Collections.Matrix 1.0.0' was restored
using '.NETFramework,Version=v4.6.1' instead of the project target
framework '.NETCoreApp,Version=v2.0'. This package may not be fully
compatible with your project.
x0,y0 (0,0) = 0
x0,y1 (0,1) = 1
x0,y2 (0,2) = 2
x0,y3 (0,3) = 3
...and so on.
```

# Practicing and exploring

Test your knowledge and understanding by answering some questions, get some hands-on practice, and explore, with deeper research into topics of this chapter.

# Exercise 7.1 – Test your knowledge

Answer the following questions:

1. What is the difference between a namespace and an assembly?
2. How do you reference another project in a `.csproj` file?
3. What is the difference between a package and a metapackage?
4. Which .NET type does the C# `float` alias represent?

5. What is the difference between the packages named `NETStandard.Library` and `Microsoft.NETCore.App`?
6. What is the difference between framework-dependent and self-contained deployments of .NET Core applications?
7. What is a RID?
8. What is the difference between the `dotnet pack` and `dotnet publish` commands?
9. What types of applications written for .NET Framework can be ported to .NET Core?
10. Can you use packages written for .NET Framework with .NET Core?

# Exercise 7.2 – Explore topics

Use the following links to read in more detail the topics covered in this chapter:

- **Porting to .NET Core from .NET Framework**: `https://docs.microsoft.com/en-us/dotnet/articles/core/porting/`
- **Packages, Metapackages and Frameworks**: `https://docs.microsoft.com/en-us/dotnet/articles/core/packages`
- **.NET Blog:** `https://blogs.msdn.microsoft.com/dotnet/`
- **What .NET Developers ought to know to start in 2017:** `https://www.hanselman.com/blog/WhatNETDevelopersOughtToKnowToStartIn2017.aspx`
- **CoreFX README.md:** `https://github.com/dotnet/corefx/blob/master/Documentation/README.md`
- **.NET Core Application Deployment**: `https://docs.microsoft.com/en-us/dotnet/articles/core/deploying/`
- **.NET Standard API Reference:** `https://github.com/dotnet/standard`

# Summary

In this chapter, you explored the relationship between assemblies and namespaces, we discussed options for porting existing .NET Framework code bases, published your apps and libraries, and deployed your code cross-platform.

In the next chapter, you will learn about some common .NET Standard 2.0 types that are included with .NET Core 2.0.

# 8
# Using Common .NET Standard Types

This chapter is about some common .NET Standard 2.0 types that are included with .NET Core 2.0. This includes types for manipulating numbers, text, collections, network access, reflection, attributes, drawing images, and internationalization.

This chapter covers the following topics:

- Working with numbers
- Working with text
- Working with collections
- Working with network resources
- Working with types and attributes
- Internationalizing your code

## Working with numbers

One of the most common types of data are numbers. The most common types in .NET Standard 2.0 for working with numbers are shown in the following table:

| Namespace | Example type(s) | Description |
|---|---|---|
| `System` | `SByte`, `Int16`, `Int32`, `Int64` | Integers, that is, positive and negative whole numbers. |
| `System` | `Byte`, `UInt16`, `UInt32`, `UInt64` | Cardinals, that is, positive whole numbers. |

| System | Single, Double | Reals, that is, floating point numbers. |
|---|---|---|
| System | Decimal | Accurate reals, that is, for use in science, engineering, or financial scenarios. |
| System .Numerics | BigInteger, Complex, Quaternion | Arbitrarily large integers, complex numbers, and quaternion numbers. |

You can read more at the following link:
https://docs.microsoft.com/en-us/dotnet/standard/numerics

Create a new console application named `WorkingWithNumbers` in a solution named `Chapter08`.

# Working with big integers

The largest whole number that can be stored in .NET Standard types that have a C# alias is about eighteen and a half quintillion, stored in an unsigned long.

In `Program.cs`, add a statement to import `System.Numerics`, as shown in the following code:

```
using System.Numerics;
```

In `Main`, add statements to output the largest value of `ulong`, and a number with 30 digits using `BigInteger`, as shown in the following code:

```
var largestLong = ulong.MaxValue;
WriteLine($"{largestLong,40:N0}");

var atomsInTheUniverse =
BigInteger.Parse("123456789012345678901234567890");
WriteLine($"{atomsInTheUniverse,40:N0}");
```

The `, 40` in the format code means right-align forty characters, so both numbers are lined up to the right hand edge.

Run the console application and view the output:

```
                    18,446,744,073,709,551,615
   123,456,789,012,345,678,901,234,567,890
```

## Working with complex numbers

A complex number can be expressed as $a + bi$, where $a$ and $b$ are real numbers, and $i$ is the imaginary unit, where $i2 = -1$. If the real part is zero it is a pure imaginary number. If the imaginary part is zero, it is a real number. Complex numbers have practical applications in many **STEM (science, technology, engineering, mathematics)** fields of study.

Complex numbers are added by separately adding the real and imaginary parts of the summands; consider this:

$(a + bi) + (c + di) = (a + c) + (b + d)i$

In `Main`, add statements to add two complex numbers, as shown in the following code:

```
var c1 = new Complex(4, 2);
var c2 = new Complex(3, 7);
var c3 = c1 + c2;
WriteLine($"{c1} added to {c2} is {c3}");
```

Run the console application and view the output:

```
(4, 2) added to (3, 7) is (7, 9)
```

Quarterions are a number system that extend complex numbers. They form a four-dimensional associative normed division algebra over the real numbers, and therefore also a domain.

Huh? Yes, I know. I don't understand that either. Don't worry, we're not going to write any code using them! Suffice to say, they are good at describing spatial rotations, so video game engines use them, as do many computer simulations and flight control systems.

# Working with text

One of the other most common types of data for variables is text. The most common types in .NET Standard 2.0 for working with text are shown in the following table:

| Namespace | Example types | Description |
|---|---|---|
| `System` | `Char` | Storage for a single text character |
| `System` | `String` | Storage for multiple text characters |
| `System.Text` | `StringBuilder` | Efficiently manipulates strings |
| `System.Text .RegularExpressions` | `Regex` | Efficiently pattern-matches strings |

## Getting the length of a string

Add a new console application project named `WorkingWithText`.

In Visual Studio 2017, set the solution's startup project to be the current selection.

Sometimes, you need to find out the length of a piece of text stored in a `string` class.

In `Main`, add statements to define a variable to store the name of the city London, and then output its name and length, as shown in the following code:

```
string city = "London";
WriteLine($"{city} is {city.Length} characters long.");
```

## Getting the characters of a string

A `string` class uses an array of `char` internally to store the text. It also has an indexer, which means that we can use the array syntax to read its characters.

Add the following statement, and then run the console application:

```
WriteLine($"First char is {city[0]} and third is {city[2]}.");
```

# Splitting a string

Sometimes, you need to split some text wherever there is a character, such as a comma.

Add more lines of code to define a single string with comma-separated city names. You can use the `Split` method and specify a character that you want to treat as the separator. An array of strings is then created that you can enumerate using a `foreach` statement:

```
string cities = "Paris,Berlin,Madrid,New York";
string[] citiesArray = cities.Split(',');
foreach (string item in citiesArray)
{
   WriteLine(item);
}
```

# Getting part of a string

Sometimes, you need to get part of some text. For example, if you had a person's full name stored in a string with a space character between the first and last name, then you could find the position of the space and extract the first name and last name as two parts, like this:

```
string fullname = "Alan Jones";
int indexOfTheSpace = fullname.IndexOf(' ');
string firstname = fullname.Substring(0, indexOfTheSpace);
string lastname = fullname.Substring(indexOfTheSpace + 1);
WriteLine($"{lastname}, {firstname}");
```

If the format of the initial full name was different, for example, `Lastname, Firstname`, then the code would be slightly different. As an optional exercise, try writing some statements that would change the input `Jones, Alan` into `Alan Jones`.

# Checking a string for content

Sometimes, you need to check whether a piece of text starts or ends with some characters or contains some characters:

```
string company = "Microsoft";
bool startsWithM = company.StartsWith("M");
bool containsN = company.Contains("N");
WriteLine($"Starts with M: {startsWithM}, contains an N:{containsN}");
```

## Other string members

Here are some other `string` members:

| Member | Description |
|---|---|
| `Trim`, `TrimStart`, and `TrimEnd` | These trim whitespaces from the beginning and/or end of the string. |
| `ToUpper` and `ToLower` | These convert the string into uppercase or lowercase. |
| `Insert` and `Remove` | These insert or remove some text in the `string` variable. |
| `Replace` | This replaces some text. |
| `string.Concat` | This concatenates two `string` variables. The + operator calls this method when used between `string` variables. |
| `string.Join` | This concatenates one or more `string` variables with a character in between each one. |
| `string.IsNullOrEmpty` | This checks whether a `string` variable is `null` or empty (`""`). |
| `string.IsNullOrWhitespace` | This checks whether a `string` variable is `null` or whitespace, that is, a mix of any number of horizontal and vertical spacing characters, for example, tab, space, carriage return, line feed, and so on. |
| `string.Empty` | This can be used instead of allocating memory each time you use a literal `string` value using an empty pair of double quotes (`""`). |
| `string.Format` | An older, alternative method to output formatted strings, that uses positioned instead of named parameters. |

Note that some of the preceding methods are **static** methods. This means that the method can only be called from the type, not from a variable instance.

For example, if I want to take an array of `string` values and combine them back together into a single `string` variable with separators, I can use the `Join` method like this:

```
string recombined = string.Join(" => ", citiesArray);
WriteLine(recombined);
```

If I want to use positioned parameters instead of interpolated `string` formatting syntax, I can use the `Format` method like this:

```
string fruit = "Apples";
decimal price = 0.39M;
DateTime when = DateTime.Today;

WriteLine($"{fruit} cost {price:C} on {when:dddd}s.");

WriteLine(string.Format("{0} cost {1:C} on {2:dddd}s.",
fruit, price, when));
```

Positioned parameters start counting at zero. Sometimes they can be more easily formatted in code compared to `string` interpolation syntax, as you can see in the previous code example.

If you run the console application and view the output, it should look like this:

```
London is 6 characters long.
First char is L and third is n.
Paris
Berlin
Madrid
New York
Jones, Alan
Starts with M: True, contains an N: False
Paris => Berlin => Madrid => New York
Apples cost £0.39 on Mondays.
Apples cost £0.39 on Mondays.
```

# Building strings efficiently

You can concatenate two strings to make a new `string` variable using the `String.Concat` method or simply using the + operator. But both of these choices are bad practice, because .NET must create a completely new `string` variable in memory. This might not be noticeable if you are only adding two `string` values, but if you concatenate inside a loop with many iterations, it can have a significant negative impact on performance and memory use.

In `Chapter 13`, *Improving Performance and Scalability Using Multitasking*, you will learn how to concatenate the `string` variables efficiently using the `StringBuilder` type.

# Pattern matching with regular expressions

Regular expressions are useful for validating input from the user. They are very powerful and can get very complicated. Almost all programming languages have support for regular expressions and use a common set of special characters to define them.

Add a new console application project named `WorkingWithRegularExpressions`.

At the top of the file, import the following namespaces:

```
using System.Text.RegularExpressions;
using static System.Console;
```

In the `Main` method, add the following statements:

```
Write("Enter your age: ");
string input = ReadLine();
var ageChecker = new Regex(@"\d");
if (ageChecker.IsMatch(input))
{
   WriteLine("Thank you!");
}
else
{
   WriteLine($"This is not a valid age: {input}");
}
```

**Good Practice**
The `@` character in front of `string` switches off the ability to use escape characters in `string`. Escape characters are prefixed with a backslash (\). For example, `\t` means a tab and `\n` means a new line. When writing regular expressions, we need to disable this feature. To paraphrase the television show *The West Wing*, "Let backslash be backslash."

Run the console application and view the output.

If you enter a whole number for the age, you will see `Thank you!`

```
Enter your age: 34
Thank you!
```

If you enter `carrots`, you will see the error message:

```
Enter your age: carrots
This is not a valid age: carrots
```

However, if you enter `bob30smith`, you will see `Thank you!`

```
Enter your age: bob30smith
Thank you!
```

The regular expression we used is `\d`, which means one digit. However, it does not specify what can be entered *before* and *after* the one digit. This regular expression could be described in English as "Enter any characters you want as long as you enter at least one digit character."

Change the regular expression to `^\d$`, like this:

```
var ageChecker = new Regex(@"^\d$");
```

Rerun the application. Now, it rejects anything except a single digit.

We want to allow one or more digits. To do this, we add a + (plus) after the `\d` expression to modify the meaning to *one or more*. Change the regular expression to look like this:

```
var ageChecker = new Regex(@"^\d+$");
```

Run the application and see how the regular expression now only allows positive whole numbers of any length.

## The syntax of a regular expression

Here are some common symbols that you can use in regular expressions:

| **Symbol** | **Meaning** | **Symbol** | **Meaning** |
|---|---|---|---|
| `^` | Start of input | `$` | End of input |
| `\d` | A single digit | `\D` | A single NON-digit |
| `\w` | Whitespace | `\W` | NON-whitespace |
| `[A-Za-z0-9]` | Range(s) of characters | `\^` | ^ (caret) character |
| `[aeiou]` | Set of characters | `[^aeiou]` | NOT in a set of characters |
| `.` | A single character | `\.` | . (dot) character |

Here are some quantifiers that affect the previous symbol in a regular expression:

| **Symbol** | **Meaning** | **Symbol** | **Meaning** |
|---|---|---|---|
| `+` | One or more | `?` | One or none |
| `{3}` | Exactly three | `{3,5}` | Three to five |
| `{3,}` | Three or more | `{,3}` | Up to three |

## Examples of regular expressions

Here are some example regular expressions:

| **Expression** | **Meaning** |
|---|---|
| `\d` | A single digit somewhere in the input |
| `a` | The `a` character somewhere in the input |
| `Bob` | The word `Bob` somewhere in the input |
| `^Bob` | The word `Bob` at the start of the input |
| `Bob$` | The word `Bob` at the end of the input |
| `^\d{2}$` | Exactly two digits |
| `^[0-9]{2}$` | Exactly two digits |

| ^[A-Z]{4,}$ | At least four uppercase letters only |
|---|---|
| ^[A-Za-z]{4,}$ | At least four upper or lowercase letters only |
| ^[A-Z]{2}\d{3}$ | Two uppercase letters and three digits only |
| ^d.g$ | The letter d, then any character, and then the letter g, so it would match both dig and dog or any single character between the d and g |
| ^d\.g$ | The letter d, then a dot (.), and then the letter g, so it would match d.g only |

**Good Practice**
Use regular expressions to validate input from the user. The same regular expressions can be reused in other languages such as JavaScript.

# Working with collections

Another of the most common types of data are collections. If you need to store multiple values in a variable, then you can use a collection.

A **collection** is a data structure in memory that can manage multiple items in different ways, although all collections have some shared functionality.

The most common types in .NET Standard 2.0 for working with collections are shown in the following table:

| **Namespace** | **Example type(s)** | **Description** |
|---|---|---|
| System .Collections | IEnumerable, IEnumerable<T> | Interfaces and base classes used by collections. |
| System .Collections .Generic | List<T>, Dictionary<T>, Queue<T>, Stack<T> | Introduced in C# 2.0 with .NET Framework 2.0. These collections allow you to specify the type you want to store using a generic type parameter (which is safer, faster, and more efficient). |
| System .Collections .Concurrent | BlockingCollection, ConcurrentDictionary, ConcurrentQueue | These collections are safe to use in multithreaded scenarios. |

| | | |
|---|---|---|
| `System .Collections .Immutable` | `ImmutableArray`, `ImmutableDictionary`, `ImmutableList`, `ImmutableQueue` | Designed for scenarios where the contents of the collection should never change. |

You can read more at the following link:

https://docs.microsoft.com/en-us/dotnet/standard/collections

# Common features of all collections

All collections implement the `ICollection` interface; this means that they must have a `Count` property to tell you how many items are in it.

For example, if we had a collection named `passengers`, we could do this:

```
int howMany = passengers.Count;
```

All collections implement the `IEnumerable` interface, which means that they must have a `GetEnumerator` method that returns an object that implements `IEnumerator`; this means that they must have a `MoveNext` method and a `Value` property so that they can be iterated using the `foreach` statement.

For example, to perform an action on all the items in the passengers' collection, we can do this:

```
foreach (var passenger in passengers)
{
   // do something with each passenger
}
```

To understand collections, it can be useful to see the most common interfaces that collections implement, as shown in the following diagram:

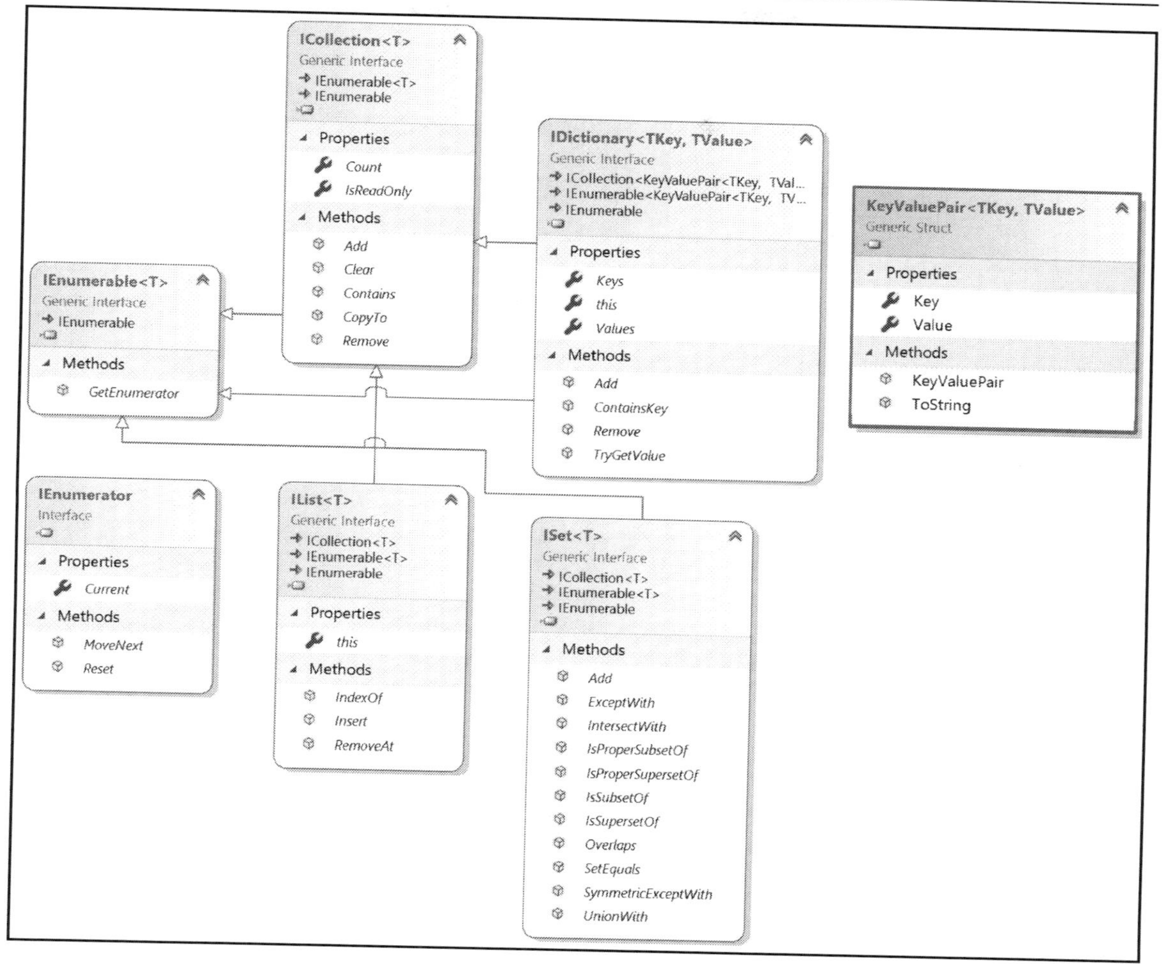


Lists, that is, a type that implements `IList`, are *ordered collections*, this means that they implement `ICollection`; so they must have a `Count` property and an `Add` method to put an item at the end of the collection, and also an `Insert` method to put an item in the list at a specified position, and `RemoveAt` to remove an item at a specified position.

# Understanding collections

There are several different collection categories: lists, dictionaries, stacks, queues, sets, and many other more specialized collections.

## Lists

**Lists** are a good choice when you want to manually control the order of items in a collection. Each item in a list has a unique index (or position) that is automatically assigned. Items can be any type (although they should all be the same type) and items can be duplicated. Indexes are `int` types and start from 0, so the first item in a list is at index 0, as shown in the following table:

| Index | Item |
|---|---|
| 0 | London |
| 1 | Paris |
| 2 | London |
| 3 | Sydney |

If a new item (for example, **Santiago**) is inserted between **London** and **Sydney**, then the index of **Sydney** is automatically incremented. Therefore, you must be aware that an item's index can change after inserting or removing items, as shown in the following table:

| Index | Item |
|---|---|
| 0 | London |
| 1 | Paris |
| 2 | London |
| 3 | Santiago |
| 4 | Sydney |

## Dictionaries

**Dictionaries** are a good choice when each value (or item) has a unique subvalue (or a made-up value) that can be used as a key to quickly find the value in the collection later. The key must be unique. If you are storing a list of people, you can use a government-issued identity number as the key.

Think of the key as being like an index entry in a real-world dictionary. It allows you to quickly find the definition of a word because the words (for example, keys) are kept sorted, and if we know we're looking for the definition of *Manatee*, we would jump to the middle of the dictionary to start looking, because the letter M is in the middle of the alphabet. Dictionaries in programming are similarly smart when looking something up.

Both the key and the value can be any type. This example uses strings for both:

| Key | Value |
|---|---|
| BSA | Bob Smith |
| MW | Max Williams |
| BSB | Bob Smith |
| AM | Amir Mohammed |

## Stacks

**Stacks** are a good choice when you want to implement the **last-in, first-out** (**LIFO**) behavior. With a stack, you can only directly access the one item at the top of the stack, although you can enumerate to read through the whole stack of items. You cannot, for example, access the second item in a stack.

For example, word processors use a stack to remember the sequence of actions you have recently performed, and then when you press *Ctrl* + *Z*, it will undo the last action in the stack, and then the next last action, and so on.

## Queues

**Queues** are a good choice when you want to implement the **first-in, first-out** (**FIFO**) behavior. With a queue, you can only directly access the one item at the front of the queue, although you can enumerate to read through the whole queue of items. You cannot, for example, access the second item in a queue.

For example, background processes use a queue to process work items in the order that they arrive, just like people standing in line at the post office.

## Sets

**Sets** are a good choice when you want to perform set operations between two collections. For example, you may have two collections of city names, and you want to know which names appear in both sets (known as the **intersect** between the sets).

# Working with lists

Add a new console application project named `WorkingWithLists`.

At the top of the file, import the following namespaces:

```
using System;
using System.Collections.Generic;
using static System.Console;
```

In the `Main` method, type the following code that illustrates some of the common ways of working with lists:

```
var cities = new List<string>();
cities.Add("London");
cities.Add("Paris");
cities.Add("Milan");
WriteLine("Initial list");
foreach (string city in cities)
{
  WriteLine($"  {city}");
}
WriteLine($"The first city is {cities[0]}.");
WriteLine($"The last city is {cities[cities.Count - 1]}.");
cities.Insert(0, "Sydney");
WriteLine("After inserting Sydney at index 0");
foreach (string city in cities)
{
  WriteLine($"  {city}");
}
cities.RemoveAt(1);
cities.Remove("Milan");
WriteLine("After removing two cities");
foreach (string city in cities)
{
  WriteLine($"  {city}");
}
```

Run the console application to see the output:

```
Initial list
  London
  Paris
  Milan
The first city is London.
The last city is Milan.
After inserting Sydney at index 0
  Sydney
```

```
  London
  Paris
  Milan
After removing two cities
  Sydney
  Paris
```

## Working with dictionaries

Add a new console application project named `WorkingWithDictionaries`.

Import the same namespaces as before.

In the `Main` method, type the following code that illustrates some of the common ways of working with dictionaries:

```
var keywords = new Dictionary<string, string>();
keywords.Add("int", "32-bit integer data type");
keywords.Add("long", "64-bit integer data type");
keywords.Add("float", "Single precision floating point number");
WriteLine("Keywords and their definitions");
foreach (KeyValuePair<string, string> item in keywords)
{
   WriteLine($"  {item.Key}: {item.Value}");
}
WriteLine($"The definition of long is {keywords["long"]}");
```

Run the application to view the output:

```
Keywords and their definitions
  int: 32-bit integer data type
  long: 64-bit integer data type
  float: Single precision floating point number
The definition of long is 64-bit integer data type
```

## Sorting collections

A `List<T>` class can be sorted by calling its `Sort` method (but remember that the indexes of each item will change).

Sorting a list of strings or other built-in types works automatically, but if you create a collection of your own type, then that type must implement an interface named `IComparable`. You learned how to do this in `Chapter 6`, *Implementing Interfaces and Inheriting Classes*.

A `Dictionary<T>`, `Stack<T>`, or `Queue<T>` collection cannot be sorted because you wouldn't usually want that functionality; for example, you would never sort a queue of guests checking into a hotel. But sometimes, you might want to sort a dictionary or a set.

The differences between these sorted collections are often subtle, but can have an impact on the memory requirements and performance of your application, so it is worth putting effort into picking the most appropriate option for your requirements.

Some common sorted collections are shown in the following table:

| **Collection** | **Description** |
|---|---|
| `SortedDictionary<TKey, TValue>` | This represents a collection of key/value pairs that are sorted on the key |
| `SortedList<TKey, TValue>` | This represents a collection of key/value pairs that are sorted by key, based on the associated `IComparer<T>` implementation |
| `SortedSet<T>` | This represents a collection of objects that is maintained in a sorted order |

# Using specialized collections

There are a few other collections for special situations:

| **Collection** | **Description** |
|---|---|
| `System.Collections.BitArray` | This manages a compact array of bit values, which are represented as Booleans, where `true` indicates that the bit is on (`1`) and `false` indicates the bit is off (`0`) |
| `System.Collections .Generics.LinkedList<T>` | This represents a doubly linked list where every item has a reference to its previous and next items |

# Using immutable collections

Sometimes you need to make a collection immutable, meaning that its members cannot change; that is, you cannot add or remove them.

If you import the `System.Collections.Immutable` namespace, then any collection that implements `IEnumerable<T>` is given six extension methods to convert it into an immutable list, dictionary, hashset, and so on.

Open the `WorkingWithLists` project, import the `System.Collections.Immutable` namespace, and add the following statements to the end of the `Main` method, as shown in the following code:

```
var immutableCities = cities.ToImmutableList();

var newList = immutableCities.Add("Rio");

Write("Immutable cities:");
foreach (string city in immutableCities)
{
   Write($" {city}");
}
WriteLine();

Write("New cities:");
foreach (string city in newList)
{
   Write($" {city}");
}
WriteLine();
```

Run the console application, view the output, and note that the immutable list of cities does not get modified when you call the `Add` method on it; instead it returns a new list with the newly added city:

```
After removing two cities
  Sydney
  Paris
Immutable cities: Sydney Paris
New cities: Sydney Paris Rio
```

# Working with network resources

Sometimes you will need to work with network resources. The most common types in .NET Standard for working with network resources are shown in the following table:

| Namespace | Example type(s) | Description |
|---|---|---|
| `System.Net` | `Dns`, `Uri`, `Cookie`, `WebClient`, `IPAddress` | These are for working with DNS servers, URIs, IP addresses, and so on |
| `System.Net` | `FtpStatusCode`, `FtpWebRequest`, `FtpWebResponse` | These are for working with FTP servers |
| `System.Net` | `HttpStatusCode`, `HttpWebRequest`, `HttpWebResponse` | These are for working with HTTP servers, that is, websites |
| `System.Net .Mail` | `Attachment`, `MailAddress`, `MailMessage`, `SmtpClient` | These are for working with SMTP servers, that is, sending email messages |
| `System.Net .NetworkInformation` | `IPStatus`, `NetworkChange`, `Ping`, `TcpStatistics` | These are for working with low-level network protocols |

## Working with URIs, DNS, and IP addresses

Add a new console application project named `WorkingWithNetworkResources`.

At the top of the file, import the following namespaces:

```
using System;
using System.Net;
using static System.Console;
```

In the `Main` method, enter statements to prompt the user to enter a website address, and then use the `Uri` type to break it down into its parts, including scheme (HTTP, FTP, and so on), port number, and host, as shown in the following code:

```
Write("Enter a valid web address: ");
string url = ReadLine();
if (string.IsNullOrWhiteSpace(url))
{
  url = "http://world.episerver.com/cms/?q=pagetype";
}

var uri = new Uri(url);
```

```
WriteLine($"Scheme: {uri.Scheme}");
WriteLine($"Port: {uri.Port}");
WriteLine($"Host: {uri.Host}");
WriteLine($"Path: {uri.AbsolutePath}");
WriteLine($"Query: {uri.Query}");
```

Run the console application, enter a valid website address, press *Enter*, and view the output:

```
Enter a valid web address:
Scheme: http
Port: 80
Host: world.episerver.com
Path: /cms/
Query: ?q=pagetype
```

Add the following statements to `Main` to get the IP address for the entered website, as shown in the following code:

```
IPHostEntry entry = Dns.GetHostEntry(uri.Host);
WriteLine($"{entry.HostName} has the following IP addresses:");
foreach (IPAddress address in entry.AddressList)
{
  WriteLine($" {address}");
}
```

Run the console application, enter a valid website address, press *Enter*, and view the output:

```
world.episerver.com has the following IP addresses: 217.114.90.249
```

# Pinging a server

In `Program.cs`, add a statement to import `System.Net.NetworkInformation`, as shown in the following code:

```
using System.Net.NetworkInformation;
```

Add the following statements to `Main` to get the IP addresses for the entered website, as shown in the following code:

```
var ping = new Ping();
PingReply reply = ping.Send(uri.Host);
WriteLine($"{uri.Host} was pinged, and replied: {reply.Status}.");
if (reply.Status == IPStatus.Success)
{
```

```
        WriteLine($"Reply from {reply.Address} took
        {reply.RoundtripTime:N0}ms");
    }
```

Run the console application, press *Enter*, view the output, and note that Episerver's developer site does not respond to ping requests (this is often done to avoid DDoS attacks):

```
world.episerver.com was pinged, and replied: TimedOut.
```

Run the console application again, and enter `http://google.com`, as shown in the following output:

```
Enter a valid web address: http://google.com
Scheme: http
Port: 80
Host: google.com
Path: /
Query:
google.com has the following IP addresses:
  216.58.206.78
  2a00:1450:4009:804::200e
google.com was pinged, and replied: Success.
Reply from 216.58.206.78 took 9ms
```

# Working with types and attributes

**Reflection** is a programming feature that allows code to understand and manipulate itself. An assembly is made up of up to four parts:

- **Assembly metadata and manifest**: Name, assembly and file version, referenced assemblies, and so on
- **Type metadata**: Information about the types, their members, and so on
- **IL code**: Implementation of methods, properties, constructors, and so on
- **Embedded Resources (optional)**: Images, strings, JavaScript, and so on

Metadata comprises of items of information about your code. Metadata is applied to your code using attributes. Attributes can be applied at multiple levels: to assemblies, to types, and to their members, as shown in the following code:

```
// an assembly-level attribute
[assembly: AssemblyTitle("Working with Reflection")]

[Serializable] // a type-level attribute
```

```
public class Person
// a member-level attribute
[Obsolete("Deprecated: use Run instead.")]
public void Walk()
{
   // ...
}
```

## Versioning of assemblies

Version numbers in .NET are a combination of three numbers, with two optional additions. If you follow the rules of semantic versioning:

- **Major**: Breaking changes
- **Minor**: Non-breaking changes, including new features and bug fixes
- **Patch**: Non-breaking bug fixes

Optionally, a version can include these:

- **Prerelease**: Unsupported preview releases
- **Build number**: Nightly builds

**Good Practice**
Follow the rules of semantic versioning, as described at the following link: `http://semver.org`

## Reading assembly metadata

Add a new console application project named `WorkingWithReflection`.

At the top of the file, import the following types and namespaces:

```
using static System.Console;
using System;
using System.Reflection;
```

In the `Main` method, enter statements to get the console apps assembly, output its name and location, and get all assembly-level attributes and output their types, as shown in the following code:

```
WriteLine("Assembly metadata:");
```

```
Assembly assembly = Assembly.GetEntryAssembly();

WriteLine($" Full name: {assembly.FullName}");
WriteLine($" Location: {assembly.Location}");

var attributes = assembly.GetCustomAttributes();

WriteLine($" Attributes:");
foreach (Attribute a in attributes)
{
   WriteLine($" {a.GetType()}");
}
```

Run the console application and view the output:

```
Assembly metadata:
  Full name: WorkingWithReflection, Version=1.0.0.0, Culture=neutral,
PublicKeyToken=null
  Location:
/Users/markjprice/Code/Chapter08/WorkingWithReflection/bin/Debug/netcoreapp
2.0/WorkingWithReflection.dll
  Attributes:
    System.Runtime.CompilerServices.CompilationRelaxationsAttribute
    System.Runtime.CompilerServices.RuntimeCompatibilityAttribute
    System.Diagnostics.DebuggableAttribute
    System.Runtime.Versioning.TargetFrameworkAttribute
    System.Reflection.AssemblyCompanyAttribute
    System.Reflection.AssemblyConfigurationAttribute
    System.Reflection.AssemblyDescriptionAttribute
    System.Reflection.AssemblyFileVersionAttribute
    System.Reflection.AssemblyInformationalVersionAttribute
    System.Reflection.AssemblyProductAttribute
    System.Reflection.AssemblyTitleAttribute
```

Now that we know some of the attributes decorating the assembly, we can ask for them specifically.

Add statements to the end of the `Main` method to get the `AssemblyInformationalVersionAttribute` and `AssemblyCompanyAttribute` classes, as shown in the following code:

```
var version =
assembly.GetCustomAttribute<AssemblyInformationalVersionAttribute>();
WriteLine($" Version: {version.InformationalVersion}");

var company = assembly.GetCustomAttribute<AssemblyCompanyAttribute>();
WriteLine($" Company: {company.Company}");
```

Run the console application and view the output:

```
Version: 1.0.0
Company: WorkingWithReflection
```

Hmm, let's explicitly set this information. The .NET Framework way to set these values is to add attributes in the C# source code file, as shown in the following code:

```
[assembly: AssemblyCompany("Packt Publishing")]
[assembly: AssemblyInformationalVersion("1.0.0")]
```

Roslyn compiler sets these attributes automatically, so we can't use the old way. Instead, they can be set in the project file.

Modify `WorkingWithReflection.csproj`, as shown in the following example:

```
<Project Sdk="Microsoft.NET.Sdk">

  <PropertyGroup>
    <OutputType>Exe</OutputType>
    <TargetFramework>netcoreapp2.0</TargetFramework>
    <Version>1.3.0</Version>
    <Company>Packt Publishing</Company>
  </PropertyGroup>

</Project>
```

Run the console application and view the output:

```
Version: 1.3.0
Company: Packt Publishing
```

# Creating custom attributes

You can define your own attributes by inheriting from the `Attribute` class.

Add a class named `CoderAttribute`, as shown in the following code:

```
using System;

[AttributeUsage(AttributeTargets.Class | AttributeTargets.Method,
                AllowMultiple = true)]
public class CoderAttribute : Attribute
{
   public string Coder { get; set; }
   public DateTime LastModified { get; set; }
```

```
    public CoderAttribute(string coder, string lastModified)
    {
        Coder = coder;
        LastModified = DateTime.Parse(lastModified);
    }
}
```

In `Program`, add a method named `DoStuff`, and decorate it with the `Coder` attribute, as shown in the following code:

```
[Coder("Mark Price", "22 August 2017")]
[Coder("Johnni Rasmussen", "13 September 2017")]
public static void DoStuff()
{

}
```

In `Program.cs`, import `System.Linq`, as shown in the following code:

```
using System.Linq;
```

In `Main`, add code to get the types, enumerate their members, read any `Coder` attributes on those members, and output the information, as shown in the following code:

```
WriteLine($"Types:");
Type[] types = assembly.GetTypes();

foreach (Type type in types)
{
    WriteLine($" Name: {type.FullName}");

    MemberInfo[] members = type.GetMembers();

    foreach (MemberInfo member in members)
    {
        WriteLine($" {member.MemberType}: {member.Name}
        ({member.DeclaringType.Name})");

        var coders = member.GetCustomAttributes<CoderAttribute>()
        .OrderByDescending(c => c.LastModified);
        foreach (CoderAttribute coder in coders)
        {
            WriteLine($" Modified by {coder.Coder} on
            {coder.LastModified.ToShortDateString()}");
        }
    }
}
```

Run the console application and view the output:

```
Types:
  Name: CoderAttribute
    Method: get_Coder (CoderAttribute)
    Method: set_Coder (CoderAttribute)
    Method: get_LastModified (CoderAttribute)
    Method: set_LastModified (CoderAttribute)
    Method: Equals (Attribute)
    Method: GetHashCode (Attribute)
    Method: get_TypeId (Attribute)
    Method: Match (Attribute)
    Method: IsDefaultAttribute (Attribute)
    Method: ToString (Object)
    Method: GetType (Object)
    Constructor: .ctor (CoderAttribute)
    Property: Coder (CoderAttribute)
    Property: LastModified (CoderAttribute)
    Property: TypeId (Attribute)
  Name: WorkingWithReflection.Program
    Method: DoStuff (Program)
      Modified by Johnni Rasmussen on 13/09/2017
      Modified by Mark Price on 22/08/2017
    Method: ToString (Object)
    Method: Equals (Object)
    Method: GetHashCode (Object)
    Method: GetType (Object)
    Constructor: .ctor (Program)
  Name: WorkingWithReflection.Program+<>c
    Method: ToString (Object)
    Method: Equals (Object)
    Method: GetHashCode (Object)
    Method: GetType (Object)
    Constructor: .ctor (<>c)
    Field: <>9 (<>c)
    Field: <>9__0_0 (<>c)
```

# Doing more with reflection

This is just a taster of what can be achieved with reflection. We only used reflection to read metadata from our code. Reflection can also do the following:

- Dynamically load assemblies that are not currently referenced
- Dynamically execute code
- Dynamically generate new code and assemblies

# Internationalizing your code

**Internationalization** is the process of enabling your code to run correctly all over the world. It has two parts: **globalization** and **localization**.

Globalization is about writing your code to accommodate multiple language and region combinations. The combination of a language and a region is known as a culture. It is important for your code to know both the language and region because the date and currency formats are different in Quebec and Paris, despite them both using the French language.

There are **International Organization for Standardization** (**ISO**) codes for all culture combinations. For example, in the code `da-DK`, `da` indicates the Danish language and `DK` indicates the Denmark region, or in the code `fr-CA`, `fr` indicates the French language and `CA` indicates the Canadian region.

ISO is not an acronym. ISO is a reference to the Greek word **isos** (which means *equal*).

Localization is about customizing the user interface to support a language, for example, changing the label of a button to be **Close** (`en`) or **Fermer** (`fr`). Since localization is more about the language, it doesn't always need to know about the region, although ironically enough, standardization (`en-US`) and standardisation (`en-GB`) suggest otherwise.

Internationalization is a huge topic on which several thousand-page books have been written. In this section, you will get a brief introduction to the basics using the `CultureInfo` type in the `System.Globalization` namespace.

# Globalizing an application

Add a new console application project named `Internationalization`.

At the top of the file, import the following types and namespaces:

```
using static System.Console;
using System;
using System.Globalization;
```

In the `Main` method, enter the following statements:

```
CultureInfo globalization = CultureInfo.CurrentCulture;
CultureInfo localization = CultureInfo.CurrentUICulture;
WriteLine($"The current globalization culture is
{globalization.Name}: {globalization.DisplayName}");
WriteLine($"The current localization culture is
{localization.Name}: {localization.DisplayName}");
WriteLine();
WriteLine("en-US: English (United States)");
WriteLine("da-DK: Danish (Denmark)");
WriteLine("fr-CA: French (Canada)");
Write("Enter an ISO culture code: ");
string newculture = ReadLine();
if (!string.IsNullOrEmpty(newculture))
{
   var ci = new CultureInfo(newculture);
   CultureInfo.CurrentCulture = ci;
   CultureInfo.CurrentUICulture = ci;
}
Write("Enter your name: ");
string name = ReadLine();
Write("Enter your date of birth: ");
string dob = ReadLine();
Write("Enter your salary: ");
string salary = ReadLine();
DateTime date = DateTime.Parse(dob);
int minutes = (int)DateTime.Today.Subtract(date).TotalMinutes;
decimal earns = decimal.Parse(salary);
WriteLine($"{name} was born on a {date:dddd} and is {minutes:N0}
minutes old and earns {earns:C}.");
```

When you run an application, it automatically sets its thread to use the culture of the operating system. I am running my code in London, UK, so the thread is already set to English (United Kingdom).

The code prompts the user to enter an alternative ISO code. This allows your applications to replace the default culture at runtime.

The application then uses standard format codes to output the day of the week, `dddd`; the number of minutes with thousand separators, `N0`; and the salary with the currency symbol, `C`. These adapt automatically, based on the thread's culture.

Run the console application and view the output. Enter `en-GB` for the ISO code and then enter some sample data. You will need to enter a date in a format valid for British English:

```
Enter an ISO culture code: en-GB
Enter your name: Alice
Enter your date of birth: 30/3/1967
Enter your salary: 23500
Alice was born on a Thursday, is 25,469,280 minutes old and earns
£23,500.00.
```

Rerun the application and try a different culture, such as Danish in Denmark (`da-DK`):

```
Enter an ISO culture code: da-DK
Enter your name: Mikkel
Enter your date of birth: 12/3/1980
Enter your salary: 34000
Mikkel was born on a onsdag, is 18.656.640 minutes old and earns kr.
34.000,00.
```

**Good Practice**
Consider whether your application needs to be internationalized and plan for that before you start coding! Write down all the pieces of text in the user interface that will need to be localized. Think about all the data that will need to be globalized (date formats, number formats, and sorting text behavior).

# Practicing and exploring

Test your knowledge and understanding by answering some questions, get some hands-on practice, and explore with deeper research into the topics of this chapter.

# Exercise 8.1 – Test your knowledge

Use the web to answer the following questions:

1. What is the maximum number of characters that can be stored in a `string` variable?
2. When and why should you use a `SecureString` class?
3. When is it appropriate to use a `StringBuilder` type?
4. When should you use a `LinkedList` class?
5. When should you use a `SortedDictionary` class rather than a `SortedList` class?
6. What is the ISO culture code for Welsh?
7. What is the difference between localization, globalization, and internationalization?
8. In a regular expression, what does `$` mean?
9. In a regular expression, how could you represent digits?
10. Why should you *not* use the official standard for email addresses to create a regular expression to validate a user's email address?

# Exercise 8.2 – Practice regular expressions

Create a console application named `Exercise02` that prompts the user to enter a regular expression, and then prompts the user to enter some input and compare the two for a match until the user presses *Esc*:

```
The default regular expression checks for at least one digit.
Enter a regular expression (or press ENTER to use the default): ^[a- z]+$
Enter some input: apples
apples matches ^[a-z]+$? True
Press ESC to end or any key to try again.
Enter a regular expression (or press ENTER to use the default): ^[a- z]+$
Enter some input: abc123xyz
abc123xyz matches ^[a-z]+$? False
Press ESC to end or any key to try again.
```

# Exercise 8.3 – Practice writing extension methods

Create extension methods that do the following:

- Extend `BigInteger` with a method named `ToWords` that returns a string describing the number, for example, 18,000,000 would be *eighteen million*, and 18,456,000,000,000,000,000 would be about *eighteen and a half quintillion*. Use the following link: `https://en.wikipedia.org/wiki/Names_of_large_numbers`

# Exercise 8.4 – Explore topics

Use the following links to read in more detail the topics covered in this chapter:

- **.NET Core API Reference**: `https://docs.microsoft.com/en-us/dotnet/core/api/index`
- **String Class**: `https://docs.microsoft.com/en-us/dotnet/core/api/system.string`
- **Regex Class**: `https://docs.microsoft.com/en-us/dotnet/core/api/system.text.regularexpressions.regex`
- **Regular expressions in .NET**: `https://docs.microsoft.com/en-us/dotnet/articles/standard/base-types/regular-expressions`
- **Regular Expression Language - Quick Reference**: `https://docs.microsoft.com/en-us/dotnet/articles/standard/base-types/quick-ref`
- **RegExr: Learn, Build, and Test RegEx**: `http://regexr.com/`
- **Collections (C# and Visual Basic)**: `https://docs.microsoft.com/en-us/dotnet/core/api/system.collections`
- **Attributes**: `https://docs.microsoft.com/en-us/dotnet/standard/attributes/`
- **Internationalization**: `https://docs.microsoft.com/en-us/dotnet/standard/globalization-localization/`

# Summary

In this chapter, you explored some choices for types to store and manipulate text, which collections to use for storing multiple items, and how to internationalize your code.

In the next chapter, we will manage files and streams, encode and decode text, and perform serialization.

# 9 Working with Files, Streams, and Serialization

This chapter is about reading and writing to files and streams, text encoding, and serialization.

This chapter will cover the following topics:

- Managing the filesystem
- Reading and writing with streams
- Encoding text
- Serializing object graphs

## Managing the filesystem

Your applications will often need to perform input and output with files and directories in different environments. The `System` and `System.IO` namespaces contain classes for this purpose.

# Handling cross-platform environments and filesystems

In Visual Studio 2017, press *Ctrl* + *Shift* + *N* or choose **File** | **New** | **Project...**.

In the **New Project** dialog, in the **Installed** list, select **.NET Core**. In the center list, select **Console App (.NET Core)**, type **Name** as `WorkingWithFileSystems`, change the location to `C:\Code`, type the solution name as `Chapter09`, and then click on **OK**.

In Visual Studio Code, in **Integrated Terminal**, make a new directory named `Chapter09` and a subdirectory named `WorkingWithFileSystems`. Open the folder and enter the `dotnet new console` command.

At the top of the `Program.cs` file, add the following import statements. Note that we will statically import the `Directory`, `Path`, and `Environment` types to simplify our code:

```
using static System.Console;
using System.IO;
using static System.IO.Directory;
using static System.IO.Path;
using static System.Environment;
```

The paths are different for Windows, macOS, and Linux, so we will start by exploring how .NET Core handles this.

Create a static `OutputFileSystemInfo` method, and write statements to the following:

- Output the path and directory separation characters
- Output the path of the current directory
- Output some special paths for system files, temporary files, and documents

```
static void OutputFileSystemInfo()
{
    WriteLine($"Path.PathSeparator: {PathSeparator}");
    WriteLine($"Path.DirectorySeparatorChar: {DirectorySeparatorChar}");
    WriteLine($"Directory.GetCurrentDirectory(): {GetCurrentDirectory()}");
    WriteLine($"Environment.CurrentDirectory: {CurrentDirectory}");
    WriteLine($"Environment.SystemDirectory: {SystemDirectory}");
    WriteLine($"Path.GetTempPath(): {GetTempPath()}");
    WriteLine($"GetFolderPath(SpecialFolder):");
    WriteLine($" System: {GetFolderPath(SpecialFolder.System)}");
    WriteLine($" ApplicationData:
    {GetFolderPath(SpecialFolder.ApplicationData)}");
```

```
    WriteLine($" MyDocuments: {GetFolderPath(SpecialFolder.MyDocuments)}");
    WriteLine($" Personal: {GetFolderPath(SpecialFolder.Personal)}");
}
```

The `Environment` type has many other useful members, including the `GetEnvironmentVariables` method and the `OSVersion` and `ProcessorCount` properties.

In the `Main` method, call `OutputFileSystemInfo`, as shown in the following code:

```
static void Main(string[] args)
{
    OutputFileSystemInfo();
}
```

## Using Windows 10

Run the console application and view the output, as shown in the following screenshot:

```
C:\WINDOWS\system32\cmd.exe
Path.PathSeparator:             ;
Path.DirectorySeparatorChar:    \
Directory.GetCurrentDirectory(): C:\Code\Chapter09\WorkingWithFileSystem
Environment.CurrentDirectory:   C:\Code\Chapter09\WorkingWithFileSystem
Environment.SystemDirectory:    C:\WINDOWS\system32
Path.GetTempPath():             C:\Users\markj\AppData\Local\Temp\
GetFolderPath(SpecialFolder):
  System:                       C:\WINDOWS\system32
  ApplicationData:              C:\Users\markj\AppData\Roaming
  MyDocuments:                  \\Mac\Home\Documents
  Personal:                     \\Mac\Home\Documents
Press any key to continue . . .
```

Windows uses a backslash for the directory separator character.

## Using macOS

Run the console application and view the output, as shown in the following screenshot:

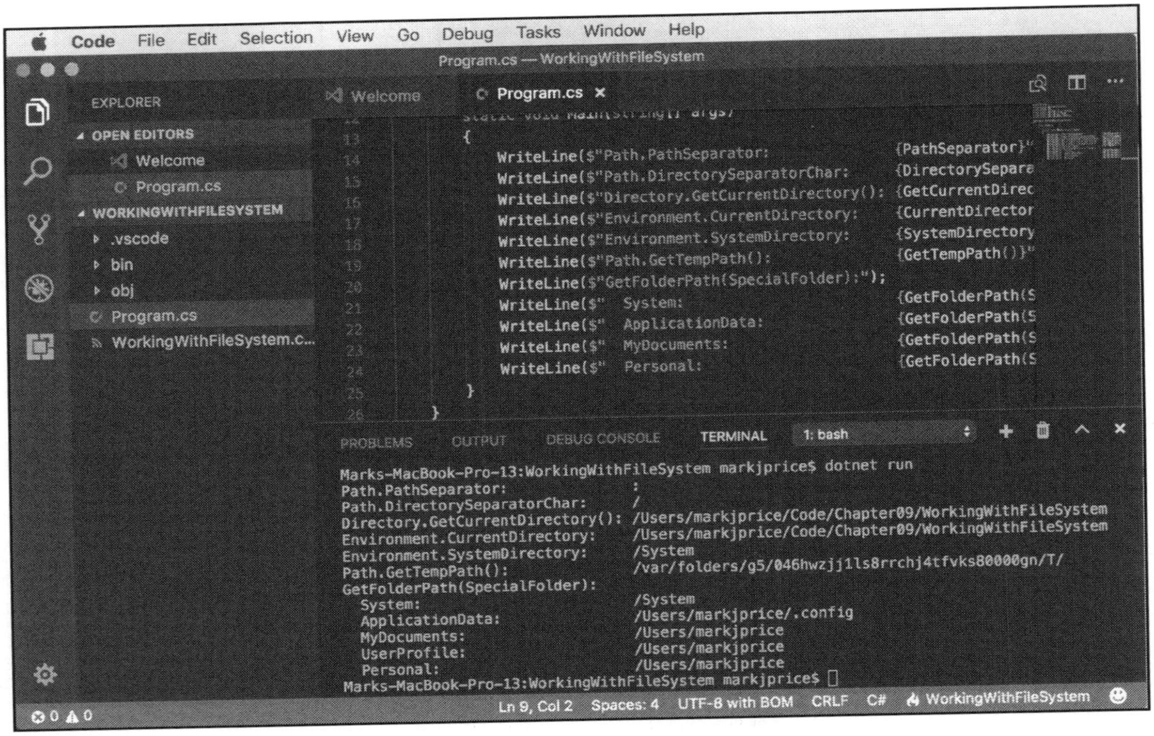

```
{
    WriteLine($"Path.PathSeparator:                {PathSeparator}"
    WriteLine($"Path.DirectorySeparatorChar:       {DirectorySepara
    WriteLine($"Directory.GetCurrentDirectory(): {GetCurrentDirec
    WriteLine($"Environment.CurrentDirectory:      {CurrentDirector
    WriteLine($"Environment.SystemDirectory:       {SystemDirectory
    WriteLine($"Path.GetTempPath():                {GetTempPath()}"
    WriteLine($"GetFolderPath(SpecialFolder):");
    WriteLine($"  System:                          {GetFolderPath(S
    WriteLine($"  ApplicationData:                 {GetFolderPath(S
    WriteLine($"  MyDocuments:                     {GetFolderPath(S
    WriteLine($"  Personal:                        {GetFolderPath(S
}
```

```
Marks-MacBook-Pro-13:WorkingWithFileSystem markjprice$ dotnet run
Path.PathSeparator:              :
Path.DirectorySeparatorChar:     /
Directory.GetCurrentDirectory(): /Users/markjprice/Code/Chapter09/WorkingWithFileSystem
Environment.CurrentDirectory:    /Users/markjprice/Code/Chapter09/WorkingWithFileSystem
Environment.SystemDirectory:     /System
Path.GetTempPath():              /var/folders/g5/046hwzjj1ls8rrchj4tfvks80000gn/T/
GetFolderPath(SpecialFolder):
  System:                        /System
  ApplicationData:               /Users/markjprice/.config
  MyDocuments:                   /Users/markjprice
  UserProfile:                   /Users/markjprice
  Personal:                      /Users/markjprice
Marks-MacBook-Pro-13:WorkingWithFileSystem markjprice$
```

macOS uses a forward slash for the directory separator character.

## Managing drives

To manage drives, use `DriveInfo`, which has a static method that returns information about all the drives connected to your computer. Each drive has a drive type.

`DriveInfo` and `DriveType` are shown in the following diagram:

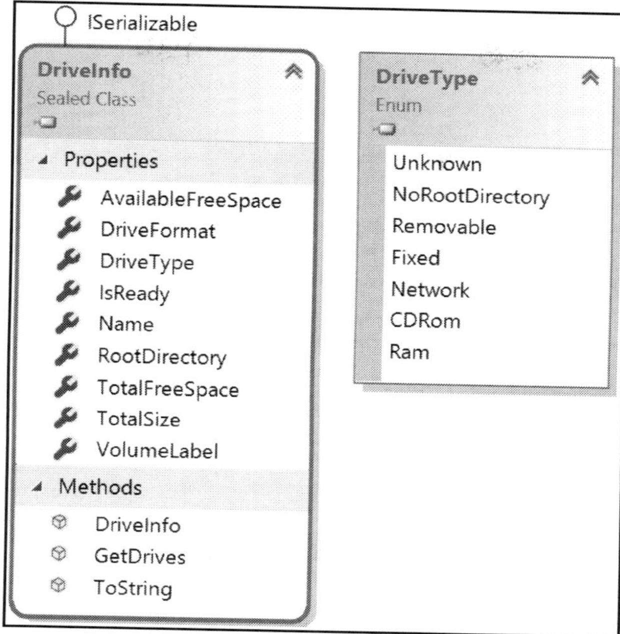


Create a `WorkWithDrives` method, and write statements to get all the drives and output their name, type, size, available free space, and format, but only if the drive is ready, as shown in the following code:

```
static void WorkWithDrives()
{
  WriteLine($"|--------------------------------|------------|
  ---------|--------------------|--------------------|");
  WriteLine($"| Name | Type | Format | Size | Free space |");
  WriteLine($"|--------------------------------|------------|
  ---------|--------------------|--------------------|");

  foreach (DriveInfo drive in DriveInfo.GetDrives())
  {
    if (drive.IsReady)
    {
      WriteLine($"| {drive.Name,-30} |
      {drive.DriveType,-10} | {drive.DriveFormat, -7} |
      {drive.TotalSize,18:N0} |
      {drive.AvailableFreeSpace,18:N0} |");
    }
```

```
        else
        {
          WriteLine($"| {drive.Name,-30} | {drive.DriveType,-10} |");
        }
      }
      WriteLine($"|--------------------------------|------------|
      ---------|---------------------|---------------------|");
    }
```

**Good Practice**
Check that a drive is ready before reading properties such as `TotalSize` or you will see an exception thrown with removable drives.

In `Main`, comment out the previous method call, and add a call to `WorkWithDrives`, as shown in the following code:

```
static void Main(string[] args)
{
  // OutputFileSystemInfo();

  WorkWithDrives();
}
```

Run the console application and view the output, as shown in the following screenshot:

| Name | Type | Format | Size | Free space |
|---|---|---|---|---|
| / | Fixed | hfs | 498,954,403,840 | 135,917,678,592 |
| /dev | Ram | devfs | 191,488 | 0 |
| /net | Network | autofs | 0 | 0 |
| /home | Network | autofs | 0 | 0 |
| /Volumes/LaCie | Fixed | hfs | 4,000,443,056,128 | 3,775,136,669,696 |
| /Volumes/[C] Windows 10.hidden | Network | smbfs | 136,844,406,784 | 43,311,140,864 |

# Managing directories

To manage directories, use the `Directory`, `Path` and `Environment` static classes, as shown in the following diagram:

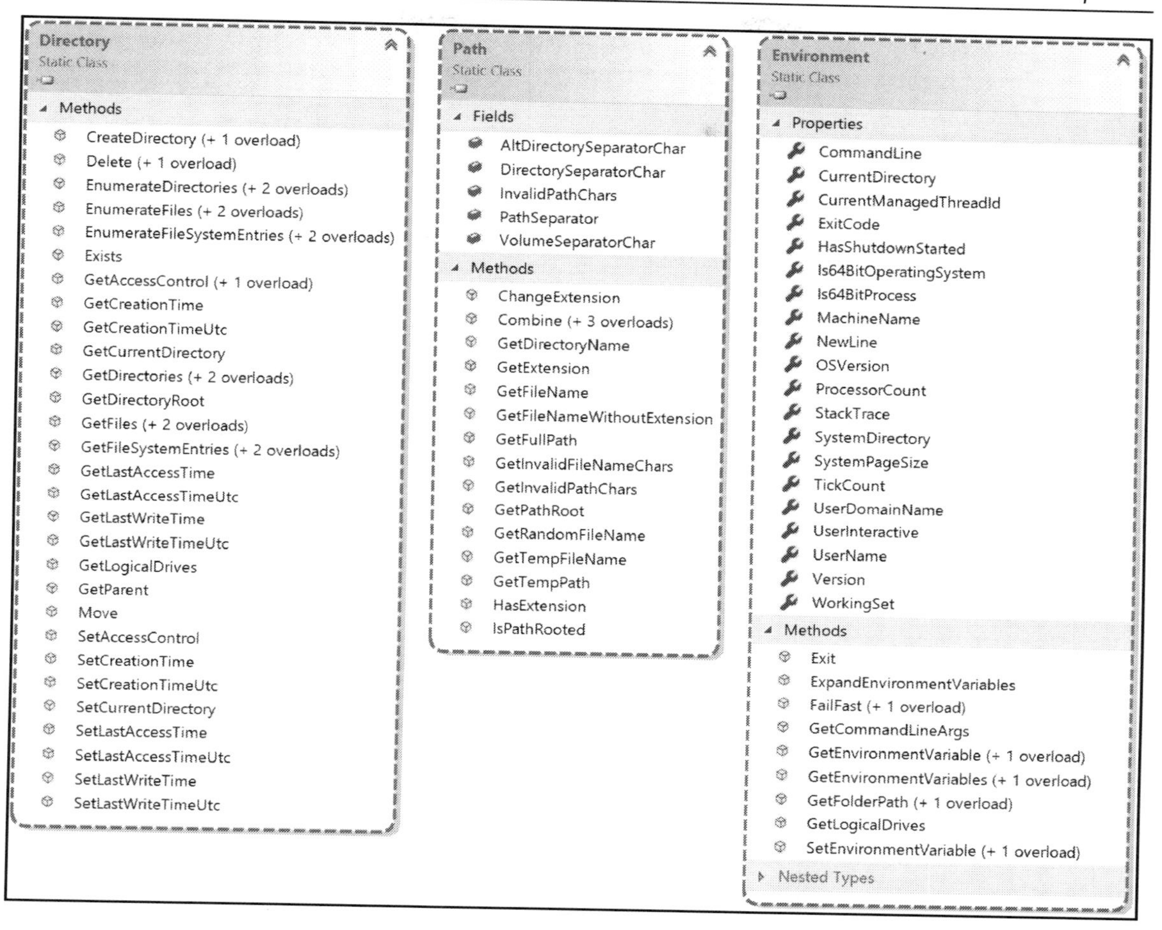


When constructing custom paths, you must be careful to write your code so that it makes no assumptions about platform, for example, what to use for the directory separator character.

Create a `WorkWithDirectories` method, and write statements to do the following:

- Define a custom path under the user's home directory by creating an array of strings for the directory names, and then properly combining them with the `Path` type's `Combine` method
- Check for the existence of the custom directory path

- Create, and then delete the directory, including files and subdirectories within it:

```
static void WorkWithDirectories()
{
    // define a custom directory path
    string userFolder = GetFolderPath(SpecialFolder.Personal);

    var customFolder = new string[]
    { userFolder, "Code", "Chapter09", "NewFolder" };
    string dir = Combine(customFolder);

    WriteLine($"Working with: {dir}");

    // check if it exists
    WriteLine($"Does it exist? {Exists(dir)}");

    // create directory
    WriteLine("Creating it...");
    CreateDirectory(dir);
    WriteLine($"Does it exist? {Exists(dir)}");

    Write("Confirm the directory exists, and then press ENTER: ");
    ReadLine();

    // delete directory
    WriteLine("Deleting it...");
    Delete(dir, recursive: true);
    WriteLine($"Does it exist? {Exists(dir)}");
}
```

In the `Main` method, comment out the previous method call, and add a call to `WorkWithDirectories`, as shown in the following code:

```
static void Main(string[] args)
{
    // OutputFileSystemInfo();
    // WorkWithDrives();

    WorkWithDirectories();
}
```

Run the console application and view the output, and use your favorite file management tool to confirm that the directory has been created before pressing *Enter* to delete it:

```
Working with: /Users/markjprice/Code/Chapter09/NewFolder
Does it exist? False
Creating it...
Does it exist? True
Confirm the directory exists, and then press ENTER:
Deleting it...
Does it exist? False
```

# Managing files

When working with files, you could statically import the `File` type, just as we did for the `Directory` type, but, for the next example, we will not, because it has some of the same methods as the `Directory` type and they would conflict. The `File` type has a short enough name not to matter in this case.

Create a `WorkWithFiles` method, and write statements to do the following:

- Check for the existence of a file
- Create a text file
- Write a line of text to the file
- Copy the file to a backup
- Delete the original file
- Read the backup file's contents

```
static void WorkWithFiles()
{
   // define a custom directory path
   string userFolder = GetFolderPath(SpecialFolder.Personal);

   var customFolder = new string[]
   { userFolder, "Code", "Chapter09", "OutputFiles" };

   string dir = Combine(customFolder);
   CreateDirectory(dir);

   // define file paths
   string textFile = Combine(dir, "Dummy.txt");
   string backupFile = Combine(dir, "Dummy.bak");

   WriteLine($"Working with: {textFile}");
```

```
    // check if a file exists
    WriteLine($"Does it exist? {File.Exists(textFile)}");

    // create a new text file and write a line to it
    StreamWriter textWriter = File.CreateText(textFile);
    textWriter.WriteLine("Hello, C#!");
    textWriter.Close(); // close file and release resources

    WriteLine($"Does it exist? {File.Exists(textFile)}");

    // copy the file, and overwrite if it already exists
    File.Copy(
      sourceFileName: textFile,
      destFileName: backupFile,
      overwrite: true);

    WriteLine($"Does {backupFile} exist? {File.Exists(backupFile)}");

    Write("Confirm the files exist, and then press ENTER: ");
    ReadLine();

    // delete file
    File.Delete(textFile);

    WriteLine($"Does it exist? {File.Exists(textFile)}");

    // read from the text file backup
    WriteLine($"Reading contents of {backupFile}:");
    StreamReader textReader = File.OpenText(backupFile);
    WriteLine(textReader.ReadToEnd());
    textReader.Close();
}
```

In .NET Standard 2.0, you can use either the `Close` or `Dispose` method when you are finished working with `StreamReader` or `StreamWriter`. In .NET Core 1.x, you could only use `Dispose`, because Microsoft had over-simplified the API.

In `Main`, comment out the previous method call, and add a call to `WorkWithFiles`.

Run the console application and view the output:

```
Working with: /Users/markjprice/Code/Chapter09/OutputFiles/Dummy.txt
Does it exist? False
Does it exist? True
Does /Users/markjprice/Code/Chapter09/OutputFiles/Dummy.bak exist? True
Confirm the files exist, and then press ENTER:
Does it exist? False
Reading contents of /Users/markjprice/Code/Chapter09/OutputFiles/Dummy.bak:
Hello, C#!
```

# Managing paths

Sometimes, you need to work with parts of a path, for example, you might want to extract just the folder name, the file name, or the extension. Sometimes, you need to generate temporary folders and file names. You can do this with the `Path` class.

Add the following statements to the end of the `WorkWithFiles` method:

```
WriteLine($"File Name: {GetFileName(textFile)}");
WriteLine($"File Name without Extension:
{GetFileNameWithoutExtension(textFile)}");
WriteLine($"File Extension: {GetExtension(textFile)}");
WriteLine($"Random File Name: {GetRandomFileName()}");
WriteLine($"Temporary File Name: {GetTempFileName()}");
```

Run the console application and view the output:

```
File Name: Dummy.txt
File Name without Extension: Dummy
File Extension: .txt
Random File Name: u45w1zki.co3
Temporary File Name:
/var/folders/tz/xx0y_wld5sx0nv0fjtq4tnpc0000gn/T/tmpyqrepP.
tmp
```

`GetTempFileName` creates a zero-byte file and returns its name, ready for you to use. `GetRandomFileName` just returns a filename; it doesn't create the file.

# Getting file information

To get more information about a file or directory, for example, its size or when it was last accessed, you can create an instance of the `FileInfo` or `DirectoryInfo` class, as shown in the following diagram:

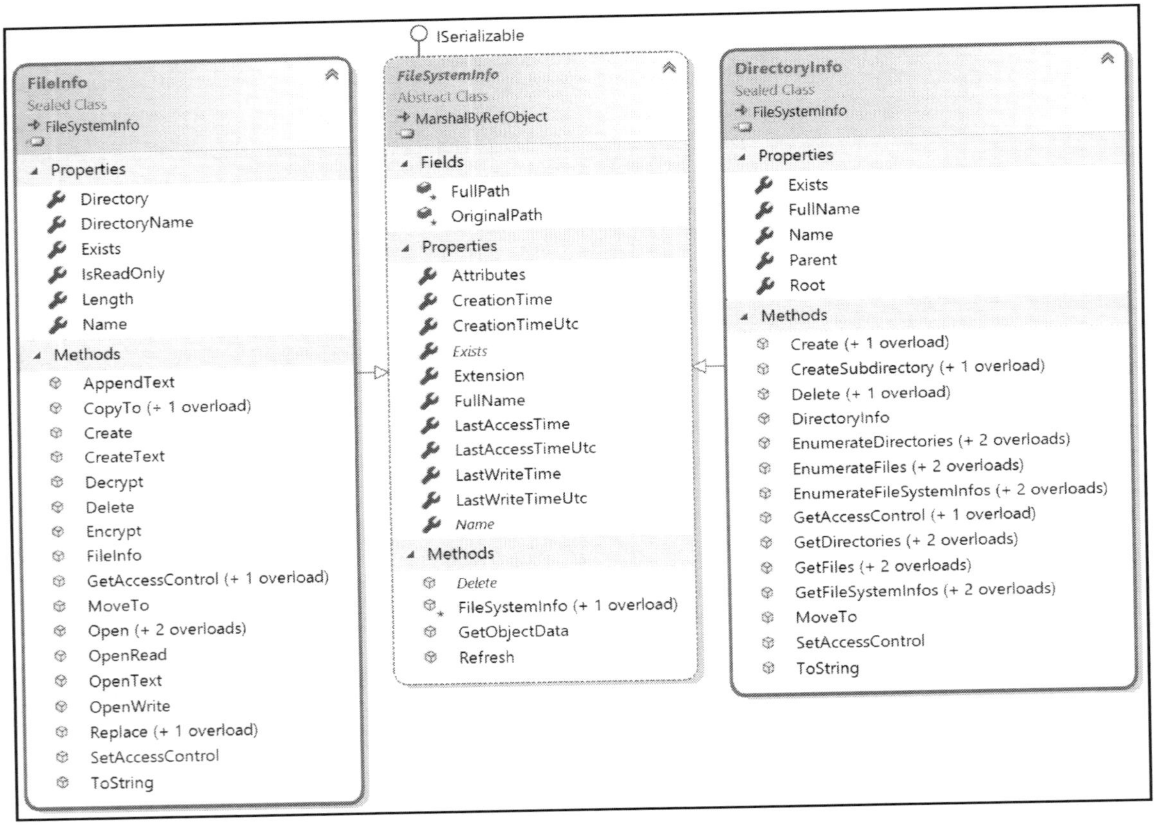

ISerializable

**FileInfo**
Sealed Class
→ FileSystemInfo

Properties
- Directory
- DirectoryName
- Exists
- IsReadOnly
- Length
- Name

Methods
- AppendText
- CopyTo (+ 1 overload)
- Create
- CreateText
- Decrypt
- Delete
- Encrypt
- FileInfo
- GetAccessControl (+ 1 overload)
- MoveTo
- Open (+ 2 overloads)
- OpenRead
- OpenText
- OpenWrite
- Replace (+ 1 overload)
- SetAccessControl
- ToString

***FileSystemInfo***
Abstract Class
→ MarshalByRefObject

Fields
- FullPath
- OriginalPath

Properties
- Attributes
- CreationTime
- CreationTimeUtc
- *Exists*
- Extension
- FullName
- LastAccessTime
- LastAccessTimeUtc
- LastWriteTime
- LastWriteTimeUtc
- *Name*

Methods
- *Delete*
- FileSystemInfo (+ 1 overload)
- GetObjectData
- Refresh

**DirectoryInfo**
Sealed Class
→ FileSystemInfo

Properties
- Exists
- FullName
- Name
- Parent
- Root

Methods
- Create (+ 1 overload)
- CreateSubdirectory (+ 1 overload)
- Delete (+ 1 overload)
- DirectoryInfo
- EnumerateDirectories (+ 2 overloads)
- EnumerateFiles (+ 2 overloads)
- EnumerateFileSystemInfos (+ 2 overloads)
- GetAccessControl (+ 1 overload)
- GetDirectories (+ 2 overloads)
- GetFiles (+ 2 overloads)
- GetFileSystemInfos (+ 2 overloads)
- MoveTo
- SetAccessControl
- ToString

`FileInfo` and `DirectoryInfo` both inherit from `FileSystemInfo`, so they both have members such as `LastAccessTime` and `Delete`.

Add the following statements to the end of the `WorkWithFiles` method:

```
var info = new FileInfo(backupFile);
WriteLine($"{backupFile}:");
WriteLine($" Contains {info.Length} bytes");
WriteLine($" Last accessed {info.LastAccessTime}");
WriteLine($" Has readonly set to {info.IsReadOnly}");
```

Run the console application and view the output:

```
/Users/markjprice/Code/Chapter09/OutputFiles/Dummy.bak:
  Contains 11 bytes
  Last accessed 26/08/2017 09:08:26
  Has readonly set to False
```

# Controlling files

When working with files, you often need to control options. To do this, use the `File.Open` method because it has overloads to specify additional options using the `enum` values as shown in the following diagram:

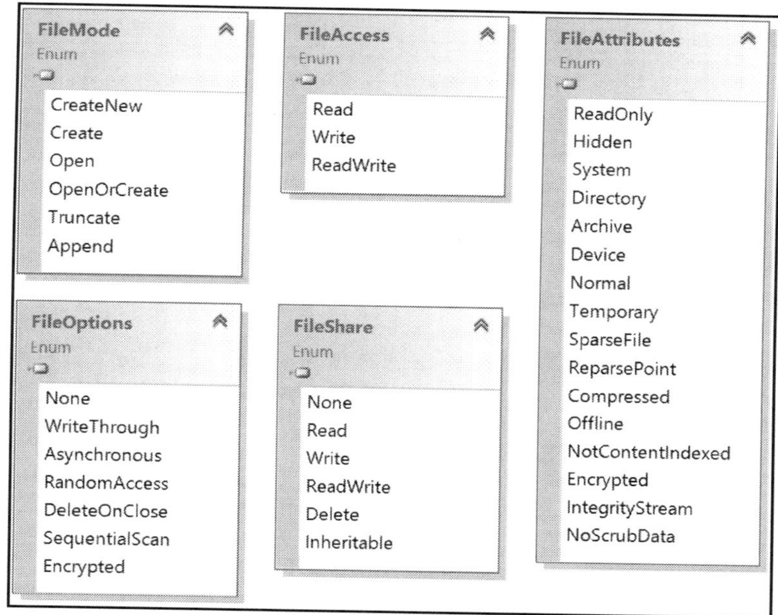

The enum types are as follows:

- FileMode: This controls what you want to do with the file
- FileAccess: This controls what level of access you need
- FileShare: This controls locks on the file to allow other processes the specified level of access
- FileOptions: This is for advanced options
- FileAttributes: This is for a FileSystemInfo-derived type, use this enum type to check its Attributes property

You might want to open a file and read from it, and allow other processes to read it too, as shown in the following code:

```
FileStream file = File.Open(pathToFile, FileMode.Open, FileAccess.Read,
FileShare.Read);
```

You might want to check a file or directory's attributes, as shown in the following code:

```
var info = new FileInfo(backupFile);
WriteLine($"Compressed?
{info.Attributes.HasFlag(FileAttributes.Compressed)}");
```

# Reading and writing with streams

A **stream** is a sequence of bytes that can be read from and written to. Although files can be processed rather like arrays, with random access provided by knowing the position of a byte within the file, it can be useful to process files as a stream in which the bytes can be accessed in sequential order.

Streams can also be used to process terminal input and output and networking resources such as sockets and ports that do not provide random access and cannot seek to a position. So you can write code to process some arbitrary bytes without knowing or caring where it comes from. Your code simply reads or writes to a stream, and another piece of code handles where the bytes are actually stored.

There is an abstract class named `Stream` that represents a stream. There are many classes that inherit from this base class, so they all work the same way, as shown in the following class diagram:

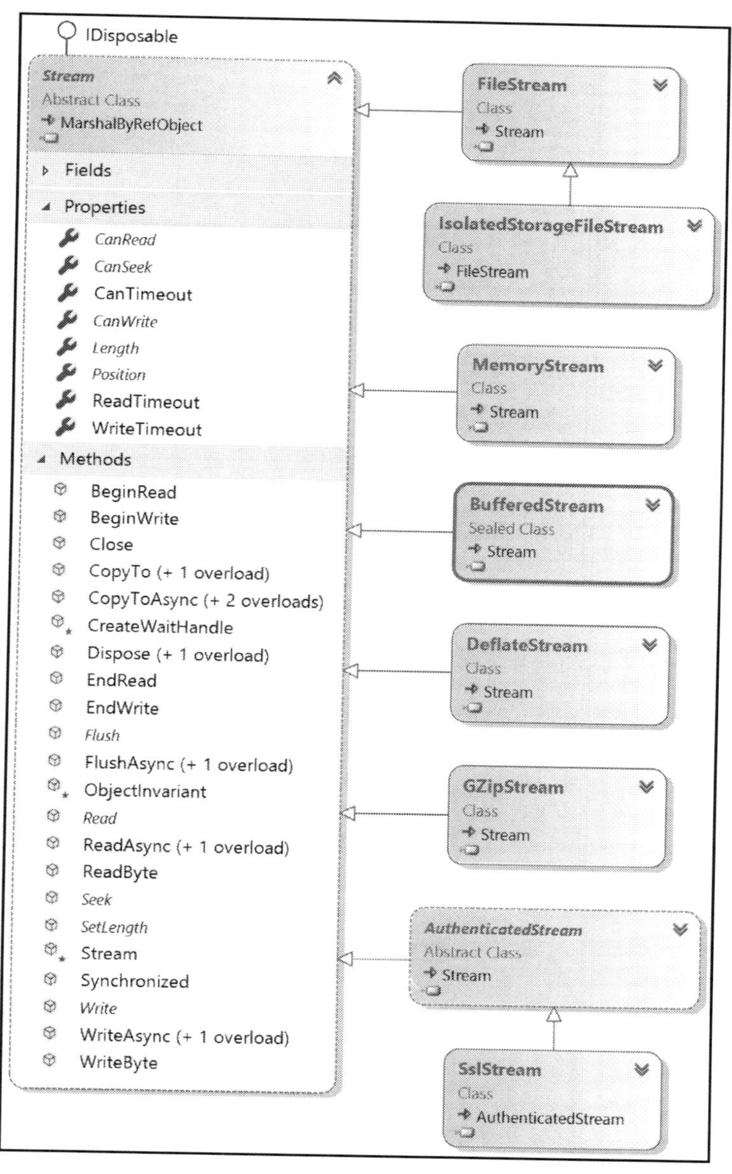

All streams implement `Disposable`, so they have a `Dispose` method to release unmanaged resources.

In the following table are some of the common members of the `Stream` class:

| Member | Description |
|---|---|
| `CanRead`, `CanWrite` | This determines whether you can read from and write to the stream |
| `Length`, `Position` | This determines the total number of bytes and the current position within the stream |
| `Dispose()` | This closes the stream and releases its resources |
| `Flush()` | If the stream has a buffer, then it is cleared and written to the underlying stream |
| `Read()`, `ReadAsync()` | This reads a specified number of bytes from the stream into a byte array and advances the position |
| `ReadByte()` | This reads the next byte from the stream and advances the position |
| `Seek()` | This moves the position to the specified position (if `CanSeek` is true) |
| `Write()`, `WriteAsync()` | This writes the contents of a byte array into the stream |
| `WriteByte()` | This writes a byte to the stream |

**Storage streams** represent a location where the bytes will be stored.

| Namespace | Class | Description |
|---|---|---|
| `System.IO` | `FileStream` | Bytes stored in the filesystem |
| `System.IO` | `MemoryStream` | Bytes stored in memory in the current process |
| `System.Net.Sockets` | `NetworkStream` | Bytes stored at a network location |

**Function streams** can only be "plugged onto" other streams to add functionality.

| Namespace | Class | Description |
|---|---|---|
| `System.Security.Cryptography` | `CryptoStream` | This encrypts and decrypts the stream |
| `System.IO.Compression` | `GZipStream`, `DeflateStream` | This compresses and decompresses the stream |
| `System.Net.Security` | `AuthenticatedStream` | This sends credentials across the stream |

Although there will be occasions where you need to work with streams at a low level, most often, you can plug helper classes into the chain to make things easier, as shown in the following diagram:

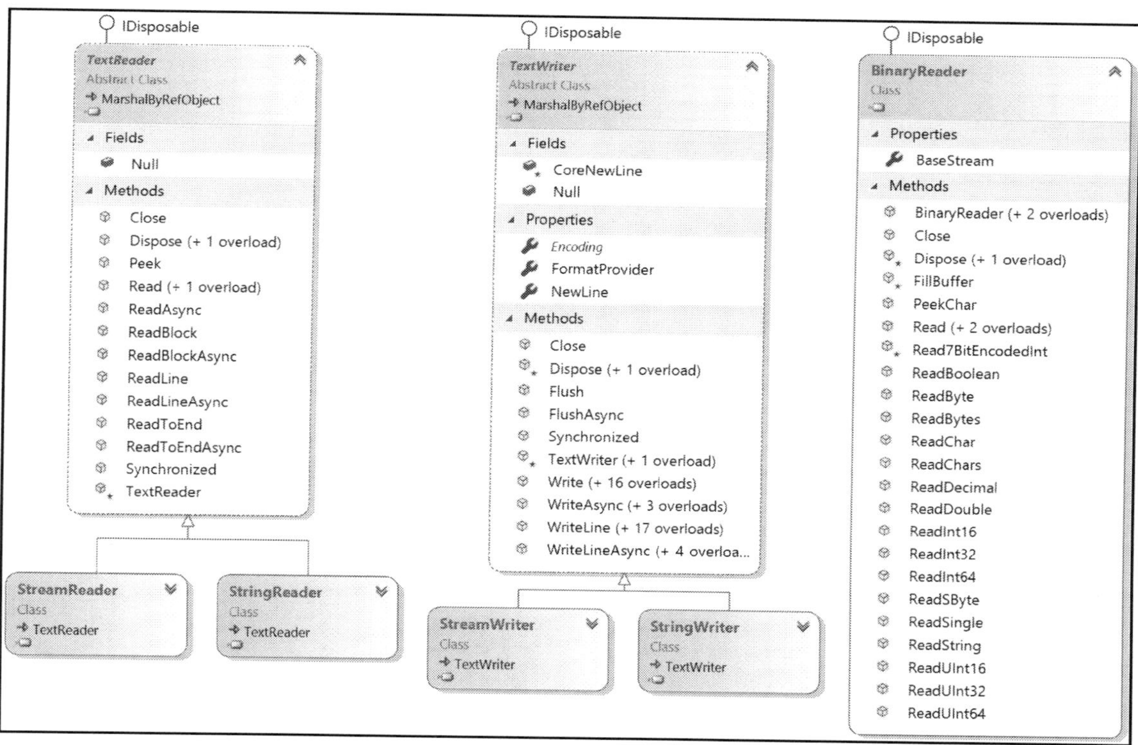

All the helper types for streams implement `IDisposable`, so they have a `Dispose` method to release unmanaged resources.

Here are some helper classes to handle common scenarios:

| Namespace | Class | Description |
|---|---|---|
| `System.IO` | `StreamReader` | This reads from streams as text |
| `System.IO` | `StreamWriter` | This writes to streams as text |
| `System.IO` | `BinaryReader` | This reads from streams as .NET types |
| `System.IO` | `BinaryWriter` | This writes to streams as .NET types |
| `System.Xml` | `XmlReader` | This reads from streams as XML |
| `System.Xml` | `XmlWriter` | This writes to streams as XML |

# Writing to text and XML streams

Add a new console application project named `WorkingWithStreams`.

In Visual Studio 2017, set the solution's start-up project to be the current selection.

## Writing to text streams

Import the `System.IO` and `System.Xml` namespaces, and statically import the `System.Console`, `System.Environment` and `System.IO.Path` types.

Define an array of Viper pilot call signs, and create a `WorkWithText` method that enumerates the call signs, writing each one into a text file, as shown in the following code:

```
// define an array of Viper pilot call signs
static string[] callsigns = new string[] { "Husker", "Starbuck",
"Apollo", "Boomer", "Bulldog", "Athena", "Helo", "Racetrack" };

static void WorkWithText()
{
    // define a file to write to
    string textFile = Combine(CurrentDirectory, "streams.txt");

    // create a text file and return a helper writer
    StreamWriter text = File.CreateText(textFile);
```

```
        // enumerate the strings, writing each one
        // to the stream on a separate line
        foreach (string item in callsigns)
        {
            text.WriteLine(item);
        }
        text.Close(); // release resources

        // output the contents of the file to the Console
        WriteLine($"{textFile} contains
        {new FileInfo(textFile).Length} bytes.");
        WriteLine(File.ReadAllText(textFile));
    }
```

In `Main`, call the `WorkWithText` method, as shown in the following code:

```
    static void Main(string[] args)
    {
        WorkWithText();
    }
```

Run the console application and view the output:

```
/Users/markjprice/Code/Chapter09/WorkingWithStreams/streams.txt contains 60
bytes.
Husker
Starbuck
Apollo
Boomer
Bulldog
Athena
Helo
Racetrack
```

Open the file that was created and check that it contains the list of call signs.

# Writing to XML streams

Create a `WorkWithXml` method that enumerates the call signs, writing each one into an XML file, as shown in the following code:

```
static void WorkWithXml()
{
   // define a file to write to
   string xmlFile = Combine(CurrentDirectory, "streams.xml");

   // create a file streams
   FileStream xmlFileStream = File.Create(xmlFile);

   // wrap the file stream in an XML writer helper
   // and automatically indent nested elements
   XmlWriter xml = XmlWriter.Create(xmlFileStream,
   new XmlWriterSettings { Indent = true });

   // write the XML declaration
   xml.WriteStartDocument();

   // write a root element
   xml.WriteStartElement("callsigns");

   // enumerate the strings writing each one to the stream
   foreach (string item in callsigns)
   {
      xml.WriteElementString("callsign", item);
   }

   // write the close root element
   xml.WriteEndElement();

   // close helper and stream
   xml.Close();
   xmlFileStream.Close();

   // output all the contents of the file to the Console
   WriteLine($"{xmlFile} contains {new FileInfo(xmlFile).Length} bytes.");
   WriteLine(File.ReadAllText(xmlFile));
}
```

In `Main`, comment the previous method call, and add a call to the `WorkWithXml` method.

Run the console application and view the output:

```
/Users/markjprice/Code/Chapter09/WorkingWithStreams/streams.xml contains
310 bytes.
<?xml version="1.0" encoding="utf-8"?>
<callsigns>
  <callsign>Husker</callsign>
  <callsign>Starbuck</callsign>
  <callsign>Apollo</callsign>
  <callsign>Boomer</callsign>
  <callsign>Bulldog</callsign>
  <callsign>Athena</callsign>
  <callsign>Helo</callsign>
  <callsign>Racetrack</callsign>
</callsigns>
```

# Disposing of file resources

When you open a file to read or write to it, you are using resources outside of .NET. These are called unmanaged resources and must be disposed of when you are done working with them. To guarantee that they are disposed of, we can call the `Dispose` method inside of a `finally` block.

## Implementing disposal with try statement

Modify the `WorkWithXml` method, as shown highlighted in the following code:

```
static void WorkWithXml()
{
    FileStream xmlFileStream = null;
    XmlWriter xml = null;
    try
    {
        // define a file to write to
        string xmlFile = Combine(CurrentDirectory, "streams.xml");

        // create a file stream
        xmlFileStream = File.Create(xmlFile);

        // wrap the file stream in an XML writer helper
        // and automatically indent nested elements
        xml = XmlWriter.Create(xmlFileStream,
        new XmlWriterSettings { Indent = true });
```

```
        // write the XML declaration
        xml.WriteStartDocument();

        // write a root element
        xml.WriteStartElement("callsigns");

        // enumerate the strings writing each one to the stream
        foreach (string item in callsigns)
        {
            xml.WriteElementString("callsign", item);
        }

        // write the close root element
        xml.WriteEndElement();

        // close helper and stream
        xml.Close();
        xmlFileStream.Close();

        // output all the contents of the file to the Console
        WriteLine($"{xmlFile} contains
        {new FileInfo(xmlFile).Length} bytes.");
        WriteLine(File.ReadAllText(xmlFile));
    }
    catch(Exception ex)
    {
        // if the path doesn't exist the exception will be caught
        WriteLine($"{ex.GetType()} says {ex.Message}");
    }
    finally
    {
        if (xml != null)
        {
            xml.Dispose();
            WriteLine("The XML writer's unmanaged
            resources have been disposed.");
        }
        if (xmlFileStream != null)
        {
            xmlFileStream.Dispose();
            WriteLine("The file stream's unmanaged
            resources have been disposed.");
        }
    }
}
```

Run the console application and view the extra output:

```
The XML writer's unmanaged resources have been disposed.
The file stream's unmanaged resources have been disposed.
```

**Good Practice**
Before calling `Dispose`, check that the object is not `null`.

## Simplifying disposal with the using statement

If you don't need to catch any exceptions, then you can simplify the code that needs to check for a non-null object and then call its `Dispose` method by using the `using` statement.

Confusingly, there are two uses for the `using` statement: importing a namespace, and generating a `finally` statement that disposes of an object.

The compiler changes your code into a full `try` and `finally` statement, but without a `catch` statement. You can use nested `try` statements; so, if you do want to catch any exceptions, you can, as shown in the following code example:

```
using (FileStream file2 = File.OpenWrite(Path.Combine(path, "file2.txt")))
{
   using (StreamWriter writer2 = new StreamWriter(file2))
   {
      try
      {
         writer2.WriteLine("Welcome, .NET Core!");
      }
      catch(Exception ex)
      {
         WriteLine($"{ex.GetType()} says {ex.Message}");
      }
   } // automatically calls Dispose if the object is not null
} // automatically calls Dispose if the object is not null
```

Many types, including `FileStream` and `StreamWriter` mentioned earlier, provide a `Close` method as well as a `Dispose` method. In .NET Standard 2.0, you can use either because they do the same thing, by literally calling each other. In .NET Core 1.1, Microsoft had over-simplified the API, so you had to use `Dispose`.

# Compressing streams

XML is relatively verbose, so it takes up more space in bytes than plain text. We can squeeze the XML using a common compression algorithm known as **GZIP**.

Import the following namespace:

```
using System.IO.Compression;
```

Add a `WorkWithCompression` method, as shown in the following code:

```
static void WorkWithCompression()
{
   // compress the XML output
   string gzipFilePath = Combine(CurrentDirectory, "streams.gzip");

   FileStream gzipFile = File.Create(gzipFilePath);
   using (GZipStream compressor =
   new GZipStream(gzipFile, CompressionMode.Compress))
   {
      using (XmlWriter xmlGzip = XmlWriter.Create(compressor))
      {
         xmlGzip.WriteStartDocument();
         xmlGzip.WriteStartElement("callsigns");
         foreach (string item in callsigns)
         {
            xmlGzip.WriteElementString("callsign", item);
         }
      }
   } // also closes the underlying stream

   // output all the contents of the compressed file to the Console
   WriteLine($"{gzipFilePath} contains
   {new FileInfo(gzipFilePath).Length} bytes.");
   WriteLine(File.ReadAllText(gzipFilePath));

   // read a compressed file
   WriteLine("Reading the compressed XML file:");
   gzipFile = File.Open(gzipFilePath, FileMode.Open);
```

```
        using (GZipStream decompressor = new GZipStream(gzipFile,
        CompressionMode.Decompress))
        {
            using (XmlReader reader = XmlReader.Create(decompressor))
            {
                while (reader.Read())
                {
                    // check if we are currently on an element node named callsign
                    if ((reader.NodeType == XmlNodeType.Element) && (reader.Name ==
                    "callsign"))
                    {
                        reader.Read(); // move to the Text node inside the element
                        WriteLine($"{reader.Value}"); // read its value
                    }
                }
            }
        }
    }
```

In `Main`, leave the call to `WorkWithXml`, and add a call to `WorkWithCompression`, as shown in the following code:

```
    static void Main(string[] args)
    {
        // WorkWithText();
        WorkWithXml();
        WorkWithCompression();
    }
```

Run the console application and compare the sizes of the XML file and the compressed XML file. It is less than half the size of the same XML without compression, as shown in the following edited output:

```
/Users/markjprice/Code/Chapter09/WorkingWithStreams/streams.xml contains
310 bytes.
/Users/markjprice/Code/Chapter09/WorkingWithStreams/streams.gzip contains
150 bytes.
```

# Encoding text

Text characters can be represented in different ways. For example, the alphabet can be encoded using Morse code into a series of dots and dashes for transmission over a telegraph line.

In a similar way, text inside a computer is stored as bits (ones and zeros). .NET uses a standard called **Unicode** to encode text internally. Sometimes, you will need to move text outside .NET for use by systems that do not use Unicode or use a variation of Unicode.

The following table lists some alternative text encodings commonly used by computers:

| Encoding | Description |
|---|---|
| ASCII | This encodes a limited range of characters using the lower seven bits of a byte |
| UTF-8 | This represents each Unicode code point as a sequence of one to four bytes |
| UTF-16 | This represents each Unicode code point as a sequence of one or two 16-bit integers |
| ANSI/ISO encodings | This provides support for a variety of code pages that are used to support a specific language or group of languages |

# Encoding strings as byte arrays

Add a new console application project named `WorkingWithEncodings`.

Import the `System.Text` namespace, statically import `Console`, and add the following statements to the `Main` method. The code encodes a string using the chosen encoding, loops through each byte, and then decodes back into a string and outputs it:

```
WriteLine("Encodings");
WriteLine("[1] ASCII");
WriteLine("[2] UTF-7");
WriteLine("[3] UTF-8");
WriteLine("[4] UTF-16 (Unicode)");
WriteLine("[5] UTF-32");
WriteLine("[any other key] Default");

// choose an encoding
Write("Press a number to choose an encoding: ");
ConsoleKey number = ReadKey(false).Key;
WriteLine();
WriteLine();

Encoding encoder;
switch (number)
{
   case ConsoleKey.D1:
```

```
      encoder = Encoding.ASCII;
      break;
    case ConsoleKey.D2:
      encoder = Encoding.UTF7;
      break;
    case ConsoleKey.D3:
      encoder = Encoding.UTF8;
      break;
    case ConsoleKey.D4:
      encoder = Encoding.Unicode;
      break;
    case ConsoleKey.D5:
      encoder = Encoding.UTF32;
      break;
    default:
      encoder = Encoding.Default;
      break;
}

// define a string to encode
string message = "A pint of milk is £1.99";

// encode the string into a byte array
byte[] encoded = encoder.GetBytes(message);

// check how many bytes the encoding needed
WriteLine($"{encoder.GetType().Name} uses {encoded.Length}
bytes.");

// enumerate each byte
WriteLine($"Byte  Hex  Char");
foreach (byte b in encoded)
{
   WriteLine($"{b,4} {b.ToString("X"),4} {(char)b,5}");
}

// decode the byte array back into a string and display it
string decoded = encoder.GetString(encoded);
WriteLine(decoded);
```

.NET Core 1.0 and 1.1 did not support `Encoding.Default`, so you had to use `GetEncoding(0)` instead.

Run the application and press 1 to choose ASCII. Notice that when outputting the bytes, the pound sign (£) cannot be represented in ASCII, so it uses a question mark (?) instead:

```
Encodings
[1] ASCII
[2] UTF-7
[3] UTF-8
[4] UTF-16 (Unicode)
[5] UTF-32
[any other key] Default
Press a number to choose an encoding: 1
ASCIIEncoding uses 23 bytes.
Byte  Hex  Char
  65   41     A
  32   20
 112   70     p
 105   69     i
 110   6E     n
 116   74     t
 32   20
 111   6F     o
 102   66     f
  32   20
 109   6D     m
 105   69     i
 108   6C     l
 107   6B     k
  32   20
 105   69     i
 115   73     s
  32   20
  63   3F     ?
  49   31     1
  46   2E     .
  57   39     9
  57   39     9
A pint of milk is ?1.99
```

Rerun the application and press 3 to choose UTF-8. Notice that, UTF-8 requires one extra byte (24 bytes instead of 23 bytes), but it can store the £ sign:

```
UTF8Encoding uses 24 bytes.
Byte  Hex  Char
  65   41     A
  32   20
 112   70     p
 105   69     i
 110   6E     n
```

```
116    74     t
 32    20
111    6F     o
102    66     f
 32    20
109    6D     m
105    69     i
108    6C     l
107    6B     k
 32    20
105    69     i
115    73     s
 32    20
194    C2     Â
163    A3     £
 49    31     1
 46    2E     .
 57    39     9
 57    39     9
A pint of milk is £1.99
```

Rerun the application and press `4` to choose Unicode (UTF-16). Notice that UTF-16 requires two bytes for every character, and it can store the £ sign:

```
UnicodeEncoding uses 46 bytes.
```

# Encoding and decoding text in files

When using stream helper classes, such as `StreamReader` and `StreamWriter`, you can specify the encoding you want to use. As you write to the helper, the strings will automatically be encoded, and as you read from the helper, the bytes will be automatically decoded.

This is how you can specify the encoding, as shown in the following code:

```
var reader = new StreamReader(stream, Encoding.UTF7);
var writer = new StreamWriter(stream, Encoding.UTF7);
```

**Good Practice**
Often, you won't have the choice of which encoding to use, because you will be generating a file for use by another system. However, if you do, pick one that uses the least number of bytes, but can store every character you need.

# Serializing object graphs

**Serialization** is the process of converting a live object into a sequence of bytes using a specified format. **Deserialization** is the reverse process.

There are dozens of formats you can choose, but the two most common ones are **eXtensible Markup Language** (**XML**) and **JavaScript Object Notation** (**JSON**).

**Good Practice**
JSON is more compact and is best for web and mobile applications. XML is more verbose, but is better supported in older systems.

.NET Standard has multiple classes that will serialize to and from XML and JSON. We will start by looking at `XmlSerializer` and `JsonSerializer`.

## Serializing with XML

Add a new console application project named `WorkingWithSerialization`.

To show a common example, we will define a custom class to store information about a person and then create an object graph using a list of `Person` instances with nesting.

Add a class named `Person` with the following definition. Notice that the `Salary` property is protected, meaning it is only accessible to itself and derived classes. To populate the salary, the class has a constructor with a single parameter to set the initial salary:

```
using System;
using System.Collections.Generic;

namespace Packt.CS7
{
   public class Person
   {
      public Person(decimal initialSalary)
      {
```

```
            Salary = initialSalary;
        }
        public string FirstName { get; set; }
        public string LastName { get; set; }
        public DateTime DateOfBirth { get; set; }
        public HashSet<Person> Children { get; set; }
        protected decimal Salary { get; set; }
    }
}
```

Back in Program.cs, import the following namespaces:

```
using System;                          // DateTime
using System.Collections.Generic; // List<T>, HashSet<T>
using System.Xml.Serialization;     // XmlSerializer
using System.IO;                       // FileStream
using Packt.CS7;                       // Person
using static System.Console;
using static System.Environment;
using static System.IO.Path;
```

Add the following statements to the Main method:

```
// create an object graph
var people = new List<Person>
{
   new Person(30000M) { FirstName = "Alice", LastName = "Smith",
   DateOfBirth = new DateTime(1974, 3, 14) },
   new Person(40000M) { FirstName = "Bob", LastName = "Jones",
   DateOfBirth = new DateTime(1969, 11, 23) },
   new Person(20000M) { FirstName = "Charlie", LastName = "Rose",
   DateOfBirth = new DateTime(1964, 5, 4),
   Children = new HashSet<Person>
   { new Person(0M) { FirstName = "Sally", LastName = "Rose",
     DateOfBirth = new DateTime(1990, 7, 12) } } }
};

// create a file to write to
string path = Combine(CurrentDirectory, "people.xml");

FileStream stream = File.Create(path);

// create an object that will format as List of Persons as XML
var xs = new XmlSerializer(typeof(List<Person>));

// serialize the object graph to the stream
xs.Serialize(stream, people);
```

```
// you must close the stream to release the file lock
stream.Close();

WriteLine($"Written {new FileInfo(path).Length} bytes of XML to
{path}");
WriteLine();

// Display the serialized object graph
WriteLine(File.ReadAllText(path));
```

Run the console application, view the output, and note that an exception is thrown:

```
Unhandled Exception: System.InvalidOperationException:
Packt.CS7.Person cannot be serialized because it does not
have a parameterless constructor.
```

Back in the `Person.cs` file, add the following statement to define a parameter-less constructor. Note that the constructor does not need to do anything, but it must exist so that the `XmlSerializer` can call it to instantiate new `Person` instances during the deserialization process:

```
public Person() { }
```

Rerun the console application and view the output.

Note that the object graph is serialized as XML and the `Salary` property is not included:

```
Written 754 bytes of XML to
/Users/markjprice/Code/Chapter09/WorkingWithSerialization/people.xml
<?xml version="1.0"?>
<ArrayOfPerson xmlns:xsi="http://www.w3.org/2001/XMLSchema-instance"
  xmlns:xsd="http://www.w3.org/2001/XMLSchema">
  <Person>
    <FirstName>Alice</FirstName>
    <LastName>Smith</LastName>
    <DateOfBirth>1974-03-14T00:00:00</DateOfBirth>
  </Person>
  <Person>
    <FirstName>Bob</FirstName>
    <LastName>Jones</LastName>
    <DateOfBirth>1969-11-23T00:00:00</DateOfBirth>
  </Person>
  <Person>
    <FirstName>Charlie</FirstName>
    <LastName>Rose</LastName>
    <DateOfBirth>1964-05-04T00:00:00</DateOfBirth>
    <Children>
      <Person>
```

```
            <FirstName>Sally</FirstName>
            <LastName>Rose</LastName>
            <DateOfBirth>1990-07-12T00:00:00</DateOfBirth>
          </Person>
        </Children>
      </Person>
    </ArrayOfPerson>
```

We could make the XML more efficient using attributes instead of elements for some fields.

In the `Person.cs` file, import the `System.Xml.Serialization` namespace and decorate all the properties, except `Children`, with the `[XmlAttribute]` attribute, setting a short name, as shown in the following code:

```
[XmlAttribute("fname")]
public string FirstName { get; set; }
[XmlAttribute("lname")]
public string LastName { get; set; }
[XmlAttribute("dob")]
public DateTime DateOfBirth { get; set; }
```

Rerun the application and notice that the XML is now more efficient:

```
Written 464 bytes of XML to C:\Code\Ch10_People.xml
<?xml version="1.0"?>
  <ArrayOfPerson xmlns:xsi="http://www.w3.org/2001/XMLSchema-instance"
    xmlns:xsd="http://www.w3.org/2001/XMLSchema">
    <Person fname="Alice" lname="Smith" dob="1974-03-14T00:00:00" />
    <Person fname="Bob" lname="Jones" dob="1969-11-23T00:00:00" />
    <Person fname="Charlie" lname="Rose" dob="1964-05-04T00:00:00">
     <Children>
        <Person fname="Sally" lname="Rose" dob="1990-07-12T00:00:00" />
     </Children>
    </Person>
  </ArrayOfPerson>
```

The size of the file has been reduced from 754 to 464 bytes, a space saving of 38%.

# Deserializing with XML

Add the following statements to the end of the `Main` method:

```
FileStream xmlLoad = File.Open(path, FileMode.Open);
// deserialize and cast the object graph into a List of Person
var loadedPeople = (List<Person>)xs.Deserialize(xmlLoad);

foreach (var item in loadedPeople)
{
   WriteLine($"{item.LastName} has {item.Children.Count}
   children.");
}
xmlLoad.Close();
```

Rerun the application and notice that the people are loaded successfully from the XML file:

```
Smith has 0 children.
Jones has 0 children.
Rose has 1 children.
```

# Customizing the XML

There are many other attributes that can be used to control the XML generated. Refer to the references at the end of this chapter for more information.

**Good Practice**
When using `XmlSerializer`, remember that only the `public` fields and properties are included, and the type must have a parameter-less constructor. You can customize the output with attributes.

# Serializing with JSON

The best library for working with JSON serialization format is **Newtonsoft.Json**.

In Visual Studio 2017, in **Solution Explorer**, in the **WorkingWithSerialization** project, right-click on **Dependencies** and choose **Manage NuGet Packages....** Search for `Newtonsoft.Json`, select the found item, and then click on **Install**.

In Visual Studio Code, edit the `WorkingWithSerialization.csproj` file to add a package reference for the latest version of `Newtonsoft.Json`, as shown in the following markup:

```
<Project Sdk="Microsoft.NET.Sdk">

  <PropertyGroup>
    <OutputType>Exe</OutputType>
    <TargetFramework>netcoreapp2.0</TargetFramework>
  </PropertyGroup>

  <ItemGroup>
    <PackageReference Include="Newtonsoft.Json" Version="10.0.3" />
  </ItemGroup>

</Project>
```

**Good Practice**
Search for NuGet packages on Microsoft's NuGet feed to discover the latest supported version, as shown at the following link: `https://www.nuget.org/packages/Newtonsoft.Json/`

Import the following namespace at the top of the `Program.cs` file:

```
using Newtonsoft.Json;
```

Add the following statements to the end of the `Main` method:

```
// create a file to write to
string jsonPath = Combine(CurrentDirectory, "people.json");

StreamWriter jsonStream = File.CreateText(jsonPath);

// create an object that will format as JSON
var jss = new JsonSerializer();

// serialize the object graph into a string
jss.Serialize(jsonStream, people);
jsonStream.Close(); // release the file lock

WriteLine();
WriteLine($"Written {new FileInfo(jsonPath).Length} bytes of
JSON to: {jsonPath}");

// Display the serialized object graph
WriteLine(File.ReadAllText(jsonPath));
```

Rerun the application and notice that JSON requires less than half the number of bytes compared to XML with elements. It's even smaller than the XML file which uses attributes, as shown in the following output:

```
Written 368 bytes of JSON to:
/Users/markjprice/Code/Chapter09/WorkingWithSerialization/people.json
[{"FirstName":"Alice","LastName":"Smith","DateOfBirth":"\/Date(132451200000
)\/","Children":null},{"FirstName":"Bob","LastName":"Jones","DateOfBirth":"
\/Date(-3369600000)\/","Children":null},{"FirstName":"Charlie","LastName":"
Rose","DateOfBirth":"\/Date(-1786788000000)\/","Children":[{"FirstName":"Sal
ly","LastName":"Rose","DateOfBirth":"\/Date(647737200000)\/","Children":nul
l}]}]
```

**Good Practice**
Use JSON to minimize the size of serialized object graphs. JSON is also a good choice when sending object graphs to web applications and mobile applications because JSON is the native serialization format for JavaScript.

## Serializing with other formats

There are many other formats available as NuGet packages that you can use for serialization. A commonly used pair are: `DataContractSerializer` (for XML) and `DataContractJsonSerializer` (for JSON), which are both in the `System.Runtime.Serialization` namespace.

# Practicing and exploring

Test your knowledge and understanding by answering some questions, get some hands-on practice, and explore this chapter's topics with deeper research.

## Exercise 9.1 – Test your knowledge

Answer the following questions:

1. What is the difference between using the `File` class and the `FileInfo` class?
2. What is the difference between the `ReadByte` method and the `Read` method of a stream?

3. When would you use the `StringReader`, `TextReader`, and `StreamReader` classes?
4. What does the `DeflateStream` type do?
5. How many bytes per character does the UTF-8 encoding use?
6. What is an object graph?
7. What is the best serialization format to choose for minimizing space requirements?
8. What is the best serialization format to choose for cross-platform compatibility?
9. What library is best for working with the JSON serialization format?
10. How many packages are available for serialization on NuGet.org?

# Exercise 9.2 – Practice serializing as XML

Create a console application named `Exercise02` that creates a list of shapes, uses serialization to save it to the filesystem using XML, and then deserializes it back:

```
// create a list of Shapes to serialize
var listOfShapes = new List<Shape>
{
   new Circle { Colour = "Red", Radius = 2.5 },
   new Rectangle { Colour = "Blue", Height = 20.0, Width = 10.0 },
   new Circle { Colour = "Green", Radius = 8 },
   new Circle { Colour = "Purple", Radius = 12.3 },
   new Rectangle { Colour = "Blue", Height = 45.0, Width = 18.0  }
};
```

Shapes should have a read-only property named `Area` so that when you deserialize, you can output a list of shapes, including their areas, as shown here:

```
List<Shape> loadedShapesXml = serializerXml.Deserialize(fileXml)
as List<Shape>;
foreach (Shape item in loadedShapesXml)
{
   WriteLine($"{item.GetType().Name} is {item.Colour} and has an
   area of {item.Area}");
}
```

This is what your output should look like when you run the application:

```
Loading shapes from XML:
Circle is Red and has an area of 19.6349540849362
Rectangle is Blue and has an area of 200
Circle is Green and has an area of 201.061929829747
Circle is Purple and has an area of 475.2915525616
Rectangle is Blue and has an area of 810
```

# Exercise 9.3 – Explore topics

Use the following links to read more on this chapter's topics:

- **File System and the Registry (C# Programming Guide)**: `https://docs.microsoft.com/en-us/dotnet/articles/csharp/programming-guide/file-system/`
- **Character encoding in .NET**: `https://docs.microsoft.com/en-us/dotnet/articles/standard/base-types/character-encoding`
- **Serialization (C#)**: `https://docs.microsoft.com/en-us/dotnet/articles/csharp/programming-guide/concepts/serialization/`
- **Serializing to Files, TextWriters, and XmlWriters**: `https://docs.microsoft.com/en-us/dotnet/articles/csharp/programming-guide/concepts/linq/serializing-to-files-textwriters-and-xmlwriters`
- **Newtonsoft Json.NET**: `http://www.newtonsoft.com/json`

# Summary

In this chapter, you learned how to read from and write to text files and XML files, how to compress and decompress files, how to encode and decode text, and how to serialize an object into JSON and XML (and deserialize it back again).

In the next chapter, you will learn how to protect data and files.

# 10
# Protecting Your Data and Applications

This chapter is about protecting your data from being viewed by malicious users using encryption, and from being manipulated or corrupted using hashing and signing.

This chapter covers the following topics:

- Understanding the vocabulary of protection
- Encrypting and decrypting data
- Hashing data
- Signing data
- Generating random numbers
- Authenticating and authorizing users

## Understanding the vocabulary of protection

There are many techniques to protect your data; some of them are as follows:

- **Encryption and decryption**: This is a two-way process to convert your data from clear-text into crypto-text and back again
- **Hashes**: This is a one-way process to generate a hash value to securely store passwords or that can be used to detect malicious changes or corruption of your data

- **Signatures**: This technique is used to ensure that data has come from someone you trust by validating a signature that has been applied to some data against someone's public key
- **Authentication**: This technique is used to identify someone by checking their credentials
- **Authorization**: This technique is used to ensure that someone has permission to perform an action or work with some data by checking the roles or groups they belong to

**Good Practice**
If security is important to you (and it should be!), then hire an experienced security expert for guidance rather than relying on advice found online. It is very easy to make small mistakes and leave your applications and data vulnerable without realizing until it is too late!

# Keys and key sizes

Protection algorithms often use a **key**. Keys can be **symmetric** (also known as shared or secret because the same key is used to encrypt and decrypt) or **asymmetric** (a public-private key pair where the public key is used to encrypt and only the private key can be used to decrypt).

**Good Practice**
Symmetric key encryption algorithms are fast and can encrypt large amounts of data using a stream. Asymmetric key encryption algorithms are slow and can only encrypt small byte arrays. In the real world, use the best of both worlds using symmetric key to encrypt your data, and asymmetric key to share the symmetric key. For example, this is how **Secure Sockets Layer** (**SSL**) encryption on the internet works.

Keys are represented by byte arrays of varying sizes.

**Good Practice**
Choose a bigger key size for stronger protection.

# IVs and block sizes

When encrypting large amounts of data, there are likely to be repeating sequences. For example, in an English document, in the sequence of characters, `the` would appear frequently and each time it might get encrypted as `hQ2`. A good cracker would use this knowledge to make it easier to crack the encryption, as shown in the following output:

```
When the wind blew hard the umbrella broke.
5:s4&hQ2aj#D f9d1d£8fh"&hQ2s0)an DF8SFd#][1
```

We can avoid repeating sequences by dividing data into **blocks**. After encrypting a block, a byte array value is generated from that block and this value is fed into the next block to adjust the algorithm so that `the` isn't encrypted in the same way. To encrypt the first block, we need a byte array to feed in. This is called the **initialization vector (IV)**.

**Good Practice**
Choose a small block size for stronger encryption.

# Salts

A **salt** is a random byte array that is used as an additional input to a one-way hash function. If you do not use a salt when generating hashes, then when many of your users register with `123456` as their password (about 8% of users still did this in 2016!), they all have the same hashed value, and their account will be vulnerable to a dictionary attack.

Dictionary Attacks 101:
`https://blog.codinghorror.com/dictionary-attacks-101/`

When a user registers, a salt should be randomly generated and concatenated with their chosen password before being hashed. The output (but not the original password) is stored with the salt in the database.

When the user next logs in and enters their password, you look up their salt, concatenate it with the entered password, regenerate a hash, and then compare its value with the hash stored in the database. If they are the same, you know they entered the correct password.

# Generating keys and IVs

Keys and IVs are byte arrays. Both of the two parties that want to exchange encrypted data need the key and IV values, but byte arrays can be difficult to exchange reliably.

You can reliably generate a key or IV using a **password-based key derivation function (PBKDF2)**. A good one is the `Rfc2898DeriveBytes` class, which takes a password, a salt, and an iteration count, and then generates keys and IVs by making calls to its `GetBytes` method.

`Rfc2898DeriveBytes` and its sister class both inherit from `DeriveBytes`, as shown in the following diagram:

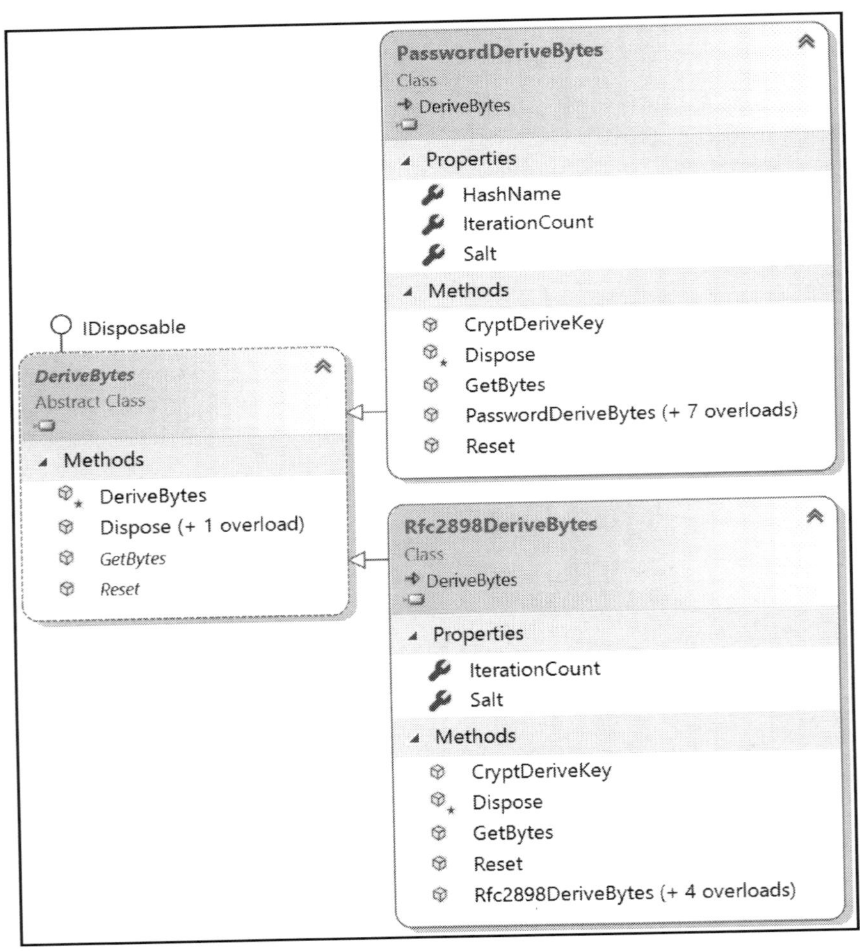

**Good Practice**
The salt size should be 8 bytes or larger and the iteration count should be greater than zero. The minimum recommended number of iterations is 1,000.

# Encrypting and decrypting data

In .NET Core, there are multiple encryption algorithms you can choose from. Some algorithms are implemented by the operating system and their names are suffixed with `CryptoServiceProvider`. Some algorithms are implemented in .NET Core and their names are suffixed with `Managed`. Some algorithms use symmetric keys, and some use asymmetric keys.

The most common symmetric encryption algorithms are shown in the following diagram:

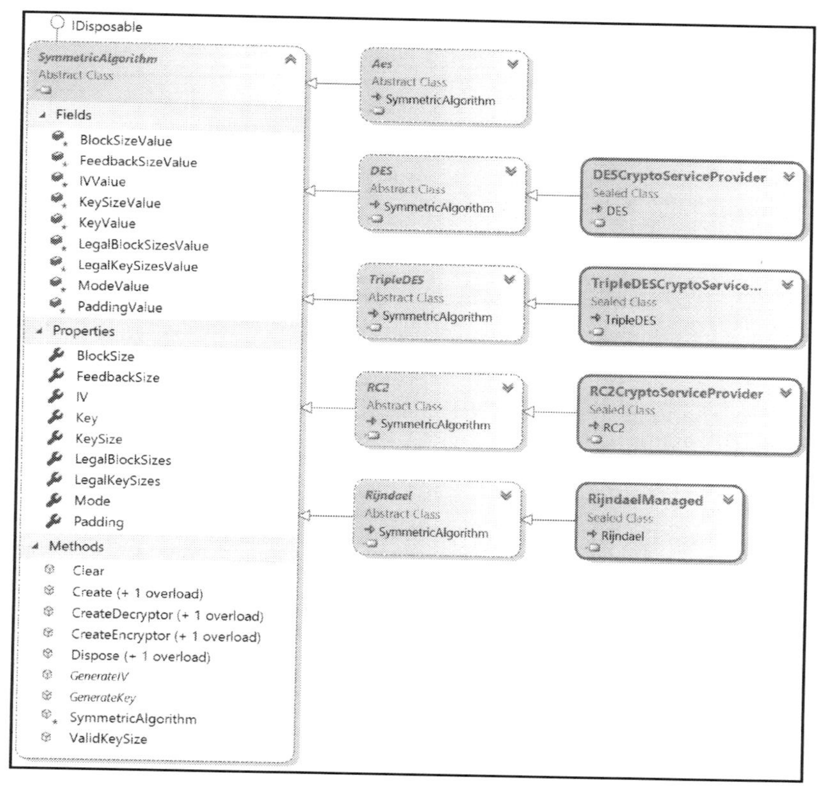

The most common asymmetric encryption algorithm is shown in the following diagram:

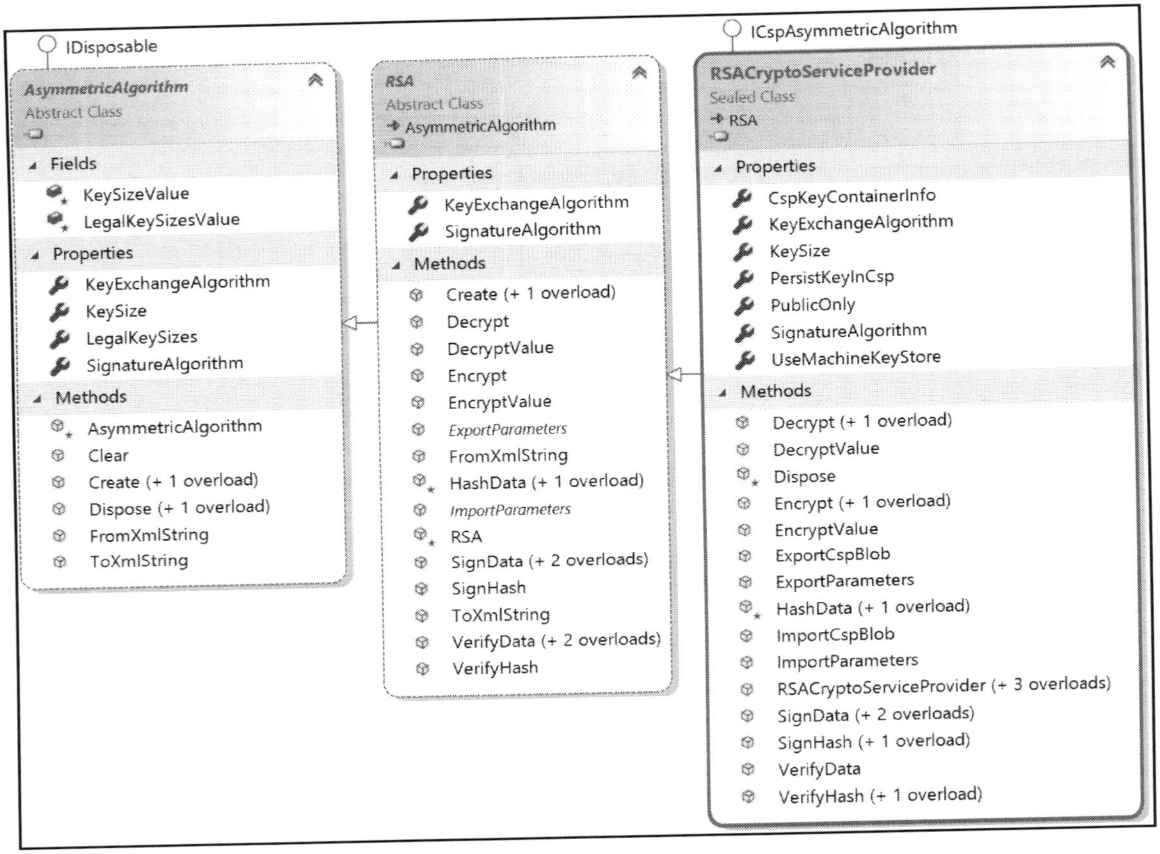

IDisposable

*AsymmetricAlgorithm*
Abstract Class

Fields
KeySizeValue
LegalKeySizesValue

Properties
KeyExchangeAlgorithm
KeySize
LegalKeySizes
SignatureAlgorithm

Methods
AsymmetricAlgorithm
Clear
Create (+ 1 overload)
Dispose (+ 1 overload)
FromXmlString
ToXmlString

*RSA*
Abstract Class
→ AsymmetricAlgorithm

Properties
KeyExchangeAlgorithm
SignatureAlgorithm

Methods
Create (+ 1 overload)
Decrypt
DecryptValue
Encrypt
EncryptValue
*ExportParameters*
FromXmlString
HashData (+ 1 overload)
*ImportParameters*
RSA
SignData (+ 2 overloads)
SignHash
ToXmlString
VerifyData (+ 2 overloads)
VerifyHash

ICspAsymmetricAlgorithm

**RSACryptoServiceProvider**
Sealed Class
→ RSA

Properties
CspKeyContainerInfo
KeyExchangeAlgorithm
KeySize
PersistKeyInCsp
PublicOnly
SignatureAlgorithm
UseMachineKeyStore

Methods
Decrypt (+ 1 overload)
DecryptValue
Dispose
Encrypt (+ 1 overload)
EncryptValue
ExportCspBlob
ExportParameters
HashData (+ 1 overload)
ImportCspBlob
ImportParameters
RSACryptoServiceProvider (+ 3 overloads)
SignData (+ 2 overloads)
SignHash (+ 1 overload)
VerifyData
VerifyHash (+ 1 overload)

**Best Practice**
Choose **Advanced Encryption Standard** (**AES**), which is based on the Rijndael algorithm for symmetric encryption. Choose RSA for asymmetric encryption. Do not confuse RSA with DSA. **Digital Signature Algorithm** (**DSA**) cannot encrypt data. It can only generate hashes and signatures.

# Encrypting symmetrically with AES

To make it easier to reuse your protection code in the future, we will create a static class named `Protector` in its own class library.

Symmetric encryption algorithms use `CryptoStream` to encrypt or decrypt large amounts of bytes efficiently. Asymmetric algorithms can only handle small amounts of bytes, stored in a byte array instead of a stream.

## Using Visual Studio 2017

In Visual Studio 2017, press *Ctrl* + *Shift* + *N* or navigate to **File** | **New** | **Project...**.

In the **New Project** dialog, go to the **Installed** list, expand **Visual C#**, and select **.NET Standard**. In the list at the center, select **Class Library (.NET Standard)**, type the name `CryptographyLib`, change the location to `C:\Code`, type the solution name as `Chapter10`, and then click on **OK**. Rename `Class1.cs` to `Protector.cs`.

In Visual Studio 2017, add a new console application project named `EncryptionApp`.

Set your solution's startup project as the current selection.

In **Solution Explorer**, in the `EncryptionApp` project, right-click on **Dependencies** and choose **Add Reference...**, select the `CryptographyLib` project, and then click on **OK**.

## Using Visual Studio Code

In Visual Studio Code, in the `Code` folder, create a folder named `Chapter10`, with two subfolders named `CryptographyLib` and `EncryptionApp`.

In Visual Studio Code, open the folder named `CryptographyLib`.

In **Integrated Terminal**, enter the following command:

```
dotnet new classlib
```

Open the folder named `EncryptionApp`.

In **Integrated Terminal**, enter the following command:

```
dotnet new console
```

Open the folder named `Chapter10`.

In the **EXPLORER** window, expand `CryptographyLib` and rename the `Class1.cs` file to `Protector.cs`.

In the `EncryptionApp` project folder, open the file named `EncryptionApp.csproj`, and add a package reference to the `CryptographyLib` library, as shown highlighted in the following markup:

```
<Project Sdk="Microsoft.NET.Sdk">

  <PropertyGroup>
    <OutputType>Exe</OutputType>
    <TargetFramework>netcoreapp2.0</TargetFramework>
  </PropertyGroup>

  <ItemGroup>
    <ProjectReference Include="..\CryptographyLib\CryptographyLib.csproj"/>
  </ItemGroup>

</Project>
```

In **Integrated Terminal**, enter the following commands:

```
cd EncryptionApp
dotnet build
```

## Creating the Protector class

In both Visual Studio 2017 and Visual Studio Code, open the `Protector.cs` file and change its contents to look like this:

```
using System;
using System.Collections.Generic;
using System.IO;
using System.Security.Cryptography;
using System.Text;
using System.Xml.Linq;

namespace Packt.CS7
{
  public static class Protector
  {
    // salt size must be at least 8 bytes, we will use 16 bytes
    private static readonly byte[] salt =
    Encoding.Unicode.GetBytes("7BANANAS");

    // iterations must be at least 1000, we will use 2000
    private static readonly int iterations = 2000;

    public static string Encrypt(string plainText,
```

```
            string password)
            {
                byte[] plainBytes = Encoding.Unicode.GetBytes(plainText);
                var aes = Aes.Create();
                var pbkdf2 = new Rfc2898DeriveBytes(password, salt,
                iterations);
                aes.Key = pbkdf2.GetBytes(32); // set a 256-bit key
                aes.IV = pbkdf2.GetBytes(16); // set a 128-bit IV
                var ms = new MemoryStream();
                using (var cs = new CryptoStream(ms, aes.CreateEncryptor(),
                CryptoStreamMode.Write))
                {
                    cs.Write(plainBytes, 0, plainBytes.Length);
                }
                return Convert.ToBase64String(ms.ToArray());
            }

            public static string Decrypt(string cryptoText,
            string password)
            {
                byte[] cryptoBytes = Convert.FromBase64String(cryptoText);
                var aes = Aes.Create();
                var pbkdf2 = new Rfc2898DeriveBytes(password, salt,
                iterations);
                aes.Key = pbkdf2.GetBytes(32);
                aes.IV = pbkdf2.GetBytes(16);
                var ms = new MemoryStream();
                using (var cs = new CryptoStream(ms, aes.CreateDecryptor(),
                CryptoStreamMode.Write))
                {
                    cs.Write(cryptoBytes, 0, cryptoBytes.Length);
                }
                return Encoding.Unicode.GetString(ms.ToArray());
            }
        }
    }
```

Note the following points:

- We used double the recommended salt size and iteration count
- Although the salt and iteration count can be hardcoded, the password *must* be passed at runtime when calling `Encrypt` and `Decrypt`
- We use a temporary `MemoryStream` type to store the results of encrypting and decrypting, and then call `ToArray` to turn the stream into a byte array
- We convert the encrypted byte arrays to and from a Base64 encoding to make them easier to read

**Good Practice**
Never hardcode a password in your source code because, even after compilation, the password can be read in the assembly by using disassembler tools.

In the `EncryptionApp` project, open the `Program.cs` file and then import the following namespace and type the following:

```
using Packt.CS7;
using static System.Console;
```

In the `Main` method, add the following statements to prompt the user for a message and a password, and then encrypt and decrypt:

```
Write("Enter a message that you want to encrypt: ");
string message = ReadLine();
Write("Enter a password: ");
string password = ReadLine();
string cryptoText = Protector.Encrypt(message, password);
WriteLine($"Encrypted text: {cryptoText}");
Write("Enter the password: ");
string password2 = ReadLine();
try
{
   string clearText = Protector.Decrypt(cryptoText, password2);
   WriteLine($"Decrypted text: {clearText}");
}
catch
{
   WriteLine(
   "Enable to decrypt because you entered the wrong password!");
}
```

Run the console application, try entering a message and password, and view the output:

```
Enter a message that you want to encrypt: Hello Bob
Enter a password: secret
Encrypted text: pV5qPDf1CCZmGzUMH2gapFSkn5731g7tMj5ajice3cQ=
Enter the password: secret
Decrypted text: Hello Bob
```

Rerun the application and try entering a message and password, but this time enter the password incorrectly after encrypting, and view the output:

```
Enter a message that you want to encrypt: Hello Bob
Enter a password: secret
Encrypted text: pV5qPDf1CCZmGzUMH2gapFSkn573lg7tMj5ajice3cQ=
Enter the password: 123456
Enable to decrypt because you entered the wrong password!
```

# Hashing data

In .NET Core, there are multiple hash algorithms you can choose from. Some do not use any key, some use symmetric keys, and some use asymmetric keys.

Some of the more common hashing algorithms are shown in the following diagram:

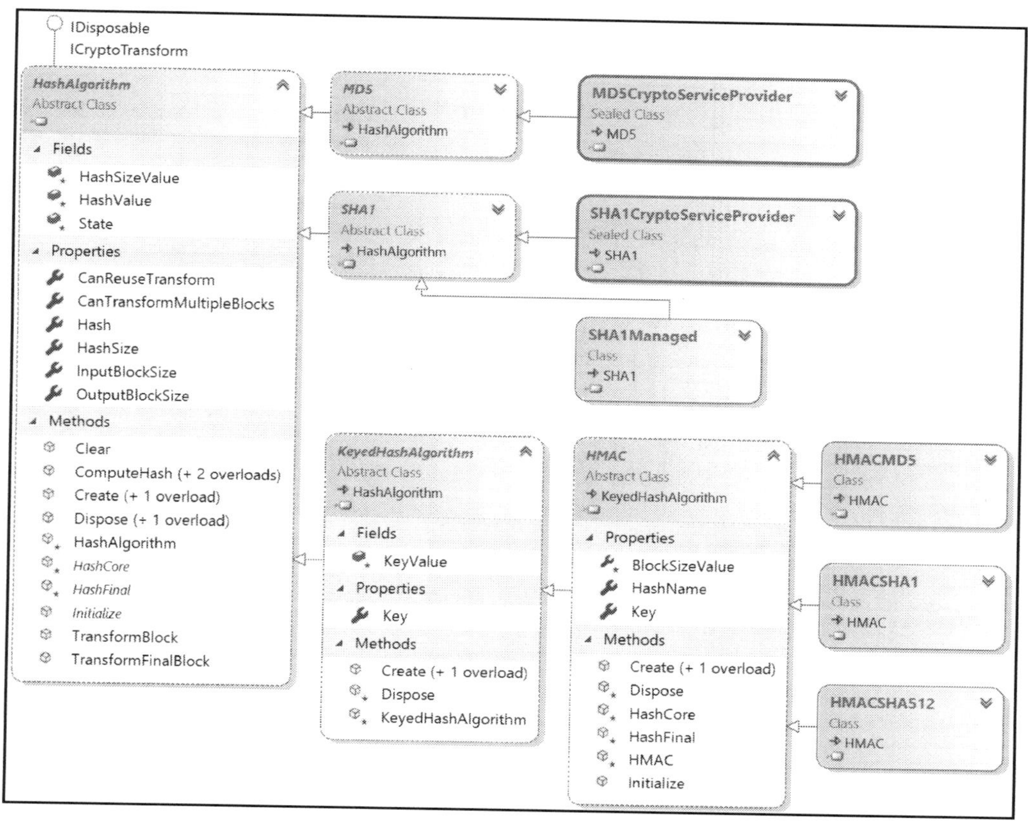

There are two important factors to consider when choosing a hash algorithm:

- **Collision resistance**: How rare is it to find two inputs that share the same hash?
- **Preimage resistance**: For a hash, how difficult would it be to find another input that shares the same hash?

Here are some common non-keyed hashing algorithms:

| Algorithm | Hash size | Description |
|---|---|---|
| MD5 | 16 bytes | This is commonly used because it is fast, but it is not collision-resistant |
| SHA1 | 20 bytes | The use of SHA1 on the internet has been deprecated since 2011 |
| SHA256<br>SHA384<br>SHA512 | 32 bytes<br>48 bytes<br>64 bytes | These are **Secure Hashing Algorithm 2nd generation (SHA2)** algorithms with different hash sizes |

**Good Practice**
Avoid MD5 and SHA1 because they have known weaknesses. Choose a larger hash size to reduce the possibility of repeated hashes. The first publicly known MD5 collision happened in 2010. The first publicly known SHA1 collision happened in 2017. You can read more at the following link: `https://arstechnica.co.uk/information-technology/2017/02/at-deaths-door-for-years-widely-used-sha1-function-is-now-dead/`

# Hashing with the commonly used SHA256

In the `CryptographyLib` class library project, add a new class named `User`. This will represent a user stored in memory, a file, or a database:

```
namespace Packt.CS7
{
   public class User
   {
      public string Name { get; set; }
      public string Salt { get; set; }
      public string SaltedHashedPassword { get; set; }
   }
}
```

Add the following code to the `Protector` class. We will use a dictionary to store multiple users in memory. There are two methods, one to register a new user and one to validate their password when they subsequently log in:

```
private static Dictionary<string, User> Users = new Dictionary<string,
User>();

public static User Register(string username, string password)
{
   // generate a random salt
   var rng = RandomNumberGenerator.Create();
   var saltBytes = new byte[16];
   rng.GetBytes(saltBytes);
   var saltText = Convert.ToBase64String(saltBytes);

   // generate the salted and hashed password
   var sha = SHA256.Create();
   var saltedPassword = password + saltText;
   var saltedhashedPassword = Convert.ToBase64String(
   sha.ComputeHash(Encoding.Unicode.GetBytes(saltedPassword)));

   var user = new User
   {
      Name = username,
      Salt = saltText,
      SaltedHashedPassword = saltedhashedPassword
   };
   Users.Add(user.Name, user);

   return user;
}

public static bool CheckPassword(string username, string password)
{
   if (!Users.ContainsKey(username))
   {
      return false;
   }
   var user = Users[username];

   // re-generate the salted and hashed password
   var sha = SHA256.Create();
   var saltedPassword = password + user.Salt;
   var saltedhashedPassword = Convert.ToBase64String(
   sha.ComputeHash(Encoding.Unicode.GetBytes(saltedPassword)));

   return (saltedhashedPassword == user.SaltedHashedPassword);
}
```

Create a new console application project named `HashingApp`. Add a reference to the `CryptographyLib` assembly as you did before, and then import the following namespace and type the following:

```
using Packt.CS7;
using static System.Console;
```

In the `Main` method, add the following statements to register a user and prompt to register a second user, and then prompt to log in as one of those users and validate the password:

```
WriteLine("A user named Alice has been registered with Pa$$w0rd as her
password.");
var alice = Protector.Register("Alice", "Pa$$w0rd");
WriteLine($"Name: {alice.Name}");
WriteLine($"Salt: {alice.Salt}");
WriteLine($"Salted and hashed password: {alice.SaltedHashedPassword}");
WriteLine();
Write("Enter a different username to register: ");
string username = ReadLine();
Write("Enter a password to register: ");
string password = ReadLine();
var user = Protector.Register(username, password);
WriteLine($"Name: {user.Name}");
WriteLine($"Salt: {user.Salt}");
WriteLine($"Salted and hashed password: {user.SaltedHashedPassword}");

bool correctPassword = false;
while (!correctPassword)
{
   Write("Enter a username to log in: ");
   string loginUsername = ReadLine();
   Write("Enter a password to log in: ");
   string loginPassword = ReadLine();
   correctPassword = Protector.CheckPassword(loginUsername,
   loginPassword);
   if (correctPassword)
   {
      WriteLine($"Correct! {loginUsername} has been logged in.");
   }
   else
   {
      WriteLine("Invalid username or password. Try again.");
   }
}
```

When using multiple projects in Visual Studio Code, remember to change to the correct console application directory by entering the `cd HashingApp` command before entering the `dotnet run` command.

Run the console application and view the output:

```
A user named Alice has been registered with Pa$$w0rd as her password.
Name: Alice
Salt: tLn3gRn9DXmp2oeuvBSxTg==
Salted and hashed password:
  w8Ub2aH5NNQ8MJarYsUgm29bbbl0lV/9dlozjWs2Ipk=
Enter a different username to register: Bob
Enter a password to register: Pa$$w0rd
Name: Bob
Salt: zPU9YyFLaz0idhQkKpzY+g==
Salted and hashed password:
  8w14w8WNHoZddEeIx2+UJhpHQqSs4EmyoazqjbmmEz0=
Enter a username to log in: Bob
Enter a password to log in: secret
Invalid username or password. Try again.
Enter a username to log in: Alice
Enter a password to log in: secret
Invalid username or password. Try again.
Enter a username to log in: Bob
Enter a password to log in: Pa$$w0rd
Correct! Bob has been logged in.
```

Even if two users register with the same password, they have randomly generated salts so that their salted and hashed passwords are different.

# Signing data

To prove that some data has come from someone we trust, it can be signed. Actually, you don't sign the data itself; instead, you sign a hash of the data. We will use the SHA256 algorithm for generating the hash, combined with the RSA algorithm for signing the hash.

We could use DSA for both hashing and signing. DSA is faster than RSA for generating a signature, but it is slower than RSA for validating a signature. Since a signature is generated once, but validated many times, it's best to have faster validation than generation.

The RSA algorithm is based on factorization of large integers, compared to the DSA algorithm, which is based on the discrete logarithm calculation. You can read more at the following link: http://mathworld.wolfram.com/RSAEncryption.html

# Signing with SHA256 and RSA

In the `CryptographyLib` class library project, add the following code to the `Protector` class:

```
public static string PublicKey;

public static string ToXmlStringExt(this RSA rsa, bool
includePrivateParameters)
{
   var p = rsa.ExportParameters(includePrivateParameters);
   XElement xml;
   if (includePrivateParameters)
   {
      xml = new XElement("RSAKeyValue"
         , new XElement("Modulus",
         Convert.ToBase64String(p.Modulus))
         , new XElement("Exponent",
         Convert.ToBase64String(p.Exponent))
         , new XElement("P", Convert.ToBase64String(p.P))
         , new XElement("Q", Convert.ToBase64String(p.Q))
         , new XElement("DP", Convert.ToBase64String(p.DP))
         , new XElement("DQ", Convert.ToBase64String(p.DQ))
         , new XElement("InverseQ",
         Convert.ToBase64String(p.InverseQ)));
   }
   else
   {
      xml = new XElement("RSAKeyValue"
         , new XElement("Modulus",
         Convert.ToBase64String(p.Modulus))
         , new XElement("Exponent",
         Convert.ToBase64String(p.Exponent)));
   }
   return xml?.ToString();
}

public static void FromXmlStringExt(this RSA rsa,
string parametersAsXml)
{
   var xml = XDocument.Parse(parametersAsXml);
```

```
        var root = xml.Element("RSAKeyValue");
        var p = new RSAParameters
        {
            Modulus =
            Convert.FromBase64String(root.Element("Modulus").Value),
            Exponent =
            Convert.FromBase64String(root.Element("Exponent").Value)
        };
        if (root.Element("P") != null)
        {
            p.P = Convert.FromBase64String(root.Element("P").Value);
            p.Q = Convert.FromBase64String(root.Element("Q").Value);
            p.DP = Convert.FromBase64String(root.Element("DP").Value);
            p.DQ = Convert.FromBase64String(root.Element("DQ").Value);
            p.InverseQ =
            Convert.FromBase64String(root.Element("InverseQ").Value);
        }
        rsa.ImportParameters(p);
    }

    public static string GenerateSignature(string data)
    {
        byte[] dataBytes = Encoding.Unicode.GetBytes(data);
        var sha = SHA256.Create();
        var hashedData = sha.ComputeHash(dataBytes);

        var rsa = RSA.Create();
        PublicKey = rsa.ToXmlStringExt(false); // exclude private key

        return Convert.ToBase64String(rsa.SignHash(hashedData,
        HashAlgorithmName.SHA256, RSASignaturePadding.Pkcs1));
    }

    public static bool ValidateSignature(string data, string signature)
    {
        byte[] dataBytes = Encoding.Unicode.GetBytes(data);
        var sha = SHA256.Create();
        var hashedData = sha.ComputeHash(dataBytes);

        byte[] signatureBytes = Convert.FromBase64String(signature);

        var rsa = RSA.Create();
        rsa.FromXmlStringExt(PublicKey);

        return rsa.VerifyHash(hashedData, signatureBytes,
        HashAlgorithmName.SHA256, RSASignaturePadding.Pkcs1);
    }
```

Note the following:

- The `RSA` type has two methods named `ToXmlString` and `FromXmlString`. These serialize and deserialize the `RSAParameters` structure that contains the public and private keys. However, .NET Core's implementations of these methods on macOS throws a `PlatformNotSupportedException` exception. I have had to re-implement them myself using **LINQ to XML** types such as `XDocument`, which you will learn about in `Chapter 12`, *Querying and Manipulating Data Using LINQ*.
- Only the public part of the public-private key pair needs to be made available to the code that is checking the signature so that we can pass the `false` value when we call the `ToXmlStringExt` method. The private part is required to sign data and must be kept secret because anyone with the private part can sign data as if they are you!
- The hash algorithm used to generate the hash from the data must match the hash algorithm set on the signer and checker. In the preceding code, we used `SHA256`.

# Testing the signing and validating

Add a new console application project named `SigningApp`. Add a reference to the `CryptographyLib` assembly, and then in `Program.cs`, import the following namespaces:

```
using static System.Console;
using Packt.CS7;
```

In the `Main` method, add the following code:

```
Write("Enter some text to sign: ");
string data = ReadLine();
var signature = Protector.GenerateSignature(data);
WriteLine($"Signature: {signature}");
WriteLine("Public key used to check signature:");
WriteLine(Protector.PublicKey);

if (Protector.ValidateSignature(data, signature))
{
   WriteLine("Correct! Signature is valid.");
}
else
{
   WriteLine("Invalid signature.");
}
```

```
// create a fake signature by replacing the
// first character with an X
var fakeSignature = signature.Replace(signature[0], 'X');
if (Protector.ValidateSignature(data, fakeSignature))
{
   WriteLine("Correct! Signature is valid.");
}
else
{
   WriteLine($"Invalid signature: {fakeSignature}");
}
```

Run the console application and enter some text, as shown in the following output (edited for length):

```
Enter some text to sign: The cat sat on the mat.
Correct! Signature is valid.
Invalid signature:
X1uDRfCDXvOyhMtqXlxqzSljhADD/81E0UonuVs9VfZ7ceuyFWh4O7rwkdc1+125DzGf64swtbX
ZsukpSupFqvkAOIJ6XqMlD92v1G1nquereiWkshYnxxVts30QJIFKKyOTBTfN/VOljlZVMxT/RA
6pggPtESlv+urDJT4z/PEtR5jdx+CTZHQc9WiceFbpuybyf/vEdddtF0T7g8NeLKEPbT6b7CHGD
M1HKbRqnSecv456QNfHNmEXxRk9MpI0DgQLnXpOhHcVwEFc6+dY6kdNnWd6NIOY3qX6FT782t01
Q2swcWxF9fUcvWVSeC84EgVK447X9Xewkrf6CF7jxg==
```

## Generating random numbers

Sometimes you need to generate random numbers, perhaps in a game that simulates rolls of a die, or for use with cryptography in encryption or signing.

There are a couple of classes that can generate random numbers in .NET Standard, as shown in the following diagram:

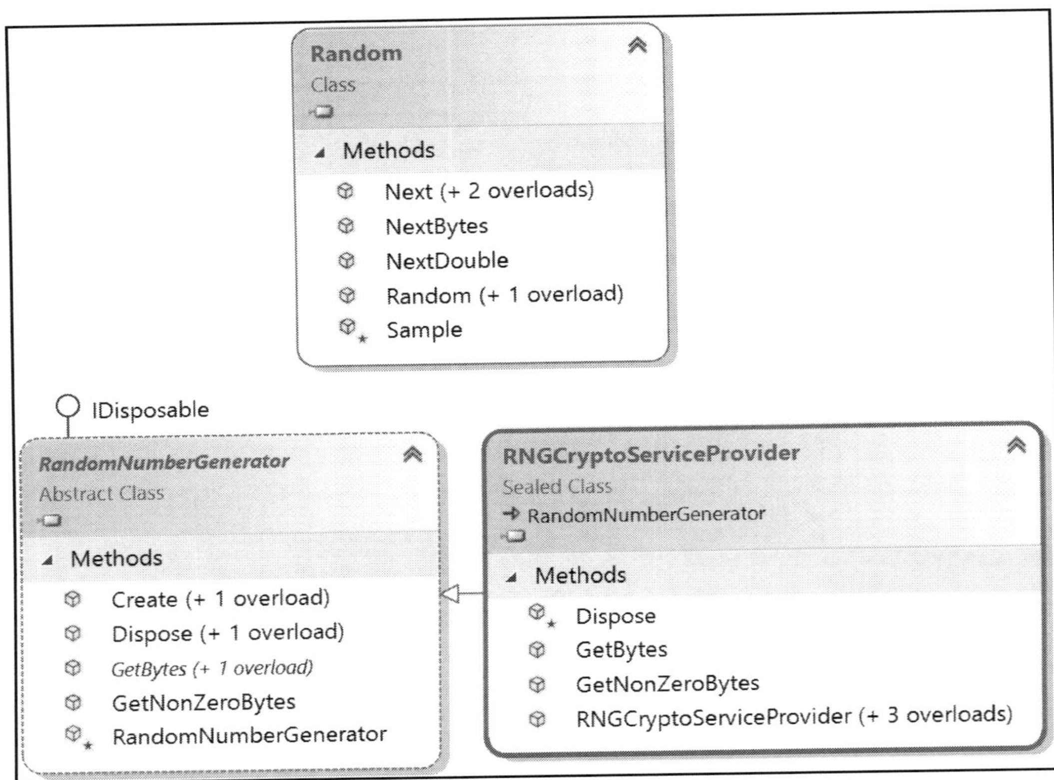


# Generating random numbers for games

In scenarios that don't need truly random numbers, you can use the `Random` class, as shown in the following code example:

```
var r = new Random();
```

`Random` has a constructor with a parameter for specifying a seed value used to initialize a pseudo-random number generator, as shown in the following code:

```
var r = new Random(Seed: 12345);
```

**Good Practice**
As you learned in Chapter 2, *Speaking C#*, parameter names should use camel case. The developer who defined the constructor for the `Random` class broke this convention! The parameter name should be `seed`, not `Seed`.

Shared seed values act as a secret key, so if you use the same random number generation algorithm with the same seed value in two applications, then they can generate the same "random" sequences of numbers. Sometimes this is necessary, for example, when synchronizing a GPS receiver with a satellite. But usually, you want to keep your seed secret.

Once you have a `Random` object, you can call its methods to generate random numbers, as shown in the following code examples:

```
int dieRoll = r.Next(minValue: 1, maxValue: 7); // returns 1 to 6
double randomReal = r.NextDouble(); // returns 0.0 to 1.0
var arrayOfBytes = new byte[256];
r.NextBytes(arrayOfBytes); // 256 random bytes in an array
```

The `Next` method takes two parameters: `minValue` and `maxValue`. `maxValue` is NOT the maximum value that the method returns! It is an *exclusive* upper-bound, meaning it is one more than the maximum value.

## Generating random numbers for cryptography

`Random` generates pseudo-random numbers. This is not good enough for cryptography! You must use a `RandomNumberGenerator` derived type, such as `RNGCryptoServiceProvider`.

In the CryptographyLib class library project, add statements to the Protector class to define a method to get a random key or IV for use in encryption, as shown in the following code:

```
public static byte[] GetRandomKeyOrIV(int size)
{
    var r = RandomNumberGenerator.Create();
    var data = new byte[size];
    r.GetNonZeroBytes(data); // array filled with cryptographically
                             // strong random bytes
    return data;
}
```

# Testing the random key or IV generation

Add a new console application project named RandomizingApp. Add a reference to the CryptographyLib assembly, and then in Program.cs, import the following namespaces:

```
using static System.Console;
using Packt.CS7;
```

In the Main method, add the following code:

```
static void Main(string[] args)
{
    Write("How big do you want the key (in bytes): ");
    string size = ReadLine();
    byte[] key = Protector.GetRandomKeyOrIV(int.Parse(size));
    WriteLine($"Key as byte array:");
    for (int b = 0; b < key.Length; b++)
    {
        Write($"{key[b]:x2} ");
        if (((b + 1) % 16) == 0) WriteLine();
    }
    WriteLine();
}
```

Run the console application, enter a typical size for the key, such as `256`, and view the output:

```
How big do you want the key (in bytes): 256
Key as byte array:
8c 93 d8 d3 b2 0f 20 45 8e de d9 79 17 1a 78 47
ab 34 e9 e5 38 89 91 58 65 d5 fe 5f 17 18 e2 b8
a4 5c f0 48 65 60 ae f1 29 c0 c2 20 9d 1b a6 9d
17 14 aa d9 25 79 19 b4 3e bd 48 84 bc a9 a0 b4
4c 4d 7c cb 9d f6 12 15 08 a4 42 93 da 46 b6 b4
68 65 6d cc 5e 9e 92 7e 04 52 22 35 65 84 76 06
11 d1 be be 5b 1f de 8e 44 ea d4 d4 ca d4 bf b0
e6 50 6d d1 69 16 8c d1 14 68 35 43 6a ee d8 a9
63 2e 4b 54 38 ef 45 c1 8b c9 f8 f1 f8 d9 d7 80
e4 c8 d3 a3 1f 3f 24 9c 1e 97 e0 55 17 ab 6d a1
b2 2a d8 59 d6 e6 06 28 f1 5c 86 9f 5a 1f d5 01
18 d7 73 bd ae 8c a1 ef ab 18 75 ba 76 65 d0 17
71 ec 68 6f fd c3 6a 0b 23 e8 ee 65 99 b2 0a af
ff c9 09 c7 7f e9 41 a1 1b e6 b8 c7 b4 0e 91 26
26 e7 e6 d0 85 0e e5 f1 48 ca 4b f8 b8 71 19 ee
ba 3b bb 6b b8 e6 2d d9 ae b8 81 fb 71 fa 98 ae
```

# Authenticating and authorizing users

**Authentication** is the process of verifying the identity of a user by validating their credentials against some authority. Credentials include a username and password combination, or a fingerprint or face scan. Once authenticated, a user can make claims, for example, what their email address is, and what groups or roles they belong to.

**Authorization** is the process of verifying membership of groups or roles before allowing access to resources such as application functions and data. Although authorization can be based on individual identity, it is good security practice to authorize based on group or role membership because that allows membership to change in future without reassigning access rights.

There are multiple authentication and authorization mechanisms to choose from. They all implement a pair of interfaces in the `System.Security.Principal` namespace: `IIdentity` and `IPrincipal`.

`IIdentity` represents a user, so it has a `Name` property and an `IsAuthenticated` property to indicate if they are anonymous or if they have been authenticated.

The most common class that implements this interface is `GenericIdentity`, which inherits from `ClaimsIdentity`, as shown in the following diagram:

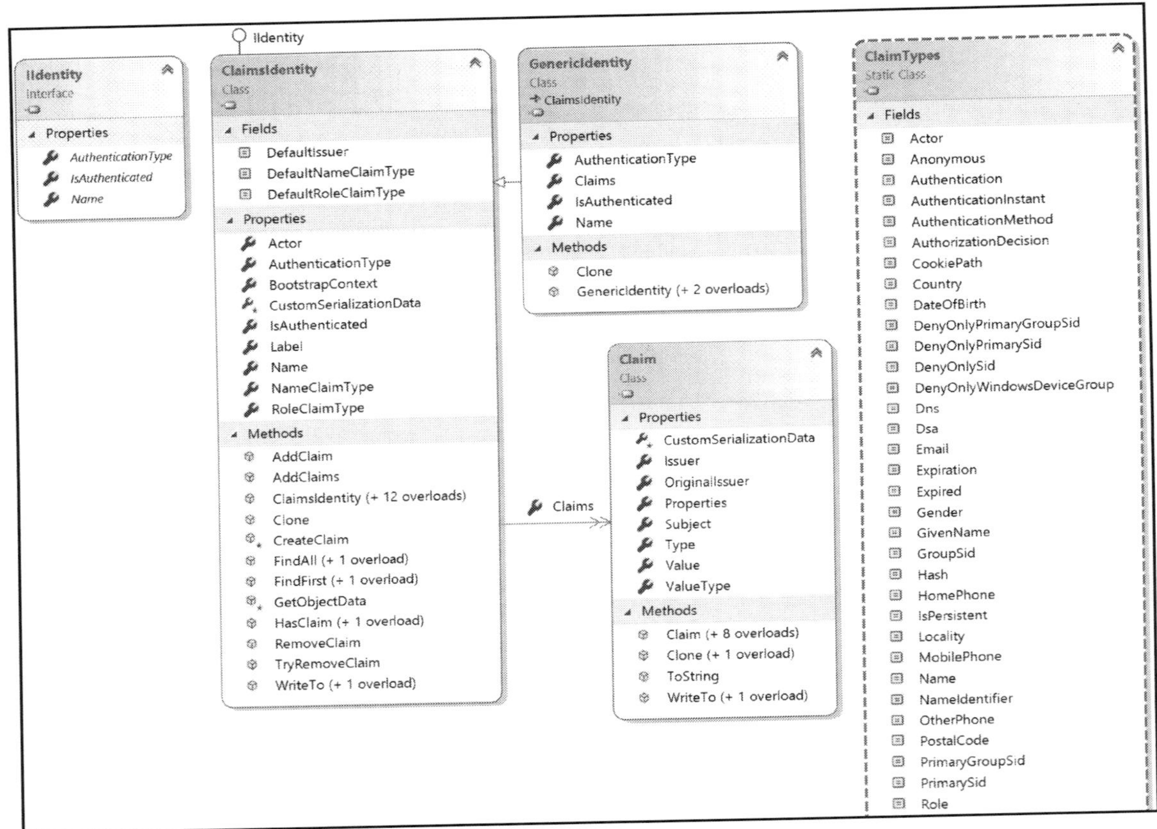


Each `ClaimsIdentity` class has a `Claims` property. The `Claim` objects have a `Type` property that indicates if the claim is for their name, their membership of a role or group, their date of birth, and so on.

`IPrincipal` is used to associate an identity with the roles and groups that they are members of, so it can be used for authorization purposes. The current thread executing your code has a `CurrentPrincipal` property that can be set to any object that implements `IPrincipal`, and it will be checked when permission is needed to perform a secure action.

The most common class that implements this interface is `GenericPrincipal`, which inherits from `ClaimsPrincipal`, as shown in the following diagram:

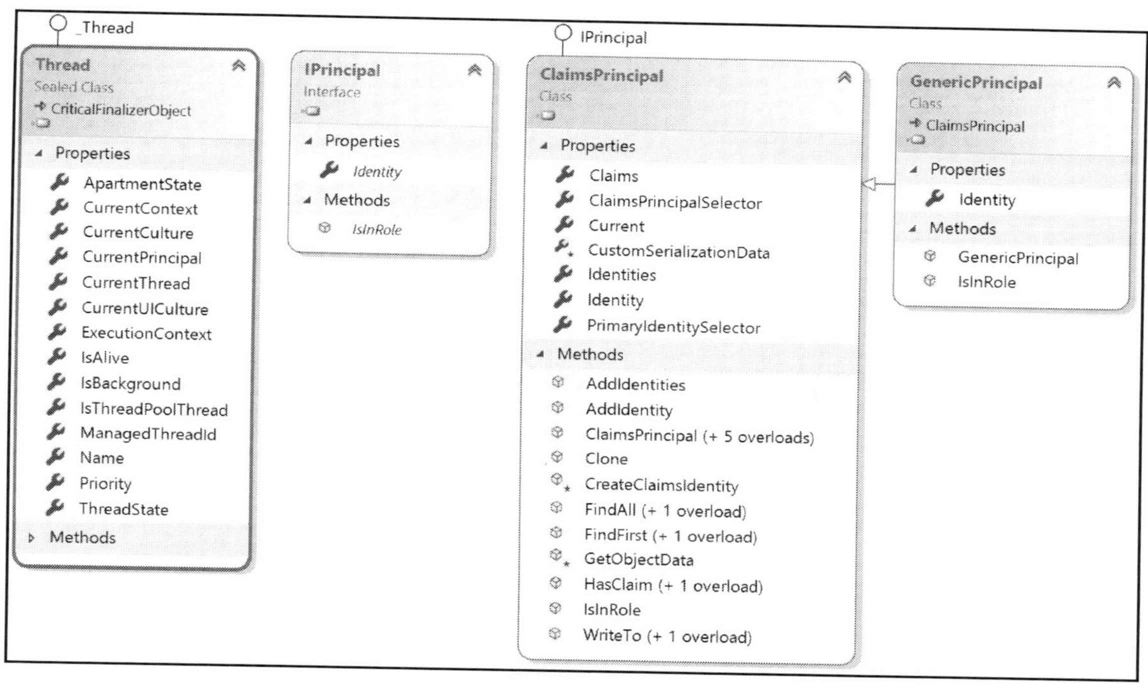


# Implementing authentication and authorization

In the `CryptographyLib` class library project, add a property to the `User` class to store an array of roles:

```
public string[] Roles { get; set; }
```

In the `CryptographyLib` class library project, modify the `Register` method in the `Protector` class to allow an array of roles to be passed as an optional parameter, as highlighted in the following code:

```
public static User Register(string username, string password, string[]
roles = null)
```

Modify the `Register` method in the `Protector` class to set the array of roles in the `User` object, as shown in the following code:

```
var user = new User
{
   Name = username,
   Salt = saltText,
   SaltedHashedPassword = saltedhashedPassword,
   Roles = roles
};
```

In the `CryptographyLib` class library project, add statements to the `Protector` class to define a method to register three users named Alice, Bob, and Eve, in various roles, as shown in the following code:

```
public static void RegisterSomeUsers()
{
   Register("Alice", "Pa$$w0rd", new[] { "Admins" });
   Register("Bob", "Pa$$w0rd", new[] { "Sales", "TeamLeads" });
   Register("Eve", "Pa$$w0rd");
}
```

**Good Practice**
To make the `Protector` class reusable with minimal complexity, it would be better to define `RegisterSomeUsers` in a separate class in a separate class library.

In the `CryptographyLib` class library project, add the following code to the `Protector` class to import `System.Security.Principal`, define a `LogIn` method to log in a user, and use generic identity and principal to assign them to the current thread, as shown in the following code:

```
public static void LogIn(string username, string password)
{
   if (CheckPassword(username, password))
   {
      var identity = new GenericIdentity(username, "PacktAuth");
      var principal = new GenericPrincipal(identity,
      Users[username].Roles);
```

```
        System.Threading.Thread.CurrentPrincipal = principal;
    }
}
```

# Testing authentication and authorization

Add a new console application project named `SecureApp`. Add a reference to the `CryptographyLib` assembly, and then in `Program.cs`, import the following namespaces:

```
using static System.Console;
using Packt.CS7;
using System.Threading;
using System.Security;
using System.Security.Permissions;
using System.Security.Principal;
using System.Security.Claims;
```

In the `Main` method, write statements to register some users, prompt the user to log in, and then output information about them, as shown in the following code:

```
Protector.RegisterSomeUsers();

Write($"Enter your user name: ");
string username = ReadLine();
Write($"Enter your password: ");
string password = ReadLine();

Protector.LogIn(username, password);
if (Thread.CurrentPrincipal == null)
{
   WriteLine("Log in failed.");
   return;
}

var p = Thread.CurrentPrincipal;

WriteLine($"IsAuthenticated: {p.Identity.IsAuthenticated}");
WriteLine($"AuthenticationType: {p.Identity.AuthenticationType}");
WriteLine($"Name: {p.Identity.Name}");
WriteLine($"IsInRole(\"Admins\"): {p.IsInRole("Admins")}");
WriteLine($"IsInRole(\"Sales\"): {p.IsInRole("Sales")}");

if (p is ClaimsPrincipal)
{
   WriteLine($"{p.Identity.Name} has the following claims:");
   foreach (Claim claim in (p as ClaimsPrincipal).Claims)
```

```
        {
            WriteLine($"  {claim.Type}: {claim.Value}");
        }
    }
```

Run the console application, log in as `Alice` with `Pa$$word`, and view the results, as shown in the following output:

```
Enter your user name: Alice
Enter your password: Pa$$w0rd
IsAuthenticated: True
AuthenticationType: PacktAuth
Name: Alice
IsInRole("Admins"): True
IsInRole("Sales"): False
Alice has the following claims:
  http://schemas.xmlsoap.org/ws/2005/05/identity/claims/name: Alice
  http://schemas.microsoft.com/ws/2008/06/identity/claims/role: Admins
```

Run the console application, log in as `Alice` with `secret`, and view the results, as shown in the following output:

```
Enter your user name: Alice
Enter your password: secret
Log in failed.
```

Run the console application, log in as `Bob` with `Pa$$word`, and view the results, as shown in the following output:

```
Enter your user name: Bob
Enter your password: Pa$$w0rd
IsAuthenticated: True
AuthenticationType: PacktAuth
Name: Bob
IsInRole("Admins"): False
IsInRole("Sales"): True
Bob has the following claims:
  http://schemas.xmlsoap.org/ws/2005/05/identity/claims/name: Bob
  http://schemas.microsoft.com/ws/2008/06/identity/claims/role: Sales
  http://schemas.microsoft.com/ws/2008/06/identity/claims/role: TeamLeads
```

## Protecting application functionality

Add a method to the `Program` class, secured by checking for permission inside the method, and throw appropriate exceptions if not, as shown in the following code:

```
static void SecureFeature()
{
   if (Thread.CurrentPrincipal == null)
   {
      throw new SecurityException("Thread.CurrentPrincipal
      cannot be null.");
   }
   if (!Thread.CurrentPrincipal.IsInRole("Admins"))
   {
      throw new SecurityException("User must be a member of Admins to
access this feature.");
   }

   WriteLine("You have access to this secure feature.");
}
```

Add statements to the end of the `Main` method to call the `SecureFeature` method in a `try...catch` statement, as shown in the following code:

```
try
{
   SecureFeature();
}
catch(System.Exception ex)
{
   WriteLine($"{ex.GetType()}: {ex.Message}");
}
```

Run the console application, log in as `Alice` with `Pa$$word`, and view the results, as shown in the following output:

```
You have access to this secure feature.
```

Run the console application, log in as `Bob` with `Pa$$word`, and view the results, as shown in the following output:

```
System.Security.SecurityException: User must be a member of Admins to
access this feature.
```

# Practicing and exploring

Test your knowledge and understanding by answering some questions, get some hands-on practice, and explore the topics covered in this chapter with deeper research.

## Exercise 10.1 – Test your knowledge

Answer the following questions:

1. Of the encryption algorithms provided by .NET, which is the best choice for symmetric encryption?
2. Of the encryption algorithms provided by .NET, which is the best choice for asymmetric encryption?
3. What is a rainbow attack?
4. For encryption algorithms, is it better to have a larger or smaller block size?
5. What is a hash?
6. What is a signature?
7. What is the difference between symmetric and asymmetric encryption?
8. What does RSA stand for?
9. Why should passwords be salted before being stored?
10. SHA1 is a hashing algorithm designed by the United States National Security Agency. Why should you never use it?

## Exercise 10.2 – Practice protecting data with encryption and hashing

Create a console application named `Exercise02` that protects an XML file, such as the following example. Note that the customer's credit card number and password are currently stored in clear text. The credit card must be encrypted so that it can be decrypted and used later, and the password must be salted and hashed:

```
<?xml version="1.0" encoding="utf-8" ?>
<customers>
  <customer>
    <name>Bob Smith</name>
```

```
        <creditcard>1234-5678-9012-3456</creditcard>
        <password>Pa$$w0rd</password>
      </customer>
    </customers>
```

## Exercise 10.3 – Practice protecting data with decryption

Create a console application named `Exercise03` that opens the XML file that you protected in the preceding code and decrypts the credit card number.

## Exercise 10.4 – Explore topics

Use the following links to read more about the topics covered in this chapter:

- **Key Security Concepts**:
  `https://msdn.microsoft.com/en-us/library/z164t8hs(v=vs.110).aspx`
- **Encrypting Data**:
  `https://msdn.microsoft.com/en-us/library/as0w18af(v=vs.110).aspx`
- **Cryptographic Signatures**:
  `https://msdn.microsoft.com/en-us/library/hk8wx38z(v=vs.110).aspx`

# Summary

In this chapter, you learned how to encrypt and decrypt using symmetric encryption, how to generate a salted hash, and how to sign data and check the signature on the data.

In the next chapter, you will learn how to work with databases using Entity Framework Core.

# 11
# Working with Databases Using Entity Framework Core

This chapter is about reading and writing to databases, such as Microsoft SQL Server, SQLite, and Azure Cosmos DB, using the object-relational mapping technology named **Entity Framework Core** (**EF Core**).

This chapter will cover the following topics:

- Understanding modern databases
- Setting up EF Core
- Defining EF Core models
- Querying an EF Core model
- Manipulating data with EF Core

## Understanding modern databases

Two of the most common places to store data are in a **Relational Database Management System** (**RDBMS**) such as Microsoft SQL Server, PostgreSQL, MySQL, and SQLite, or in a **NoSQL** data store such as Microsoft Azure Cosmos DB, Redis, MongoDB, and Apache Cassandra.

This chapter will focus on RDBMSes such as SQL Server and SQLite. To learn more about NoSQL databases such as Cosmos DB and MongoDB and how to use them with EF Core, follow these links:

- **Introduction to Cosmos DB**: `https://docs.microsoft.com/en-us/azure/cosmos-db/introduction`
- **Using NoSQL databases with EF Core**: `https://docs.microsoft.com/en-us/dotnet/standard/microservices-architecture/microservice-ddd-cqrs-patterns/nosql-database-persistence-infrastructure`
- **What is MongoDB?** `https://www.mongodb.com/what-is-mongodb`
- **EF Core MongoDB Provider**: `https://github.com/crhairr/EntityFrameworkCore.MongoDb`

# Using a sample relational database

To learn how to manage an RDBMS using .NET Core, it would be useful to have a sample one to practice on that has a medium complexity and a decent amount of sample records. Microsoft offers several sample databases, most of which are too complex for our needs. So, we will use a database that was first created in the early 1990s known as **Northwind**.

Use the `https://github.com/markjprice/cs7dotnetcore2/tree/master/sql-scripts/` link to download `Northwind4SQLServer.sql` for use with Microsoft SQL Server, or `Northwind4SQLite.sql` for use with SQLite.

Here is a diagram of the Northwind database that you can refer to as we write queries:

You will write code to work with the `Categories` and `Products` tables later in this chapter.

# Using Microsoft SQL Server

Microsoft offers various editions of its popular and capable SQL Server product for Windows, Linux, and Docker containers, that you can learn more about by following this link:

`https://www.microsoft.com/en-us/sql-server/sql-server-2017`

We will use a free version that can run standalone, known as **SQL Server LocalDB**. The latest version of SQL Server LocalDB is included with all editions of Visual Studio 2017.

## Connecting to SQL Server

When you write code to connect to an SQL Server database, you need to know its **server name**. The name depends on the version you choose to use. Here are some examples:

- **Visual Studio 2017 installs SQL Server LocalDB 2016:** `(localdb)\mssqllocaldb`
- **Visual Studio 2015 installs SQL Server LocalDB 2014:** `(localdb)\mssqllocaldb`
- **Visual Studio 2012/2013 installs SQL Server LocalDB 2012:** `(localdb)\v11.0`
- **If you install SQL Server Express:** `.\sqlexpress`
- **If you install full SQL Server:** `.`

The dot in the last two connection strings is shorthand for the local computer name. Server names for SQL Server are made of two parts: the name of the computer and the name of a SQL Server instance. The full version does not need an instance name, although you can provide one during installation.

### Creating the Northwind sample database for SQL Server

Download a script to create the Northwind database for Microsoft SQL Server from the following link:

`https://github.com/markjprice/cs7dotnetcore2/sql-scripts/Northwind4SQLServer.sql`

In Visual Studio 2017, go to **File** | **Open** | **File...** or press *Ctrl* + *O*.

Browse to select the `Northwind4SQLServer.sql` file and choose **Open**.

In the editor window, right-click and choose **Execute** or press *Ctrl* + *Shift* + *E*.

In the dialog box, enter the server name as `(localdb)\mssqllocaldb` and click on **Connect**, as shown in the following screenshot:

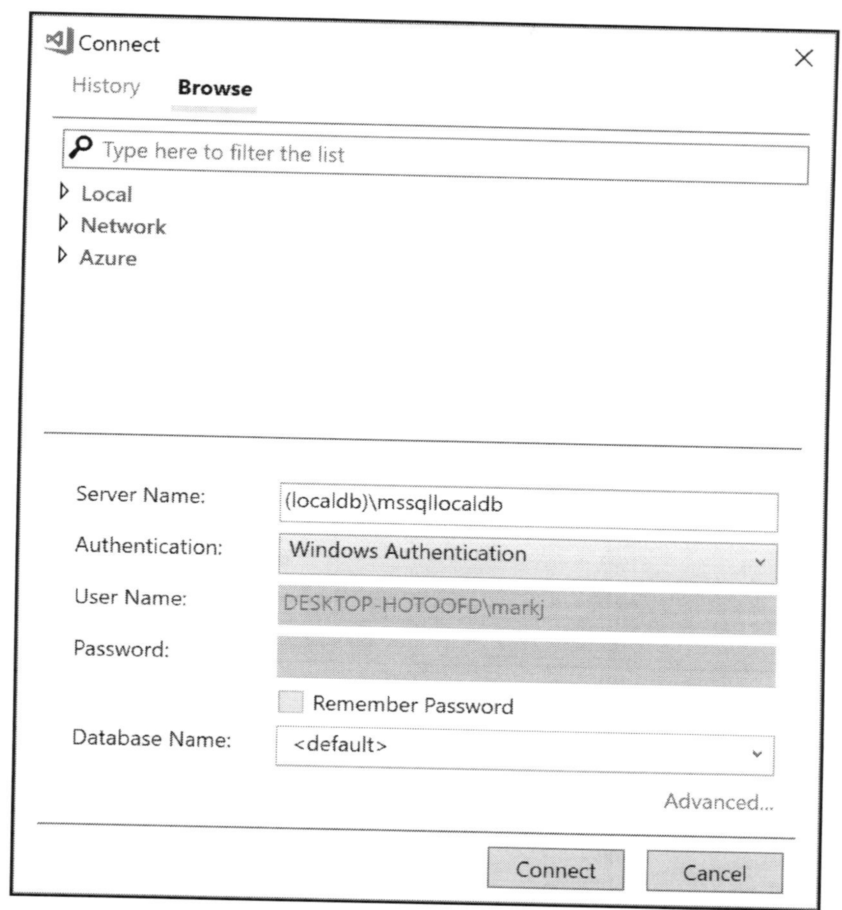


When you see the **Command(s) completed successfully** message, then the `Northwind` database has been created, and we can connect to it.

LocalDB sometimes takes too long to start the first time, and you might see a timeout error. Simply click on **Connect** again, and it should work.

## Managing the Northwind sample database with Server Explorer

In Visual Studio 2017, choose **View** | **Server Explorer** or press *Ctrl* + *W* + *L*.

In the **Server Explorer** window, right-click on **Data Connections** and choose **Add Connection...**.

If you see the **Choose Data Source** dialog, as shown in the following screenshot, then select **Microsoft SQL Server** and click on **Continue**:

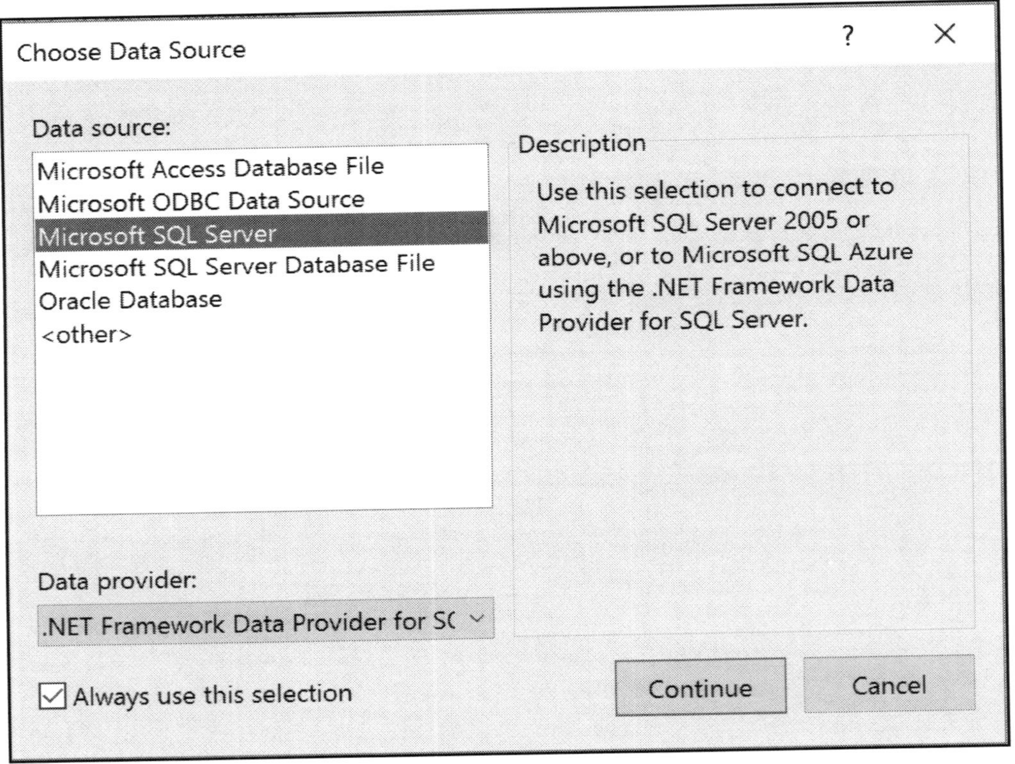

In the **Add Connection** dialog, enter the server name as `(localdb)\mssqllocaldb`, enter the database name as `Northwind`, and click on **OK**, as shown in the following screenshot:

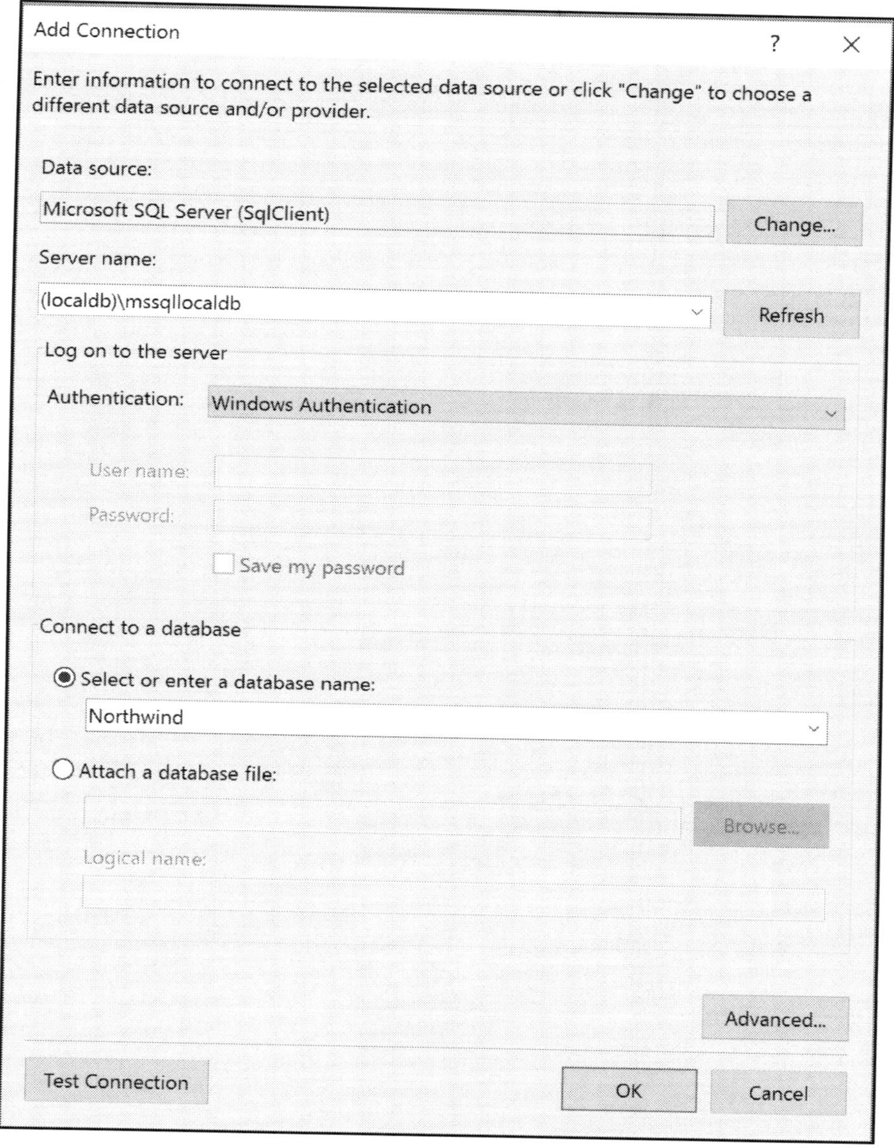

In the **Server Explorer**, expand the data connection and its tables. You should see 13 tables, including the **Categories** and **Products** tables, as shown in the following screenshot:

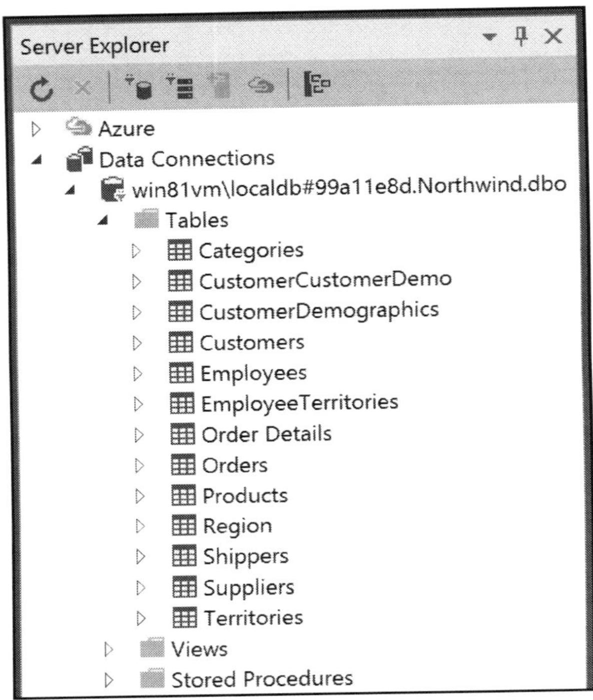


Right-click on the **Products** table and choose **Show Table Data**, as shown in the following screenshot:

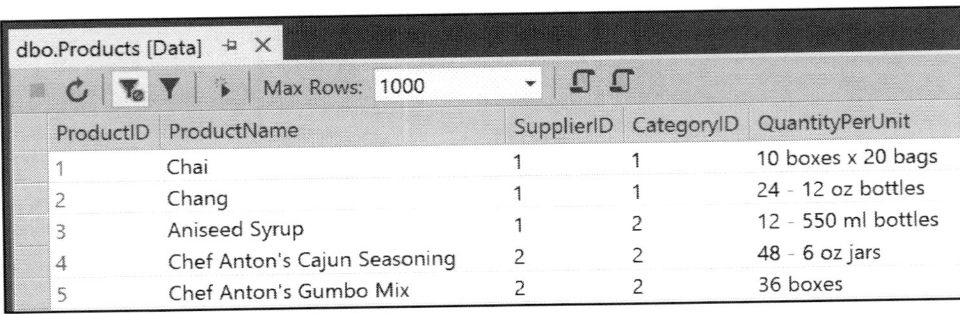

To see the details of the **Products** table columns and types, right-click on **Products** and choose **Open Table Definition**, as shown in the following screenshot:

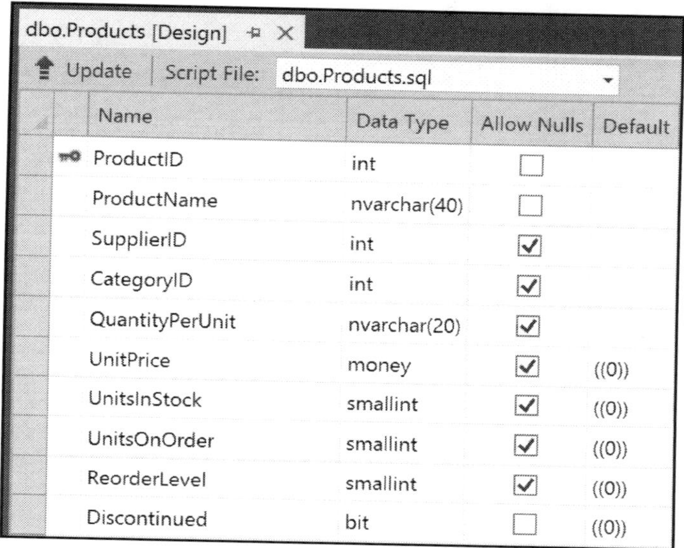


# Using SQLite

SQLite is a small, cross-platform, self-contained RDBMS that is available in the public domain. It is the most common RDBMS for mobile platforms such as iOS (iPhone and iPad) and Android.

SQLite is included in macOS in the `/usr/bin/` directory as a command-line application named `sqlite3`.

If you are using Visual Studio Code on Windows, then you must install SQLite yourself, or use SQL Server instead. These instructions assume Visual Studio Code for macOS.

You can download a graphical database manager named SQLiteStudio for SQLite at the following link:

`http://sqlitestudio.pl`

You can read about the SQL statements supported by SQLite at the following link:

`https://sqlite.org/lang.html`

## Creating the Northwind sample database for SQLite

Create a folder named `Chapter11` with a subfolder named `WorkingWithEFCore`.

Download a script to create the `Northwind` database for SQLite from the following link:

`https://github.com/markjprice/cs7dotnetcore2/blob/master/sql-scripts/Northwind4SQLite.sql`

Copy `Northwind4SQLite.sql` into the `WorkingWithEFCore` folder.

Start **Terminal** (or use Visual Studio Code's Integrated Terminal).

Enter commands to change to the `Code` folder, change to the directory named `Chapter11`, and run the SQLite script to create the `Northwind.db` database, as shown in the following commands:

```
cd Code/Chapter11/WorkingWithEFCore
sqlite3 Northwind.db < Northwind4SQLite.sql
```

## Managing the Northwind sample database with SQLiteStudio

Launch **SQLiteStudio**, or some other graphical tool for managing SQLite databases.

If you see a warning about not being able to run the application, hold down *Shift* while opening it, and then click on **Open**.

In **SQLiteStudio**, on the **Database** menu, choose **Add a database**, or press *Cmd* + *O*.

In the **Database** dialog, click on the folder button to browse for an existing database file on the local computer. Select the `Northwind.db` file. Optionally, click on **Test connection** to see the green tick, as shown in the following screenshot, and then click on **OK**:

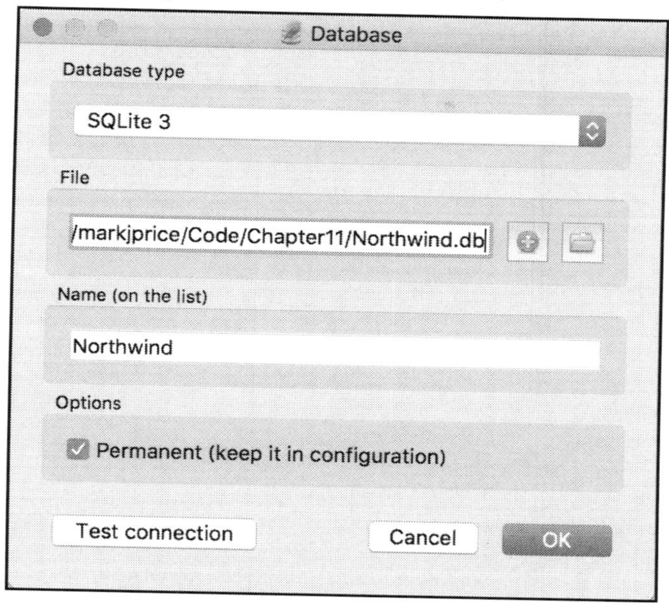


Right-click on the **Northwind** database and choose **Connect to the database**, as shown here:

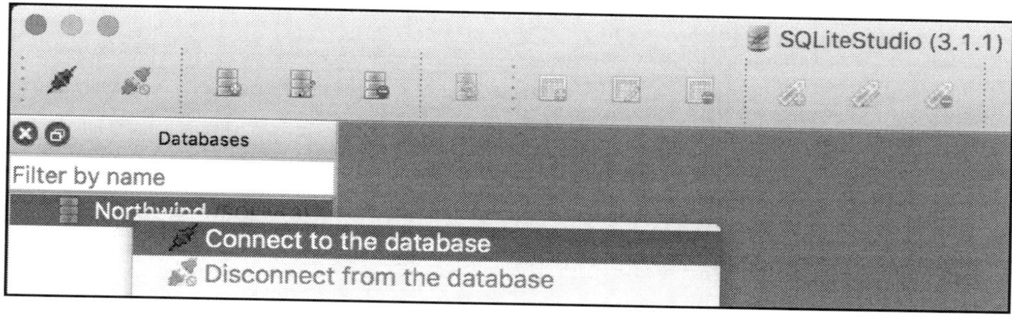

You will see the ten tables that were created by the script, as shown in the following screenshot:

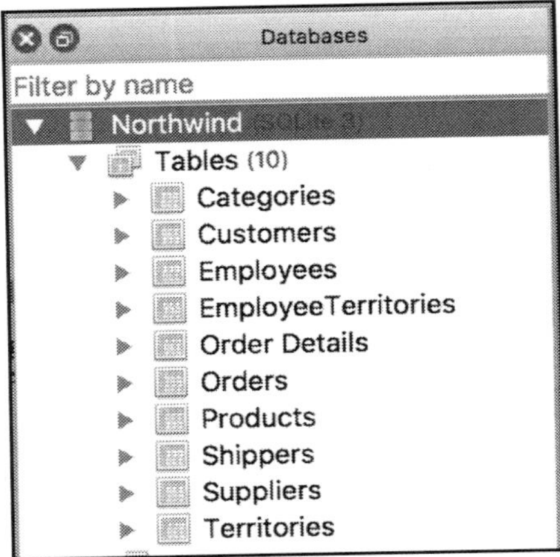


Right-click on the **Products** table and choose **Edit the table**:

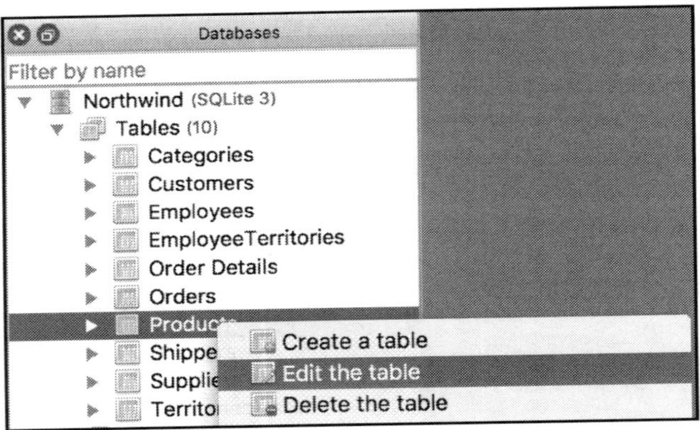

In the table editor window, you will see the structure of the **Products** table, including column names, data types, keys, and constraints, as shown in the following screenshot:

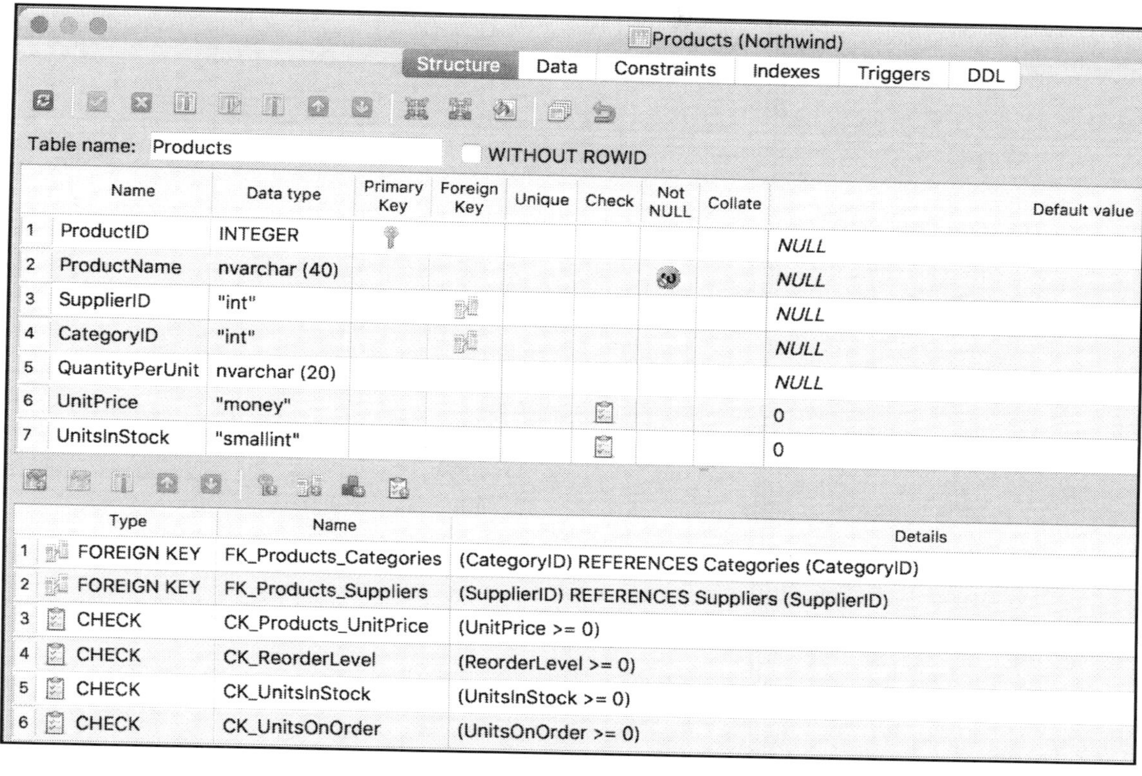

In the table editor window, click the **Data** tab. You will see 77 products:

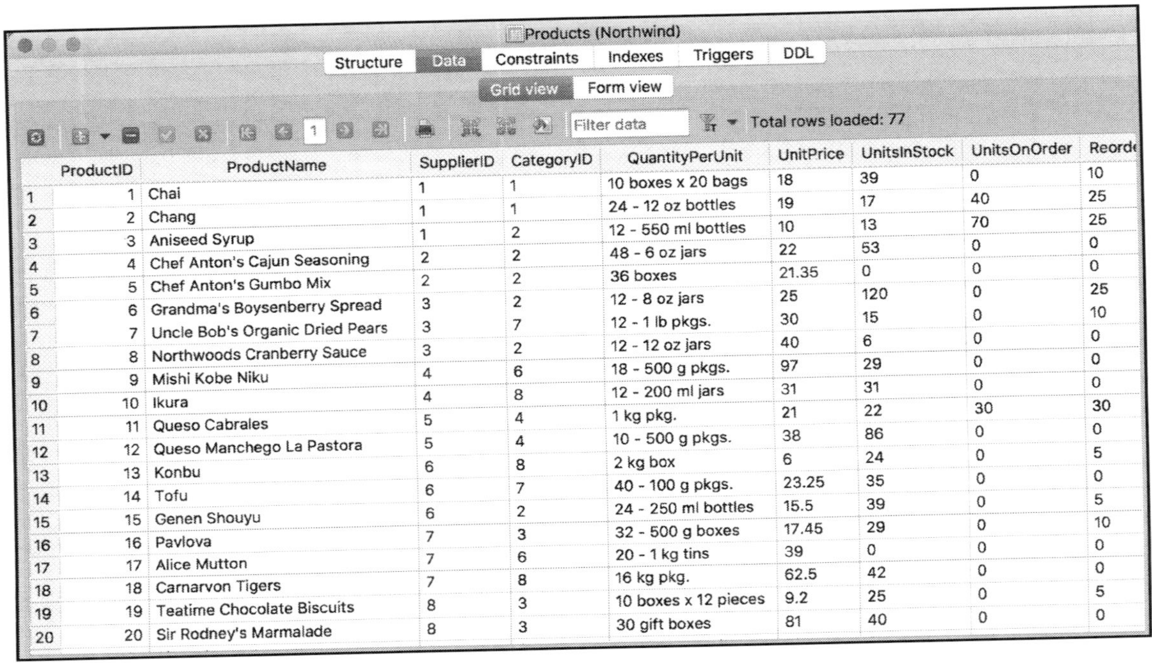


| | ProductID | ProductName | SupplierID | CategoryID | QuantityPerUnit | UnitPrice | UnitsInStock | UnitsOnOrder | Reord |
|---|---|---|---|---|---|---|---|---|---|
| 1 | 1 | Chai | 1 | 1 | 10 boxes x 20 bags | 18 | 39 | 0 | 10 |
| 2 | 2 | Chang | 1 | 1 | 24 - 12 oz bottles | 19 | 17 | 40 | 25 |
| 3 | 3 | Aniseed Syrup | 1 | 2 | 12 - 550 ml bottles | 10 | 13 | 70 | 25 |
| 4 | 4 | Chef Anton's Cajun Seasoning | 2 | 2 | 48 - 6 oz jars | 22 | 53 | 0 | 0 |
| 5 | 5 | Chef Anton's Gumbo Mix | 2 | 2 | 36 boxes | 21.35 | 0 | 0 | 0 |
| 6 | 6 | Grandma's Boysenberry Spread | 3 | 2 | 12 - 8 oz jars | 25 | 120 | 0 | 25 |
| 7 | 7 | Uncle Bob's Organic Dried Pears | 3 | 7 | 12 - 1 lb pkgs. | 30 | 15 | 0 | 10 |
| 8 | 8 | Northwoods Cranberry Sauce | 3 | 2 | 12 - 12 oz jars | 40 | 6 | 0 | 0 |
| 9 | 9 | Mishi Kobe Niku | 4 | 6 | 18 - 500 g pkgs. | 97 | 29 | 0 | 0 |
| 10 | 10 | Ikura | 4 | 8 | 12 - 200 ml jars | 31 | 31 | 0 | 0 |
| 11 | 11 | Queso Cabrales | 5 | 4 | 1 kg pkg. | 21 | 22 | 30 | 30 |
| 12 | 12 | Queso Manchego La Pastora | 5 | 4 | 10 - 500 g pkgs. | 38 | 86 | 0 | 0 |
| 13 | 13 | Konbu | 6 | 8 | 2 kg box | 6 | 24 | 0 | 5 |
| 14 | 14 | Tofu | 6 | 7 | 40 - 100 g pkgs. | 23.25 | 35 | 0 | 0 |
| 15 | 15 | Genen Shouyu | 6 | 2 | 24 - 250 ml bottles | 15.5 | 39 | 0 | 5 |
| 16 | 16 | Pavlova | 7 | 3 | 32 - 500 g boxes | 17.45 | 29 | 0 | 10 |
| 17 | 17 | Alice Mutton | 7 | 6 | 20 - 1 kg tins | 39 | 0 | 0 | 0 |
| 18 | 18 | Carnarvon Tigers | 7 | 8 | 16 kg pkg. | 62.5 | 42 | 0 | 0 |
| 19 | 19 | Teatime Chocolate Biscuits | 8 | 3 | 10 boxes x 12 pieces | 9.2 | 25 | 0 | 5 |
| 20 | 20 | Sir Rodney's Marmalade | 8 | 3 | 30 gift boxes | 81 | 40 | 0 | 0 |

# Setting up Entity Framework Core

**Entity Framework** (**EF**) was first released as part of the **.NET Framework 3.5 with Service Pack 1** back in late 2008. Since then, it has evolved, as Microsoft has observed how programmers use an **object-relational mapping** (**ORM**) tool in the real world.

ORMs use a mapping definition to associate columns in tables to properties in classes. Then, a programmer can just interact with objects of different types in a way that they are familiar, instead of having to deal with knowing how to store the values in a table structure.

The version included with .NET Framework is **Entity Framework 6** (**EF6**). It is mature, stable, and supports an old EDMX (XML file) way of defining the model as well as complex inheritance models, and a few other advanced features. However, EF6 is only supported by .NET Framework, not by .NET Core.

The cross-platform version, EF Core, is different. Microsoft has named it that way to emphasize that it is a reset of functionality. Although EF Core has a similar name, you should be aware that it currently varies from EF6.

Look at its pros and cons:

- Pros
    - EF Core is available for .NET Core as well as .NET Framework, which means it can be used cross-platform on Linux and macOS, as well as Windows
    - EF Core supports modern cloud-based, nonrelational, schema-less data stores, such as Microsoft Azure Cosmos DB, MongoDB, and Redis
- Cons
    - EF Core will never support the EDMX design-time XML file format
    - EF Core does not (yet) support complex inheritance models and other advanced features of EF6

## Choosing an EF Core data provider

Before we dive into the practicalities of managing data using EF Core, let's briefly talk about choosing between **EF Core data providers**.

Although EF Core 2.0 is part of .NET Standard 2.0, to manage data in a specific database, we need classes that know how to efficiently *talk* to that database. EF Core data providers are sets of classes that are optimized for a specific database. They are distributed as NuGet packages.

SQL Server, SQLite, and in-memory database providers are included in the ASP.NET Core 2.0 metapackage. If you create web applications or web services with ASP.NET Core, then installing the packages given in the following table won't be necessary. Since we are building a console application, we must add them manually.

| To manage this database | Install this NuGet package |
|---|---|
| Microsoft SQL Server 2008 or later | `Microsoft.EntityFrameworkCore.SqlServer` |
| SQLite 3.7 or later | `Microsoft.EntityFrameworkCore.SQLite` |
| MySQL | `MySQL.Data.EntityFrameworkCore` |
| In-memory (for unit testing) | `Microsoft.EntityFrameworkCore.InMemory` |

Devart is a third party that offers EF Core providers for a wide range of databases. Find out more at the following link: `https://www.devart.com/dotconnect/entityframework.html`

## Connecting to the database

To connect to SQLite, we just need to know the database filename.

To connect to Microsoft SQL Server, we need to know some information about it:

- The name of the server computer that is running the RDBMS
- The name of the database
- Security information, such as username and password, or if we should pass the currently logged-on user's credentials automatically

We specify this information in a connection string. For backward compatibility, there are multiple possible keywords we can use. Here are some examples:

- **Data Source or server or addr**: These keywords are the name of the server (and an optional instance)
- **Initial Catalog or database**: These keywords are the name of the database
- **Integrated Security or trusted_connection**: These keywords are set to `true` or `SSPI` to pass the thread's current user credentials
- **MultipleActiveResultSets**: This keyword is set to `true` to enable a single connection to be used to work with multiple tables simultaneously to improve efficiency

## Using Visual Studio 2017

In Visual Studio 2017, press *Ctrl* + *Shift* + *N* or go to **File** | **New** | **Project...**.

In the **New Project** dialog, in the **Installed** list, expand **Visual C#**, and select **.NET Core**. In the center list, select **Console App (.NET Core)**, type the name as `WorkingWithEFCore`, change the location to `C:\Code`, type the solution name as `Chapter11`, and then click on **OK**.

Right-click on **Dependencies** and choose **Manage NuGet packages...**. In **NuGet Package Manager**, click on the **Browse** tab and, in the search box, enter `Microsoft.EntityFrameworkCore.SqlServer`, and click on **Install**:

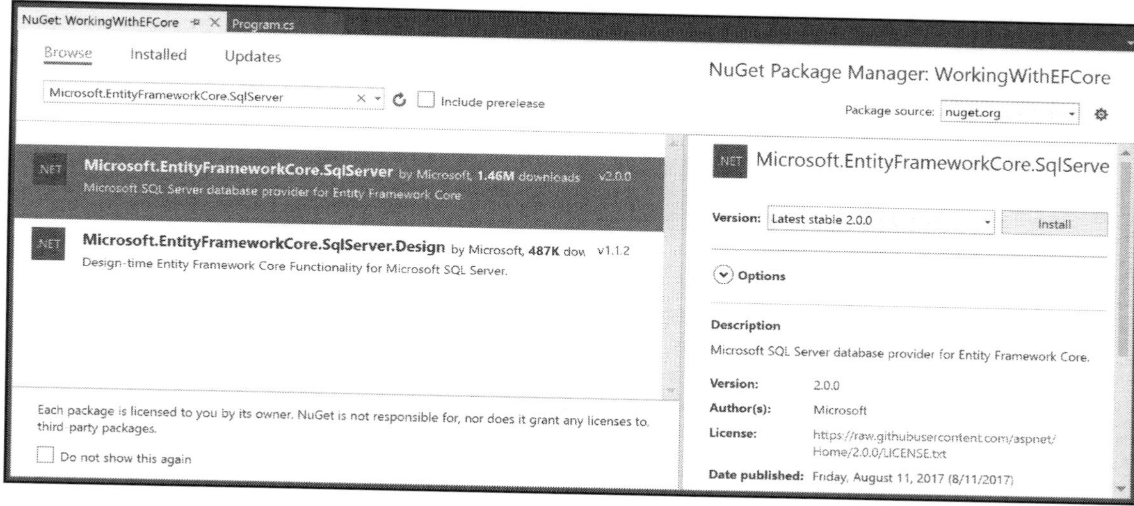

Review the changes, as shown in the following screenshot:

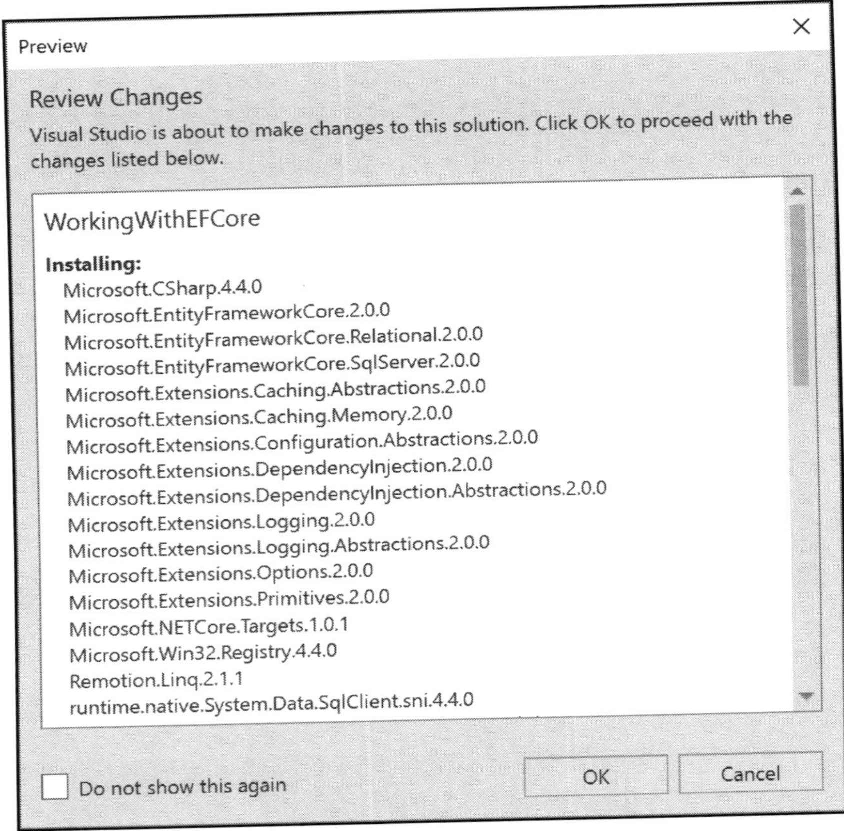


Accept the license agreement.

## Using Visual Studio Code

In Visual Studio Code, open the `WorkingWithEFCore` folder that you created earlier.

In **Integrated Terminal**, enter the `dotnet new console` command.

In the **EXPLORER** pane, click on the `WorkingWithEFCore.csproj` file.

Add a package reference to EF Core data provider for SQLite, as shown highlighted in the following markup:

```
<Project Sdk="Microsoft.NET.Sdk">

  <PropertyGroup>
    <OutputType>Exe</OutputType>
    <TargetFramework>netcoreapp2.0</TargetFramework>
  </PropertyGroup>

  <ItemGroup>
    <PackageReferenceInclude=
     "Microsoft.EntityFrameworkCore.Sqlite" Version="2.0.0" />
  </ItemGroup>

</Project>
```

You can check the most recent version at the following link: `https://www.nuget.org/packages/Microsoft.EntityFrameworkCore.Sqlite/`

# Defining Entity Framework Core models

EF Core uses a combination of **conventions**, **annotation attributes**, and **Fluent API** statements to build an entity model at runtime so that any actions performed on the classes can later be automatically translated into actions performed on the actual database. An entity class represents a row in a table.

## EF Core conventions

The code we will write will use the following conventions:

- The name of a table is assumed to match the name of a `DbSet<T>` property in the `DbContext` class, for example, `Products`
- The names of the columns are assumed to match the names of properties in the class, for example, `ProductID`
- The `string` .NET type is assumed to be an `nvarchar` type in the database

- The `int` .NET type is assumed to be an `int` type in the database
- A property that is named `ID` or the name of the class with `ID` as the suffix is assumed to be a primary key. If this property is any integer type or the `Guid` type, then it is also assumed to be `IDENTITY` (automatically assigned value when inserting).

There are many other conventions, and you can even define your own, but that is beyond the scope of this book. You can read about them at the following link:
`https://docs.microsoft.com/en-us/ef/core/modeling/`

# EF Core annotation attributes

Conventions often aren't enough to completely map the classes to the database objects. A simple way of adding more smarts to your model is to apply annotation attributes.

For example, in the database, the maximum length of a product name is `40`, and the value cannot be null (empty). In a `Product` class, we could apply attributes to specify this:

```
[Required]
[StringLength(40)]
public string ProductName { get; set; }
```

When there isn't an obvious map between .NET types and database types, an attribute can be used. For example, in the database, the column type of `UnitPrice` for the `Products` table is `money`. .NET does not have a `money` type, so it should use `decimal` instead:

```
[Column(TypeName = "money")]
public decimal? UnitPrice { get; set; }
```

In the `Category` table, the `Description` column can be longer than the 8,000 characters that can be stored in an `nvarchar` variable, so it needs to map to `ntext` instead:

```
[Column(TypeName = "ntext")]
public string Description { get; set; }
```

## EF Core Fluent API

The last way that the model can be defined is using the **Fluent API**. It can be used instead of attributes and in addition to them. For example, look at the following two attributes in a `Product` class:

```
[Required]
[StringLength(40)]
public string ProductName { get; set; }
```

The attributes could be removed from the class to keep it simpler, and replaced with a Fluent API statement in the `OnModelBuilding` method of the `Northwind` class, as shown in the following code:

```
modelBuilder.Entity<Product>()
  .Property(product => product.ProductName)
  .IsRequired()
  .HasMaxLength(40);
```

# Building an EF Core model

In both Visual Studio 2017 and Visual Studio Code, add three class files to the project named `Northwind.cs`, `Category.cs`, and `Product.cs`. To make the classes more reusable, we will define them in the `Packt.CS7` namespace.

These three classes will refer to each other, so to avoid confusion, create the three classes without any members first, as shown in the following three class files.

Create a class file named `Category.cs`, as shown in the following code:

```
namespace Packt.CS7
{
   public class Category
   {
   }
}
```

Create a class file named `Product.cs`, as shown here:

```
namespace Packt.CS7
{
   public class Product
   {
   }
}
```

Create a class file named `Northwind.cs`, as shown here:

```
namespace Packt.CS7
{
   public class Northwind
   {
   }
}
```

## Defining the Category entity class

`Category` will be used to represent a row in the `Categories` table, which has four columns, as shown in the following screenshot:

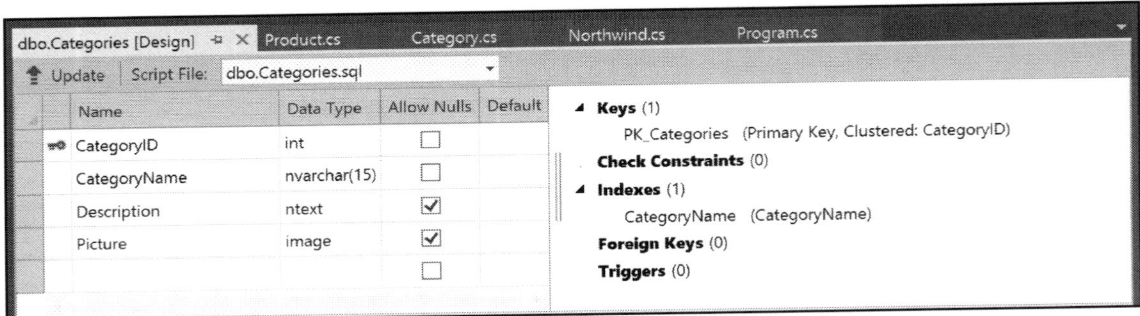


We will use conventions to define the four properties, the primary key, and the one-to-many relationship to the `Products` table, but to map the `Description` column to the correct database type, we will need to decorate the `string` property with the `Column` attribute.

Later, we will use Fluent API to define that `CategoryName` cannot be `null` and is limited to a maximum of 40 characters.

You do not need to include all columns from a table as properties on a class. We will not map the `Picture` column.

Modify the class file named `Category.cs`, as shown in the following code:

```
using System.Collections.Generic;
using System.ComponentModel.DataAnnotations.Schema;

namespace Packt.CS7
{
   public class Category
   {
      // these properties map to columns in the database
      public int CategoryID { get; set; }

      public string CategoryName { get; set; }

      [Column(TypeName = "ntext")]
      public string Description { get; set; }

      // defines a navigation property for related rows
      public virtual ICollection<Product> Products { get; set; }

      public Category()
      {
         // to enable developers to add products to a Category we must
         // initialize the navigation property to an empty list
         this.Products = new List<Product>();
      }
   }
}
```

## Defining the Product entity class

`Product` will be used to represent a row in the `Products` table, which has ten columns, as shown in the following screenshot:

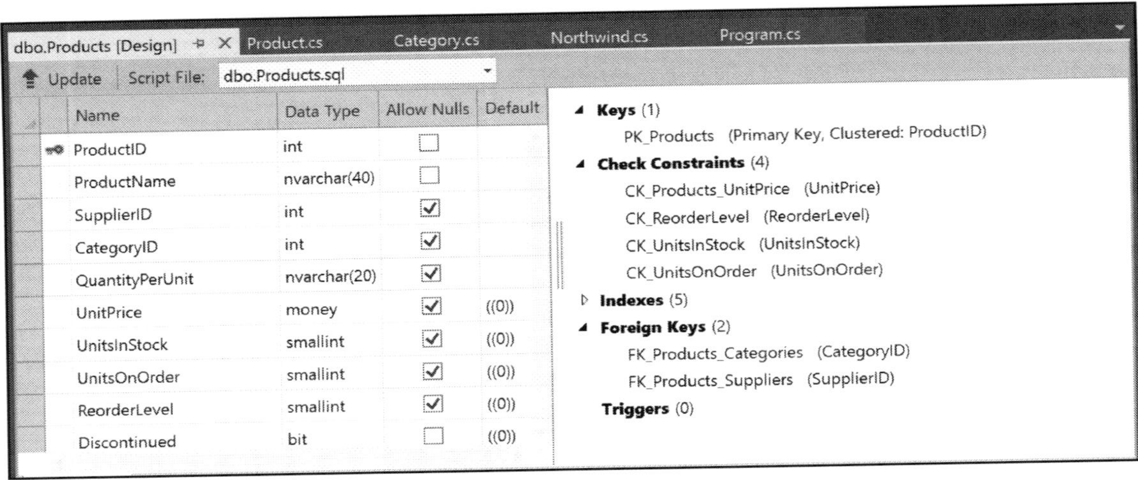


We will only map six properties: `ProductID`, `ProductName`, `UnitPrice`, `UnitsInStock`, `Discontinued`, and `CategoryID`.

`CategoryID` is associated with a `Category` property that will be used to map each product to its parent category.

Modify the class file named `Product.cs`, as shown in the following code:

```
using System.ComponentModel.DataAnnotations;
using System.ComponentModel.DataAnnotations.Schema;

namespace Packt.CS7
{
   public class Product
   {
      public int ProductID { get; set; }

      [Required]
      [StringLength(40)]
      public string ProductName { get; set; }

      [Column("UnitPrice", TypeName = "money")]
      public decimal? Cost { get; set; }
```

```
        [Column("UnitsInStock")]
        public short? Stock { get; set; }

        public bool Discontinued { get; set; }

        // these two define the foreign key relationship
        // to the Categories table
        public int CategoryID { get; set; }
        public virtual Category Category { get; set; }
    }
}
```

The two properties that relate the two entities, `Category.Products` and `Product.Category`, are both marked as `virtual`. This allows EF Core to inherit and override the properties to provide extra features, such as lazy loading. Lazy loading is not implemented in .NET Core 2.0 or earlier. Hopefully, it will be implemented in .NET Core 2.1 or later.

## Defining the Northwind database context class

`Northwind` will be used to represent the database. To use EF Core, the class must inherit from `DbContext`. This class understands how to communicate with databases and dynamically generate SQL statements to query and manipulate data.

Inside your `DbContext`-derived class, you must define at least one property of the `DbSet<T>` type. These properties represent tables. To tell EF Core what columns each table has, the `DbSet` properties use generics to specify a class that represents a row in the table, with properties that represent its columns.

Your `DbContext`-derived class should have an overridden method named `OnConfiguring`. This will set the database connection string. If you want to use SQL Server, then you must uncomment the `UseSqlServer` method call. If you want to use SQLite, then you must uncomment the `UseSqlite` method call.

Your `DbContext`-derived class can optionally have an overridden method named `OnModelCreating`. This is where you can write Fluent API statements as an alternative to decorating your entity classes with attributes.

Modify the class file named `Northwind.cs`, as shown in the following code:

```
using Microsoft.EntityFrameworkCore;

namespace Packt.CS7
{
  // this manages the connection to the database
  public class Northwind : DbContext
  {
    // these properties map to tables in the database
    public DbSet<Category> Categories { get; set; }
    public DbSet<Product> Products { get; set; }

    protected override void OnConfiguring(DbContextOptionsBuilder
    optionsBuilder)
    {
      // to use Microsoft SQL Server, uncomment the following
      // optionsBuilder.UseSqlServer(
      //   @"Data Source=(localdb)\mssqllocaldb;" +
      //   "Initial Catalog=Northwind;" +
      //   "Integrated Security=true;" +
      //   "MultipleActiveResultSets=true;");

      // to use SQLite, uncomment the following
      // string path = System.IO.Path.Combine(
      //   System.Environment.CurrentDirectory, "Northwind.db");
      // optionsBuilder.UseSqlite($"Filename={path}");
    }

    protected override void OnModelCreating(ModelBuilder modelBuilder)
    {
      // example of using Fluent API instead of attributes
      // to limit the length of a category name to under 40
      modelBuilder.Entity<Category>()
        .Property(category => category.CategoryName)
        .IsRequired()
        .HasMaxLength(40);
    }
  }
}
```

Before continuing, make sure that you have uncommented the appropriate method to use the connection string for either SQL Server or SQLite.

# Querying an EF Core model

Open the `Program.cs` file and import the following namespaces:

```
using static System.Console;
using Packt.CS7;
using Microsoft.EntityFrameworkCore;
using System.Linq;
```

In `Program`, define a `QueryingCategories` method, and add the following statements to do these:

- Create an instance of the `Northwind` class that will manage the database
- Create a query for all categories that includes their related products
- Enumerate through the categories, outputting the name and number of products for each one:

```
static void QueryingCategories()
{
    using (var db = new Northwind())
    {
        WriteLine("Categories and how many products they have:");

        // a query to get all categories and their related products
        IQueryable<Category> cats = db.Categories.Include(c => c.Products);

        foreach (Category c in cats)
        {
            WriteLine($"{c.CategoryName} has {c.Products.Count} products.");
        }
    }
}
```

You will learn much more about writing LINQ queries in `Chapter 12`, *Querying and Manipulating Data Using LINQ*. For now, just write the code and view the results.

In `Main`, call the `QueryingCategories` method, as shown in the following code:

```
static void Main(string[] args)
{
   QueryingCategories();
}
```

Run the console application and view the output:

```
Categories and how many products they have:
Beverages has 12 products.
Condiments has 12 products.
Confections has 13 products.
Dairy Products has 10 products.
Grains/Cereals has 7 products.
Meat/Poultry has 6 products.
Produce has 5 products.
Seafood has 12 products.
```

In `Program`, define a `QueryingProducts` method, and add the following statements to do these:

- Create an instance of the `Northwind` class that will manage the database
- Prompt the user for a price for products
- Create a query for products that cost more than the price using LINQ
- Loop through the results, outputting the ID, name, cost (formatted with US dollars), and number of units in stock:

```
static void QueryingProducts()
{
   using (var db = new Northwind())
   {
      WriteLine("Products that cost more than a price, and sorted.");
      string input;
      decimal price;
      do
      {
         Write("Enter a product price: ");
         input = ReadLine();
      } while(!decimal.TryParse(input, out price));

      IQueryable<Product> prods = db.Products
        .Where(product => product.Cost > price)
        .OrderByDescending(product => product.Cost);

      foreach (Product item in prods)
      {
```

```
            WriteLine($"{item.ProductID}: {item.ProductName}
            costs {item.Cost:$#,##0.00} and
            has {item.Stock} units in stock.");
        }
    }
}
```

In `Main`, comment the previous method, and call the method, as shown in the following code:

```
static void Main(string[] args)
{
    //QueryingCategories();
    QueryingProducts();
}
```

Run the console program, enter `50` when prompted to enter a product price, and view the output:

```
Products that cost more than a price, and sorted.
Enter a product price: 50
38: Côte de Blaye costs $263.50 and has 17 units in stock.
29: Thüringer Rostbratwurst costs $123.79 and has 0 units in stock.
9: Mishi Kobe Niku costs $97.00 and has 29 units in stock.
20: Sir Rodney's Marmalade costs $81.00 and has 40 units in stock.
18: Carnarvon Tigers costs $62.50 and has 42 units in stock.
59: Raclette Courdavault costs $55.00 and has 79 units in stock.
51: Manjimup Dried Apples costs $53.00 and has 20 units in stock.
```

There is a limitation with the console provided by Microsoft on versions of Windows before the Windows 10 Fall Creators Update. By default, they cannot display Unicode characters. Unfortunately, UTF-8 is a second-class citizen in old versions of Windows. You can temporarily change the code page (character set) in a console to Unicode UTF-8 by entering the following command at the prompt before running the app:
`chcp 65001`

# Logging EF Core

To monitor the interaction between EF Core and the database, we can enable logging. This requires the following:

- The registering of a **logging provider**
- The implementation of a **logger**

In Visual Studio 2017 or Visual Studio Code, add a class file to your project named `ConsoleLogger.cs`.

Modify the file to define two classes, one to implement `ILoggerProvider` and one to implement `ILogger`, as shown in the following code, and note the following:

- `ConsoleLoggerProvider` returns an instance of `ConsoleLogger`. It does not need any unmanaged resources, so the `Dispose` method does not do anything, but it must exist.
- `ConsoleLogger` is disabled for log levels `None`, `Trace`, and `Information`. It is enabled for all other log levels.
- `ConsoleLogger` implements its `Log` method by writing to `Console`:

```
using Microsoft.Extensions.Logging;
using System;
using static System.Console;

namespace Packt.CS7
{
   public class ConsoleLoggerProvider : ILoggerProvider
   {
      public ILogger CreateLogger(string categoryName)
      {
         return new ConsoleLogger();
      }

      // if your logger uses unmanaged resources,
      // you can release the memory here
      public void Dispose() { }
   }

   public class ConsoleLogger : ILogger
   {
      // if your logger uses unmanaged resources, you can
      // return the class that implements IDisposable here
      public IDisposable BeginScope<TState>(TState state)
      {
         return null;
      }

      public bool IsEnabled(LogLevel logLevel)
      {
         // to avoid overlogging, you can filter
         // on the log level
         switch (logLevel)
         {
```

```
            case LogLevel.Trace:
            case LogLevel.Information:
            case LogLevel.None:
              return false;
            case LogLevel.Debug:
            case LogLevel.Warning:
            case LogLevel.Error:
            case LogLevel.Critical:
            default:
              return true;
        };
      }

      public void Log<TState>(LogLevel logLevel,EventId eventId,
      TState state, Exception exception, Func<TState, Exception, string>
      formatter)
      {
        // log the level and event identifier
        Write($"Level: {logLevel}, Event ID: {eventId}");

        // only output the state or exception if it exists
        if (state != null)
        {
          Write($", State: {state}");
        }
        if (exception != null)
        {
          Write($", Exception: {exception.Message}");
        }
        WriteLine();
      }
    }
  }
```

At the top of the `Program.cs` file, add the following statements to import namespaces:

```
using System;
using Microsoft.EntityFrameworkCore.Infrastructure;
using Microsoft.Extensions.DependencyInjection;
using Microsoft.Extensions.Logging;
```

To both the `QueryingCategories` and `QueryingProducts` methods, add the following statements immediately inside the `using` block for the `Northwind` database context:

```
using (var db = new Northwind())
{
    var loggerFactory = db.GetService<ILoggerFactory>();
    loggerFactory.AddProvider(new ConsoleLoggerProvider());
```

Run the console application and view the output, which is partially shown in the following screenshot:

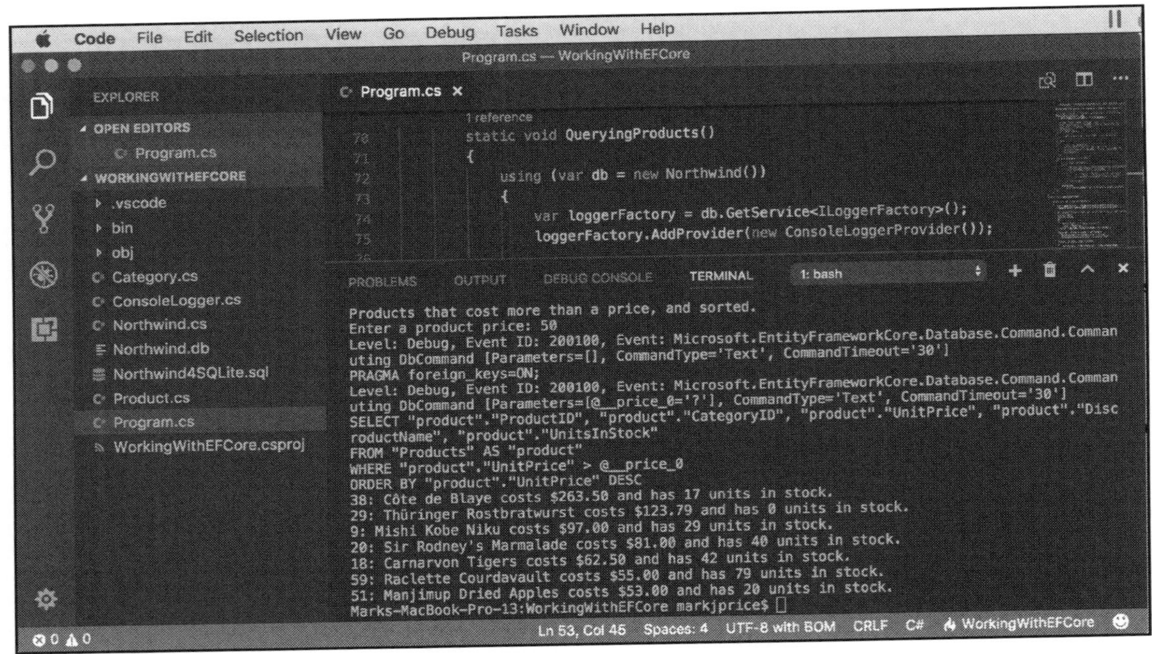

The event ID values and what they mean will be specific to the .NET data provider. If we want to know how the LINQ query has been translated into SQL statements, then the `Event ID` to output has an `Id` value of `200100` and it is named `Microsoft.EntityFrameworkCore.Database.Command.CommandExecuting`.

Modify the `Log` method in `ConsoleLogger` to only output events with `Id` of `200100`, as highlighted in the following code:

```
public void Log<TState>(LogLevel logLevel,EventId eventId,
TState state, Exception exception,Func<TState, Exception, string>
formatter)
{
    if (eventId.Id == 200100)
    {
        // log the level and event identifier
        Write($"Level: {logLevel}, Event ID: {eventId.Id},
        Event: {eventId.Name}");

        // only output the state or exception if it exists
        if (state != null)
        {
            Write($", State: {state}");
        }
        if (exception != null)
        {
            Write($", Exception: {exception.Message}");
        }
        WriteLine();
    }
}
```

In `Main`, uncomment the `QueryingCategories` method so that we can monitor the SQL statements that are generated.

One of the improvements in EF Core 2.0 are the SQL statements that are generated. They are more efficient than in EF Core 1.0 and 1.1.

Run the console application, and note the following SQL statements that were logged, as shown in the following edited output:

```
SELECT "c"."CategoryID", "c"."CategoryName", "c"."Description"
FROM "Categories" AS "c"
ORDER BY "c"."CategoryID"

SELECT "c.Products"."ProductID", "c.Products"."CategoryID",
"c.Products"."UnitPrice", "c.Products"."Discontinued",
"c.Products"."ProductName", "c.Products"."UnitsInStock"
FROM "Products" AS "c.Products"
INNER JOIN (
    SELECT "c0"."CategoryID"
```

```
        FROM "Categories" AS "c0"
    ) AS "t" ON "c.Products"."CategoryID" = "t"."CategoryID"
    ORDER BY "t"."CategoryID"

    SELECT "product"."ProductID", "product"."CategoryID",
    "product"."UnitPrice", "product"."Discontinued", "product"."ProductName",
    "product"."UnitsInStock"
    FROM "Products" AS "product"
    WHERE "product"."UnitPrice" > @__price_0
    ORDER BY "product"."UnitPrice" DESC
```

# Pattern matching with Like

One of the new features in EF Core 2.0 is support for SQL statements including `Like` for pattern matching.

In `Program`, add a method named `QueryingWithLike`, as shown in the following code:

```
static void QueryingWithLike()
{
   using (var db = new Northwind())
   {
      var loggerFactory = db.GetService<ILoggerFactory>();
      loggerFactory.AddProvider(new ConsoleLoggerProvider());

      Write("Enter part of a product name: ");
      string input = ReadLine();

      IQueryable<Product> prods = db.Products
      .Where(p => EF.Functions.Like(p.ProductName, $"%{input}%"));

      foreach (Product item in prods)
      {
         WriteLine($"{item.ProductName} has {item.Stock}
         units in stock. Discontinued? {item.Discontinued}");
      }
   }
}
```

In `Main`, comment the existing methods, and call `QueryingWithLike`, as shown in the following code:

```
static void Main(string[] args)
{
   // QueryingCategories();
   // QueryingProducts();
   QueryingWithLike();
}
```

Run the console application, enter a partial product name such as `che`, and view the output:

```
Enter part of a product name: che
Level: Debug, Event ID: 200100, Event:
Microsoft.EntityFrameworkCore.Database.Command.CommandExecuting, State:
Executing DbCommand [Parameters=[], CommandType='Text',
CommandTimeout='30']
PRAGMA foreign_keys=ON;
Level: Debug, Event ID: 200100, Event:
Microsoft.EntityFrameworkCore.Database.Command.CommandExecuting, State:
Executing DbCommand [Parameters=[@__Format_1='?'], CommandType='Text',
CommandTimeout='30']
SELECT "p"."ProductID", "p"."CategoryID", "p"."UnitPrice",
"p"."Discontinued", "p"."ProductName", "p"."UnitsInStock"
FROM "Products" AS "p"
WHERE "p"."ProductName" LIKE @__Format_1
Chef Anton's Cajun Seasoning has 53 units in stock. Discontinued? False
Chef Anton's Gumbo Mix has 0 units in stock. Discontinued? True
Queso Manchego La Pastora has 86 units in stock. Discontinued? False
Gumbär Gummibärchen has 15 units in stock. Discontinued? False
```

# Defining global filters

Another new feature in EF Core 2.0 are global filters.

The `Northwind` products can be discontinued, so it might be useful to ensure that discontinued products are never returned in results, even if the programmer forgets to use `Where` to filter them out, as we did in the previous example (Chef Anton's Gumbo Mix is discontinued, which is sad, because it's very flavorful).

Modify the `OnModelCreating` method in the `Northwind` class to add a global filter to remove discontinued products, as shown in the following code:

```
protected override void OnModelCreating(ModelBuilder modelBuilder)
{
   // example of using Fluent API instead of attributes
   // to limit the length of a category name to under 40
   modelBuilder.Entity<Category>()
      .Property(category => category.CategoryName)
      .IsRequired()
      .HasMaxLength(40);

   // global filter to remove discontinued products
   modelBuilder.Entity<Product>().HasQueryFilter(p => !p.Discontinued);
}
```

Run the console application, enter a partial product name such as `che`, view the output, and note that Chef Anton's Gumbo Mix is now missing, because the SQL statement generated includes a filter for the `Discontinued` column:

```
SELECT "p"."ProductID", "p"."CategoryID", "p"."UnitPrice",
"p"."Discontinued", "p"."ProductName", "p"."UnitsInStock"
FROM "Products" AS "p"
WHERE ("p"."Discontinued" = 0) AND "p"."ProductName" LIKE @__Format_1
Chef Anton's Cajun Seasoning has 53 units in stock. Discontinued? False
Queso Manchego La Pastora has 86 units in stock. Discontinued? False
Gumbär Gummibärchen has 15 units in stock. Discontinued? False
```

# Loading patterns with EF Core

There are three **loading patterns** that are commonly used with EF: **lazy loading**, **eager loading**, and **explicit loading**, but not all of them are supported in EF Core.

## Eager and lazy loading entities

In the `QueryingCategories` method, the code currently uses the `Categories` property to loop through each category, outputting the category name and the number of products in that category. This works because when we wrote the query, we used the `Include` method to use eager loading (aka **early loading**) for the related products.

Modify the query to comment out the `Include` method call, as shown in the following code:

```
IQueryable<Categories> cats = db.Categories; //.Include(c => c.Products);
```

In `Main`, comment all methods except `QueryingCategories`, as shown in the following code:

```
static void Main(string[] args)
{
   QueryingCategories();
   // QueryingProducts();
   // QueryingWithLike();
}
```

Run the console application and view the output:

```
Beverages has 0 products.
Condiments has 0 products.
Confections has 0 products.
Dairy Products has 0 products.
Grains/Cereals has 0 products.
Meat/Poultry has 0 products.
Produce has 0 products.
Seafood has 0 products.
```

Each item in `foreach` is an instance of the `Category` class, which has a property named `Products`, that is, the list of products in that category. Since the original query is only selected from the `Categories` table, this property is empty for each category.

When lazy loading is finally implemented in EF Core, every time the loop enumerates and an attempt is made to read the `Products` property, EF Core will automatically check if they are loaded. If not, EF Core will load them for us "lazily" by executing a `SELECT` statement to load just that set of products for the current category, and then the correct count would be returned to the output.

The problem with lazy loading is that multiple round trips to the database server are required to eventually fetch all the data. Therefore, it has not been a priority for the EF Core team.

## Explicit loading entities

Another type of loading is explicit loading. It works like lazy loading, but you are in control of exactly which related data is loaded and when. You can think of lazy loading as explicit loading that happens automatically for all related entities.

In the `QueryingCategories` method, modify your query statements to prompt the user if they want to enable eager loading and explicit loading, as shown in the following code:

```
IQueryable<Category> cats;
// = db.Categories;//.Include(c => c.Products);

Write("Enable eager loading? (Y/N): ");
bool eagerloading = (ReadKey().Key == ConsoleKey.Y);
bool explicitloading = false;
WriteLine();
if (eagerloading)
{
   cats = db.Categories.Include(c => c.Products);
}
else
{
   cats = db.Categories;
   Write("Enable explicit loading? (Y/N): ");
   explicitloading = (ReadKey().Key == ConsoleKey.Y);
   WriteLine();
}
```

Inside the `foreach` loop, before the `WriteLine` method call, add statements to check if explicit loading is enabled, and if so, prompt the user if they want to explicitly load each individual category, as shown in the following code:

```
if (explicitloading)
{
   Write($"Explicitly load products for {c.CategoryName}? (Y/N):");
   if (ReadKey().Key == ConsoleKey.Y)
   {
      var products = db.Entry(c).Collection(c2 => c2.Products);
      if (!products.IsLoaded) products.Load();
   }
   WriteLine();
}
```

Run the console application; press *N* to disable eager loading, and press *Y* to enable explicit loading.

For each category, press *Y* or *N* to load its products as you wish. In the following example output, I chose to load products for only two of the eight categories, `Beverages` and `Seafood`:

```
Categories and how many products they have:
Enable eager loading? (Y/N): n
Enable explicit loading? (Y/N): y
Level: Debug, Event ID: 200100, Event:
Microsoft.EntityFrameworkCore.Database.Command.CommandExecuting, State:
Executing DbCommand [Parameters=[], CommandType='Text',
CommandTimeout='30']
PRAGMA foreign_keys=ON;
Level: Debug, Event ID: 200100, Event:
Microsoft.EntityFrameworkCore.Database.Command.CommandExecuting, State:
Executing DbCommand [Parameters=[], CommandType='Text',
CommandTimeout='30']
SELECT "c"."CategoryID", "c"."CategoryName", "c"."Description"
FROM "Categories" AS "c"
Explicitly load products for Beverages? (Y/N):yLevel: Debug, Event ID:
200100, Event:
Microsoft.EntityFrameworkCore.Database.Command.CommandExecuting, State:
Executing DbCommand [Parameters=[@__get_Item_0='?'], CommandType='Text',
CommandTimeout='30']
SELECT "e"."ProductID", "e"."CategoryID", "e"."UnitPrice",
"e"."Discontinued", "e"."ProductName", "e"."UnitsInStock"
FROM "Products" AS "e"
WHERE "e"."CategoryID" = @__get_Item_0

Beverages has 12 products.
Explicitly load products for Condiments? (Y/N):n
Condiments has 0 products.
Explicitly load products for Confections? (Y/N):n
Confections has 0 products.
Explicitly load products for Dairy Products? (Y/N):n
Dairy Products has 0 products.
Explicitly load products for Grains/Cereals? (Y/N):n
Grains/Cereals has 0 products.
Explicitly load products for Meat/Poultry? (Y/N):n
Meat/Poultry has 0 products.
Explicitly load products for Produce? (Y/N):n
Produce has 0 products.
Explicitly load products for Seafood? (Y/N):yLevel: Debug, Event ID:
200100, Event:
Microsoft.EntityFrameworkCore.Database.Command.CommandExecuting, State:
```

```
Executing DbCommand [Parameters=[@__get_Item_0='?'], CommandType='Text',
CommandTimeout='30']
SELECT "e"."ProductID", "e"."CategoryID", "e"."UnitPrice",
"e"."Discontinued", "e"."ProductName", "e"."UnitsInStock"
FROM "Products" AS "e"
WHERE "e"."CategoryID" = @__get_Item_0

Seafood has 12 products.
```

**Good Practice**
Carefully consider which loading pattern is best for your code. In the future, if lazy loading is the default as it is with EF6, then it could literally make you a lazy database developer!

# Manipulating data with EF Core

Inserting, updating, and deleting entities using EF Core is easy.

## Inserting entities

In `Program`, create a new method named `AddProduct`, as shown in the following code:

```
static bool AddProduct(int categoryID, string productName, decimal? price)
{
   using (var db = new Northwind())
   {
      var newProduct = new Product
      {
         CategoryID = categoryID,
         ProductName = productName,
         Cost = price
      };

      // mark product as added in change tracking
      db.Products.Add(newProduct);
      // save tracked changes to database
      int affected = db.SaveChanges();
      return (affected == 1);
   }
}
```

In Program, create a new method named ListProducts, as shown in the following code:

```
static void ListProducts()
{
   using (var db = new Northwind())
   {
      WriteLine("------------------------------------------------------------
---------------");
      WriteLine("| ID | Product Name | Cost | Stock | Disc. |");
      WriteLine("------------------------------------------------------------
---------------");
      foreach (var item in db.Products.OrderByDescending(p => p.Cost))
      {
         WriteLine($"| {item.ProductID:000} |
                     {item.ProductName,-35} |
                     {item.Cost,8:$#,##0.00} |
                     {item.Stock, 5} |
                     {item.Discontinued} |");
      }
      WriteLine("------------------------------------------------------------
---------------");
   }
}
```

In Main, comment previous method calls, and then call AddProduct and ListProducts, as shown in the following code:

```
static void Main(string[] args)
{
   // QueryingCategories();
   // QueryingProducts();
   // QueryingWithLike();

   AddProduct(6, "Bob's Burgers", 500M);
   ListProducts();
}
```

Run the application, view the output, and note the product has been inserted, as shown in the following screenshot:

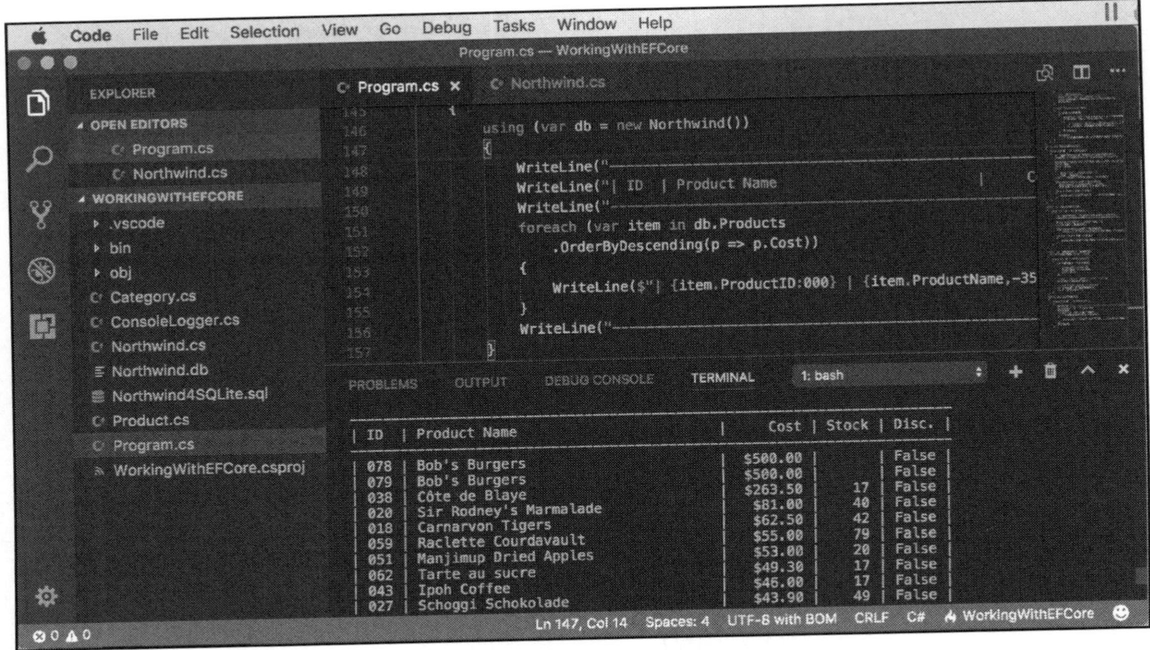


# Updating entities

In `Program`, add a method to increase the price of the first product with a name that begins with `Bob` by $20, as shown in the following code:

```
static bool IncreaseProductPrice(string name, decimal amount)
{
   using (var db = new Northwind())
   {
      Product updateProduct = db.Products.First(
      p => p.ProductName.StartsWith(name));
      updateProduct.Cost += amount;
      int affected = db.SaveChanges();
      return (affected == 1);
   }
}
```

In Main, comment the call to AddProduct, and add a call to IncreaseProductPrice:

```
static void Main(string[] args)
{
    // QueryingCategories();
    // QueryingProducts();
    // QueryingWithLike();

    // AddProduct(6, "Bob's Burgers", 500M);

    IncreaseProductPrice("Bob", 20M);
    ListProducts();
}
```

Run the console application, view the output, and note that the existing entity for Bob's Burgers has increased in price by $20:

```
-----------------------------------------------------------
| ID  | Product Name                        |      Cost |
-----------------------------------------------------------
| 078 | Bob's Burgers                       |   $520.00 |
```

# Deleting entities

In Program, import System.Collections.Generic, and then add a method to delete all products with a name that begins with Bob, as shown in the following code:

```
static int DeleteProducts(string name)
{
    using (var db = new Northwind())
    {
        IEnumerable<Product> products = db.Products.Where(
        p => p.ProductName.StartsWith(name));
        db.Products.RemoveRange(products);
        int affected = db.SaveChanges();
        return affected;
    }
}
```

You can remove individual entities with the Remove method. RemoveRange is more efficient when you want to delete multiple entities.

In `Main`, comment the call to `AddProduct`, and add a call to `DeleteProducts`, as shown in the following code:

```
static void Main(string[] args)
{
    // QueryingCategories();
    // QueryingProducts();
    // QueryingWithLike();

    // AddProduct(6, "Bob's Burgers", 500M);
    // IncreaseProductPrice("Bob", 20M);

    int deleted = DeleteProducts("Bob");
    WriteLine($"{deleted} product(s) were deleted.");
    ListProducts();
}
```

Run the console application, view the output, and note if multiple product names start with `Bob`, then they are all deleted, as shown in the following output:

```
2 product(s) were deleted.
-----------------------------------------------------------------
| ID  | Product Name                          |    Cost | Stock | Disc. |
-----------------------------------------------------------------
| 038 | Côte de Blaye                         | $263.50 |    17 | False |
```

# Pooling database contexts

A feature of ASP.NET Core 2.0 that is related to EF Core 2.0 is that it makes your code more efficient by pooling database contexts when building web applications and web services. This allows you to create and dispose as many `DbContext`-derived objects as you want, knowing your code is still very efficient.

# Transactions

Every time you call the `SaveChanges` method, an **implicit transaction** is started so that if something goes wrong, it would automatically rollback all the changes. If every operation succeeds, then the transaction is committed.

Transactions maintain the integrity of your database by applying locks to prevent reads and writes while a sequence of operations is occurring.

Transactions are ACID, which is explained here:

- **A** is for atomic. Either all the operations in the transaction commit or none of them do.
- **C** is for consistent. The state of the database before and after a transaction is consistent. This is dependent on your code logic.
- **I** is for isolated. During a transaction, changes are hidden from other processes. There are multiple isolation levels that you can pick from (refer to the following table). The stronger the level, the better the integrity of the data. However, more locks must be applied, which will negatively affect other processes. Snapshot is a special case because it creates multiple copies of rows to avoid locks, but this will increase the size of your database while transactions occur.
- **D** is for durable. If a failure occurs during a transaction, it can be recovered. The opposite of durable is volatile:

| **Isolation level** | **Lock(s)** | **Integrity problems allowed** |
|---|---|---|
| `ReadUncommitted` | None | Dirty reads, nonrepeatable reads, and phantom data |
| `ReadCommitted` | When editing, it applies read lock(s) to block other users from reading the record(s) until the transaction ends | Nonrepeatable reads and phantom data |
| `RepeatableRead` | When reading, it applies edit lock(s) to block other users from editing the record(s) until the transaction ends | Phantom data |
| `Serializable` | Applies key-range locks to prevent any action that would affect the results, including inserts and deletes | None |
| `Snapshot` | None | None |

## Defining an explicit transaction

You can control explicit transactions using the `Database` property of the database context.

Import the following namespace in `Program.cs` to use the `IDbContextTransaction` interface:

```
using Microsoft.EntityFrameworkCore.Storage;
```

In the `DeleteProducts` method, after the instantiation of the `db` variable, add the following statements to start an explicit transaction and output its isolation level. At the bottom of the method, commit the transaction, and close the brace, as shown in the following code:

```
static int DeleteProducts(string name)
{
    using (var db = new Northwind())
    {
        using (IDbContextTransaction t =
        db.Database.BeginTransaction())
        {
            WriteLine($"Transaction started with
            this isolation level: {t.GetDbTransaction().IsolationLevel}");

            var products = db.Products.Where(
            p => p.ProductName.StartsWith(name));
            db.Products.RemoveRange(products);
            int affected = db.SaveChanges();
            t.Commit();
            return affected;
        }
    }
}
```

Run the console application and view the output.

When using Microsoft SQL Server, you will see the following isolation level:

```
Transaction started with this isolation level: ReadCommitted
```

When using SQLite, you will see the following isolation level:

```
Transaction started with this isolation level: Serializable
```

# Practicing and exploring

Test your knowledge and understanding by answering some questions, get some hands-on practice, and explore this chapter's topics with deeper research.

## Exercise 11.1 – Test your knowledge

Answer the following questions:

1. What type would you use for the property that represents a table, for example, the `Products` property of a `Northwind` database context?
2. What type would you use for the property that represents a one-to-many relationship, for example, the `Products` property of a `Category` entity?
3. What is the EF Core convention for primary keys?
4. When would you use an annotation attribute in an entity class?
5. Why might you choose the Fluent API in preference to annotation attributes?
6. What does a transaction isolation level of `Serializable` mean?
7. What does the `DbContext.SaveChanges()` method return?
8. What is the difference between eager loading and explicit loading?
9. How should you define an EF Core entity class to match the following table?

```
CREATE TABLE Employees(
  EmpID INT IDENTITY,
  FirstName NVARCHAR(40) NOT NULL,
  Salary MONEY
)
```

10. What benefit do you get from declaring entity properties as `virtual`?

## Exercise 11.2 – Practice exporting data using different serialization formats

Create a console application named `Exercise02` that queries the Northwind database for all the categories and products, and then serializes the data using at least three formats of serialization available to .NET Core.

Which format of serialization uses the least number of bytes?

## Exercise 11.3 – Explore the EF Core documentation

Go to the following website and read the official Entity Framework Core documentation. Follow the tutorials to create Windows desktop, and web applications and services. If you have a macOS or a Linux virtual machine, follow the tutorials to use EF Core on those alternative platforms:

`https://docs.microsoft.com/en-us/ef/core/index`

# Summary

In this chapter, you learned how to connect to a database, how to execute a simple LINQ query and process the results, and how to build entity data models for an existing database, such as Northwind.

In the next chapter, you will learn how to write more advanced LINQ queries to select, filter, sort, join, and group.

# 12
# Querying and Manipulating Data Using LINQ

This chapter is about **Language Integrated Query** (**LINQ**), a set of language extensions that add the ability to work with sequences of items and then filter, sort, and project them into different outputs.

This chapter covers the following topics:

- Writing LINQ queries
- Working with sets
- Using LINQ with EF Core
- Sweetening the syntax with syntactic sugar
- Using multiple threads with parallel LINQ
- Creating your own LINQ extension methods
- Working with LINQ to XML

# Writing LINQ queries

Although we wrote a few LINQ queries in `Chapter 11`, *Working with Databases Using Entity Framework Core*, I didn't properly explain how LINQ works.

LINQ has several parts; some are required and some are optional:

- **Extension methods (required)**: These include examples such as `Where`, `OrderBy`, and `Select`. These are what provide the functionality of LINQ.
- **LINQ providers (required)**: These include LINQ to Objects, LINQ to Entities, LINQ to XML, LINQ to OData, and LINQ to Amazon. These are what convert standard LINQ operations into specific commands for different types of data.
- **Lambda expressions (optional)**: These can be used instead of named methods to simplify LINQ extension method calls.
- **LINQ query comprehension syntax (optional)**: These include `from`, `in`, `where`, `orderby`, `descending`, and `select`. These are C# keywords that are aliases for some of the LINQ extension methods, and their use can simplify the queries you write, especially if you already have experience with other query languages, such as **Structured Query Language** (**SQL**).

When programmers are first introduced to LINQ, they often believe that LINQ query comprehension syntax is LINQ, but ironically, that is one of the parts of LINQ that is optional!

# Extending sequences with the enumerable class

The LINQ extension methods, such as `Where` and `Select`, are appended by the `Enumerable` static class to any type, known as a **sequence**, that implements `IEnumerable<T>`. The `Enumerable` class is shown in the following diagram:

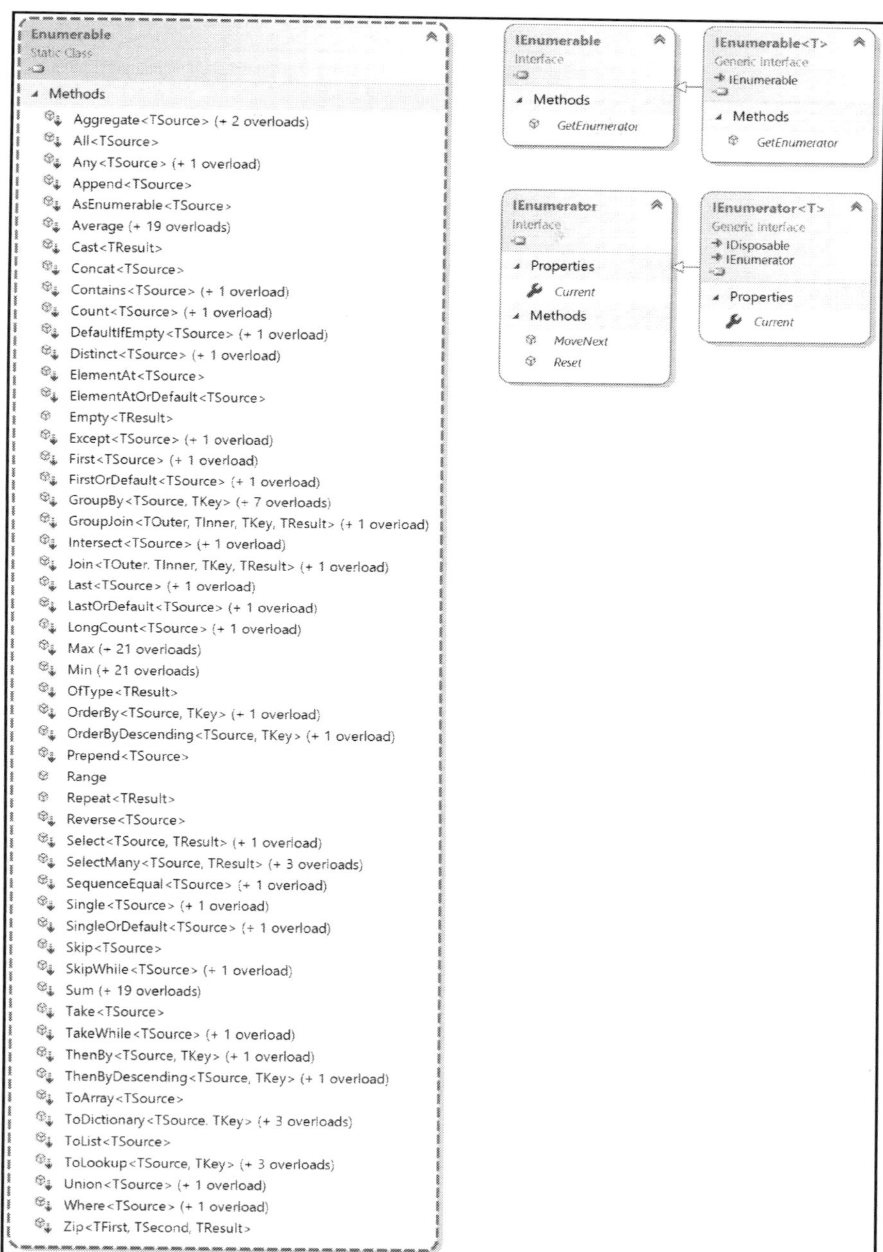
Enumerable
Static Class
Methods
Aggregate<TSource> (+ 2 overloads)
All<TSource>
Any<TSource> (+ 1 overload)
Append<TSource>
AsEnumerable<TSource>
Average (+ 19 overloads)
Cast<TResult>
Concat<TSource>
Contains<TSource> (+ 1 overload)
Count<TSource> (+ 1 overload)
DefaultIfEmpty<TSource> (+ 1 overload)
Distinct<TSource> (+ 1 overload)
ElementAt<TSource>
ElementAtOrDefault<TSource>
Empty<TResult>
Except<TSource> (+ 1 overload)
First<TSource> (+ 1 overload)
FirstOrDefault<TSource> (+ 1 overload)
GroupBy<TSource, TKey> (+ 7 overloads)
GroupJoin<TOuter, TInner, TKey, TResult> (+ 1 overload)
Intersect<TSource> (+ 1 overload)
Join<TOuter, TInner, TKey, TResult> (+ 1 overload)
Last<TSource> (+ 1 overload)
LastOrDefault<TSource> (+ 1 overload)
LongCount<TSource> (+ 1 overload)
Max (+ 21 overloads)
Min (+ 21 overloads)
OfType<TResult>
OrderBy<TSource, TKey> (+ 1 overload)
OrderByDescending<TSource, TKey> (+ 1 overload)
Prepend<TSource>
Range
Repeat<TResult>
Reverse<TSource>
Select<TSource, TResult> (+ 1 overload)
SelectMany<TSource, TResult> (+ 3 overloads)
SequenceEqual<TSource> (+ 1 overload)
Single<TSource> (+ 1 overload)
SingleOrDefault<TSource> (+ 1 overload)
Skip<TSource>
SkipWhile<TSource> (+ 1 overload)
Sum (+ 19 overloads)
Take<TSource>
TakeWhile<TSource> (+ 1 overload)
ThenBy<TSource, TKey> (+ 1 overload)
ThenByDescending<TSource, TKey> (+ 1 overload)
ToArray<TSource>
ToDictionary<TSource, TKey> (+ 3 overloads)
ToList<TSource>
ToLookup<TSource, TKey> (+ 3 overloads)
Union<TSource> (+ 1 overload)
Where<TSource> (+ 1 overload)
Zip<TFirst, TSecond, TResult>
IEnumerable
Interface
Methods
GetEnumerator
IEnumerable<T>
Generic Interface
IEnumerable
Methods
GetEnumerator
IEnumerator
Interface
Properties
Current
Methods
MoveNext
Reset
IEnumerator<T>
Generic Interface
IDisposable
IEnumerator
Properties
Current

For example, an array of any type implements the `IEnumerable<T>` class, where `T` is the type of item in the array, so all arrays support LINQ to query and manipulate them.

All generic collections, such as `List<T>`, `Dictionary<TKey, TValue>`, `Stack<T>`, and `Queue<T>`, implement `IEnumerable<T>`, so they can be queried and manipulated with LINQ.

`DbSet<T>` implements `IEnumerable<T>`, so LINQ can be used to query and manipulate entity models built for EF Core.

# Filtering entities with Where

The most common reason for using LINQ is to filter items in a sequence using the `Where` extension method.

In **Visual Studio 2017**, press *Ctrl* + *Shift* + *N* or navigate to **File** | **New** | **Project....** In the **New Project** dialog, in the **Installed** list, expand **Visual C#**, and select **.NET Core**. In the list at the center, select **Console App (.NET Core)**, type the name `LinqWithObjects`, change the location to `C:\Code`, type the solution name `Chapter12`, and then click on **OK**.

In **Visual Studio Code**, make a directory named `Chapter12` with a subfolder named `LinqWithObjects`. Open the `LinqWithObjects` folder and execute the `dotnet new console` command in the Terminal.

In the `Program` class, add a `LinqWithArrayOfStrings` method, that defines an array of strings, and then attempts to call the `Where` extension method on it, as shown in the following code:

```
static void LinqWithArrayOfStrings()
{
   var names = new string[] { "Michael", "Pam", "Jim",
       "Dwight", "Angela", "Kevin", "Toby", "Creed" };
   var query = names.
```

As you try to type the `Where` method, note that it is missing from the IntelliSense list of members of a `string` array, as shown in the following screenshot:

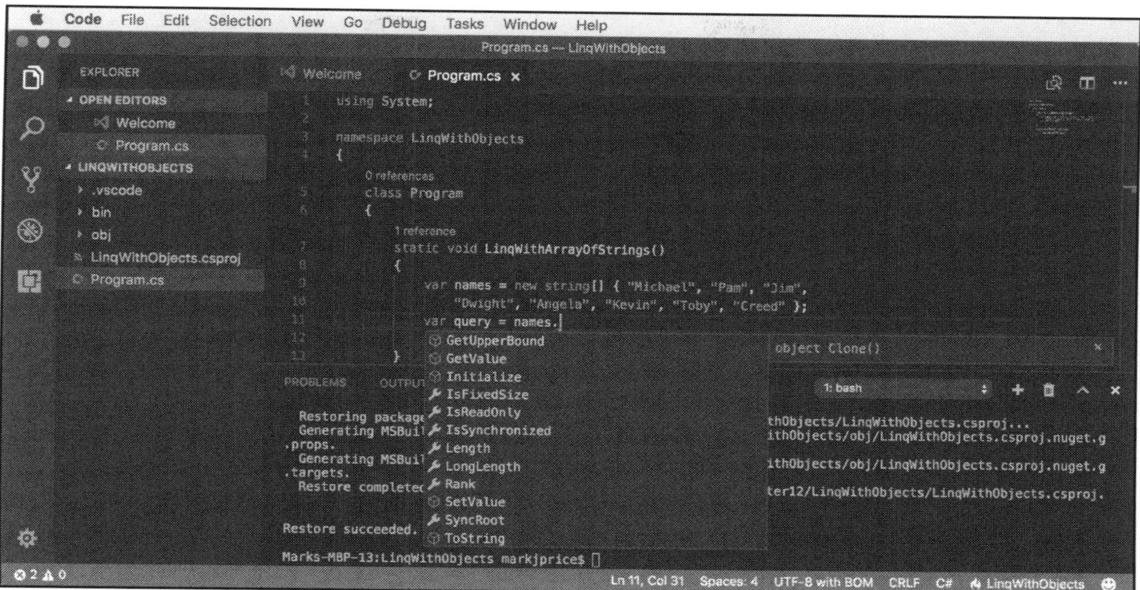

This is because the `Where` method is an **extension method**. It does not exist on the array type. To make the `Where` extension method available, we must import the `System.Linq` namespace.

Add the following statement to the top of the `Program.cs` file:

```
using System.Linq;
```

Now, as you type the `W`, note the IntelliSense list shows the three members that contain a letter W. The IntelliSense also tells us that to call `Where`, we must pass in an instance of a `Func<string, bool>` delegate, as shown in the following screenshot:

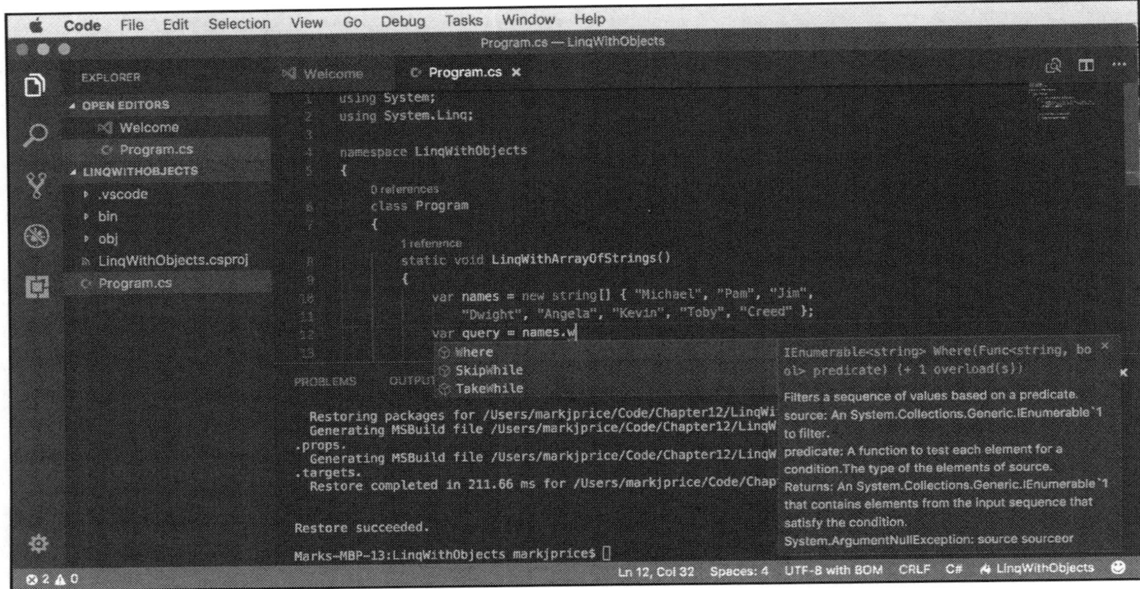


Enter the following code to create a new delegate instance:

```
var query = names.Where(new Func<string, bool>())
```

Note the IntelliSense shown in Visual Studio 2017 (but not in Visual Studio Code). This tells us that the `target` method must have a single input parameter of type `string`, and a return of type `bool`, as shown in the following screenshot:

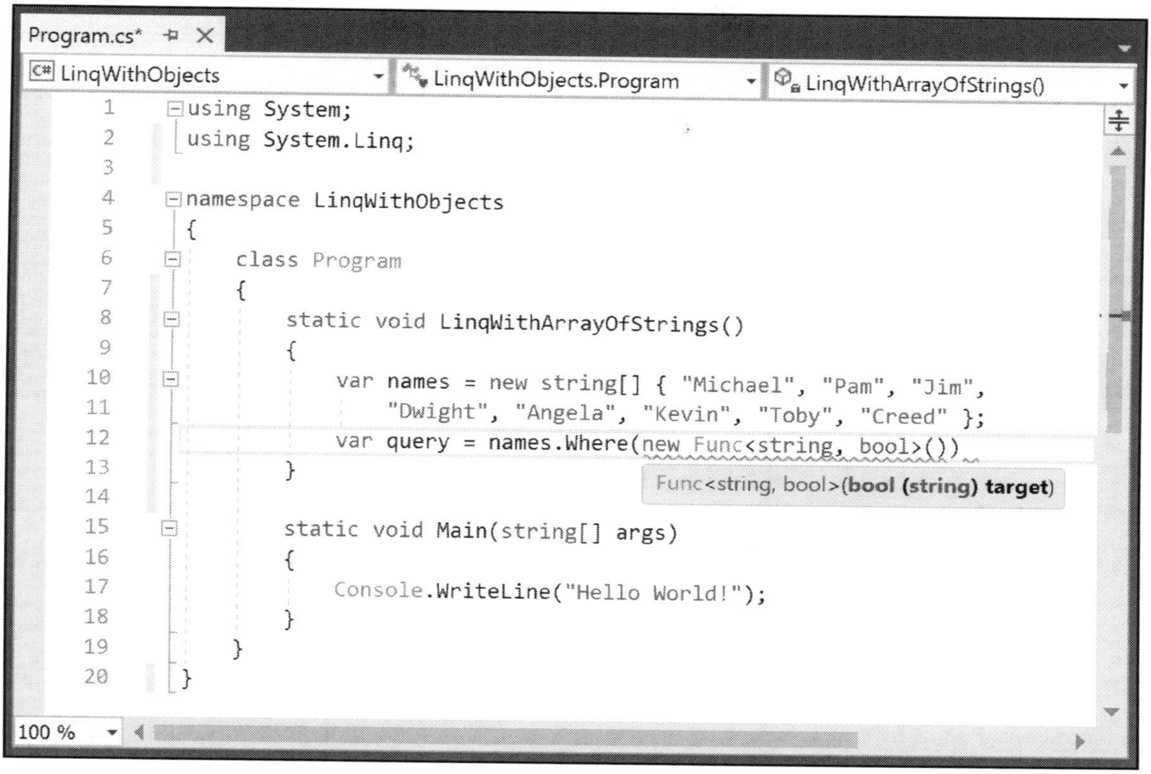

```
Program.cs*
LinqWithObjects | LinqWithObjects.Program | LinqWithArrayOfStrings()

using System;
using System.Linq;

namespace LinqWithObjects
{
    class Program
    {
        static void LinqWithArrayOfStrings()
        {
            var names = new string[] { "Michael", "Pam", "Jim",
                "Dwight", "Angela", "Kevin", "Toby", "Creed" };
            var query = names.Where(new Func<string, bool>())
        }
                                    Func<string, bool>(bool (string) target)
        static void Main(string[] args)
        {
            Console.WriteLine("Hello World!");
        }
    }
}

100 %
```

For each `string` variable passed to the method, the method must return a Boolean value. If the method returns `true`, it indicates that we should include the `string` in the results, and if the method returns `false`, it indicates that we should exclude it.

## Targeting a named method

Let's define a method that only includes names that are longer than four characters.

Statically import the `Console` class, and then add the following method to the `Program` class:

```
static bool NameLongerThanFour(string name)
{
   return name.Length > 4;
}
```

Pass the method's name into the `Func<string, bool>` delegate, and then loop through the query items, as shown in the following code:

```
var query = names.Where(new Func<string, bool>(NameLongerThanFour));
foreach (string item in query)
{
   WriteLine(item);
}
```

In the `Main` method, call the `LinqWithArrayOfStrings` method, as shown in the following code:

```
static void Main(string[] args)
{
   LinqWithArrayOfStrings();
}
```

Run the console application and view the output:

```
Michael
Dwight
Angela
Kevin
Creed
```

## Simplifying the code by removing the explicit delegate instantiation

We can simplify the code by deleting the explicit instantiation of the `Func<string, bool>` delegate. The C# compiler will instantiate the `Func<string, bool>` delegate for us, so you never need to explicitly do it.

Copy and paste the query, comment the first example, and modify the copy to remove the explicit instantiation of the `Func<string, bool>` delegate, as shown in the following code:

```
// var query = names.Where(new Func<string, bool>(NameLongerThanFour));

var query = names.Where(NameLongerThanFour);
```

Rerun the application and note that it has the same behavior.

## Targeting a lambda expression

We can simplify our code even further using a **lambda expression** in place of the named method.

Although it can look complicated at first, a lambda expression is simply a *nameless function*. It uses the => (read as "goes to") symbol to indicate the return value.

Copy and paste the query, comment the second example, and modify the query to look like the following statement:

```
var query = names.Where(name => name.Length > 4);
```

Note that the syntax for a lambda expression includes all the important parts of the `NameLongerThanFour` method, but nothing more. A lambda expression only needs to define the following:

- The names of input parameters
- A return value expression

The type of the `name` input parameter is inferred from the fact that the sequence contains `string` values, and the return type must be a `bool` value for `Where` to work, so the expression after the => symbol must return a `bool` value.

The compiler does most of the work for us, so our code can be as concise as possible.

Rerun the application and note that it has the same behavior.

## Sorting entities

`Where` is just one of about 30 extension methods provided by the `Enumerable` type. Other extension methods are `OrderBy` and `ThenBy`. Extension methods can be chained if the previous method returns another sequence, that is, a type that implements the `IEnumerable<T>` interface.

### Sorting by a single property using OrderBy

Append a call to `OrderBy` to the end of the existing query, as shown here:

```
var query = names.Where(name => name.Length > 4)
    .OrderBy(name => name.Length);
```

**Good Practice**
Format the LINQ statement so that each extension method call happens on its own line to make them easier to read.

Rerun the application and note that the names are now sorted with shortest first:

```
Kevin
Creed
Dwight
Angela
Michael
```

To put the longest name first, you will use `OrderByDescending`.

### Sorting by a subsequent property using ThenBy

We might want to sort by more than one property.

Append a call to ThenBy to the end of the existing query, as shown here:

```
var query = names.Where(name => name.Length > 4)
    .OrderBy(name => name.Length).ThenBy(name => name);
```

Rerun the application and note the slight difference in the following sort order. Within a group of names of the same length, the names are sorted alphabetically by the full value of the string, so Creed comes before Kevin, and Angela comes before Dwight:

```
Creed
Kevin
Angela
Dwight
Michael
```

# Filtering by type

The Where extension method is great for filtering by values, such as text and numbers. But what if the sequence contains multiple types, and you want to filter by a specific type, and respect any inheritance hierarchy?

Imagine that you have a sequence of exceptions, as shown in the following code example:

```
var errors = new Exception[]
{
    new ArgumentException(),
    new SystemException(),
    new IndexOutOfRangeException(),
    new InvalidOperationException(),
    new NullReferenceException(),
    new InvalidCastException(),
    new OverflowException(),
    new DivideByZeroException(),
    new ApplicationException()
};
```

Exceptions have a complex hierarchy, as shown in the following diagram:

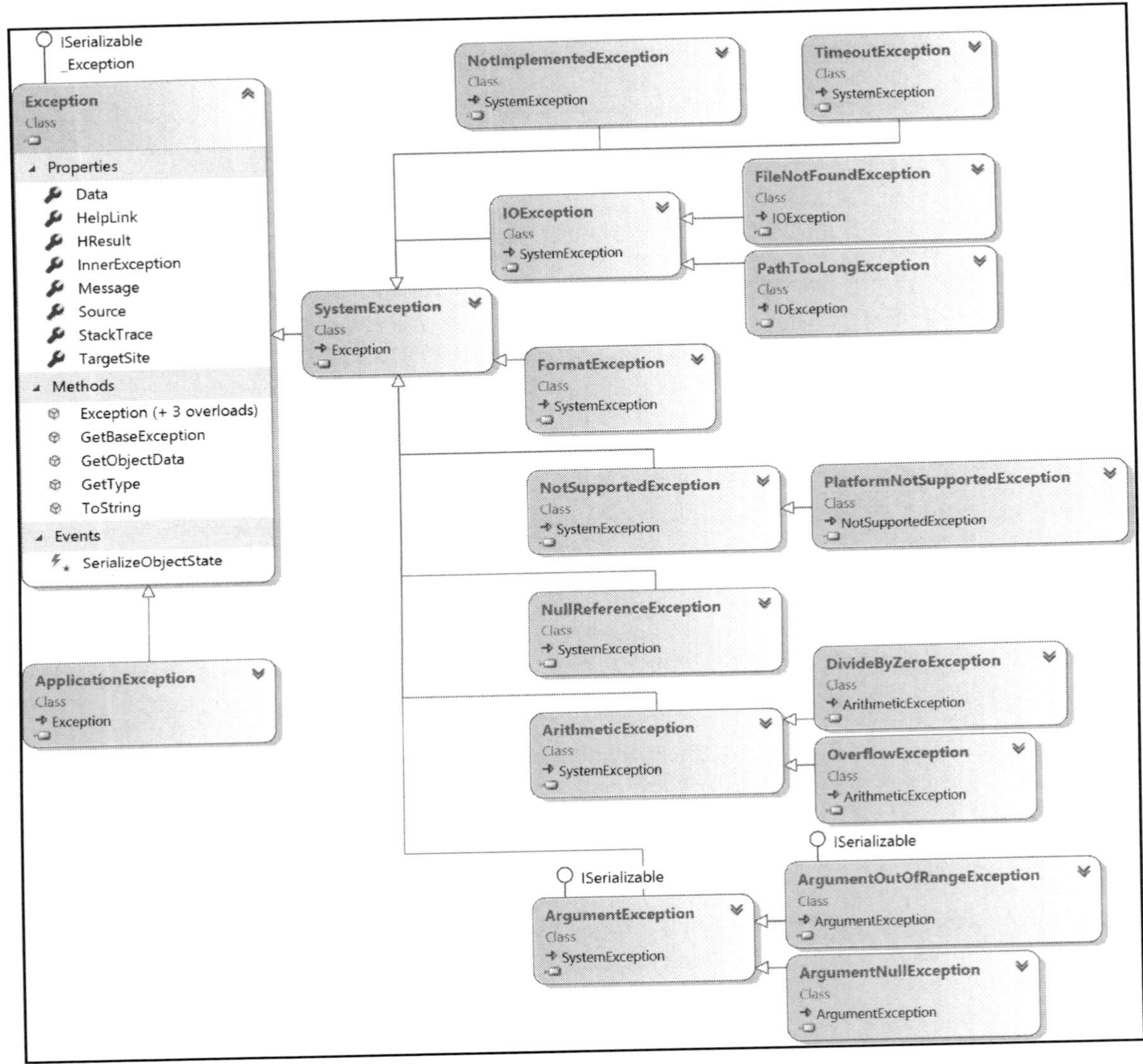

To filter by type, we could write statements using the `OfType<T>` extension method, as shown in the following code example:

```
var numberErrors = errors.OfType<ArithmeticException>();

foreach (var error in numberErrors)
{
   WriteLine(error);
}
```

The results would only include exceptions of the `ArithmeticException` type, or the `ArithmeticException`-derived types, as shown in the following output:

```
System.OverflowException: Arithmetic operation resulted in an overflow.
System.DivideByZeroException: Attempted to divide by zero.
```

# Working with sets

Sets are one of the most fundamental concepts in mathematics. A **set** is a collection of one or more objects. You might remember being taught about Venn diagrams in school. Common set operations include the **intersect** or **union** between sets.

Add a new console application project named `LinqWithSets` in either Visual Studio 2017 or Visual Studio Code.

In Visual Studio 2017, set the solution's start up project to be the current selection.

This application will define three arrays of strings for cohorts of apprentices and then perform some common set operations.

Import the following additional namespaces:

```
using System.Collections.Generic; // for IEnumerable<T>
using System.Linq; // for LINQ extension methods
```

Inside the `Program` class, before the `Main` method, add the following method that outputs any sequence of `string` variables as a comma-separated single string to the console output, along with an optional description:

```
private static void Output(IEnumerable<string> cohort,
string description = "")
{
   if (!string.IsNullOrEmpty(description))
   {
      WriteLine(description);
```

```
        }
        Write("    ");
        WriteLine(string.Join(", ", cohort.ToArray()));
    }
```

In the `Main` method, write the following statements:

```
    var cohort1 = new string[]
      { "Rachel", "Gareth", "Jonathan", "George" };
    var cohort2 = new string[]
      { "Jack", "Stephen", "Daniel", "Jack", "Jared" };
    var cohort3 = new string[]
      { "Declan", "Jack", "Jack", "Jasmine", "Conor" };

    Output(cohort1, "Cohort 1");
    Output(cohort2, "Cohort 2");
    Output(cohort3, "Cohort 3");
    WriteLine();

    Output(cohort2.Distinct(),"cohort2.Distinct(): removes duplicates");

    Output(cohort2.Union(cohort3),"cohort2.Union(cohort3):
    combines and removes duplicates");

    Output(cohort2.Concat(cohort3),"cohort2.Concat(cohort3):
    combines but leaves duplicates");

    Output(cohort2.Intersect(cohort3),"cohort2.Intersect(cohort3):
    items that are in both sequences");
    Output(cohort2.Except(cohort3),"cohort2.Except(cohort3):
    removes items from the first sequence that are in the second sequence");
    Output(cohort1.Zip(cohort2,(c1, c2) => $"{c1} matched with {c2}"),
          "cohort1.Zip(cohort2, (c1, c2) => $\"{c1} matched with {c2}\")" +
          ": matches items based on position in the sequence");
```

Run the console application and view the output:

```
    Cohort 1
      Rachel, Gareth, Jonathan, George
    Cohort 2
      Jack, Stephen, Daniel, Jack, Jared
    Cohort 3
      Declan, Jack, Jack, Jasmine, Conor
    cohort2.Distinct(): removes duplicates
      Jack, Stephen, Daniel, Jared
    cohort2.Union(cohort3): combines two sequences and removes any
    duplicates
      Jack, Stephen, Daniel, Jared, Declan, Jasmine, Conor
```

```
cohort2.Concat(cohort3): combines two sequences but leaves in any
duplicates
  Jack, Stephen, Daniel, Jack, Jared, Declan, Jack, Jack, Jasmine,
  Conor
cohort2.Intersect(cohort3): returns items that are in both sequences
  Jack
cohort2.Except(cohort3): removes items from the first sequence that
are in the second sequence
  Stephen, Daniel, Jared
cohort1.Zip(cohort2, (c1, c2) => $"{c1} matched with {c2}"): matches
items based on position in the sequence
  Rachel matched with Jack, Gareth matched with Stephen, Jonathan
  matched with Daniel, George matched with Jack
```

With `Zip`, if there are unequal numbers of items in the two sequences, then some items will not have a matching partner.

# Using LINQ with EF Core

To learn about **projection**, it is best to have some more complex sequences to work with; so, in the next project, we will use the `Northwind` sample database.

## Projecting entities with Select

Add a new console application project named `LinqWithEFCore`.

In **Visual Studio 2017**, in the **LinqWithEFCore** project, right-click on **Dependencies** and choose **Manage NuGet Packages....** Search for the `Microsoft.EntityFrameworkCore.SqlServer` package and install it.

If you did not complete `Chapter 11`, *Working with Databases Using Entity Framework Core*, then open the `Northwind4SQLServer.sql` file, and right-click and choose **Execute** to create the `Northwind` database on the server named `(localdb)\mssqllocaldb`.

In **Visual Studio Code**, modify the `LinqWithEFCore.csproj` file as highlighted in the following markup:

```
<Project Sdk="Microsoft.NET.Sdk">

  <PropertyGroup>
    <OutputType>Exe</OutputType>
    <TargetFramework>netcoreapp1.1</TargetFramework>
  </PropertyGroup>

  <ItemGroup>
    <PackageReference
        Include="Microsoft.EntityFrameworkCore.Sqlite"
        Version="2.0.0" />
    </ItemGroup>

</Project>
```

Copy the `Northwind4SQLite.sql` file into the `LinqWithEFCore` folder, and then use **Integrated Terminal** to create the `Northwind` database by executing the following command:

```
sqlite3 Northwind.db < Northwind4SQLite.sql
```

## Building an EF Core model

In both Visual Studio 2017 and Visual Studio Code, add three class files to the project named `Northwind.cs`, `Category.cs`, and `Product.cs`.

Your `DbContext`-derived class should have an overridden method named `OnConfiguring`. This will set the database connection string. If you want to use SQL Server, then you must uncomment the `UseSqlServer` method call. If you want to use SQLite, then you must uncomment the `UseSqlite` method call.

Modify the class file named `Northwind.cs`, as shown in the following code:

```
using Microsoft.EntityFrameworkCore;

namespace Packt.CS7
{
   // this manages the connection to the database
   public class Northwind : DbContext
   {
      // these properties map to tables in the database
      public DbSet<Category> Categories { get; set; }
```

```
        public DbSet<Product> Products { get; set; }

        protected override void OnConfiguring(
        DbContextOptionsBuilder optionsBuilder)
        {
            // to use Microsoft SQL Server, uncomment the following
            // optionsBuilder.UseSqlServer(
            //    @"Data Source=(localdb)\mssqllocaldb;" +
            //    "Initial Catalog=Northwind;" +
            //    "Integrated Security=true;" +
            //    "MultipleActiveResultSets=true;");

            // to use SQLite, uncomment the following
            // string path = System.IO.Path.Combine(
            //    System.Environment.CurrentDirectory, "Northwind.db");
            // optionsBuilder.UseSqlite($"Filename={path}");
        }
    }
}
```

`Category.cs` should look like this:

```
using System.ComponentModel.DataAnnotations;

namespace Packt.CS7
{
    public class Category
    {
        public int CategoryID { get; set; }
        [Required]
        [StringLength(15)]
        public string CategoryName { get; set; }
        public string Description { get; set; }
    }
}
```

`Product.cs` should look like this:

```
using System.ComponentModel.DataAnnotations;

namespace Packt.CS7
{
    public class Product
    {
        public int ProductID { get; set; }
        [Required]
        [StringLength(40)]
        public string ProductName { get; set; }
```

```
        public int? SupplierID { get; set; }
        public int? CategoryID { get; set; }
        [StringLength(20)]
        public string QuantityPerUnit { get; set; }
        public decimal? UnitPrice { get; set; }
        public short? UnitsInStock { get; set; }
        public short? UnitsOnOrder { get; set; }
        public short? ReorderLevel { get; set; }
        public bool Discontinued { get; set; }
    }
}
```

We have not defined relationships between the two entity classes. This is deliberate. Later, you will use LINQ to join the two entity sets.

Open the `Program.cs` file and import the following namespaces:

```
using static System.Console;
using Packt.CS7;
using Microsoft.EntityFrameworkCore;
using System.Linq;
```

In the `Main` method, write the following statements:

```
using (var db = new Northwind())
{
   var query = db.Products
        .Where(product => product.UnitPrice < 10M)
        .OrderByDescending(product => product.UnitPrice);

   WriteLine("Products that cost less than $10:");
   foreach (var item in query)
   {
      WriteLine($"{item.ProductID}: {item.ProductName}
      costs {item.UnitPrice:$#,##0.00}");
   }
   WriteLine();
}
```

Run the console application and view the output:

```
Products that cost less than $10:
41: Jack's New England Clam Chowder costs $9.65
45: Rogede sild costs $9.50
47: Zaanse koeken costs $9.50
19: Teatime Chocolate Biscuits costs $9.20
```

```
23: Tunnbröd costs $9.00
75: Rhönbräu Klosterbier costs $7.75
54: Tourtière costs $7.45
52: Filo Mix costs $7.00
13: Konbu costs $6.00
24: Guaraná Fantástica costs $4.50
33: Geitost costs $2.50
```

Although this query outputs the information we want, it does so inefficiently because it returns all columns from the Products table instead of just the three columns we need, which is the equivalent of the following SQL statement:

```
SELECT * FROM Products;
```

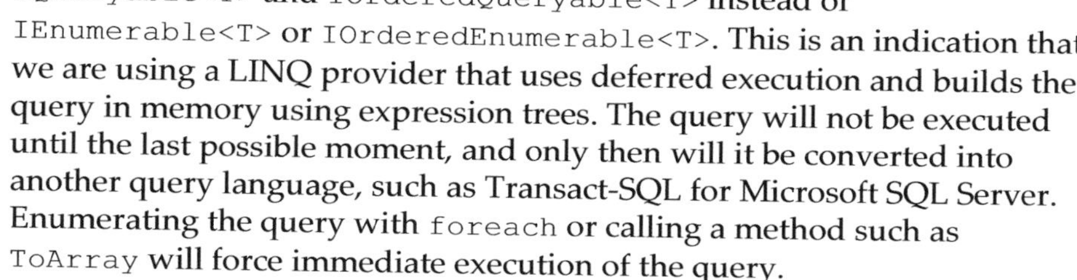

You might have also noticed that the sequences implement IQueryable<T> and IOrderedQueryable<T> instead of IEnumerable<T> or IOrderedEnumerable<T>. This is an indication that we are using a LINQ provider that uses deferred execution and builds the query in memory using expression trees. The query will not be executed until the last possible moment, and only then will it be converted into another query language, such as Transact-SQL for Microsoft SQL Server. Enumerating the query with foreach or calling a method such as ToArray will force immediate execution of the query.

In the Main method, modify the LINQ query to use the Select method to return only the three properties (table columns) that we need, as shown in the following statements:

```
var query = db.Products
    .Where(product => product.UnitPrice < 10M)
    .OrderByDescending(product => product.UnitPrice)
    .Select(product => new
    {
       product.ProductID,
       product.ProductName,
       product.UnitPrice
    });
```

Run the console application and confirm that the output is the same as before.

## Joining and grouping

There are two extension methods for joining and grouping:

- `Join`: This method has four parameters: the sequence that you want to join with, the property or properties on the *left* sequence to match on, the property or properties on the *right* sequence to match on, and a projection
- `GroupJoin`: This method has the same parameters, but it combines the matches into a group object with a `Key` property for the matching value and an `IEnumerable<T>` type for the multiple matches

In the `Main` method, write the following statements:

```
// create two sequences that we want to join together
var categories = db.Categories.Select(
    c => new { c.CategoryID, c.CategoryName }).ToArray();

var products = db.Products.Select(
    p => new { p.ProductID, p.ProductName,
    p.CategoryID }).ToArray();

// join every product to its category to return 77 matches
var queryJoin = categories.Join(products,
    category => category.CategoryID,
    product => product.CategoryID,
    (c, p) => new { c.CategoryName, p.ProductName,
    p.ProductID });

foreach (var item in queryJoin)
{
   WriteLine($"{item.ProductID}: {item.ProductName} is in
   {item.CategoryName}.");
}
```

Run the console application and view the output.

Note that there is a single line output for each of the 77 products, and the results show all products in the `Beverages` category first, then the `Condiments` category, and so on:

```
1: Chai is in Beverages.
2: Chang is in Beverages.
24: Guaraná Fantástica is in Beverages.
34: Sasquatch Ale is in Beverages.
35: Steeleye Stout is in Beverages.
38: Côte de Blaye is in Beverages.
39: Chartreuse verte is in Beverages.
```

```
43: Ipoh Coffee is in Beverages.
67: Laughing Lumberjack Lager is in Beverages.
70: Outback Lager is in Beverages.
75: Rhönbräu Klosterbier is in Beverages.
76: Lakkalikööri is in Beverages.
3: Aniseed Syrup is in Condiments.
4: Chef Anton's Cajun Seasoning is in Condiments.
```

Change the query to sort by `ProductID`:

```
var queryJoin = categories.Join(products,
    category => category.CategoryID,
    product => product.CategoryID,
    (c, p) => new { c.CategoryName, p.ProductName,
    p.ProductID }).OrderBy(cp => cp.ProductID);
```

Rerun the application and view the output:

```
1: Chai is in Beverages.
2: Chang is in Beverages.
3: Aniseed Syrup is in Condiments.
4: Chef Anton's Cajun Seasoning is in Condiments.
5: Chef Anton's Gumbo Mix is in Condiments.
6: Grandma's Boysenberry Spread is in Condiments.
7: Uncle Bob's Organic Dried Pears is in Produce.
8: Northwoods Cranberry Sauce is in Condiments.
9: Mishi Kobe Niku is in Meat/Poultry.
10: Ikura is in Seafood.
11: Queso Cabrales is in Dairy Products.
12: Queso Manchego La Pastora is in Dairy Products.
13: Konbu is in Seafood.
14: Tofu is in Produce.
15: Genen Shouyu is in Condiments.
```

Add some new statements, as shown in the following code, to the bottom of the `Main` method to show the use of the `GroupJoin` method, and in the output, show the group name and then all the items within each group:

```
// group all products by their category to return 8 matches
var queryGroup = categories.GroupJoin(products,
    category => category.CategoryID,
    product => product.CategoryID,
    (c, Products) => new { c.CategoryName,
    Products = Products.OrderBy(p => p.ProductName) });

  foreach (var item in queryGroup)
  {
     WriteLine($"{item.CategoryName} has
```

```
        {item.Products.Count()} products.");
        foreach (var product in item.Products)
        {
          WriteLine($"  {product.ProductName}");
        }
    }
```

Rerun the console application and view the output.

Note that the products inside each category have been sorted by their name, as the query asked:

```
Beverages has 12 products.
  Chai
  Chang
  Chartreuse verte
  Côte de Blaye
  Guaraná Fantástica
  Ipoh Coffee
  Lakkalikööri
  Laughing Lumberjack Lager
  Outback Lager
  Rhönbräu Klosterbier
  Sasquatch Ale
  Steeleye Stout
Condiments has 12 products.
  Aniseed Syrup
  Chef Anton's Cajun Seasoning
  Chef Anton's Gumbo Mix
```

# Aggregating sequences

There are LINQ extension methods to perform aggregation functions, such as `Average` and `Sum`.

Add some new statements, as shown in the following code, to the bottom of the `Main` method to show the use of the aggregation extension methods:

```
WriteLine("Products");
WriteLine($" Count:
{db.Products.Count()}");
WriteLine($" Sum of units in stock:
{db.Products.Sum(p => p.UnitsInStock):N0}");
WriteLine($" Sum of units on order:
{db.Products.Sum(p => p.UnitsOnOrder):N0}");
WriteLine($" Average unit price:
```

```
{db.Products.Average(p => p.UnitPrice):$#,##0.00}");
WriteLine($" Value of units in stock:
{db.Products.Sum(p => p.UnitPrice * p.UnitsInStock):$#,##0.00}");
```

Run the console application and view the output:

```
Products
  Count: 77
  Sum of units in stock: 3,119
  Sum of units on order: 780
  Average unit price: $28.87
  Value of units in stock: $74,050.85
```

# Sweetening the syntax with syntactic sugar

C# 3 introduced some new keywords in 2008 to make it easier for programmers with experience in SQL to write LINQ queries. This *syntactic sugar* is sometimes called the **LINQ query comprehension syntax**.

The LINQ query comprehension syntax is limited in functionality. You must use extension methods to access all the features of LINQ.

Consider the following code:

```
var names = new string[] { "Michael", "Pam", "Jim",
    "Dwight", "Angela", "Kevin", "Toby", "Creed" };

var query = names.Where(name => name.Length > 4)
    .OrderBy(name => name.Length).ThenBy(name => name);
```

Instead of writing the preceding code using **extension methods** and **lambda expressions**, you can write the following code using **query comprehension syntax**:

```
var query = from name in names where name.Length > 4
    orderby name.Length, name select name;
```

The compiler changes the query comprehension syntax to the extension method and lambda expression equivalent for you.

The `select` keyword is always required for LINQ query comprehension syntax. The `Select` extension method is optional when using extension methods and lambda expressions.

Not all extension methods have a C# keyword equivalent, for example, the `Skip` and `Take` extension methods that are commonly used to implement paging for lots of data. The following query cannot be written using only the query syntax:

```
var query = names.Where(name => name.Length > 4)
    .OrderBy(name => name.Length)
    .ThenBy(name => name).Skip(80).Take(10);
```

Luckily, you can wrap query comprehension syntax in parentheses and then switch to using extension methods, as shown in the following code:

```
var query = (from name in names
    where name.Length > 4
    orderby name.Length, name
    select name).Skip(80).Take(10);
```

**Good Practice**
Learn both extension methods with lambda expressions and the query comprehension syntax ways of writing LINQ queries, because you are likely to have to maintain code that uses both.

# Using multiple threads with parallel LINQ

By default, only one thread is used to execute a LINQ query. **Parallel LINQ (PLINQ)** is an easy way to enable multiple threads to execute a LINQ query.

**Good Practice**
Do not assume that using parallel threads will improve the performance of your applications. Always measure real-world timings and resource usage.

To see it in action, we will start with some code that only uses a single thread to double 200 million integers. We will use the `StopWatch` type to measure the change in performance. We will use operating system tools to monitor CPU and CPU core usage.

Use either Visual Studio 2017 or Visual Studio Code to add a new console application project named `LINQingInParallel`.

Import the `System.Diagnostics` namespace so that we can use the `StopWatch` type; `System.Collections.Generic` so that we can use the `IEnumerable<T>` type, `System.Linq`; and statically import the `System.Console` type.

Add the following statements to the `Main` method to create a stopwatch to record timings, wait for a key press before starting the timer, create 200 million integers, square each of them, stop the timer, and display the elapsed milliseconds:

```
var watch = Stopwatch.StartNew();
Write("Press ENTER to start: ");
ReadLine();
watch.Start();

IEnumerable<int> numbers = Enumerable.Range(1, 200_000_000);
var squares = numbers.Select(number => number * 2).ToArray();
watch.Stop();
WriteLine(
$"{watch.ElapsedMilliseconds:#,##0} elapsed milliseconds.");
```

Run the console application, but *do not* press *Enter* to start yet.

In Windows 10, right-click on the Windows **Start** button or press *Ctrl* + *Alt* + *Delete*, and then click on **Task Manager**.

At the bottom of the **Task Manager** window, click on the **More details** button. At the top of the **Task Manager** window, click on the **Performance** tab.

Right-click on the **CPU Utilisation** graph, choose **Change graph to**, and then **Logical processors**, as you can see in the following screenshot:

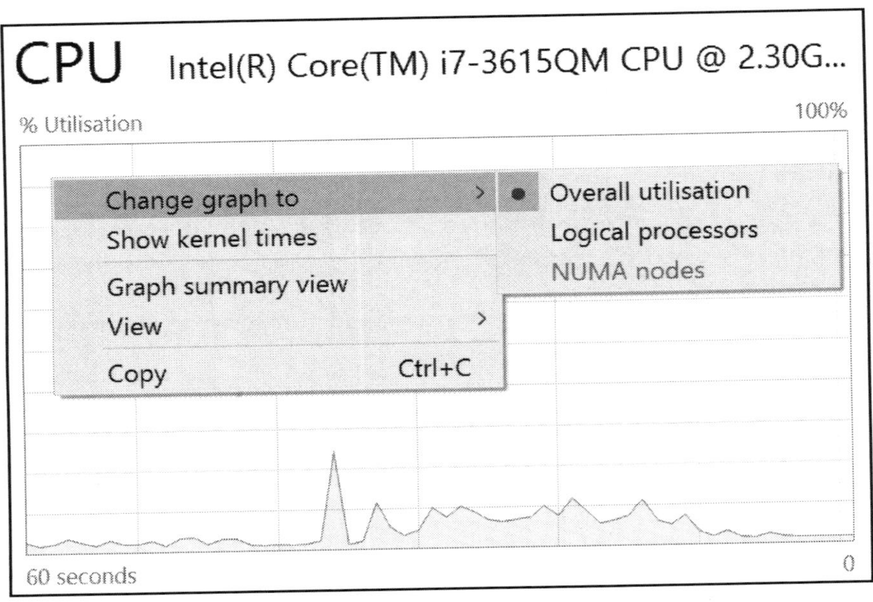


In macOS, run **Activity Monitor**.

Navigate to **View** | **Update Frequency** | **Very often (1 sec)**.

To see the CPU graphs, navigate to **Window** | **CPU History**.

If you do not have multiple CPUs, then this exercise won't show much!

Rearrange **Task Manager** and your console application, or **CPU History** and Visual Studio Code's **Integrated Terminal**, so that they are side by side, as shown in the following screenshot:

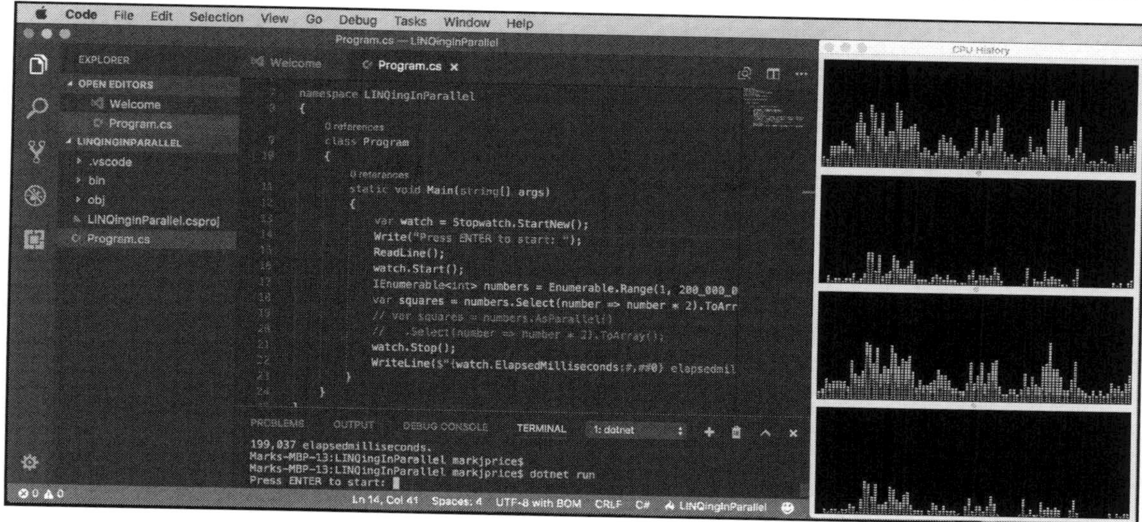

Wait for the CPUs to settle and then press *Enter* to start the stopwatch and run the query. Your output should look like this:

```
Press ENTER to start.
31,230 elapsed milliseconds.
```

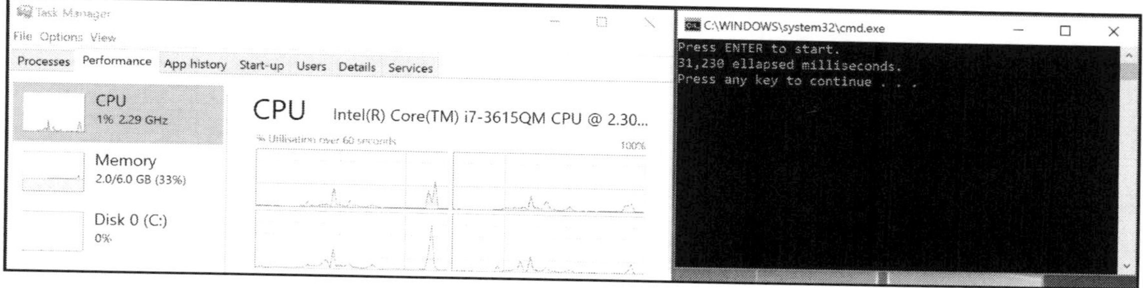

The **Task Manager** or **CPU History** windows should show that one or two CPUs were used the most. Others may execute background tasks at the same time, such as the garbage collector, so the others CPUs won't be completely flat, but the work certainly is not being evenly spread amongst all possible CPUs.

Back in the `Main` method, modify the query to make a call to the `AsParallel` extension method, as follows:

```
var squares = numbers.AsParallel().Select(number => number * 2).ToArray();
```

Run the application again. Wait for the **Task Manager** or **CPU History** windows to settle and then press *Enter* to start the stopwatch and run the query.

This time, the application should complete in less time (although it might not be as less as you might hope for—managing those multiple threads takes extra effort!):

```
Press ENTER to start.
26,830 elapsed milliseconds.
```

The **Task Manager** or **CPU History** windows should show that all CPUs were used equally to execute the LINQ query, as shown in the following screenshot for Windows 10:

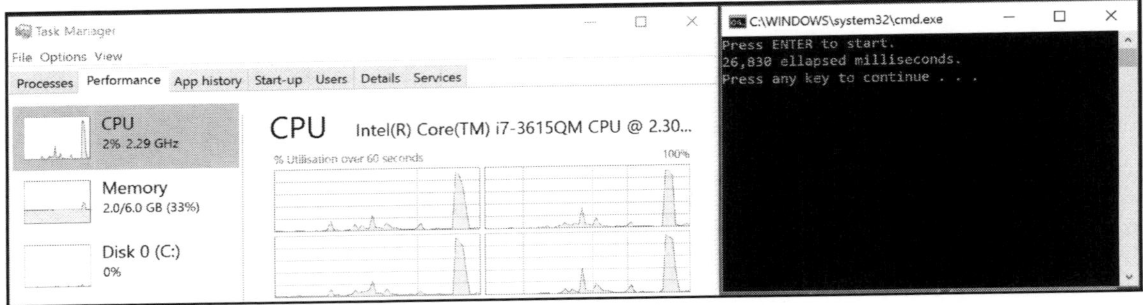

For macOS, you should see something like this:

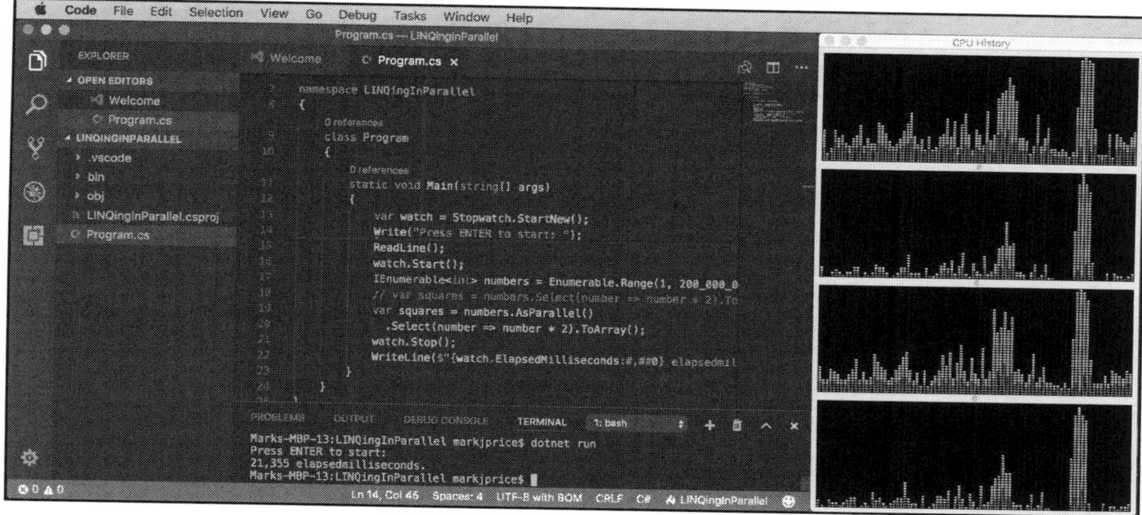

You will learn more about managing multiple threads in `Chapter 13`, *Improving Performance and Scalability Using Multitasking*.

# Creating your own LINQ extension methods

In `Chapter 6`, *Implementing Interfaces and Inheriting Classes*, you learned how to create your own extension methods. To create LINQ extension methods, all you must do is extend the `IEnumerable<T>` type.

**Good Practice**
Put your own extension methods in a separate class library so that they can be easily deployed as their own assembly or NuGet package.

In either Visual Studio 2017 or Visual Studio Code, open the `LinqWithEFCore` project or folder, and add a new class file named `MyLINQExtensions.cs`.

We will look at the `Average` extension method as an example. Any school child will tell you that *average* can mean one of three things:

- **Mean:** Sum the numbers and divide by the count
- **Mode:** The most common number
- **Median:** The number in the middle of the numbers when ordered

The `Average` extension method actually calculates the mean. We might want to define our own extension methods for mode and median.

Modify the class to look like the following code:

```
using System.Collections.Generic;

namespace System.Linq
{
   public static class MyLINQExtensions
   {
      // this is a chainable LINQ extension method
      public static IEnumerable<T> ProcessSequence<T>(
      this IEnumerable<T> sequence)
      {
         return sequence;
      }

      // these are scalar LINQ extension methods
      public static int? Median(this IEnumerable<int?> sequence)
      {
         var ordered = sequence.OrderBy(item => item);
         int middlePosition = ordered.Count() / 2;
         return ordered.ElementAt(middlePosition);
      }

      public static int? Median<T>(
      this IEnumerable<T> sequence, Func<T, int?> selector)
      {
         return sequence.Select(selector).Median();
      }

      public static decimal? Median(this IEnumerable<decimal?> sequence)
      {
         var ordered = sequence.OrderBy(item => item);
         int middlePosition = ordered.Count() / 2;
         return ordered.ElementAt(middlePosition);
      }

      public static decimal? Median<T>(
```

```
        this IEnumerable<T> sequence, Func<T, decimal?> selector)
        {
            return sequence.Select(selector).Median();
        }

        public static int? Mode(this IEnumerable<int?> sequence)
        {
            var grouped = sequence.GroupBy(item => item);
            var orderedGroups = grouped.OrderBy(group => group.Count());
            return orderedGroups.FirstOrDefault().Key;
        }

        public static int? Mode<T>(
        this IEnumerable<T> sequence, Func<T, int?> selector)
        {
            return sequence.Select(selector).Mode();
        }

        public static decimal? Mode(this IEnumerable<decimal?> sequence)
        {
            var grouped = sequence.GroupBy(item => item);
            var orderedGroups = grouped.OrderBy(group => group.Count());
            return orderedGroups.FirstOrDefault().Key;
        }

        public static decimal? Mode<T>(
        this IEnumerable<T> sequence, Func<T, decimal?> selector)
        {
            return sequence.Select(selector).Mode();
        }
    }
}
```

Note that the `ProcessSequence` extension method doesn't modify the sequence. We've created it only as an example. It would be up to you to process the sequence in whatever manner you want.

To use your LINQ extension methods, you simply need to reference the class library assembly because the `System.Linq` namespace is usually already imported.

In `Main`, modify the LINQ query for `Products` to call your custom chainable extension method, as shown in the following code:

```
static void Main(string[] args)
{
    using (var db = new Northwind())
    {
```

```
var query = db.Products
    .ProcessSequence()
    .Where(product => product.UnitPrice < 10M)
    .OrderByDescending(product => product.UnitPrice)
    .Select(product => new
    {
       product.ProductID,
       product.ProductName,
       product.UnitPrice
    });
```

If you run the console application, then you will see the same output as before because your method doesn't modify the sequence. But, you now know how to extend LINQ with your own functionality.

In `Main`, at the end of the method, add statements to output the mean, median, and mode, for `UnitsInStock` and `UnitPrice` for products, using your custom extension methods and the built-in `Average` extension method, as shown in the following code:

```
WriteLine("Custom LINQ extension methods:");
WriteLine($" Mean units in stock:
{db.Products.Average(p => p.UnitsInStock):N0}");
WriteLine($" Mean unit price:
{db.Products.Average(p => p.UnitPrice):$#,##0.00}");
WriteLine($" Median units in stock:
{db.Products.Median(p => p.UnitsInStock)}");
WriteLine($" Median unit price:
{db.Products.Median(p => p.UnitPrice):$#,##0.00}");
WriteLine($" Mode units in stock:
{db.Products.Mode(p => p.UnitsInStock)}");
WriteLine($" Mode unit price:
{db.Products.Mode(p => p.UnitPrice):$#,##0.00}");
```

Run the console application and view the output:

```
Custom LINQ extension methods:
  Mean units in stock: 41
  Mean unit price: $28.87
  Median units in stock: 26
  Median unit price: $19.50
  Mode units in stock: 13
  Mode unit price: $22.00
```

# Working with LINQ to XML

**LINQ to XML** is a LINQ provider that allows you to query and manipulate XML.

## Generating XML using LINQ to XML

Open the console application project or folder named `LinqWithEFCore`.

In the `Program.cs` file, import the `System.Xml.Linq` namespace.

In the `Main` method, at the bottom, write the following statements:

```
var productsForXml = db.Products.ToArray();

var xml = new XElement("products",
    from p in productsForXml
    select new XElement("product",
    new XAttribute("id", p.ProductID),
    new XAttribute("price", p.UnitPrice),
    new XElement("name", p.ProductName)));

WriteLine(xml.ToString());
```

Run the console application and view the output.

Note the structure of the XML generated matches the elements and attributes that the LINQ to XML statement declaratively described in the preceding code:

```
<products>
  <product id="1" price="18.0000">
    <name>Chai</name>
  </product>
  <product id="2" price="19.0000">
    <name>Chang</name>
  </product>
  <product id="3" price="10.0000">
    <name>Aniseed Syrup</name>
  </product>
```

# Reading XML using LINQ to XML

You might want to use LINQ to XML to easily query XML files.

In the `LinqWithEFCore` project, add an XML file named `settings.xml`. Modify its contents to look like this:

```
<?xml version="1.0" encoding="utf-8" ?>
  <appSettings>
    <add key="color" value="red" />
    <add key="size" value="large" />
    <add key="price" value="23.99" />
  </appSettings>
```

Back in the `Program` class, add the following statements to do these:

- Load the XML file
- Use LINQ to XML to search for an element named `appSettings` and its descendants named `add`
- Project the XML into an array of an anonymous type with a `Key` and `Value` property
- Enumerate through the array to show the results:

```
XDocument doc = XDocument.Load("settings.xml");

var appSettings =
doc.Descendants("appSettings").Descendants("add").Select(node => new
{
   Key = node.Attribute("key").Value,
   Value = node.Attribute("value").Value
}).ToArray();

foreach (var item in appSettings)
{
   WriteLine($"{item.Key}: {item.Value}");
}
```

Run the console application and view the output:

```
color: red
size: large
price: 23.99
```

# Practicing and exploring

Test your knowledge and understanding by answering some questions, get some hands-on practice, and explore with deeper research into the topics covered in this chapter.

## Exercise 12.1 – Test your knowledge

Answer the following questions:

1. What are the two required parts of LINQ?
2. Which LINQ extension method would you use to return a subset of properties from a type?
3. Which LINQ extension method would you use to filter a sequence?
4. List five LINQ extension methods that perform aggregation.
5. What is the difference between the `Select` and `SelectMany` extension methods?

## Exercise 12.2 – Practice querying with LINQ

Create a console application, named `Exercise02`, that prompts the user for a city and then lists the company names for Northwind customers in that city:

```
Enter the name of a city: London
There are 6 customers in London:
Around the Horn
B's Beverages
Consolidated Holdings
Eastern Connection
North/South
Seven Seas Imports
```

Enhance the application by displaying a list of all unique cities that customers already reside in as a prompt to the user before they enter their preferred city:

```
Aachen, Albuquerque, Anchorage, Århus, Barcelona, Barquisimeto,
Bergamo, Berlin, Bern, Boise, Bräcke, Brandenburg, Bruxelles, Buenos
Aires, Butte, Campinas, Caracas, Charleroi, Cork, Cowes, Cunewalde,
Elgin, Eugene, Frankfurt a.M., Genève, Graz, Helsinki, I. de
Margarita, Kirkland, Kobenhavn, Köln, Lander, Leipzig, Lille, Lisboa,
London, Luleå, Lyon, Madrid, Mannheim, Marseille, México D.F.,
```

```
Montréal, München, Münster, Nantes, Oulu, Paris, Portland, Reggio
Emilia, Reims, Resende, Rio de Janeiro, Salzburg, San Cristóbal, San
Francisco, Sao Paulo, Seattle, Sevilla, Stavern, Strasbourg,
Stuttgart, Torino, Toulouse, Tsawassen, Vancouver, Versailles, Walla
Walla, Warszawa
```

# Exercise 12.3 – Explore topics

Use the following links to read more details about the topics covered in this chapter:

- **LINQ in C#**: `https://docs.microsoft.com/en-us/dotnet/articles/csharp/linq/linq-in-csharp`
- **101 LINQ Samples**: `https://code.msdn.microsoft.com/101-LINQ-Samples-3fb9811b`
- **Parallel LINQ (PLINQ)**: `https://msdn.microsoft.com/en-us/library/dd460688(v=vs.110).aspx`
- **LINQ to XML (C#)**: `https://docs.microsoft.com/en-us/dotnet/articles/csharp/programming-guide/concepts/linq/linq-to-xml`
- **LINQPad - The .NET Programmer's Playground**: `https://www.linqpad.net/`

# Summary

In this chapter, you learned how to write LINQ queries to select, project, filter, sort, join, and group data in many different formats, including XML, which are tasks you will perform every day.

In the next chapter, you will use the `Task` type to improve the performance of your applications.

# 13
# Improving Performance and Scalability Using Multitasking

This chapter is about allowing multiple actions to occur at the same time to improve performance, scalability, and user productivity.

In this chapter, we will cover the following topics:

- Monitoring performance and resource usage
- Understanding processes, threads, and tasks
- Running tasks asynchronously
- Synchronizing access to shared resources
- Understanding `async` and `await`

## Monitoring performance and resource usage

Before we can improve the performance of some code, we need to be able to monitor its speed and efficiency to record a baseline we can start measuring from.

# Evaluating the efficiency of types

What is the best type to use for a scenario? To answer this question, we need to carefully consider what we mean by best. We should consider the following factors:

- **Functionality**: This can be decided by checking whether the type provides the features you need
- **Memory size**: This can be decided by the number of bytes of memory the type takes up
- **Performance**: This can be decided by how fast the type is
- **Future needs**: This depends on the changes in requirements and maintainability

There will be scenarios, such as storing numbers, where multiple types have the same functionality, so we will need to consider the memory and performance to make a choice.

If we need to store millions of numbers, then the best type to use would be the one that requires the least number of bytes of memory. If we only need to store a few numbers, but we need to perform lots of calculations on them, then the best type to use would be the one that runs fastest on a CPU.

You have seen the use of the `sizeof()` function to show the number of bytes a single instance of a type uses in memory. When we are storing lots of values in more complex data structures, such as arrays and lists, then we need a better way of measuring memory usage.

You can read lots of advice online and in books, but the only way to know for sure what the best type would be for your code is to compare the types yourself. In the next section, you will learn how to write the code to monitor the actual memory requirements and the actual performance when using different types.

Today a `short` variable might be the best choice, but it might be a better choice to use an `int` variable even though it takes twice as much space in memory, because we might need a wider range of values to be stored in the future.

There is another metric we should consider: maintenance. This is a measure of how much effort another programmer would have to put in to understand and modify your code. If you use a nonobvious type choice, it might confuse the programmer who comes along later and needs to fix a bug or add a feature. There are analyzing tools that will generate a report that shows how easily maintainable your code is.

# Monitoring performance and memory use

The `System.Diagnostics` namespace has lots of useful types for monitoring your code. The first one we will look at is the `Stopwatch` type.

## Using Visual Studio 2017

In Visual Studio 2017, press *Ctrl* + *Shift* + *N* or navigate to **File** | **New** | **Project....**

In the **New Project** dialog, in the **Installed** list, expand **Visual C#**, and select **.NET Standard**. In the list at the center, select **Class Library (.NET Standard)**, type the name `MonitoringLib`, change the location to `C:\Code`, type the solution name as `Chapter13`, and then click on **OK**. Rename `Class1.cs` to `Recorder.cs`.

In Visual Studio 2017, add a new console application project named `MonitoringApp`.

Set your solution's startup project as the current selection.

In **Solution Explorer**, in the `MonitoringApp` project, right-click on **Dependencies** and choose **Add Reference...**, select the `MonitoringLib` project, and then click on **OK**.

## Using Visual Studio Code

In Visual Studio Code, in the `Code` folder, create a folder named `Chapter13`, with two subfolders named `MonitoringLib` and `MonitoringApp`.

In Visual Studio Code, open the folder named `MonitoringLib`.

In **Integrated Terminal**, enter the following command:

```
dotnet new classlib
```

Open the folder named `MonitoringApp`.

In **Integrated Terminal**, enter the following command:

```
dotnet new console
```

Open the folder named `Chapter13`.

In the **EXPLORER** window, expand `MonitoringLib` and rename the `Class1.cs` file as `Recorder.cs`.

In the `MonitoringApp` project folder, open the file named `MonitoringApp.csproj`, and add a package reference to the `MonitoringLib` library, as shown highlighted in the following markup:

```
<Project Sdk="Microsoft.NET.Sdk">

  <PropertyGroup>
    <OutputType>Exe</OutputType>
    <TargetFramework>netcoreapp2.0</TargetFramework>
  </PropertyGroup>

  <ItemGroup>
    <ProjectReference Include="..\MonitoringLib\MonitoringLib.csproj"
    />
  </ItemGroup>

</Project>
```

In **Integrated Terminal**, enter the following commands:

```
cd MonitoringApp
dotnet build
```

## Creating the Recorder class

In both Visual Studio 2017 and Visual Studio Code, open the `Recorder.cs` file and change its contents to look like this:

```
using System;
using System.Diagnostics;
using static System.Console;
using static System.Diagnostics.Process;

namespace Packt.CS7
{
   public static class Recorder
   {
      static Stopwatch timer = new Stopwatch();
      static long bytesPhysicalBefore = 0;
      static long bytesVirtualBefore = 0;

      public static void Start()
      {
```

```
            GC.Collect();
            GC.WaitForPendingFinalizers();
            GC.Collect();
            bytesPhysicalBefore = GetCurrentProcess().WorkingSet64;
            bytesVirtualBefore = GetCurrentProcess().VirtualMemorySize64;
            timer.Restart();
        }

        public static void Stop()
        {
            timer.Stop();
            long bytesPhysicalAfter = GetCurrentProcess().WorkingSet64;
            long bytesVirtualAfter = GetCurrentProcess().VirtualMemorySize64;
            WriteLine("Stopped recording.");
            WriteLine($"{bytesPhysicalAfter - bytesPhysicalBefore:N0}
            physical bytes used.");
            WriteLine($"{bytesVirtualAfter - bytesVirtualBefore:N0}
            virtual bytes used.");
            WriteLine($"{timer.Elapsed} time span ellapsed.");
            WriteLine($"{timer.ElapsedMilliseconds:N0}
            total milliseconds ellapsed.");
        }
    }
}
```

The `Start` method of the `Recorder` class uses the **garbage collector (GC)** type to ensure that all the currently allocated memory is collected before recording the amount of used memory. This is an advanced technique that you should almost never use in production code.

In the `Program` class, in the `Main` method, write statements to start and stop the `Recorder` while generating an array of ten thousand integers, as shown in the following code:

```
using System.Linq;
using Packt.CS7;
using static System.Console;

namespace MonitoringApp
{
    class Program
    {
        static void Main(string[] args)
        {
            Write("Press ENTER to start the timer: ");
            ReadLine();
            Recorder.Start();
            int[] largeArrayOfInts = Enumerable.Range(1, 10000).ToArray();
```

```
            Write("Press ENTER to stop the timer: ");
            ReadLine();
            Recorder.Stop();
            ReadLine();
        }
    }
}
```

You have created a class named `Recorder` with two methods to start and stop recording the time and memory used by any code you run. The `Main` method starts recording when the user presses *Enter*, creates an array of ten thousand `int` variables, and then stops recording when the user presses *Enter* again.

The `Stopwatch` type has some useful members, as shown in the following table:

| Member | Description |
|---|---|
| The `Restart` method | This resets the elapsed time to zero and then starts the stopwatch |
| The `Stop` method | This stops the stopwatch |
| The `Elapsed` property | This is the elapsed time stored as a `TimeSpan` format (*hours:minutes:seconds*) |
| The `ElapsedMilliseconds` property | This is the elapsed time in milliseconds stored as a long integer |

The `Process` type has some useful members, as shown in the following table:

| Member | Description |
|---|---|
| `VirtualMemorySize64` | This displays the amount of virtual memory, in bytes, allocated for the process |
| `WorkingSet64` | This displays the amount of physical memory, in bytes, allocated for the process |

Run the console application without the debugger attached. The application will start recording the time and memory used when you press *Enter*, and then stop recording when you press *Enter* again. Wait for a few seconds between pressing *Enter* twice, as you can see that I did with the following output:

```
Press ENTER to start the timer:
Press ENTER to stop the timer:
Stopped recording.
942,080 physical bytes used.
```

```
0 virtual bytes used.
00:00:03.1166037 time span ellapsed.
3,116 total milliseconds ellapsed.
```

## Measuring the efficiency of processing strings

Now that you've seen how the `Stopwatch` and `Process` types can be used to monitor your code, we will use them to evaluate the best way to process string variables.

Comment out the previous code in the `Main` method by wrapping it in `/* */`.

Add the following code to the `Main` method. It creates an array of fifty thousand `int` variables and then concatenates them with commas for separators using a `string` and `StringBuilder` class:

```
int[] numbers = Enumerable.Range(1, 50000).ToArray();
Recorder.Start();
WriteLine("Using string");
string s = "";
for (int i = 0; i < numbers.Length; i++)
{
   s += numbers[i] + ", ";
}
Recorder.Stop();
Recorder.Start();
WriteLine("Using StringBuilder");
var builder = new System.Text.StringBuilder();
for (int i = 0; i < numbers.Length; i++)
{
   builder.Append(numbers[i]);
   builder.Append(", ");
}
Recorder.Stop();
ReadLine();
```

Run the console application and view the output:

```
Using string
Stopped recording.
12,447,744 physical bytes used.
1,347,584 virtual bytes used.
00:00:03.4700170 time span ellapsed.
3,470 total milliseconds ellapsed.

Using StringBuilder
Stopped recording.
```

```
12,288 physical bytes used.
0 virtual bytes used.
00:00:00.0051490 time span ellapsed.
5 total milliseconds ellapsed.
```

We can summarize the results as follows:

- The `string` class used about 12.5 MB of memory and took 3.5 seconds
- The `StringBuilder` class used 12.3 KB of memory and took 5 milliseconds

In this scenario, `StringBuilder` is about seven hundred times faster and about one thousand times more memory efficient when concatenating text!

**Good Practice**
Avoid using the `String.Concat` method or the + operator inside loops. Avoid using C# `$` string interpolation inside loops. It uses less physical memory but twice as much virtual memory, and it takes more than 30 seconds! Instead, use `StringBuilder`.

Now that you've learned how to measure performance and resource efficiency of your code, let's learn about processes, threads, and tasks.

# Understanding processes, threads, and tasks

A **process**, for example, each of the console applications we have created, has resources allocated to it like memory and threads. A **thread** executes your code, statement by statement. By default, each process only has one thread, and this can cause problems when we need to do more than one **task** at the same time.

Threads are also responsible for keeping track of things like the currently authenticated user and any internationalization rules that should be followed for the current language and region.

Windows and most other modern operating systems use preemptive multitasking, which simulates the parallel execution of tasks. It divides the processor time among the threads, allocating a *time slice* to each thread one after another. The current thread is suspended when its time slice finishes. The processor allows another thread to run for a time slice.

When Windows switches from one thread to another, it saves the context of the thread and reloads the previously saved context of the next thread in the thread queue. This takes time and resources.

Threads have a `Priority` property and a `ThreadState` property, and there is a `ThreadPool` class for managing a pool of background worker threads, as shown in the following diagram:

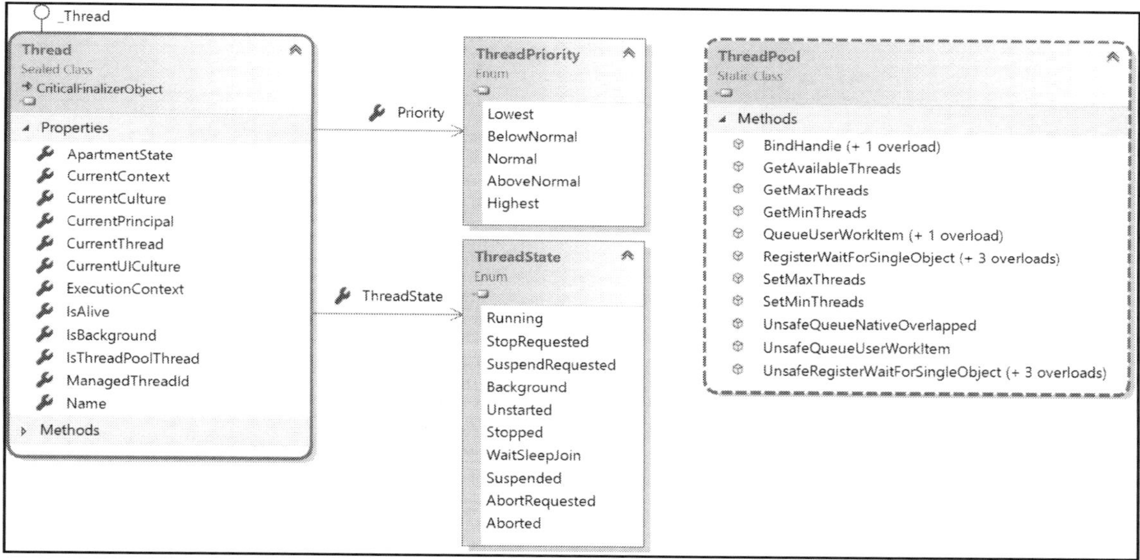


Threads may have to compete for, and wait for access to, shared resources, such as variables, files, and database objects.

Depending on the task, doubling the number of threads (workers) to perform a task does not halve the number of seconds the task will take. In fact, it can *increase* the duration of the task, as pointed out by the following tweet:

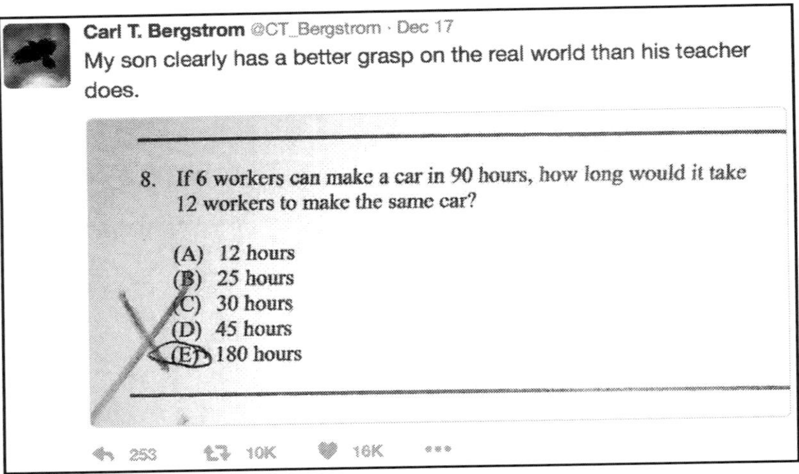

**Good Practice**
Never assume that more threads (workers) will improve performance. Run performance tests on a baseline code implementation *without* multiple threads, and then again on a code implementation *with* multiple threads. Run performance tests in a staging environment that is as close as possible to the production environment.

# Running tasks asynchronously

First, we will write a simple console application that needs to execute three methods, and execute them synchronously (one after the other).

## Running multiple actions synchronously

In Visual Studio 2017, press *Ctrl* + *Shift* + *N* or go to **File** | **Add** | **New Project...**.

In the **New Project** dialog, in the **Installed** list, expand **Visual C#**, and select **.NET Core**. In the center list, select **Console App (.NET Core)**, type the name as `WorkingWithTasks`, change the location to `C:\Code`, type the solution name as `Chapter13`, and then click on **OK**.

In Visual Studio Code, create a directory named `Chapter13` with a subfolder named `WorkingWithTasks`, and open the `WorkingWithTasks` folder. In **Integrated Terminal**, execute the command: `dotnet new console`.

In both Visual Studio 2017 and Visual Studio Code, ensure that the following namespaces have been imported:

```
using System;
using System.Threading;
using System.Threading.Tasks;
using System.Diagnostics;
using static System.Console;
```

There will be three methods that need to be executed: the first takes 3 seconds, the second takes 2 seconds, and the third takes 1 second. To simulate that work, we can use the `Thread` class to tell the current thread to go to sleep for a specified number of milliseconds.

Inside the `Program` class, add the following code:

```
static void MethodA()
{
   WriteLine("Starting Method A...");
   Thread.Sleep(3000); // simulate three seconds of work
   WriteLine("Finished Method A.");
}

static void MethodB()
{
   WriteLine("Starting Method B...");
   Thread.Sleep(2000); // simulate two seconds of work
   WriteLine("Finished Method B.");
}

static void MethodC()
{
   WriteLine("Starting Method C...");
   Thread.Sleep(1000); // simulate one second of work
   WriteLine("Finished Method C.");
}
```

In the `Main` method, add the following statements:

```
static void Main(string[] args)
{
   var timer = Stopwatch.StartNew();

   WriteLine("Running methods synchronously on one thread.");
```

```
        MethodA();
        MethodB();
        MethodC();

        WriteLine($"{timer.ElapsedMilliseconds:#,##0}ms elapsed.");

        WriteLine("Press ENTER to end.");
        ReadLine();
    }
```

The calls to `WriteLine` and `ReadLine` at the end of the `Main` method prompting the user to press *Enter* are only necessary when using Visual Studio 2017 with the debugger attached, because Visual Studio 2017 will automatically terminate the application at the end of `Main`! By calling `ReadLine`, the console application stays running until the user presses *Enter*. For Visual Studio Code, you can leave out those two statements.

Run the console application and view the output, and note that as there is only one thread, the total time required is just over 6 seconds:

```
Running methods synchronously on one thread.
Starting Method A...
Finished Method A.
Starting Method B...
Finished Method B.
Starting Method C...
Finished Method C.
6,047ms elapsed.
Press ENTER to end.
```

## Running multiple actions asynchronously using tasks

The `Thread` class has been available since the first version of C# and can be used to create new threads and manage them, but it can be tricky to work with directly.

C# 4 introduced the `Task` class, which is a wrapper around a thread that enables easier creating and management. Creating multiple threads wrapped in tasks will allow our code to execute asynchronously (at the same time).

Each `Task` has a `Status` property and a `CreationOptions` property, has a `ContinueWith` method that can be customized with the `TaskContinuationOptions` enum, and can be managed with the `TaskFactory` class, as shown in the following diagram:

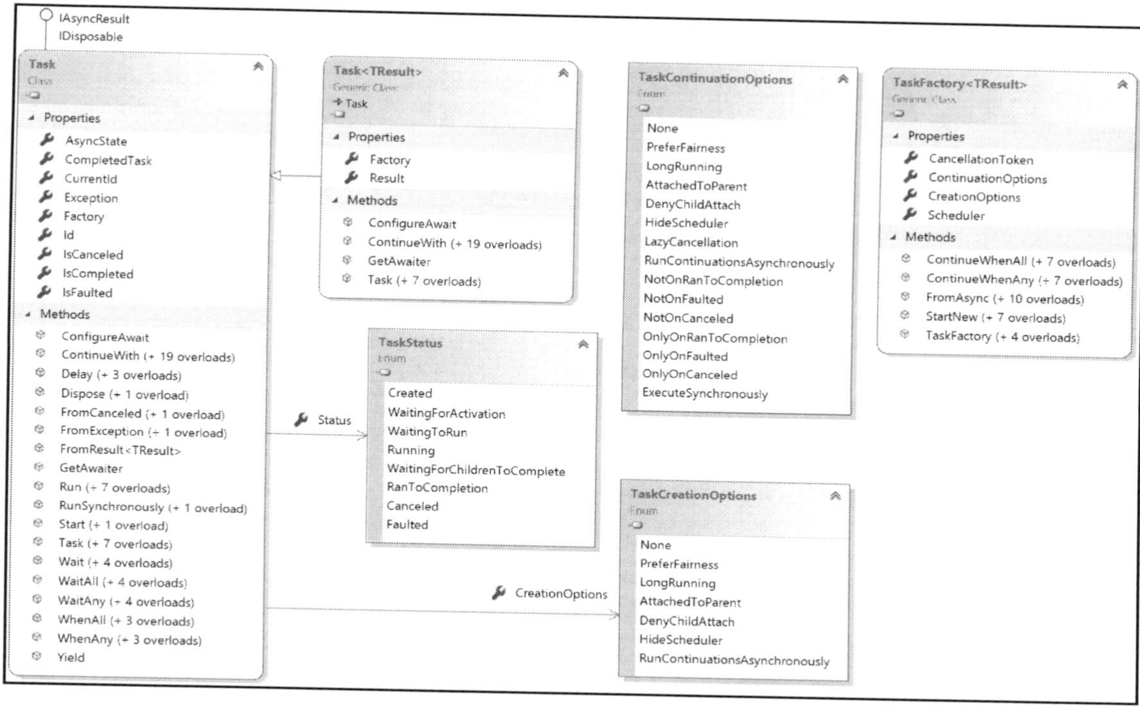


We will look at three ways to start the methods using `Task` instances. Each has a slightly different syntax, but they all define a `Task` and start it.

Comment out the calls to the three methods and the associated console message, and then add the new statements, as shown highlighted in the following code:

```
static void Main(string[] args)
{
   var timer = Stopwatch.StartNew();
   //WriteLine("Running methods synchronously on one thread.");
   //MethodA();
   //MethodB();
   //MethodC();
   WriteLine("Running methods asynchronously on multiple threads.");
   Task taskA = new Task(MethodA);
   taskA.Start();
   Task taskB = Task.Factory.StartNew(MethodB);
```

```
        Task taskC = Task.Run(new Action(MethodC));
        WriteLine($"{timer.ElapsedMilliseconds:#,##0}ms elapsed.");
        WriteLine("Press ENTER to end.");
        ReadLine();
    }
```

Run the console application and view the output, and note the elapsed milliseconds will depend on the performance of your CPU, so you are likely to see a different value than shown in the following example output:

```
Running methods asynchronously on multiple threads.
Starting Method A...
Starting Method B...
Starting Method C...
23ms elapsed.
Press ENTER to end.
Finished Method C.
Finished Method B.
Finished Method A.
```

Note the elapsed time is output almost immediately, because each of the three methods are now being executed by three *new* threads. The *original* thread continues executing until it reaches the `ReadLine` call at the end of the `Main` method.

Meanwhile, the three new threads execute their code simultaneously, and they start in any order. `MethodC` will usually finish first, because it takes only 1 second, then `MethodB`, and finally `MethodA`, because it takes 3 seconds.

However, the actual CPU used has a big effect on the results. It is the CPU that allocates time slices to each process to allow them to execute their threads. You have no control over when the methods run.

# Waiting for tasks

Sometimes, you need to wait for a task to complete before continuing. To do this, you can use the `Wait` method on a `Task` instance, or the `WaitAll` or `WaitAny` static methods on an array of tasks, as described in the following table:

| Method | Description |
|---|---|
| `t.Wait()` | This waits for the task instance named `t` to complete execution |
| `Task.WaitAny(Task[])` | This waits for any of the tasks in the array to complete execution |
| `Task.WaitAll(Task[])` | This waits for all the tasks in the array to complete execution |

Add the following statements to the `Main` method immediately after creating the three tasks and before outputting the elapsed time. This will combine references to the three tasks into an array and pass them to the `WaitAll` method. Now, the original thread will pause on that statement, waiting for all three tasks to finish before outputting the elapsed time:

```
Task[] tasks = { taskA, taskB, taskC };
Task.WaitAll(tasks);
```

Rerun the console application and view the output:

```
Running methods asynchronously on multiple threads.
Starting Method A...
Starting Method B...
Starting Method C...
Finished Method C.
Finished Method B.
Finished Method A.
3,024 milliseconds elapsed.
Press ENTER to end.
```

Notice that the total time is now slightly more than the time to run the longest method. If all three tasks can be performed at the same time, then this will be all we need to do.

However, often a task is dependent on the output from another task. To handle this scenario, we need to define **continuation tasks**.

# Continuing with another task

Add the following methods to the `Program` class:

```
static decimal CallWebService()
{
    WriteLine("Starting call to web service...");
    Thread.Sleep((new Random()).Next(2000, 4000));
    WriteLine("Finished call to web service.");
    return 89.99M;
}

static string CallStoredProcedure(decimal amount)
{
    WriteLine("Starting call to stored procedure...");
    Thread.Sleep((new Random()).Next(2000, 4000));
    WriteLine("Finished call to stored procedure.");
    return $"12 products cost more than {amount:C}.";
}
```

These methods simulate a call to a web service that returns a monetary amount that then needs to be used to retrieve how many products cost more than that amount in a database. The result returned from the first method needs to be fed into the input of the second method.

I used the `Random` class to wait for a random interval of between 2 and 4 seconds for each method call to simulate the work.

Inside the `Main` method, comment out the previous tasks by wrapping them in multiline comment characters `/* */`.

Then, add the following statements before the existing statement that outputs the total time elapsed and then calls `ReadLine` to wait for the user to press *Enter*:

```
WriteLine("Passing the result of one task as an input into another.");

var taskCallWebServiceAndThenStoredProcedure =
Task.Factory.StartNew(CallWebService).
ContinueWith(previousTask => CallStoredProcedure(previousTask.Result));

WriteLine($"{taskCallWebServiceAndThenStoredProcedure.Result}");
```

Run the console application and view the output:

```
Passing the result of one task as an input into another.
Starting call to web service...
Finished call to web service.
Starting call to stored procedure...
Finished call to stored procedure.
12 products cost more than £89.99.
5,971 milliseconds elapsed.
Press ENTER to end.
```

# Nested and child tasks

Add a new console application project named `NestedAndChildTasks`.

In Visual Studio 2017, in the solution's **Properties**, remember to change **Startup Project** to **Current selection**.

Ensure the following namespaces have been imported:

```
using System;
using System.Threading;
using System.Threading.Tasks;
using System.Diagnostics;
using static System.Console;
```

Inside the `Main` method, add the following statements:

```
var outer = Task.Factory.StartNew(() =>
{
   WriteLine("Outer task starting...");
   var inner = Task.Factory.StartNew(() =>
   {
      WriteLine("Inner task starting...");
      Thread.Sleep(2000);
      WriteLine("Inner task finished.");
   });
});
outer.Wait();
WriteLine("Outer task finished.");
WriteLine("Press ENTER to end.");
ReadLine();
```

Run the console application and view the output:

```
Outer task starting...
Outer task finished.
Inner task starting...
Inner task finished.
Press ENTER to end.
```

Note that, although we wait for the outer task to finish, its inner task does not have to finish as well. To link the two tasks, we must use a special option.

Modify the existing code that defines the inner task to add a `TaskCreationOption` value of `AttachedToParent`:

```
var inner = Task.Factory.StartNew(() =>
{
   WriteLine("Inner task starting...");
   Thread.Sleep(2000);
   WriteLine("Inner task finished.");
}, TaskCreationOptions.AttachedToParent);
```

Rerun the console application and view the output. Note that the inner task must finish before the outer task can:

```
Outer task starting...
Inner task starting...
Inner task finished.
Outer task finished.
Press ENTER to end.
```

# Synchronizing access to shared resources

When you have multiple threads executing at the same time, there is a possibility that two or more threads may access the same variable or another resource at the same time and cause a problem.

For this reason, you should carefully consider how to make your code *thread safe*.

The simplest mechanism for implementing thread safety is to use an object variable as a *flag* or *traffic light* to indicate when a shared resource has an exclusive lock applied.

In William Golding's *Lord of the Flies*, Piggy and Ralph spot a conch shell and use it to call a meeting. The boys impose a "rule of the conch" on themselves, deciding that no one can speak unless he's holding the conch. I like to name the object variable I use the "conch." When a thread has the conch, no other thread can access the shared resource(s) represented by that conch.

We will explore some types that can be used to synchronize access to resources, as shown in the following diagram:

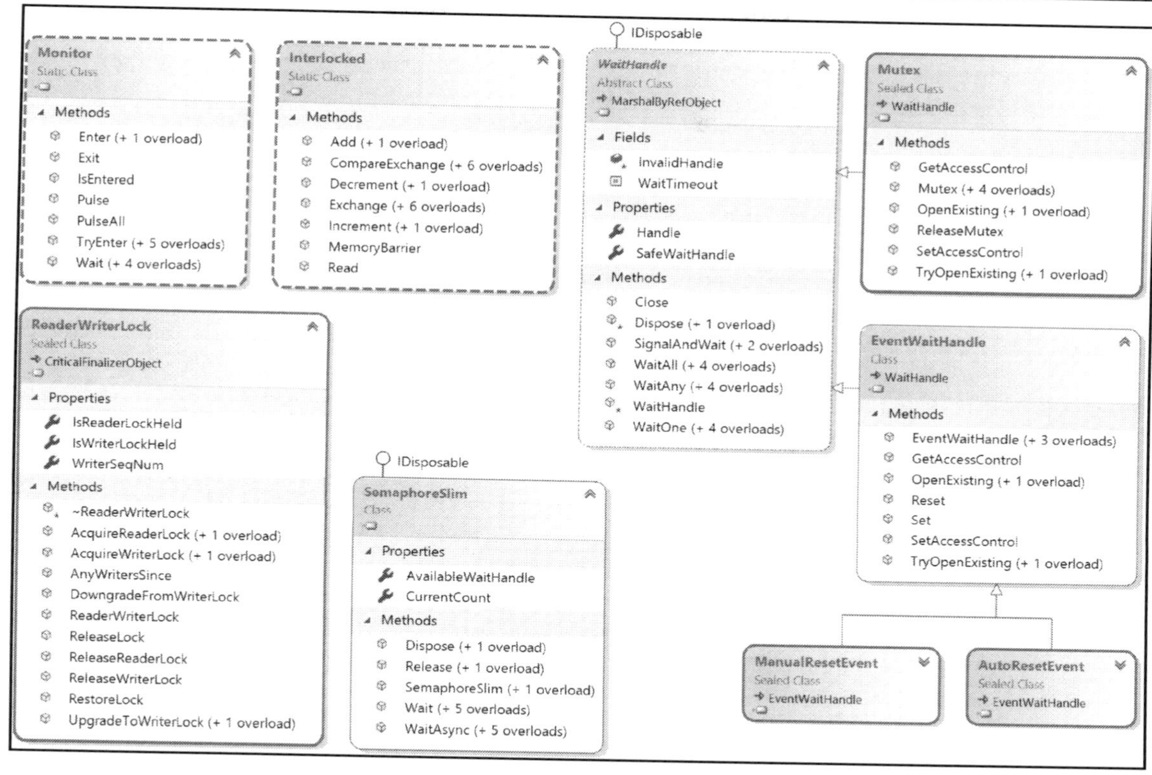


# Accessing a resource from multiple threads

Add a new console application project named `SynchronizingResourceAccess`.

Ensure that the following namespaces have been imported:

```
using System;
using System.Threading;
using System.Threading.Tasks;
using System.Diagnostics;
using static System.Console;
```

Inside the `Program` class, add the following statements to do the following:

- Declare and instantiate an object to generate random wait times
- Declare a `string` variable to store a message (this is the shared resource)
- Declare two methods that add a letter, `A` or `B`, to the shared `string` five times in a loop, and wait for a random interval of up to 2 seconds for each iteration
- A `Main` method that executes both methods on separate threads using a pair of tasks and waits for them to complete before outputting the elapsed milliseconds it took

```
static Random r = new Random();
static string Message; // a shared resource

static void MethodA()
{
   for (int i = 0; i < 5; i++)
   {
      Thread.Sleep(r.Next(2000));
      Message += "A";
      Write(".");
   }
}

static void MethodB()
{
   for (int i = 0; i < 5; i++)
   {
      Thread.Sleep(r.Next(2000));
      Message += "B";
      Write(".");
   }
}

static void Main(string[] args)
{
   WriteLine("Please wait for the tasks to complete.");
   Stopwatch watch = Stopwatch.StartNew();

   Task a = Task.Factory.StartNew(MethodA);
   Task b = Task.Factory.StartNew(MethodB);

   Task.WaitAll(new Task[] { a, b });
```

```
        WriteLine();
        WriteLine($"Results: {Message}.");
        WriteLine($"{watch.ElapsedMilliseconds:#,##0} elapsed
        milliseconds.");
    }
```

Run the console application and view the output:

```
Please wait for the tasks to complete.
..........
Results: BABBABBAAA.
6,099 elapsed milliseconds.
```

Note that the results show that both threads were modifying the message concurrently. In an actual application, this could be a problem. We can prevent concurrent access by applying a mutually exclusive lock.

# Applying a mutually exclusive lock to a resource

In the `Program` class, define an object variable instance to act as a *conch*:

```
static object conch = new object();
```

In both `MethodA` and `MethodB`, add a `lock` statement around the `for` statement:

```
lock (conch)
{
    for (int i = 0; i < 5; i++)
    {
        Thread.Sleep(r.Next(2000));
        Message += "A";
        Write(".");
    }
}
```

Rerun the console application and view the output:

```
Please wait for the tasks to complete.
..........
Results: AAAAABBBBB.
9,751 elapsed milliseconds.
```

Although the time elapsed was longer, only one method at a time could access the shared resource. Once a method has finished its work on the shared resource, then the conch gets released, and the other method has a chance to do its work.

Either `MethodA` or `MethodB` could start first.

# Understanding the lock statement

You might wonder how the `lock` statement works when it *locks* an object variable. The compiler changes this:

```
lock (conch)
{
   // access shared resource
}
```

The preceding code block is changed into this:

```
try
{
   Monitor.Enter(conch);
   // access shared resource
}
finally
{
   Monitor.Exit(conch);
}
```

Knowing how the `lock` statement works internally is important, because using the `lock` statement can cause a deadlock.

Deadlocks occur when there are two or more shared resources (and therefore conches) and the following sequence of events happens:

- Thread X locks conch A
- Thread Y locks conch B
- Thread X attempts to lock conch B but is blocked because thread Y already has it
- Thread Y attempts to lock conch A but is blocked because thread X already has it

A proven way to prevent deadlocks is to specify a timeout when attempting to get a lock. To do this, you must manually use the `Monitor` class instead of using the `lock` statement.

Modify your code to replace the `lock` statements with code that tries to enter the conch with a timeout like this:

```
try
{
   Monitor.TryEnter(conch, TimeSpan.FromSeconds(15));
   for (int i = 0; i < 5; i++)
   {
      Thread.Sleep(r.Next(2000));
      Message += "A";
      Write(".");
   }
}
finally
{
   Monitor.Exit(conch);
}
```

Rerun the console application and view the output. It should return the same results as before, but is better code because it will avoid potential deadlocks.

**Good Practice**
Never use the `lock` keyword. Always use the `Monitor.TryEnter` method instead, in combination with a `try` statement, so that you can supply a timeout and avoid a potential deadlock scenario.

# Making operations atomic

Look at the following increment operation:

```
int x = 3;
x++; // is this an atomic CPU operation?
```

**Atomic**: This is from Greek *atomos, undividable.*

It is not atomic! Incrementing an integer requires the following three CPU operations:

1. Load a value from an instance variable into a register.
2. Increment the value.
3. Store the value in the instance variable.

A thread could be preempted after executing the first two steps. A second thread could then execute all three steps. When the first thread resumes execution, it will overwrite the value in the variable, and the effect of the increment or decrement performed by the second thread will be lost!

There is a type named `Interlocked` that can perform atomic actions on value types, such as integers and floats.

Declare another shared resource that will count how many operations have occurred:

```
static int Counter; // another shared resource
```

In both methods, inside the `for` statement, after modifying `string`, add the following statement to safely increment the counter:

```
Interlocked.Increment(ref Counter);
```

After outputting the elapsed time, output the counter:

```
WriteLine($"{Counter} string modifications.");
```

Rerun the console application and view the output:

```
10 string modifications.
```

## Applying other types of synchronization

`Monitor` and `Interlocked` are mutually exclusive locks that are simple and effective, but sometimes, you need more advanced options to synchronize access to shared resources:

| Type | Description |
|---|---|
| `ReaderWriterLock` and `ReaderWriterLockSlim` (recommended) | These allow multiple threads to be in **read mode**, one thread to be in the **write mode** with exclusive ownership of the lock, and one thread that has read access to be in the **upgradeable read mode**, from which the thread can upgrade to the write mode without having to relinquish its read access to the resource |
| `Mutex` | Like `Monitor`, this provides exclusive access to a shared resource, except it is used for **inter-process** synchronization |
| `Semaphore` and `SemaphoreSlim` | These limit the number of threads that can access a resource or pool of resources concurrently by defining **slots** |
| `AutoResetEvent` and `ManualResetEvent` | Event wait handles allow threads to synchronize activities by **signaling** each other and by waiting for each other's signals |

## Understanding async and await

C# 5 introduced two keywords to simplify working with the `Task` type. They are especially useful for the following:

- Implementing multitasking for a **graphical user interface** (GUI)
- Improving the scalability of web applications and web services

In `Chapter 15`, *Building Web Sites Using ASP.NET Core MVC*, and in `Chapter 16`, *Building Web Services and Applications Using ASP.NET Core*, we will explore how the `async` and `await` keywords can improve scalability in websites, web services, and web applications.

In `Chapter 17`, *Building Windows Apps Using XAML and Fluent Design*, and in `Chapter 18`, *Building Mobile Apps Using XAML and Xamarin.Forms*, we will explore how the `async` and `await` keywords can implement multitasking with a GUI running on Universal Windows Platform and Xamarin.

For now, let's learn the theory of why these two C# keywords were introduced, and then later you will see them used in practice.

# Improving responsiveness for console apps

One of the limitations with console applications is that you can only use the `await` keyword inside methods that are marked as `async...`, and C# 7 and earlier do not allow the `Main` method to be marked as `async`!

Luckily, a new feature in C# 7.1 is support for `async` on `Main`.

Create a new console app named `AsyncConsole`.

Import the `System.Net.Http` and `System.Threading.Tasks` namespaces, and statically import `System.Console`, as shown in the following code:

```
using System.Net.Http;
using System.Threading.Tasks;
using static System.Console;
```

Add statements to the `Main` method to create an `HttpClient` instance, make a request for Apple's home page, and output how many bytes it has, as shown in the following code:

```
var client = new HttpClient();
HttpResponseMessage response = await
client.GetAsync("http://www.apple.com/");
WriteLine($"Apple's home page has
{response.Content.Headers.ContentLength:N0} bytes.");
```

Build the project, and note the error message, as shown in the following output:

```
Program.cs(12,44): error CS4033: The 'await' operator can only be used
within an async method. Consider marking this method with the 'async'
modifier and changing its return type to 'Task'.
[/Users/markjprice/Code/Chapter13/AsyncConsole/AsyncConsole.csproj]
```

Add the `async` keyword to the `Main` method, change its return type to `Task`, build the project, and note the error message, as shown in the following output:

```
Program.cs(10,22): error CS8107: Feature 'async main' is not available in
C# 7. Please use language version 7.1 or greater.
[/Users/markjprice/Code/Chapter13/AsyncConsole/AsyncConsole.csproj]
CSC : error CS5001: Program does not contain a static 'Main' method
suitable for an entry point
[/Users/markjprice/Code/Chapter13/AsyncConsole/AsyncConsole.csproj]
```

Modify `AsyncConsole.csproj` to specify C# 7.1, as shown highlighted in the following markup:

```
<Project Sdk="Microsoft.NET.Sdk">

  <PropertyGroup>
    <OutputType>Exe</OutputType>
    <TargetFramework>netcoreapp2.0</TargetFramework>
    <LangVersion>7.1</LangVersion>
  </PropertyGroup>

</Project>
```

Build the project, and note that it now builds successfully.

Run the console application and view the output:

```
Apple's home page has 42,740 bytes.
```

# Improving responsiveness for GUI apps

So far we have only built console applications. Life for a programmer gets more complicated when building web applications, web services, and apps with GUIs such as UWP and mobile apps.

One reason for this is that for a GUI app, there is a special thread: the **user interface (UI)** thread.

There are two rules for working in GUIs:

- Do not perform long-running tasks on the UI thread
- Do not access UI elements on any thread except the UI thread

To handle these rules, programmers used to have to write complex code to ensure that long-running tasks were executed by a nonUI thread, but once complete, the results of the task were safely passed to the UI thread to present to the user. It could quickly get messy!

Luckily, with C# 5 and later, you have the use of `async` and `await`. They allow you to continue to write your code as if it is synchronous, which keeps your code clean and easy to understand, but underneath, the C# compiler creates a complex state machine and keeps track of running threads. It's kind of magical!

# Improving scalability for web applications and web services

The `async` and `await` keywords can also be applied on the server side when building websites, applications, and services. From the client application's point of view, nothing changes (or they might even notice a small increase in the time for a request to return). So, from a single client's point of view, the use of `async` and `await` to implement multitasking on the server side makes their experience worse!

On the server side, additional, cheaper worker threads are created to wait for long-running tasks to finish so that expensive IO threads can handle other client's requests instead of being blocked. This improves the overall scalability of a web application or service. More clients can be supported simultaneously.

# Common types that support multitasking

Here are some common types that have asynchronous methods that you can await:

| Type | Methods |
|---|---|
| `DbContext<T>` | `AddAsync`, `AddRangeAsync`, `FindAsync`, and `SaveChangesAsync` |
| `DbSet<T>` | `AddAsync`, `AddRangeAsync`, `ForEachAsync`, `SumAsync`, `ToListAsync`, `ToDictionaryAsync`, `AverageAsync`, and `CountAsync` |
| `HttpClient` | `GetAsync`, `PostAsync`, `PutAsync`, `DeleteAsync`, and `SendAsync` |
| `StreamReader` | `ReadAsync`, `ReadLineAsync`, and `ReadToEndAsync` |
| `StreamWriter` | `WriteAsync`, `WriteLineAsync`, and `FlushAsync` |

**Good Practice**
Any time you see a method that ends in the suffix `Async`, check to see whether it returns `Task` or `Task<T>`. If it does, then you should use it instead of the synchronous non `Async` suffixed method. Remember to call it using `await` and decorate your method with `async`.

## await in catch blocks

In C# 5, it was only possible to use the `await` keyword in a `try` exception handling block, but not in a `catch` block. In C# 6 or later, it is now possible to use `await` in both the `try` and `catch` blocks.

# Practicing and exploring

Test your knowledge and understanding by answering some questions, get some hands-on practice, and explore this chapter's topics with deeper research.

## Exercise 13.1 – Test your knowledge

Answer the following questions:

1. Which information can you find out about a process?
2. How accurate is the `Stopwatch` type?
3. By convention, what suffix should be applied to a method that returns `Task` or `Task<T>`?
4. To use the `await` keyword inside a method, what keyword must be applied to the method declaration?
5. How do you create a child task?
6. Why should you avoid the `lock` keyword?
7. When should you use the `Interlocked` class?
8. When should you use the `Mutex` class instead of the `Monitor` class?
9. Does using `async` and `await` in a web application or web service improve performance? If not, why do it?
10. Can you cancel a `Task` instance? How?

## Exercise 13.2 – Explore topics

Use the following links to read more about this chapter's topics:

- **Threads and threading**: `https://docs.microsoft.com/en-us/dotnet/standard/threading/threads-and-threading`
- **Async in depth**: `https://docs.microsoft.com/en-us/dotnet/standard/async-in-depth`
- **await (C# reference)**: `https://docs.microsoft.com/en-us/dotnet/csharp/language-reference/keywords/await`
- **Parallel Programming in the .NET Framework**: `https://docs.microsoft.com/en-us/dotnet/standard/parallel-programming/`
- **Overview of Synchronization Primitives**: `https://docs.microsoft.com/en-us/dotnet/standard/threading/overview-of-synchronization-primitives`

# Summary

In this chapter, you learned how to define and start a task, how to wait for one or more tasks to finish, and how to control task completion order. You also learned how to synchronize access to shared resources, and the theory behind `async` and `await`.

In the next part, you will learn how to create applications for the App Models supported by .NET Core, such as web applications, web services, and Universal Windows Platform apps, and App Models, such as Xamarin, that are supported by .NET Standard.

# Part 3

## App Models

This part of the book is about **App Models**: platforms for building complete applications such as websites, web services, web applications, Windows apps, and mobile apps. Since this book is about C# 7.1 and .NET Core 2.0 (and .NET Standard 2.0), we will focus on App Models that use those technologies to implement the majority of a solution.

**Websites** are made up of multiple web pages loaded statically from the filesystem or generated dynamically by a server-side technology, such as ASP.NET Core. A web browser makes `GET` requests using URLs that identify each page, and can manipulate data stored on the server using the `POST`, `PUT`, and `DELETE` requests, as shown in the following diagram:

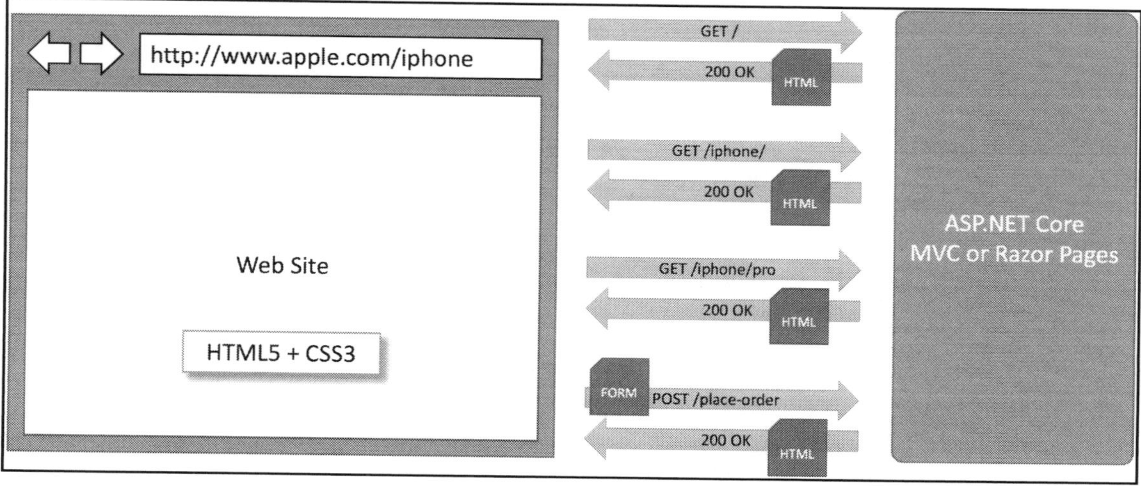

With websites, the web browser is treated as a presentation layer, with almost all of the processing performed on the server side. A small amount of JavaScript might be used on the client side to implement some presentation features, such as carousels.

**Web applications** are made up of a single web page, and a web service that a frontend technology such as Angular or React can make requests to for further interactions, exchanging data using common serialization formats, such as XML and JSON, as shown in the following diagram:

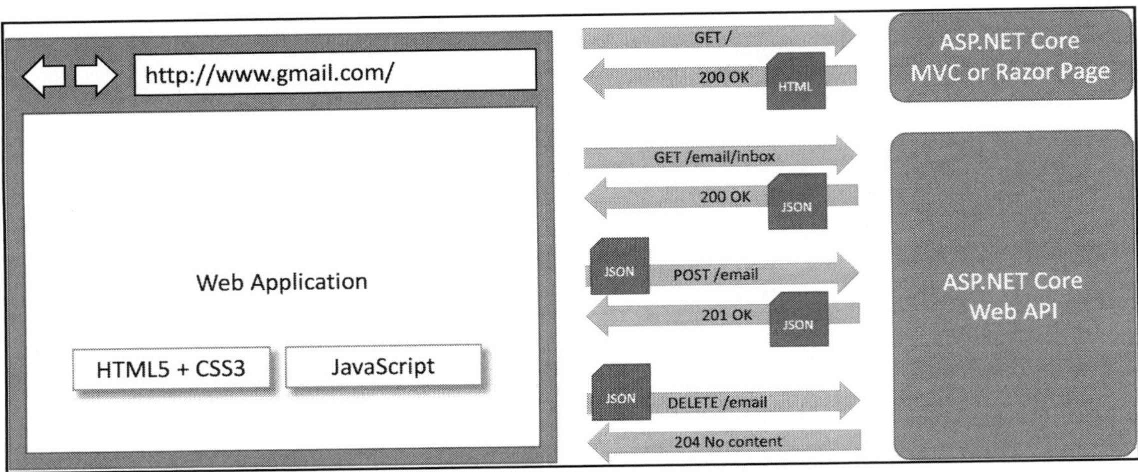


With a web application, known as a **Single Page Application** (**SPA**), the client-side uses advanced JavaScript libraries such as Angular and React to implement more sophisticated user interactions, but all of the important processing still happens on the server-side, because the web browser has limited access to local system resources.

In Q1 2018, on the server side, you will be able to use ASP.NET Core Sockets (the new name for SignalR) to implement web applications with real-time communication, but it was not ready in time for the release of ASP.NET Core 2.0.

**Windows apps** can only execute on the Windows 10 platform using C#, and can run on devices from phones and tablets, through desktops and laptops, to XBOX and mixed reality headsets. The apps can exist on their own, but they usually call web services to provide an experience that spans across all of your devices, as shown in the following diagram:

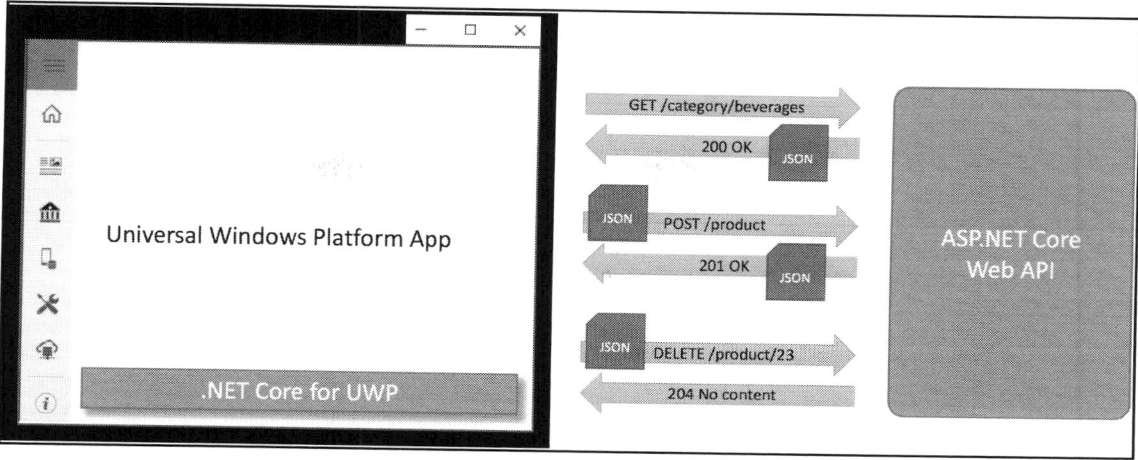


With Windows apps, the client side can provide extremely sophisticated user interactions, and has full access to all local system resources; so the app only needs the server side if the app needs to implement cross-device functionality, for example, creating a document on a tablet device, and continuing to work on the document on a desktop device, or having game playing progress shared across devices.

**Mobile apps** can be built once for the Xamarin.Forms platform using C#, and can run on iOS, Android, and other operating systems. The apps can exist on their own, but they usually call web services to provide an experience that spans across all of your mobile devices, as shown in the following diagram:

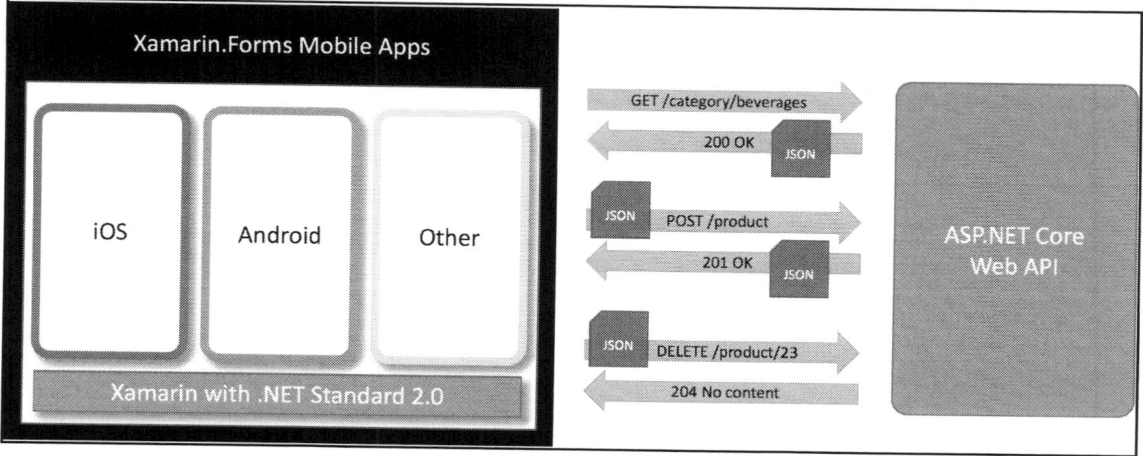

Mobile apps have similar benefits as Windows apps, except they are cross-platform, not just cross-device. Technologies for defining the user interface such as XAML can be shared with Windows apps.

Microsoft has extensive guidance for implementing App Models such as ASP.NET Web Applications, Xamarin Mobile Apps, and UWP Apps in its .NET Application Architecture Guidance documentation, that you can read at the following link:
`https://www.microsoft.com/net/learn/architecture`

In the following chapters, you will learn how to build the following:

14. Simple websites with Razor Pages.
15. Complex websites with MVC.
16. Web services with Web API and SPAs with Angular.
17. Windows apps with XAML and Fluent Design.
18. Mobile apps with Xamarin.Forms.

# 14
# Building Web Sites Using ASP.NET Core Razor Pages

This chapter is about building websites with a modern HTTP architecture on the server side using Microsoft ASP.NET Core. You will learn about building simple websites using the new ASP.NET Core 2.0 Razor Pages feature.

This chapter will cover the following topics:

- Understanding web development
- Understanding ASP.NET Core
- Exploring Razor Pages
- Using Entity Framework Core with ASP.NET Core

## Understanding web development

Developing for the web is developing with HTTP.

## Understanding HTTP

To communicate with a web server, the client, aka **user agent**, makes calls over the network using a protocol known as **Hypertext Transfer Protocol** (**HTTP**). HTTP is the technical underpinning of the *web*. So, when we talk about web applications or web services, we mean that they use HTTP to communicate between a client (often a web browser) and a server.

A client makes an HTTP request for a resource, such as a page identified by a **Uniform Resource Locator** (**URL**), and the server sends back an HTTP response, as shown in the following diagram:

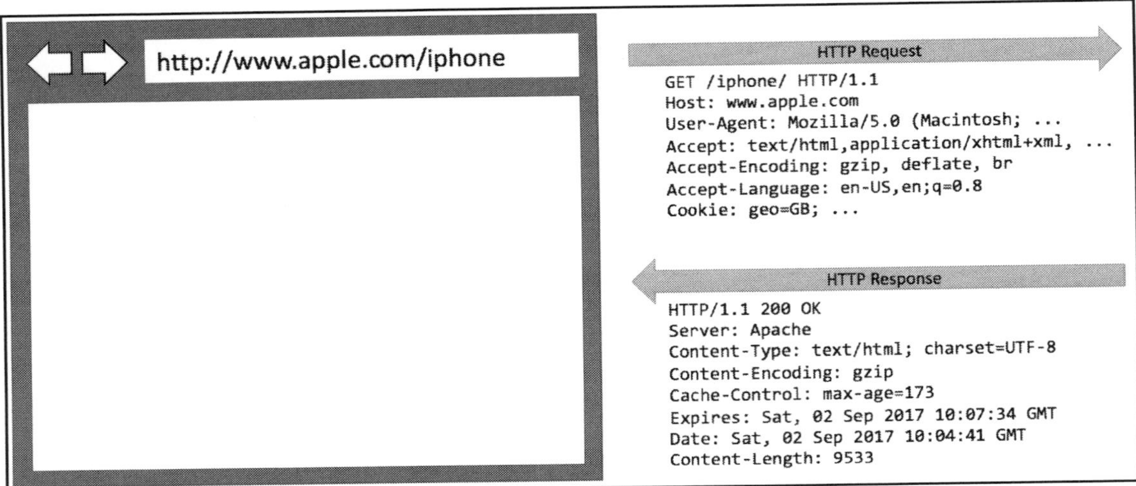


You can use Google Chrome and other browsers to record requests and responses.

**Good Practice**
**Google Chrome** is available on more operating systems than any other browser, and it has powerful, built-in developer tools, so it is a good first choice of browser. Always test your web application with Chrome and at least two other browsers, for example, **Firefox** and either **Microsoft Edge** for Windows 10 or **Safari** for macOS.

Start **Google Chrome**. To show developer tools in Chrome, do the following:

- On macOS, press *Alt* + *Cmd* + *I*
- On Windows, press *F12* or *Ctrl* + *Shift* + *I*

Click on the **Network** tab. Chrome should immediately start recording the network traffic between your browser and any web servers, as shown in the following screenshot:

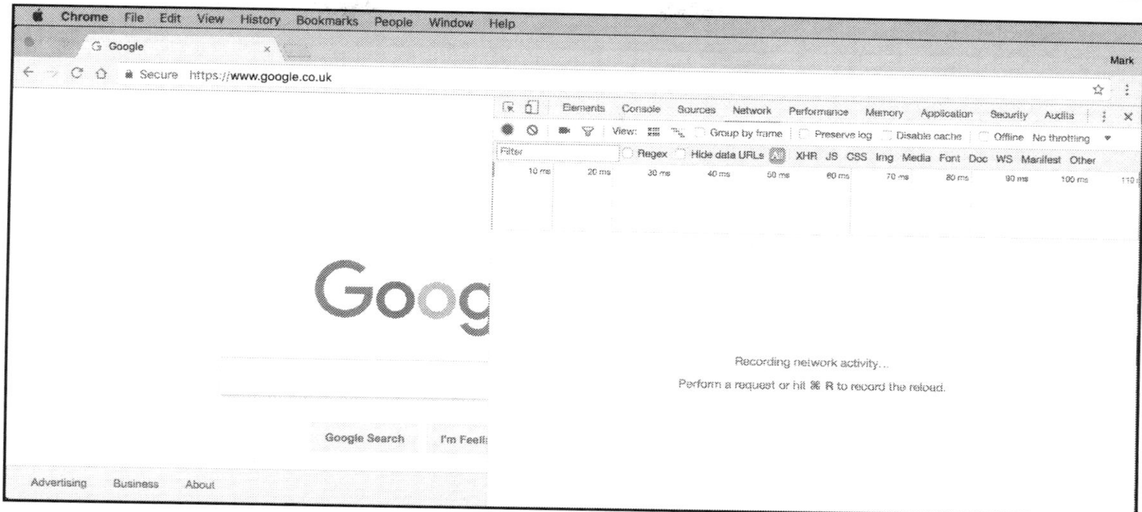


In Chrome's address box, enter the following URL:
`https://www.asp.net/get-started`

In the **Developer tools** window, in the list of recorded requests, click on the first entry, as shown in the following screenshot:

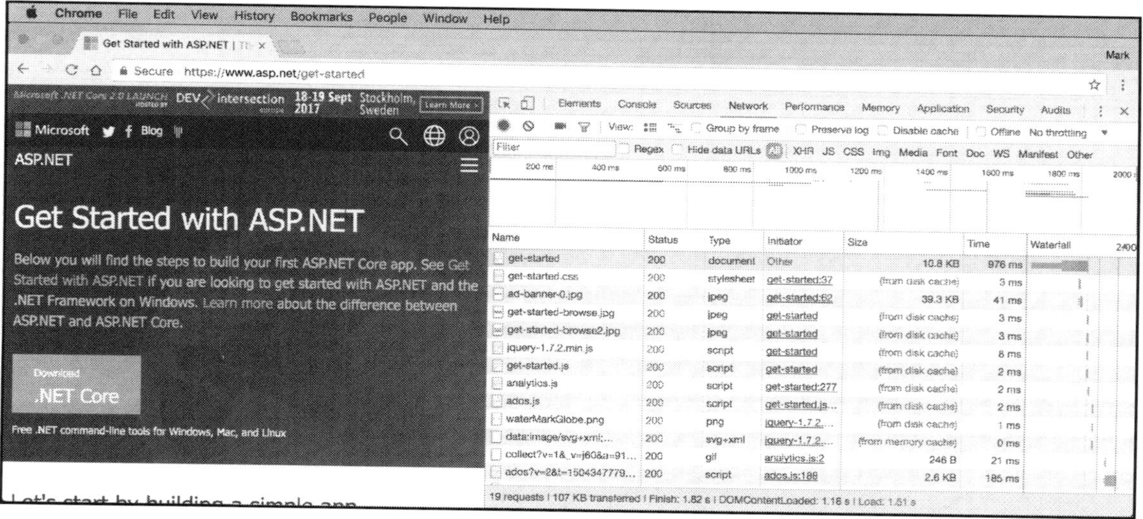

On the right-hand side, click on the **Headers** tab, and you will see details about the request and the response, as shown in the following screenshot:

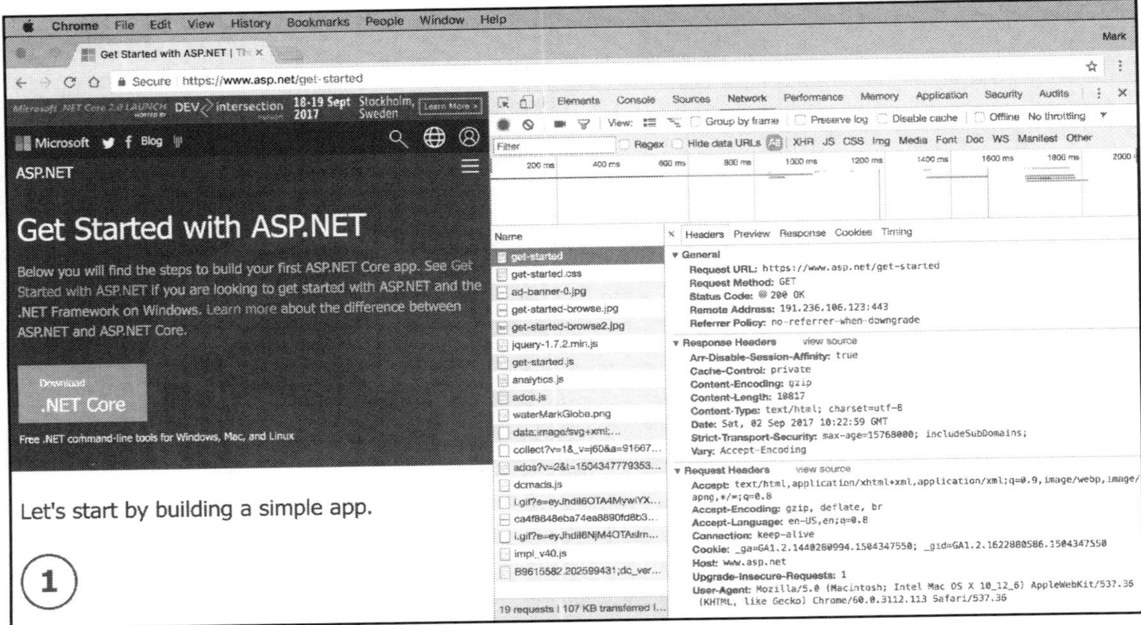

Note the following aspects:

- **Request Method** is `GET`. Other methods that HTTP defines include `POST`, `PUT`, `DELETE`, `HEAD`, and `PATCH`.
- **Status Code** is `200 OK`. This means that the server found the resource that the browser requested. Other status codes include `404 Missing`.
- **Request Headers** include **Accept**, which lists what formats the browser accepts. In this case, the browser is saying it understands HTML, XHTML, XML, and others.
- **Accept-Encoding** header means the browser has told the server that it understands the GZIP and DEFLATE compression algorithms.
- The browser has also told the server which human languages it would prefer: US English and then any dialect of English (with a quality value of `0.8`).
- I must have been to this site before because a Google Analytics cookie, named `_ga`, is being sent to the server so that it can track me.
- The server has sent back the response compressed using the GZIP algorithm because it knows that the client can decompress that format.

# Client-side web development

When building web applications, a developer needs to know more than just C# and .NET Core. On the client (that is, in the web browser), you will use a combination of the following components:

- **HTML5**: This is used for the content and structure of a web page
- **CSS3**: This is used for the styles applied to elements on the web page
- **JavaScript**: This is used for the procedural actions of the web page

Although HTML5, CSS3, and JavaScript are the fundamental components of frontend web development, there are many libraries that can make frontend web development more productive, including the following:

- **Bootstrap:** This is a CSS3 library for implementing responsive design in web pages. Optionally, it can use jQuery to add some advanced dynamic features.
- **jQuery**: This is a popular JavaScript library.
- **TypeScript**: This is a language created by Microsoft and embraced by Google, that adds C# type features to the JavaScript language. TypeScript files (`*.ts`) can be compiled into JavaScript files (`*.js`) during the build process.
- **Angular**: This is a popular library for building **single page applications (SPAs)** using TypeScript.
- **React:** This is another popular library for building SPAs.
- **Redux:** This is a library for managing state.

As part of the build and deploy process, you will likely use a combination of these technologies:

- **Node.js**: This is a server-side JavaScript library.
- **NPM**: This is the **Node Package Manager**, and has become the de facto package manager for JavaScript and many other web development modules.
- **Bower**: This is a client-side package manager for the web.
- **Gulp**: This is a toolkit for automating painful or time-consuming tasks.
- **Webpack**: This is a popular module bundler, a tool for compiling, transforming, and bundling application source code.

This book is about C# and .NET Core, so we will cover some of the basics of frontend web development, but for more detail, try *HTML5 Web Application Development By Example* at: `https://www.packtpub.com/web-development/html5-web-application-development-example-beginners-guide`, and *ASP.NET Core and Angular 2* at: `https://www.packtpub.com/application-development/aspnet-core-and-angular-2`

To make it easier to work with HTML5, CSS3, and JavaScript, both Visual Studio 2017 and Visual Studio Code have extensions such as the ones listed here:

- Mads Kristensen's extensions for Visual Studio: `https://marketplace.visualstudio.com/search?term=publisher%3A%22Mads%20Kristensen%22&target=VS&sortBy=Relevance`
- HTML Programming in VS Code: `https://code.visualstudio.com/Docs/languages/html`
- Microsoft's Visual Studio Code extensions: `https://marketplace.visualstudio.com/search?term=publisher%3A%22Microsoft%22&target=VSCode&sortBy=Relevance`

Mads Kristensen wrote one of the most popular extensions for web development with Visual Studio 2010, and later named it *Web Essentials*. It has now been broken up into smaller extensions that can be individually installed.

# Understanding ASP.NET Core

Microsoft ASP.NET Core is part of a history of Microsoft technologies used to build web applications and services that have evolved over the years:

- **Active Server Pages** (**ASP**) was released in 1996, and was Microsoft's first attempt at a platform for dynamic server-side execution of web application code. ASP files are written in the VBScript language.
- **ASP.NET Web Forms** was released in 2002 with the .NET Framework, and is designed to enable nonweb developers, such as those familiar with Visual Basic, to quickly create web applications by dragging and dropping visual components and writing event-driven code in Visual Basic or C#. Web Forms can only be hosted on Windows, but it is still used today in products such as Microsoft SharePoint. It should be avoided for new web projects in favor of ASP.NET Core.

- **Windows Communication Foundation** (**WCF**) was released in 2006, and enables developers to build SOAP and REST services. SOAP is powerful but complex, so it should be avoided unless you need advanced features, such as distributed transactions and complex messaging topologies.
- **ASP.NET MVC** was released in 2009, and is designed to cleanly separate the concerns of web developers between the *models* that temporarily store the data, the *views* that present the data using various formats in the UI, and the *controllers* that fetch the model and pass it to a view. This separation enables improved reuse and unit testing.
- **ASP.NET Web API** was released in 2012, and enables developers to create HTTP aka REST services that are simpler and more scalable than SOAP services.
- **ASP.NET SignalR** was released in 2013, and enables real-time communication in web applications by abstracting underlying technologies and techniques, such as *Web Sockets* and *Long Polling*.
- **ASP.NET Core** was released in 2016 and combines MVC, Web API, and SignalR, running on .NET Core. Therefore, it can execute cross-platform. ASP.NET Core 2.0 adds many templates to get you started with both server-side coding with .NET Core, and client-side coding with Angular or React or other frontend technologies.

**Good Practice**
Choose ASP.NET Core to develop web applications and services because it includes web-related technologies that are modern and cross-platform.

ASP.NET Core is .NET Standard 2.0-compliant so it can execute on .NET Framework 4.6.1 or later (Windows only) as well as .NET Core 2.0 or later (cross-platform).

# Classic ASP.NET versus modern ASP.NET Core

ASP.NET celebrates its 15th birthday in 2017. It's a teenager!

Until now, it has been built on top of a large assembly in the .NET Framework named `System.Web.dll`. Over the years, this assembly has accumulated a lot of features, many of which are not suitable for modern cross-platform development.

ASP.NET Core is a major redesign of ASP.NET. It removes the dependency on the `System.Web.dll` assembly and is composed of modular lightweight packages, just like the rest of .NET Core.

You can develop and run ASP.NET Core applications cross-platform on Windows, macOS, and Linux. Microsoft has even created a cross-platform, super performant web server named **Kestrel**. The entire stack is open source, and it is designed to integrate with a variety of client-side tools and frameworks, including Bower, Gulp, Grunt, Angular, jQuery, and Bootstrap.

All of the projects in `Part 3`, *App Models*, will be created in a `Part3` folder instead of individual chapter folders for convenience. I recommend that you work through the chapters in `Part 3`, *App Models* sequentially because later chapters will reference projects in earlier chapters.

# Creating an ASP.NET Core project with Visual Studio 2017

In Visual Studio 2017, press *Ctrl* + *Shift* + *N* or go to **File** | **New** | **Project...**.

In the **New Project** dialog, in the **Installed** list, expand **Visual C#**, and select **.NET Core**. In the center list, select **ASP.NET Core Web Application**, type the name as `NorthwindWeb`, type the location as `C:\Code`, type the solution name as `Part3`, and then click on **OK**.

In the **New ASP.NET Core Web Application - NorthwindWeb** dialog, select **.NET Core**, select **ASP.NET Core 2.0**, and select the **Empty** template. The **Enable Docker Support** box should be left unchecked. Click on **OK**, as shown in the following screenshot:

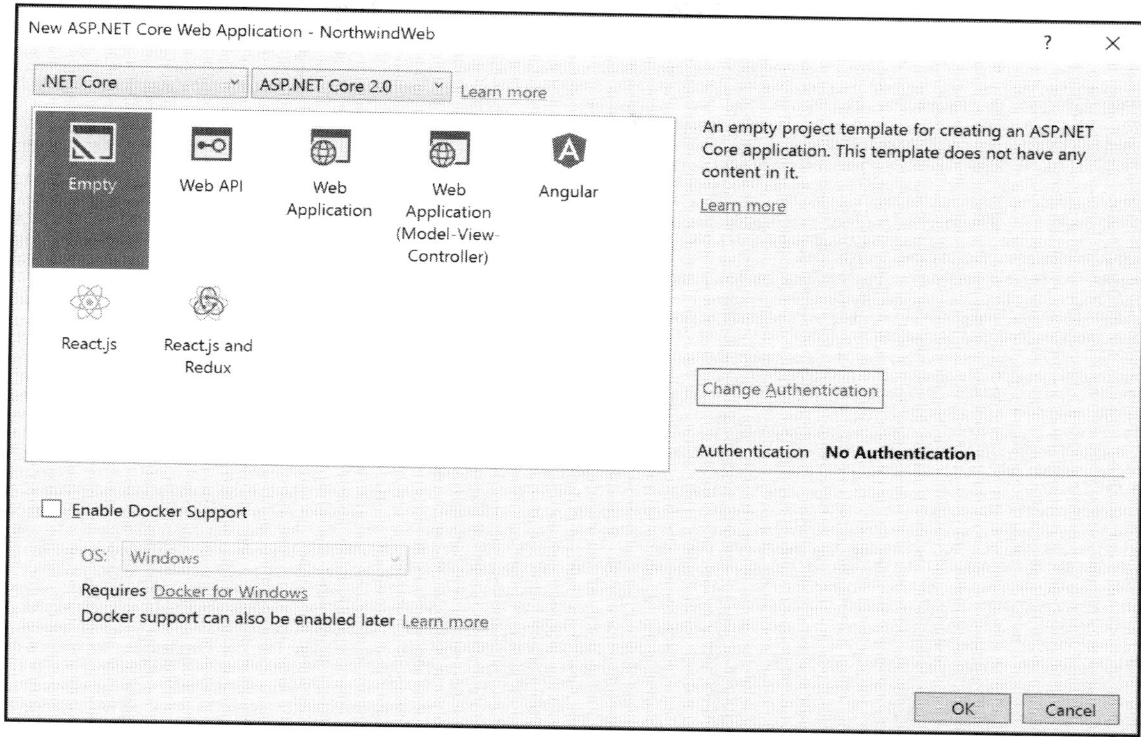


# Creating an ASP.NET Core project with Visual Studio Code

Create a folder named `Part3` with a subfolder named `NorthwindWeb`.

In Visual Studio Code, open the `NorthwindWeb` folder. In **Integrated Terminal**, enter the following command to create an ASP.NET Core Empty website:

```
dotnet new web
```

# Reviewing the ASP.NET Core Empty project template

In both Visual Studio 2017 and Visual Studio Code, edit `NorthwindWeb.csproj`, and note the following:

- The target framework is .NET Core 2.0.
- When published, the contents of the folder name `wwwroot\` will be included.
- A single package reference named `Microsoft.AspNetCore.All`. In older versions of ASP.NET Core, you would need to include lots of references. With ASP.NET Core 2.0 and later, you can use this special reference:

```
<Project Sdk="Microsoft.NET.Sdk.Web">

  <PropertyGroup>
    <TargetFramework>netcoreapp2.0</TargetFramework>
  </PropertyGroup>

  <ItemGroup>
    <Folder Include="wwwroot\" />
  </ItemGroup>

  <ItemGroup>
    <PackageReference
      Include="Microsoft.AspNetCore.All" Version="2.0.0" />
  </ItemGroup>

</Project>
```

`Microsoft.AspNetCore.All` is a metapackage that includes all ASP.NET Core packages, all **Entity Framework Core** (**EF Core**) packages, and all dependencies of ASP.NET Core and EF Core. Read more about the .NET Core Runtime Package Store at the following link: `https://docs.microsoft.com/en-us/dotnet/core/deploying/runtime-store`

Open `Program.cs`, and note the following:

- It is like a console application, with a static `Main` method
- The `WebHost` specifies a startup class. This is used to configure the website:

```
public class Program
{
   public static void Main(string[] args)
   {
      BuildWebHost(args).Run();
   }

    public static IWebHost BuildWebHost(string[] args) =>
      WebHost.CreateDefaultBuilder(args)
      .UseStartup<Startup>()
      .Build();
}
```

You can see exactly what the `CreateDefaultBuilder` method does at the following link:
https://github.com/aspnet/MetaPackages/blob/dev/src/Microsoft.AspNetCore/WebHost.cs

Open `Startup.cs`, and note the following:

- The `ConfigureServices` method is used to add services to the host container
- The `Configure` method is used to configure the HTTP request pipeline. The method currently does two things: when developing, any unhandled exceptions will be shown in the browser window for the developer to see its details, and it runs, waits for requests, and responds to all requests by returning the plain text, `Hello World!`:

```
public class Startup
{
   public void ConfigureServices(IServiceCollection services)
   {
   }

   public void Configure(
   IApplicationBuilder app, IHostingEnvironment env)
   {
      if (env.IsDevelopment())
      {
         app.UseDeveloperExceptionPage();
      }
```

```
        app.Run(async (context) =>
        {
            await context.Response.WriteAsync("Hello World!");
        });
    }
}
```

# Testing the empty website

In Visual Studio 2017, press *Ctrl* + *F5*, or go to **Debug** | **Start Without Debugging**.

In Visual Studio Code, in **Integrated Terminal**, enter the `dotnet run` command.

With Visual Studio 2017, a browser will run and make a request for the website, as shown in the following screenshot:

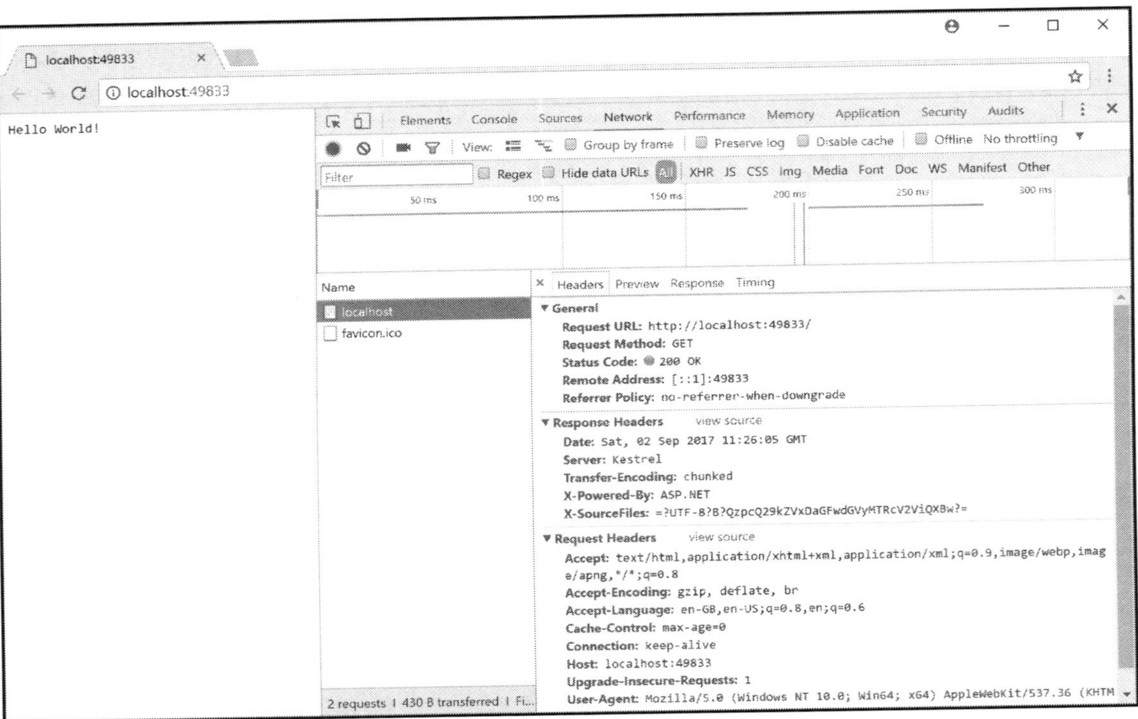

In Visual Studio 2017, go to **View** | **Output**, choose to show output from the **ASP.NET Core Web Server**, and note the requests being handled, as shown in the following screenshot:

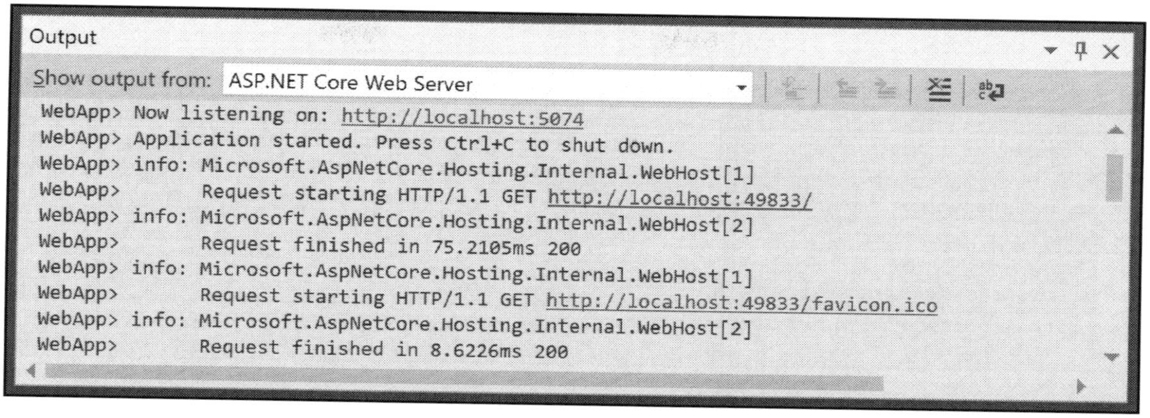

```
Output
Show output from: ASP.NET Core Web Server
WebApp> Now listening on: http://localhost:5074
WebApp> Application started. Press Ctrl+C to shut down.
WebApp> info: Microsoft.AspNetCore.Hosting.Internal.WebHost[1]
WebApp>       Request starting HTTP/1.1 GET http://localhost:49833/
WebApp> info: Microsoft.AspNetCore.Hosting.Internal.WebHost[2]
WebApp>       Request finished in 75.2105ms 200
WebApp> info: Microsoft.AspNetCore.Hosting.Internal.WebHost[1]
WebApp>       Request starting HTTP/1.1 GET http://localhost:49833/favicon.ico
WebApp> info: Microsoft.AspNetCore.Hosting.Internal.WebHost[2]
WebApp>       Request finished in 8.6226ms 200
```

In Visual Studio Code, note the messages in **Integrated Terminal**, as shown in the following output:

```
Hosting environment: Production
Content root path: /Users/markjprice/Code/Chapter14/WebApp
Now listening on: http://localhost:5000
Application started. Press Ctrl+C to shut down.
```

With Visual Studio Code, you must run a browser manually.

Start Chrome, enter the address: `http://localhost:5000/`, and note that you get the same response as shown in the previous screenshots for Visual Studio 2017.

In Visual Studio Code, press *Ctrl* + *C* to stop the web server. Remember to do this whenever you have finished testing a website.

Close your browser.

# Enabling static files

A website that only ever returns a single plain text message isn't very useful! At a minimum, it ought to return static HTML pages, CSS stylesheets the web pages use, and any other static resources such as images and videos.

In both Visual Studio 2017 and Visual Studio Code, add a new file to the `wwwroot` folder named `index.html`, and modify its content to link to CDN-hosted Bootstrap, and use modern good practices such as setting the viewport, as shown in the following markup:

Make sure that you put the `index.html` file in the `wwwroot` folder!

```
<!DOCTYPE html>
<html lang="en">
<head>
  <meta charset="utf-8" />
  <meta name="viewport" content=
   "width=device-width, initial-scale=1, shrink-to-fit=no" />
  <link rel="stylesheet"
href="https://maxcdn.bootstrapcdn.com/bootstrap/4.0.0-beta/css/bootstrap.mi
n.css"
    integrity="sha384-
/Y6pD6FV/Vv2HJnA6t+vslU6fwYXjCFtcEpHbNJ0lyAFsXTsjBbfaDjzALeQsN6M"
    crossorigin="anonymous" />
  <title>Welcome ASP.NET Core!</title>
</head>
<body>
   <div class="container">
     <div class="jumbotron">
       <h1 class="display-3">Welcome to Northwind!</h1>
       <p class="lead">We supply products to our customers.</p>
       <hr />
       <p>Our customers include restaurants, hotels, and cruise lines.</p>
       <p>
       <a class="btn btn-primary"
         href="https://www.asp.net/">Learn more</a>
     </p>
    </div>
  </div>
</body>
</html>
```

To understand the Bootstrap classes that I have used to style the page, read the documentation at this link:
`https://getbootstrap.com/docs/4.0/components/jumbotron/`

If you were to start the website, and enter `/index.html` in the address box, the website would continue to return the plain text `Hello World!`.

To enable the website to return static files such as `index.html`, we must explicitly configure those features.

In `Startup.cs`, in the `Configure` method, comment the statements that return the `Hello World!` response, and add a statement to enable static files, as shown in the following code:

```
public void Configure(
  IApplicationBuilder app, IHostingEnvironment env)
  {
     if (env.IsDevelopment())
     {
        app.UseDeveloperExceptionPage();
     }

     // app.Run(async (context) =>
     // {
     //    await context.Response.WriteAsync("Hello World!");
     // });

    app.UseStaticFiles();
  }
```

Start the website, and note the `404` error for the website, as shown in the following screenshot:

With Visual Studio Code, you must manually start the browser and enter this:
`http://localhost:5000`

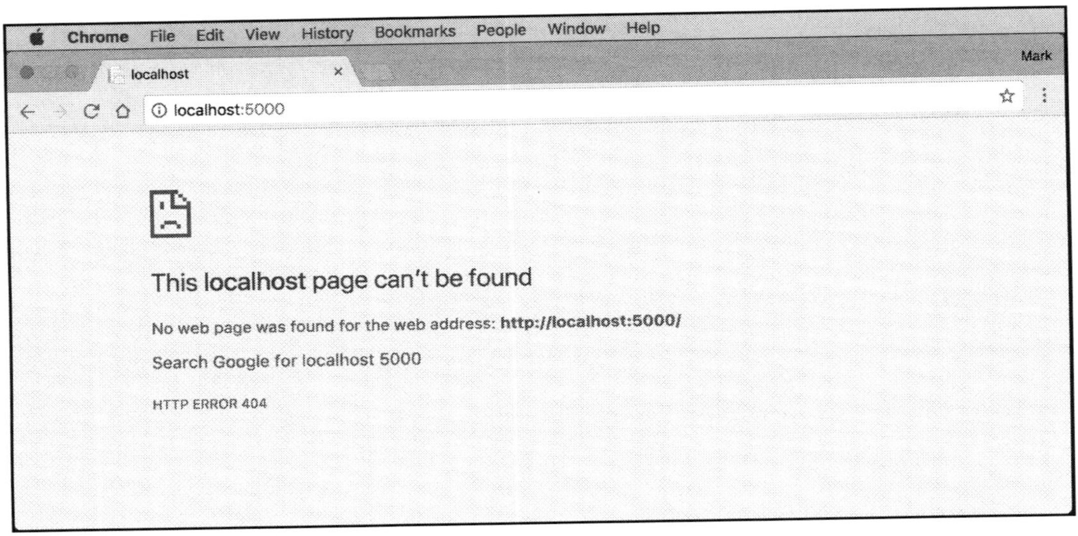


In the address box, enter `/index.html`, and note that the `index.html` web page is found and returned, as shown in the following screenshot:

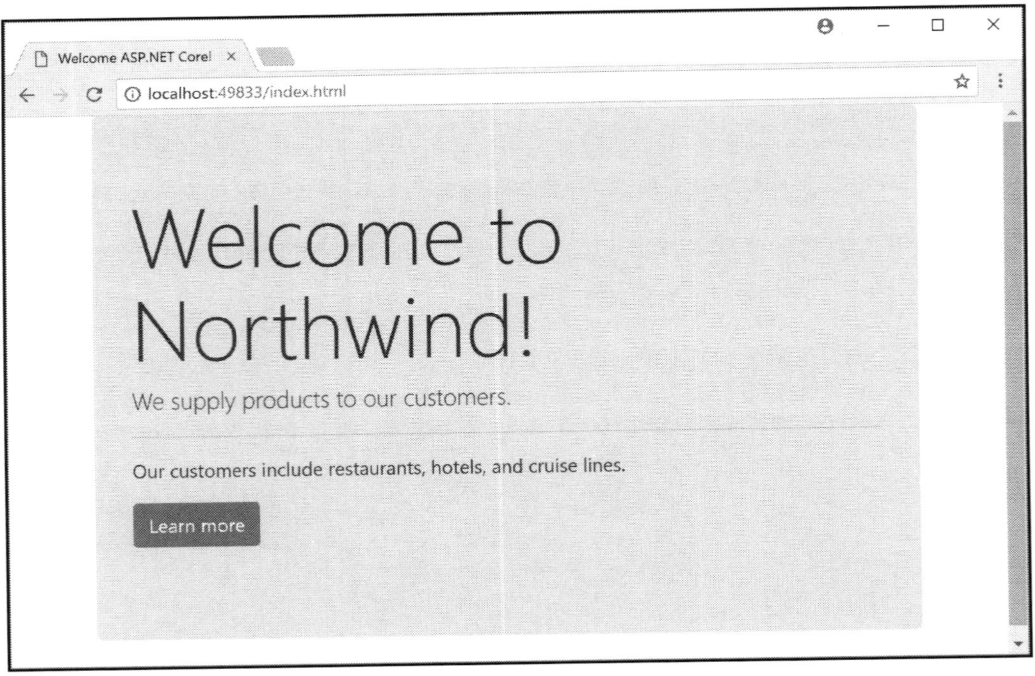

## Enabling default files

If the `index.html` file was returned as the default response for the website instead of having to enter its filename, it would be better.

In `Startup.cs`, add a statement to the `Configure` method to enable default files, as shown in the following code:

```
app.UseDefaultFiles(); // index.html, default.html, and so on
```

The call to `UseDefaultFiles` must be before the call to `UseStaticFiles`, or it won't work!

Start the website, and note that the `index.html` file is now returned immediately because it is the default web page for this website.

If all web pages are static, that is, they only get changed manually by a web editor, then our website programming work is complete. But, almost all websites need dynamic content. For example, a web page that is generated at runtime by executing code. The easiest way to do that is to use a new feature of ASP.NET Core named **Razor Pages**.

## Exploring Razor Pages

Razor Pages allow a developer to easily mix HTML markup with C# code statements. That is why they use the `.cshtml` file extension. The Razor syntax is indicated by the `@` symbol.

In the `NorthwindWeb` project, create a folder named `Pages`.

ASP.NET Core runtime looks for Razor Pages in the `Pages` folder by default.

Move the `index.html` file into the `Pages` folder, and rename the file extension from `.html` to `.cshtml`.

# Enabling Razor Pages

To enable Razor Pages, we must add and enable a service named MVC, because Razor Pages is a part of MVC.

In `Startup.cs`, in the `ConfigureServices` method, add statements to add MVC, as shown in the following code:

```
public void ConfigureServices(IServiceCollection services)
{
   services.AddMvc();
}
```

In `Startup.cs`, in the `Configure` method, after the existing statements to use default files and static files, add a statement to use MVC, as shown in the following code:

```
app.UseDefaultFiles(); // index.html, default.html, and so on
app.UseStaticFiles();
app.UseMvc(); // includes Razor Pages
```

# Defining a Razor Page

Razor Pages can be described as follows:

- They require the `@page` directive at the top of the file
- They can have a `@functions` section that defines these:
    - Properties for storing data values, just like a class
    - Methods named `OnGet`, `OnPost`, `OnDelete`, and so on, that execute when HTTP requests are made such as `GET`, `POST`, and `DELETE`

Modify `index.cshtml`, by adding C# statements to the top of the file to define this file as a Razor Page with `@page`, and define a property to store the current day name, and a method to set it that executes when a HTTP GET request is made for the page, as shown in the following code:

```
@page
@functions {
  public string DayName { get; set; }
  public void OnGet()
  {
```

```
            Model.DayName = DateTime.Now.ToString("dddd");
        }
    }
```

Modify `index.cshtml` to output the day name inside one of the paragraphs, as shown in the following markup:

```
<p>It's @Model.DayName! Our customers include restaurants, hotels, and
cruise lines.</p>
```

Start the website, and note the current day name is output on the page, as shown in the following screenshot:

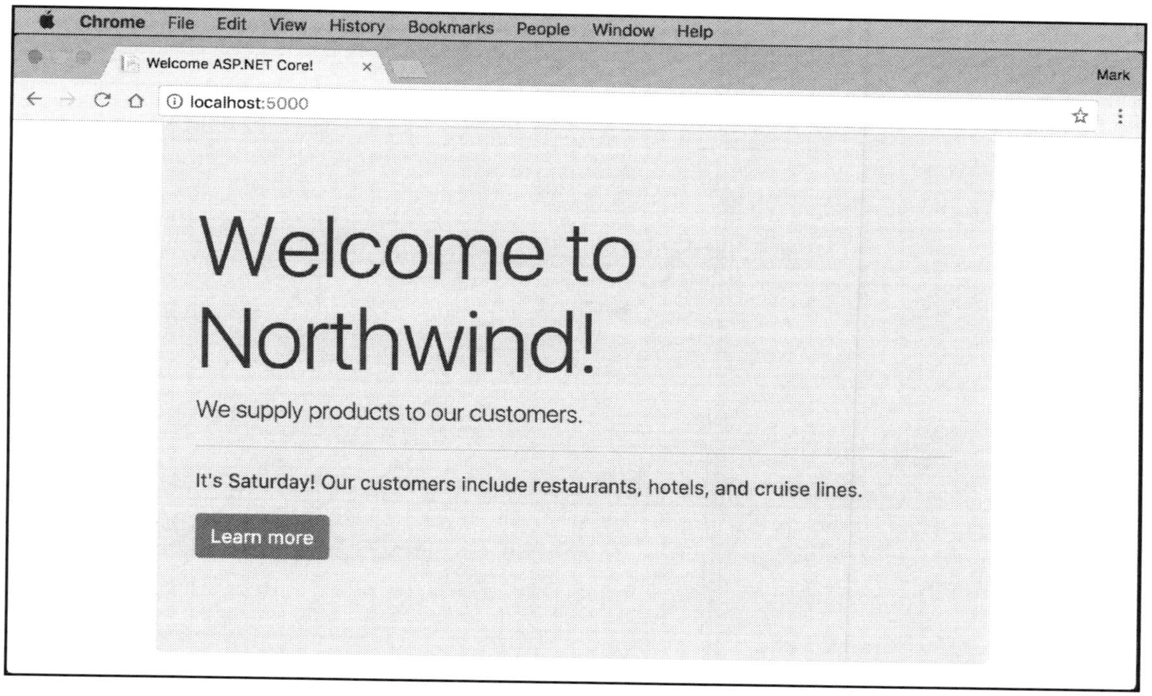


# Using shared layouts with Razor Pages

Most websites have more than one page. If every page had to contain all of the boilerplate markup that is currently in `index.cshtml`, that would become a pain to manage. So, ASP.NET Core has **layouts**.

## Setting a shared layout

To use layouts, we must first create a specially named file to set a default layout for all Razor Pages (and all MVC views). The name of this file must be `_ViewStart.cshtml`.

In Visual Studio 2017, in the `Pages` folder, add a new **MVC View Start Page** item, as shown in the following screenshot:

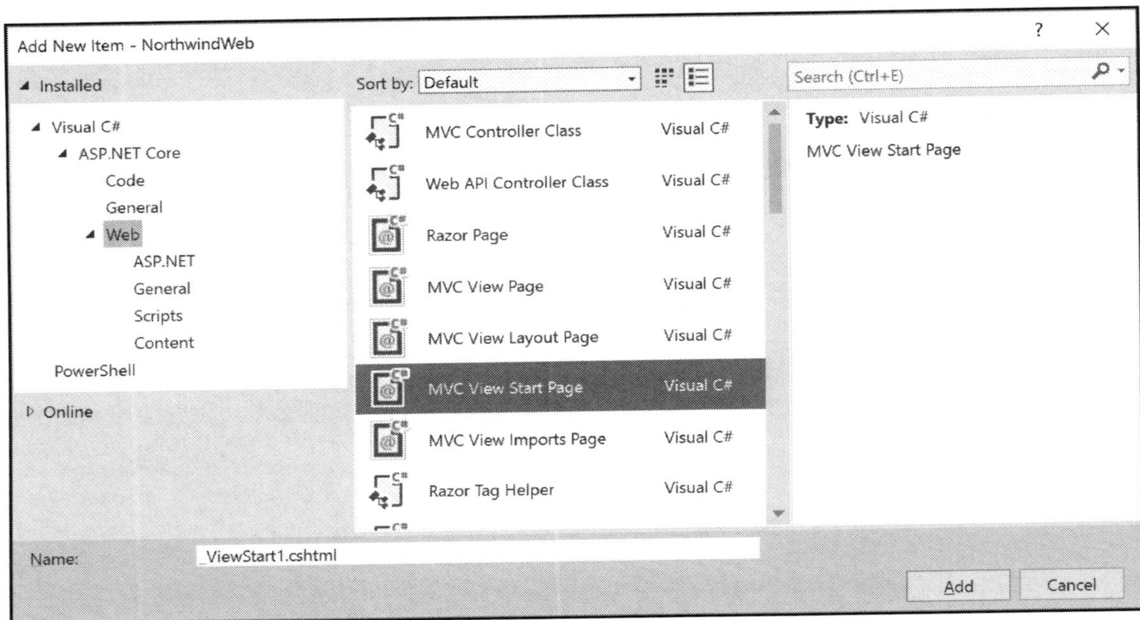


In Visual Studio Code, in the `Pages` folder, create a file named `_ViewStart.cshtml`, and modify its content, as shown in the following markup:

```
@{
   Layout = "_Layout";
 }
```

## Defining a shared layout

To use layouts, we must next create a Razor `.cshtml` file to define the default layout for all Razor Pages (and all MVC views). The name of this file can be anything, but `_Layout.cshtml` is good practice, so that is the name that you previously set in the `_ViewStart.cshtml` file.

In Visual Studio 2017, in the `Pages` folder, add a new **MVC View Layout Page** item.

In Visual Studio Code, in the `Pages` folder, create a file named `_Layout.cshtml`.

In both Visual Studio 2017 and Visual Studio Code, modify the content of `_Layout.cshtml`, as shown in the following markup (it is similar to `index.cshtml`, so you can copy and paste it from there):

```
<!DOCTYPE html>
<html lang="en">
<head>
<meta charset="utf-8" />
<meta name="viewport" content=
  "width=device-width, initial-scale=1, shrink-to-fit=no" />
  <link rel="stylesheet"
href="https://maxcdn.bootstrapcdn.com/bootstrap/4.0.0-beta/css/bootstrap.mi
n.css"
     integrity="sha384-
/Y6pD6FV/Vv2HJnA6t+vslU6fwYXjCFtcEpHbNJ0lyAFsXTsjBbfaDjzALeQsN6M"
     crossorigin="anonymous" />
  <title>@ViewData["Title"]</title>
</head>
<body>
  <div class="container">
     @RenderBody()
     <hr />
     <footer>
       <p>Copyright &copy; 2017 - @ViewData["Title"]</p>
     </footer>
  </div>
  <script src="https://code.jquery.com/jquery-3.2.1.slim.min.js"
     integrity="sha384-
KJ3o2DKtIkvYIK3UENzmM7KCkRr/rE9/Qpg6aAZGJwFDMVNA/GpGFF93hXpG5KkN"
     crossorigin="anonymous"></script>
  <script
src="https://cdnjs.cloudflare.com/ajax/libs/popper.js/1.11.0/umd/popper.min
.js"
     integrity="sha384-
b/U6ypiBEHpOf/4+1nzFpr53nxSS+GLCkfwBdFNTxtclqqenISfwAzpKaMNFNmj4"
     crossorigin="anonymous"></script>
  <script
src="https://maxcdn.bootstrapcdn.com/bootstrap/4.0.0-beta/js/bootstrap.min.
js"
     integrity="sha384-
```

```
h0AbiXch4ZDo7tp9hKZ4TsHbi047NrKGLO3SEJAg45jXxnGIfYzk4Si90RDIqNm1"
        crossorigin="anonymous"></script>
    @RenderSection("Scripts", required: false)
</body>
</html>
```

The layout we will use for all of the pages on the site is similar to that originally used in `index.cshtml`, but with some scripts at the bottom to implement some dynamic features of Bootstrap that we will use later.

Modify `index.cshtml`, remove all HTML markup except `<div class="jumbotron">` and its contents, add a statement to the `OnGet` method to store a page title in the `ViewData` dictionary, and modify the button to navigate to a suppliers page (which we will create in the next topic), as shown in the following markup:

```
@page
@functions {
  public string DayName { get; set; }

  public void OnGet()
  {
     ViewData["Title"] = "Northwind Web Site";
     Model.DayName = DateTime.Now.ToString("dddd");
  }
}
<div class="jumbotron">
  <h1 class="display-3">Welcome to Northwind!</h1>
  <p class="lead">We supply products to our customers.</p>
  <hr />
  <p>
     It's @Model.DayName! Our customers include restaurants,
     hotels, and cruise lines.
  </p>
  <p>
    <a class="btn btn-primary" href="suppliers">
       Learn more about our suppliers
    </a>
  </p>
</div>
```

`ViewData` is a dictionary that uses the `string` values for its keys. It is handy for passing values between Razor Pages and a shared layout without needing to define a property on the model as we did for `DayName`. Note that `ViewData["Title"]` is set in the Razor Page, and read in the shared layout.

Start the website, and note that it has similar behavior as before.

When using Visual Studio Code, remember to stop the web server with *Ctrl* + *C* and then restart with `dotnet run` to see changes.

# Using code-behind files with Razor Pages

Sometimes, it is better to separate the HTML markup from the data and executable code, so Razor Pages allows **code-behind** class files.

In Visual Studio 2017, right-click on the **Pages** folder, select **Add** | **New Item....** In the **Add New Item** dialog, select **Razor Page**, change the name to `Suppliers.cshtml`, and click on **Add**.

In Visual Studio Code, add two files to the `Pages` folder named `Suppliers.cshtml` and `Suppliers.cshtml.cs`.

Modify the contents of `Suppliers.cshtml.cs`, as shown in the following code, and note the following:

- `SuppliersModel` inherits from `PageModel`, so it has members such as `ViewData`
- `SuppliersModel` defines a property for storing a collection of string values
- When a HTTP GET request is made for this Razor Page, the `Suppliers` property is populated with some example supplier names:

```
using Microsoft.AspNetCore.Mvc.RazorPages;
using System.Collections.Generic;

namespace NorthwindWeb.Pages
{
   public class SuppliersModel : PageModel
   {
      public IEnumerable<string> Suppliers { get; set; }

      public void OnGet()
```

```
        {
            ViewData["Title"] = "Northwind Web Site - Suppliers";
            Suppliers = new[]
            { "Alpha Co", "Beta Limited", "Gamma Corp" };
        }
    }
}
```

In this example, we are focusing on learning about code-behind files. In the next topic, we will load the list of suppliers from a database, but for now, we will simulate that with a hard-coded array of the `string` values.

Modify the contents of `Suppliers.cshtml`, as shown in the following code, and note the following:

- The model for this Razor Page is set to `SuppliersModel`
- The page outputs an HTML table with Bootstrap styles
- The data rows in the table are generated by looping through the `Suppliers` property of `Model`

```
@page
@model NorthwindWeb.Pages.SuppliersModel
<div class="row">
  <h1 class="display-2">Suppliers</h1>
  <table class="table">
     <thead class="thead-inverse">
        <tr><th>Company Name</th></tr>
     </thead>
           <tbody>
              @foreach(string name in Model.Suppliers)
              {
                 <tr><td>@name</td></tr>
              }
           </tbody>
   </table>
</div>
```

Start the website, click on the button to learn more about suppliers, and note the table of suppliers, as shown in the following screenshot:

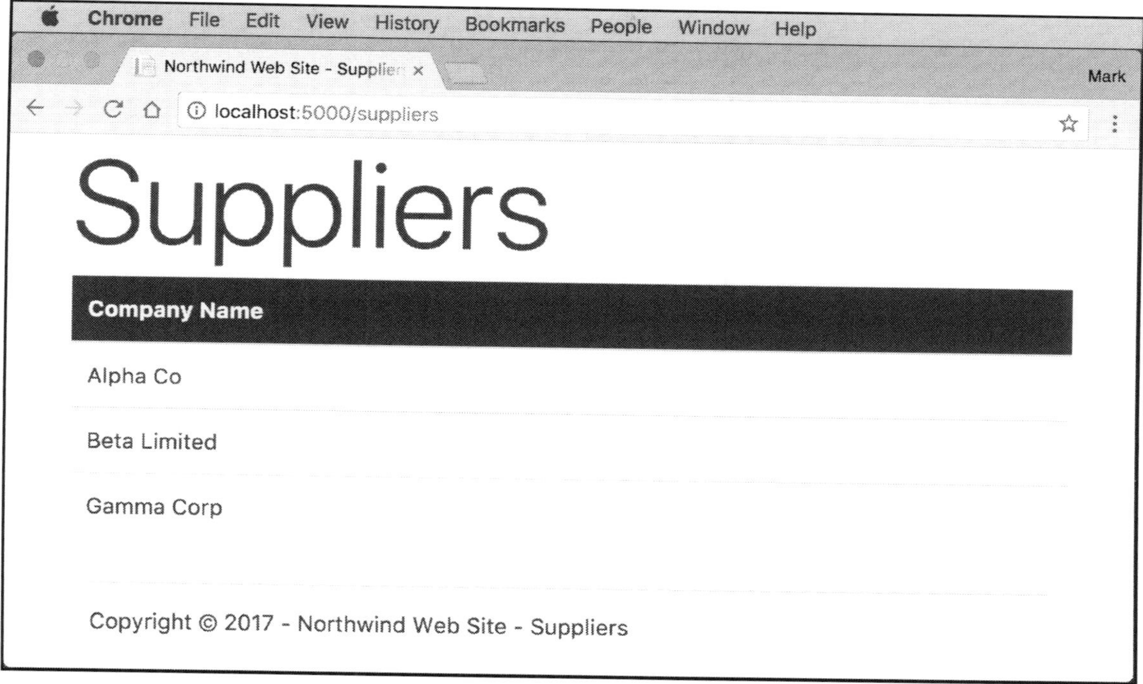


# Using Entity Framework Core with ASP.NET Core

Entity Framework Core 2.0 is included with ASP.NET Core 2.0, so it is a natural way to get real data into a website.

## Creating Entity models for Northwind

Creating entity data models in separate class libraries that are .NET Standard 2.0-compatible so that they can be reused in other types of projects is good practice.

## Creating a class library for the Northwind entity classes

In Visual Studio 2017, choose **File** | **Add** | **New Project...**.

In the **Add New Project** dialog, in the **Installed** list, expand **Visual C#**, and select **.NET Standard**. In the center list, select **Class Library (.NET Standard)**, type the name as `NorthwindEntitiesLib`, type the location as `C:\Code\Part3`, and then click on **OK**, as shown in the following screenshot:

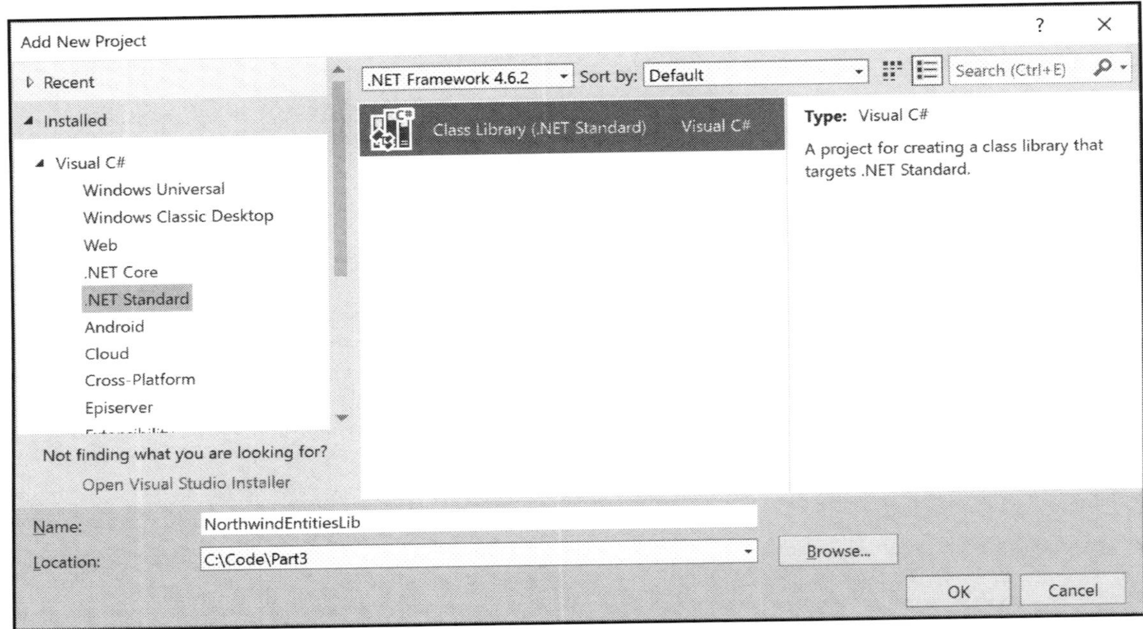


In Visual Studio Code, in the `Part3` folder, create a folder named `NorthwindEntitiesLib`, and open it with Visual Studio Code.

In the **Integrated Terminal**, enter the command: `dotnet new classlib`.

In Visual Studio Code, open the `Part3` folder, and in the **Integrated Terminal**, enter the command: `cd NorthwindWeb`.

## Defining the entity classes

In both Visual Studio 2017 and Visual Studio Code, add the following class files to the `NorthwindEntitiesLib` project: `Category.cs`, `Customer.cs`, `Employee.cs`, `Order.cs`, `OrderDetail.cs`, `Product.cs`, `Shipper.cs`, and `Supplier.cs`.

`Category.cs` should look like this:

```
using System.Collections.Generic;

namespace Packt.CS7
{
   public class Category
   {
      public int CategoryID { get; set; }
      public string CategoryName { get; set; }
      public string Description { get; set; }
      public ICollection<Product> Products { get; set; }
   }
}
```

`Customer.cs` should look like this:

```
using System.Collections.Generic;

namespace Packt.CS7
{
   public class Customer
   {
      public string CustomerID { get; set; }
      public string CompanyName { get; set; }
      public string ContactName { get; set; }
      public string ContactTitle { get; set; }
      public string Address { get; set; }
      public string City { get; set; }
      public string Region { get; set; }
      public string PostalCode { get; set; }
      public string Country { get; set; }
      public string Phone { get; set; }
      public string Fax { get; set; }
      public ICollection<Order> Orders { get; set; }
   }
}
```

`Employee.cs` should look like this:

```
using System;
using System.Collections.Generic;

namespace Packt.CS7
{
   public class Employee
   {
      public int EmployeeID { get; set; }
      public string LastName { get; set; }
      public string FirstName { get; set; }
      public string Title { get; set; }
      public string TitleOfCourtesy { get; set; }
      public DateTime? BirthDate { get; set; }
      public DateTime? HireDate { get; set; }
      public string Address { get; set; }
      public string City { get; set; }
      public string Region { get; set; }
      public string PostalCode { get; set; }
      public string Country { get; set; }
      public string HomePhone { get; set; }
      public string Extension { get; set; }
      public string Notes { get; set; }
      public int ReportsTo { get; set; }
      public Employee Manager { get; set; }
      public ICollection<Order> Orders { get; set; }
   }
}
```

`Order.cs` should look like this:

```
using System;
using System.Collections.Generic;

namespace Packt.CS7
{
   public class Order
   {
      public int OrderID { get; set; }
      public string CustomerID { get; set; }
      public Customer Customer { get; set; }
      public int EmployeeID { get; set; }
      public Employee Employee { get; set; }
      public DateTime? OrderDate { get; set; }
      public DateTime? RequiredDate { get; set; }
      public DateTime? ShippedDate { get; set; }
      public int ShipVia { get; set; }
```

```
        public Shipper Shipper { get; set; }
        public decimal? Freight { get; set; } = 0;
        public ICollection<OrderDetail> OrderDetails { get; set; }
    }
}
```

`OrderDetail.cs` should look like this:

```
namespace Packt.CS7
{
    public class OrderDetail
    {
        public int OrderID { get; set; }
        public Order Order { get; set; }
        public int ProductID { get; set; }
        public Product Product { get; set; }
        public decimal UnitPrice { get; set; } = 0;
        public short Quantity { get; set; } = 1;
        public double Discount { get; set; } = 0;
    }
}
```

`Product.cs` should look like this:

```
namespace Packt.CS7
{
    public class Product
    {
        public int ProductID { get; set; }
        public string ProductName { get; set; }
        public int? SupplierID { get; set; }
        public Supplier Supplier { get; set; }
        public int? CategoryID { get; set; }
        public Category Category { get; set; }
        public string QuantityPerUnit { get; set; }
        public decimal? UnitPrice { get; set; } = 0;
        public short? UnitsInStock { get; set; } = 0;
        public short? UnitsOnOrder { get; set; } = 0;
        public short? ReorderLevel { get; set; } = 0;
        public bool Discontinued { get; set; } = false;
    }
}
```

`Shipper.cs` should look like this:

```
using System.Collections.Generic;

namespace Packt.CS7
{
   public class Shipper
   {
      public int ShipperID { get; set; }
      public string ShipperName { get; set; }
      public string Phone { get; set; }
      public ICollection<Order> Orders { get; set; }
   }
}
```

`Supplier.cs` should look like this:

```
using System.Collections.Generic;

namespace Packt.CS7
{
   public class Supplier
   {
      public int SupplierID { get; set; }
      public string CompanyName { get; set; }
      public string ContactName { get; set; }
      public string ContactTitle { get; set; }
      public string Address { get; set; }
      public string City { get; set; }
      public string Region { get; set; }
      public string PostalCode { get; set; }
      public string Country { get; set; }
      public string Phone { get; set; }
      public string Fax { get; set; }
      public string HomePage { get; set; }
      public ICollection<Product> Products { get; set; }
   }
}
```

**Good Practice**
You should create a separate class library project for your entity data models that does not have a dependency on anything except .NET Standard 2.0. This allows easier sharing between backend servers and frontend clients.

## Creating a class library for Northwind database context

With Visual Studio 2017, you will use the EF Core data provider for SQL Server.

With Visual Studio Code, you will use the EF Core data provider for SQLite.

### Using Visual Studio 2017

In Visual Studio 2017, go to **File** | **Add** | **New Project....**

In the **Add New Project** dialog, in the **Installed** list, expand **Visual C#**, and select **.NET Standard**. In the center list, select **Class Library (.NET Standard)**, type the name as `NorthwindContextLib`, type the location as `C:\Code\Part3`, and then click on **OK**.

In the **NorthwindContextLib** project, right-click on **Dependencies**, and select **Add Reference....**

In the **Reference Manager - NorthwindContextLib** dialog, select **NorthwindEntitiesLib**, and click on **OK**, as shown in the following screenshot:

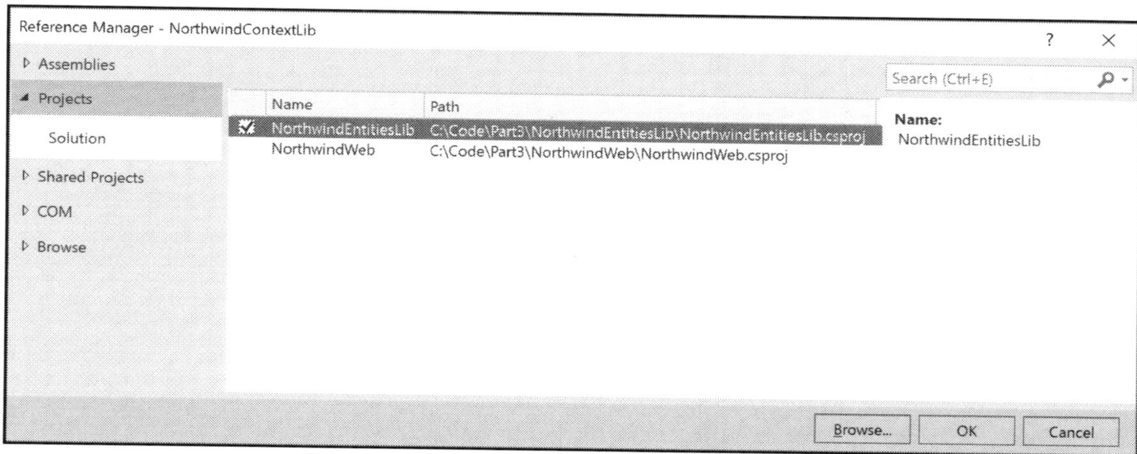


In the **NorthwindContextLib** project, right-click on **Dependencies**, and select **Manage NuGet Packages....**

In **NuGet Package Manager: NorthwindContextLib**, select **Browse**, search for and install `w`, and click on **OK**.

### Using Visual Studio Code

In Visual Studio Code, in the `Part3` folder, create a folder named `NorthwindContextLib`, and open it with Visual Studio Code.

In **Integrated Terminal**, enter the command: `dotnet new classlib`.

In Visual Studio Code, modify `NorthwindContextLib.csproj` to add a reference to the `NorthwindEntitiesLib` project, and the Entity Framework Core 2.0 package for SQLite, as shown in the following markup:

```
<Project Sdk="Microsoft.NET.Sdk">

  <PropertyGroup>
    <TargetFramework>netstandard2.0</TargetFramework>
  </PropertyGroup>

  <ItemGroup>
    <ProjectReference
       Include="..\NorthwindEntitiesLib\NorthwindEntitiesLib.csproj" />
    <PackageReference
       Include="Microsoft.EntityFrameworkCore.SQLite" Version="2.0.0" />
  </ItemGroup>

</Project>
```

In Visual Studio Code, open the `Part3` folder, and in **Integrated Terminal**, enter the command: `cd NorthwindWeb`.

## Defining the database context class

In both Visual Studio 2017 and Visual Studio Code, in the `NorthwindContextLib` project, rename the `Class1.cs` class file as `Northwind.cs`.

`Northwind.cs` should look like this:

```
using Microsoft.EntityFrameworkCore;

namespace Packt.CS7
{
  public class Northwind : DbContext
  {
     public DbSet<Category> Categories { get; set; }
     public DbSet<Customer> Customers { get; set; }
     public DbSet<Employee> Employees { get; set; }
     public DbSet<Order> Orders { get; set; }
```

```
    public DbSet<OrderDetail> OrderDetails { get; set; }
    public DbSet<Product> Products { get; set; }
    public DbSet<Shipper> Shippers { get; set; }
    public DbSet<Supplier> Suppliers { get; set; }

    public Northwind(DbContextOptions options)
        : base(options) { }

    protected override void OnModelCreating(ModelBuilder modelBuilder)
    {
        base.OnModelCreating(modelBuilder);

        modelBuilder.Entity<Category>()
          .Property(c => c.CategoryName)
          .IsRequired()
          .HasMaxLength(15);

        // define a one-to-many relationship
        modelBuilder.Entity<Category>()
          .HasMany(c => c.Products)
          .WithOne(p => p.Category);

        modelBuilder.Entity<Customer>()
          .Property(c => c.CustomerID)
          .IsRequired()
          .HasMaxLength(5);

        modelBuilder.Entity<Customer>()
          .Property(c => c.CompanyName)
          .IsRequired()
          .HasMaxLength(40);

        modelBuilder.Entity<Customer>()
          .Property(c => c.ContactName)
          .HasMaxLength(30);

        modelBuilder.Entity<Customer>()
          .Property(c => c.Country)
          .HasMaxLength(15);

        modelBuilder.Entity<Employee>()
          .Property(c => c.LastName)
          .IsRequired()
          .HasMaxLength(20);

        modelBuilder.Entity<Employee>()
          .Property(c => c.FirstName)
          .IsRequired()
```

```
            .HasMaxLength(10);

        modelBuilder.Entity<Employee>()
            .Property(c => c.Country)
            .HasMaxLength(15);

        modelBuilder.Entity<Product>()
            .Property(c => c.ProductName)
            .IsRequired()
            .HasMaxLength(40);

        modelBuilder.Entity<Product>()
            .HasOne(p => p.Category)
            .WithMany(c => c.Products);

        modelBuilder.Entity<Product>()
            .HasOne(p => p.Supplier)
            .WithMany(s => s.Products);

        modelBuilder.Entity<OrderDetail>()
            .ToTable("Order Details");

        // define multi-column primary key
        // for Order Details table
        modelBuilder.Entity<OrderDetail>()
            .HasKey(od => new { od.OrderID, od.ProductID });

        modelBuilder.Entity<Supplier>()
            .Property(c => c.CompanyName)
            .IsRequired()
            .HasMaxLength(40);

        modelBuilder.Entity<Supplier>()
            .HasMany(s => s.Products)
            .WithOne(p => p.Supplier);
    }
  }
}
```

We will set the database connection string in the ASP.NET Core startup so that it does not need to be done in the `Northwind` class, but the class derived from `DbContext` must have a constructor with a `DbContextOptions` parameter.

## Creating the Northwind database in the website

Follow the instructions in `Chapter 11`, *Working with Databases Using Entity Framework Core,* to create the `Northwind` database, as summarized in the following bullet points:

- To use SQL Server on Windows, create the database in the `(local)\mssqllocaldb` server. If you completed the earlier chapters, then you have already done this.
- To use SQLite on macOS or other operating systems, create the `Northwind.db` file by copying the `Northwind4SQLite.sql` file into the `Part3` folder, and then enter the following command in **TERMINAL**:

```
sqlite3 Northwind.db < Northwind4SQLite.sql
```

## Configure Entity Framework Core as a service

Services such as the Entity Framework Core, that are needed by ASP.NET Core, must be registered as a service during startup.

In Visual Studio 2017, in **NorthwindWeb** project, right-click on **Dependencies**, and add a reference to the `NorthwindContextLib` project.

In Visual Studio Code, in the `NorthwindWeb` project, modify `NorthwindWeb.csproj`, and add a reference to the `NorthwindContextLib` project, as shown in the following markup:

```
<Project Sdk="Microsoft.NET.Sdk.Web">

  <PropertyGroup>
    <TargetFramework>netcoreapp2.0</TargetFramework>
  </PropertyGroup>

  <ItemGroup>
    <Folder Include="wwwroot\" />
  </ItemGroup>

  <ItemGroup>
    <PackageReference Include="Microsoft.AspNetCore.All" Version="2.0.0" />
    <ProjectReference
       Include="..\NorthwindContextLib\NorthwindContextLib.csproj" />
  </ItemGroup>

</Project>
```

In both Visual Studio 2017 and Visual Studio Code, open the `Startup.cs` file, and import the `Microsoft.EntityFrameworkCore` and `Packt.CS7` namespaces, as shown in the following code:

```
using Microsoft.EntityFrameworkCore;
using Packt.CS7;
```

Add the following statement to the `ConfigureServices` method.

For SQL Server LocalDB, use this statement:

```
services.AddDbContext<Northwind>(options => options.UseSqlServer(
"Server=(localdb)\\mssqllocaldb;Database=Northwind;
Trusted_Connection=True;MultipleActiveResultSets=true"));
```

For SQLite, use this one:

```
services.AddDbContext<Northwind>(options => options.UseSqlite("Data
Source=../Northwind.db"));
```

In the `NorthwindWeb` project, in the `Pages` folder, open `Suppliers.cshtml.cs`, and import the `Packt.CS7` and `System.Linq` namespaces, as shown in the following code:

```
using System.Linq;
using Packt.CS7;
```

In the `SuppliersModel` class, add a private field and a constructor to get the `Northwind` database context, as shown in the following code:

```
private Northwind db;

public SuppliersModel(Northwind injectedContext)
{
   db = injectedContext;
}
```

In the `OnGet` method, modify the statements to use `Northwind` to get the names of suppliers, as shown in the following code:

```
public void OnGet()
{
   ViewData["Title"] = "Northwind Web Site - Suppliers";

   Suppliers = db.Suppliers.Select(s => s.CompanyName).ToArray();
}
```

Start the website, and note that the supplier table now loads from the database, as shown in the following screenshot:

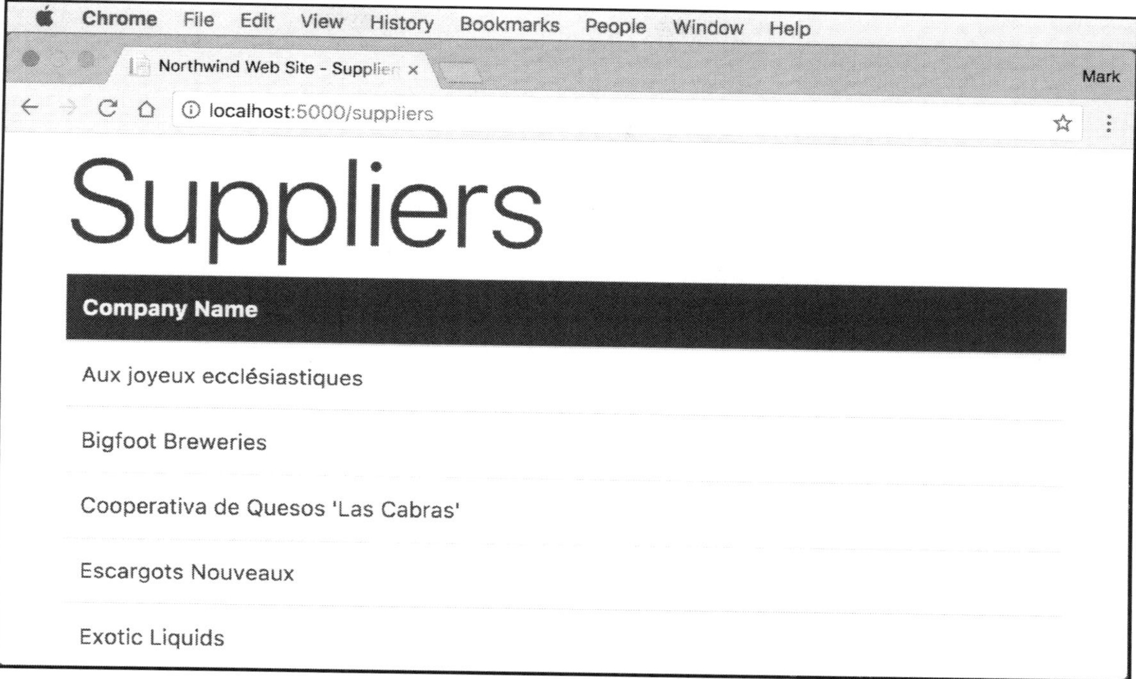


# Manipulating data

Let's add the functionality to insert a new supplier.

Open `Suppliers.cshtml.cs`, and import the following namespace:

```
using Microsoft.AspNetCore.Mvc;
```

In the `SuppliersModel` class, add a property to store a supplier, and a method named `OnPost` that adds the supplier if its model is valid, as shown in the following code:

```
[BindProperty]
public Supplier Supplier { get; set; }

public IActionResult OnPost()
{
  if (ModelState.IsValid)
```

```
    {
        db.Suppliers.Add(Supplier);
        db.SaveChanges();
        return RedirectToPage("/suppliers");
    }
    return Page();
}
```

Open `Suppliers.cshtml`, and add tag helpers, as shown in the following markup:

```
@addTagHelper *, Microsoft.AspNetCore.Mvc.TagHelpers
```

At the bottom of the `.cshtml` file, add a form to insert a new supplier, and use the `asp-for` tag helper to connect the `CompanyName` property of the `Supplier` class to the input box, as shown in the following markup:

```
<div class="row">
  <p>Enter a name for a new supplier:</p>
  <form method="POST">
    <div><input asp-for="Supplier.CompanyName" /></div>
    <input type="submit" />
  </form>
</div>
```

Start the website, click on **Learn more about our suppliers**, scroll down to the form to add a new supplier, enter `Bob's Burgers`, and click on **Submit**:

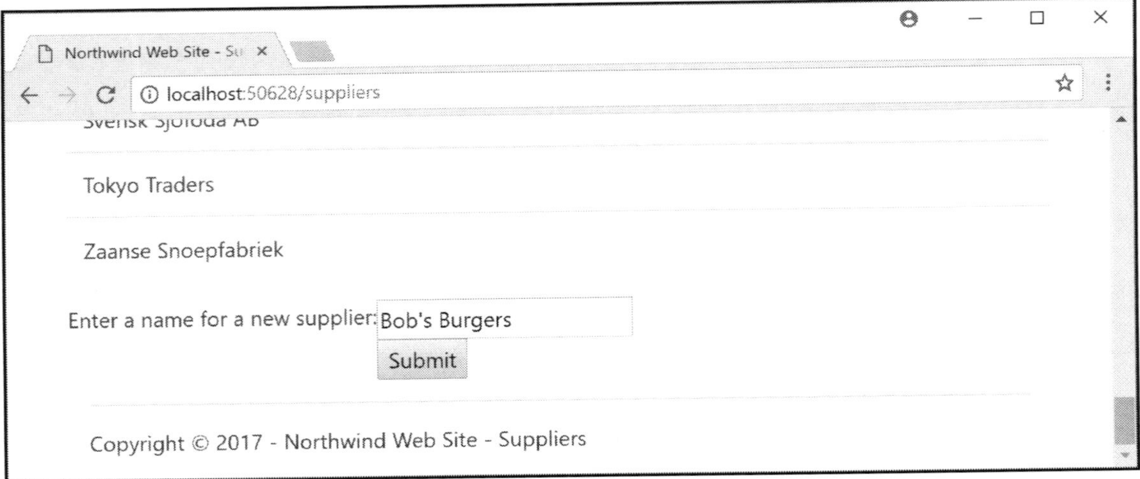

If you were to set a breakpoint inside the `OnPost` method and add a watch expression for the `Supplier` property, you would see that its properties have been populated automatically, as shown here:

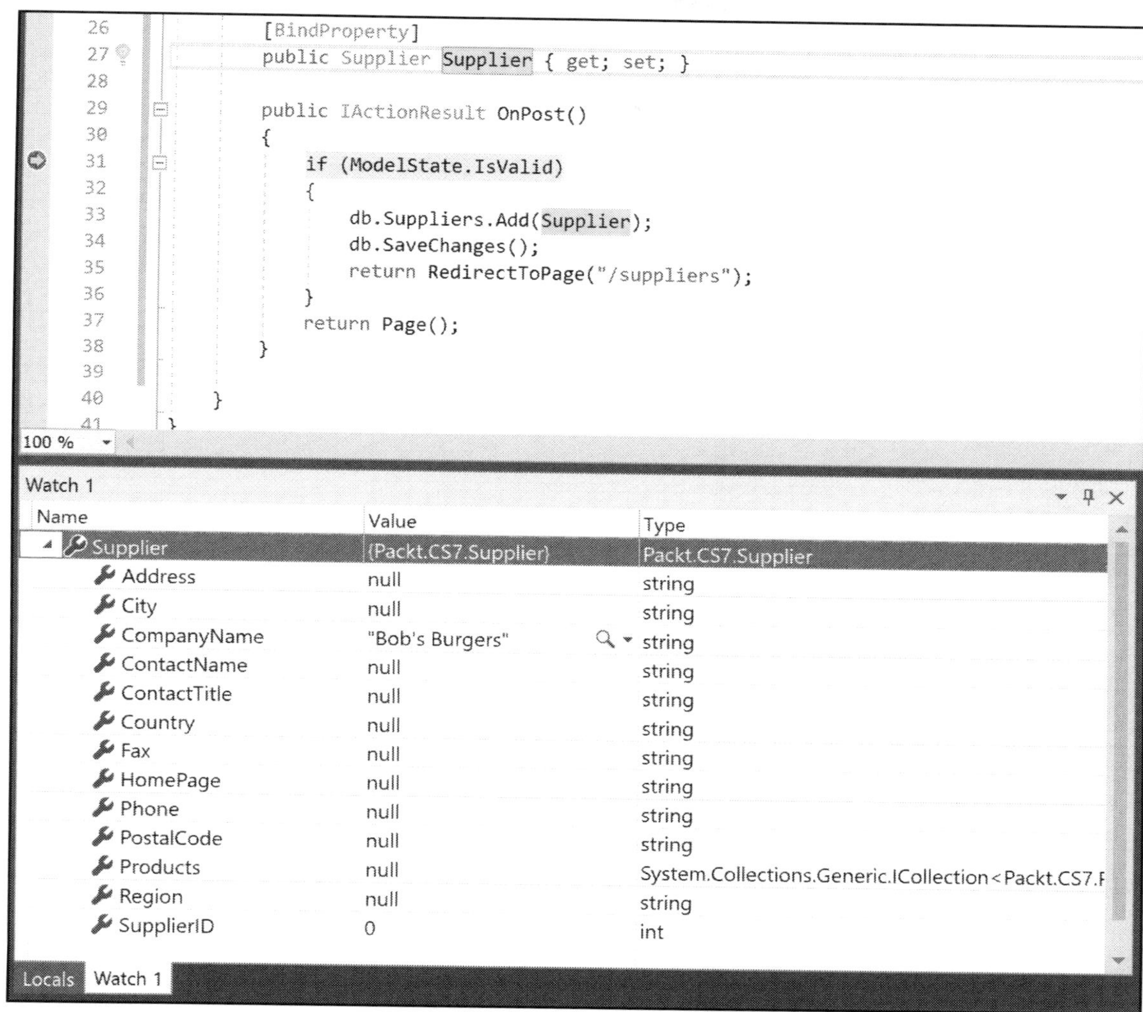

After clicking on **Submit**, you will be redirected back to the **Suppliers** list, as shown in the following screenshot:

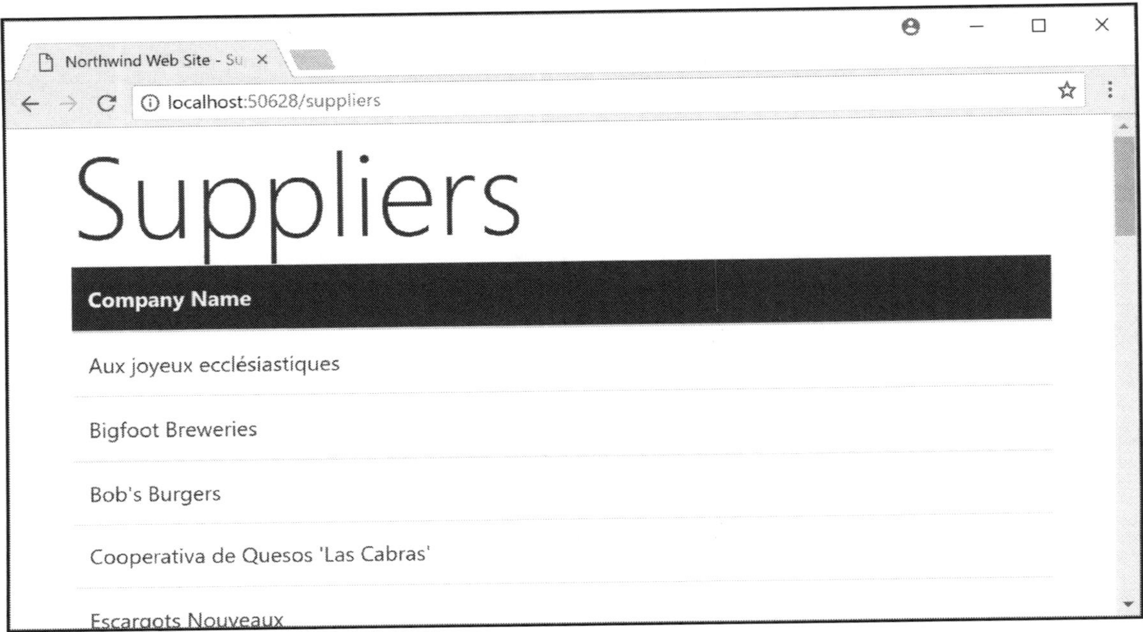


# Practicing and exploring

Get some hands-on practice and explore this chapter's topics with deeper research.

## Exercise 14.1 – Practice building a data-driven website

Add a Razor Page to the **NorthwindWeb** website that enables the user to see a list of customers grouped by country. When the user clicks on a customer record, they then see a page showing the full contact details of that customer, and a list of their orders.

## Exercise 14.2 – Explore topics

Use the following links to read more details about this chapter's topics:

- **ASP.NET Core**: `https://www.asp.net/core`
- **Introduction to working with static files in ASP.NET Core**: `https://docs.microsoft.com/en-us/aspnet/core/fundamentals/static-files`
- **Introduction to Razor Pages in ASP.NET Core**: `https://docs.microsoft.com/en-us/aspnet/core/mvc/razor-pages/`
- **Working with Data in ASP.NET Core**: `https://docs.microsoft.com/en-gb/aspnet/core/data/`
- **ASP.NET Core Schedule and Roadmap**: `https://github.com/aspnet/Home/wiki/Roadmap`

# Summary

In this chapter, you learned how to build a simple website that returns static files, and used ASP.NET Core Razor Pages and Entity Framework Core to create web pages dynamically generated from a database.

In the next chapter, you will learn how to build more complex websites using ASP.NET Core MVC, which separates concerns into models, views, and controllers.

# 15
# Building Web Sites Using ASP.NET Core MVC

This chapter is about building websites with a modern HTTP architecture on the server-side using Microsoft ASP.NET Core MVC, including the startup configuration, authentication, authorization, routes, models, views, and controllers that make up ASP.NET Core MVC.

This chapter will cover the following topics:

- Setting up an ASP.NET Core MVC website
- Understanding an ASP.NET Core MVC website

## Setting up an ASP.NET Core MVC website

ASP.NET Core Razor Pages are great for simple websites. For more complex websites, it would be better to have a more formal structure to manage that complexity.

This is where the Model-View-Controller design pattern is useful. It uses technologies similar to Razor Pages, but allows a cleaner separation between concerns, as shown in the following list:

- **Models**: A folder that contains classes that represent the data used in the websites.
- **Views**: A folder that contains Razor files, that is, the `.cshtml` files, that convert models into HTML pages.

- **Controllers**: A folder that contains classes that execute code when an HTTP request arrives. The code usually creates a model and passes it to a view.

The best way to understand MVC is to see a working example.

# Creating an ASP.NET Core MVC website

Visual Studio 2017 has a graphical way to create an MVC website and Visual Studio Code has a command-line way. It's worth looking at both to see the similarities and differences.

## Using Visual Studio 2017

In Visual Studio 2017, open the `Part3` solution, and press *Ctrl* + *Shift* + *N* or go to **File** | **Add** | **New Project...**.

In the **Add New Project** dialog, in the **Installed** list, expand **Visual C#**, and select **.NET Core**. In the center list, select **ASP.NET Core Web Application**, type the name as `NorthwindMvc`, and then click on **OK**.

In the **New ASP.NET Core Web Application - NorthwindMvc** dialog, select **.NET Core**, select **ASP.NET Core 2.0**, and select the **Web Application (Model-View-Controller)** template.

Click on **Change Authentication**, select **Individual User Accounts**, select **Store user accounts in-app**, and click on **OK**, as shown in the following screenshot:

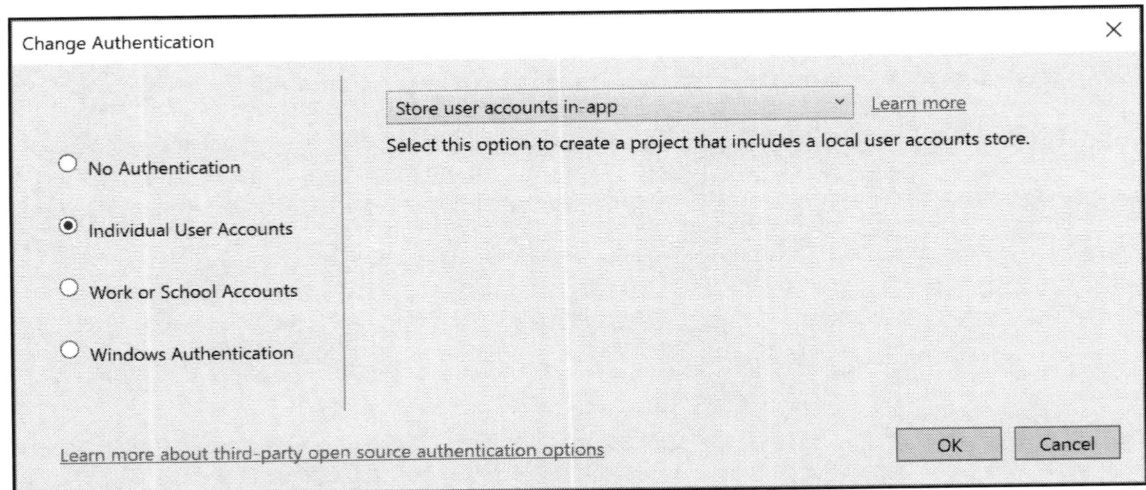

In the **New ASP.NET Core Web Application - NorthwindMvc** dialog, leave the **Enable Docker Support** box unchecked, and then click on **OK**, as shown in the following screenshot:

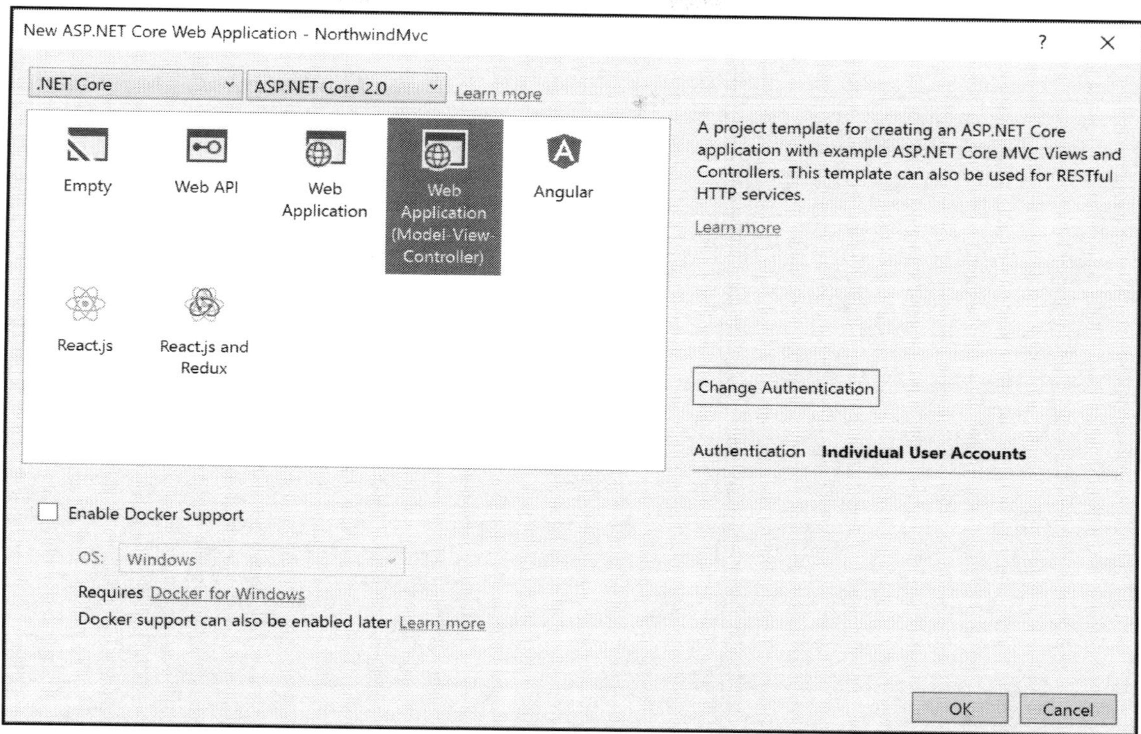


## Using Visual Studio Code

In the folder named `Part3`, create a folder named `NorthwindMvc`.

In Visual Studio Code, open the `NorthwindMvc` folder.

In the **Integrated Terminal**, enter the following command to create an ASP.NET Core MVC application with a database for authenticating and authorizing users:

```
dotnet new mvc --auth Individual
```

The MVC project template uses **Bower** to manage client-side packages, for example, Bootstrap and jQuery. Bower are not installed with Visual Studio Code by default, so we need to install it now.

In Visual Studio Code, go to **View** | **Extensions** or press *Shift* + *Cmd* + *X*.

Search for `bower` to find the most popular Bower extension, and click on **Install**, as shown in the following screenshot:

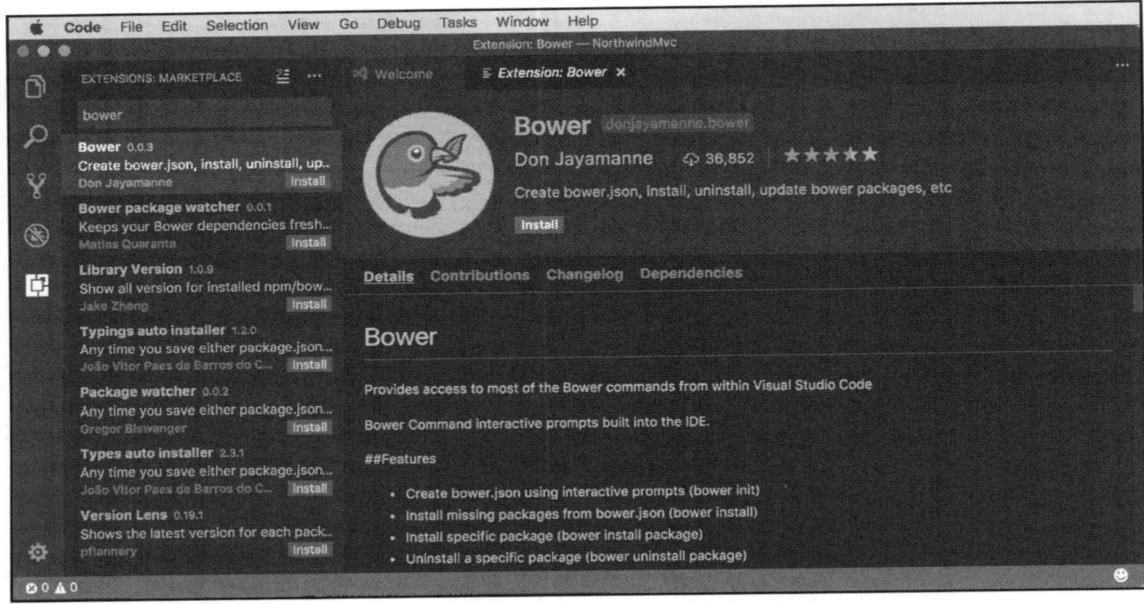


Once Bower has installed, click on **Reload**, and then **Reload Window** to reload Visual Studio Code.

Navigate to **View** | **Command Palette...**, or press *Shift* + *Cmd* + *P*.

Enter the `Bower` command, and then choose **Bower Install** to restore client-side packages such as Bootstrap, as shown in the following screenshot:

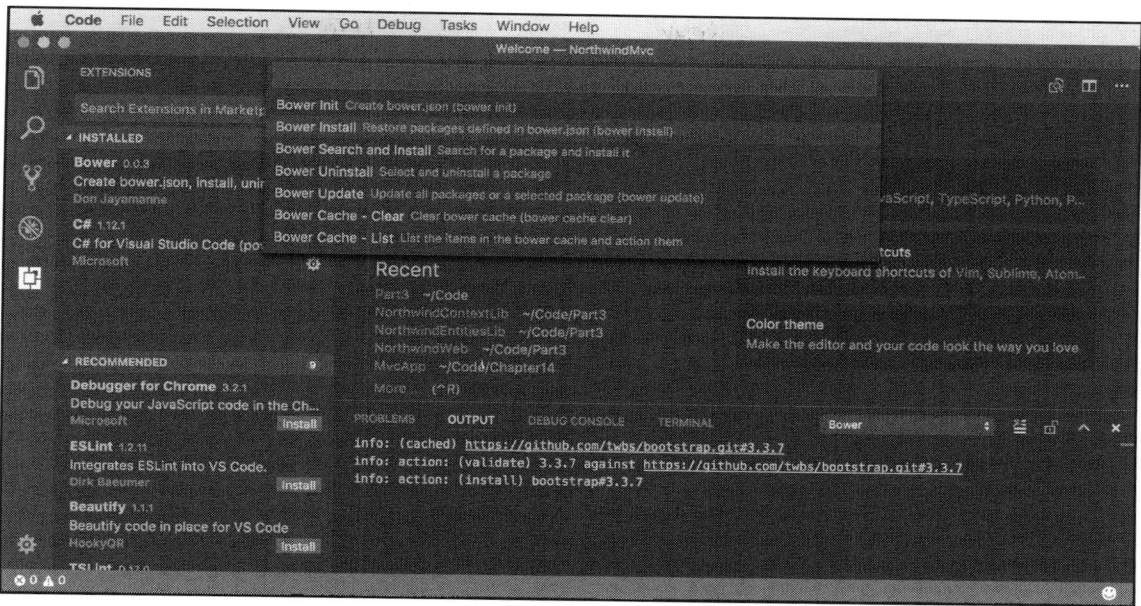

Navigate to **View** | **Explorer...**, or press *Shift* + *Cmd* + *E*.

Expand `wwwroot` and note that the `lib` folder has been created with four subfolders for the packages that are specified in the `bower.json` file, as shown in the following code:

```
{
  "name": "webapplication",
  "private": true,
  "dependencies": {
    "bootstrap": "3.3.7",
    "jquery": "2.2.0",
    "jquery-validation": "1.14.0",
    "jquery-validation-unobtrusive": "3.2.6"
  }
}
```

# Reviewing the ASP.NET Core MVC project template

In Visual Studio 2017, look at the **Solution Explorer**. In Visual Studio Code, look at the **EXPLORER** pane, as shown in the following screenshot:

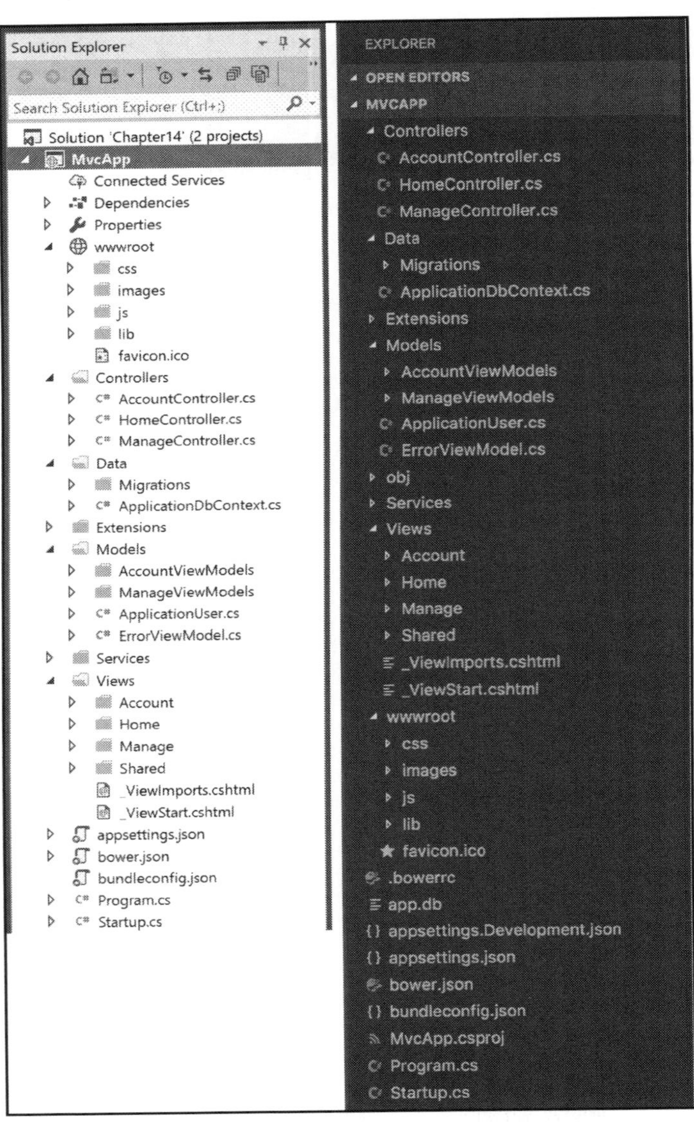

Note the following:

- `wwwroot`: This folder contains static content, such as CSS for styles, images, JavaScript, and a `favicon.ico` file.
- `Data`: This folder contains Entity Framework Core classes used by the **ASP.NET Identity** system to provide authentication and authorization.
- `Dependencies` (*Visual Studio 2017 only*): This folder contains a graphical representation of `NuGet` for modern package management. The actual NuGet references are in `MvcApp.csproj`. In Visual Studio 2017, you can edit the project manually by right-clicking on the project and choosing **Edit MvcApp.csproj**.
- `NorthwindMvc.csproj` (*Visual Studio Code only*): This file contains a list of NuGet packages that your project requires.
- `.vscode/launch.json` (*Visual Studio Code only*) and `Properties/launchSettings.json` (*Visual Studio 2017 only*): These files configure options for starting the web application from inside your development environment.
- `Controllers`: This folder contains C# classes that have methods (known as actions) that fetch a *model* and pass it to a *view*.
- `Models`: This folder contains C# classes that represent all of the data required to respond to an HTTP request.
- `Views`: This folder contains the `.cshtml` Razor files that combine HTML and C# code to enable the dynamic generation of an HTML response.
- `Services`: This folder contains C# interfaces and classes for integrating with external services, such as sending email messages.
- `Extensions`: This folder contains extension methods for the project.
- `appsettings.json`: This file contains settings that your web application can load at runtime, for example, the database connection string for the ASP.NET Identity system.
- `bower.json`: This file contains client-side packages that combine resources such as jQuery and Bootstrap.

- `Program.cs`: This file is a console application that contains the `Main` entry point that performs initial configuration, compilation, and executes the web application. It can call the `UseStartup<T>()` method to specify another class that can perform additional configuration.
- `Startup.cs`: This optional file performs additional configuration of the services, for example, ASP.NET Identity for authentication, SQLite for data storage, and so on, and routes for your application.

# Performing database migrations

Before we test the web application, we need to ensure that the database migrations have been executed to create the tables used by ASP.NET Identity, an authentication and authorization system.

## Using Visual Studio 2017

Open the `appsettings.json` file and note the database connection string. It will look something like this:

```
Server=(localdb)\\mssqllocaldb;Database=aspnet-NorthwindMvcApp-584f323f-
a60e-4933-9845-f67225753337;
Trusted_Connection=True;MultipleActiveResultSets=true
```

When the database migrations execute, it will create a database with the preceding name in Microsoft SQL Server LocalDB.

From the Windows Start menu, start **Developer Command Prompt for VS 2017**.

Change to the project directory and execute the database migrations by entering the following commands:

```
cd C:\Code\Part3\NorthwindMvc
dotnet ef database update
```

You should see output, as shown in the following screenshot:

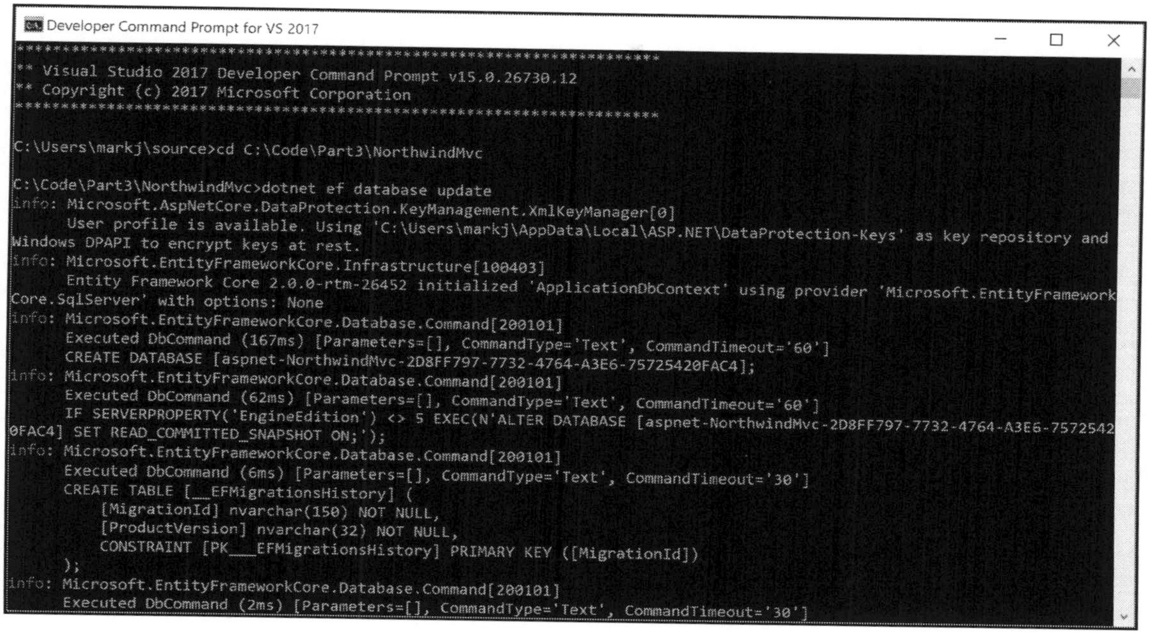

```
Developer Command Prompt for VS 2017
**********************************************************************
** Visual Studio 2017 Developer Command Prompt v15.0.26730.12
** Copyright (c) 2017 Microsoft Corporation
**********************************************************************

C:\Users\markj\source>cd C:\Code\Part3\NorthwindMvc

C:\Code\Part3\NorthwindMvc>dotnet ef database update
info: Microsoft.AspNetCore.DataProtection.KeyManagement.XmlKeyManager[0]
      User profile is available. Using 'C:\Users\markj\AppData\Local\ASP.NET\DataProtection-Keys' as key repository and
Windows DPAPI to encrypt keys at rest.
info: Microsoft.EntityFrameworkCore.Infrastructure[100403]
      Entity Framework Core 2.0.0-rtm-26452 initialized 'ApplicationDbContext' using provider 'Microsoft.EntityFramework
Core.SqlServer' with options: None
info: Microsoft.EntityFrameworkCore.Database.Command[200101]
      Executed DbCommand (167ms) [Parameters=[], CommandType='Text', CommandTimeout='60']
      CREATE DATABASE [aspnet-NorthwindMvc-2D8FF797-7732-4764-A3E6-75725420FAC4];
info: Microsoft.EntityFrameworkCore.Database.Command[200101]
      Executed DbCommand (62ms) [Parameters=[], CommandType='Text', CommandTimeout='60']
      IF SERVERPROPERTY('EngineEdition') <> 5 EXEC(N'ALTER DATABASE [aspnet-NorthwindMvc-2D8FF797-7732-4764-A3E6-7572542
0FAC4] SET READ_COMMITTED_SNAPSHOT ON;');
info: Microsoft.EntityFrameworkCore.Database.Command[200101]
      Executed DbCommand (6ms) [Parameters=[], CommandType='Text', CommandTimeout='30']
      CREATE TABLE [__EFMigrationsHistory] (
          [MigrationId] nvarchar(150) NOT NULL,
          [ProductVersion] nvarchar(32) NOT NULL,
          CONSTRAINT [PK___EFMigrationsHistory] PRIMARY KEY ([MigrationId])
      );
info: Microsoft.EntityFrameworkCore.Database.Command[200101]
      Executed DbCommand (2ms) [Parameters=[], CommandType='Text', CommandTimeout='30']
```

Close the **Developer Command Prompt for VS 2017** window.

## Using Visual Studio Code

Open the `appsettings.json` file and note the database connection string. It will be something like this:

```
Data Source=app.db
```

When the database migrations execute, it will create a database with the preceding name in the current folder using SQLite.

In the **Integrated Terminal**, enter the following command to execute the database migrations:

```
dotnet ef database update
```

In the **EXPLORER** pane, note that the SQLite database named `app.db` has been created.

If you installed an SQLite tool such as **SQLiteStudio**, then you can open the database and see the tables that the ASP.NET Identity system uses to register users and roles, as shown in the following screenshot:

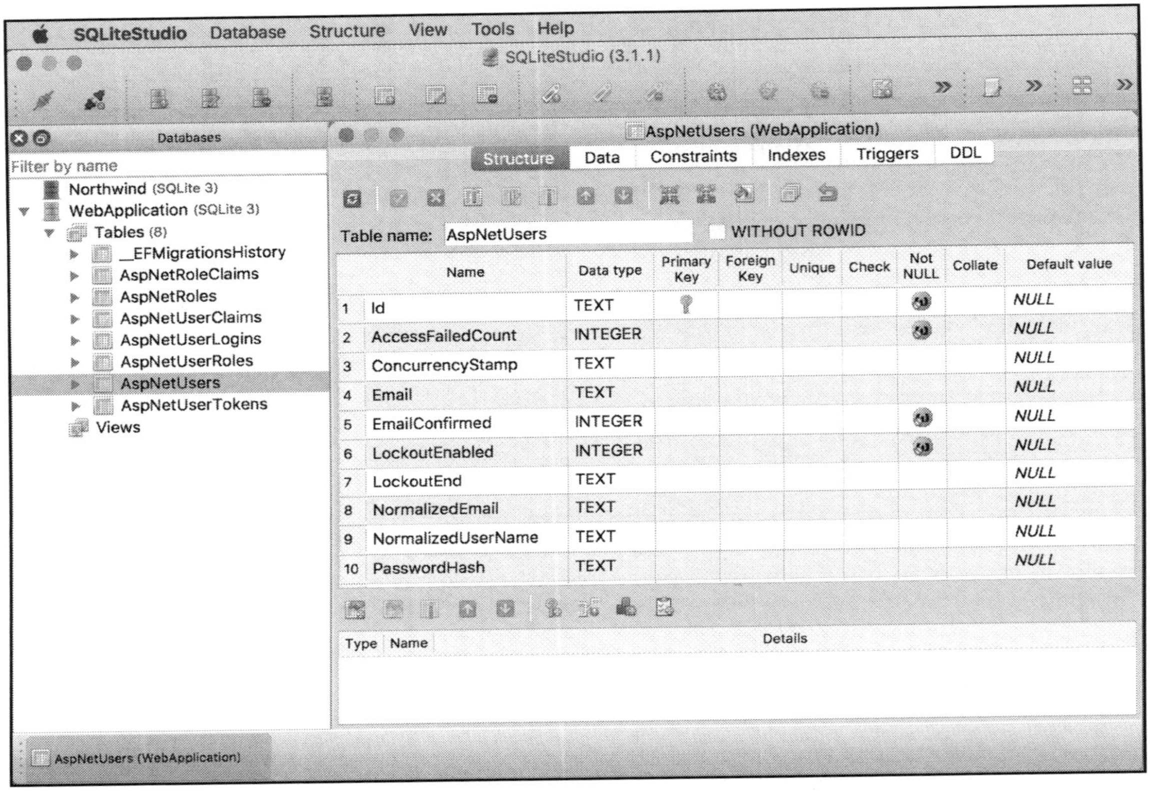

## Testing the ASP.NET MVC website

In both Visual Studio 2017 and Visual Studio Code, start the website.

With Visual Studio 2017, a web browser will start automatically. With Visual Studio Code, you must start your browser manually and enter the following address:
`http://localhost:5000/`
For Visual Studio 2017, if you are prompted to trust the self-signed certificate that IIS Express has generated for SSL, click on **Yes**.

Note that your ASP.NET Core application is hosted in a cross-platform web server named **Kestrel** (when using Visual Studio 2017, it is integrated with IIS Express) using a random port number for local testing. Also note that the ASP.NET Core MVC project is a site with half a dozen pages, including **Home**, **About**, **Contact**, **Register**, and **Log in**, as shown in the following screenshot:

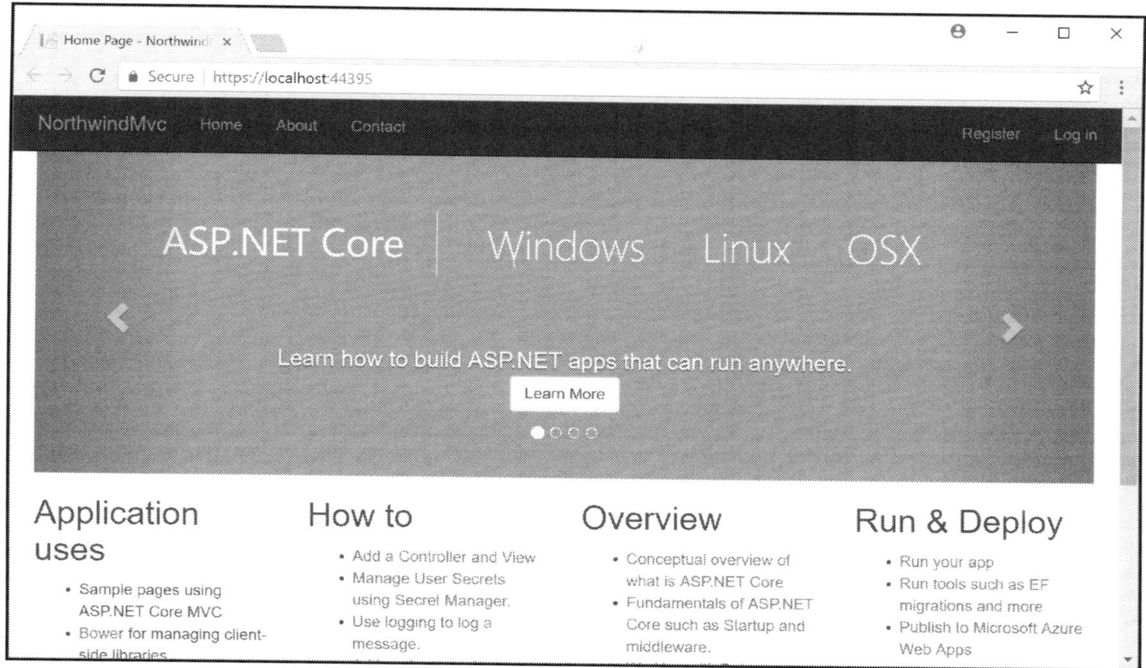

Click on the **Register** link and then complete the form to create a new account in the database that was created by the migration, as shown in the following screenshot:

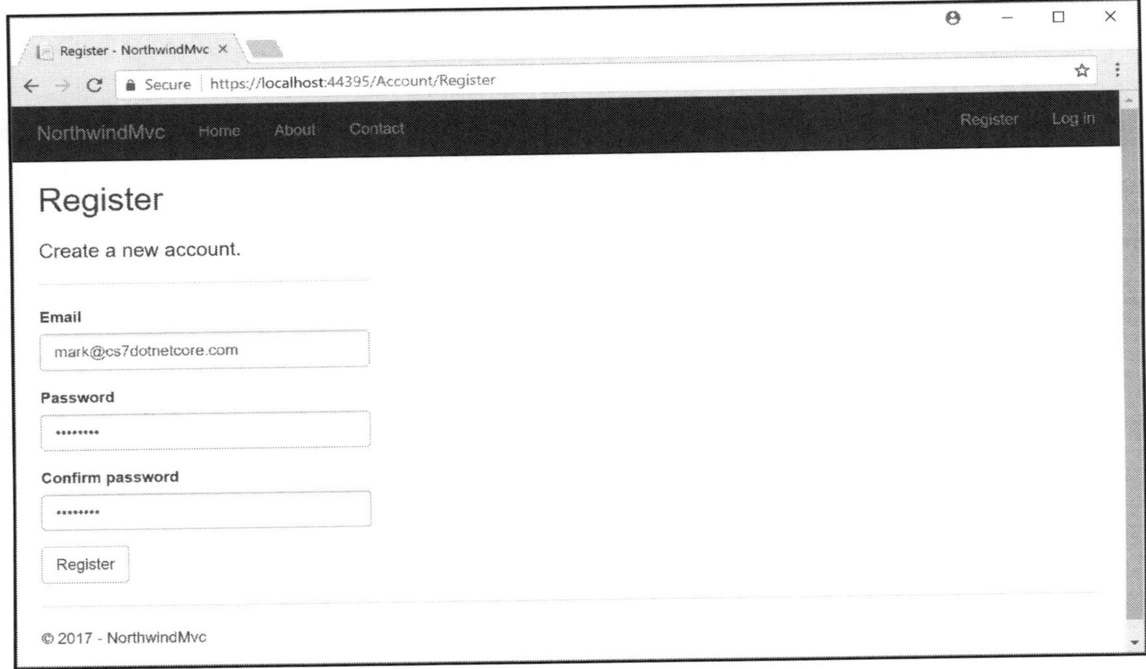


Note that if you enter a password that is not strong enough, there is built-in validation.

Click on **Register**, and note that you are now registered and logged in, as shown in the following screenshot:

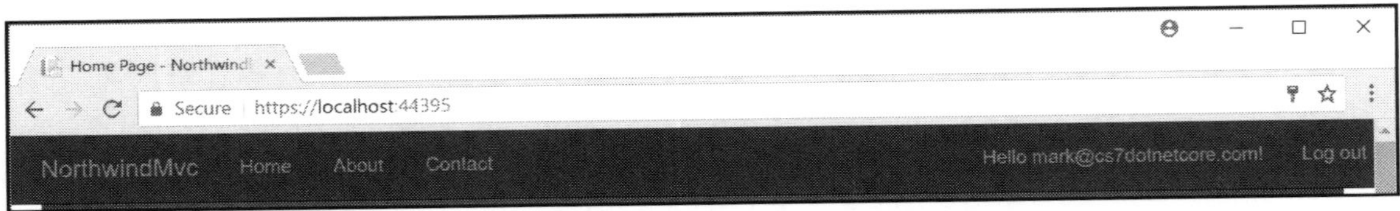


Close Chrome.

In Visual Studio Code, in **Integrated Terminal**, press *Ctrl* + *C* to stop the console application and shut down the Kestrel web server that is hosting your ASP.NET Core website.

# Reviewing authentication with ASP.NET Identity

In Visual Studio 2017, go to **View** | **Server Explorer**.

Right-click on **Data Connections**, and select **Add Connection...**.

In the **Add Connection** dialog, enter a **Server name** of `(localdb)\mssqllocaldb`, and select the **aspnet-NorthwindMvc-GUID** database from the drop-down list, as shown in the following screenshot:

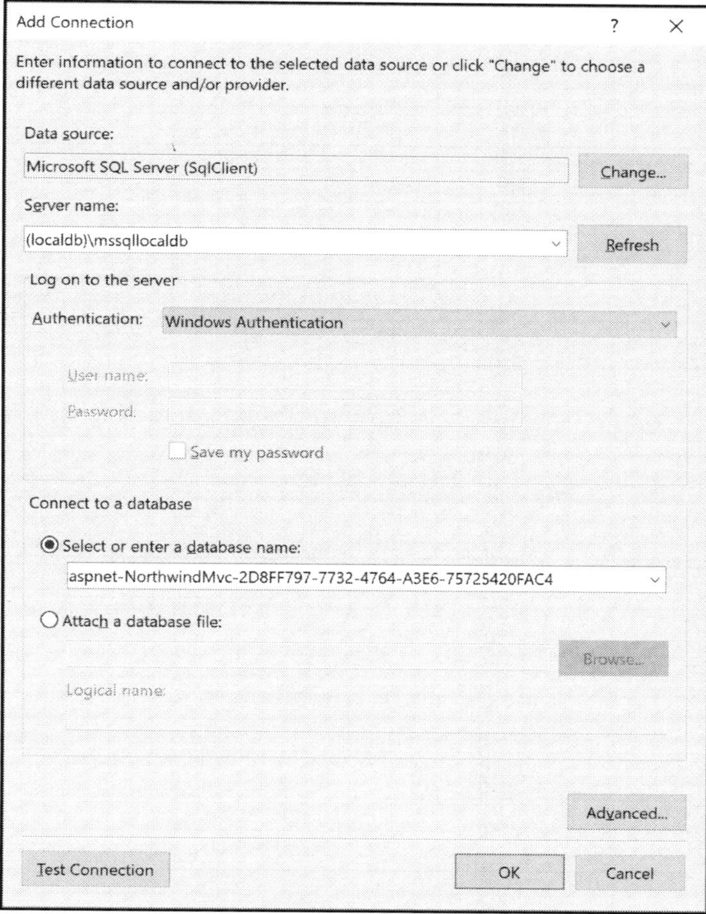

In **Server Explorer**, expand **Tables**, right-click on the **AspNetUsers** table, select **Show Table Data**, and note the row that was added to the database when you completed the register form:

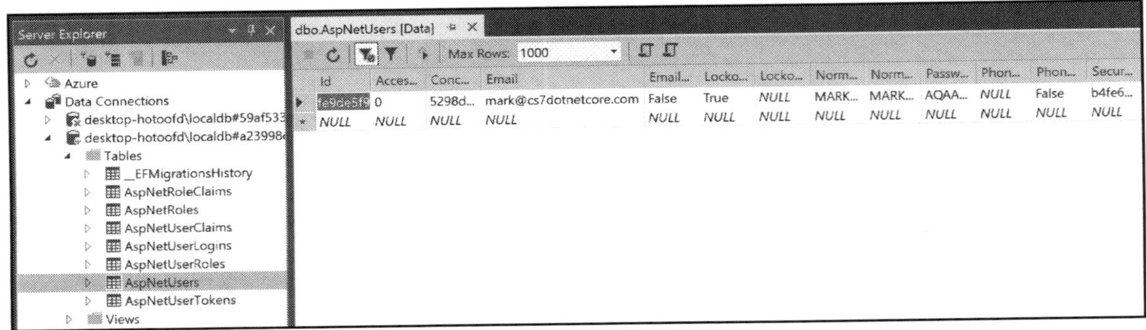

**Good Practice**
The ASP.NET Core web application project follows good practice by storing a hash of the password instead of the password itself, as you learned how to do in `Chapter 10`, *Protecting Your Data and Applications*. The ASP.NET Core Identity system can be extended to support two-factor authentication.

Close the table, and in **Server Explorer**, right-click on the database connection, and select **Close Connection**.

# Understanding an ASP.NET Core MVC website

Let's walk through the parts that make up a modern ASP.NET Core MVC application.

## ASP.NET Core startup

Open the `Startup.cs` file.

Note that the `ConfigureServices` method adds support for MVC along with other frameworks and services such as ASP.NET Identity, as shown in the following code:

```
public void ConfigureServices(IServiceCollection services)
{
    services.AddDbContext<ApplicationDbContext>(options =>
     options.UseSqlServer(Configuration
     .GetConnectionString("DefaultConnection")));

    services.AddIdentity<ApplicationUser, IdentityRole>()
     .AddEntityFrameworkStores<ApplicationDbContext>()
     .AddDefaultTokenProviders();

    // Add application services.
    services.AddTransient<IEmailSender, EmailSender>();

    services.AddMvc();
}
```

Next, we have the `Configure` method, as shown in the following code:

```
public void Configure(IApplicationBuilder app, IHostingEnvironment env)
{
    if (env.IsDevelopment())
    {
        app.UseDeveloperExceptionPage();
        app.UseDatabaseErrorPage();
    }
    else
    {
        app.UseExceptionHandler("/Home/Error");
    }

    app.UseStaticFiles();

    app.UseAuthentication();

    app.UseMvc(routes =>
    {
        routes.MapRoute(
          name: "default",
          template: "{controller=Home}/{action=Index}/{id?}");
    });
}
```

Note the following:

- If the website is running in the development environment, then these two things happen:
    - When an exception is thrown, a rich error page showing source code is displayed.
    - Also, a database error page is enabled.
- If the website is running in a production environment, the visitor will be redirected to `/Home/Error`.
- Static files are enabled to allow CSS, JavaScript, and so on, to be served from the filesystem.
- ASP.NET Identity is enabled for authentication and authorization.
- The most important statement here is the one that calls `UseMvc` and maps a default route. This route is very flexible, because it will map to almost any incoming URL, as you will see in the next section.

# Understanding the default route

The default route looks at any URL entered by the user in the address bar and matches it to extract the name of a controller, the name of an action, and an optional `id` value (the `?` symbol makes it optional). If the user hasn't entered these names, it uses defaults of `Home` for the controller and `Index` for the action (the `=` assignment sets a default for a named segment).

Contents in curly-brackets `{}` are called **segments**, and they are like a named parameter of a method. The value of these segments can be any string.

The responsibility of a route is to discover the name of a controller and an action.

The following table contains example URLs and how MVC would work out the names:

| URL | Controller | Action | ID |
|---|---|---|---|
| `/` | `Home` | `Index` | |
| `/Muppet` | `Muppet` | `Index` | |
| `/Muppet/Kermit` | `Muppet` | `Kermit` | |
| `/Muppet/Kermit/Green` | `Muppet` | `Kermit` | `Green` |
| `/Products` | `Products` | `Index` | |

| | | | |
|---|---|---|---|
| /Products/Detail | Products | Detail | |
| /Products/Detail/3 | Products | Detail | 3 |

Note that if the user does not supply a name, then the defaults, `Home` and `Index`, are used as specified when the route was registered. You could change these defaults if you wanted.

# Understanding ASP.NET Core MVC controllers

From the route and an incoming URL, ASP.NET Core MVC knows the name of the controller and action, so it will look for a class that implements an interface named `IController`. To simplify the requirements, Microsoft supplies a class named `Controller` that your classes can inherit from.

The responsibilities of a controller are as follows:

- To extract parameters from the HTTP request
- To use the parameters to fetch the correct model and pass it to the correct view client as an HTTP response
- To return the results from the view to the client as an HTTP response

Expand the `Controllers` folder and double-click on the file named `HomeController.cs`:

```
public class HomeController : Controller
{
    public IActionResult Index()
    {
        return View();
    }

    public IActionResult About()
    {
        ViewData["Message"] = "Your application description page.";
        return View();
    }

    public IActionResult Contact()
    {
        ViewData["Message"] = "Your contact page.";
        return View();
    }

    public IActionResult Error()
    {
```

```
        return View(new ErrorViewModel {
          RequestId = Activity.Current?.Id ??
          HttpContext.TraceIdentifier });
    }
}
```

If the user enters / or /Home, then it is the equivalent of /Home/Index because those were the defaults.

Note the following:

- None of the action methods use a model
- Two of the action methods use the dictionary named ViewData to store a string item named Message that can then be read inside a view
- All of the action methods call a method named View() and return the results as an IActionResult interface to the client

# Understanding ASP.NET Core MVC models

In ASP.NET Core MVC, the model represents the data required for a request. For example, an HTTP GET request for http://www.example.com/products/details/3 might mean that the browser is asking for the details of product number 3.

The controller would need to use the ID value 3 to retrieve the record for that product and pass it to a view that can then turn the model into HTML for display in the browser.

## Configuring an EF Core entity data model

We will reference the Entity Framework Core entity data model for the Northwind database that you created in Chapter 14, *Building Web Sites Using ASP.NET Core Razor Pages*.

In Visual Studio 2017, in the **NorthwindMvc** project, right-click on **Dependencies**, and select **Add Reference...**. Select **NorthwindContextLib**, and click on **OK**.

In Visual Studio Code, in the NorthwindMvc project, modify NorthwindMvc.csproj, and add a project reference to NorthwindContextLib.

In both Visual Studio 2017 and Visual Studio Code, modify `Startup.cs`, to add the following statement to the `ConfigureServices` method.

For SQL Server LocalDB, add this statement:

```
services.AddDbContext<Packt.CS7.Northwind>(options =>
  options.UseSqlServer("Server=(localdb)\\mssqllocaldb;" +
  "Database=Northwind;Trusted_Connection=True;" +
  "MultipleActiveResultSets=true"));
```

For SQLite, add this one:

```
services.AddDbContext<Packt.CS7.Northwind>(options =>
  options.UseSqlite("Data Source=../Northwind.db"));
```

# Creating view models for requests

Imagine that when a user comes to our website, we want to show them a carousel of categories, a list of products, and a count of the number of visitors we have had this month. All of the data that we want to show in response to a request is the MVC model, sometimes called a **view model**, because it is a *model* that is passed to a *view*.

Add a class to the `Models` folder and name it `HomeIndexViewModel`.

Modify the class definition, as shown in the following code:

```
using System.Collections.Generic;

namespace Packt.CS7
{
   public class HomeIndexViewModel
   {
      public int VisitorCount;
      public IList<Category> Categories { get; set; }
      public IList<Product> Products { get; set; }
   }
}
```

# Fetch the model in the controller

Open the `HomeController` class.

Import the `Packt.CS7` namespace.

Add a field to store a reference to a `Northwind` instance, and initialize it in a constructor, as shown in the following code:

```
private Northwind db;

public HomeController(Northwind injectedContext)
{
   db = injectedContext;
}
```

Modify the contents of the `Index` action method, as shown in the following code:

```
var model = new HomeIndexViewModel
{
   VisitorCount = (new Random()).Next(1, 1001),
   Categories  = db.Categories.ToList(),
   Products = db.Products.ToList()
};
return View(model); // pass model to view
```

We have simulated a visitor count using the `Random` class to generate a number between 1 and 1000.

# Understanding ASP.NET Core MVC views

The responsibility of a view is to transform a model into HTML or other formats. There are multiple **view engines** that can be used to do this. The default view engine for ASP.NET MVC 3 and later is called **Razor**, and it uses the `@` symbol to indicate server-side code execution.

The new Razor Pages feature in ASP.NET Core 2.0 uses the same view engine and so can use the same Razor syntax.

## Rendering the Home controller's views

Expand the `Views` folder, and then expand the `Home` folder. Note the three files with the `.cshtml` file extension.

The `.cshtml` file extension means that this is a file that mixes C# and HTML.

When the `View()` method is called in a controller's action method, ASP.NET Core MVC looks in the `Views` folder for a subfolder with the same name as the current controller, that is, `Home`. It then looks for a file with the same name as the current action, that is, `Index`, `About`, or `Contact`.

In the `Index.cshtml` file, note the block of C# code wrapped in `@{ }`. This will execute first and can be used to store data that needs to be passed into a shared layout file:

```
@{
    ViewData["Title"] = "Home Page";
}
```

Note the static HTML content in several `<div>` elements that uses Bootstrap for styling.

**Good Practice**
As well as defining your own styles, base your styles on a common library, such as Bootstrap, that implements responsive design. To learn more about CSS3 and responsive design, read the book *Responsive Web Design with HTML5 and CSS3 - Second Edition* by *Packt Publishing* at the following link:
`https://www.packtpub.com/web-development/responsive-web-design-html5-and-css3-second-edition`

## Sharing layouts between views

Just as with Razor Pages, there is a file named `_ViewStart.cshtml` that gets executed by the `View()` method. It is used to set defaults that apply to all views.

For example, it sets the `Layout` property of all views to a shared layout file:

```
@{
    Layout = "_Layout";
 }
```

In the `Shared` folder, open the `_Layout.cshtml` file. Note that the title is being read from the `ViewData` dictionary that was set earlier in the `Index.cshtml` view.

Note the rendering of common styles to support Bootstrap and the two sections. During *development*, the fully commented and nicely formatted versions of CSS files will be used. For *staging* and *release*, the minified versions will be used:

```
<environment include="Development">
  <link rel="stylesheet" href="~/lib/bootstrap/dist/css/bootstrap.css" />
  <link rel="stylesheet" href="~/css/site.css" />
</environment>
<environment exclude="Development">
  <link rel="stylesheet" href="https://ajax.aspnetcdn.com/ajax/
    bootstrap/3.3.5/css/bootstrap.min.css"
    asp-fallback-href="~/lib/bootstrap/dist/css/bootstrap.min.css"
    asp-fallback-test-class="sr-only"
    asp-fallback-test-property="position"
    asp-fallback-test-value="absolute" />
  <link rel="stylesheet" href="~/css/site.min.css"
    asp-append-version="true" />
</environment>
```

Here, ~ means the `wwwroot` folder.

Note the rendering of hyperlinks to allow users to click between pages using the navigation bar at the top of every page. The <a> elements use *tag helper* attributes to specify the controller name and action name that will execute when the link is clicked on:

```
<div class="navbar-collapse collapse">
  <ul class="nav navbar-nav">
    <li><a asp-controller="Home" asp-action="Index">Home</a></li>
    <li><a asp-controller="Home" asp-action="About">About</a></li>
    <li><a asp-controller="Home" asp-action="Contact">Contact</a></li>
  </ul>
</div>
```

Note the rendering of the body:

```
@RenderBody()
```

Note the rendering of script blocks at the bottom of the page so that it doesn't slow down the display of the page:

```
<environment include="Development">
  <script src="~/lib/jquery/dist/jquery.js"></script>
  <script src="~/lib/bootstrap/dist/js/bootstrap.js"></script>
  <script src="~/js/site.js" asp-append-version="true"></script>
</environment>
<environment exclude="Development">
  <script src="https://ajax.aspnetcdn.com/ajax/jquery/jquery-2.1.4.min.js"
      asp-fallback-src="~/lib/jquery/dist/jquery.min.js"
      asp-fallback-test="window.jQuery">
  </script>
  <script
src="https://ajax.aspnetcdn.com/ajax/bootstrap/3.3.5/bootstrap.min.js"
      asp-fallback-src="~/lib/bootstrap/dist/js/bootstrap.min.js"
      asp-fallback-test="window.jQuery && window.jQuery.fn &&
      window.jQuery.fn.modal">
  </script>
    <script src="~/js/site.min.js" asp-append-version="true">
  </script>
</environment>
```

You can add your own script blocks into an optional defined section named `scripts`:

```
@RenderSection("scripts", required: false)
```

## Defining custom styles

In the `wwwroot\css` folder, open the `site.css` file.

Add a new style that will apply to an element with the `newspaper` ID, like this:

```
#newspaper {
  column-count: 3;
}
```

In Visual Studio Code, you will need to add the style to `site.min.css` too. Usually, you would have a build step to minify your `site.css` into a `site.min.css`, but for now, just do it manually.

## Defining a typed view

To improve the IntelliSense when writing a view, you can define the type the view can expect using a `@model` directive at the top.

In the `Views\Home` folder, open `Index.cshtml` view, and add a statement to set the model type to use the `HomeIndexViewModel` as the first line of the file, as shown in the following code:

```
@model Packt.CS7.HomeIndexViewModel
```

Now, whenever we type `Model` in this view, the IntelliSense will know the correct type and will provide IntelliSense.

To declare the type for the model, use `@model` (with lowercase `m`).

To interact with the model, use `@Model` (with uppercase `M`).

In `Index.cshtml`, modify the carousel `<div>` element, delete all of the other `<div>` elements, and replace them with the new markup to output products as an unordered list, as shown in the following markup:

```
@model Packt.CS7.HomeIndexViewModel
@{
    ViewData["Title"] = "Home Page";
 }
 <div id="myCarousel" class="carousel slide" data-ride="carousel"
  data-interval="6000">
    <ol class="carousel-indicators">
      @for (int c = 0; c < Model.Categories.Count; c++)
      {
          if (c == 0)
          {
              <li data-target="#myCarousel" data-slide-to="@c"
               class="active"></li>
          }
          else
          {
              <li data-target="#myCarousel" data-slide-to="@c"></li>
          }
      }
    </ol>
    <div class="carousel-inner" role="listbox">
      @for (int c = 0; c < Model.Categories.Count; c++)
      {
          if (c == 0)
          {
              <div class="item active">
                <img src="~/images/category@
                 (Model.Categories[c].CategoryID).jpeg"
                  alt="@Model.Categories[c].CategoryName"
                  class="img-responsive" />
                <div class="carousel-caption" role="option">
                  <p>
                    @Model.Categories[c].Description
                    <a class="btn btn-default" href="/category/
                     @Model.Categories[c].CategoryID">
                       @Model.Categories[c].CategoryName
                    </a>
                  </p>
                </div>
              </div>
          }
          else
          {
              <div class="item">
```

```
              <img src="~/images/category@
               (Model.Categories[c].CategoryID).jpeg"
                alt="@Model.Categories[c].CategoryName"
                class="img-responsive" />
                <div class="carousel-caption" role="option">
                  <p>
                    @Model.Categories[c].Description
                    <a class="btn btn-default" href="/category/
                     @Model.Categories[c].CategoryID">
                       @Model.Categories[c].CategoryName
                    </a>
                  </p>
                </div>
            </div>
        }
      }
    </div>
    <a class="left carousel-control" href="#myCarousel" role="button"
     data-slide="prev">
      <span class="glyphicon glyphicon-chevron-left"
       aria-hidden="true"></span>
      <span class="sr-only">Previous</span>
    </a>
    <a class="right carousel-control" href="#myCarousel" role="button"
     data-slide="next">
      <span class="glyphicon glyphicon-chevron-right"
       aria-hidden="true">
      </span>
      <span class="sr-only">Next</span>
    </a>
  </div>
  <div class="row">
    <div class="col-md-12">
      <h1>Northwind</h1>
      <p class="lead">
        We have had @Model.VisitorCount
        visitors this month.
      </p>
      <h2>Products</h2>
      <div id="newspaper">
        <ul>
          @foreach (var item in @Model.Products)
          {
             <li>
               <a asp-controller="Home"
                asp-action="ProductDetail"
                asp-route-id="@item.ProductID">
                @item.ProductName costs
```

```
                @item.UnitPrice.Value.ToString("C")
              </a>
            </li>
        }
      </ul>
    </div>
  </div>
</div>
```

Note how easy it is to mix static HTML elements such as `<ul>` and `<li>` with C# code to output the list of product names.

Note the `<div>` element with the `id` attribute of `newspaper`. This will use the custom style that we defined earlier, so all of the content in that element will display in three columns.

In the `wwwroot` folder, in the `images` folder, add eight image files named `category1.jpeg`, `category2.jpeg`, and so on, up to `category8.jpeg`.

You can download images from the Github repository for this book at the following link:
`https://github.com/markjprice/cs7dotnetcore2/tree/master/Assets`
To find suitable images for the eight categories, I searched on a site that has free stock photos for commercial use with no attribution required, at the following link:
`https://www.pexels.com`

In Visual Studio 2017, press *Ctrl* + *F5*.

In Visual Studio Code, enter the `dotnet run` command, and then run Chrome and navigate to `http://localhost:5000/`.

The home page will have a rotating carousel showing categories, and a list of products in three columns, as shown in the following screenshot:

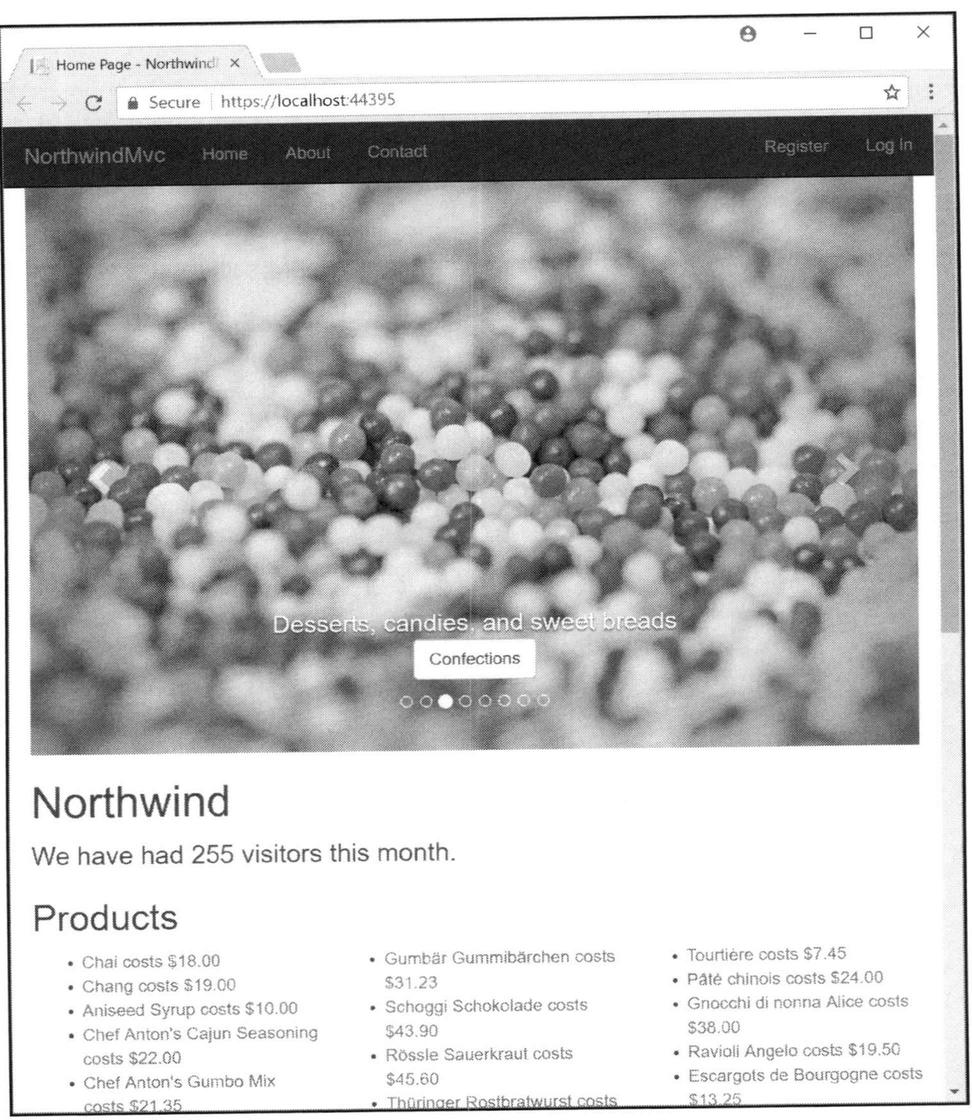

At the moment, clicking on any of the product links gives a `404` error, as shown in the following screenshot:

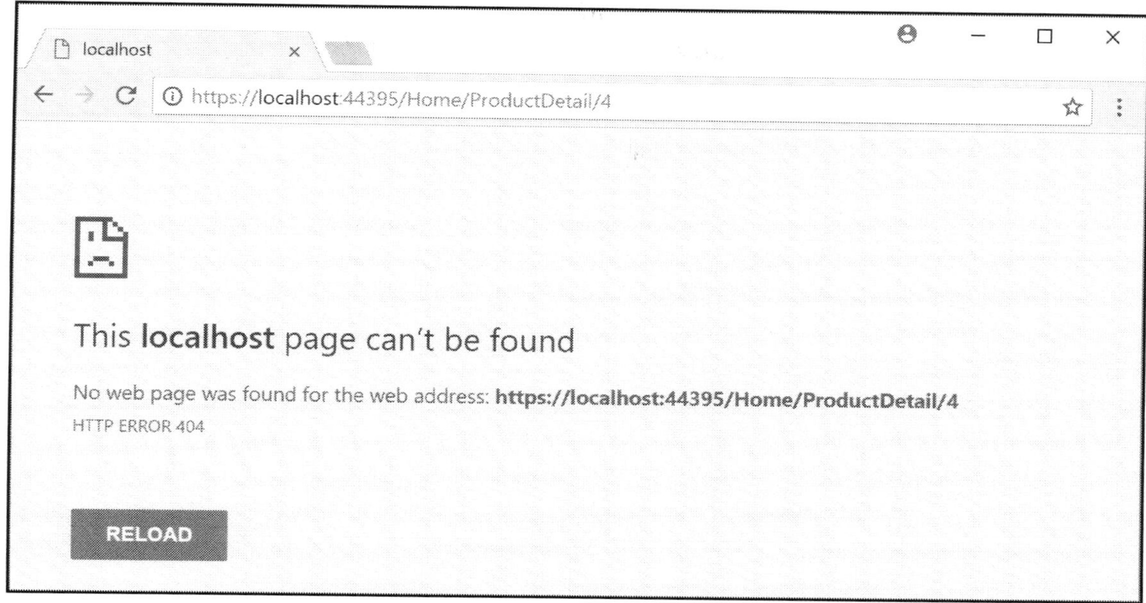


Now that you've seen the basics of how models, views, and controllers work together to provide a web application, let's look at some common scenarios, such as passing parameters, so that we can see the details of a product.

# Passing parameters using a route value

Back in the `HomeController` class, add an action method named `ProductDetail`, as shown in the following code:

```
public IActionResult ProductDetail(int? id)
{
   if (!id.HasValue)
   {
      return NotFound("You must pass a product ID in the route, for
      example, /Home/ProductDetail/21");
   }
   var model = db.Products.SingleOrDefault(p => p.ProductID == id);
   if (model == null)
   {
      return NotFound($"A product with the ID of {id} was not found.");
```

```
        }
        return View(model); // pass model to view
    }
```

Note the following:

- This method uses a feature of ASP.NET Core called **model binding** to automatically match the `id` passed in the route to the parameter named `id` in the method
- Inside the method, we check to see whether `id` is null, and if so, it returns a `404` status code and message
- Otherwise, we can connect to the database and try to retrieve a product using the `id` variable
- If we find a product, we pass it to a view; otherwise, we return a different `404` status code and message

Model binders are very powerful, and the default one does a lot for you. For advanced scenarios, you can create your own by implementing the `IModelBinder` interface, but that is beyond the scope of this book.

Now, we need to create a view for this request.

In Visual Studio 2017, inside the `Views` folder, right-click on **Home** and choose **Add** | **New Item....** Choose **MVC View Page** and name it `ProductDetail.cshtml`.

In Visual Studio Code, inside the `Views/Home` folder, add a new file named `ProductDetail.cshtml`.

Modify the contents, as shown in the following markup:

```
@model Packt.CS7.Product
@{
    ViewData["Title"] = "Product Detail - " + Model.ProductName;
}
<h2>Product Detail</h2>
<hr />
<div>
  <dl class="dl-horizontal">
    <dt>Product ID</dt>
    <dd>@Model.ProductID</dd>
    <dt>Product Name</dt>
    <dd>@Model.ProductName</dd>
```

```
        <dt>Category ID</dt>
        <dd>@Model.CategoryID</dd>
        <dt>Unit Price</dt>
        <dd>@Model.UnitPrice.Value.ToString("C")</dd>
        <dt>Units In Stock</dt>
        <dd>@Model.UnitsInStock</dd>
      </dl>
    </div>
```

Run the web application, and when the home page appears with the list of products, click on one of them, for example, the second product, **Chang**. The result should look as shown in the following screenshot:

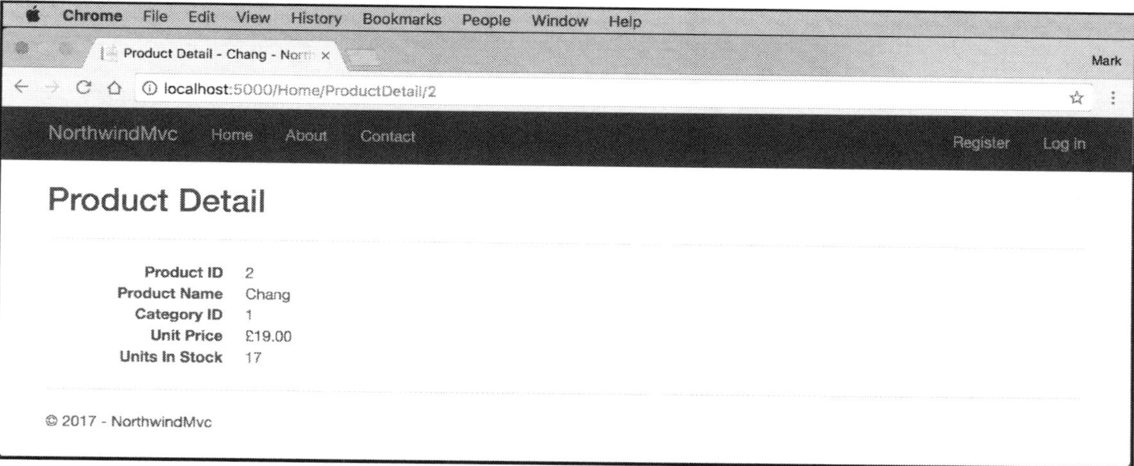


# Passing parameters using a query string

In the `HomeController` class, import the `Microsoft.EntityFrameworkCore` namespace. We need this to add the `Include` extension method so that we can include related entities.

Add a new action method, as shown in the following code:

```
public IActionResult ProductsThatCostMoreThan(decimal? price)
{
   if (!price.HasValue)
   {
      return NotFound("You must pass a product price in the query
      string, for example, /Home/ProductsThatCostMoreThan?price=50");
   }
   var model = db.Products.Include(p => p.Category).Include(
```

```
        p => p.Supplier).Where(p => p.UnitPrice > price).ToArray();
        if (model.Count() == 0)
        {
            return NotFound($"No products cost more than {price:C}.");
        }
        ViewData["MaxPrice"] = price.Value.ToString("C");
        return View(model); // pass model to view
    }
```

Inside the `Views/Home` folder, add a new file named `ProductsThatCostMoreThan.cshtml`.

Modify the contents, as shown in the following code:

```
@model IEnumerable<Packt.CS7.Product>
@{
    ViewData["Title"] =
      "Products That Cost More Than " + ViewData["MaxPrice"];
}
<h2>Products That Cost More Than @ViewData["MaxPrice"]</h2>
<table class="table">
  <tr>
    <th>Category Name</th>
    <th>Supplier's Company Name</th>
    <th>Product Name</th>
    <th>Unit Price</th>
    <th>Units In Stock</th>
  </tr>
  @foreach (var item in Model)
  {
     <tr>
       <td>
         @Html.DisplayFor(modelItem => item.Category.CategoryName)
       </td>
       <td>
         @Html.DisplayFor(modelItem => item.Supplier.CompanyName)
       </td>
       <td>
         @Html.DisplayFor(modelItem => item.ProductName)
       </td>
       <td>
         @Html.DisplayFor(modelItem => item.UnitPrice)
       </td>
       <td>
         @Html.DisplayFor(modelItem => item.UnitsInStock)
```

```
            </td>
          </tr>
      }
    </table>
```

In the `Views/Home` folder, open `Index.cshtml`, and add the following `form` element near the bottom of the file, but above the `Products` heading and its listing of products. This will provide a form for the user to enter a price. The user can then click on a `submit` button to call the action method that shows only products that cost more than the entered price:

```
<form asp-action="ProductsThatCostMoreThan" method="get">
  <input name="price" placeholder="Enter a product price" />
  <input type="submit" />
</form>
```

Run the web application, and on the home page, scroll down and enter a price in the form, for example, `50`, and then click on **Submit**, as shown in the following screenshot:

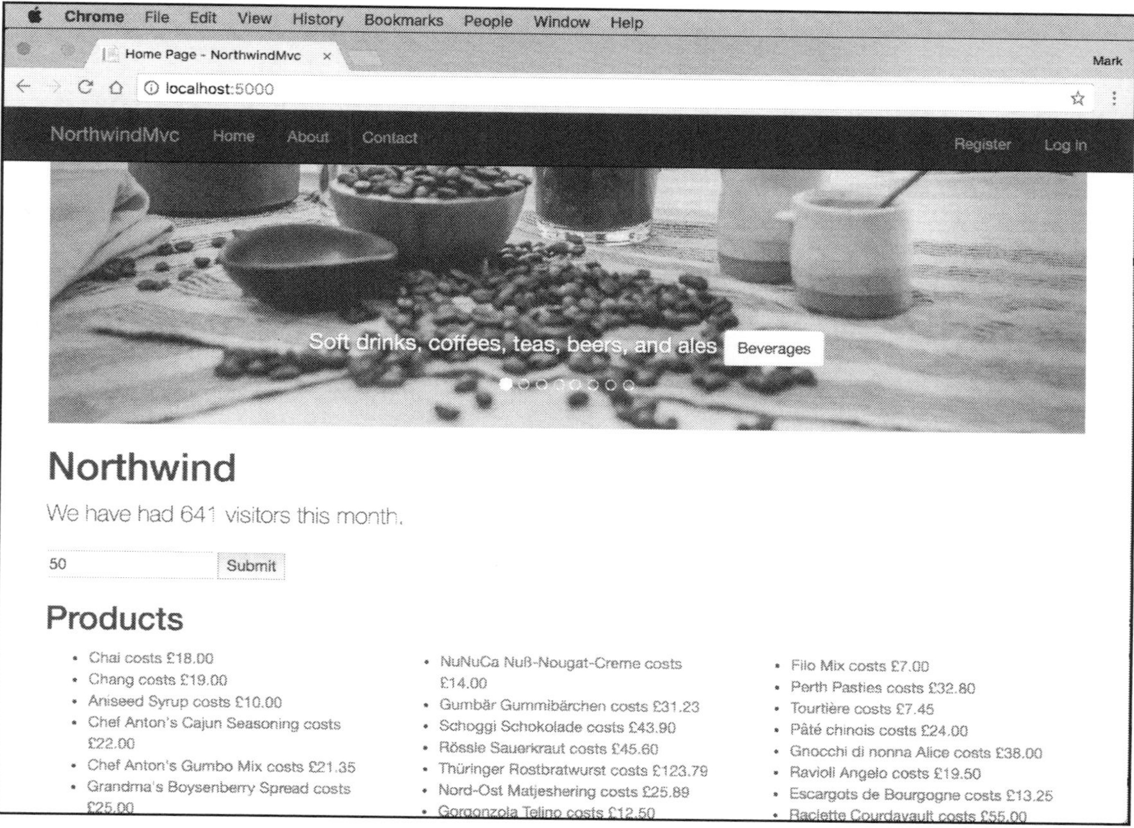

You will see a table of the products that cost more than the price that you entered, as shown in the following screenshot:

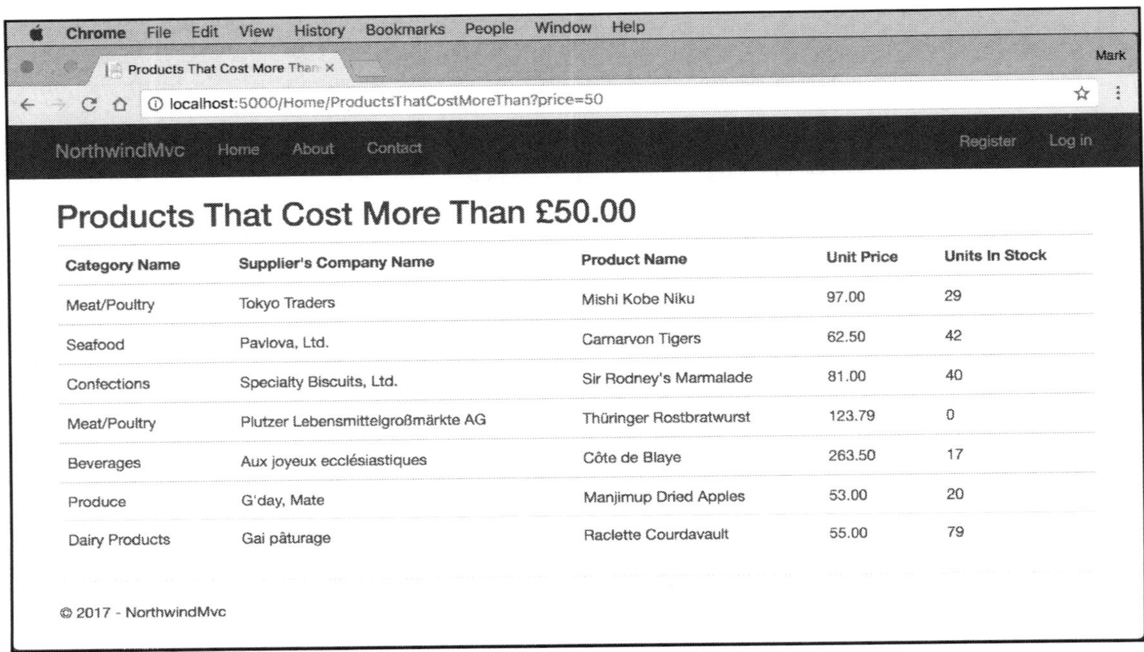


# Practicing and exploring

Get some hands-on practice and explore this chapter's topics with deeper research.

## Exercise 15.1 – Practice improving scalability by understanding and implementing async action methods

A few years ago, Stephen Cleary wrote an excellent article for MSDN Magazine explaining the benefits to scalability of implementing async action methods for ASP.NET. The same principles apply to ASP.NET Core, but even more so because unlike old ASP.NET as described in the article, ASP.NET Core supports asynchronous filters and other components.

Read the article at the following link and change the application that you created in this chapter to use async action methods in the controller:
https://msdn.microsoft.com/en-us/magazine/dn802603.aspx

# Exercise 15.2 – Explore topics

Use the following links to read more details about this chapter's topics:

- **Overview of ASP.NET Core MVC**: https://docs.microsoft.com/en-us/aspnet/core/mvc/overview
- **Getting started with ASP.NET Core MVC and Entity Framework Core using Visual Studio**: https://docs.microsoft.com/en-us/aspnet/core/data/ef-mvc/intro
- **Handling request with controllers in ASP.NET Core MVC**: https://docs.microsoft.com/en-us/aspnet/core/mvc/controllers/actions
- **Model Binding**: https://docs.microsoft.com/en-us/aspnet/core/mvc/models/model-binding
- **Views in ASP.NET Core MVC**: https://docs.microsoft.com/en-us/aspnet/core/mvc/views/overview

# Summary

In this chapter, you learned how to build more complex websites using ASP.NET Core MVC.

In the next chapter, you will learn how to build web applications using backend web services built with ASP.NET Core Web API, and using frontend technologies including Angular and React.

# 16

# Building Web Services and Applications Using ASP.NET Core

This chapter is about learning how to build web applications using a combination of backend web services using ASP.NET Core Web API and frontend **Single Page Applications (SPAs)** with Angular or React.

In this chapter, we will cover the following topics:

- Building web services using ASP.NET Core Web API
- Documenting and testing web services using Swagger
- Building SPAs using Angular
- Using other project templates

# Building web services using ASP.NET Core Web API

Although HTTP was originally designed to request and respond with HTML and other resources for humans to look at, it is also good for building services. Roy Fielding stated in his doctoral dissertation, describing the **Representational State Transfer (REST)** architectural style, that the HTTP standard defines the following:

- URLs to uniquely identify resources
- Methods to perform common tasks, such as `GET`, `POST`, `PUT`, and `DELETE`
- The ability to negotiate media formats, such as XML and JSON

**Web services** are services that use the HTTP communication standard, so they are sometimes called HTTP or RESTful services.

## Understanding ASP.NET Core controllers

To allow the easy creation of web services, ASP.NET Core has combined what used to be two types of controller.

In earlier versions of ASP.NET, you would derive web services from `ApiController` to create a Web API service and then register API routes in the same route table that MVC uses.

With ASP.NET Core, you use the same `Controller` base class as you used with MVC, except the routes are configured on the controller itself, using attributes, rather than in the route table.

## Creating an ASP.NET Core Web API project

We will build a web service that provides a way to work with data in the `Northwind` database using ASP.NET Core so that the data can be used on any platform that can make HTTP requests and receive HTTP responses.

### Using Visual Studio 2017

In Visual Studio 2017, open the `Part3` solution, and press *Ctrl* + *Shift* + *N* or go to **File** | **Add** | **New Project...**.

In the **Add New Project** dialog, in the **Installed** list, expand **Visual C#**, and select **.NET Core**. In the center list, select **ASP.NET Core Web Application**, type the name as `NorthwindService`, and then click on **OK**.

In the **New ASP.NET Core Web Application - NorthwindService** dialog, select **.NET Core**, select **ASP.NET Core 2.0**, and then select the **Web API** template. Make sure that **No Authentication** is selected, with no Docker support. Click on **OK**.

## Using Visual Studio Code

In the folder named `Part3`, create a folder named `NorthwindService`.

In Visual Studio Code, open the `NorthwindService` folder.

In **Integrated Terminal**, enter the following command to create a new ASP.NET Core Web API project:

```
dotnet new webapi
```

## Using Visual Studio 2017 and Visual Studio Code

In the `Controllers` folder, open `ValuesController.cs`, and note the following:

- The `[Route]` attribute registers the `/api/values` relative URL for clients to use to make HTTP requests that will be handled by this controller. The `/api/` base route followed by a controller name is a convention to differentiate between MVC and Web API. You do not have to use it. If you use `[controller]` as shown, it uses the characters before `Controller` in the class name, or you can simply enter a different name without the brackets.
- The `[HttpGet]` attribute registers the `Get` method to respond to HTTP GET requests, and it returns an array of `string` values.
- The `[HttpGet]` attribute with a parameter registers the `Get` method with an `id` parameter to respond to HTTP GET requests that include a parameter value in the route.

- The `[HttpPost]`, `[HttpPut]`, and `[HttpDelete]` attributes register three other methods to respond to the equivalent HTTP methods, but currently do nothing:

```
using System.Collections.Generic;
using Microsoft.AspNetCore.Mvc;

namespace NorthwindService.Controllers
{
   [Route("api/[controller]")]
   public class ValuesController : Controller
   {
      // GET api/values
      [HttpGet]
      public IEnumerable<string> Get()
      {
         return new string[] { "value1", "value2" };
      }

      // GET api/values/5
      [HttpGet("{id}")]
      public string Get(int id)
      {
         return "value";
      }

      // POST api/values
      [HttpPost]
      public void Post([FromBody]string value)
      {
      }

      // PUT api/values/5
      [HttpPut("{id}")]
      public void Put(int id, [FromBody]string value)
      {
      }

      // DELETE api/values/5
      [HttpDelete("{id}")]
      public void Delete(int id)
      {
      }
   }
}
```

If you have used older versions of ASP.NET Web API for .NET Framework, then you know that you could create C# methods that begin with any HTTP method (`GET`, `POST`, `PUT`, and so on), and the controller would automatically execute the correct one. In ASP.NET Core, this doesn't happen anymore because we are not inheriting from `ApiController`. So, you must apply an attribute such as `[HttpGet]` to explicitly map HTTP methods to C# methods. Although this requires more code, it allows us to use any name we like for the controller's methods.

Modify the second `Get` method to return a message telling the client what `id` value they sent, as shown in the following code:

```
// GET api/values/5
[HttpGet("{id}")]
public string Get(int id)
{
   return $"You sent me the id: {id}";
}
```

Start the website.

In Visual Studio 2017, press *Ctrl* + *F5*.

In Visual Studio Code, enter `dotnet run`, and then start Chrome. Navigate to `http:/localhost:5000/api/values`.

In Chrome, show the **Developer tools**, and press *F5* to refresh.

The Web API service should return a JSON document, as shown in the following screenshot:

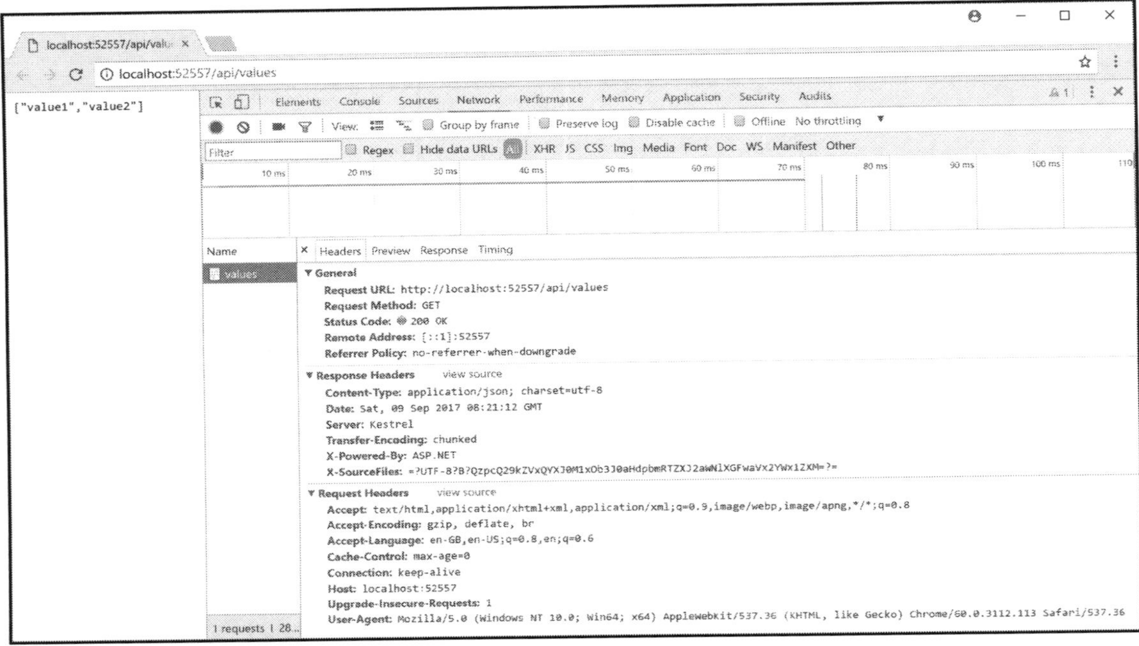

In Visual Studio 2017, you do not need to enter the `/api/values` relative URL because the project's **Debug** properties have been configured to do that for you, as shown in the following screenshot:

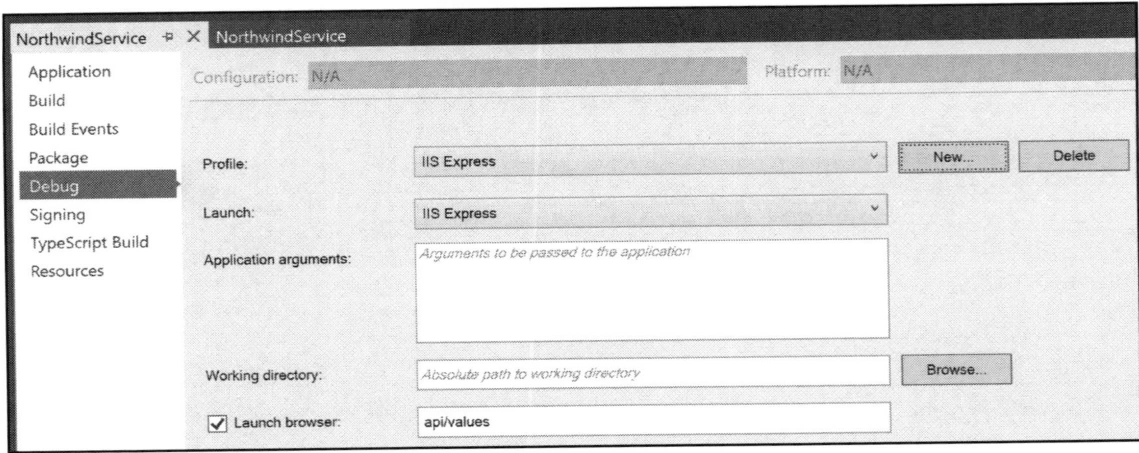

Navigate to `http:/localhost:5000/api/values/42`, and note the response, as shown in the following screenshot:

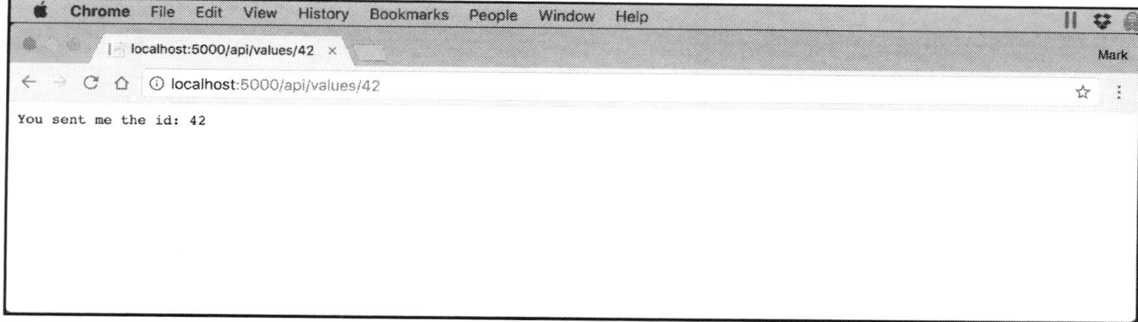


Close Google Chrome.

In Visual Studio Code, in **Integrated Terminal**, press *Ctrl* + *C* to stop the console application and shut down the Kestrel web server that is hosting your ASP.NET Core web service.

# Creating a web service for the Northwind database

Unlike controllers for MVC, controllers for Web API do not call Razor views to return HTML responses for humans to see in browsers. Instead, they use **content negotiation** with the client application that made the HTTP request to return data in formats such as XML, JSON, or X-WWW-FORMURLENCODED in the HTTP response.

The client application must then deserialize the data from the negotiated format. The most commonly used format for modern web services is **JavaScript Object Notation** (**JSON**) because it is compact and works natively with JavaScript in a browser.

We will reference the Entity Framework Core entity data model for the `Northwind` database that you created in `Chapter 14`, *Building Web Sites Using ASP.NET Core Razor Pages*.

## Using Visual Studio 2017

In Visual Studio 2017, in the **NorthwindService** project, right-click on **Dependencies**, and select **Add Reference....** Select **NorthwindContextLib**, and click on **OK**.

## Using Visual Studio Code

In Visual Studio Code, in the **NorthwindService** project, open `NorthwindService.csproj`, and add a project reference to `NorthwindContextLib`, as shown in the following markup:

```
<ItemGroup>
  <PackageReference Include="Microsoft.AspNetCore.All" Version="2.0.0" />
  <ProjectReference
   Include="..\NorthwindContextLib\NorthwindContextLib.csproj" />
</ItemGroup>
```

## Using Visual Studio 2017 and Visual Studio Code

In both Visual Studio 2017 and Visual Studio Code, modify `Startup.cs`, import the `Microsoft.EntityFrameworkCore` and `Packt.CS7` namespaces, and add the following statement to the `ConfigureServices` method before the call to `AddMvc`.

For SQL Server LocalDB, add this statement:

```
services.AddDbContext<Northwind>(options => options.UseSqlServer(
"Server=(localdb)\\mssqllocaldb;Database=Northwind;Trusted_Connection=True;
MultipleActiveResultSets=true"));
```

For SQLite, add this one:

```
services.AddDbContext<Northwind>(options =>
options.UseSqlite("Data Source=../Northwind.db"));
```

# Creating data repositories for entities

Defining and implementing a data repository to provide CRUD operations is good practice:

- C for Create
- R for Retrieve (or Read)
- U for Update
- D for Delete

We will create a data repository for the `Customers` table in `Northwind`. We will follow modern good practice and make the repository API asynchronous.

In the `NorthwindService` project, create a `Repositories` folder.

Add two class files to the `Repositories` folder named `ICustomerRepository.cs` and `CustomerRepository.cs`.

`ICustomerRepository` should look like this:

```
using Packt.CS7;
using System.Collections.Generic;
using System.Threading.Tasks;

namespace NorthwindService.Repositories
{
   public interface ICustomerRepository
   {
      Task<Customer> CreateAsync(Customer c);

      Task<IEnumerable<Customer>> RetrieveAllAsync();

      Task<Customer> RetrieveAsync(string id);

      Task<Customer> UpdateAsync(string id, Customer c);

      Task<bool> DeleteAsync(string id);
   }
}
```

`CustomerRepository` should look like this:

```
using Microsoft.EntityFrameworkCore.ChangeTracking;
using Packt.CS7;
using System.Collections.Generic;
using System.Collections.Concurrent;
using System.Linq;
using System.Threading.Tasks;

namespace NorthwindService.Repositories
{
   public class CustomerRepository : ICustomerRepository
   {
      // cache the customers in a thread-safe dictionary
      // to improve performance
      private static ConcurrentDictionary<string, Customer> customersCache;

      private Northwind db;

      public CustomerRepository(Northwind db)
      {
         this.db = db;
```

```
            // pre-load customers from database as a normal
            // Dictionary with CustomerID is the key,
            // then convert to a thread-safe ConcurrentDictionary
            if (customersCache == null)
            {
                customersCache = new ConcurrentDictionary<string, Customer>(
                db.Customers.ToDictionary(c => c.CustomerID));
            }
        }

        public async Task<Customer> CreateAsync(Customer c)
        {
            // normalize CustomerID into uppercase
            c.CustomerID = c.CustomerID.ToUpper();

            // add to database using EF Core
            EntityEntry<Customer> added = await db.Customers.AddAsync(c);

            int affected = await db.SaveChangesAsync();

            if (affected == 1)
            {
                // if the customer is new, add it to cache, else
                // call UpdateCache method
                return customersCache.AddOrUpdate(c.CustomerID, c,
                UpdateCache);
            }
            else
            {
                return null;
            }
        }

        public async Task<IEnumerable<Customer>> RetrieveAllAsync()
        {
            // for performance, get from cache
            return await Task.Run<IEnumerable<Customer>>(
            () => customersCache.Values);
        }

        public async Task<Customer> RetrieveAsync(string id)
        {
            return await Task.Run(() =>
            {
                // for performance, get from cache
                id = id.ToUpper();
                Customer c;
                customersCache.TryGetValue(id, out c);
```

```
            return c;
         });
      }

      private Customer UpdateCache(string id, Customer c)
      {
         Customer old;
         if (customersCache.TryGetValue(id, out old))
         {
            if (customersCache.TryUpdate(id, c, old))
            {
               return c;
            }
         }
         return null;
      }

      public async Task<Customer> UpdateAsync(string id, Customer c)
      {
         return await Task.Run(() =>
         {
            // normalize customer ID
            id = id.ToUpper();
            c.CustomerID = c.CustomerID.ToUpper();

            // update in database
            db.Customers.Update(c);
            int affected = db.SaveChanges();

            if (affected == 1)
            {
               // update in cache
               return Task.Run(() => UpdateCache(id, c));
            }
            return null;
         });
      }

      public async Task<bool> DeleteAsync(string id)
      {
         return await Task.Run(() =>
         {
            id = id.ToUpper();

            // remove from database
            Customer c = db.Customers.Find(id);
            db.Customers.Remove(c);
            int affected = db.SaveChanges();
```

```
                if (affected == 1)
                {
                    // remove from cache
                    return Task.Run(() => customersCache.TryRemove(id, out c));
                }
                else
                {
                    return null;
                }
            });
        }
    }
}
```

## Configuring and registering the customers repository

Open the `Startup.cs` file, and import the following namespace:

```
using NorthwindService.Repositories;
```

Add the following statement to the bottom of the `ConfigureServices` method that will register the `CustomerRepository` for use at runtime by ASP.NET Core, as shown in the following code:

```
services.AddScoped<ICustomerRepository, CustomerRepository>();
```

## Creating the Web API controller

In the `Controllers` folder, add a new class named `CustomersController.cs`.

We could delete the `ValuesController.cs` file, but it is good to have a simple Web API controller with minimal dependencies in a service for testing purposes.

In the `CustomersController` class, add the following code, and note the following:

- The controller class registers a route that starts with `api` and includes the name of the controller, that is, `api/customers`.
- The constructor uses dependency injection to get the registered repository for customers.
- There are five methods to perform CRUD operations on customers—two `GET` methods (all customers or one customer), `POST` (create), `PUT` (update), and `DELETE`.
- `GetCustomers` can have a `string` parameter passed with a country name. If it is missing, all customers are returned. If it is present, it is used to filter customers by country.
- `GetCustomer` has a route explicitly named `GetCustomer` so that it can be used to generate a URL after inserting a new customer:

```
using Microsoft.AspNetCore.Mvc;
using Packt.CS7;
using NorthwindService.Repositories;
using System.Collections.Generic;
using System.Linq;
using System.Threading.Tasks;

namespace NorthwindService.Controllers
{
   // base address: api/customers
   [Route("api/[controller]")]
   public class CustomersController : Controller
   {
      private ICustomerRepository repo;

      // constructor injects registered repository
      public CustomersController(ICustomerRepository repo)
      {
         this.repo = repo;
      }

      // GET: api/customers
      // GET: api/customers/?country=[country]
      [HttpGet]
      public async Task<IEnumerable<Customer>> GetCustomers(string country)
      {
         if (string.IsNullOrWhiteSpace(country))
         {
            return await repo.RetrieveAllAsync();
         }
```

```
        else
        {
            return (await repo.RetrieveAllAsync())
            .Where(customer => customer.Country == country);
        }
    }

    // GET: api/customers/[id]
    [HttpGet("{id}", Name = "GetCustomer")]
    public async Task<IActionResult> GetCustomer(string id)
    {
        Customer c = await repo.RetrieveAsync(id);
        if (c == null)
        {
            return NotFound(); // 404 Resource not found
        }
        return new ObjectResult(c); // 200 OK
    }

    // POST: api/customers
    // BODY: Customer (JSON, XML)
    [HttpPost]
    public async Task<IActionResult> Create([FromBody] Customer c)
    {
        if (c == null)
        {
            return BadRequest(); // 400 Bad request
        }
        Customer added = await repo.CreateAsync(c);
        return CreatedAtRoute("GetCustomer", // use named route
        new { id = added.CustomerID.ToLower() }, c); // 201 Created
    }

    // PUT: api/customers/[id]
    // BODY: Customer (JSON, XML)
    [HttpPut("{id}")]
    public async Task<IActionResult> Update(string id, [FromBody]
    Customer c)
    {
        id = id.ToUpper();
        c.CustomerID = c.CustomerID.ToUpper();

        if (c == null || c.CustomerID != id)
        {
            return BadRequest(); // 400 Bad request
        }

        var existing = await repo.RetrieveAsync(id);
```

```
            if (existing == null)
            {
                return NotFound(); // 404 Resource not found
            }

            await repo.UpdateAsync(id, c);
            return new NoContentResult(); // 204 No content
        }

        // DELETE: api/customers/[id]
        [HttpDelete("{id}")]
        public async Task<IActionResult> Delete(string id)
        {
            var existing = await repo.RetrieveAsync(id);
            if (existing == null)
            {
                return NotFound(); // 404 Resource not found
            }

            bool deleted = await repo.DeleteAsync(id);

            if (deleted)
            {
                return new NoContentResult(); // 204 No content
            }
            else
            {
                return BadRequest();
            }
        }
    }
}
```

# Documenting and testing web services using Swagger

You can easily test a web service by making GET requests, using a browser.

# Testing GET requests with any browser

Start the web service.

In Chrome, in the address bar, enter the following URL:

```
http://localhost:5000/api/customers
```

You should see a JSON document returned, containing all the 91 customers in the `Northwind` database, as shown in the following screenshot:

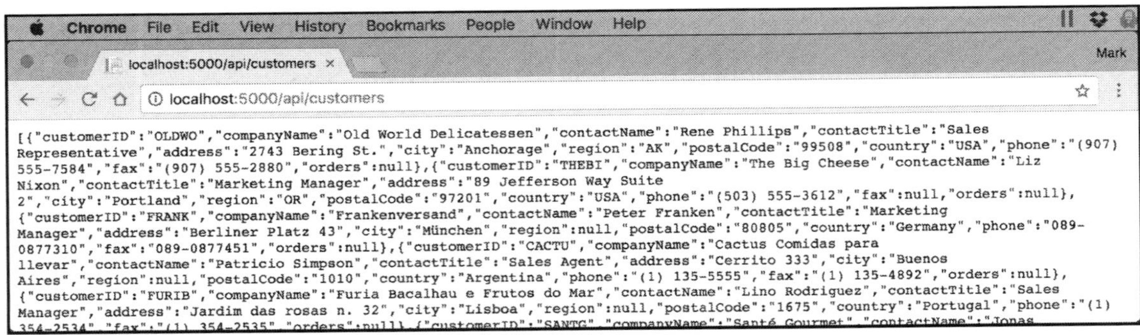


In the address bar, enter the following URL:

```
http://localhost:5000/api/customers/alfki
```

You should see a JSON document returned containing only the customer named **Alfreds Futterkiste**, as shown in the following screenshot:

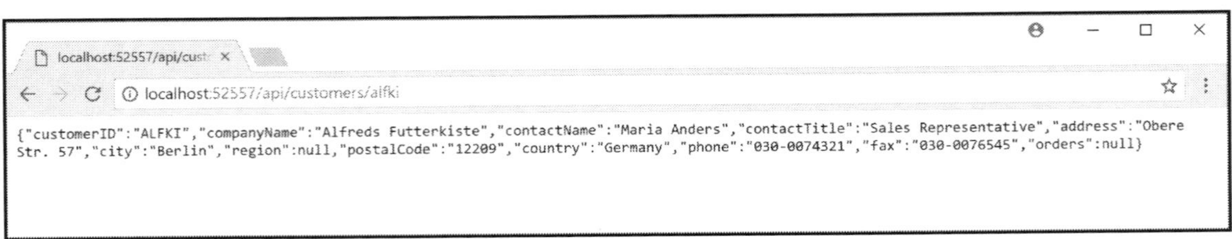

In the address bar, enter the following URL:

```
http://localhost:5000/api/customers/?country=Germany
```

You should see a JSON document returned, containing the customers in Germany, as shown in the following screenshot:

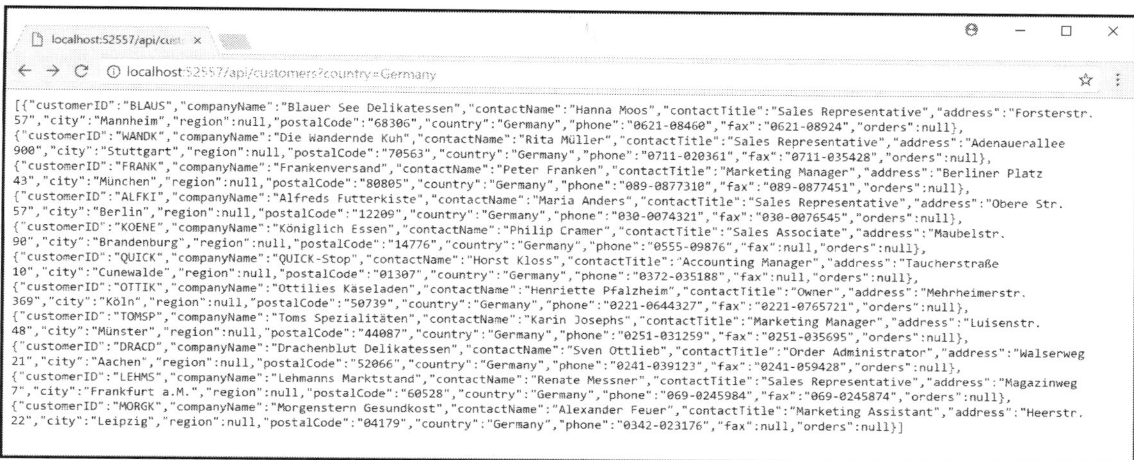

But how can we test the other HTTP methods, such as `POST`, `PUT`, and `DELETE`? And how can we document our web service so it's easy for anyone to understand how to interact with it?

# Testing POST, PUT, and DELETE requests with Swagger

**Swagger** is the world's most popular technology for documenting and testing HTTP APIs.

The most important part of Swagger is the **OpenAPI Specification** that defines a REST-style contract for your API, *detailing all of its resources and operations in a human and machine readable format for easy development, discovery, and integration.*

For us, another useful feature is Swagger UI, because it automatically generates documentation for your API with built-in visual testing capabilities.

Read more about Swagger at the following link:
`https://swagger.io`

## Installing a Swagger package

To use Swagger, we must install a Swagger implementation package. The most popular for ASP.NET Core is named Swashbuckle.

### Using Visual Studio 2017

In **Solution Explorer**, in **NorthwindService**, right-click on **Dependencies**, and select **Manage NuGet Packages...**.

Select **Browse**, and enter `Swashbuckle.AspNetCore` in the search box, and click on **Install**, as shown in the following screenshot:

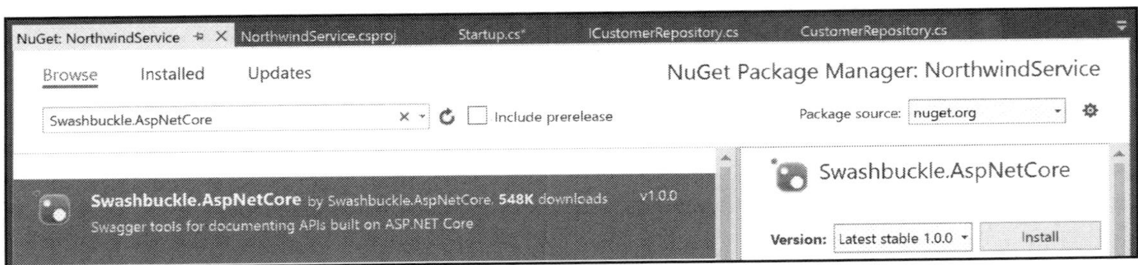


### Using Visual Studio Code

Edit `NorthwindService.csproj`, and add a package reference for `Swashbuckle.AspNetCore`, as shown highlighted in the following markup:

```
<ItemGroup>
  <PackageReference Include="Microsoft.AspNetCore.All" Version="2.0.0" />
  <ProjectReference
   Include="..\NorthwindContextLib\NorthwindContextLib.csproj" />
  <PackageReference Include="Swashbuckle.AspNetCore" Version="1.0.0" />
</ItemGroup>
```

## Using Visual Studio 2017 and Visual Studio Code

Open `Startup.cs`, and import the Swashbuckle's `Swagger` namespace, as shown in the following code:

```
using Swashbuckle.AspNetCore.Swagger;
```

In the `ConfigureServices` method, add a statement to add Swagger support with documentation for the Northwind service, as shown in the following code:

```
// Register the Swagger generator, and define a Swagger document
//for Northwind service
services.AddSwaggerGen(c =>
{
    c.SwaggerDoc("v1", new Info { Title = "Northwind Service API",
    Version = "v1" });
});
```

In the `Configure` method, add a statement to use Swagger and Swagger UI, and define an endpoint for the OpenAPI specification JSON document, as shown in the following code:

```
app.UseSwagger();

app.UseSwaggerUI(c =>
{
    c.SwaggerEndpoint("/swagger/v1/swagger.json",
    "Northwind Service API V1");
});
```

# Testing GET requests with Swagger UI

Start the website, and navigate to `/swagger/`; note that both the **Customers** and **Values** controllers have been discovered and documented, as shown in the following screenshot:

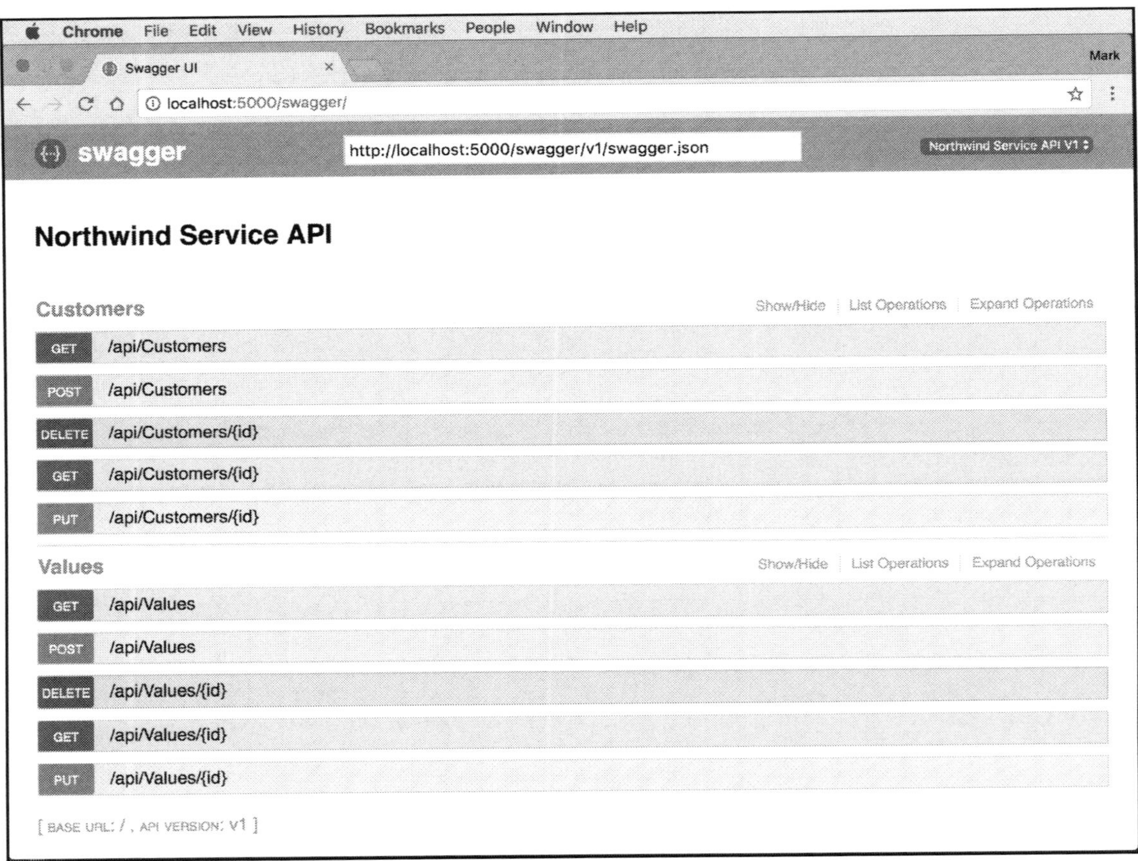


Click on **GET /api/Customers/{id}**, and note the required parameter for the ID of a customer, as shown in the following screenshot:

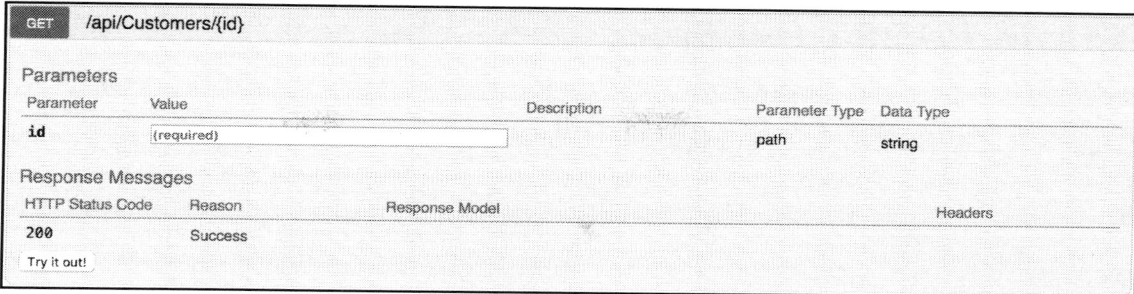


Enter an ID of `ALFKI`, select **Try it out!**, and note the **Request URL**, **Response Body**, **Response Code**, and **Response Headers**, as shown in the following screenshot:

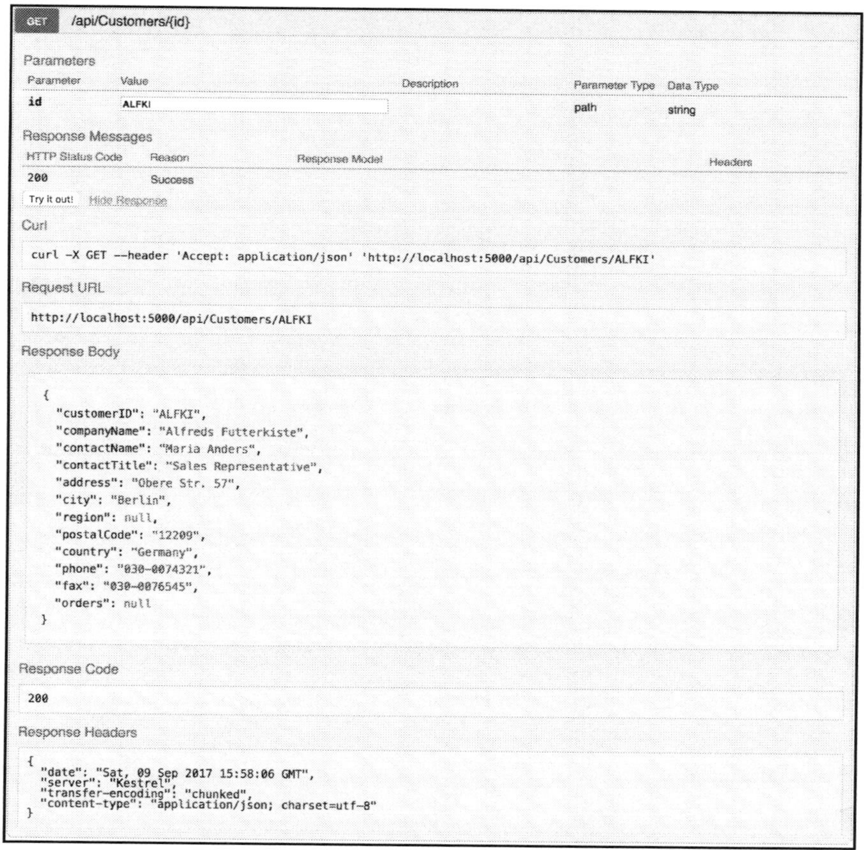

# Testing POST requests with Swagger UI

Click on **POST /api/Customers**.

Click on the body of the **Example Value** to copy it to the **c** parameter value box, and modify the JSON to define a new customer, as shown in the following JSON and screenshot:

```
{
  "customerID": "SUPER",
  "companyName": "Super Company",
  "contactName": "Rasmus Ibensen",
  "contactTitle": "Sales Leader",
  "address": "Rotterslef 23",
  "city": "Billund",
  "region": null,
  "postalCode": "4371",
  "country": "Denmark",
  "phone": "31 21 43 21",
  "fax": "31 21 43 22",
  "orders": null
}
```

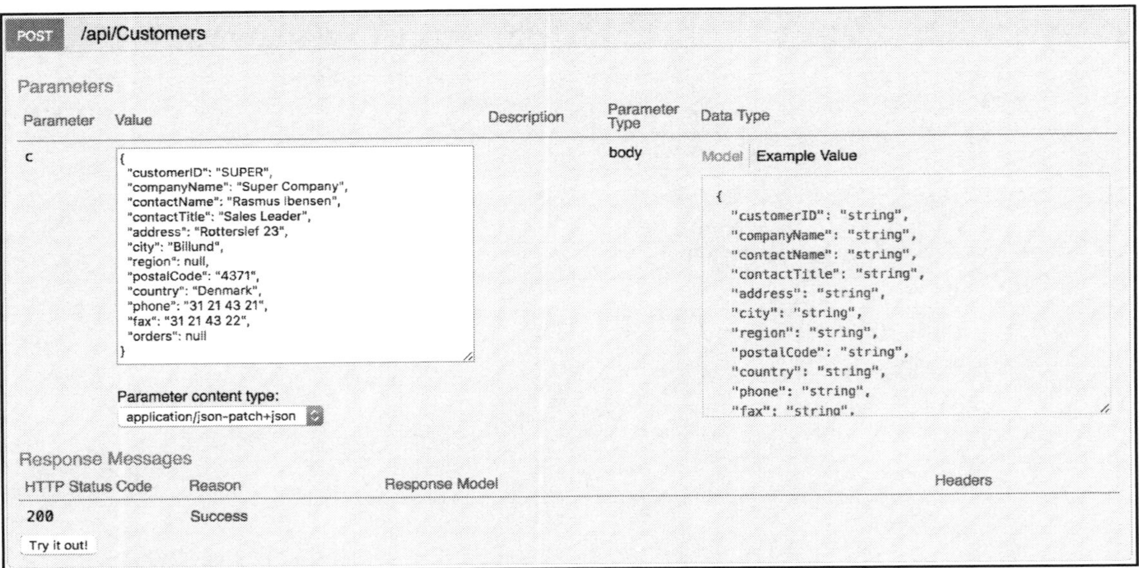

Click on **Try it out!**, and note the **Request URL**, **Response Body**, **Response Code**, and **Response Headers**, as shown in the following screenshot:

Request URL

```
http://localhost:5000/api/Customers
```

Response Body

```
{
  "customerID": "SUPER",
  "companyName": "Super Company",
  "contactName": "Rasmus Ibensen",
  "contactTitle": "Sales Leader",
  "address": "Rotterslef 23",
  "city": "Billund",
  "region": null,
  "postalCode": "4371",
  "country": "Denmark",
  "phone": "31 21 43 21",
  "fax": "31 21 43 22",
  "orders": null
}
```

Response Code

```
201
```

Response Headers

```
{
  "location": "http://localhost:5000/api/Customers/super",
  "date": "Sat, 09 Sep 2017 16:10:19 GMT",
  "server": "Kestrel",
  "transfer-encoding": "chunked",
  "content-type": "application/json; charset=utf-8"
}
```

A response code of `201` means the customer was created successfully.

Click on the **GET /api/Customers** method, enter `Denmark` for the **country** parameter, and click on **Try it out!**, to confirm that the new customer was added to the database, as shown in the following screenshot:

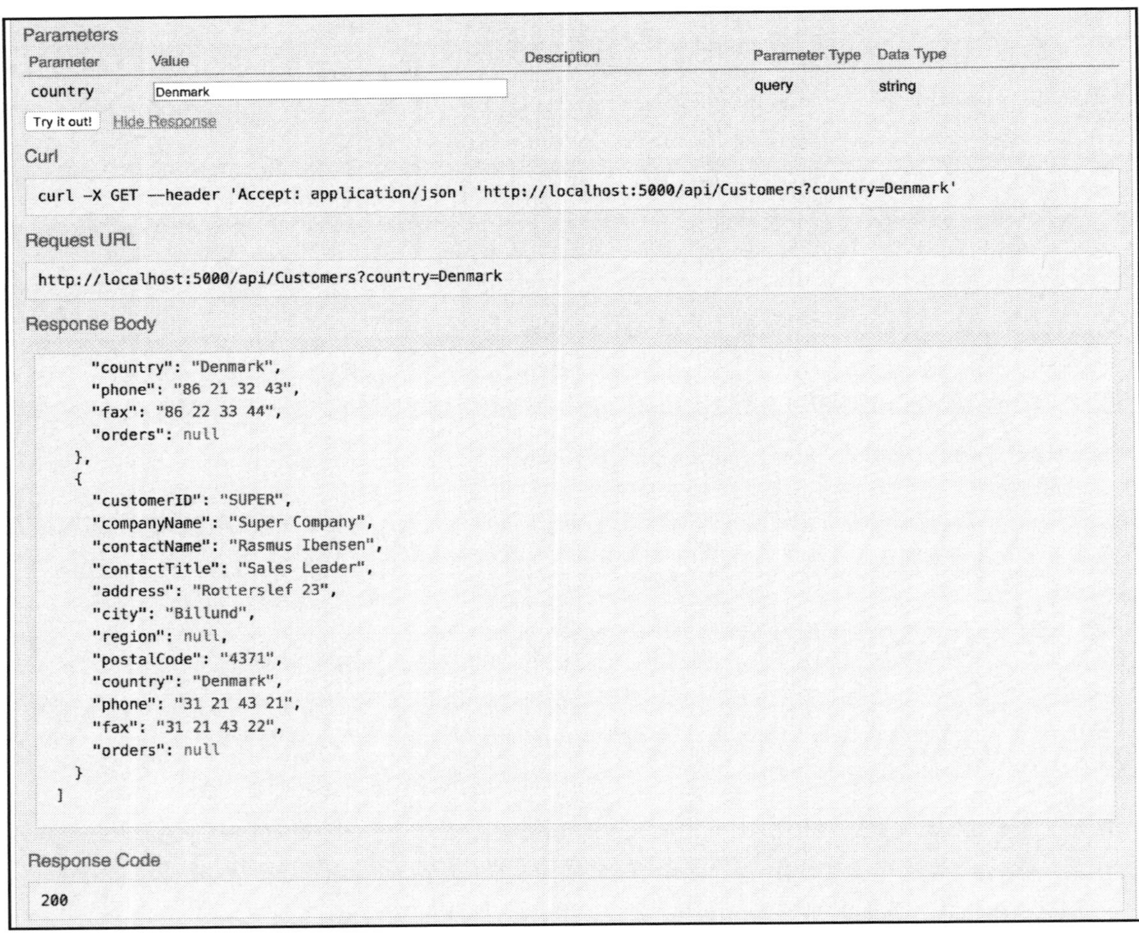


Click on **DELETE /api/Customers/{id}**, enter `super` for the ID, click on **Try it out!**, and note that the Response Code is `204`, indicating it was successfully deleted, as shown in the following screenshot:

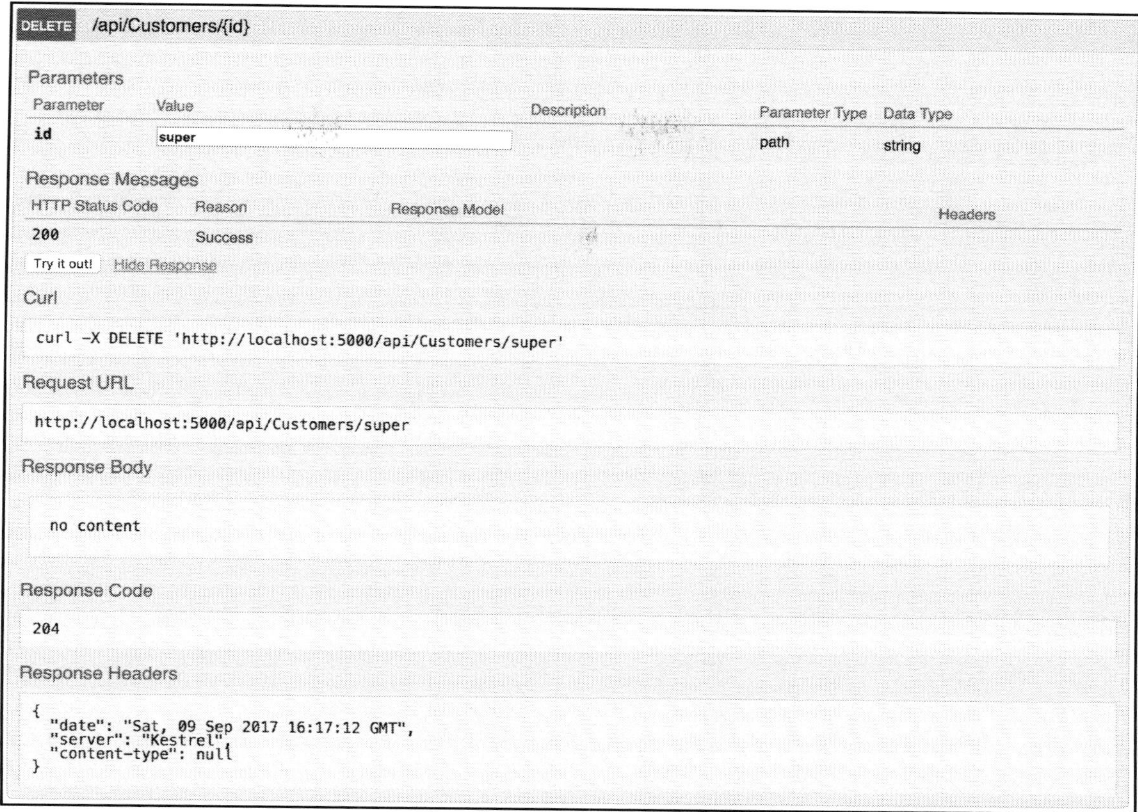


Click on **Try it out!** again, and note that the **Response Code** is `404`, indicating the customer does not exist any more.

Use the `GET` methods to confirm that the new customer has been deleted from the database.

I will leave testing updates using `PUT`, to the reader.

Close Chrome.

In **Integrated Terminal**, press *Ctrl* + *C* to stop the console application and shut down the Kestrel web server that is hosting your ASP.NET Core web service.

You are now ready to build a web application that calls the web service.

# Building SPAs using Angular

Angular is a popular frontend framework for building web and mobile applications. It uses TypeScript, a Microsoft-created, strongly-typed language that compiles into JavaScript.

## Understanding the Angular project template

ASP.NET Core has a project template specifically for Angular. Let's see what it includes.

### Using Visual Studio 2017

In Visual Studio 2017, open the `Part3` solution, and press *Ctrl* + *Shift* + *N* or go to **File** | **Add** | **New Project...**.

In the **Add New Project** dialog, in the **Installed** list, expand **Visual C#**, and select **.NET Core**. In the center list, select **ASP.NET Core Web Application**, type the name as `ExploreAngular`, and then click on **OK**.

In the **New ASP.NET Core Web Application - ExploreAngular** dialog; select **.NET Core**, **ASP.NET Core 2.0**, and the **Angular** template; and click on **OK**.

### Using Visual Studio Code

In the folder named `Part3`, create a folder named `ExploreAngular`.

In Visual Studio Code, open the `ExploreAngular` folder.

In **Integrated Terminal**, enter the following commands to create a new ASP.NET Core Web API project, and then use Node Package Manager to install dependent packages:

```
dotnet new angular
npm install
```

On the first build, NuGet and NPM will download all package dependencies, which can take some time. Annoyingly, the tooling gives no feedback about what's happening, so you might think it's broken!

## Using Visual Studio 2017 and Visual Studio Code

Start the website, as shown in the following screenshot:

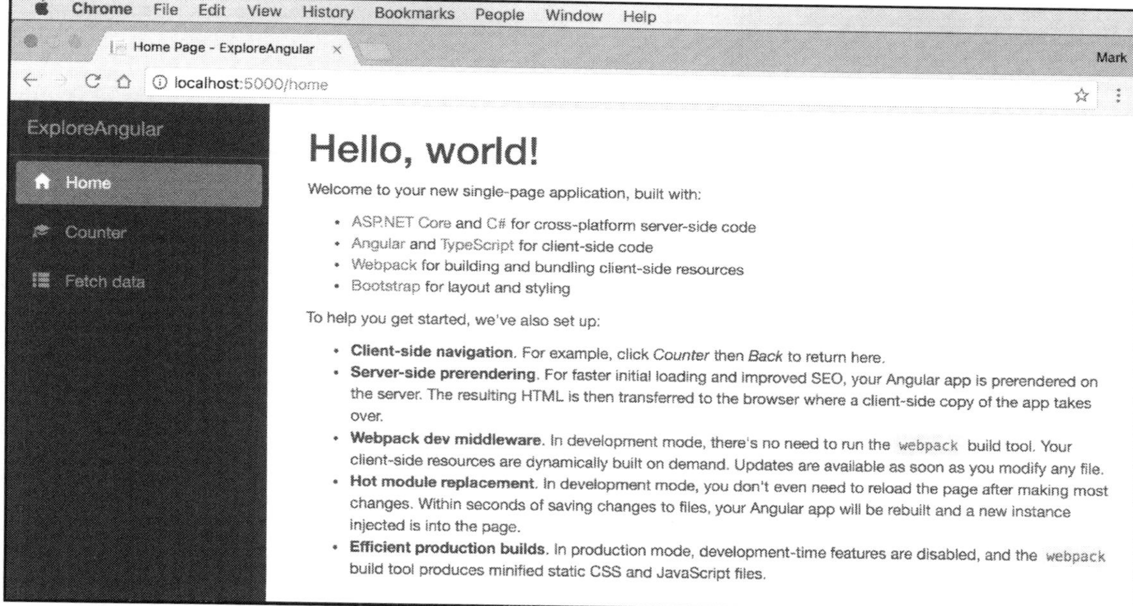

Click on **Fetch data**, as shown in the following screenshot:

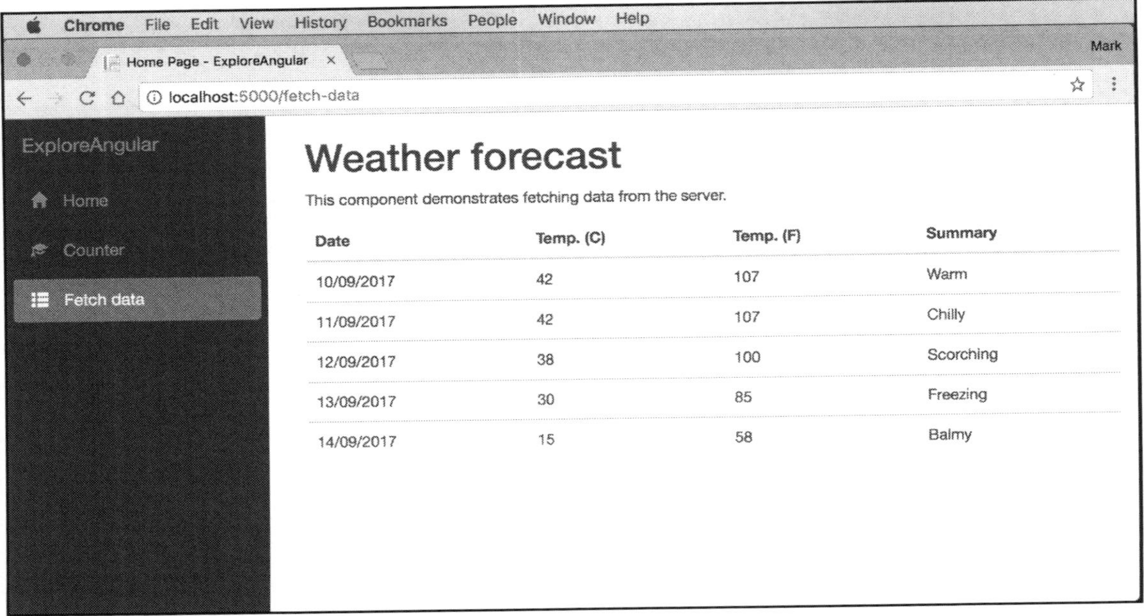


Close Chrome, and let's see how this works.

Open `Startup.cs`, and note that it is mostly similar to the MVC project template, except that it also does the following:

- It uses Webpack middleware to support hot module replacement, meaning that if a developer makes a change to an Angular module while a website is running, that module's changes can be immediately pushed to the client and used
- It adds a fallback route if the SPA fails to show the `Home` controller's `Index` view

In the `Controllers` folder, open `HomeController.cs`, and note that the `Index` method does nothing special.

In the `Views` folder, in the `Home` folder, open `Index.cshtml`, and note the `<app>` element that references the `ClientApp/dist/main-server` folder that contains server-side code, and the `<script>` element that references the `dist` folder's `main-client.js` file that contains client-side code, as shown in the following markup:

```
@{
    ViewData["Title"] = "Home Page";
}

<app asp-prerender-module="ClientApp/dist/main-server">Loading...</app>

<script src="~/dist/vendor.js" asp-append-version="true"></script>
@section scripts {
  <script src="~/dist/main-client.js"
    asp-append-version="true"></script>
}
```

The JavaScript code for server-side and client-side is generated by Webpack from the TypeScript code that you write in the `ClientApp` folder.

In the `Controllers` folder, open `SampleDataController.cs`, and note that it is a Web API service with a single `GET` method that returns random weather forecast data using a simple `WeatherForecast` model class.

In the `ClientApp` folder, note the `boot.browser.ts` file that contains TypeScript statements that import an AppModule from `app/app.module.browser`, as shown in the following code:

```
import { AppModule } from './app/app.module.browser';
```

In the `ClientApp` folder, expand the `app` folder, open `app.module.brower.ts`, and note that it has a statement to import `AppModuleShared`, as shown in the following code:

```
import { AppModuleShared } from './app.module.shared';
```

Open `app.module.shared.ts`, and note that it imports five components, as shown in the following code:

```
import { AppComponent } from './components/app/app.component';
import { NavMenuComponent } from './components/navmenu/navmenu.component';
import { HomeComponent } from './components/home/home.component';
import { FetchDataComponent } from
'./components/fetchdata/fetchdata.component';
import { CounterComponent } from './components/counter/counter.component';
```

In the `ClientApp` folder, expand the `app` folder and the `components` folder, to see the five Angular components for this SPA, as shown in the following screenshot, and note the following:

- `app` is the main application component that has a menu on the left and a client-side router in the main part on the right
- `counter` is a component with a simple button that increments
- `fetchdata` is a component that requests data from the weather service
- `home` is the default component, and it shows some static HTML content
- `navmenu` is a component that allows client-side routing between the other components:

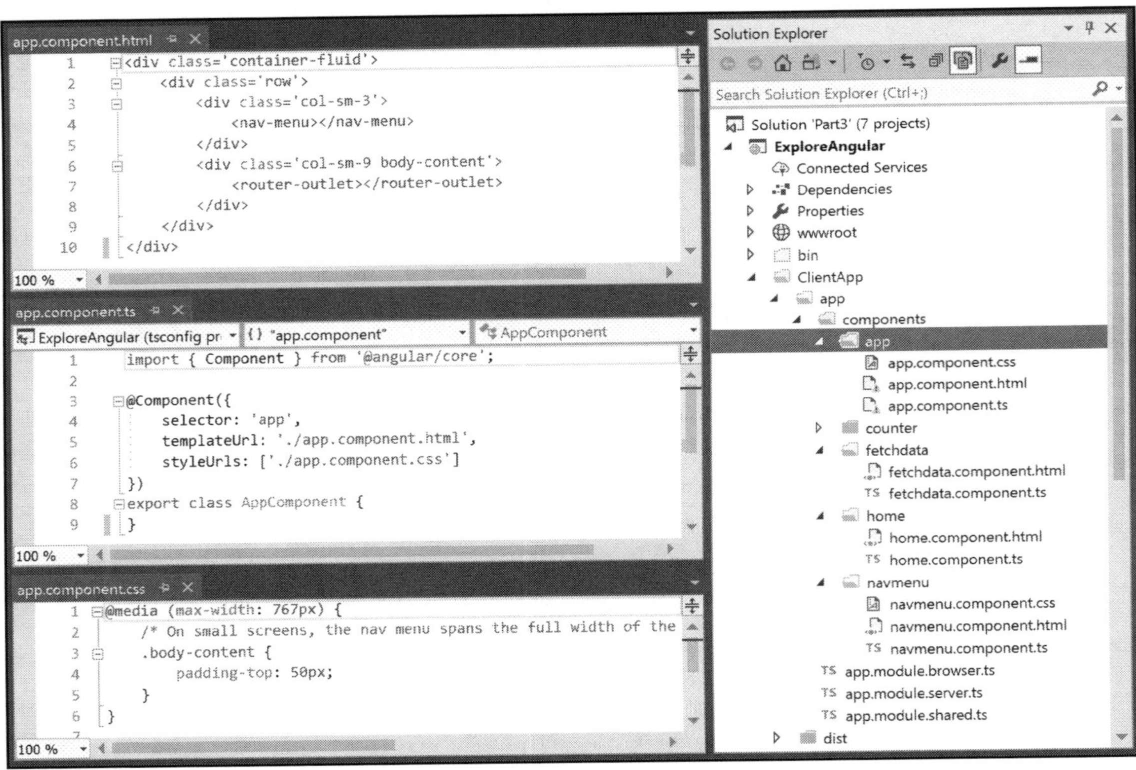

Open `home.component.ts` and `fetchdata.component.ts`, compare the two, as shown in the following code, and note the following:

- The `home` component has no code, but just static HTML content
- The `fetchdata` component imports the `Http` namespace, uses it in its constructor to make an HTTP `GET` request to the weather service, and stores the response in a public array of `WeatherForecast` objects, defined by an interface:

```
// home.component.ts
import { Component } from '@angular/core';

@Component({
    selector: 'home',
    templateUrl: './home.component.html'
})
export class HomeComponent {
}

// fetchdata.component.ts
import { Component, Inject } from '@angular/core';
import { Http } from '@angular/http';

@Component({
    selector: 'fetchdata',
    templateUrl: './fetchdata.component.html'
})
export class FetchDataComponent {
public forecasts: WeatherForecast[];

constructor(http: Http, @Inject('BASE_URL') baseUrl: string) {
    http.get(baseUrl + 'api/SampleData/WeatherForecasts')
    .subscribe(result => {
         this.forecasts = result.json() as WeatherForecast[];
          }, error => console.error(error));
     }
}

interface WeatherForecast {
    dateFormatted: string;
    temperatureC: number;
    temperatureF: number;
    summary: string;
}
```

# Calling NorthwindService

Now that you understand a little of how Angular components fit together and can fetch data from services, we will modify the `home` component to load a list of customers from `NorthwindService`.

But first, it would be useful to explicitly specify the port numbers for the `NorthwindService` and `ExploreAngular` websites, and to enable **Cross-Origin Resource Sharing (CORS)** so that `ExploreAngular` can call `NorthwindService`.

Default browser same-origin policy prevents code downloaded from one origin from accessing resources downloaded from a different origin to improve security. CORS can be enabled to allow requests from specified domains. Learn more about CORS and ASP.NET Core at the following link:
`https://docs.microsoft.com/en-us/aspnet/core/security/cors`

## Using Visual Studio 2017

In **Solution Explorer**, right-click on **NorthwindService**, and select **Properties**.

Select **Debug** tab, in **Web Server Settings**, modify the **App URL** port number to `5001`, as shown in the following code:

```
http://localhost:5001/
```

In **Solution Explorer**, right-click on **ExploreAngular**, and select **Properties**.

Select the **Debug** tab, in **Web Server Settings**, modify the **App URL** port number to `5002`.

## Using Visual Studio Code

In `NorthwindService`, open `Program.cs`, and in the `BuildWebHost` method, add an extension method call to `UseUrls`, to specify port number `5001`, as shown highlighted in the following code:

```
public static IWebHost BuildWebHost(string[] args) =>
    WebHost.CreateDefaultBuilder(args)
    .UseStartup<Startup>()
    .UseUrls("http://localhost:5001")
    .Build();
```

In ExploreAngular, open Program.cs, and in the BuildWebHost method, add an extension method call to UseUrls, to specify port number 5002, as shown highlighted in the following code:

```
public static IWebHost BuildWebHost(string[] args) =>
    WebHost.CreateDefaultBuilder(args)
    .UseStartup<Startup>()
    .UseUrls("http://localhost:5002")
    .Build();
```

## Using Visual Studio 2017 and Visual Studio Code

In NorthwindService, open Startup.cs, and add a statement to the top of the ConfigureServices method, to add support for CORS, as shown highlighted in the following code:

```
public void ConfigureServices(IServiceCollection services)
{
   services.AddCors();
```

Add a statement to the Configure method, before calling UseMvc, to use CORS and allow requests from the ExploreAngular site, as shown highlighted in the following code:

```
public void Configure(IApplicationBuilder app, IHostingEnvironment env)
{
   if (env.IsDevelopment())
   {
      app.UseDeveloperExceptionPage();
   }

   app.UseCors(c => c.WithOrigins("http://localhost:5002"));

   app.UseMvc();
```

CORS must be used before MVC or it will not work!

## Modifying the home component to call NorthwindService

Open `home.component.ts`, and modify it, as shown in the following code:

```
import { Component, Inject } from '@angular/core';
import { Http } from '@angular/http';

@Component({
    selector: 'home',
    templateUrl: './home.component.html'
})
export class HomeComponent {
    public customers: Customer[];

constructor(http: Http, @Inject('BASE_URL') baseUrl: string) {
     http.get('http://localhost:5001/api/customers').subscribe(result => {
          this.customers = result.json() as Customer[];
           }, error => console.error(error));
       }
   }

interface Customer {
    customerID: string;
    companyName: string;
    contactName: string;
    contactTitle: string;
    address: string;
    city: string;
    region: string;
    postalCode: string;
    country: string;
    phone: string;
    fax: string;
}
```

Open `home.component.html`, and modify it, as shown in the following code:

```
<h1>Customers</h1>
<p>These customers have been loaded from the NorthwindService.</p>
<p *ngIf="!customers"><em>Loading customers... please wait.</em></p>
<table class='table' *ngIf="customers">
  <thead>
    <tr>
      <th>ID</th>
      <th>Company Name</th>
      <th>Contact Name</th>
```

```
        <th>City</th>
        <th>Country</th>
      </tr>
    </thead>
    <tbody>
    <tr *ngFor="let customer of customers">
      <td>{{ customer.customerID }}</td>
      <td>{{ customer.companyName }}</td>
      <td>{{ customer.contactName }}</td>
      <td>{{ customer.city }}</td>
      <td>{{ customer.country }}</td>
    </tr>
  </tbody>
  </table>
```

# Testing the Angular component calling the service

To test our changes, we should start the websites: `NorthwindService` and then `ExploreAngular`.

## Using Visual Studio 2017

In **Solution Explorer**, select **NorthwindService**, and go to **Debug** | **Start Without Debugging**, or press *Ctrl* + *F5*.

Chrome will start and show the JSON document with all the customers from the `Northwind` database.

Leave Chrome running.

In **Solution Explorer**, select **ExploreAngular**, and go to **Debug** | **Start Without Debugging**, or press *Ctrl* + *F5*.

## Using Visual Studio Code

In Visual Studio Code, open the `NorthwindService` folder, and in **Integrated Terminal**, enter the following command to set the hosting environment and start the website:

```
ASPNETCORE_ENVIRONMENT=Development dotnet run
```

In Visual Studio Code, go to **File** | **New Window**, open the `ExploreAngular` folder, and in **Integrated Terminal**, enter the following command to set the hosting environment and start the website:

```
ASPNETCORE_ENVIRONMENT=Development dotnet run
```

Start Chrome, and enter the address: `http://localhost:5002`.

## Using Visual Studio 2017 and Visual Studio Code

The Angular component will execute first on the server and send a pre-rendered HTML page with all the customers, and then an asynchronous call will be made to `NorthwindService`. While it waits, the **Loading** message will briefly show, and then the table updates with the JSON response, as shown in the following screenshot:

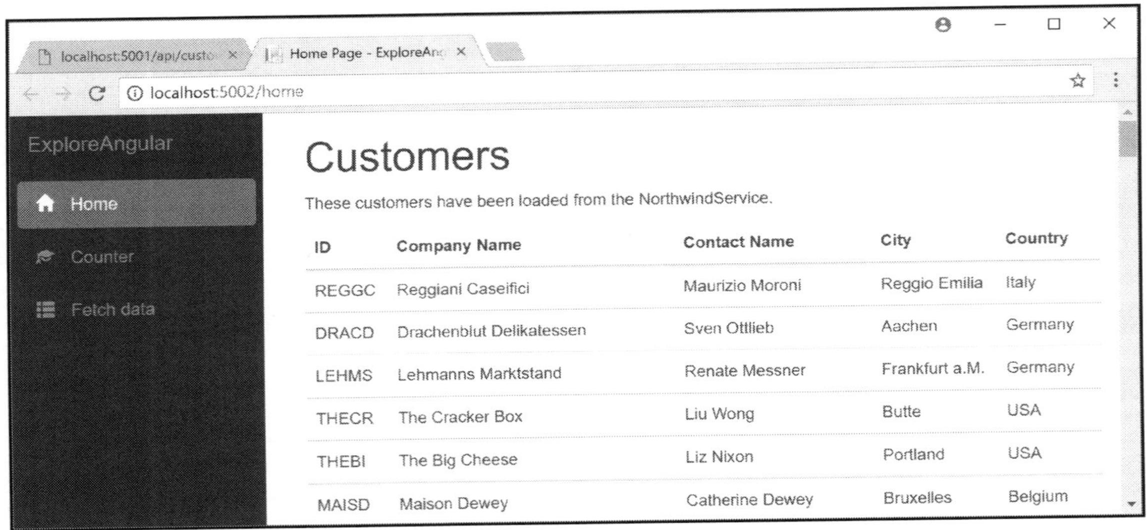

# Using other project templates

When you install .NET Core SDK 2.0, there are many project templates included.

At Command Prompt or Terminal, enter the following command:

```
dotnet new --help
```

You will see a list of currently installed templates, as shown in the following screenshot:

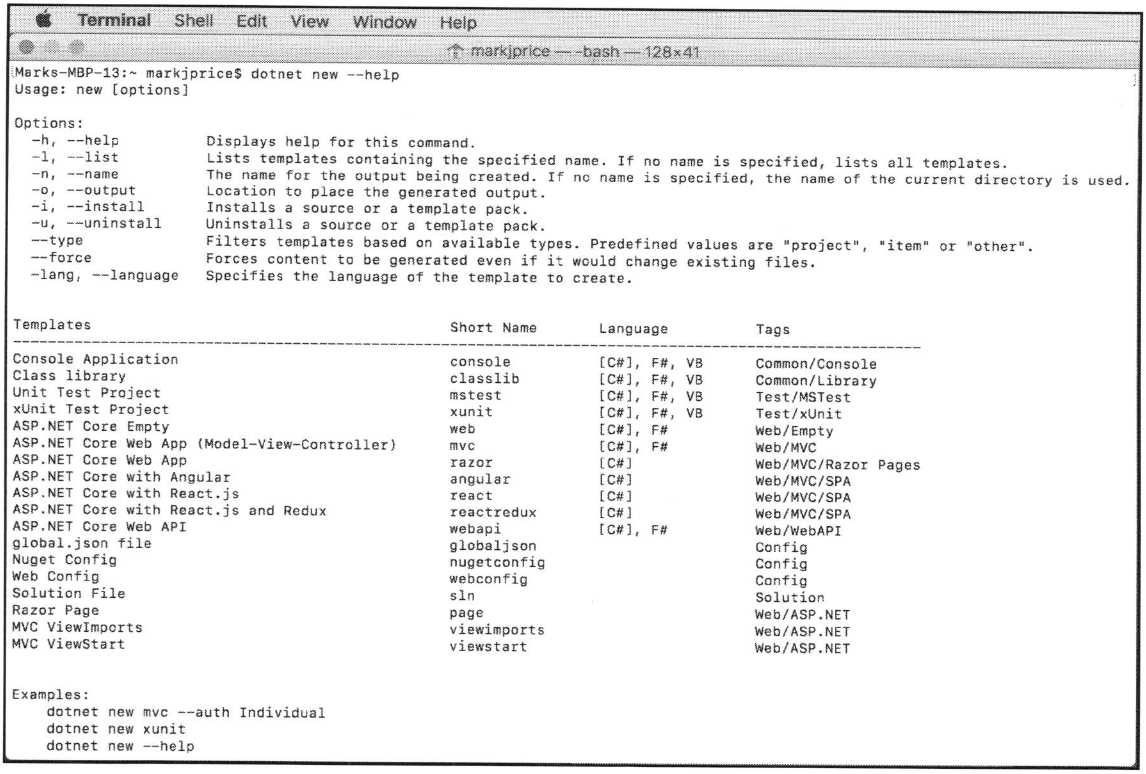

```
Terminal  Shell  Edit  View  Window  Help
markjprice — -bash — 128×41
Marks-MBP-13:~ markjprice$ dotnet new --help
Usage: new [options]

Options:
  -h, --help          Displays help for this command.
  -l, --list          Lists templates containing the specified name. If no name is specified, lists all templates.
  -n, --name          The name for the output being created. If no name is specified, the name of the current directory is used.
  -o, --output        Location to place the generated output.
  -i, --install       Installs a source or a template pack.
  -u, --uninstall     Uninstalls a source or a template pack.
  --type              Filters templates based on available types. Predefined values are "project", "item" or "other".
  --force             Forces content to be generated even if it would change existing files.
  -lang, --language   Specifies the language of the template to create.


Templates                                         Short Name       Language          Tags
--------------------------------------------------------------------------------------------------------
Console Application                               console          [C#], F#, VB      Common/Console
Class library                                     classlib         [C#], F#, VB      Common/Library
Unit Test Project                                 mstest           [C#], F#, VB      Test/MSTest
xUnit Test Project                                xunit            [C#], F#, VB      Test/xUnit
ASP.NET Core Empty                                web              [C#], F#          Web/Empty
ASP.NET Core Web App (Model-View-Controller)      mvc              [C#], F#          Web/MVC
ASP.NET Core Web App                              razor            [C#]              Web/MVC/Razor Pages
ASP.NET Core with Angular                         angular          [C#]              Web/MVC/SPA
ASP.NET Core with React.js                        react            [C#]              Web/MVC/SPA
ASP.NET Core with React.js and Redux              reactredux       [C#]              Web/MVC/SPA
ASP.NET Core Web API                              webapi           [C#], F#          Web/WebAPI
global.json file                                  globaljson                         Config
Nuget Config                                      nugetconfig                        Config
Web Config                                        webconfig                          Config
Solution File                                     sln                                Solution
Razor Page                                        page                               Web/ASP.NET
MVC ViewImports                                   viewimports                        Web/ASP.NET
MVC ViewStart                                     viewstart                          Web/ASP.NET


Examples:
    dotnet new mvc --auth Individual
    dotnet new xunit
    dotnet new --help
```

## Installing additional template packs

Start a browser, and navigate to the `http://dotnetnew.azurewebsites.net` link, to see a searchable list of available templates, as shown in the following screenshot:

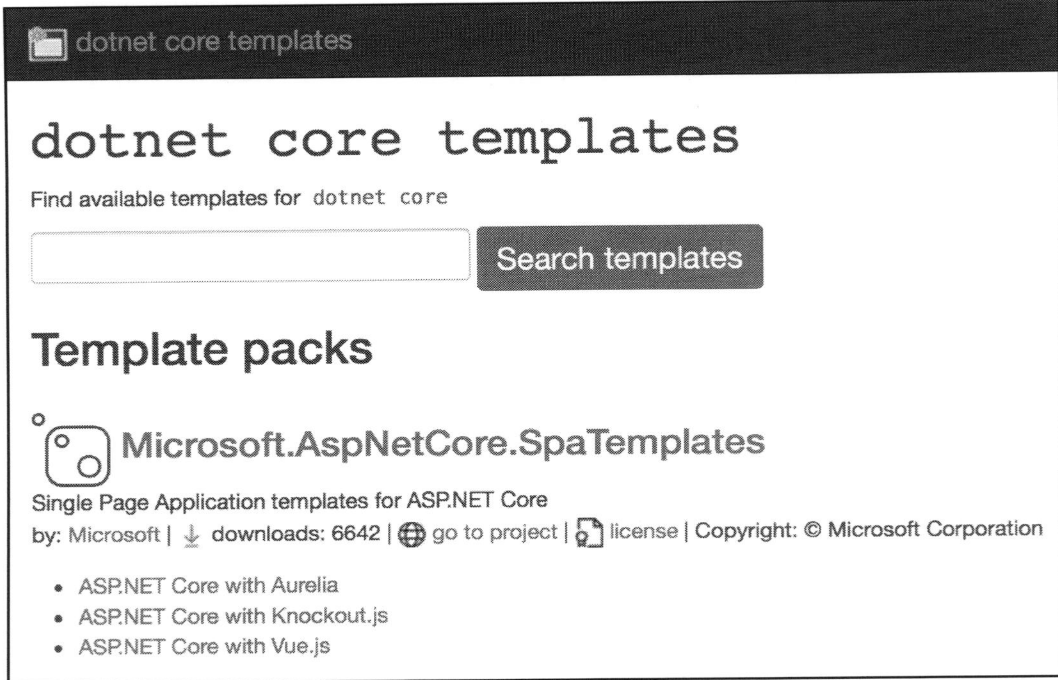


Click on **ASP.NET Core with Aurelia**, and note the instructions for installing and using this template, as shown in the following screenshot:

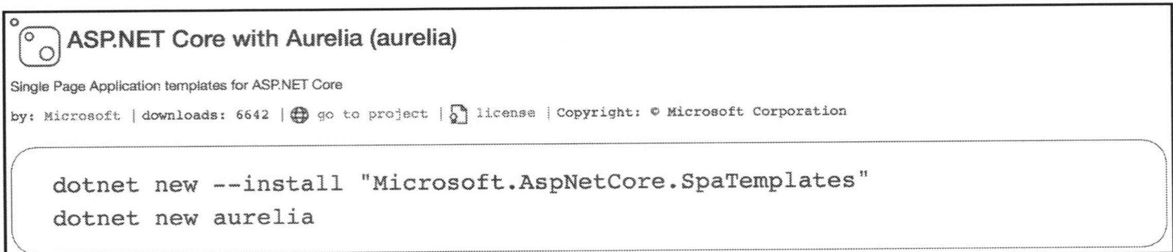

# Practicing and exploring

Get some hands-on practice and explore this chapter's topics with deeper research.

## Exercise 16.1 – Practice with React and Redux

Create a new project using the **React.js** and **Redux** project template, and then attempt to modify its code to call the `NorthwindService`, as we did for Angular:

```
dotnet new reactredux
```

## Exercise 16.2 – Explore topics

Use the following links to read more about this chapter's topics:

- **Building Web APIs:** `https://docs.microsoft.com/en-us/aspnet/core/mvc/web-api/`
- **Swagger Tools:** `https://swagger.io/tools/`
- **Swashbuckle for ASP.NET Core:** `https://github.com/domaindrivendev/Swashbuckle.AspNetCore`
- **Angular:** `https://angular.io`
- **TypeScript:** `https://www.typescriptlang.org`
- **React:** `https://facebook.github.io/react/`
- **Redux:** `http://redux.js.org`

# Summary

In this chapter, you learned how to build an ASP.NET Core Web API service that can be hosted cross-platform. You also learned how to test and document web service APIs with Swagger, and how to build a Single Page Application (SPA) using Angular that calls a web service, even if the service is on another domain.

In the next chapter, you will learn how to build cross-device apps for the Universal Windows Platform using XAML.

# 17
# Building Windows Apps Using XAML and Fluent Design

This chapter is about seeing what can be achieved with XAML when defining the user interface for a graphical app, in particular, for **Universal Windows Platform** (**UWP**). You will explore some of the new user interface features of Fluent Design, available in the Fall Creators Update of Windows 10.

In a single chapter, we will only be able to scratch the surface of everything that can be done with XAML and UWP. However, I hope to excite you into wanting to learn more about this cool technology and platform.

Think of this chapter as a whistle-stop tour of the coolest parts of XAML, UWP, and Fluent Design, including *template-able* controls, data binding, and animation!

**Some important points about this chapter**
UWP apps are not cross-platform, but they are cross-device if those devices run a modern flavor of Windows. You will need Windows 10 Fall Creators Update and Visual Studio 2017 version 15.4 or later to create the examples in this chapter. UWP supports .NET Native, which means that your code is compiled to native CPU instructions for a smaller memory footprint and faster execution.

In this chapter, we will cover the following topics:

- Understanding the modern Windows platform
- Creating a modern Windows app
- Using resources and templates
- Data binding
- Building apps using Windows Template Studio

# Understanding the modern Windows platform

Microsoft continues to improve their Windows platform, which includes multiple technologies for building modern apps:

- Universal Windows Platform 6.0
- Fluent Design System
- XAML Standard 1.0

## Understanding Universal Windows Platform

UWP is Microsoft's latest technology solution to build applications for its Windows suite of operating systems.

UWP provides a guaranteed API layer across multiple device types. You can create a single app package that can be uploaded to a single store to be distributed to reach all the device types your app can run on. These devices include Windows 10, Windows 10 Mobile, Xbox One, and Microsoft HoloLens.

Windows 10 Fall Creators Update, released on October 17, 2017, includes UWP 6.0, which is built on a custom-forked implementation of .NET Core 2.0.

XAML and UWP provide layout panels that adapt how they display their child controls to make the most of the device they are currently running on. It is the Windows app equivalent of web page responsive design.

XAML and UWP provide visual state triggers to alter the layout based on dynamic changes, such as the horizontal or vertical orientation of a tablet.

UWP provides standard mechanisms to detect the capabilities of the current device, and then activate additional features of your app to fully take advantage of them.

## Understanding Fluent Design System

Microsoft's Fluent Design System will be delivered in multiple waves, rather than as a "Big Bang" all in one go, to help developers slowly migrate from traditional styles of user interface to more modern ones.

Wave 1, available in Windows 10 Fall Creators Update, includes the following features:

- Acrylic material
- Connected animations
- Parallax views
- Reveal lighting

## Filling user interface elements with acrylic brushes

Acrylic material is a semi-transparent blur-effect brush that can be used to fill user interface elements to add depth and perspective to your apps. Acrylic can show through what is in the background behind the app, or elements within the app that are behind a pane. Acrylic material can be customized with varying colors and transparencies.

Learn about how and when to use Acrylic material at the following link: `https://docs.microsoft.com/en-gb/windows/uwp/style/acrylic`

## Connecting user interface elements with animations

When navigating around a user interface, animating elements to draw connections between screens helps users to understand where they are and how to interact with your app.

Learn about how and when to use Connected animations at the following link: `https://docs.microsoft.com/en-gb/windows/uwp/style/connected-animation`

## Parallax views and Reveal lighting

Parallax views give your apps a modern feel, and Reveal lighting helps the user understand what is an interactive element by *lighting up* the user interface to draw their focus as they move around it.

Learn about how and when to use Reveal to bring focus to user interface elements at the following link: `https://docs.microsoft.com/en-gb/windows/uwp/style/reveal`

# Understanding XAML Standard 1.0

In 2006, Microsoft released **Windows Presentation Foundation** (**WPF**), which was the first technology to use XAML. WPF is still used today to create Windows desktop applications, for example, Microsoft Visual Studio 2017 is a WPF application.

**XAML** can be used to create these:

- **Windows Store apps** for Windows 10, Windows 10 Mobile, Xbox One, and Microsoft HoloLens
- **WPF applications** for the Windows desktop, including Windows 7 and later

In a similar fashion to .NET, XAML has fragmented, with slight variations in capabilities between XAML for different platforms. So just as .NET Standard 2.0 is an initiative to bring various platforms of .NET together, XAML Standard 1.0 is an initiative to do the same for XAML.

## Simplifying code using XAML

XAML simplifies C# code, especially when building a user interface.

Imagine that you need two or more buttons laid out horizontally to create a toolbar. In C#, you might write this code:

```
var toolbar = new StackPanel();
toolbar.Orientation = Orientation.Horizontal;
var newButton = new Button();
newButton.Content = "New";
newButton.Background = new SolidColorBrush(Colors.Pink);
toolbar.Children.Add(newButton);
var openButton = new Button();
openButton.Content = "Open";
openButton.Background = new SolidColorBrush(Colors.Pink);
toolbar.Children.Add(openButton);
```

In XAML, this could be simplified to the following lines of code. When this XAML is processed, the equivalent properties are set, and methods are called to achieve the same goal as the preceding C# code:

```
<StackPanel Name="toolbar" Orientation="Horizontal">
  <Button Name="newButton" Background="Pink">New</Button>
  <Button Name="OpenButton" Background="Pink">Open</Button>
</StackPanel>
```

XAML is an alternative (better) way of declaring and instantiating .NET types.

## Choosing common controls

There are lots of predefined controls that you can choose from for common user interface scenarios. Almost all versions of XAML support these controls:

| Controls | Description |
|---|---|
| `Button`, `Menu`, `Toolbar` | Executing actions |
| `CheckBox`, `RadioButton` | Choosing options |
| `Calendar`, `DatePicker` | Choosing dates |
| `ComboBox`, `ListBox`, `ListView`, `TreeView` | Choosing items from lists and hierarchical trees |
| `Canvas`, `DockPanel`, `Grid`, `StackPanel`, `WrapPanel` | Layout containers that affect their children in different ways |
| `Label`, `TextBlock` | Displaying read-only text |
| `RichTextBox`, `TextBox` | Editing text |
| `Image`, `MediaElement` | Embedding images, videos, and audio files |
| `DataGrid` | Viewing and editing bound data |
| `Scrollbar`, `Slider`, `StatusBar` | Miscellaneous user interface elements |

# Creating a modern Windows app

We will start by creating a simple Windows app, with some common controls and modern features of Fluent Design like acrylic material.

To be able to create apps for UWP, you must enable developer mode in Windows 10.

# Enabling developer mode

Go to **Start** | **Settings** | **Update & Security** | **For developers**, and then click on **Developer mode**, as shown in the following screenshot:

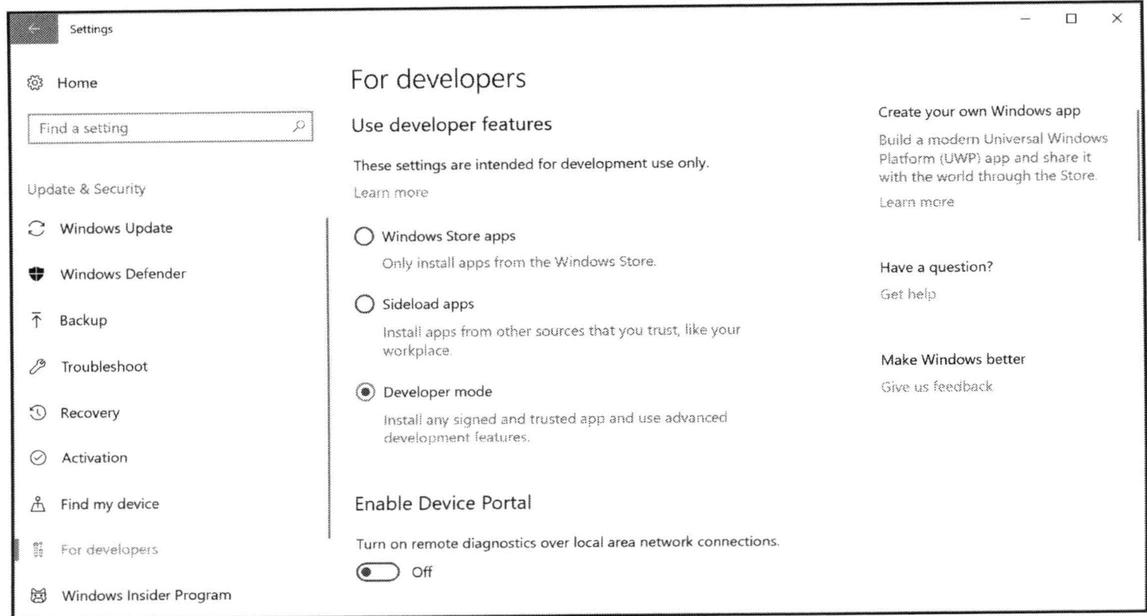


Accept the warning about how it "could expose your device and personal data to security risk or harm your device," and then close the **Settings** app. You might need to restart your PC.

# Creating a UWP project

In Visual Studio 2017, open the `Part3` solution, and choose **File** | **Add** | **New Project...**.

In the **Add New Project** dialog, in the **Installed** list, select **Visual C#** | **Windows Universal**. In the center list, select **Blank App (Universal Windows)**, type the name as `FluentUwpApp`, and then click on **OK**.

In the **New Universal Windows Platform Project** dialog, choose the latest version of Windows 10 for **Target Version** and **Minimum Version**, and click on **OK**, as shown in the following screenshot:

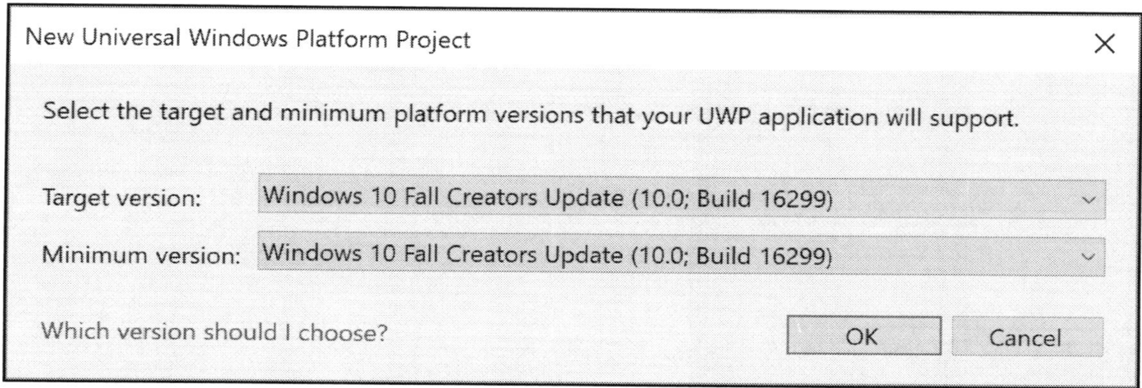

**Good Practice**
Developers writing UWP apps for a general audience should choose one of the latest builds of Windows 10 for **Minimum Version**. Developers writing enterprise apps should choose an older **Minimum Version**. Build 10240 was released in July 2015 and is a good choice for maximum compatibility, but you will not have access to modern features such as Fluent Design System.

In the **Solution Explorer** window, double-click on the **MainPage.xaml** file to open it for editing. You will see the XAML design window showing a graphical view and a XAML view. You will be able to make the following observations:

- The XAML designer is split horizontally, but you can toggle to a vertical split and collapse one side by clicking on the buttons on the right edge of the divider
- You can swap views by clicking on the double-arrow button in the divider

- You can scroll and zoom in both views:

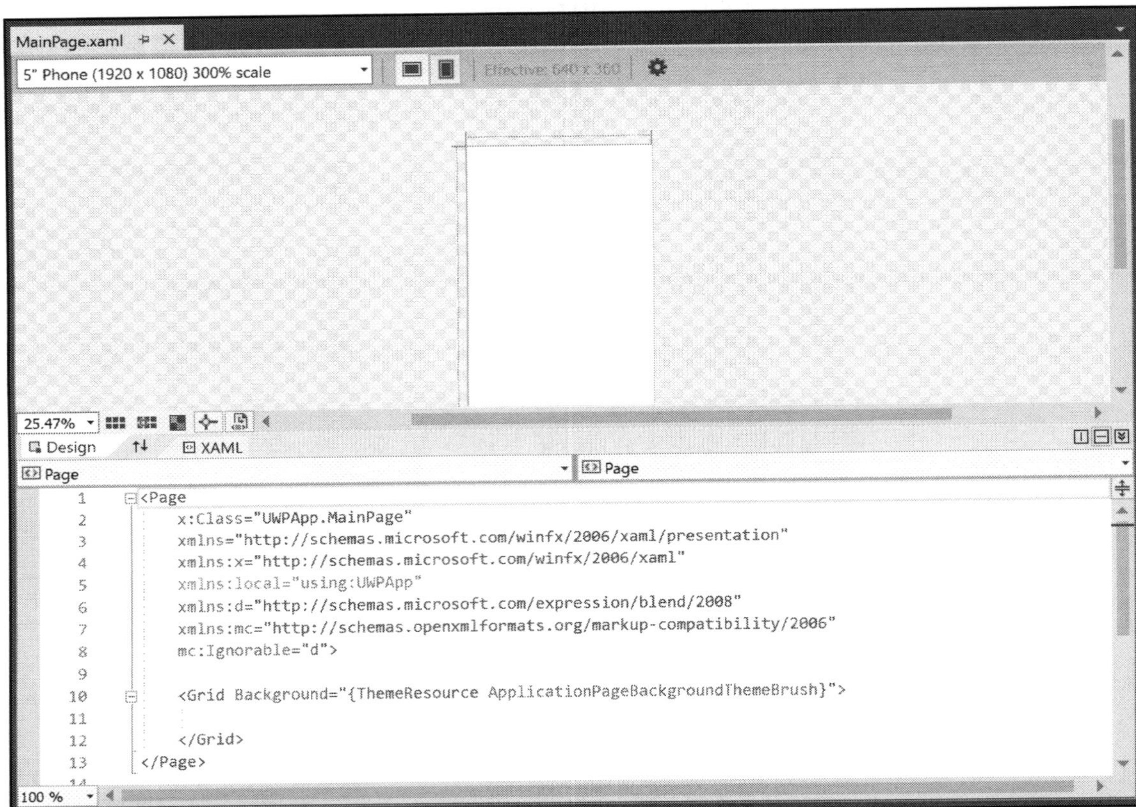

Change the zoom to 100%. Navigate to **View** | **Toolbox** or press *Ctrl* + *W*, *X*. Note that the toolbox has sections for **Common XAML Controls**, **All XAML Controls**, and **General**. At the top of the toolbox is a search box.

Enter the letters `bu`, and note that the list of controls is filtered.

Drag and drop the **Button** control from the toolbox onto the **Design** view. Resize it by clicking, holding, and dragging any of the eight square resize handles on each edge and in each corner. Note that the button is given a fixed width and height, and fixed left (30 units) and top (40 units) margins, to position and size it absolutely inside the grid, as shown in the following screenshot:

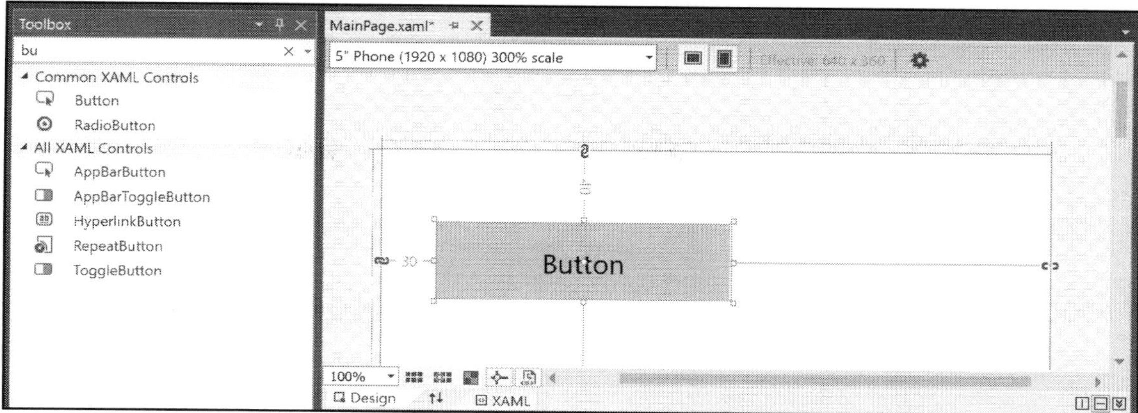


Although you can drag and drop controls, it is better to use the XAML view for layout so that you can position items relatively and implement more of a responsive design.

In the XAML view, find the `Button` element and delete it.

In the XAML view, inside the `Grid` element, enter the following markup:

```
<Button Margin="6" Padding="6" Name="clickMeButton">
  Click Me
</Button>
```

Change the zoom to 50%, and note that the button is automatically sized to its content, `Click Me`, aligned vertically in the center and aligned horizontally to the left, even if you toggle between vertical and horizontal phone layouts, as shown in the following screenshot:

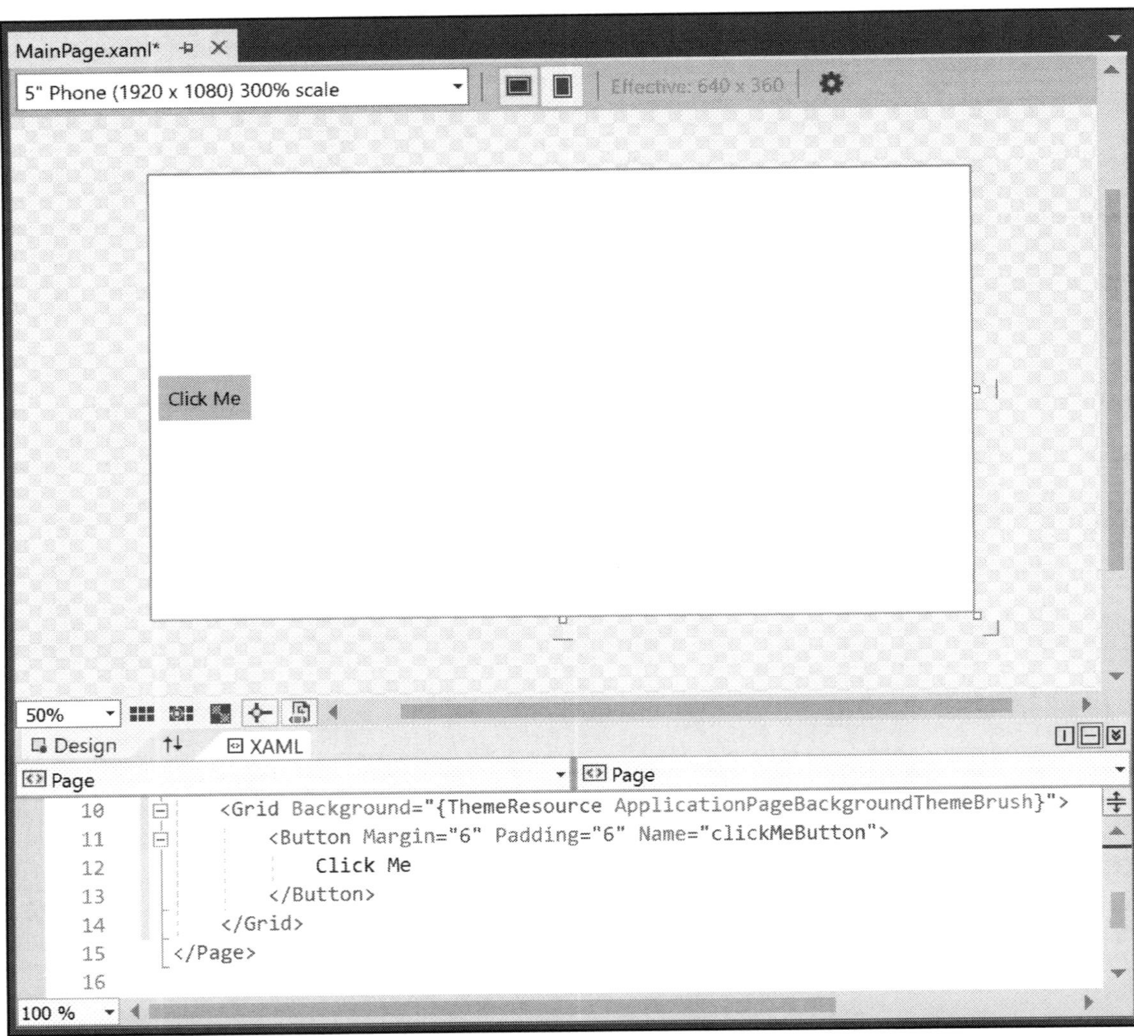

Modify the XAML to wrap the `Button` element inside a horizontally-orientated `StackPanel` with a light-gray background, that is inside a vertically orientated (by default) `StackPanel`, and note the change in its layout to be in the top-left of the available space:

```
<StackPanel>
  <StackPanel Orientation="Horizontal" Padding="4"
              Background="LightGray" Name="toolbar">
    <Button Margin="6" Padding="6" Name="clickMeButton">
      Click Me
    </Button>
  </StackPanel>
</StackPanel>
```

Modify the `Button` element to give it a new event handler for its `Click` event. When you see the IntelliSense showing `<New Event Handler>`, press *Enter*, as shown in the following screenshot:

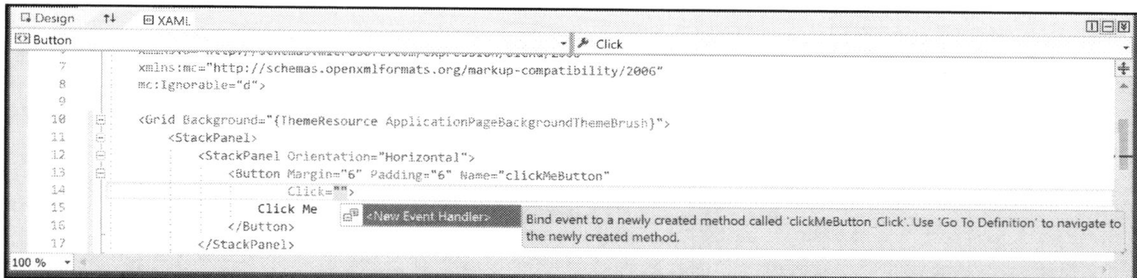


Navigate to **View** | **Code**, or press *F7*.

In the `MainPage.xaml.cs` file, add a statement to the event handler that sets the content of the button to the current time, as shown highlighted in the following code:

```
private void clickMeButton_Click(object sender, RoutedEventArgs e)
{
   clickMeButton.Content = DateTime.Now.ToString("hh:mm:ss");
}
```

Navigate to **Build** | **Configuration Manager...**, for the **FluentUwpApp** project, select the **Build** and **Deploy** checkboxes, select **Platform** of **x64**, and then select **Close**, as shown in the following screenshot:

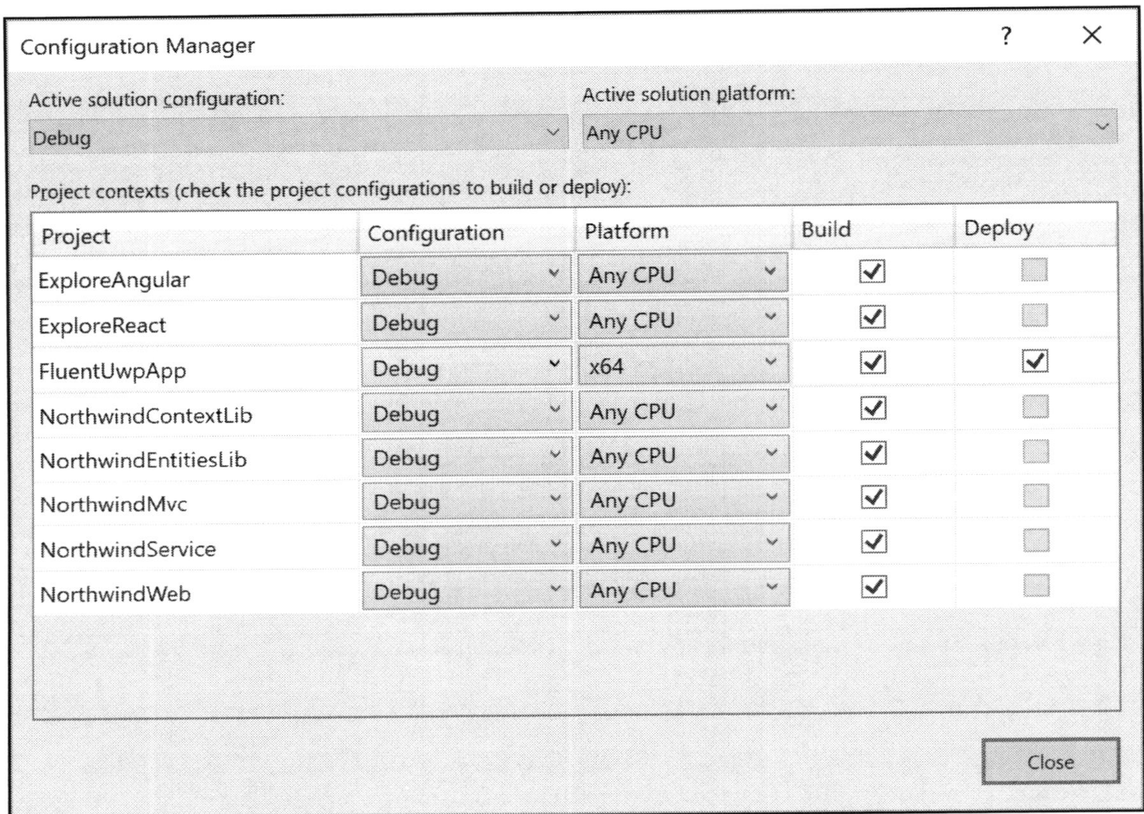

Run the application by navigating to **Debug** | **Start Without Debugging**, or pressing *Ctrl* + *F5*.

Click on the **Click Me** button.

Every time you click on the button, the button's content changes to show the current time.

# Exploring common controls and acrylic brushes

Open `MainPage.xaml`, set the grid's background to use the acrylic system window brush, and add some elements to the stack panel after the button for the user to enter their name and toggle acrylic material, as shown highlighted in the following markup:

```
<Grid Background="{ThemeResource SystemControlAcrylicWindowBrush}">
  <StackPanel>
    <StackPanel Orientation="Horizontal" Padding="4"
                Background="LightGray" Name="toolbar">
      <Button Margin="6" Padding="6" Name="clickMeButton"
              Click="clickMeButton_Click">
        Click Me
      </Button>
      <TextBlock Text="First name:"
                 VerticalAlignment="Center" Margin="4" />
      <TextBox PlaceholderText="Enter your name"
               VerticalAlignment="Center" Width="200" />
      <CheckBox IsChecked="True" Content="Enable acrylic background"
                Margin="20,0,0,0" Name="enableAcrylic" />
    </StackPanel>
  </StackPanel>
</Grid>
```

Run the application by navigating to **Debug** | **Start Without Debugging**, or pressing *Ctrl* + *F5*, and note the user interface, including the tinted acrylic material showing the orange rocks and blue sky through the app window background, as shown in the following screenshot:

Acrylic uses a lot of system resources, so if an app loses the focus, or your device is low on battery, then acrylic is disabled automatically.

# Exploring Reveal

Reveal is built in to some controls, such as `ListView` and `NavigationView`, that you will see later. For other controls, you can enable it by applying a theme style.

Open `MainPage.xaml`, add a new horizontal stack panel under the one used as a toolbar, and add a grid with buttons to define a calculator, as shown in the following markup:

```
<StackPanel Orientation="Horizontal">
  <Grid Background="DarkGray" Margin="10"
        Padding="5" Name="gridCalculator">
    <Grid.ColumnDefinitions>
      <ColumnDefinition/>
      <ColumnDefinition/>
      <ColumnDefinition/>
      <ColumnDefinition/>
    </Grid.ColumnDefinitions>
    <Grid.RowDefinitions>
      <RowDefinition/>
      <RowDefinition/>
      <RowDefinition/>
      <RowDefinition/>
    </Grid.RowDefinitions>
    <Button Grid.Row="0" Grid.Column="0" Content="X" />
    <Button Grid.Row="0" Grid.Column="1" Content="/" />
    <Button Grid.Row="0" Grid.Column="2" Content="+" />
    <Button Grid.Row="0" Grid.Column="3" Content="-" />
    <Button Grid.Row="1" Grid.Column="0" Content="7" />
    <Button Grid.Row="1" Grid.Column="1" Content="8" />
    <Button Grid.Row="1" Grid.Column="2" Content="9" />
    <Button Grid.Row="1" Grid.Column="3" Content="0" />
    <Button Grid.Row="2" Grid.Column="0" Content="4" />
    <Button Grid.Row="2" Grid.Column="1" Content="5" />
    <Button Grid.Row="2" Grid.Column="2" Content="6" />
    <Button Grid.Row="2" Grid.Column="3" Content="." />
    <Button Grid.Row="3" Grid.Column="0" Content="1" />
    <Button Grid.Row="3" Grid.Column="1" Content="2" />
    <Button Grid.Row="3" Grid.Column="2" Content="3" />
    <Button Grid.Row="3" Grid.Column="3" Content="=" />
  </Grid>
</StackPanel>
```

In the `Page` element, add an event handler for `Loaded`, as shown highlighted in the following markup:

```
<Page
  x:Class="FluentUwpApp.MainPage"
  xmlns="http://schemas.microsoft.com/winfx/2006/xaml/presentation"
  xmlns:x="http://schemas.microsoft.com/winfx/2006/xaml"
  xmlns:local="using:FluentUwpApp"
  xmlns:d="http://schemas.microsoft.com/expression/blend/2008"
  xmlns:mc="http://schemas.openxmlformats.org/markup-compatibility/2006"
```

```
    mc:Ignorable="d"
    Loaded="Page_Loaded">
```

In `MainPage.xaml.cs`, add statements to the `Page_Loaded` method to loop through all of the calculator buttons, setting them to be the same size, and apply the Reveal style, as shown in the following code:

```
private void Page_Loaded(object sender, RoutedEventArgs e)
{
   foreach (Button b in gridCalculator.Children.OfType<Button>())
   {
      b.FontSize = 24;
      b.Width = 54;
      b.Height = 54;
      b.Style = Resources.ThemeDictionaries["ButtonRevealStyle"] as Style;
   }
}
```

Run the application by navigating to **Debug** | **Start Without Debugging**, or pressing *Ctrl* + *F5*, and note the calculator starts with a flat gray user interface, as shown in the following screenshot:

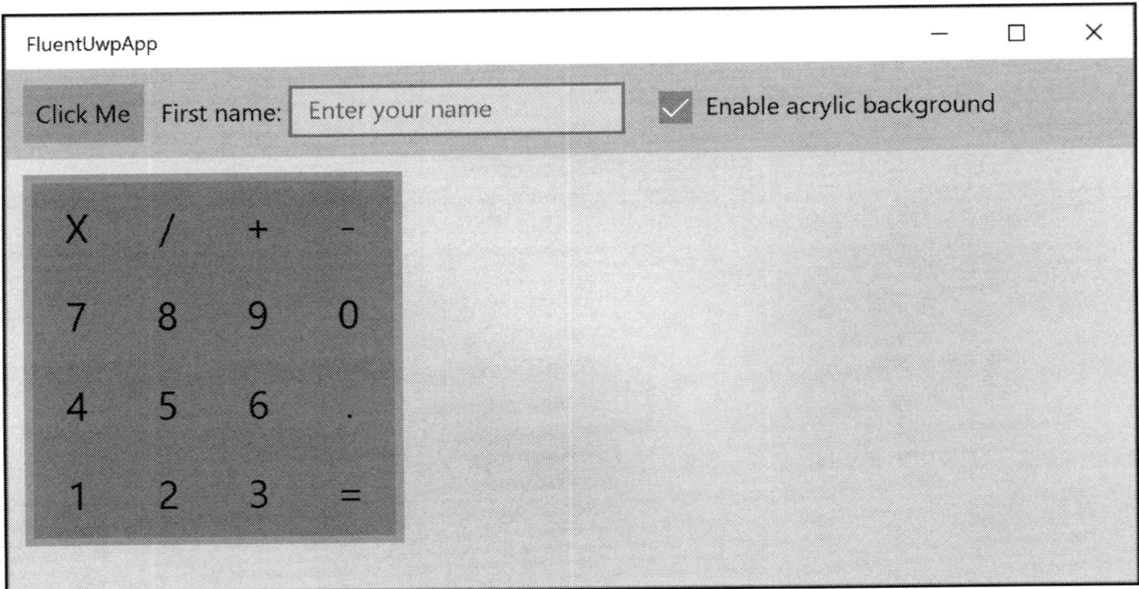

When the user moves their mouse pointer over the calculator, Reveal lights it up, as shown in the following screenshot:

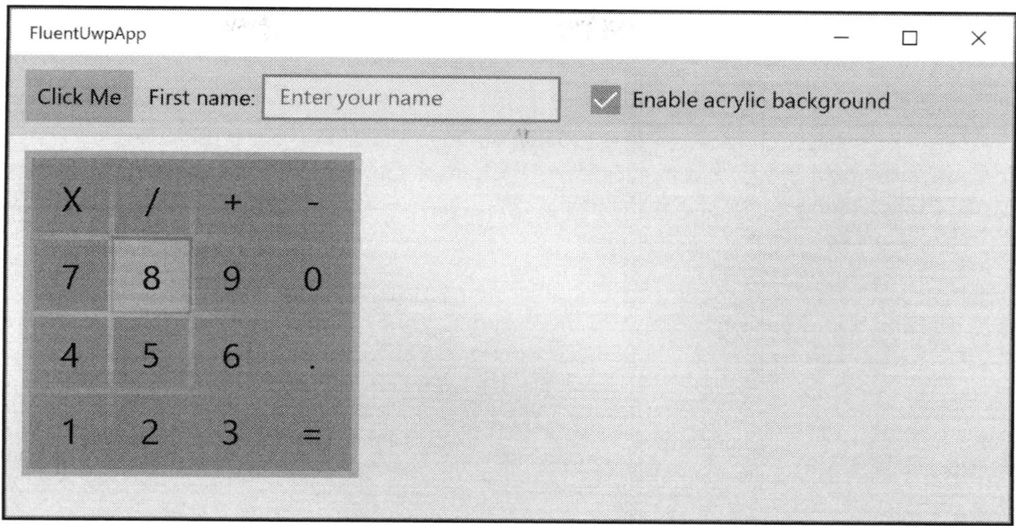


## Installing more controls

In addition to dozens of built-in controls, you can install additional ones as NuGet packages. One of the best is the UWP Community Toolkit, which you can read more about at the following link:

`http://www.uwpcommunitytoolkit.com/`

In the **FluentUwpApp** project, right-click on **References**, and select **Manage NuGet Packages....** Click on **Browse**, search for `Microsoft.Toolkit.Uwp.UI.Controls`, and click on **Install**, as shown in the following screenshot:

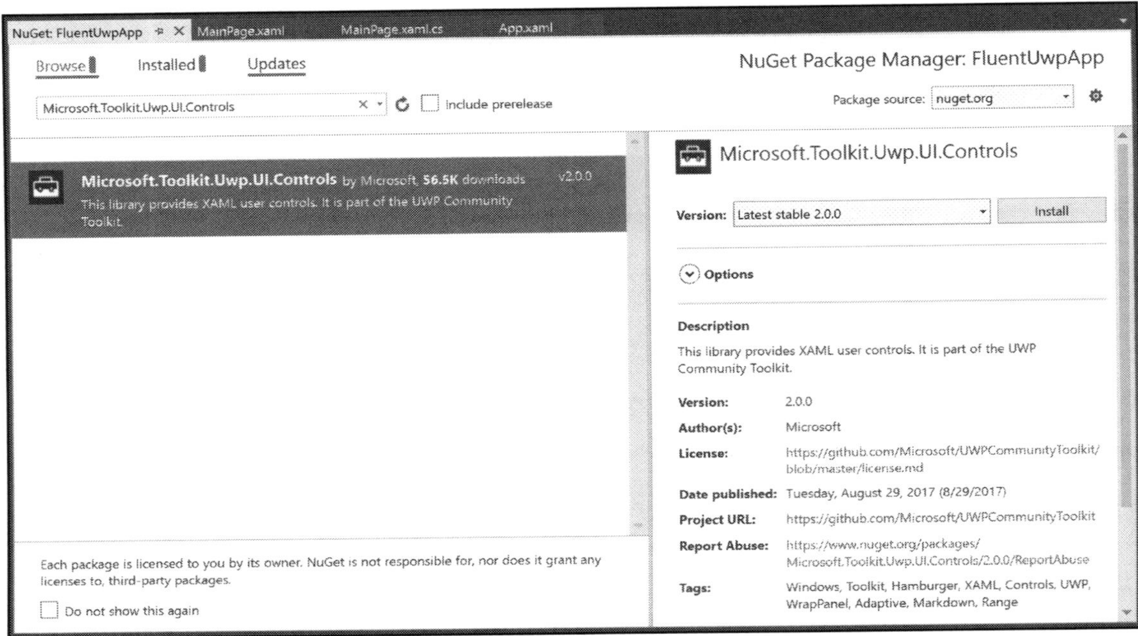


Review the changes and accept the license agreement.

Open `MainPage.xaml`, and in the `Page` element, import the toolkit namespace as a prefix named `kit`, as shown in the following markup:

```
<Page
  x:Class="FluentUwpApp.MainPage"
  xmlns="http://schemas.microsoft.com/winfx/2006/xaml/presentation"
  xmlns:x="http://schemas.microsoft.com/winfx/2006/xaml"
  xmlns:local="using:FluentUwpApp"
  xmlns:d="http://schemas.microsoft.com/expression/blend/2008"
  xmlns:mc="http://schemas.openxmlformats.org/markup-compatibility/2006"
  xmlns:kit="using:Microsoft.Toolkit.Uwp.UI.Controls"
  mc:Ignorable="d"
  Loaded="Page_Loaded">
```

After the calculator grid, add a textbox and a markdown text block, as shown in the following markup:

```
<TextBox Name="markdownSource" Text="# Welcome"
         Header="Enter some Markdown text:"
         VerticalAlignment="Stretch" Margin="5"
         AcceptsReturn="True" />
<kit:MarkdownTextBlock
         Text="{Binding ElementName=markdownSource, Path=Text}"
         VerticalAlignment="Stretch"
         HorizontalAlignment="Stretch" Margin="5"/>
```

Run the application by navigating to **Debug** | **Start Without Debugging**, or pressing *Ctrl* + *F5*, and note that the user can enter Markdown syntax in the textbox, and it is rendered in the Markdown text block, as shown in the following screenshot:

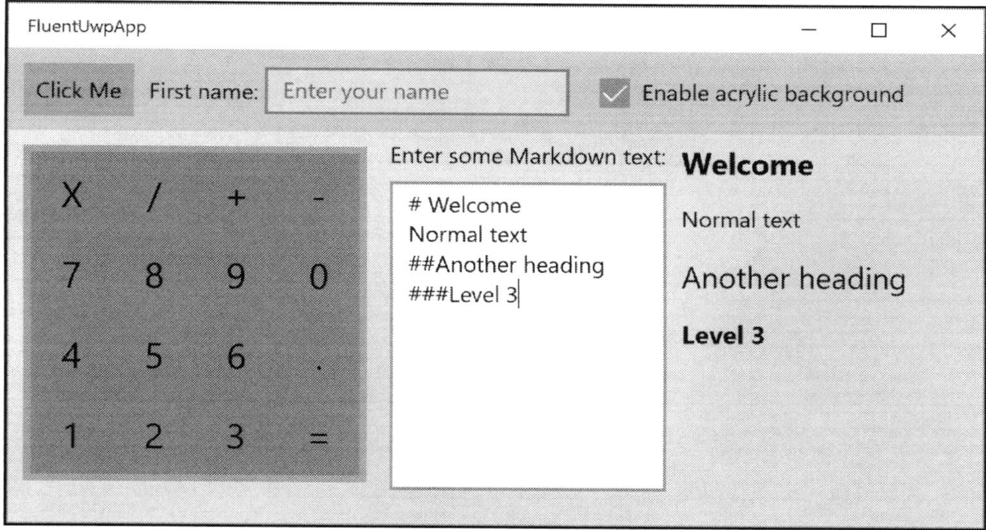


The UWP Community Toolkit includes dozens of controls, animations, extensions, and services.

# Using resources and templates

When building graphical user interfaces, you will often want to use a resource, such as a brush, to paint the background of controls. These resources can be defined in a single place and shared throughout the app.

## Sharing resources

In **Solution Explorer**, double-click on the **App.xaml** file, as shown in the following screenshot:

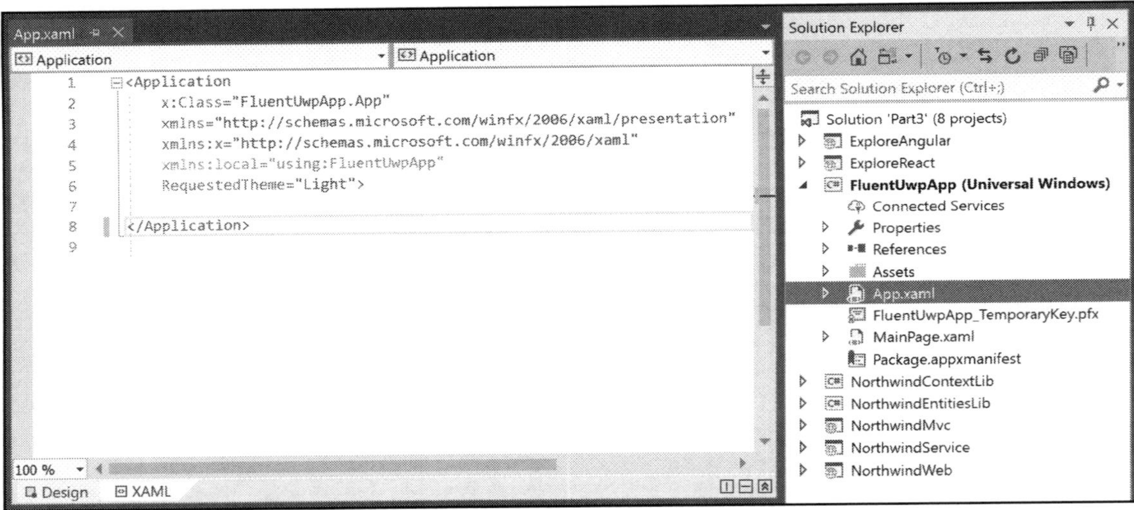


Add the following markup inside the existing `<Application>` element:

```
<Application.Resources>
  <LinearGradientBrush x:Key="rainbow">
    <GradientStop Color="Red" Offset="0" />
    <GradientStop Color="Orange" Offset="0.1" />
    <GradientStop Color="Yellow" Offset="0.3" />
    <GradientStop Color="Green" Offset="0.5" />
    <GradientStop Color="Blue" Offset="0.7" />
    <GradientStop Color="Indigo" Offset="0.9" />
    <GradientStop Color="Violet" Offset="1" />
  </LinearGradientBrush>
</Application.Resources>
```

In the `MainPage.xaml` file, modify the toolbar `StackPanel` element to have its background set to the `rainbow` brush that you just defined, as shown in the following markup:

```
<StackPanel Orientation="Horizontal" Padding="4"
            Background="{StaticResource rainbow}" Name="toolbar">
```

Design view will show your `rainbow` resource and the built-in resources in IntelliSense, as shown in the following screenshot:

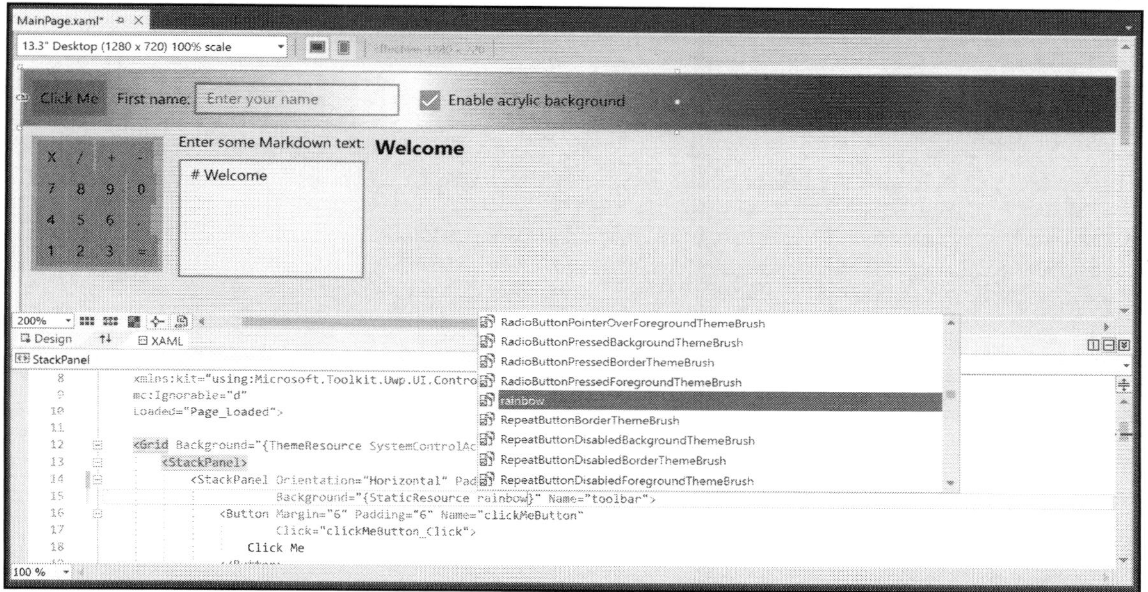

**Good Practice**
A resource can be an instance of any object. To share it within an application, define it in the `App.xaml` file and give it a unique key. To set an element's property to apply the resource, use `StaticResource` with the key.

Resources can be defined and stored inside any element of XAML, not just at the app level. So, for example, if a resource is only needed on `MainPage`, it can be defined there. You can also dynamically load XAML files at runtime.

# Replacing a control template

You can redefine how a control looks by replacing its default template. The default control template for a button is flat and transparent.

One of the most common resources is a style that can set multiple properties at once. If a style has a unique key then it must be explicitly set, like we did earlier with the linear gradient. If it doesn't have a key then it will be automatically applied based on the `TargetType` property.

In the `App.xaml` file, add the following markup inside the `<Application.Resources>` element, and note that the `<Style>` element will automatically set the `Template` property of all controls that are `TargetType`, that is, buttons, to use the defined control template.

```
<ControlTemplate x:Key="DarkGlassButton" TargetType="Button">
  <Border BorderBrush="#FFFFFFFF"
          BorderThickness="1,1,1,1" CornerRadius="4,4,4,4">
    <Border x:Name="border" Background="#7F000000"
            BorderBrush="#FF000000" BorderThickness="1,1,1,1"
            CornerRadius="4,4,4,4">
      <Grid>
        <Grid.RowDefinitions>
          <RowDefinition Height="*"/>
          <RowDefinition Height="*"/>
        </Grid.RowDefinitions>
        <Border Opacity="0" HorizontalAlignment="Stretch"
                x:Name="glow" Width="Auto" Grid.RowSpan="2"
                CornerRadius="4,4,4,4">
        </Border>
        <ContentPresenter HorizontalAlignment="Center"
                          VerticalAlignment="Center" Width="Auto"
                          Grid.RowSpan="2" Padding="4"/>
        <Border HorizontalAlignment="Stretch" Margin="0,0,0,0"
                x:Name="shine" Width="Auto"
                CornerRadius="4,4,0,0">
          <Border.Background>
            <LinearGradientBrush EndPoint="0.5,0.9"
                                 StartPoint="0.5,0.03">
              <GradientStop Color="#99FFFFFF" Offset="0"/>
              <GradientStop Color="#33FFFFFF" Offset="1"/>
            </LinearGradientBrush>
          </Border.Background>
        </Border>
      </Grid>
    </Border>
  </Border>
</ControlTemplate>
```

```
<Style TargetType="Button">
  <Setter Property="Template"
          Value="{StaticResource DarkGlassButton}" />
  <Setter Property="Foreground" Value="White" />
</Style>
```

Rerun the application and view the results. Note the *black glass* effect on the button in the toolbar, as shown in the following screenshot:

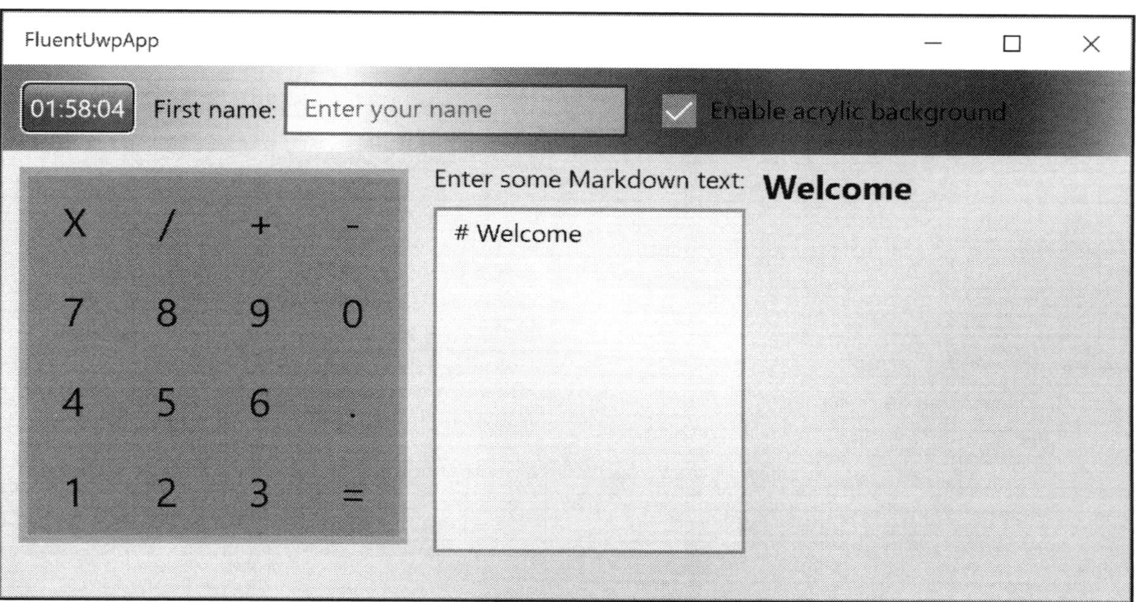

The calculator buttons are not affected at runtime by this *black glass* effect because we replace their styles using code after the page has loaded.

# Data binding

When building graphical user interfaces, you will often want to bind a property of one control to another or to some data.

## Binding to elements

In the `MainPage.xaml` file, add a text block for instructions, a slider for selecting a rotation, a grid containing stack panel and text blocks to show the selected rotation in degrees, a radial gauge from the UWP Community Toolkit, and a red square to rotate, as shown in the following markup:

```
<TextBlock Grid.ColumnSpan="2" Margin="10">
  Use the slider to rotate the square:</TextBlock>
<Slider Value="180" Minimum="0" Maximum="360"
        Name="sliderRotation" Margin="10,0" />
<Grid>
  <Grid.ColumnDefinitions>
    <ColumnDefinition/>
    <ColumnDefinition/>
    <ColumnDefinition/>
  </Grid.ColumnDefinitions>
  <StackPanel Orientation="Horizontal"
              VerticalAlignment="Center"
              HorizontalAlignment="Center">
    <TextBlock
    Text="{Binding ElementName=sliderRotation, Path=Value}"
               FontSize="30" />
    <TextBlock Text="degrees" FontSize="30" Margin="10,0" />
  </StackPanel>
  <kit:RadialGauge Grid.Column="1" Minimum="0"
                   Maximum="360"
                   Value="{Binding ElementName=sliderRotation,
                   Path=Value}"
                   Height="200" Width="200" />
  <Rectangle Grid.Column="2" Height="100" Width="100" Fill="Red">
    <Rectangle.RenderTransform>
      <RotateTransform
        Angle="{Binding ElementName=sliderRotation, Path=Value}" />
      </Rectangle.RenderTransform>
  </Rectangle>
</Grid>
```

Note that the text of the text block, the value of the radial gauge, and the angle of the rotation transform are all data bound to the slider's value.

Run the app, and click, hold, and drag the slider to rotate the red square, as shown in the following screenshot:

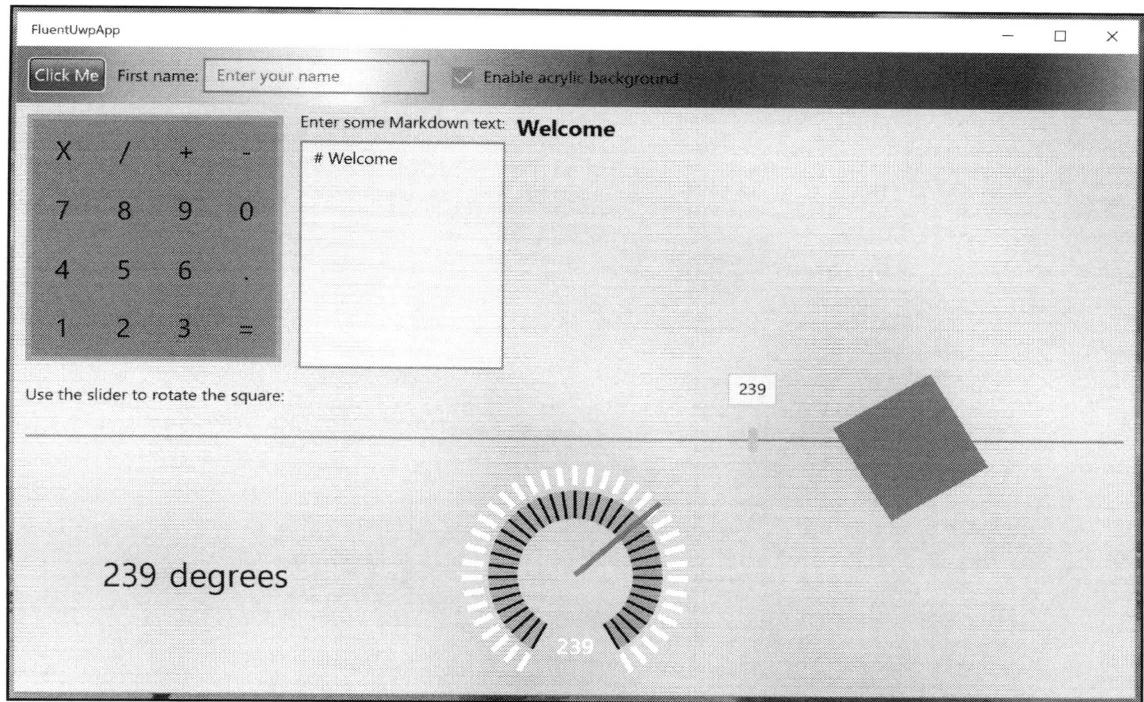


# Binding to data sources

To illustrate binding to data sources, we will create an app for the `Northwind` database that shows categories and products.

## Modifying the NorthwindService

Open the `Part3` solution, and expand the **NorthwindService** project.

In the **Controllers** folder, right-click and choose **Add | New Item...**, select **Web API Controller Class**, name it as `CategoriesController.cs`, and modify it to have two `HttpGet` methods that use the `Northwind` database context to retrieve all categories, or a single category using its ID, as shown in the following code:

```
using Microsoft.AspNetCore.Mvc;
using Packt.CS7;
using System.Collections.Generic;
using System.Linq;

namespace NorthwindService.Controllers
{
   [Route("api/[controller]")]
   public class CategoriesController : Controller
   {
      private readonly Northwind db;

      public CategoriesController(Northwind db)
      {
         this.db = db;
      }

      // GET: api/categories
      [HttpGet]
      public IEnumerable<Category> Get()
      {
         var categories = db.Categories.ToArray();
         return categories;
      }

      // GET api/categories/5
      [HttpGet("{id}")]
      public Category Get(int id)
      {
         var category = db.Categories.Find(id);
         return category;
      }
   }
}
```

In the **Controllers** folder, right-click and choose **Add** | **New Item...**, select **Web API Controller Class**, name it as `ProductsController.cs`, and modify it to have two `HttpGet` methods that use the `Northwind` database context to retrieve all products, or the products in a category using the category ID, as shown in the following code:

```
using Microsoft.AspNetCore.Mvc;
using Packt.CS7;
using System.Collections.Generic;
using System.Linq;

namespace NorthwindService.Controllers
{
   [Route("api/[controller]")]
   public class ProductsController : Controller
   {
      private readonly Northwind db;

      public ProductsController(Northwind db)
      {
         this.db = db;
      }

      // GET: api/products
      [HttpGet]
      public IEnumerable<Product> Get()
      {
         var products = db.Products.ToArray();
         return products;
      }

      // GET api/products/5
      [HttpGet("{id}")]
      public IEnumerable<Product> GetByCategory(int id)
      {
         var products = db.Products.Where(
             p => p.CategoryID == id).ToArray();
             return products;
      }
   }
}
```

Test `NorthwindService` by entering the relative URL `/api/products/1`, and ensuring the service returns only beverages.

## Creating the Northwind app

Open the `Part3` solution, and choose **File** | **Add** | **New Project....**

In the **New Project** dialog, in the **Installed** list, select **Visual C#** | **Windows Universal**. In the center list, select **Blank App (Universal Windows)**, type the location as `C:\Code\Part3\`, type the name as `NorthwindFluent`, and click on **OK**.

Select the latest Windows 10 build for both **Target Version** and **Minimum Version**.

In the `NorthwindFluent` project, add a **Blank Page** item named `NotImplementedPage`, and, inside the existing `Grid` element, add a text block saying, `"Not yet implemented"`, centered on the page, as shown in the following markup:

```
<Grid Background="{ThemeResource ApplicationPageBackgroundThemeBrush}">
  <TextBlock Text="Not yet implemented." VerticalAlignment="Center"
             HorizontalAlignment="Center" FontSize="20" />
</Grid>
```

In the `NorthwindFluent` project, add a reference to the `NorthwindEntities` project.

In the `NorthwindFluent` project, add some images to the `Assets` folder, named like this:

- `categories.jpeg`
- `category1-small.jpeg`
- `category2-small.jpeg`, and so on.

In the `NorthwindFluent` project, add a class named `CategoriesViewModel`, and populate its `Categories` property using the `Northwind` database context, as shown in the following markup:

```
using Packt.CS7;
using System;
using System.Collections.Generic;
using System.Collections.ObjectModel;
using System.Linq;
using System.Net.Http;
using System.Runtime.Serialization.Json;

namespace NorthwindFluent
{
   public class CategoriesViewModel
   {
      public class CategoryJson
      {
         public int categoryID;
```

```
            public string categoryName;
            public string description;
        }

        public ObservableCollection<Category> Categories { get; set; }

        public CategoriesViewModel()
        {
            using (var http = new HttpClient())
            {
                http.BaseAddress = new Uri("http://localhost:5001/");

                var serializer = new
                DataContractJsonSerializer(typeof(List<CategoryJson>));

                var stream = http.GetStreamAsync("api/categories").Result;

                var cats = serializer.ReadObject(stream) as List<CategoryJson>;

                var categories = cats.Select(c => new Category
                          { CategoryID = c.categoryID,
                            CategoryName = c.categoryName,
                            Description = c.description });

                Categories = new ObservableCollection<Category>(categories);
            }
        }
    }
}
```

We had to define a class named `CategoryJson` because the `DataContractJsonSerializer` class is not smart enough to understand camel casing used in JSON and convert automatically to title casing used in C#. So the simplest solution is to do the conversion manually using LINQ projection.

In the `NorthwindFluent` project, add a class named `CategoryIDToImageConverter`, implement the `IValueConverter` interface, and convert the integer value for the category ID into a valid path to the appropriate image file, as shown in the following code:

```
using System;
using Windows.UI.Xaml.Data;
using Windows.UI.Xaml.Media.Imaging;

namespace NorthwindFluent
{
    public class CategoryIDToImageConverter : IValueConverter
```

```
    {
        public object Convert(object value, Type targetType,
                      object parameter, string language)
        {
            int n = (int)value;
            string path =
            $"{Environment.CurrentDirectory}/Assets/category{n}-small.jpeg";
            var image = new BitmapImage(new Uri(path));
            return image;
        }

        public object ConvertBack(object value, Type targetType,
                      object parameter, string language)
        {
            throw new NotImplementedException();
        }
    }
}
```

In the `NorthwindFluent` project, add a **Blank Page** item named `CategoriesPage`, as shown in the following markup:

```
<Page
  x:Class="NorthwindFluent.CategoriesPage"
  xmlns="http://schemas.microsoft.com/winfx/2006/xaml/presentation"
  xmlns:x="http://schemas.microsoft.com/winfx/2006/xaml"
  xmlns:local="using:NorthwindFluent"
  xmlns:nw="using:Packt.CS7"
  xmlns:d="http://schemas.microsoft.com/expression/blend/2008"
  xmlns:mc="http://schemas.openxmlformats.org/markup-compatibility/2006"
  mc:Ignorable="d">
  <Page.Resources>
    <local:CategoryIDToImageConverter x:Key="id2image" />
  </Page.Resources>

  <Grid Background="{ThemeResource ApplicationPageBackgroundThemeBrush}">
    <ParallaxView Source="{x:Bind ForegroundElement}" VerticalShift="50">
      <Image x:Name="BackgroundImage" Source="Assets/categories.jpeg"
             Stretch="UniformToFill"/>
    </ParallaxView>
    <ListView x:Name="ForegroundElement"
              ItemsSource="{x:Bind ViewModel.Categories}">
      <ListView.Header>
        <Grid Padding="20"
              Background="{ThemeResource
SystemControlAcrylicElementBrush}">
          <TextBlock Style="{StaticResource TitleTextBlockStyle}"
                     FontSize="24"
```

```
                    VerticalAlignment="Center"
                    Margin="12,0"
                    Text="Categories"/>
      </Grid>
    </ListView.Header>
    <ListView.ItemTemplate>
      <DataTemplate x:DataType="nw:Category">
        <Grid Margin="4">
          <Grid.ColumnDefinitions>
            <ColumnDefinition />
            <ColumnDefinition />
          </Grid.ColumnDefinitions>
          <Image Source="{x:Bind CategoryID,
                 Converter={StaticResource id2image}}"
                 Stretch="UniformToFill" Height="200"
                 Width="300" />
          <StackPanel
                 Background=
                 "{ThemeResource
SystemControlAcrylicElementMediumHighBrush}"
                 Padding="10" Grid.Column="1">
            <TextBlock Text="{x:Bind CategoryName}" FontSize="20" />
            <TextBlock Text="{x:Bind Description}" FontSize="16" />
          </StackPanel>
        </Grid>
      </DataTemplate>
    </ListView.ItemTemplate>
  </ListView>
</Grid>
</Page>
```

Note that the code does the following:

- Imports the `Packt.CS7` namespace using `nw` as the element prefix
- Defines a page resource that instantiates a converter for category IDs to images
- Uses a Parallax view to provide a large image as a scrolling background for the foreground element, which is the list view of categories, so when the list scrolls, the large background image moves slightly too
- Binds the list view to the view model's categories collection
- Gives the list view an in-app acrylic header
- Gives the list view an item template for rendering each category using its name, description, and image based on converting its ID into an image loaded from a path

Open `CategoriesPage.xaml.cs`, and add statements to define a `ViewModel` property, and then set it in the constructor, as shown in the following code:

```
public sealed partial class CategoriesPage : Page
{
   public CategoriesViewModel ViewModel { get; set; }

   public CategoriesPage()
   {
      this.InitializeComponent();
      ViewModel = new CategoriesViewModel();
   }
}
```

Open `MainPage.xaml` and add elements to define a navigation view, that automatically uses the new Acrylic material and Reveal highlight in its pane, as shown in the following markup:

```
<Page
  x:Class="NorthwindFluent.MainPage"
  xmlns="http://schemas.microsoft.com/winfx/2006/xaml/presentation"
  xmlns:x="http://schemas.microsoft.com/winfx/2006/xaml"
  xmlns:local="using:NorthwindFluent"
  xmlns:d="http://schemas.microsoft.com/expression/blend/2008"
  xmlns:mc="http://schemas.openxmlformats.org/markup-compatibility/2006"
  mc:Ignorable="d">

  <NavigationView x:Name="NavView"
                  ItemInvoked="NavView_ItemInvoked"
                  Loaded="NavView_Loaded">

  <NavigationView.AutoSuggestBox>
    <AutoSuggestBox x:Name="ASB" QueryIcon="Find"/>
  </NavigationView.AutoSuggestBox>

  <NavigationView.HeaderTemplate>
    <DataTemplate>
      <Grid>
        <Grid.ColumnDefinitions>
          <ColumnDefinition Width="Auto"/>
          <ColumnDefinition/>
        </Grid.ColumnDefinitions>
        <TextBlock Style="{StaticResource TitleTextBlockStyle}"
                   FontSize="28"
                   VerticalAlignment="Center"
                   Margin="12,0"
                   Text="Northwind Fluent"/>
          <CommandBar Grid.Column="1"
```

```
                        HorizontalAlignment="Right"
                        DefaultLabelPosition="Right"
                        Background=
                   "{ThemeResource SystemControlBackgroundAltHighBrush}">
              <AppBarButton Label="Refresh" Icon="Refresh"
                     Name="RefreshButton" Click="RefreshButton_Click"/>
            </CommandBar>
          </Grid>
        </DataTemplate>
      </NavigationView.HeaderTemplate>

      <Frame x:Name="ContentFrame">
        <Frame.ContentTransitions>
          <TransitionCollection>
            <NavigationThemeTransition/>
          </TransitionCollection>
        </Frame.ContentTransitions>
      </Frame>

    </NavigationView>
  </Page>
```

Open `MainPage.xaml.cs`, and modify its contents, as shown in the following code:

```
using System;
using Windows.UI.Xaml;
using Windows.UI.Xaml.Controls;

namespace NorthwindFluent
{
   public sealed partial class MainPage : Page
   {
      public MainPage()
      {
         this.InitializeComponent();
      }

      private void NavView_Loaded(object sender, RoutedEventArgs e)
      {
         NavView.MenuItems.Add(new NavigationViewItem
         { Content = "Categories",
           Icon = new SymbolIcon(Symbol.BrowsePhotos),
           Tag = "categories" });
         NavView.MenuItems.Add(new NavigationViewItem
         { Content = "Products",
           Icon = new SymbolIcon(Symbol.AllApps),
           Tag = "products" });
         NavView.MenuItems.Add(new NavigationViewItem
```

```
      { Content = "Suppliers",
        Icon = new SymbolIcon(Symbol.Contact2),
        Tag = "suppliers" });
      NavView.MenuItems.Add(new NavigationViewItemSeparator());
      NavView.MenuItems.Add(new NavigationViewItem
      { Content = "Customers",
        Icon = new SymbolIcon(Symbol.People),
        Tag = "customers" });
      NavView.MenuItems.Add(new NavigationViewItem
      { Content = "Orders",
        Icon = new SymbolIcon(Symbol.PhoneBook),
        Tag = "orders" });
      NavView.MenuItems.Add(new NavigationViewItem
      { Content = "Shippers",
        Icon = new SymbolIcon(Symbol.PostUpdate),
        Tag = "shippers" });
  }

  private void NavView_ItemInvoked(
    NavigationView sender, NavigationViewItemInvokedEventArgs args)
  {
      switch (args.InvokedItem.ToString())
      {
          case "Categories":
                 ContentFrame.Navigate(typeof(CategoriesPage));
                 break;

          default:
                ContentFrame.Navigate(typeof(NotImplementedPage));
                break;
      }
  }

  private async void RefreshButton_Click(
          object sender, RoutedEventArgs e)
  {
      var notImplementedDialog = new ContentDialog
      {
          Title = "Not implemented",
          Content =
              "The Refresh functionality has not yet been implemented.",
              CloseButtonText = "OK"
      };
```

```
            ContentDialogResult result =
                        await notImplementedDialog.ShowAsync();
        }
    }
}
```

The **Refresh** button has not yet been implemented, so we can display a dialog. Like most APIs in UWP, the method to show a dialog is asynchronous.

We can use the `await` keyword for any `Task`. This means that the main thread will not be blocked while we wait, but will remember its current position within the statements so that, once the `Task` has completed, the main thread continues executing from that same point. This allows us to write code that looks as simple as synchronous, but underneath it is much more complex.

Internally, `await` creates a state machine to manage the complexity of passing state between any worker threads and the user interface thread.

Note that, to use the `await` keyword, we must mark the `await` containing method with the `async` keyword. They always work as a pair.

Make sure that the web service is running and that you have configured the `NorthwindFluent` app to deploy, and then run the application by navigating to **Debug | Start Without Debugging**, or pressing *Ctrl* + *F5*.

Resize the window to show its responsive design, as explained in the following bullets:

- When narrow, the navigation hides and the user must click on the hamburger menu to show the navigation pane
- When mid-width, the navigation is thin and only shows the icons, and has a non-acrylic background
- When wide, the navigation shows with an acrylic background

As you move your mouse over the navigation, note the Reveal lighting, and when you click on a menu item, such as **Orders**, the highlight bar stretches and animates as it moves, and the **Not yet implemented** message appears, as shown in the following screenshot:

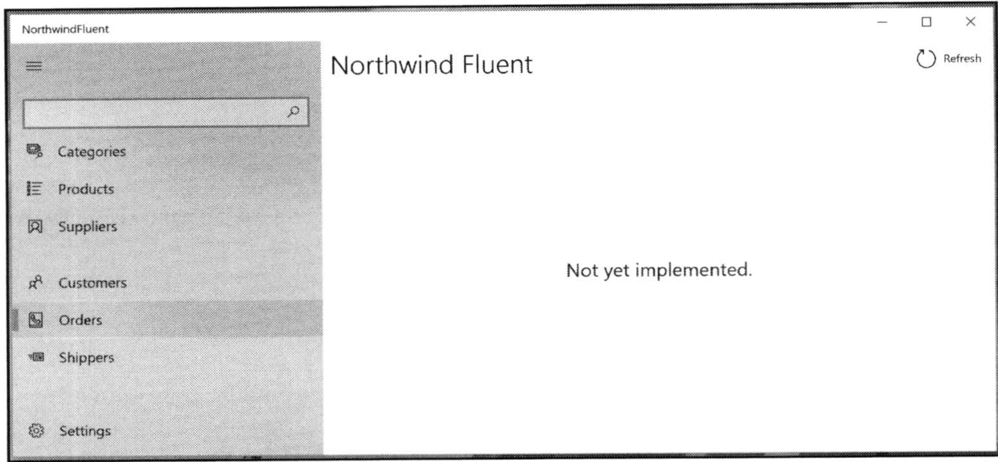


Click on **Categories**, and note the in-app acrylic of the **Categories** header, and the Parallax effect on the background image when scrolling up and down the list of categories, as shown in the following screenshot:

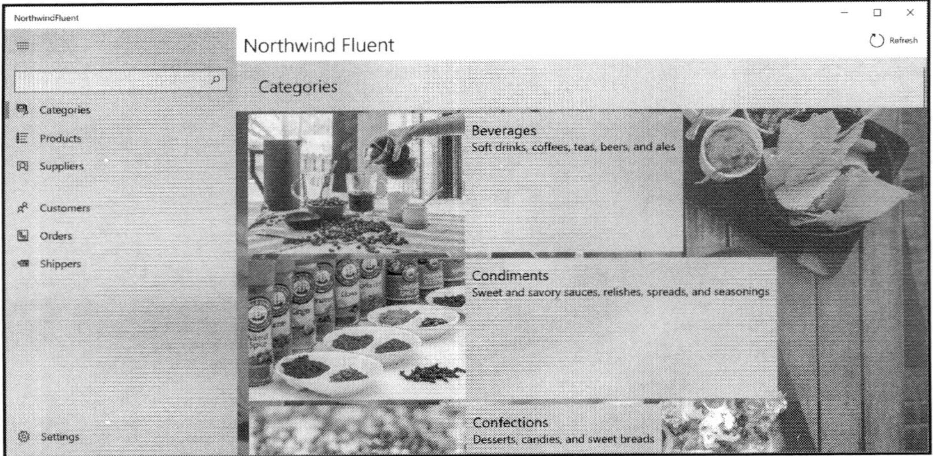

Click on the hamburger menu to collapse the navigation view and give more space for the categories list, as shown in the following screenshot:

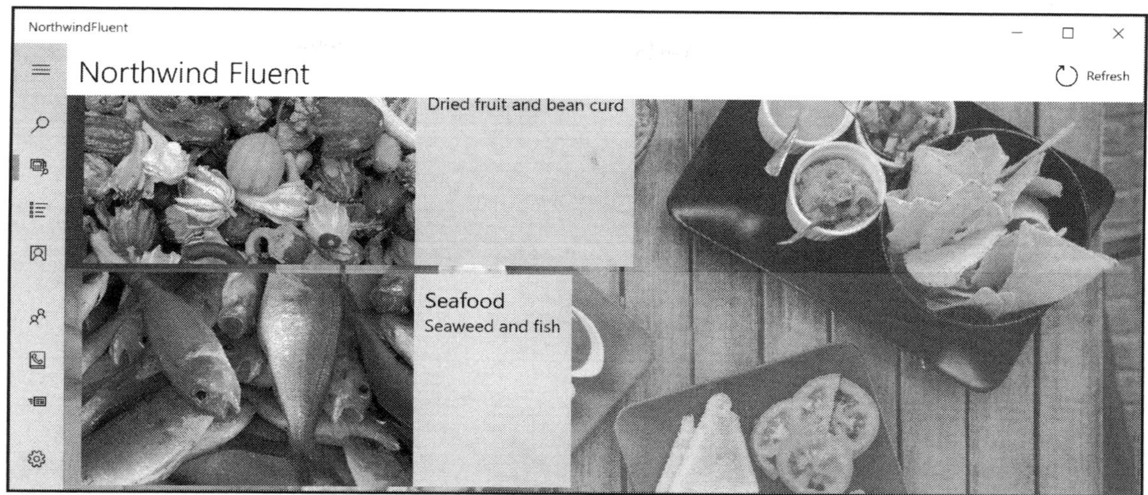


I will leave it as an exercise, for the reader to implement a page for products that is shown when a user clicks on each category.

# Building apps using Windows Template Studio

To quickly get started building UWP apps, Microsoft has created the Windows Template Studio extension for Visual Studio. We will use it to create a new app that shows some of its features and good practices.

# Installing Windows Template Studio

Navigate to **Tools** | **Extensions and Updates...**, select **Online**, enter `Windows Template Studio` in the search box, and click on **Download**, and then **Close**, as shown in the following screenshot:

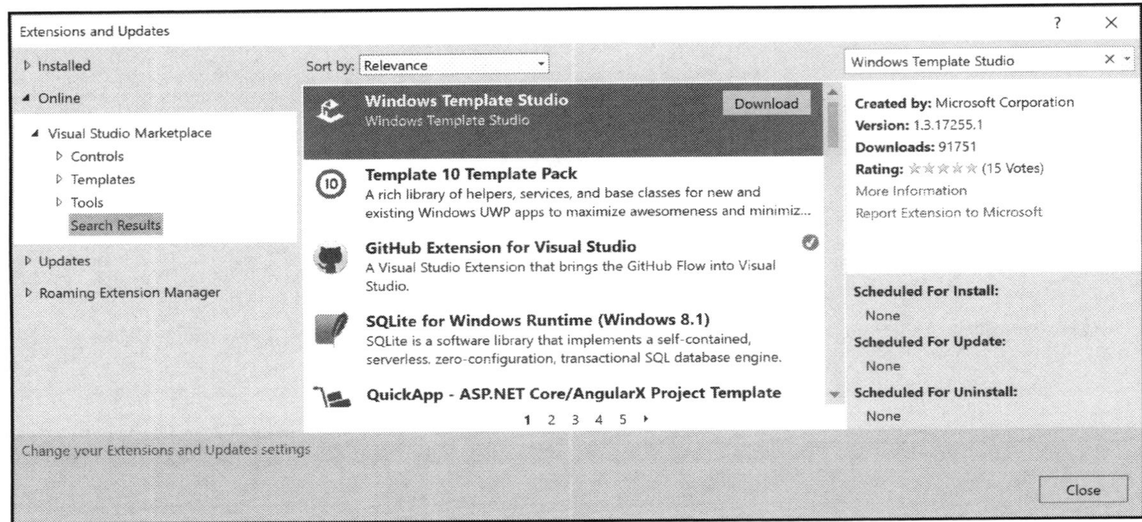


Exit Visual Studio 2017, and wait for the extension to install using the VSIX Installer.

Currently, Windows Template Studio gets confused when used in a solution with multiple projects, so I recommend that you always create projects with it in a new solution. After the project is created, you can then manually add it to another solution.

# Selecting project types, frameworks, pages, and features

Start Visual Studio 2017, open the `Part3` solution, and go to **File** | **New** | **Project...**.

In the **New Project** dialog, in the **Installed** list, select **Visual C# | Windows Universal**. In the center list, select **Windows Template Studio (Universal Windows)**, type the location as `C:\Code\Part3\`, type the name as `NorthwindUwp`, and click on **OK**.

In the **Select project type and framework** dialog, select **Navigation Pane** and **MVVM Basic**, and then click on **Next**, as shown in the following screenshot:

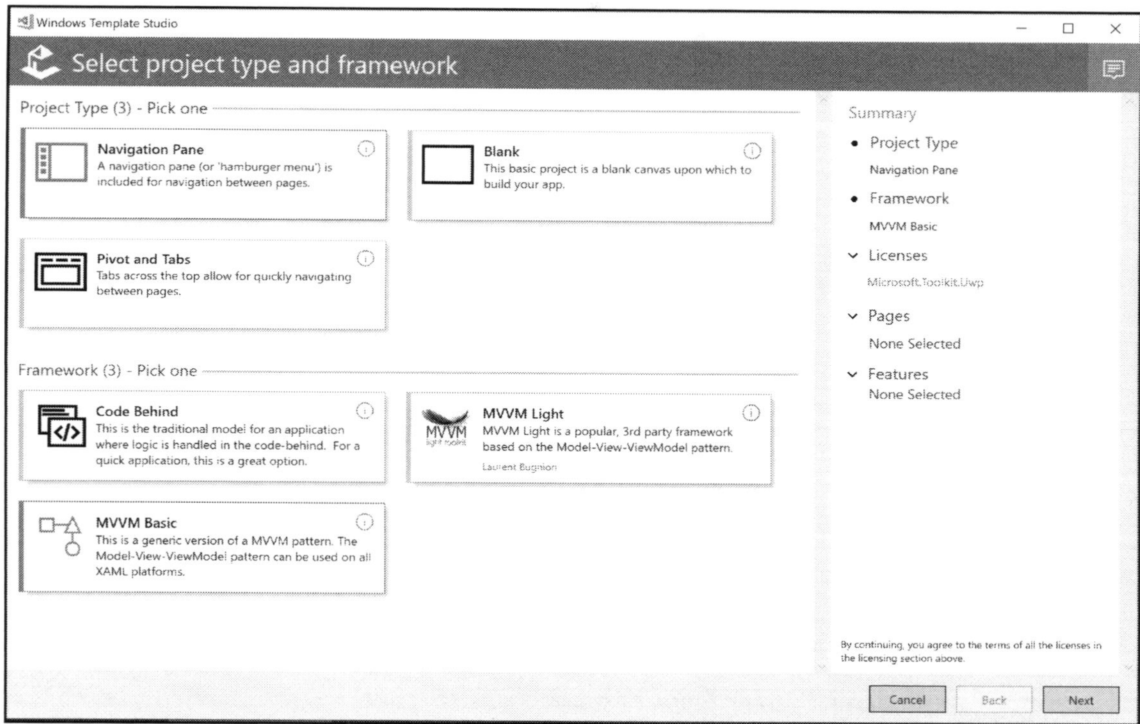

In the **Select pages and features** dialog, select the circle with a plus button in the **Settings** pane, leave its name as **Settings**, and then click on the tick button, as shown in the following screenshot:

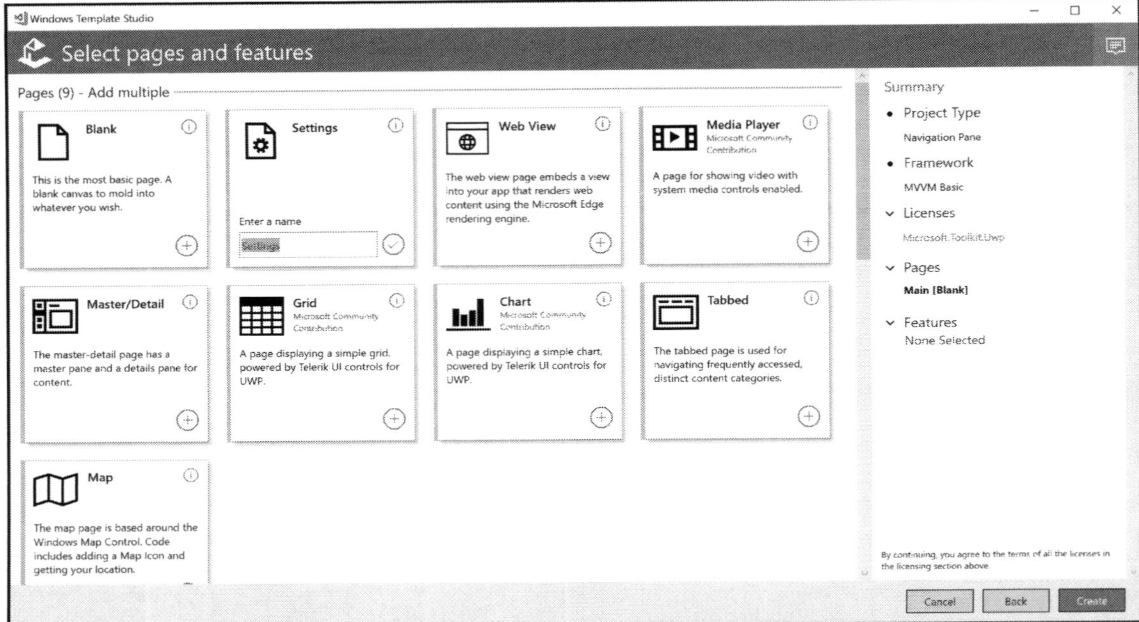


Repeat for the following panes:

- Add a **Blank** page named `AboutNorthwindApp`
- Add a **Web View** page named `AngularWebView`
- Add a **Master/Detail** page named `CategoryMasterDetail`
- Add a **Grid** page named `CustomersGrid`
- Add a **Map** page named `CustomerMap`
- Add **First Run Prompt**

In **Summary**, confirm you have created the pages, and click on **Create**, as shown in the following screenshot:

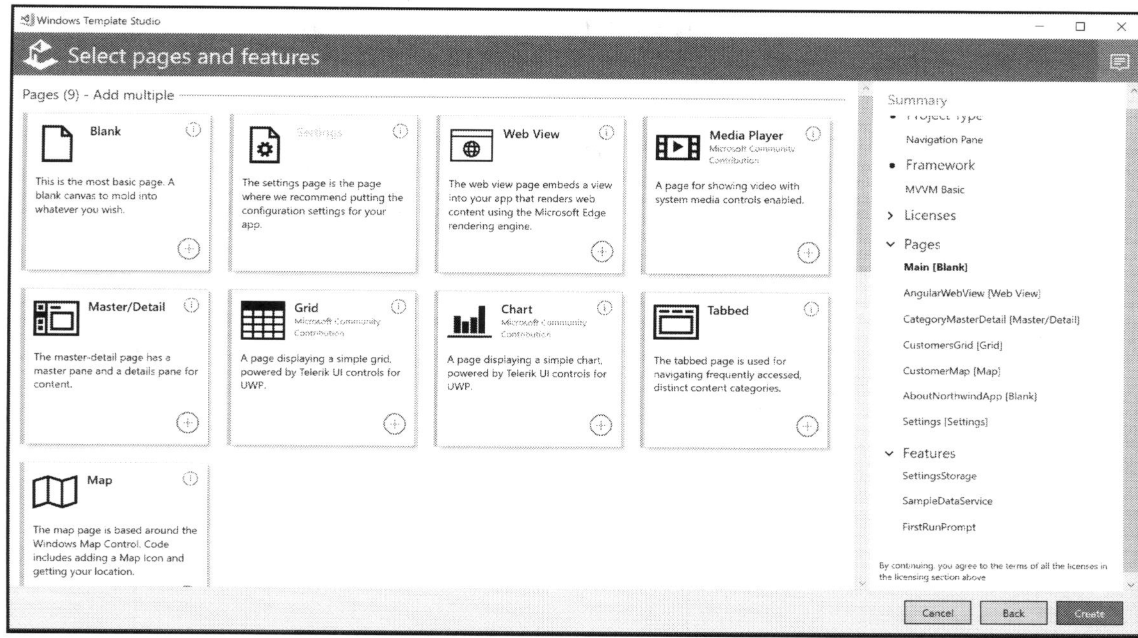


Once the new project has been successfully created, close the solution, and open the `Part3` solution.

Navigate to **File** | **Add** | **Existing Project**, and select **NorthwindUwp.csproj**.

# Retargeting the project

In **Solution Explorer**, in **NorthwindUwp** project, open **Properties**, and change **Target version** and **Min version** to the latest build.

In **Solution Explorer**, right-click on the **Part3** solution, and choose **Properties**, or press *Alt* + *Enter*.

Set **Multiple startup projects**, with **ExploreAngular** set to **Start** first, then the **NorthwindService** project, and finally the **NorthwindUwp** project, as shown in the following screenshot:

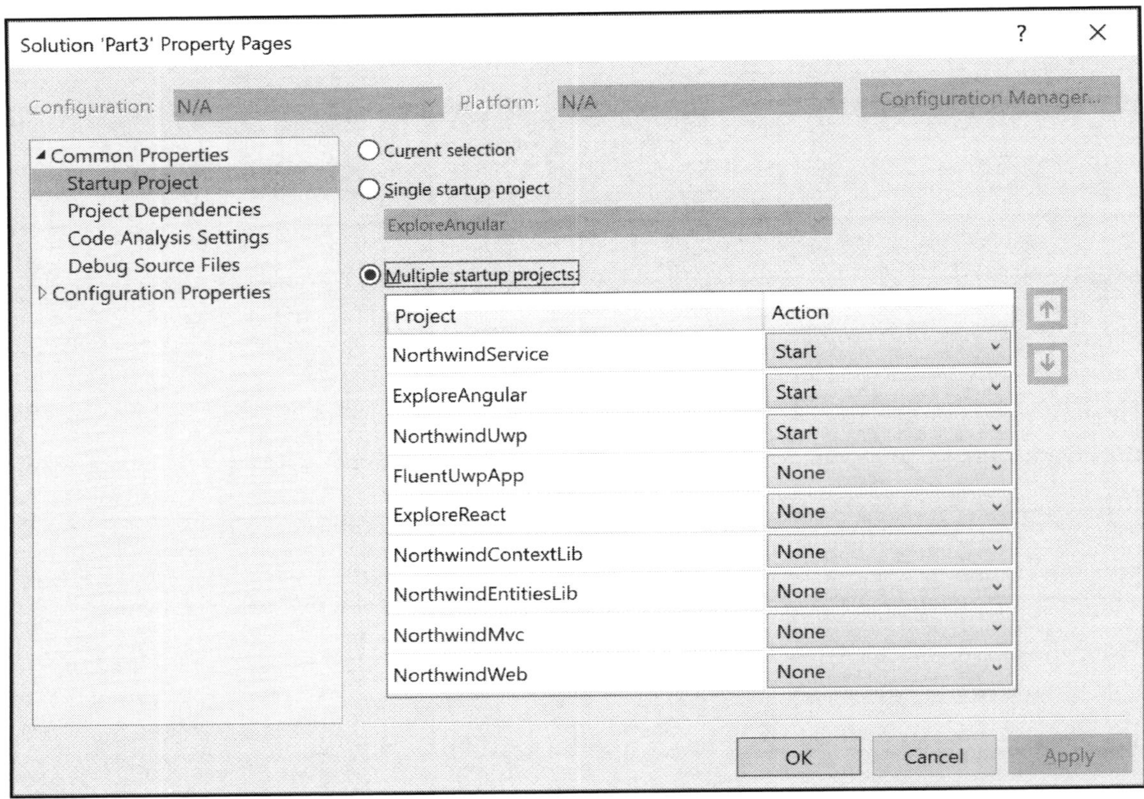


## Customizing some views

In **Solution Explorer**, expand the `NorthwindUwp` project and the `ViewModels` folder, open `AngularWebViewViewModel.cs`, and modify the `DefaultUrl` string constant to use the Angular web application that you created earlier, which listens on port `5002`, as shown in the following code:

```
private const string DefaultUrl = "http://localhost:5002";
```

In **Solution Explorer**, expand the `NorthwindUwp` project and the `ViewModels` folder, open `SHellViewModel.cs`, and modify the `PopulateNavItems` method to use some different symbols, as shown highlighted in the following code:

```
_primaryItems.Add(ShellNavigationItem.FromType<MainPage>("Shell_Main".GetLocalized(), Symbol.Home));
_primaryItems.Add(ShellNavigationItem.FromType<AngularWebViewPage>("Shell_AngularWebView".GetLocalized(), Symbol.Globe));
_primaryItems.Add(ShellNavigationItem.FromType<CategoryMasterDetailPage>("Shell_CategoryMasterDetail".GetLocalized(), Symbol.ContactInfo));
_primaryItems.Add(ShellNavigationItem.FromType<CustomersGridPage>("Shell_CustomersGrid".GetLocalized(), Symbol.PhoneBook));
_primaryItems.Add(ShellNavigationItem.FromType<CustomerMapPage>("Shell_CustomerMap".GetLocalized(), Symbol.Map));
_primaryItems.Add(ShellNavigationItem.FromType<AboutNorthwindAppPage>("Shell_AboutNorthwindApp".GetLocalized(), Symbol.Help));
```

Expand the `Strings` and `en-us` folders, and open `Resources.resw`.

At the bottom of the grid, modify the **Value** for the resources that begin with the word `Shell` to be more appropriate, as shown in the following screenshot:

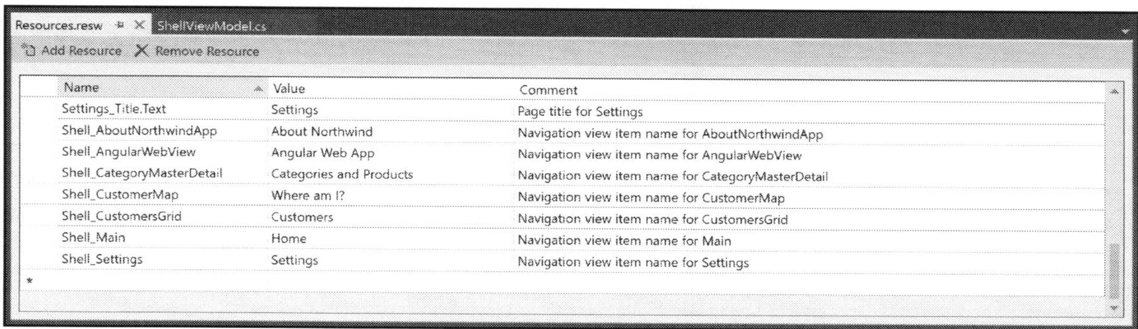

| Name | Value | Comment |
|---|---|---|
| Settings_Title.Text | Settings | Page title for Settings |
| Shell_AboutNorthwindApp | About Northwind | Navigation view item name for AboutNorthwindApp |
| Shell_AngularWebView | Angular Web App | Navigation view item name for AngularWebView |
| Shell_CategoryMasterDetail | Categories and Products | Navigation view item name for CategoryMasterDetail |
| Shell_CustomerMap | Where am I? | Navigation view item name for CustomerMap |
| Shell_CustomersGrid | Customers | Navigation view item name for CustomersGrid |
| Shell_Main | Home | Navigation view item name for Main |
| Shell_Settings | Settings | Navigation view item name for Settings |

Navigate to **Build** | **Configuration Manager**, and select the **Build** and **Deploy** checkboxes for the **NorthwindUwp** project.

# Testing the app's functionality

Start the app by navigating to **Debug** | **Start**, or press *F5*.

When the app has started, click on the hamburger menu, click on **Angular Web App**, and note that the web application is loaded, as shown in the following screenshot:

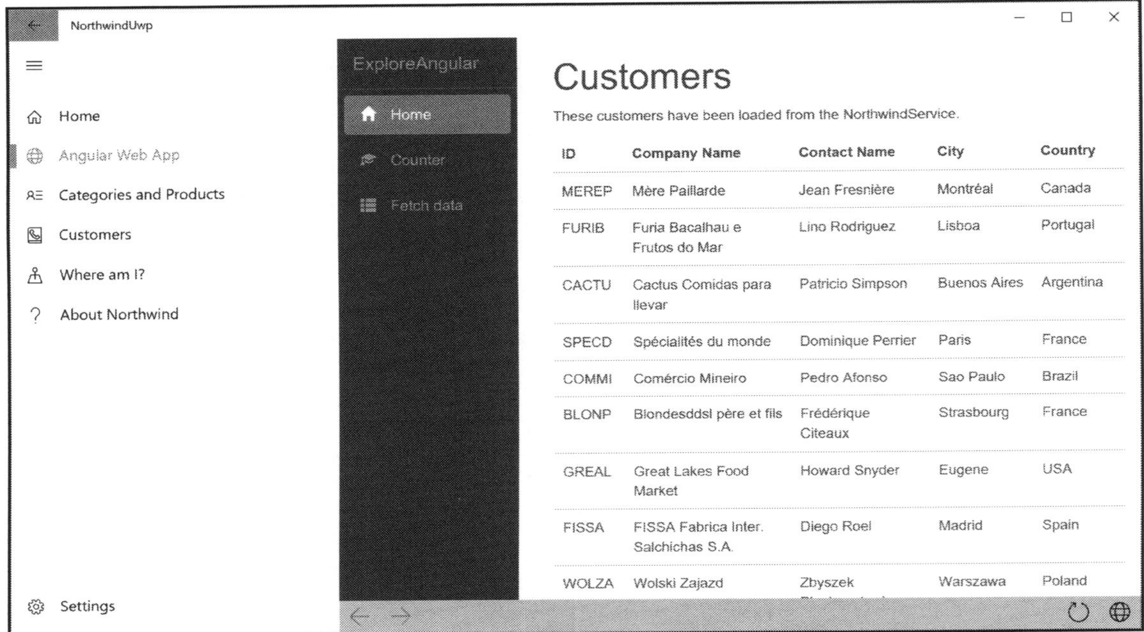


Click on **Where am I?**, and click on **Yes** to allow the app to access your precise location, as shown in the following screenshot:

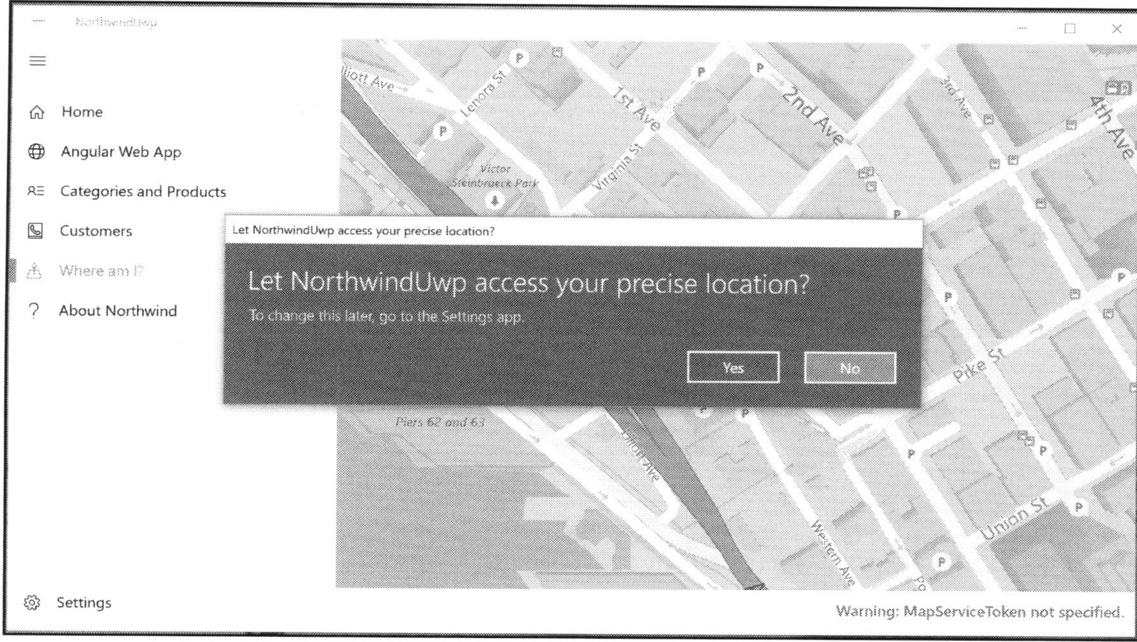


Note the back arrow button that navigates the user back to previous screens.

Click on **Settings** and select the **Dark** theme.

Click on **Customers** and note the grid of sample data.

Click on **Categories and Products** and note the sample data.

Close the app.

# Practicing and exploring

Explore this chapter's topics with deeper research.

# Exercise 17.1 – Explore topics

Use the following links to read more about this chapter's topics.

- **Enable your device for development**: `https://docs.microsoft.com/en-us/windows/uwp/get-started/enable-your-device-for-development`
- **Intro to the Universal Windows Platform:** `https://docs.microsoft.com/en-us/windows/uwp/get-started/universal-application-platform-guide`
- **UWP Community Toolkit**: `https://docs.microsoft.com/en-gb/windows/uwpcommunitytoolkit/Getting-Started`
- **Design UWP and Fluent Design System**: `https://developer.microsoft.com/en-us/windows/apps/design`
- **How-to articles for UWP apps on Windows 10**: `https://developer.microsoft.com/en-us/windows/apps/develop`

# Summary

In this chapter, you learned how to build a graphical user interface using XAML and the new Fluent Design System, including features such as Acrylic material, Reveal lighting, and Parallax view. You also learned how to share resources in an app, how to replace a control's template, how to bind to data and controls, and how to prevent thread blocking with multitasking and the C# `async` and `await` keywords.

In the next chapter, you will learn how to build mobile apps using Xamarin.Forms.

# 18

# Building Mobile Apps Using XAML and Xamarin.Forms

This chapter is about learning how to take C# mobile by building a cross-platform mobile app for iOS, Android, and other mobile platforms. The mobile app will allow the listing and management of customers in the Northwind database.

The mobile app will call the Northwind service that you built with ASP.NET Core Web API in `Chapter 16`, *Building Web Services and Applications Using ASP.NET Core*. If you have not built the Northwind service, go back and build it now.

The client-side Xamarin.Forms mobile app will be written with **Visual Studio for Mac**.

You will need a computer with macOS, Xcode, and Visual Studio for Mac to complete this chapter.

In this chapter, we will cover the following topics:

- Understanding Xamarin and Xamarin.Forms
- Building mobile apps using Xamarin.Forms

# Understanding Xamarin and Xamarin.Forms

**Xamarin** enables developers to build mobile apps for Apple iOS (iPhone and iPad), Google Android, and Windows Mobile using C#. It is based on a third-party open source implementation of .NET known as Mono. Business logic layer can be written once and shared between all mobile platforms. User interface interactions and APIs are different on various mobile platforms, so the user experience layer is often custom for each platform.

## How Xamarin.Forms extends Xamarin

**Xamarin.Forms** extends Xamarin to make cross-platform mobile development even easier by sharing most of the user experience layer, as well as the business logic layer.

Like Universal Windows Platform apps, Xamarin.Forms uses XAML to define the user interface once for all platforms using abstractions of platform-specific user interface components. Applications built with Xamarin.Forms draw the user interface using native platform widgets, so the app's look-and-feel fits naturally with the target mobile platform.

A user experience built using Xamarin.Forms will never perfectly fit a specific platform as one custom built with Xamarin, but for enterprise mobile apps, it is more than good enough.

# Mobile first, cloud first

Mobile apps are often supported by services in the cloud. Satya Nadella, CEO of Microsoft, famously said this:

> *To me, when we say mobile first, it's not the mobility of the device, it's actually the mobility of the individual experience. [...] The only way you are going to be able to orchestrate the mobility of these applications and data is through the cloud.*

As you have seen earlier in this book, to create the ASP.NET Core Web API service to support the mobile app, we can use any of the Visual Studio family of IDEs.

To create Xamarin.Forms apps, developers can use either Visual Studio 2017 or Visual Studio for Mac.

To compile Windows Mobile apps, you will require Windows and Visual Studio 2017. To compile iOS apps, you will require a Mac, Visual Studio for Mac, and Xcode. So, why did I choose the Mac platform for mobile development in this chapter?

Android runs on six times as many mobile phones compared to iOS; however, consider these things:

- For every dollar an Android user spends on apps, an iOS user spends ten dollars
- For every hour an Android user spends browsing the web, an iOS user spends two hours

So, market share numbers should be taken in the context that iOS users engage far more with their devices, which is important for monetizing mobile apps, either through up-front sales, in-app purchases, or advertising.

A summary of which IDE can be used to create and compile which type of app is shown in the following table:

| | **iOS** | **Android** | **Windows Mobile** | **ASP.NET Core Web API** |
|---|---|---|---|---|
| Smartphone Market Share | 14% | 86% | < 0.1% | n/a |
| Visual Studio Code | No | No | No | Yes |
| Visual Studio for Mac | Yes | Yes | No | Yes |
| Visual Studio 2017 | No | Yes | Yes | Yes |

If you would like to learn more about Xamarin, then I recommend the *Xamarin: Cross-Platform Mobile Application Development* Learning Path, by *Jonathan Peppers, George Taskos*, and *Can Bilgin*, that you can read more about at the following link: `https://www.packtpub.com/application-development/xamarin-cross-platform-mobile-application-development`

# Building mobile apps using Xamarin.Forms

We will build a mobile app that runs on either iOS or Android for managing customers in Northwind.

If you have never run Xcode, run it now to ensure that all its required components are installed and registered.

# Adding Android SDKs

To target Android, you must install at least one Android SDK. A default installation of Visual Studio for Mac already includes one Android SDK, but it is often an older version to support as many Android devices as possible. To use the latest features of Xamarin.Forms, you must install a more recent Android SDK.

Start Visual Studio for Mac, and navigate to **Visual Studio Community** | **Preferences**.

In **Preferences**, navigate to **Projects** | **SDK Locations**, and select the **Platforms** you want, for example, **Android 8.0 - Oreo**, as shown in the following screenshot:

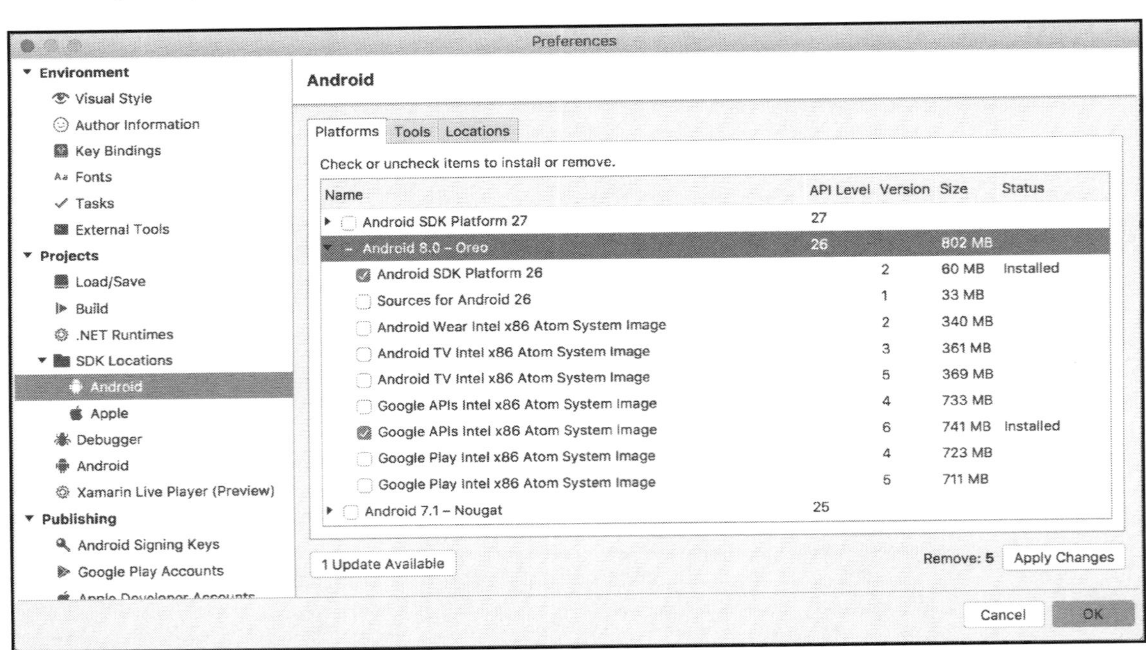

When installing an Android SDK, you must select at least one **System Image** to use as a virtual machine emulator for testing.

# Creating a Xamarin.Forms solution

Navigate to **File** | **New Solution...**.

In the **New Project** dialog, choose **Multiplatform** | **App** in the left-hand column.

Choose **Xamarin.Forms** | **Blank Forms App** in the middle column, as shown in the following screenshot:

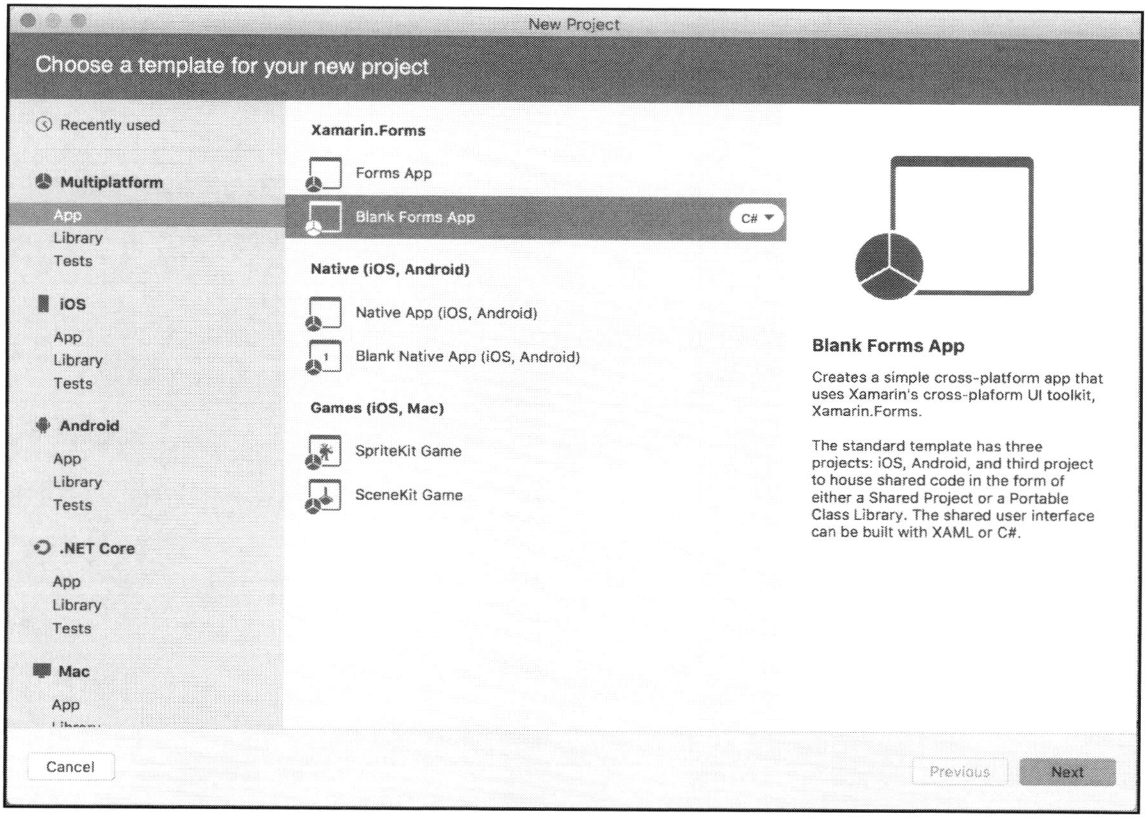

Click on **Next**.

Enter **App Name** as `NorthwindMobile` and **Organization Identifier** as `com.packt`, select **Shared Code** to **Use Shared Library**, and ensure that you use XAML for the user interface files, as shown in the following screenshot:

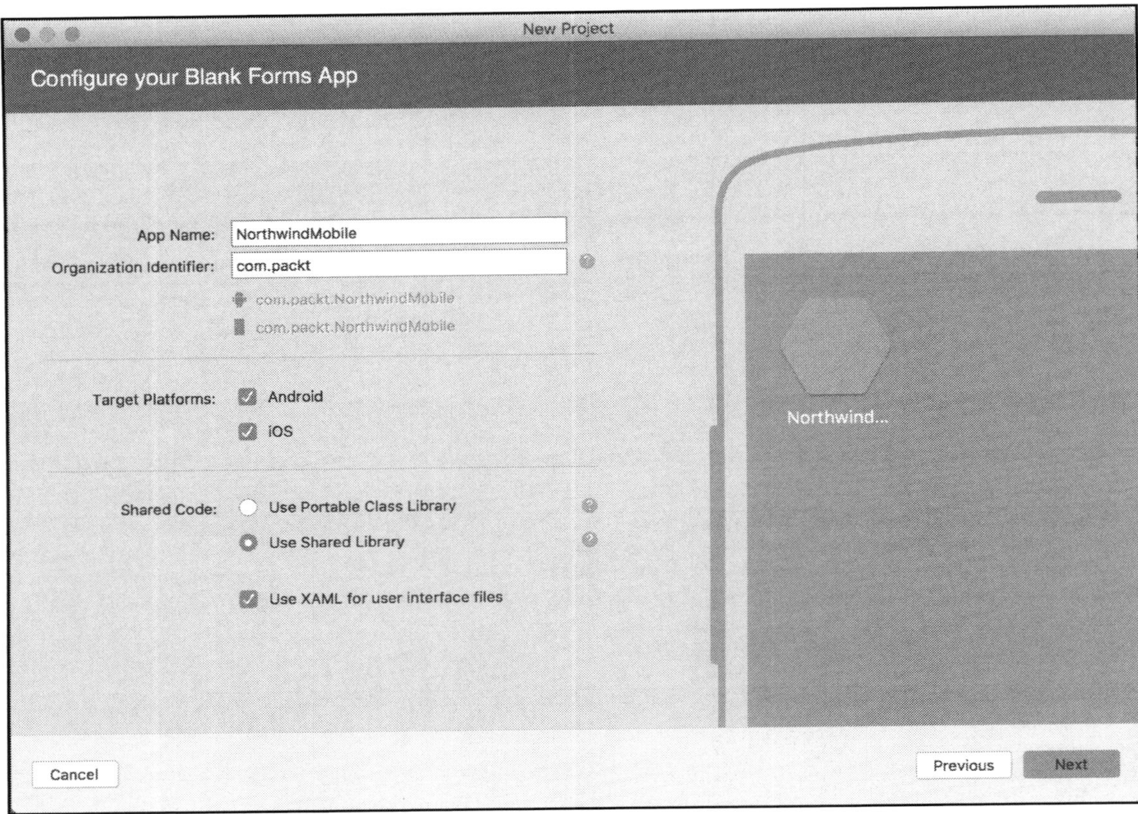


Click on **Next**.

Change **Solution Name** to `Part3Mobile`, and **Location** to `/Users/[user_folder]/Code`, as shown in the following screenshot:

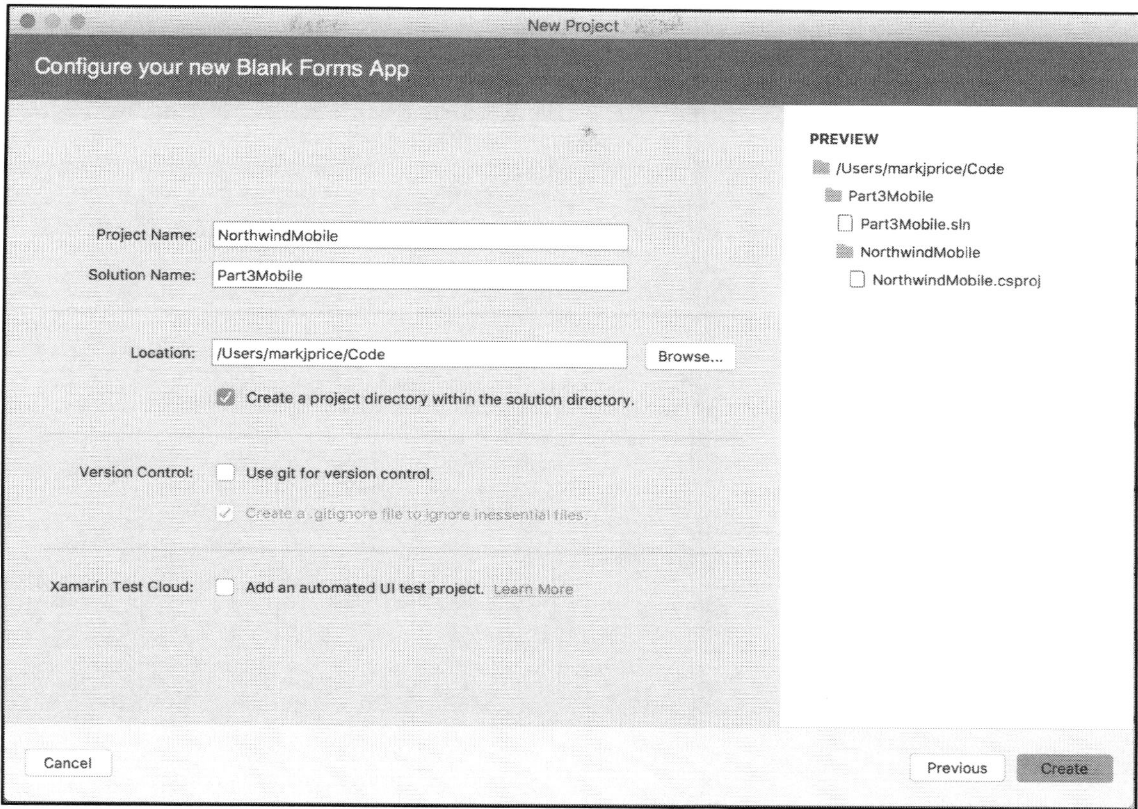


Click on **Create**.

After a few moments, the solution and all three projects will be created. In Visual Studio for Mac, navigate to **Build | Build All**, and wait for the solution to download any updated packages and build the projects, as shown in the following screenshot:

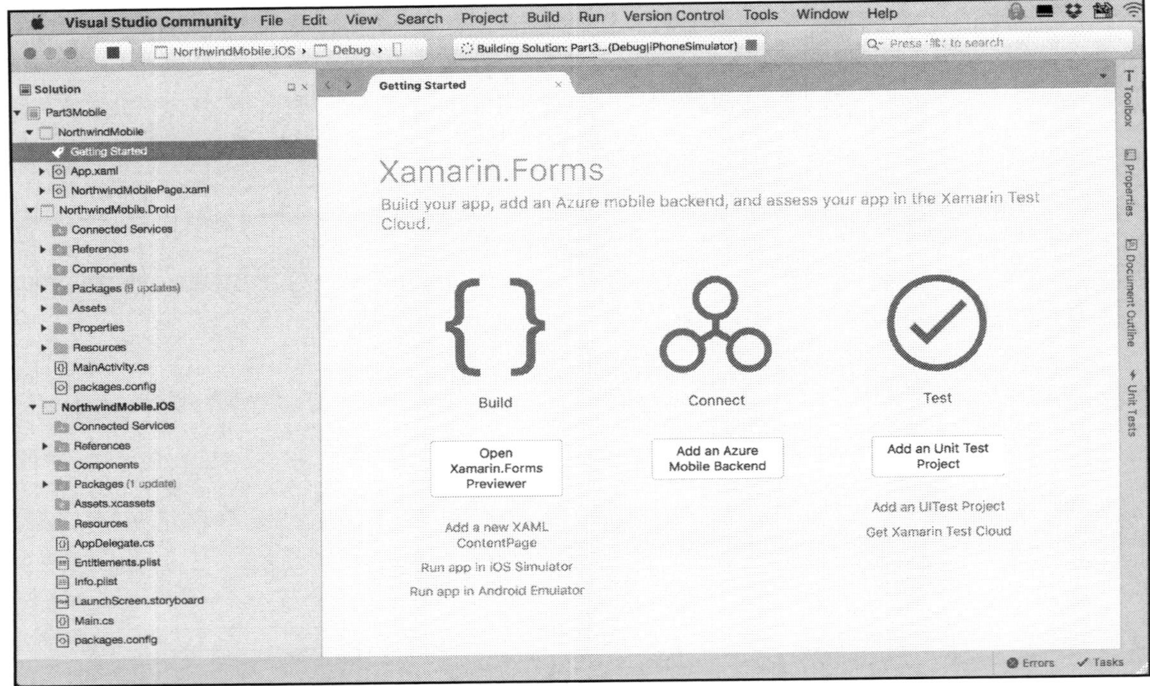

Right-click on **Part3Mobile**, and choose **Update NuGet Packages**.

# Creating a model

Although we could reuse the .NET Standard 2.0 entity data model library that you created earlier, we want to implement two-way data binding, so we will create a new class to represent customer entities in the mobile app.

Right-click on the project named `NorthwindMobile`, go to **Add | New Folder**, and name it `Models`.

Right-click on the `Models` folder and go to **Add | New File...**.

In the **New File** dialog, go to **General** | **Empty Class**, enter the name `Customer`, as shown in the following screenshot, and click on **New**:

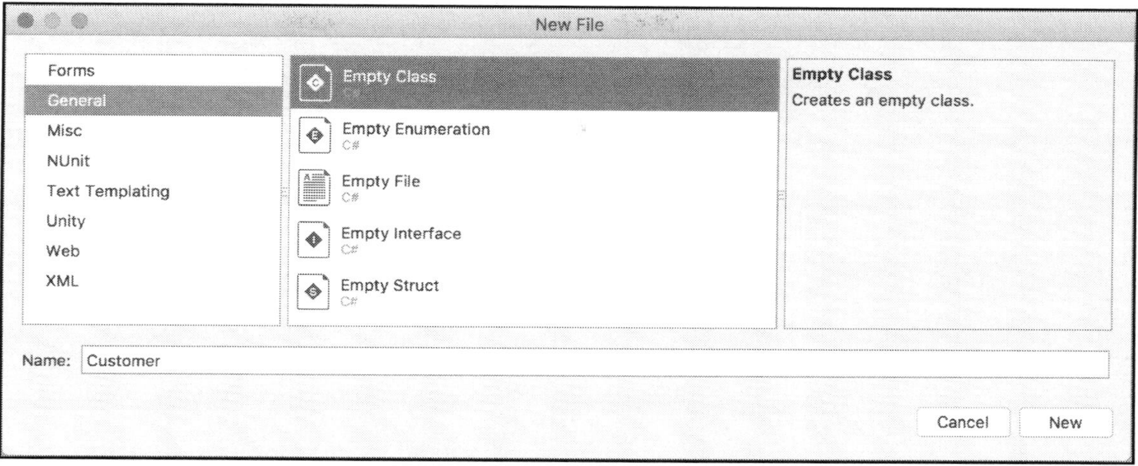


Modify the statements, as shown in the following code:

```
using System.Collections.Generic;
using System.Collections.ObjectModel;
using System.ComponentModel;

namespace NorthwindMobile.Models
{
   public class Customer : INotifyPropertyChanged
   {
      public static IList<Customer> Customers;

      static Customer()
      {
         Customers = new ObservableCollection<Customer>();
      }

      public event PropertyChangedEventHandler PropertyChanged;

      private string customerID;
      private string companyName;
      private string contactName;
      private string city;
      private string country;
      private string phone;

      public string CustomerID
```

```
{
   get { return customerID; }
   set
   {
      customerID = value;
      PropertyChanged?.Invoke(this,
      new PropertyChangedEventArgs("CustomerID"));
   }
}

public string CompanyName
{
   get { return companyName; }
   set
   {
      companyName = value;
      PropertyChanged?.Invoke(this,
      new PropertyChangedEventArgs("CompanyName"));
   }
}

public string ContactName
{
   get { return contactName; }
   set
   {
      contactName = value;
      PropertyChanged?.Invoke(this,
      new PropertyChangedEventArgs("ContactName"));
   }
}
public string City
{
   get { return city; }
   set
   {
      city = value;
      PropertyChanged?.Invoke(this,
      new PropertyChangedEventArgs("City"));
   }
}

public string Country
{
   get { return country; }
   set
   {
      country = value;
```

```
            PropertyChanged?.Invoke(this,
            new PropertyChangedEventArgs("Country"));
        }
    }

    public string Phone
    {
        get { return phone; }
        set
        {
            phone = value;
            PropertyChanged?.Invoke(this,
            new PropertyChangedEventArgs("Phone"));
        }
    }

    public string Location
    {
        get
        {
            return string.Format("{0}, {1}", City, Country);
        }
    }

    // for testing before calling web service
    public static void SampleData()
    {
        Customers.Clear();

        Customers.Add(new Customer
        {
            CustomerID = "ALFKI",
            CompanyName = "Alfreds Futterkiste",
            ContactName = "Maria Anders",
            City = "Berlin",
            Country = "Germany",
            Phone = "030-0074321"
        });

        Customers.Add(new Customer
        {
            CustomerID = "FRANK",
            CompanyName = "Frankenversand",
            ContactName = "Peter Franken",
            City = "München",
            Country = "Germany",
            Phone = "089-0877310"
        });
```

```
            Customers.Add(new Customer
            {
                CustomerID = "SEVES",
                CompanyName = "Seven Seas Imports",
                ContactName = "Hari Kumar",
                City = "London",
                Country = "UK",
                Phone = "(171) 555-1717"
            });
        }
    }
}
```

Note the following:

- The class implements `INotifyPropertyChanged`, so a two-way bound user interface components such as `Editor` will update the property and vice versa. There is a `PropertyChanged` event that is raised whenever one of the properties is modified.
- After loading from the service, the customers will be cached locally in the mobile app using `ObservableCollection`. This supports notifications to any bound user interface components, such as `ListView`.
- In addition to properties for storing values retrieved from the REST service, the class defines a read-only `Location` property. This will be used to bind to, in a summary list of customers.
- For testing purposes, when the REST service is not available, there is a method to populate three sample customers.

# Creating an interface for dialing phone numbers

Right-click on the `NorthwindMobile` folder and choose **New File...**.

Go to **General** | **Empty Interface**, name the file `IDialer`, and click on **New**.

Modify the `IDialer` contents, as shown in the following code:

```
namespace NorthwindMobile
{
   public interface IDialer
   {
      bool Dial(string number);
   }
}
```

# Implement the phone dialer for iOS

Right-click on the `NorthwindMobile.iOS` folder and choose **New File...**.

Go to **General** | **Empty Class**, name the file as `PhoneDialer`, and click on **New**.

Modify its contents, as shown in the following code:

```
using Foundation;
using NorthwindMobile.iOS;
using UIKit;
using Xamarin.Forms;

[assembly: Dependency(typeof(PhoneDialer))]
namespace NorthwindMobile.iOS
{
   public class PhoneDialer : IDialer
   {
      public bool Dial(string number)
      {
         return UIApplication.SharedApplication.OpenUrl(
         new NSUrl("tel:" + number));
      }
   }
}
```

## Implement the phone dialer for Android

Right-click on the `NorthwindMobile.Droid` folder and choose **New File...**.

Choose **General | Empty Class**, name the file as `PhoneDialer`, and click on **New**.

Modify its contents, as shown in the following code:

```
using Android.Content;
using Android.Telephony;
using NorthwindMobile.Droid;
using System.Linq;
using Xamarin.Forms;
using Uri = Android.Net.Uri;

[assembly: Dependency(typeof(PhoneDialer))]
namespace NorthwindMobile.Droid
{
   public class PhoneDialer : IDialer
   {
      public bool Dial(string number)
      {
         var context = Forms.Context;
         if (context == null)
         return false;

         var intent = new Intent(Intent.ActionCall);
         intent.SetData(Uri.Parse("tel:" + number));

         if (IsIntentAvailable(context, intent))
         {
            context.StartActivity(intent);
            return true;
         }

         return false;
      }

      public static bool IsIntentAvailable(Context context, Intent
      intent)
      {
         var packageManager = context.PackageManager;

         var list = packageManager.QueryIntentServices(intent, 0)
         .Union(packageManager.QueryIntentActivities(intent, 0));

         if (list.Any())
         return true;
```

```
            var manager = TelephonyManager.FromContext(context);
            return manager.PhoneType != PhoneType.None;
        }
    }
}
```

In NorthwindMobile.Droid, expand **Properties**, and open AndroidManifest.xml.

In **Required permissions**, check the **CallPhone** permission, as shown in the following screenshot:

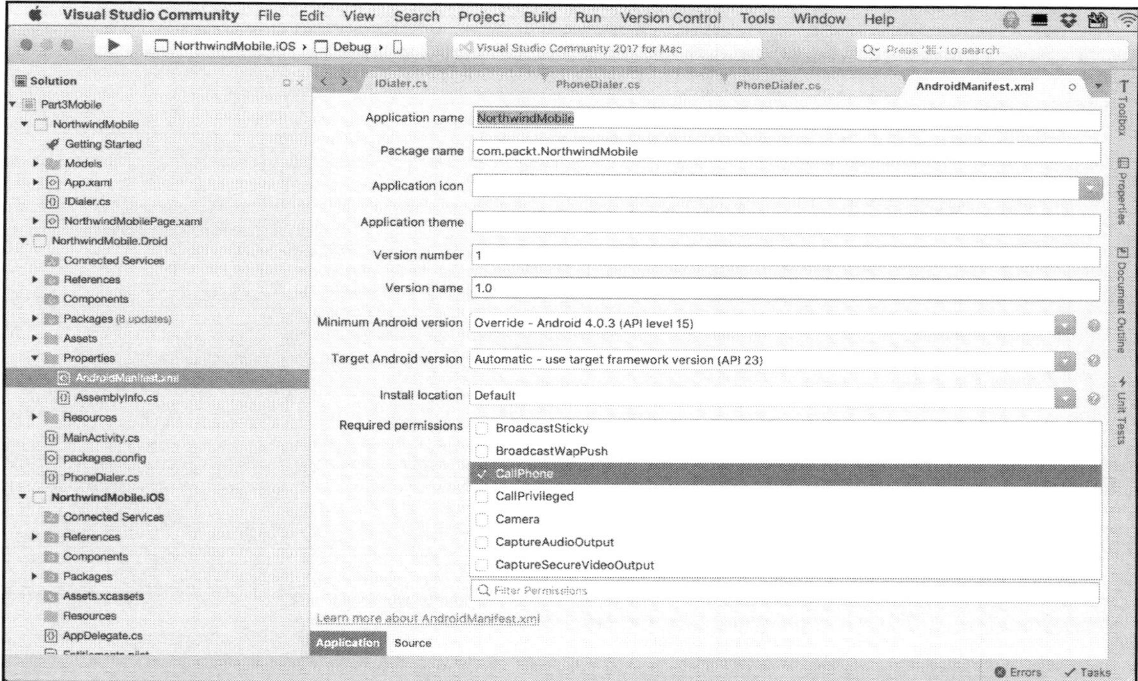

# Creating views for the customers list and customer details

Right-click on `NorthwindMobilePage.xaml`, click on **Remove**, and then click on **Remove from Project**.

Right-click on the project named `NorthwindMobile`, go to **Add | New Folder**, and name it `Views`.

Right-click on the `Views` folder and choose **New File...**.

Go to **Forms | Forms ContentPage Xaml**, name the file as `CustomersList`, and click on **New**, as shown in the following screenshot:

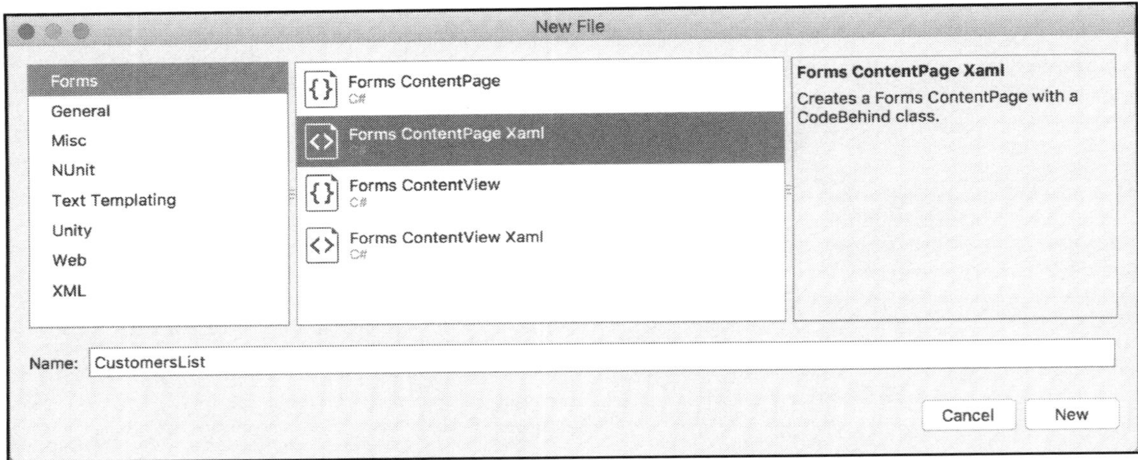


## Creating the view for the list of customers

In `NorthwindMobile`, open `CustomersList.xaml`, and modify its contents, as shown in the following markup:

```
<?xml version="1.0" encoding="UTF-8"?>
<ContentPage xmlns="http://xamarin.com/schemas/2014/forms"
 xmlns:x="http://schemas.microsoft.com/winfx/2009/xaml"
 x:Class="NorthwindMobile.Views.CustomersList"
 Title="List">
  <ContentPage.Content>
    <ListView ItemsSource="{Binding .}"
     VerticalOptions="Center" HorizontalOptions="Center"
```

```
        IsPullToRefreshEnabled="True"
        ItemTapped="Customer_Tapped"
        Refreshing="Customers_Refreshing">
         <ListView.Header>
           <Label Text="Northwind Customers"
            BackgroundColor="Silver" />
         </ListView.Header>
         <ListView.ItemTemplate>
           <DataTemplate>
             <TextCell Text="{Binding CompanyName}"
              Detail="{Binding Location}">
               <TextCell.ContextActions>
                 <MenuItem Clicked="Customer_Phoned" Text="Phone" />
                 <MenuItem Clicked="Customer_Deleted"
                   Text="Delete" IsDestructive="True" />
               </TextCell.ContextActions>
             </TextCell>
           </DataTemplate>
         </ListView.ItemTemplate>
       </ListView>
     </ContentPage.Content>
     <ContentPage.ToolbarItems>
       <ToolbarItem Text="Add" Activated="Add_Activated"
        Order="Primary" Priority="0" />
     </ContentPage.ToolbarItems>
   </ContentPage>
```

Note the following:

- The `ContentPage` element has had its `Title` attribute set to `List`
- Event handlers have been written for this: loading the customers when the view appears, a customer being tapped (to show detail), the list being swiped down to refresh, and a customer being deleted by swiping left and then clicking on a **Delete** button
- A data template defines how to display each customer: large text for the company name and smaller text for the location underneath
- An **Add** button is displayed so that users can navigate to a detail view to add a new customer

Modify the contents of `CustomersList.xaml.cs`, as shown in the following code:

```
using System;
using System.Threading.Tasks;
using NorthwindMobile.Models;
using Xamarin.Forms;
```

```
namespace NorthwindMobileApp.Views
{
   public partial class CustomersList : ContentPage
   {
      public CustomersList()
      {
         InitializeComponent();
         Customer.SampleData();
         BindingContext = Customer.Customers;
      }

      async void Customer_Tapped(object sender, ItemTappedEventArgs e)
      {
         Customer c = e.Item as Customer;
         if (c == null) return;
         // navigate to the detail view and show the tapped customer
         await Navigation.PushAsync(new CustomerDetails(c));
      }

      async void Customers_Refreshing(object sender, EventArgs e)
      {
         ListView listView = sender as ListView;
         listView.IsRefreshing = true;
         // simulate a refresh
         await Task.Delay(1500);
         listView.IsRefreshing = false;
      }

      void Customer_Deleted(object sender, EventArgs e)
      {
         MenuItem menuItem = sender as MenuItem;
         Customer c = menuItem.BindingContext as Customer;
         Customer.Customers.Remove(c);
      }

      async void Customer_Phoned(object sender, EventArgs e)
      {
         MenuItem menuItem = sender as MenuItem;
         Customer c = menuItem.BindingContext as Customer;
         if (await this.DisplayAlert("Dial a Number",
             "Would you like to call " + c.Phone + "?",
             "Yes", "No"))
         {
            var dialer = DependencyService.Get<IDialer>();
            if (dialer != null)
            dialer.Dial(c.Phone);
         }
      }
```

```
        async void Add_Activated(object sender, EventArgs e)
        {
            await Navigation.PushAsync(new CustomerDetails());
        }
    }
}
```

Note the following:

- `BindingContext` is set to the sample list of `Customers` in the constructor of the page
- When a customer in the list view is tapped, the user is taken to a details view (that you will create in the next step)
- When the list view is pulled down, it triggers a simulated refresh that takes one and a half seconds
- When a customer is deleted in the list view, it is removed from the bound collection of customers
- When a customer in the list view is swiped, and the **Phone** button is tapped, a dialog prompts the user if they want to dial the number, and if so, the platform-specific implementation will be retrieved using the dependency resolver and then used to dial the number
- When the **Add** button is tapped, the user is taken to the customer detail page to enter details for a new customer

## Creating the view for the customer details

Add another **Forms ContentPage Xaml** file named `CustomerDetails`.

Open `CustomerDetails.xaml`, and modify its contents, as shown in the following markup, and note the following:

- `Title` of the `ContentPage` element has been set to `Edit Customer`
- `Grid` with two columns and six rows is used for the layout
- `Editor` elements are two-way bound to properties of the `Customer` class

```
<?xml version="1.0" encoding="UTF-8"?>
<ContentPage xmlns="http://xamarin.com/schemas/2014/forms"
 xmlns:x="http://schemas.microsoft.com/winfx/2009/xaml"
 x:Class="NorthwindMobile.Views.CustomerDetails" Title="Edit Customer">
  <ContentPage.Content>
    <StackLayout VerticalOptions="Fill"
     HorizontalOptions="Fill">
```

```
    <Grid BackgroundColor="Silver">
      <Grid.ColumnDefinitions>
        <ColumnDefinition/> <ColumnDefinition/>
      </Grid.ColumnDefinitions>
      <Grid.RowDefinitions>
        <RowDefinition/> <RowDefinition/> <RowDefinition/>
        <RowDefinition/> <RowDefinition/> <RowDefinition/>
      </Grid.RowDefinitions>
      <Label Text="Customer ID"
       VerticalOptions="Center" Margin="6" />
      <Editor Text="{Binding CustomerID, Mode=TwoWay}"
       Grid.Column="1" />
      <Label Text="Company Name" Grid.Row="1"
       VerticalOptions="Center" Margin="6" />
      <Editor Text="{Binding CompanyName, Mode=TwoWay}"
       Grid.Column="1" Grid.Row="1" />
      <Label Text="Contact Name" Grid.Row="2"
       VerticalOptions="Center" Margin="6" />
      <Editor Text="{Binding ContactName, Mode=TwoWay}"
       Grid.Column="1" Grid.Row="2" />
      <Label Text="City" Grid.Row="3"
       VerticalOptions="Center" Margin="6" />
      <Editor Text="{Binding City, Mode=TwoWay}"
       Grid.Column="1" Grid.Row="3" />
      <Label Text="Country" Grid.Row="4"
       VerticalOptions="Center" Margin="6" />
      <Editor Text="{Binding Country, Mode=TwoWay}"
       Grid.Column="1" Grid.Row="4" />
      <Label Text="Phone" Grid.Row="5"
       VerticalOptions="Center" Margin="6" />
      <Editor Text="{Binding Phone, Mode=TwoWay}"
       Grid.Column="1" Grid.Row="5" />
    </Grid>
    <Button x:Name="InsertButton" Text="Insert Customer"
     Clicked="InsertButton_Clicked" />
    </StackLayout>
  </ContentPage.Content>
</ContentPage>
```

Open `CustomerDetails.xaml.cs`, and modify its contents, as shown in the following code:

```
using System;
using NorthwindMobile.Models;
using Xamarin.Forms;

namespace NorthwindMobile.Views
{
```

```
    public partial class CustomerDetails : ContentPage
    {
        private bool newCustomer = false;

        public CustomerDetails()
        {
            InitializeComponent();
            BindingContext = new Customer();
            newCustomer = true;
            Title = "Add Customer";
        }

        public CustomerDetails(Customer customer)
        {
            InitializeComponent();
            BindingContext = customer;
            InsertButton.IsVisible = false;
        }

        async void InsertButton_Clicked(object sender, EventArgs e)
        {
            if (newCustomer)
            {
                Customer.Customers.Add((Customer)BindingContext);
            }
            await Navigation.PopAsync(animated: true);
        }
    }
}
```

Open `App.xaml.cs`.

Import the `NorthwindMobile.Views` namespace.

Modify the statement that sets `MainPage` to create an instance of `CustomersList` wrapped in `NavigationPage`, as shown in the following code:

```
MainPage = new NavigationPage(new CustomersList());
```

# Testing the mobile app with iOS

Click on the mobile phone icon in the **Debug** toolbar, and select **iPhone X iOS 11.0**, as shown in the following screenshot:

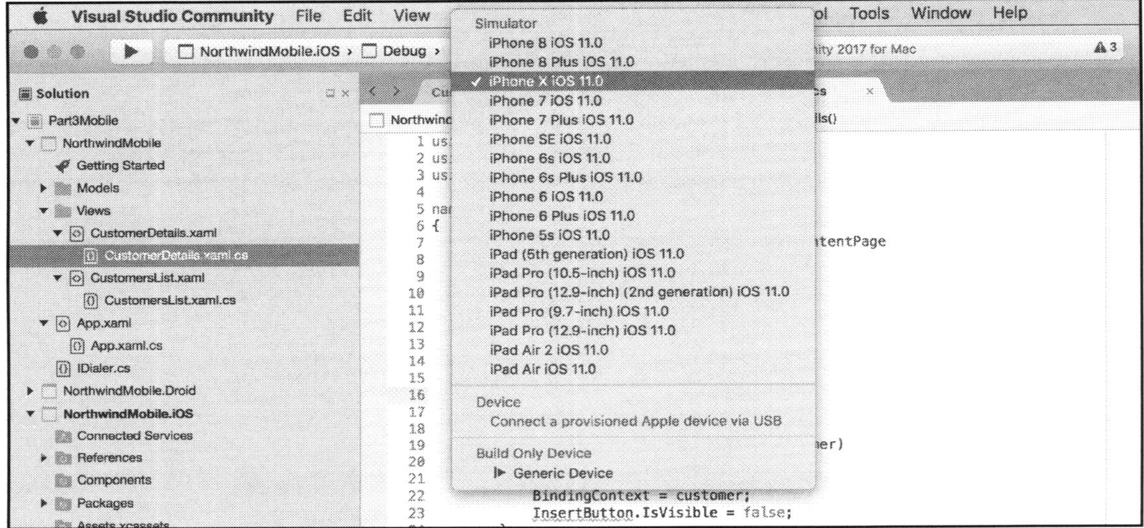


Click on the **Start** button in the toolbar, or go to **Run** | **Start Debugging**.

After a few moments, **Simulator** will show your running mobile app, as shown in the following screenshot:

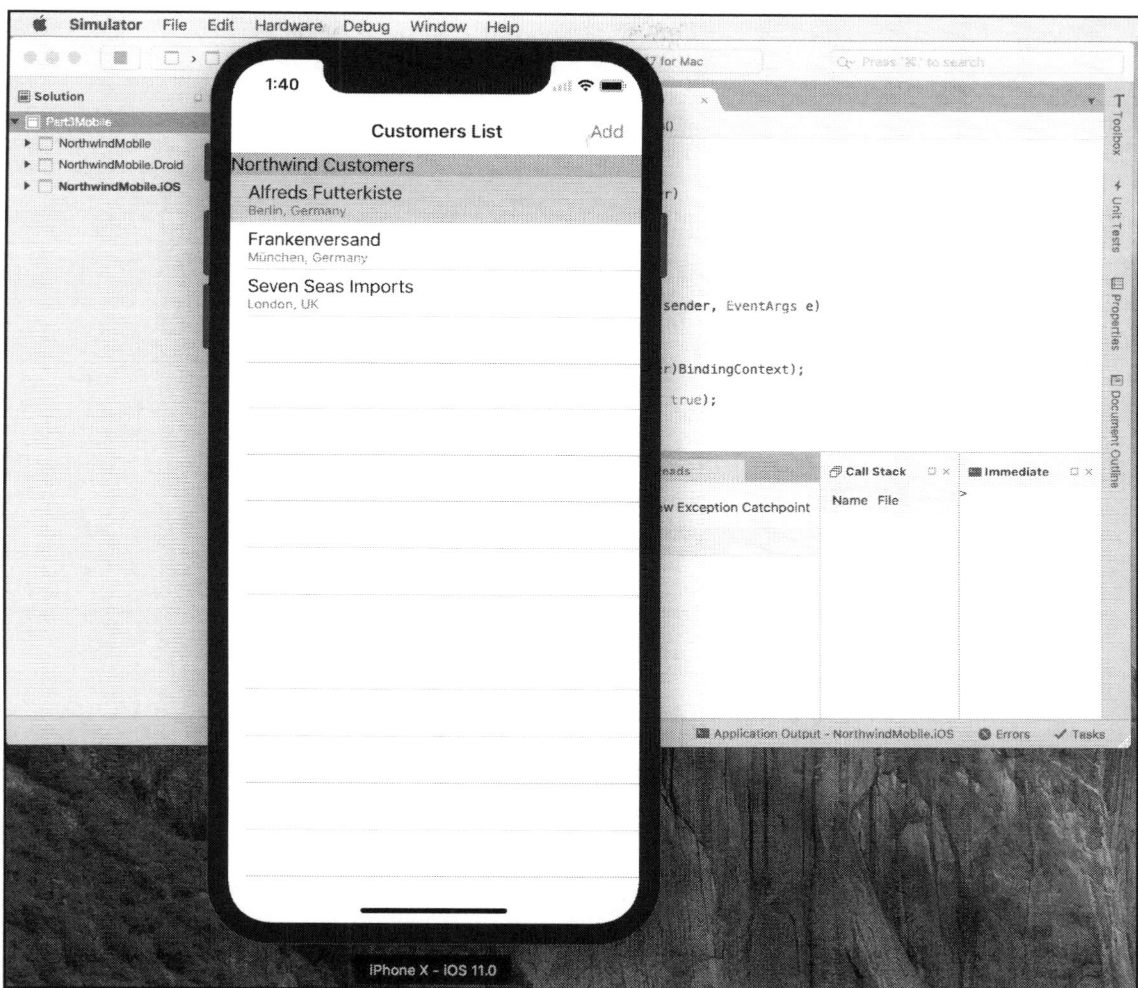

Click on a customer and modify its **Company Name**:

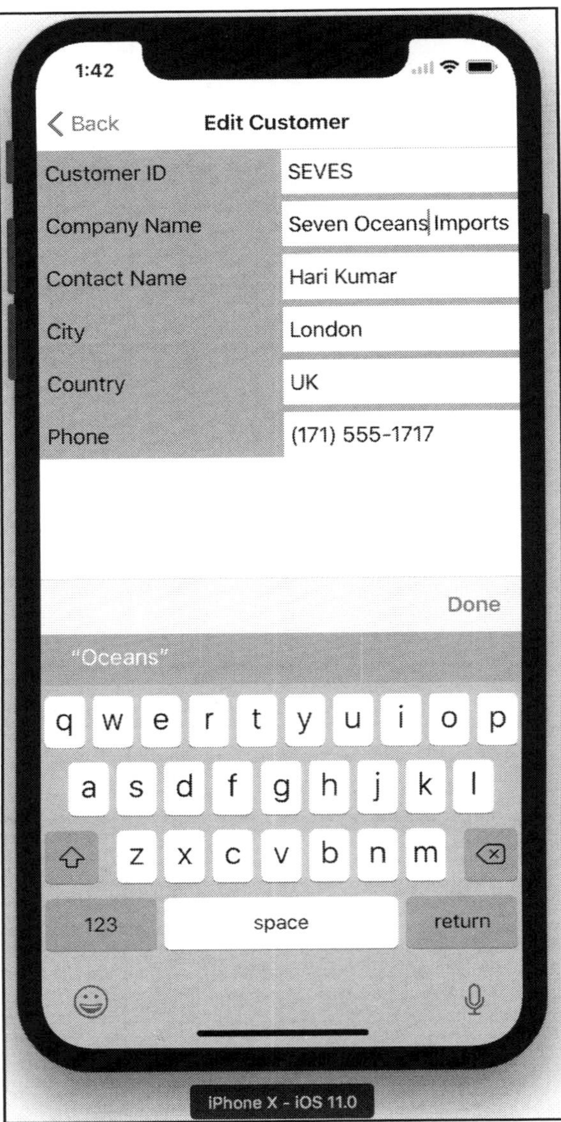


Click on **Back** to return to the list of customers and note that the company name has been updated.

Click on **Add**.

Fill in the fields for a new customer, as shown in the following screenshot:

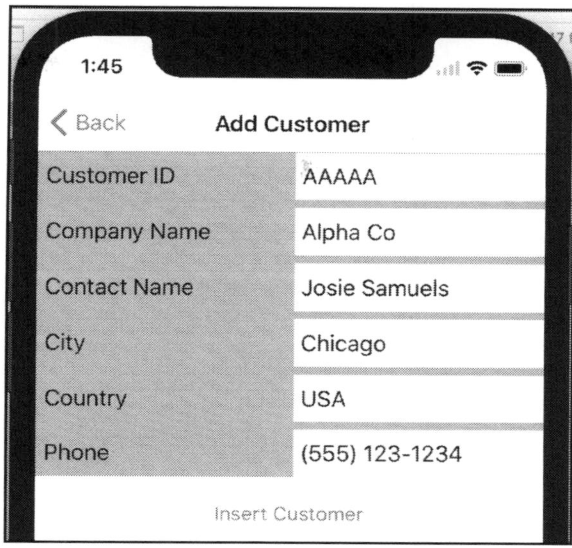


Click on **Insert Customer** and note that the new customer has been added to the list.

Slide one of the customers to the left to reveal two action buttons, **Phone** and **Delete**:

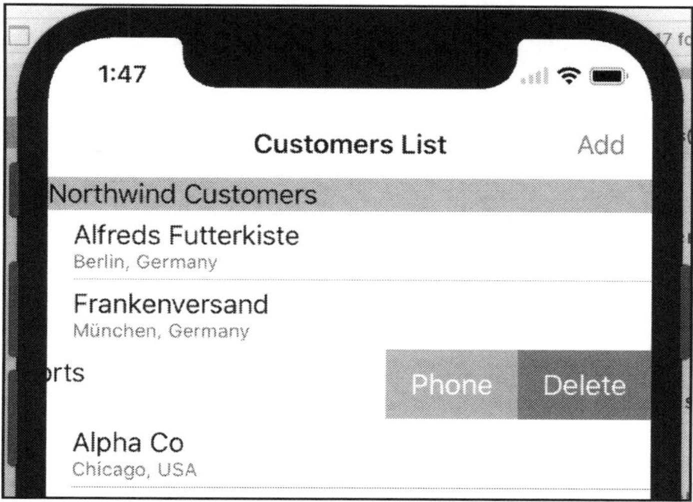

Click on **Phone** and note the prompt to the user, as shown here:

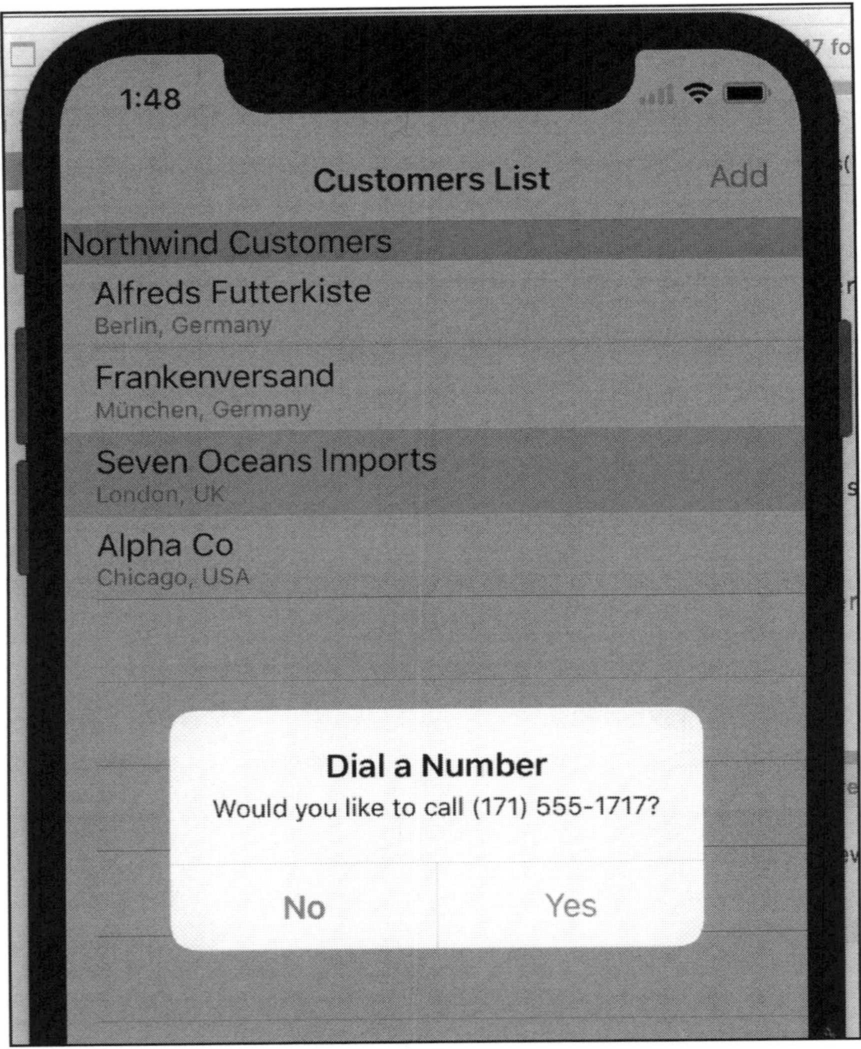


Slide one of the customers to the left to reveal two action buttons, **Phone** and **Delete**, and click on **Delete**, and note that the customer is removed.

Quit **Simulator**.

# Adding NuGet packages for calling a REST service

In the project named `NorthwindMobile.iOS`, right-click on the folder named `Packages` and choose **Add Packages...**.

In the **Add Packages** dialog, enter `System.Net.Http` in the **Search** box. Select the package named **System.Net.Http** and click on **Add Package**, as shown in the following screenshot:

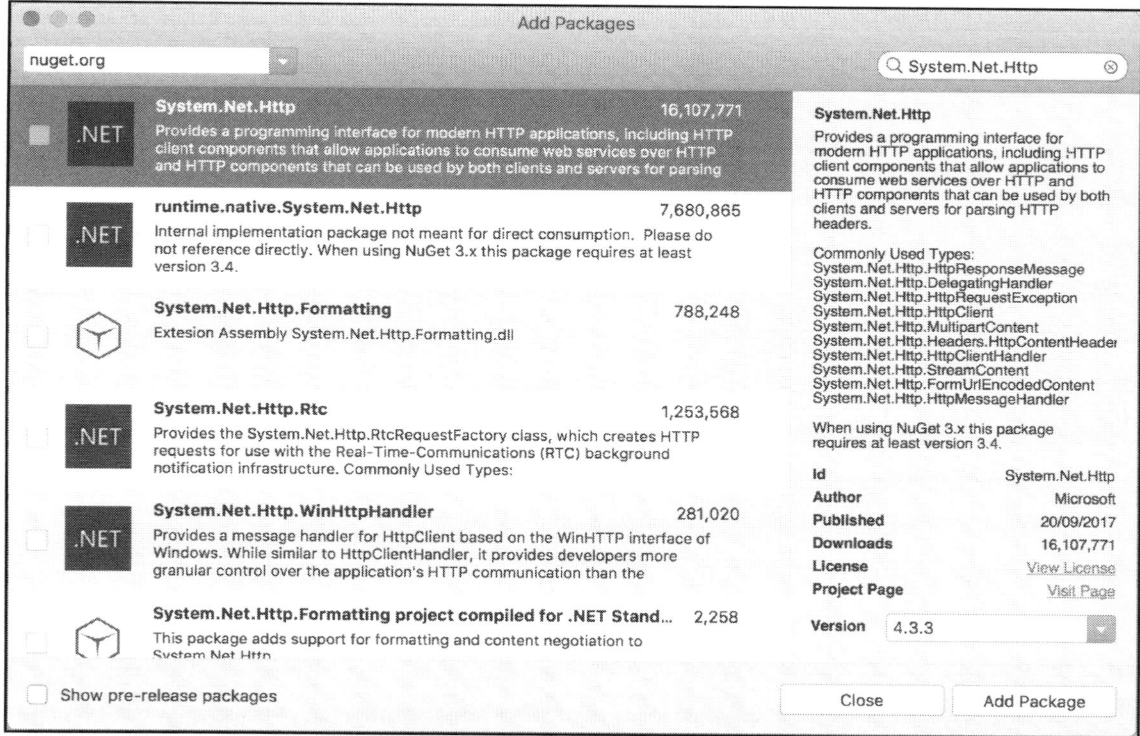


In the **License Acceptance** dialog, click on **Accept**.

In the project named `NorthwindMobile.iOS`, right-click on the folder named `Packages` and choose **Add Packages...**.

In the **Add Packages** dialog, enter `Json.NET` in the **Search** box. Select the package named **Json.NET** and click on **Add Package**, as shown in the following screenshot:

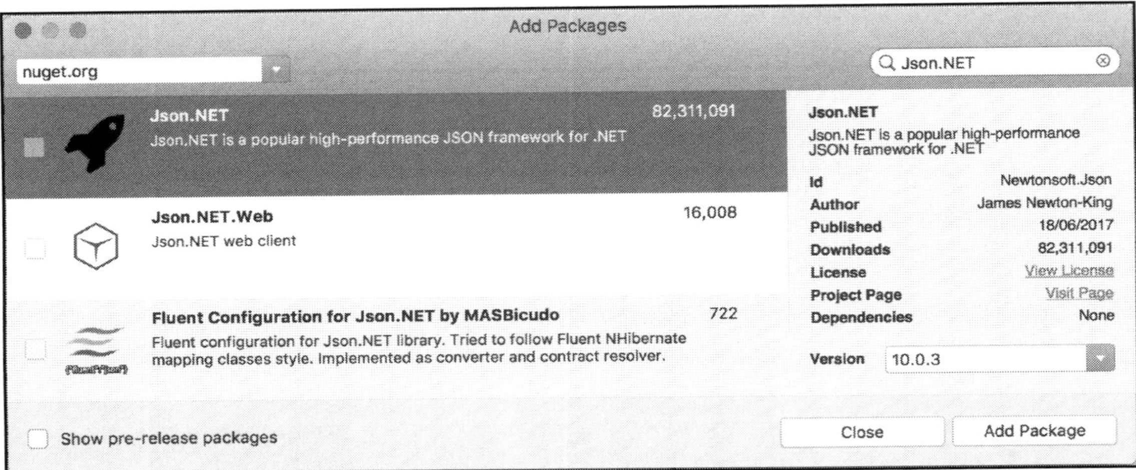


Accept the license.

Repeat these steps to add the same two NuGet packages to the project named `NorthwindMobile.Android`.

# Getting customers from the service

Open `CustomersList.xaml.cs`, and import the following highlighted namespaces:

```
using System.Threading.Tasks;
using NorthwindMobile.Models;
using Xamarin.Forms;
using System;
using System.Linq;
using System.Collections.Generic;
using System.Net.Http;
using System.Net.Http.Headers;
using Newtonsoft.Json;
```

Modify the `CustomersList` constructor to load the list of customers using the service proxy instead of the `SampleData` method, as shown in the following code:

```
public CustomersList()
{
   InitializeComponent();

   //Customer.SampleData();

   var client = new HttpClient();
   client.BaseAddress = new Uri(
     "http://localhost:5001/api/customers");

   client.DefaultRequestHeaders.Accept.Add(
     new MediaTypeWithQualityHeaderValue("application/json"));

   HttpResponseMessage response = client.GetAsync("").Result;

   response.EnsureSuccessStatusCode();

   string content =
     response.Content.ReadAsStringAsync().Result;
   var customersFromService = JsonConvert.DeserializeObject
   <IEnumerable<Customer>>(content);

   foreach (Customer c in customersFromService
     .OrderBy(customer => customer.CompanyName)
   {
      Customer.Customers.Add(c);
   }

   BindingContext = Customer.Customers;
}
```

In Visual Studio Code, run the `NorthwindService` project.

In Visual Studio for Mac, run the `NorthwindMobile` project, and note that 91 customers are loaded from the web service, as shown in the following screenshot:

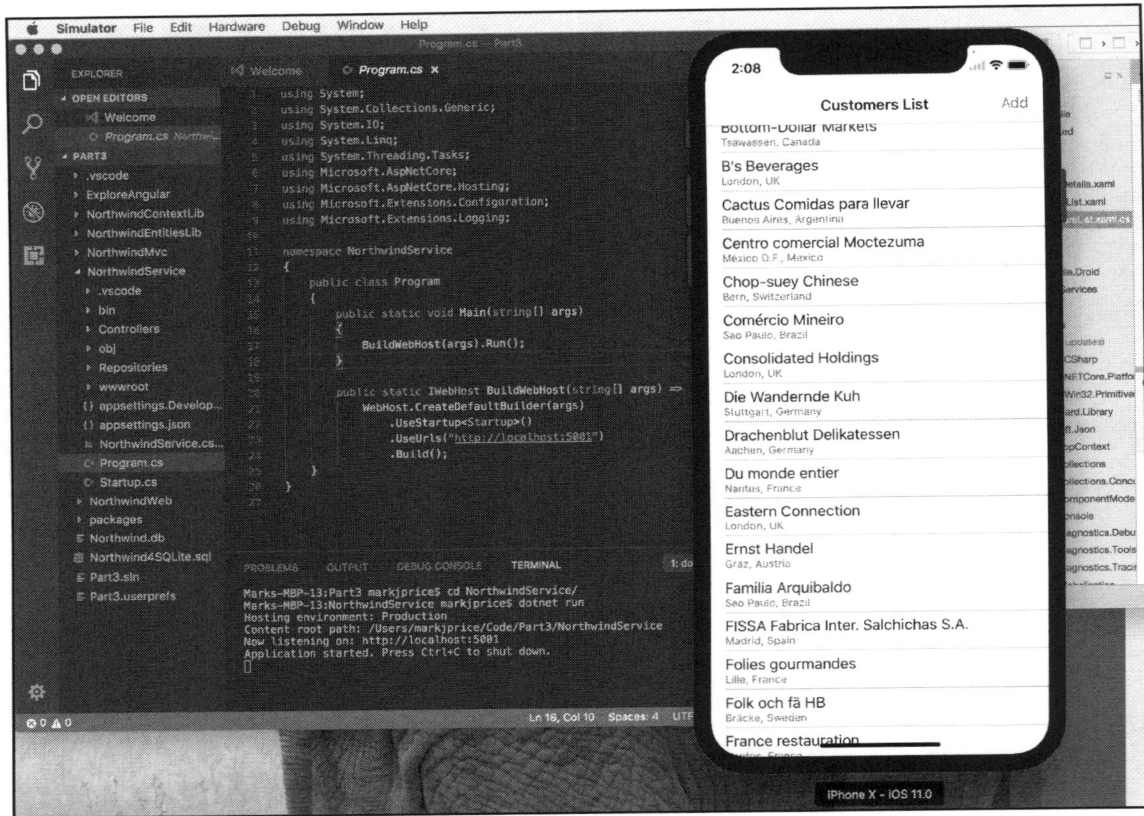

# Practicing and exploring

Explore this chapter's topics with deeper research.

# Exercise 18.1 - Explore topics

Use the following links to read more about this chapter's topics:

- **Visual Studio Code for Mac developers**: `https://channel9.msdn.com/Series/Visual-Studio-Code-for-Mac-Developers`
- **Xamarin.Forms:** `https://www.xamarin.com/forms`
- **Xamarin Developer Center**: `https://developer.xamarin.com`

# Summary

In this chapter, you learned how to build a mobile app using Xamarin.Forms, which is cross-platform for iOS and Android (and potentially other platforms), and consumes a REST/HTTP service using the `HttpClient` and `Newtonsoft.Json` packages.

# Summary

## Good luck!

Hopefully, your experience with this book about the C# 7.1 language and .NET Core 2.0 APIs has inspired you to think about how you can use C# and .NET Core to build well-architected and modern applications that run cross-platform on Windows, macOS, and Linux.

Use the links to references at the end of each chapter to build on what you learned in the book. Some additional references to take your learning further include the following links:

- **Transitioning to .NET Core on Red Hat Enterprise Linux**: `https://developers.redhat.com/promotions/dot-net-core/`
- **Azure Functions Documentation**: `https://docs.microsoft.com/en-us/azure/azure-functions/`
- **.NET on Google Cloud Platform**: `https://cloud.google.com/dotnet/`
- **Xamarin University**: `https://www.xamarin.com/university`

With C# and .NET Core in your arsenal of tools and technologies, you can conquer the universe of cross-platform development and build any type of application that you need.

# Answers to the Test Your Knowledge Questions

This appendix has the answers to the questions in the *Test Your Knowledge* section at the end of each chapter.

## Chapter 1 – Hello, C#! Welcome, .NET Core!

1. Why can a programmer use different languages, for example C# and F#, to write applications that run on .NET Core?

   **Answer**: Multiple languages are supported on .NET Core because each one has a compiler that translates the source code into IL (intermediate language) code. This IL code is then compiled to native CPU instructions at runtime by the CLR.

2. What do you type at the prompt to build and execute C# source code?

   **Answer:** Using .NET Core CLI in a folder with a `ProjectName.csproj` file, we type `dotnet run`.

3. What is the Visual C# developer settings keyboard shortcut to save, compile, and run an application without attaching the debugger?

   **Answer**: *Ctrl* + *F5*.

4. What is the Visual Studio Code keyboard shortcut to view the Integrated Terminal?

   **Answer:** *Ctrl* + ` (back tick).

5. Is Visual Studio 2017 better than Visual Studio Code?

   **Answer**: No. Each is optimized for different tasks. Visual Studio 2017 is large, heavy-weight, and can create applications with graphical user interfaces, for example WPF, UWP, and Xamarin mobile apps, but is only available on Windows. Visual Studio Code is smaller, lighter-weight, command-line and code-focused, and available cross-platform.

6. Is .NET Core better than .NET Framework?

   **Answer:** It depends on what you need. .NET Core is a slimmed down, cross-platform version of the more full-featured, mature .NET Framework.

7. How is .NET Native different from .NET Core?

   **Answer:** .NET Native is an ahead-of-time compiler that can produce native code assemblies that have better performance and reduced memory footprints, and it has its .NET assemblies statically linked, which removes its dependency on CoreCLR.

8. What is .NET Standard and why is it important?

   **Answer:** .NET Standard defines an API that a .NET platform can implement. Current versions of .NET Framework, .NET Core, and Xamarin implement .NET Standard 2.0 to provide a single, standard API that developers can learn and target.

9. What is the difference between Git and GitHub?

   **Answer:** Git is a source code management platform. GitHub is a popular web service that implements Git.

10. What is the name of the entry point method of a .NET console application and how should it be declared?

    **Answer**: The entry point of a .NET console application is the `Main` method and the following code is how it is declared. An optional `string` array for command-line arguments and a return type of `int` are recommended, but they are not required:

```
public static void Main() // minimum
public static int Main(string[] args) // recommended
```

# Chapter 2 – Speaking C#

What type would you choose for the following "numbers?"

1. A person's telephone number.

   **Answer:** `string`.

2. A person's height.

   **Answer:** `float` or `double`.

3. A person's age.

   **Answer:** `int` for performance or `byte` (0 to 255) for size.

4. A person's salary.

   **Answer:** `decimal`.

5. A book's ISBN.

   **Answer:** `string`.

6. A book's price.

   **Answer:** `decimal`.

7. A book's shipping weight.

   **Answer:** `float` or `double`.

8. A country's population.

   **Answer:** `uint` (0 to about 4 billion).

9. The number of stars in the universe.

   **Answer:** `ulong` (0 to about 18 quadrillion) or `System.Numerics.BigInteger` (allows an arbitrarily large integer).

10. The number of employees in each of the small or medium businesses in the UK (up to about 50,000 employees per business).

    **Answer:** Since there are hundreds of thousands of small or medium businesses, we need to take memory size as the determining factor, so choose `ushort`, because it only takes 2 bytes compared to an `int`, which takes 4 bytes.

# Chapter 3 – Controlling the Flow and Converting Types

1. Where would you look for help about a C# keyword?

   **Answer:** `https://docs.microsoft.com/en-us/dotnet/articles/csharp/language-reference/keywords/`

2. Where would you look for solutions to common programming problems?

   **Answer:** `http://stackoverflow.com`

3. What happens when you divide an `int` variable by 0?

   **Answer:** `DivideByZeroException` is thrown when dividing an integer or decimal.

4. What happens when you divide a `double` variable by `0`?

   **Answer:** The `double` type contains a special value of `Infinity`. Instances of floating-point numbers can have the `NaN` (not a number), `PositiveInfinity`, and `NegativeInfinity` special values.

5. What happens when you overflow an `int` variable, that is, set it to a value beyond its range?

   **Answer:** It will loop unless you wrap the statement in a `checked` block, in which case, `OverflowException` will be thrown.

6. What is the difference between `x = y++;` and `x = ++y;`?

   **Answer:** In `x = y++;`, `y` will be assigned to `x` and then `y` will be incremented, but in `x = ++y;`, `y` will be incremented and then the result will be assigned to `x`.

7. What is the difference between `break`, `continue`, and `return` when used inside a loop statement?

   **Answer:** The `break` statement will end the whole loop and continue executing after the loop, the `continue` statement will end the current iteration of the loop and continue executing at the start of the loop block for the next iteration, and the `return` statement will end the current method call and continue executing after the method call.

8. What are the three parts of a `for` statement and which of them are required?

   **Answer:** The three parts of a `for` statement are the initializer, condition, and incrementer. The condition is required to be an expression that returns `true` or `false`, but the other two are optional.

9. What is the difference between the `=` and `==` operators?

   **Answer:** The `=` operator is the assignment operator for assigning values to variables, while the `==` operator is the equality check operator that returns `true` or `false`.

10. Does the following statement compile? `for ( ; true; ) ;`

 **Answer:** Yes. The `for` statement only requires a Boolean expression. The `initializer` and `incrementer` statements are optional. This `for` statement will execute the empty `;` statement forever. It is an example of an infinite loop.

### Exercise 3.2

1. What will happen if this code executes?

```
int max = 500;
for (byte i = 0; i < max; i++)
{
    WriteLine(i);
}
```

 **Answer:**

 - The code will loop non-stop because the value of `i` can only be between `0` and `255`, so once it gets incremented beyond `255`, it goes back to `0` and therefore will always be less than `max` (`500`).
 - To prevent it from looping non-stop, you can add a checked statement around the code. This would cause an exception to be thrown after `255`, like this:

```
254
255
System.OverflowException says Arithmetic operation resulted in an
overflow.
```

# Chapter 4 – Writing, Debugging, and Testing Functions

1. What does the C# keyword `void` mean?

 **Answer:** It indicates that a method has no return value.

2. How many parameters can a method have?

   **Answer:** A method with 16,383 parameters can be compiled, run, and called. Any more than that and an unstated exception is thrown at runtime. IL has predefined opcodes to load up to four parameters and a special opcode to load up to 16-bit (65,536) parameters. The best practice is to limit your methods to three or four parameters. You can combine multiple parameters into a new class to encapsulate them into a single parameter. You can find more information on this at the following site:
   `http://stackoverflow.com/questions/12658883/what-is-the-maximum-number-of-parameters-that-a-c-sharp-method-can-be-defined-as`

3. In Visual Studio 2017, what is the difference between pressing *F5, Ctrl + F5, Shift + F5,* and *Ctrl + Shift + F5?*

   **Answer:** *F5* saves; compiles; runs; and attaches the debugger, *Ctrl + F5* saves; compiles; and runs the debugger, *Shift + F5* stops the debugger, and *Ctrl + Shift + F5* restarts the debugger.

4. Where does the `Trace.WriteLine` method write its output to?

   **Answer:** `Trace.WriteLine` writes its output to any configured trace listeners. By default, this includes Visual Studio 2017's Output window, but can be configured to be the console, a text file, or any custom listener.

5. What are the five trace levels?

   **Answer**: 0 = None, 1 = Error, 2 = Warning, 3 = Info, and 4 = Verbose.

6. What is the difference between `Debug` and `Trace`?

   **Answer:** `Debug` is active only during development. `Trace` is active during development and after release into production.

7. When writing a unit test, what are the three As?

   **Answer:** Arrange, Act, Assert.

8. When writing a unit test using xUnit, what attribute must you decorate the test methods with?

   **Answer:** `[Fact]`

9. What `dotnet` command executes xUnit test?

   **Answer:** `dotnet test`

10. What is TDD?

    **Answer:** Test Driven Development. Read more at the following link: `https://docs.microsoft.com/en-us/dotnet/core/testing/`

# Chapter 5 – Building Your Own Types with Object-Oriented Programming

1. What are the four access modifiers and what do they do?

   **Answer:** The four access modifiers and their effect are described here:

   - `private`: This modifier makes a member only visible inside the class
   - `internal`: This modifier makes a member only visible inside the class or within the same assembly
   - `protected`: This modifier makes a member only visible inside the class or derived classes
   - `public`: This modifier makes a member visible everywhere

2. What is the difference between the `static`, `const`, and `readonly` keywords?

   **Answer:** The difference between the `static`, `const`, and `readonly` keywords is:

   - `static`: This keyword makes the member shared by all instances and accessed through the type
   - `const`: This keyword makes a field a fixed literal value that should never change
   - `readonly`: This keyword makes a field that can only be assigned at runtime using a constructor

3. What does a constructor do?

   **Answer:** A constructor allocates memory and initializes field values.

4. Why do you need to apply the `[Flags]` attribute to an `enum` type when you want to store combined values?

   **Answer:** If you don't apply the `[Flags]` attribute to an `enum` type when you want to store combined values, then a stored `enum` value that is a combination will return as the stored integer value instead of a comma-separated list of text values.

5. Why is the `partial` keyword useful?

   **Answer:** You can use the `partial` keyword to split the definition of a type over multiple files.

6. What is a tuple?

   **Answer:** A data structure consisting of multiple parts.

7. What does the C# `ref` keyword do?

   **Answer:** The C# `ref` keyword converts a parameter passed by its current value into a parameter passed as a pointer aka reference.

8. What does overloading mean?

   **Answer:** Overloading is when you define more than one method with the same method name and different input parameters.

9. What is the difference between a field and a property?

   **Answer:** A field is a data storage location that can be referenced. A property is one or a pair of methods that get and/or set a value. The value is often stored in a private field.

10. How do you make a method parameter optional?

    **Answer:** You make a method parameter optional by assigning a default value to it.

# Chapter 6 – Implementing Interfaces and Inheriting Classes

1. What is a delegate?

   **Answer:** A delegate is a type-safe method reference. It can be used to execute any method with a matching signature.

2. What is an event?

   **Answer:** An event is a field that is a delegate having the `event` keyword applied. The keyword ensures that only += and -= are used; this safely combines multiple delegates without replacing any existing event handlers.

3. How is a base class and a derived class related?

   **Answer:** A derived class (or subclass) is a class that inherits from a base class (or superclass).

4. What is the difference between the `is` and `as` operators?

   **Answer:** The `is` operator returns `true` if an object can be cast to the type. The `as` operator returns a reference if an object can be cast to the type; otherwise, it returns `null`.

5. Which keyword is used to prevent a class from being derived from, or a method from being overridden?

   **Answer:** `sealed`.
   Find more information on the `sealed` keyword at:
   `https://msdn.microsoft.com/en-us/library/88c54tsw.aspx`

6. Which keyword is used to prevent a class from being instantiated with the `new` keyword?

   **Answer:** `abstract`.
   Find more information on the `abstract` keyword at:
   `https://msdn.microsoft.com/en-us/library/sf985hc5.aspx`

7. Which keyword is used to allow a member to be overridden?

   **Answer:** `virtual`.
   Find more information on the `virtual` keyword at:
   `https://msdn.microsoft.com/en-us/library/9fkccyh4.aspx`

8. What's the difference between a destructor and a deconstructor?

   **Answer:** A destructor, also known as a finalizer, must be used to release resources owned by the object. A deconstructor is a new feature of C# 7 or later that allows a complex object to be broken down into smaller parts.

9. What are the signatures of the constructors that all exceptions should have?

   **Answer:** The following are the signatures of the constructors that all exceptions should have:

   - A constructor with no parameters
   - A constructor with a `string` parameter, usually named `message`
   - A constructor with a `string` parameter, usually named `message`, and an `Exception` parameter, usually named `innerException`

10. What is an extension method and how do you define one?

    **Answer:** An extension method is a compiler trick that makes a static method of a static class appear to be one of the members of a type. You define which type you want to extend by prefixing the type with `this`.

# Chapter 7 – Understanding and Packaging .NET Standard Types

1. What is the difference between a namespace and an assembly?

   **Answer:** A namespace is a logical container for a type. An assembly is a physical container for a type.

2. How do you reference another project in a `.csproj` file?

```
<ItemGroup>
  <ProjectReference Include="..\Calculator\Calculator.csproj" />
</ItemGroup>
```

3. What is the difference between a package and a metapackage?

   **Answer:** A metapackage is a grouping of packages.

4. Which .NET type does the C# `float` alias represent?

   **Answer:** `System.Single`.

5. What is the difference between the packages named `NETStandard.Library` and `Microsoft.NETCore.App`?

   **Answer:** `Microsoft.NETCore.App` is a superset of `NETStandard.Library`; this means that it implements all of .NET Standard 2.0 and extra APIs specific to .NET Core 2.0.

6. What is the difference between framework-dependent and self-contained deployments of .NET Core applications?

   **Answer:** Framework-dependent .NET Core applications require .NET Core to exist for an operating system to execute. Self-contained .NET Core applications include everything necessary to execute in their own.

7. What is a RID?

   **Answer:** Runtime Identifier. RID values are used to identify target platforms where a .NET Core application runs.

8. What is the difference between the `dotnet pack` and `dotnet publish` commands?

   **Answer:** The `dotnet pack` command creates a NuGet package. The `dotnet publish` command puts the application and its dependencies into a folder for deployment to a hosting system.

9. What types of applications written for .NET Framework can be ported to .NET Core?

   **Answer:** Console, ASP.NET MVC, ASP.NET Web API.

10. Can you use packages written for .NET Framework with .NET Core?

    **Answer:** Yes, as long as they only call APIs in .NET Standard 2.0.

# Chapter 8 – Using Common .NET Standard Types

1. What is the maximum number of characters that can be stored in a `string` variable?

   **Answer:** The maximum size of a `string` variable is 2 GB or about 1 billion characters, because each `char` variable uses 2 bytes due to the internal use of Unicode (UTF-16) encoding for characters.

2. When and why should you use a `SecureString` type?

   **Answer:** The `string` type leaves text data in the memory for too long and it's too visible. The `SecureString` type encrypts the text and ensures that the memory is released immediately. WPF's `PasswordBox` control stores the password as a `SecureString` variable, and when starting a new process, the `Password` parameter must be a `SecureString` variable. For more discussion, visit: `http://stackoverflow.com/questions/141203/when-would-i-need-a-securestring-in-net`

3. When is it appropriate to use a `StringBuilder` class?

   **Answer:** When concatenating more than about three `string` variables, you will use less memory and get improved performance using `StringBuilder` than using the `string.Concat` method or the + operator.

4. When should you use `LinkedList<T>`?

   **Answer:** Each item in a linked list has a reference to its previous and next siblings as well as the list itself, so a linked list should be used when items need to be inserted and removed from positions in the list without actually moving the items in memory.

5. When should you use a `SortedDictionary` variable rather than a `SortedList` variable?

   **Answer:** The `SortedList` class uses lesser memory than `SortedDictionary`; `SortedDictionary` has faster insertion and removal operations for unsorted data. If the list is populated all at once from sorted data, `SortedList` is faster than `SortedDictionary`. For more discussion, visit: `http://stackoverflow.com/questions/935621/whats-the-difference-between-sortedlist-and-sorteddictionary`

6. What is the ISO culture code for Welsh?

   **Answer:** `cy-GB`. For a complete list of culture codes, visit: `http://timtrott.co.uk/culture-codes/`

7. What is the difference between localization, globalization, and internationalization?

   **Answer**: **Localization** affects the user interface of your application. Localization is controlled by a neutral (language only) or specific (language and region) culture. You provide multiple language versions of text and other values. For example, the label of a text box might be **First name** in English, and **Prénom** in French. **Globalization** affects the data of your application. Globalization is controlled by a specific (language and region) culture, for example, `en-GB` for British English, or `fr-CA` for Canadian French. The culture must be specific because a decimal value formatted as currency must know to use Canadian dollars instead of French euros. **Internationalization** is the combination of localization and globalization.

8. In a regular expression, what does `$` mean?

   **Answer:** `$` represents the end of the input.

9. In a regular expression, how would you represent digits?

   **Answer**: `\d+` or `[0-9]+`

10. Why should you not use the official standard for email addresses to create a regular expression to validate a user's email address?

    **Answer:** The effort is not worth the pain for you or your users. Validating an email address using the official specification doesn't check whether that address actually exists or whether the person entering the address is its owner. For more discussion, visit:
    `http://davidcel.is/posts/stop-validating-email-addresses-with-regex/` or
    `http://stackoverflow.com/questions/201323/using-a-regular-expression-to-validate-an-email-address`

# Chapter 9 – Working with Files, Streams, and Serialization

1. What is the difference between using the `File` class and the `FileInfo` class?

   **Answer:** The `File` class has static methods, so it cannot be instantiated. It is best used for one-off tasks such as copying a file. The `FileInfo` class requires the instantiation of an object that represents a file. It is best used when you need to perform multiple operations on the same file.

2. What is the difference between the `ReadByte` method and the `Read` method of a stream?

   **Answer:** The `ReadByte` method returns a single byte each time it is called and the `Read` method fills a temporary array with bytes up to a specified length. It is generally best to use `Read` to process blocks of bytes at once.

3. When would you use the `StringReader`, `TextReader`, and `StreamReader` classes?

   **Answer:** `StringReader` is used for efficiently reading from a string stored in memory. `TextReader` is an abstract class that `StringReader` and `StreamReader` both inherit from, for their shared functionality. `StreamReader` is used for reading strings from a stream that can be any type of text file, including XML and JSON.

4. What does the `DeflateStream` type do?

   **Answer:** `DeflateStream` implements the same compression algorithm as GZIP, but without a cyclical redundancy check; so, although it produces smaller compressed files, it cannot perform integrity checks when decompressing.

5. How many bytes per character does the UTF-8 encoding use?

   **Answer:** It depends on the character. Most Western alphabet characters are stored using a single byte. Other characters may need two or more bytes.

6. What is an object graph?

   **Answer:** An object graph is any instance of classes in memory that reference each other, thereby forming a set of related objects. For example, a `Customer` object may have a property that references a set of `Order` instances.

7. What is the best serialization format to choose for minimizing space requirements?

   **Answer:** JavaScript Object Notation (JSON).

8. What is the best serialization format to choose for cross-platform compatibility?

   **Answer:** eXtensible Markup Language (XML), although JSON is even better these days.

9. What library is best for working with the JSON serialization format?

   **Answer:** `Newtonsoft.JSON`

10. How many packages are available for serialization on NuGet.org?

    **Answer:** 778 packages are available for serialization.

# Chapter 10 – Protecting Your Data and Applications

1. Of the encryption algorithms provided by .NET, which is the best choice for symmetric encryption?

   **Answer:** The AES algorithm is the best choice for symmetric encryption.

2. Of the encryption algorithms provided by .NET, which is the best choice for asymmetric encryption?

   **Answer:** The RSA algorithm is the best choice for asymmetric encryption.

3. What is a rainbow attack?

   **Answer:** A rainbow attack uses a table of precalculated hashes of passwords. When a database of password hashes is stolen, the attacker can compare against the rainbow table hashes quickly and determine the original passwords. You can learn more at the following link: `https://learncryptography.com/hash-functions/rainbow-tables`

4. For encryption algorithms, is it better to have a larger or smaller block size?

   **Answer:** For encryption algorithms, it is better to have a smaller block size.

5. What is a hash?

   **Answer:** A hash is a fixed-size output that results from an input of arbitrary size being processed by a hash function. Hash functions are one-way, which means that the only way to recreate the original input is to brute-force all possible inputs and compare the results.

6. What is a signature?

   **Answer:** A signature is a value appended to a digital document to prove its authenticity. A valid signature tells the recipient that the document was created by a known sender.

7. What is the difference between symmetric and asymmetric encryption?

   **Answer:** Symmetric encryption uses a secret shared key to both encrypt and decrypt. Asymmetric encryption uses a public key to encrypt and a private key to decrypt.

8. What does RSA stand for?

   **Answer:** Rivest-Shamir-Adleman, the surnames of the three men who publicly described the algorithm in 1978.

9. Why should passwords be salted before being stored?

   **Answer:** To slow down rainbow dictionary attacks.

10. SHA-1 is a hashing algorithm designed by the United States National Security Agency. Why should you never use it?

    **Answer:** SHA-1 is no longer secure. All modern browsers have stopped accepting SHA-1 SSL certificates.

# Chapter 11 – Working with Databases Using Entity Framework Core

1. What type would you use for the property that represents a table, for example, the `Products` property of a `Northwind` database context?

   **Answer:** `DbSet<T>`, where `T` is the entity type, for example, `Product`.

2. What type would you use for the property that represents a one-to-many relationship, for example, the `Products` property of a `Category` entity?

   **Answer:** `ICollection<T>`, where `T` is the entity type, for example, `Product`.

3. What is the EF convention for primary keys?

   **Answer:** The property named `ID` or `ClassNameID` is assumed to be the primary key. If the type of that property is any of the following, then the property is also marked as being an `IDENTITY` column: `tinyint`, `smallint`, `int`, `bigint`, `guid`.

4. When would you use an annotation attribute in an entity class?

   **Answer:** You would use an annotation attribute in an entity class when the conventions cannot work out the correct mapping between the classes and tables. For example, if a class name does not match a table name or a property name does not match a column name.

5. Why might you choose fluent API in preference to annotation attributes?

   **Answer:** You might choose fluent API in preference to annotation attributes when the conventions cannot work out the correct mapping between the classes and tables, and you do not want to use annotation attributes because you want to keep your entity classes clean and free from extraneous code.

6. What does a transaction isolation level of `Serializable` mean?

   **Answer:** Maximum locks are applied to ensure complete isolation from any other processes working with the affected data.

7. What does the `DbContext.SaveChanges()` method return?

   **Answer:** An integer value for the number of entities affected.

8. What is the difference between eager loading and explicit loading?

   **Answer:** Eager loading means related entities are included in the original query to the database so that they do not have to be loaded later. Explicit loading means related entities are not included in the original query to the database and they must be explicitly loaded just before they are needed.

9. How should you define an EF Core entity class to match the following table?

```
CREATE TABLE Employees(
    EmpID INT IDENTITY,
    FirstName NVARCHAR(40) NOT NULL,
    Salary MONEY
)
```

   **Answer:** Use the following class:

```
public class Employee
{
   [Column("EmpID")]
   public int EmployeeID { get; set; }

   [Required]
   [StringLength(40)]
   public string FirstName { get; set; }

   [Column(TypeName = "money")]
   public decimal? Salary { get; set; }
}
```

10. What benefit do you get from declaring entity properties as `virtual`?

    **Answer:** The next version of EF Core is expected to support lazy loading if you declare entity properties as `virtual`.

# Chapter 12 – Querying and Manipulating Data Using LINQ

1. What are the two required parts of LINQ?

   **Answer:** A LINQ provider and the LINQ extension methods. You must import the `System.Linq` namespace to make the LINQ extension methods available and reference a LINQ provider assembly for the type of data that you want to work with.

2. Which LINQ extension method would you use to return a subset of properties from a type?

   **Answer:** The `Select` method allows projection (selection) of properties.

3. Which LINQ extension method would you use to filter a sequence?

   **Answer:** The `Where` method allows filtering by supplying a delegate (or lambda expression) that returns a Boolean to indicate whether the value should be included in the results.

4. List five LINQ extension methods that perform aggregation.

   **Answer**: Any five of the following: `Max`, `Min`, `Count`, `LongCount`, `Average`, `Sum`, and `Aggregate`.

5. What is the difference between the `Select` and `SelectMany` extension methods?

   **Answer:** `Select` returns exactly what you specify to return. `SelectMany` checks that the items you have selected are themselves `IEnumerable<T>` and then breaks them down into smaller parts. For example, if the type you select is a string value (which is `IEnumerable<char>`), `SelectMany` will break each string value returned into their individual `char` values.

# Chapter 13 – Improving Performance and Scalability Using Multitasking

1. Which information can you find out about a process?

   **Answer:** The `Process` class has many properties including: `ExitCode`, `ExitTime`, `Id`, `MachineName`, `PagedMemorySize64`, `ProcessorAffinity`, `StandardInput`, `StandardOutput`, `StartTime`, `Threads`, and `TotalProcessorTime`. You can find more information about **Process Properties** at: `https://msdn.microsoft.com/en-us/library/System.Diagnostics.Process_properties(v=vs.110).aspx`

2. How accurate is the `Stopwatch` class?

   **Answer:** The `Stopwatch` class can be accurate to within a nanosecond (a billionth of a second), but you shouldn't rely on that. You can improve accuracy by setting processor affinity, as shown in the article at the following link: `http://www.codeproject.com/Articles/61964/Performance-Tests-Precise-Run-Time-Measurements-wi`

3. By convention, what suffix should be applied to a method that returns `Task` or `Task<T>`?

   **Answer**: Add the suffix `Async` to the method name, for example, `OpenAsync` for a method named `Open`.

4. To use the `await` keyword inside a method, which keyword must be applied to the method declaration?

   **Answer:** The `async` keyword must be applied to the method declaration.

5. How do you create a child task?

   **Answer:** Call the `Task.Factory.StartNew` method with the `TaskCreationOptions.AttachToParent` option to create a child task.

6. Why should you avoid the `lock` keyword?

   **Answer:** The `lock` keyword does not allow you to specify a timeout; this can cause deadlocks. Use `Monitor.Enter` with `TimeSpan` and `Monitor.Exit` instead.

7. When should you use the `Interlocked` class?

   **Answer:** If you have integers and floating point numbers that are shared between multiple threads, you should use the `Interlocked` class.

8. When should you use the `Mutex` class instead of the `Monitor` class?

   **Answer:** Use `Mutex` when you need to share a resource across process boundaries.

9. Does using `async` and `await` in a web application or web service improve performance? If not, why do it?

   **Answer:** No. In a web application or web service, using `async` and `await` improves scalability, but not performance of a specific request, because extra work of handling over work between threads is required.

10. Can you cancel a task? How?

    **Answer:** Yes, you can cancel a task, as described at the following link: `https://docs.microsoft.com/en-us/dotnet/csharp/programming-guide/concepts/async/cancel-an-async-task-or-a-list-of-tasks`

# Index

# B



# C

# D

# E

# F

# N

# O



# P

# Q



# R

## S

# T

# U



# V

# W

# X

Printed in Great Britain
by Amazon